The Hong Kong Diaries

BY THE SAME AUTHOR

First Confession: A Sort of Memoir

What Next?: Surviving the Twenty-First Century

Not Quite the Diplomat: Home Truths about World Affairs

East and West: The Last Governor of Hong Kong on Power, Freedom and the Future

CHRIS PATTEN

The Hong Kong Diaries

ALLEN LANE
an imprint of
PENGUIN BOOKS

ALLEN LANE

UK | USA | Canada | Ireland | Australia
India | New Zealand | South Africa

Allen Lane is part of the Penguin Random House group of companies
whose addresses can be found at global.penguinrandomhouse.com.

Penguin Random House UK

First published by Allen Lane 2022
001

Set in 10.2/13.5pt Sabon LT Std
Typeset by Jouve (UK), Milton Keynes
Printed and bound in Great Britain by Clays Ltd, Elcograf S.p.A.

The authorized representative in the EEA is Penguin Random House Ireland,
Morrison Chambers, 32 Nassau Street, Dublin D02 YH68

A CIP catalogue record for this book is available from the British Library

ISBN: 978-0-241-56049-5

www.greenpenguin.co.uk

FSC
www.fsc.org
MIX
Paper from
responsible sources
FSC® C018179

Penguin Random House is committed to a
sustainable future for our business, our readers
and our planet. This book is made from Forest
Stewardship Council® certified paper.

To Lavender,
who gave up her career so that I could go to Hong Kong,
who helped me hugely in my work as Governor,
and who loved Hong Kong as much as I did.

Contents

Acknowledgements

Sadly, in the light of circumstances in Hong Kong today, I cannot in their own interest name many people in the city who have helped to keep me in touch with what has happened there, a story of broken promises and totalitarian vandalism. In London, I am particularly grateful to Hugh Davies and Charles Parton for their regular insights into what is happening in Hong Kong and in China as a whole. Johnny Patterson of Hong Kong Watch has helped to provide me with information and has checked some of my facts, and I've also benefited from the ubiquitous advocacy of human rights of Ben Rogers, who helped to found this excellent organization.

My agent, Jim Gill, has been professionally helpful and supportive once again. Above all, I have benefited from the wisdom of Stuart Proffitt, the prince of editors, who makes me work hard despite my grumbles. At Penguin, Alice Skinner has been incredibly diligent and encouraging in moments when I have been sharing my study with the black dog. Alice's sister, Lucy, came heroically to my aid at a difficult time to decipher and type my gnomic handwriting. I'd also like to express my gratitude to Ania Gordon, Mark Handsley, Rebecca Lee, Emma Lubega and Pen Vogler. Twenty-five years ago, when my writing was bad but not quite as awful as it is today, the original diaries were typed up either from my manuscripts or from tapes by two former PAs, Dame Shirley Oxenbury and the Rev. Freda Evans; they did tremendous work.

All the members of my family as ever have been terrific. Kate and Alice have helped me to acquire some vague notion of how to use the technology on which I have been obliged to depend. Laura has cheered us all up and helped to keep everyone but me quite fit. Lavender has read every word of these diaries and has been available with advice 24 hours a day, seven days a week, as my technological and moral backup as I have shouted and raged at clouds, dragons, laptops, iPads and all the rest of this twenty-first-century stuff, which was very competently installed and humoured by Chris Edwards. Martin Dinham and Edward Llewellyn, who shared these years, have read a lot of the text of my edited diary, but any errors or solecisms are my responsibility alone.

Penny Rankin and Anna Alcraft have looked after what has been left of the rest of my life, public and private.

My most profound thanks go above all to those who worked with me in Hong Kong to try to protect and preserve what their city had been promised by a malevolent Communist Party. The people of Hong Kong were kind to me and my family; they made us welcome in their own homes; and I hope that one day they will be able to read these diaries and see how much their future mattered to so many of those of us who were given responsibility for them by events of an earlier age which no one today would seek to defend or condone.

Maps

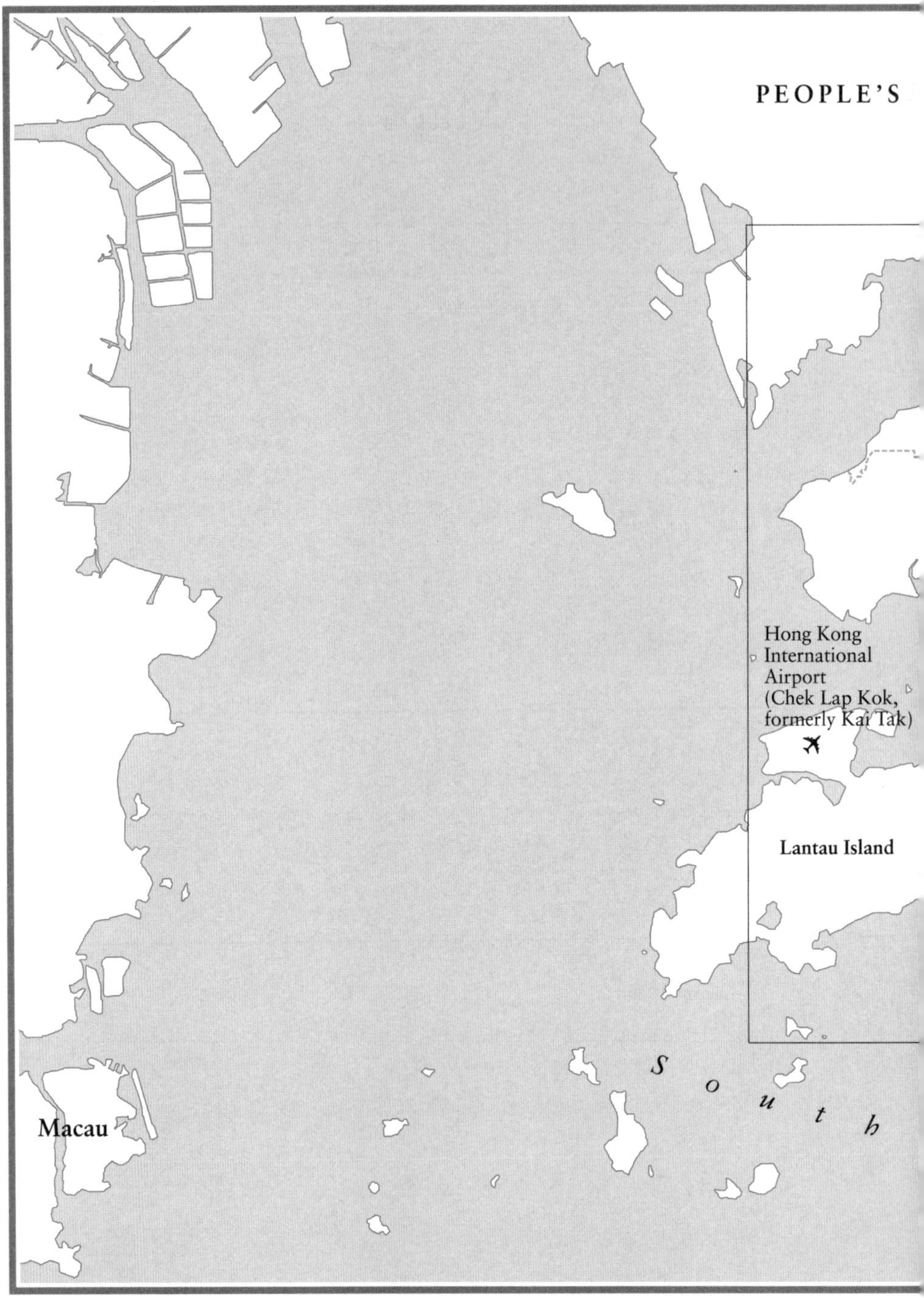
PEOPLE'S
Hong Kong
International
Airport
(Chek Lap Kok,
formerly Kai Tak)
Lantau Island
S o u t h
Macau

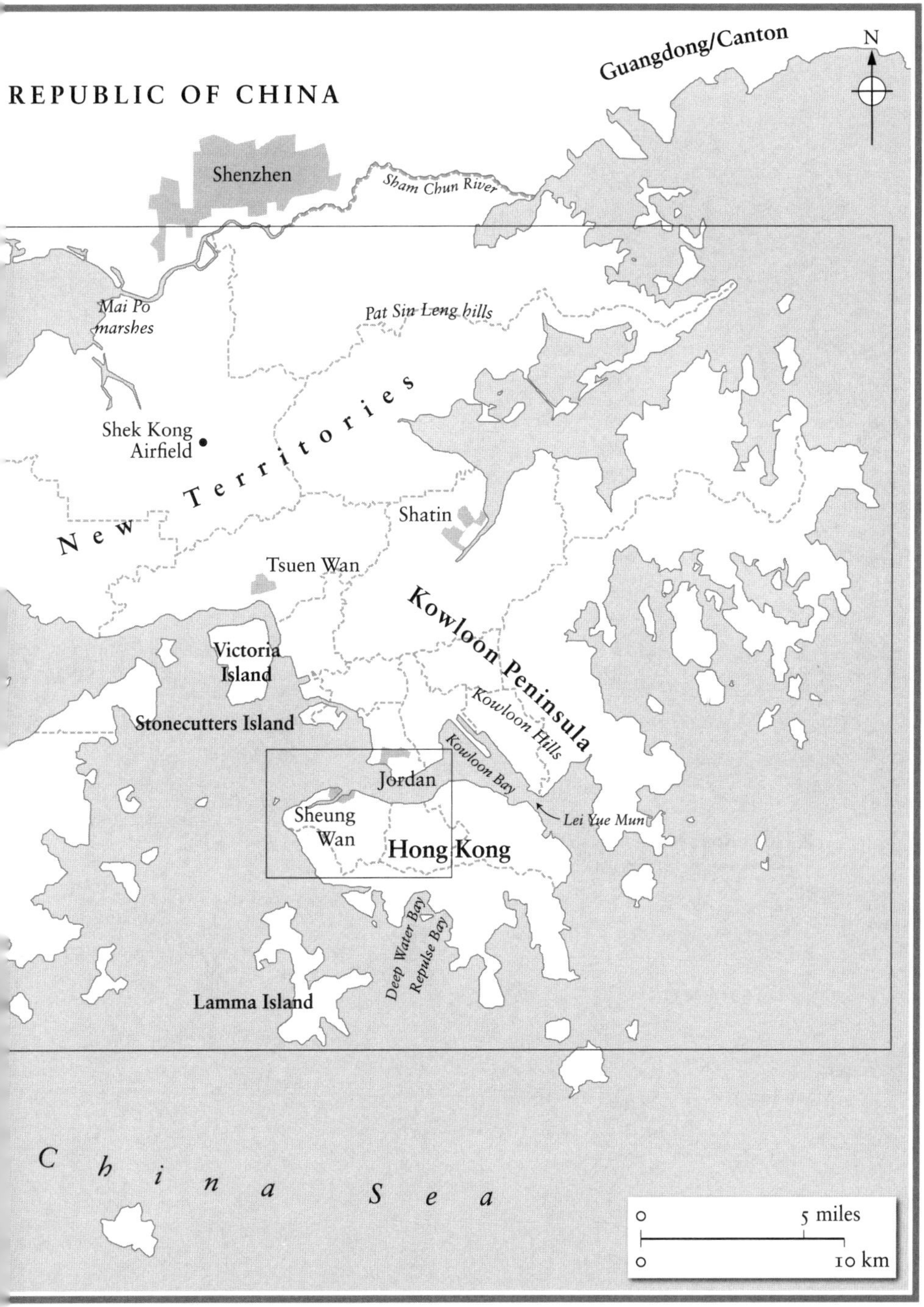
REPUBLIC OF CHINA
Guangdong/Canton
N
Shenzhen
Sham Chun River
Mai Po marshes
Pat Sin Leng hills
Shek Kong Airfield
New Territories
Shatin
Tsuen Wan
Kowloon Peninsula
Victoria Island
Stonecutters Island
Kowloon Hills
Kowloon Bay
Jordan
Lei Yue Mun
Sheung Wan
Hong Kong
Deep Water Bay
Repulse Bay
Lamma Island
China Sea
0 5 miles
0 10 km

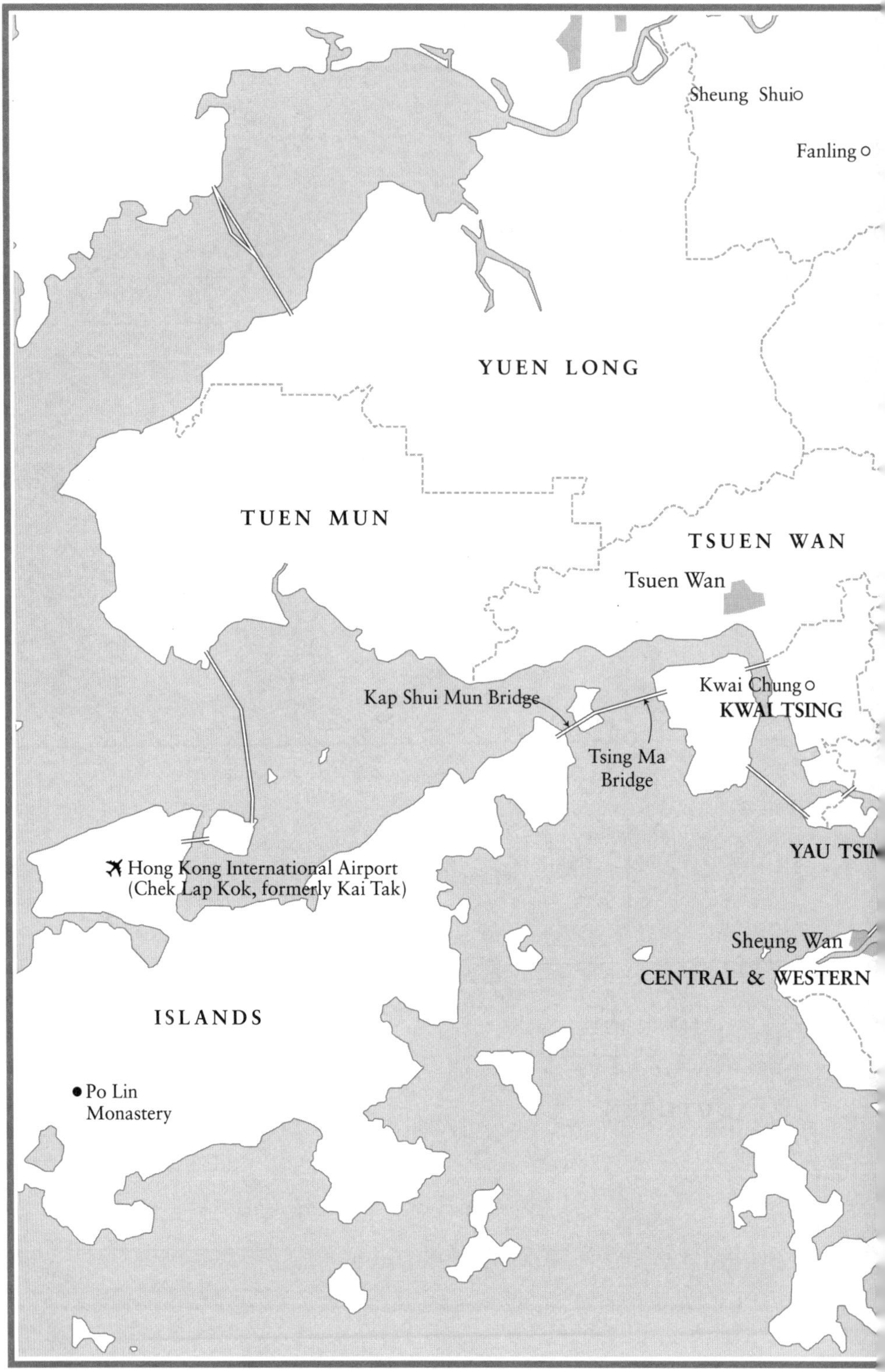
Sheung Shui
Fanling
YUEN LONG
TUEN MUN
TSUEN WAN
Tsuen Wan
Kwai Chung
KWAI TSING
Kap Shui Mun Bridge
Tsing Ma
Bridge
YAU TSIM
Hong Kong International Airport
(Chek Lap Kok, formerly Kai Tak)
Sheung Wan
CENTRAL & WESTERN
ISLANDS
Po Lin
Monastery

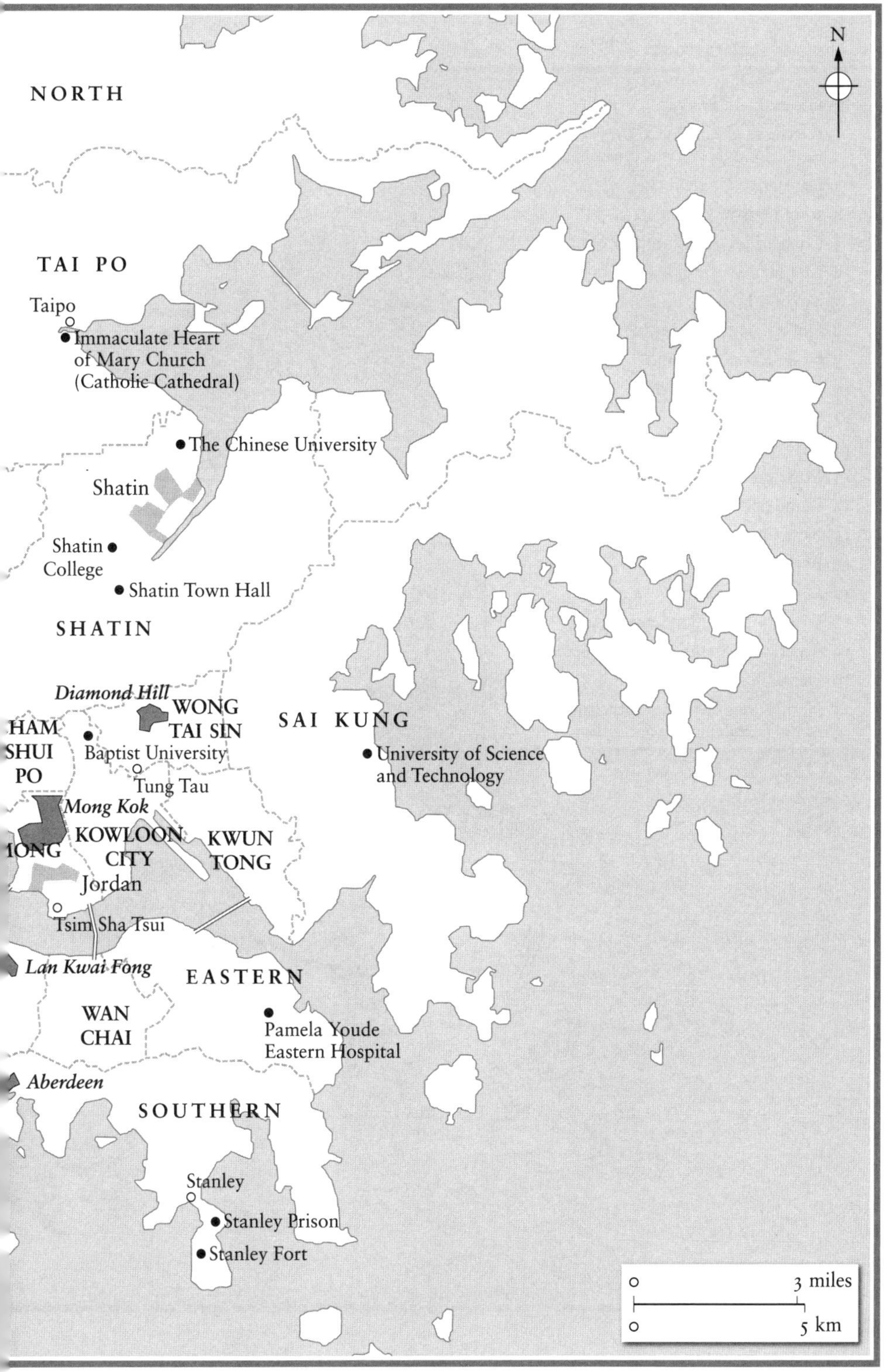
N
NORTH
TAI PO
Taipo
Immaculate Heart of Mary Church (Catholic Cathedral)
The Chinese University
Shatin
Shatin College
Shatin Town Hall
SHATIN
Diamond Hill
WONG TAI SIN
HAM SHUI PO
Baptist University
Tung Tau
SAI KUNG
University of Science and Technology
Mong Kok
KOWLOON CITY
KWUN TONG
Jordan
Tsim Sha Tsui
Lan Kwai Fong
EASTERN
WAN CHAI
Pamela Youde Eastern Hospital
Aberdeen
SOUTHERN
Stanley
Stanley Prison
Stanley Fort
0 3 miles
0 5 km

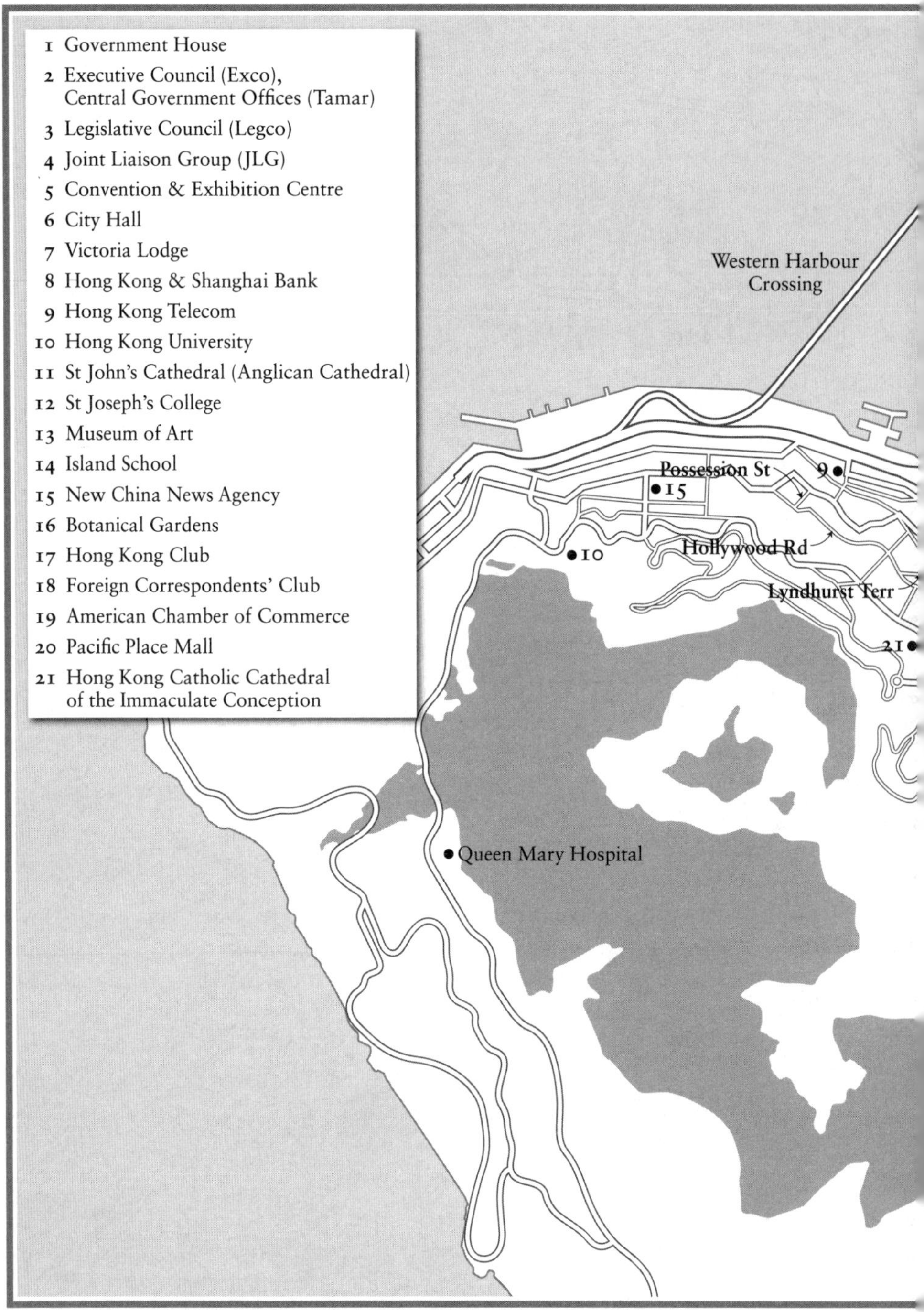
1 Government House
2 Executive Council (Exco), Central Government Offices (Tamar)
3 Legislative Council (Legco)
4 Joint Liaison Group (JLG)
5 Convention & Exhibition Centre
6 City Hall
7 Victoria Lodge
8 Hong Kong & Shanghai Bank
9 Hong Kong Telecom
10 Hong Kong University
11 St John's Cathedral (Anglican Cathedral)
12 St Joseph's College
13 Museum of Art
14 Island School
15 New China News Agency
16 Botanical Gardens
17 Hong Kong Club
18 Foreign Correspondents' Club
19 American Chamber of Commerce
20 Pacific Place Mall
21 Hong Kong Catholic Cathedral of the Immaculate Conception
Western Harbour Crossing
Possession St
9
15
Hollywood Rd
10
Lyndhurst Terr
21
Queen Mary Hospital

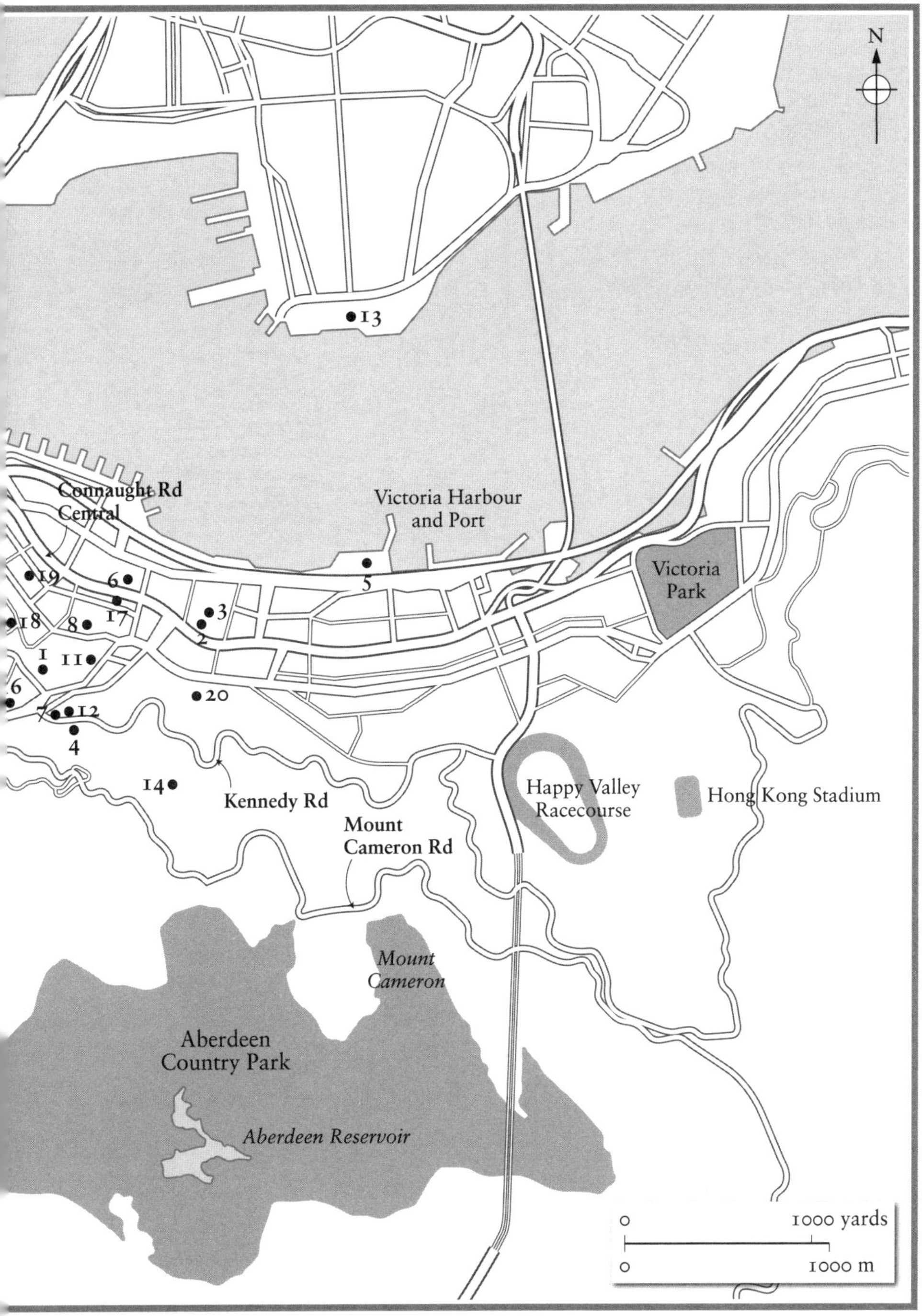
N
13
Connaught Rd Central
Victoria Harbour and Port
5
19
6
18
8
17
3
2
1
11
6
20
7
12
4
14
Kennedy Rd
Mount Cameron Rd
Victoria Park
Happy Valley Racecourse
Hong Kong Stadium
Mount Cameron
Aberdeen Country Park
Aberdeen Reservoir
0
1000 yards
0
1000 m

List of Illustrations

Every effort has been made to contact all copyright holders. The publisher will be pleased to amend in future printings any errors or omissions brought to their attention. Numbers refer to plates.

All other photographs are from the collection of the author and the Patten family.

Foreword

As one of Britain's and America's leading historians, Simon Schama, contends, 'History is an argument.' The pity is that it is an argument that too often reflects attitudes and even prejudices already held rather than a balanced scrutiny of evidence and narrative. This is even more so when our interpretation of the past has critical significance for the present. The story of Hong Kong, where I spent five years as the last British Governor, has some bearing on a contemporary argument about Empire which carries the battle scars of preconceptions and facile generalizations. No one today (as I said in my farewell speech in Hong Kong on 30 June 1997) would seek to justify imperialism – though even as I write these words, I think of the narrative that communist China weaves around its repressive rule in Xinjiang and Tibet. More relevant now is not whether we can justify colonial rule, applying contemporary values to past millennia, or even enumerate some of its benign consequences, but how and why empires have been assembled. Britain's Empire is widely believed to have ended formally with our handover of the Hong Kong colony (or 'territory' as we liked to call it, covering our embarrassment at the use of the other word) to China, a quarter of a century ago. What created it?

The 19th-century liberal historian and defender of imperialism Sir John Seeley famously remarked that 'the British Empire was acquired in a fit of absence of mind', mostly a result of mistakes, accidents and unintended consequences and the reactions to them. This was the opinion too of Jan Morris, who not only wrote a masterly history of Empire but also the best descriptive book on Hong Kong. Looking at the history of this colony, it certainly bears out her argument that imperial history was 'all bits and pieces'. But the 'bits and pieces' on the southern China shore, just south of the Tropic of Cancer and close to the Pearl River Delta, were very different to those that were assembled into Empire elsewhere.

The archipelago south of the Kowloon Hills – peninsula, islands, rocks and 'fragrant Harbour' – was the territorial booty of a war fought with the declining Qing Empire to allow the British trading houses (forerunners of the famous hongs) based in Macau and Guangzhou to sell the opium produced in India into China at will. The expenses of the Raj were to be partly allayed by drugs sold and consumed in China, a great civilization no longer able to halt this pernicious example of globalization by requiring the Western barbarians to 'tremble and obey'. Gunboat diplomacy in the early 1840s ended with China's defeat and the grant of spoils in the Treaty of Nanjing of 1842. Britain's man on the spot, Captain Charles Elliot, the chief superintendent of trade in China, extracted as a prize for this naval bullying what seemed to many, including Britain's Foreign Secretary, Lord Palmerston, the inadequate pickings of a harbour, some islands and a lot of rocks. Disappointment at the modest scale of the plunder perhaps contributed to Captain Elliot's subsequent appointment as chargé d'affaires in the newly created Republic of Texas, later capped by his governorship of St Helena.

Victory in a second opium war led to a further grant of land, the tip of the Kowloon Peninsula across the harbour from Victoria Island, which was to become the heart of the territory. But the real settlement of Hong Kong's destiny was still to come. At the tail end of the century, joining with other imperial powers – Japan, Germany, Russia, Portugal, France – in seizing desirable chunks of China from the increasingly enfeebled Qing dynasty, Britain took, not with sovereignty but on a long lease, the hinterland to the north of the harbour and islands. Beyond Kowloon, the so-called New Territories were acquired on a lease for 99 years. In 1898, when the lease was agreed, who would have imagined the day when it would terminate? But the days, months, years went by; the pages of the calendar turned and yellowed. Hong Kong's history was lived in the growing shadow of its finite destiny: never to stand on its own feet but to return on 30 June 1997 to the embrace of the motherland.

The government of this motherland twisted and turned from rule by a Qing Emperor to attempts at democracy, from warlords to civil war, from Japanese invaders to war between nationalist Kuomintang and communist revolutionaries, and finally to Leninist totalitarianism which at one time seemed to thaw before it froze again. This is the implacable reality that always confronted Hong Kong, changed though it was from rocks and harbour to a great international commercial hub. It was never to become an independent city state but must always remain a city in China trying to make its peace with whatever and whoever held sway in Beijing and beyond.

As the clock ticked on, some were to argue that Britain could legally hold on to the land which it had been granted and simply give back what was held on a lease. But, as Hong Kong grew, this was never actually an option. The burgeoning city needed the water, the land, the space and the agriculture of the New Territories, where in time seven new cities were built. Moreover, the price that Britain would pay in terms of international opprobrium would have been too high: it would have been an apparent reprise of those 'unequal treaties' of the 19th century. China could always squeeze the city at will or take it by force if it was so minded, and the only bunkers in Hong Kong were on the golf courses. Yet so long as Hong Kong thrived, so long as it was a valuable conduit for money, goods and expertise from the outside world into China and in the other direction, it was permitted to continue. This was true during the Korean War, in the grim days of Maoist economics and on to the days that saw the steady reconnection of China to the world under Deng Xiaoping and later.

Hong Kong's development, especially after the Second World War, saw the growth of an educated Chinese middle class, the usually successful competition from Chinese entrepreneurs for the old British masters of the China trade, and a growing and healthy population with its own increasingly explicit notion of citizenship. Without the ticking clock, all this would have pointed in one direction. Like virtually every other British colony, as the imperial appetite and capacity faded, Hong Kong would be prepared with all the hardware and software of British political and constitutional practice for independence: the rule of law, an independent judiciary, a politically neutral civil service and a democratically elected government. In preparation for independent self-determination, politicians would be elected by the citizens of the new country which had taken control of itself and would be charged with the accountable responsibility of running it. The fact that this was never to be Hong Kong's destiny gave the communist regime in Beijing a powerful argument, one actually accepted with some relief by Britain and by those in the colony who feared the establishment in Hong Kong of even the first stages of democratization. Begin to give Hong Kong the democratic institutions put in place in other colonies, Beijing's communist rulers said, and Hong Kong would start to think that sooner or later it was to become like Singapore or Malaysia, an independent state. That was something Beijing could never contemplate.

Such Chinese constraint was perhaps not, as I say, unwelcome to the British government or to the British business community in Hong Kong. A Governor who flirted with ideas of democracy, shortly after the Second World War, was given short shrift. The reasons for this attitude weakened as the years passed. In the 1940s and '50s there were worries that the battle between the Kuomintang and the communists might simply be played out in Hong Kong's own political arena. Then there were the anxieties about the violent politics of Chinese communists during and after the Cultural Revolution transferring to the colony. There were always patronizing assumptions that people in Hong Kong were not interested in politics but only in making money. These were undoubtedly infused with the anxiety that democratic politics would inevitably lead to more welfare spending, more government interference and regulation, and even (perish the thought) higher taxes than Hong Kong's rock bottom imposts. Would it be remotely possible to run one of the freest and most open economies in the world if elected politicians could interfere with the free flow of market forces? Yet as education did its benign work; as men and women joined professions and studied at universities the works of Karl Popper and other advocates of open societies; as the community read in its newspapers and saw on its televisions what was happening in South Korea and Taiwan and all around the world; and as the people of Hong Kong were encouraged to take their own economic decisions; as all this happened, it became difficult to argue that they should be denied any say in the biggest issues affecting their lives. Then they had the disagreeable and very worrying experience, while listening to the ticking clock, of wondering what the corpses in and around Tiananmen Square in 1989 told them about their imminent future. Their demands were surprising for their moderation; their behaviour astonishing for its restraint. What was to happen to them?

It had seemed in the mid-1980s that a foundation had not only been discovered for their future well-being, but a formula too which could provide assurance and satisfaction all round. When Britain began to negotiate with Beijing about Hong Kong's future after 1997, Deng Xiaoping made a proposal already offered to Taiwan to encourage its reunification with mainland China. The mantra which encompassed it was 'one country, two systems'. At the end of the lease, Hong Kong would become once again a part of China under Chinese sovereignty. Yet it would be allowed to retain a high degree of autonomy, in all areas except foreign policy and defence, and would be allowed to preserve its existing way of life and the manner in which it ran its affairs: capitalism, private ownership, the rule of law, the freedoms associated with an open society (the press, assembly, religion, enquiry), a politically neutral civil service, and the accountability of government to the legislature. And so it came to pass: all this was set out very clearly in an international treaty between China and Britain. The Sino-British Joint Declaration was lodged at the United Nations in 1985 and its principal promises were turned into a constitution for Hong Kong: 160 articles and three annexes were drafted by China with the input of some Hong Kong citizens, which was called the Basic Law.

The genius of this formula was that it accommodated the political and moral embarrassment of both the British and Chinese sides and it did so, moreover, in a fashion that appeared to satisfy the citizens of Hong Kong, who, unlike those in other colonies, were not actually going to be given their independence. The embarrassment for Britain was moral because of precisely this point, and political because we could not help being reminded of the circumstances in which Hong Kong – albeit now a flourishing international city – had been acquired. The political embarrassment was for China partly this reminder of the years of the so-called (not unreasonably) 'unequal treaties', but also the knowledge (which must have given pause for thought to all but the most ignorant and ideologically hidebound communists) that the large majority of Hong Kong citizens were themselves refugees from the brutalities of modern communist history.

Alongside the ticking clock, the fact that Hong Kong is a refugee community is the second most significant of its defining characteristics. The population of Hong Kong, which was 5.8 million when I arrived in 1992, has been drawn from all around the world – from Iraq, South Asia, the United States, Australia, Canada, New Zealand, Japan, Britain and other European countries. You can check this global personality by ticking off any list of international schools in the city. However, apart from the descendants of a tiny indigenous number of people, the population is above all drawn from elsewhere in China. First-, second- and third-generation refugees were the relatives of those who fought for the Kuomintang and of the business leaders who fled from Shanghai after the communist takeover in 1949, bringing industries such as garments and watchmaking to this British colony. They were from families who swam, stowed away on ships and clambered over razor wire to get away from the persecution of landowners, from the Great Leap Forward, from the starvation (even cannibalism) of the great famine and its tombstone politics, from the ubiquitous horrors and brutalities of modern Chinese crackdowns on any dissent. The flow of immigrants to this redoubt of British imperialist oppression in the 1970s was so great that the authorities introduced a 'touch base' policy. If you could get across the border, reach an urban area and find a relative there, you could have a Hong Kong identity card. These were the people who had been told that if they were to love China they must also make clear that they loved the Communist Party; the lethal consubstantiality of Chinese Leninist theology.

So here was a city of refugees with an end date to its certainties, with promises about its future, but no say in what that future should be, and with a usually well-meaning government – albeit one whose colonial masters in London often gave the impression that they thought it was a distraction from the greater game of Sino-British trade and global partnership in solving the more important problems of the day. A pebble in the shoe. But there is one other inescapable reality about this extraordinary place, this imperial oddball. In a real sense it was made by China – by the totalitarianism that drove so many of its business class from Shanghai, which drove wave after wave of refugees to its Archipelago and Islands, to its slums, temporary housing areas and before too long its high-rise blocks of flats, and to its sampans and dragon boat races, and its common law courts and its liberties, and a police force that used to be called 'Asia's finest'. That was then. These are the people who having fled communist China then helped in the extraordinary opening up of China to the world's marketplace, to assist in China's real and so far sustained great leap forward. And their reward? That same communist China is now set on demolishing their way of life and their freedom, stone by stone and broken promise by broken promise.

The outrage and the arguments around the world that this has provoked encouraged me to publish this diary, which I kept while I was Governor of Hong Kong from 1992 to 1997; perhaps this account of my experiences is now worth putting on the public record. I have added at the end of this foreword a short note listing the main institutions and arrangements that provided the infrastructure of official life in Hong Kong. At the end of the diary I have added a brief cast list of those principally involved in running Hong Kong and policy concerning the handover of Hong Kong in both London and Beijing, and finally a short essay giving a brief account of recent events in what has turned out to be the demolition of a free society.

I have not used any material from government archives, neither those kept at Kew nor those which reside separately with other colonial papers. Nor have I used any private correspondence. I have from time to time borrowed the description of events from the meticulously kept diary of my wife, Lavender, and occasionally have cross-checked dates and events with her accounts. We both intend to give our original diaries – in my own case principally the transcription of tape recordings and the large exercise books in which I wrote down every evening what was happening during the last part of my governorship – to the Bodleian Library in Oxford and ask that they should be made available, warts and all, to scholars who wish to read them. In some places the text has been reformulated for publication and to cope with the reduction of the total day-by-day diary by several hundred thousand words. I have not excised passages where occasionally my frustration may, with hindsight, have got the better of me, since they are a true reflection of the tensions that from time to time surfaced as we navigated an unprecedented series of events. But looking back now there is nothing material that I would have done differently. My only self-censorship has been to avoid the use of names from time to time, particularly those of people who are still in Hong Kong and might suffer because of the brutal and authoritarian communist regime which now holds a city I love in its handcuffs.

What, When, Who, How?

What was to become the heart of Hong Kong, the harbour and main island (Victoria), was ceded to Britain in the Treaty of Nanjing of 1842, which ended the First Opium War. The southern part of the Kowloon Peninsula and Stonecutters Island were later ceded to Britain in 1860 in the Convention of Peking at the conclusion of the Second Opium War. The so-called New Territories, covering more than 85 per cent of Hong Kong's land mass, stretching from Kowloon to the China border on the Sham Chun River and including most of the outlying islands, were leased to Britain for 99 years in the Second Convention of Peking, signed in 1898. This was part of the carve-up of China by colonial powers which followed China's defeat in the First Sino–Japanese War.

The return to China of the ceded and leased territories of Hong Kong was negotiated in the Sino-British Joint Declaration (JD), signed in 1984 by the Chinese Premier, Zhao Ziyang, and the UK Prime Minister, Margaret Thatcher. It was ratified and lodged at the UN in the following year.

The Basic Law (BL) is a Chinese national law adopted by the National People's Congress in 1990 in order to implement the Joint Declaration. Some Hong Kong citizens gave advice in the drafting of the law, which came into effect on 1 July 1997 as the de facto constitution of Hong Kong.

Until 1997, Hong Kong was run by a Governor, appointed by and responsible to the government and Parliament of the United Kingdom. There were 28 governors of Hong Kong in all. I was the last, from 1992 to 1997. After 1997 the Governor's role was taken by a Chief Executive.

The Hong Kong government was run by a mixture of expatriate and local Chinese civil servants. By 1997 all these senior civil servants were Hong Kong Chinese except for the Attorney General. The Chief Justice (CJ) was also Hong Kong Chinese. The senior member of the government under the Governor was the Chief Secretary (CS). The Financial Secretary (FS) was in charge of financial and economic affairs. The secretaries of individual government departments acting under the Governor and the Chief

Secretary were more like ministers than British permanent secretaries. The garrison was commanded by the Commander British Forces (CBF).

The Governor was advised by an Executive Council (Exco), which he appointed, and was broadly representative of (mostly) establishment opinion in the community. There were usually between a dozen and 16 members of Exco, for example 16 in 1992 became 13 in 1993. By the 1990s the Legislature Council (Legco) included both elected and appointed members. The Basic Law laid down that there should be 60 members on the council, 20 elected from geographical constituencies through direct elections, 10 returned by an election committee, and 30 elected by functional constituencies. The Bill of Rights was enacted by Legco in 1991 to incorporate the provisions of the International Covenant on Civil and Political Rights into Hong Kong law before the handover.

The Governor had his office and home in Government House (GH). He had a private office of civil servants, a spokesman, two personal advisers brought from Britain and an ADC, as well as bodyguards drawn from the Royal Hong Kong Police Force. He also had a Central Policy Unit (CPU). There was a housekeeper who ran Government House, and the Governor's wife had a social secretary. At weekends there was a house at Fanling, quite close to the border, for the Governor's use.

As Governor, I discussed most big decisions, especially concerning China and transitional issues involving the change of sovereignty, with a group which was called for prosaic reasons the Ad Hoc Group. This typically would include the Chief Secretary, the Financial Secretary, relevant heads of Hong Kong government departments, my Foreign Office (FCO) political adviser and his deputy, the head of the CPU, my spokesman and the senior team from the Joint Liaison Group (JLG). The JLG was set up under the Joint Declaration to consult on its implementation , to discuss issues related to the smooth transfer of government in 1997, and to exchange information and have consultations on subjects agreed by both sides. The British side was led by an FCO official of ambassadorial rank and there was a similar team on the Chinese side. The JLG was where most of the spade work was done regarding the transition , on the British side by an outstanding team of very hard-working and superhumanly patient officials.

We had regular contact with the British Embassy in Beijing and were supported by the Hong Kong department in London, which worked under the senior diplomats responsible for policy on China and East Asia. They, in turn, worked to a minister of state and the Foreign Secretary himself. The Governor was required to take major decisions with the advice and agreement of the Prime Minister and senior ministers , especially the Foreign Secretary.

On the Chinese side there was an office called the Hong Kong and Macau Affairs Office (HKMAO), whose responsibilities were as the title describes. The Chinese Foreign Ministry would also intervene directly from time to time with the FCO. Within Hong Kong the primary coordinator of United Front (that is, pro-Chinese communist) activity was the New China News Agency (NCNA), which also acted frequently as a spokesman for the Chinese Communist Party on Hong Kong matters. Its head was a not very diplomatic diplomat. The Hang Seng index was a benchmark for the principal stocks traded on the Hong Kong stock exchange. It was clearly sometimes manipulated by politically well-informed Chinese investors and mainland companies.

Many UN members had Consulates-General or the equivalent in Hong Kong, since it was frequently a larger trade partner for their countries than most sovereign states. A regular feature of the weekly life of the Governor and his wife was attendance at national-day celebrations, where an observant Governor would be able to acquire an encyclopaedic knowledge of national flags. Dogs were not a traditional part of the Governor's entourage, but Lavender and I introduced them, as readers will see.

Democracy and the Dragon: April 1992–April 1993

Friday 10 April

I woke up after about four hours' sleep to the *Today* programme. Predictable headlines. Major wins surprising victory, party chairman loses seat. I don't feel particularly depressed by what has happened. That's partly because while I predicted that John* would win the general election – I told him this last Monday – I also thought it was inevitable that I would lose my own seat because of tactical voting by Labour. When I also told John this, he thought I was simply being characteristically pessimistic. My relatively sanguine feelings are also in part the result of the unsavoury and unpleasant behaviour of the crowd outside Bath's Guildhall when the result was announced. I think I would have felt worse if my opponents had behaved better. For millions of viewers the resulting pictures were obviously pretty disturbing. It all left a nasty taste in the mouth and must have been an awful shock for Laura and Alice, who were in Bath at our headquarters, and for Kate, who heard all this on the World Service in Latin America. They were all upset. But as Nelson Polsby, our American friend from Berkeley, said on the telephone earlier today – 'Why are you worried that your kids are concerned about you? Most parents don't have kids who care that much. You shouldn't be worried. You should be grateful.'

The nasty stuff was much worse for Lavender and Freda.† While I was trying to run the national campaign for at least part of each day, Lavender had fought the whole election on the ground in Bath with Freda and three marvellous young helpers, including Magnus Goodlad, the very engaging

* John Major was Prime Minister and leader of the Conservative Party from 1990 to 1997.

† Freda Evans had been my parliamentary constituency secretary for two full terms and had worked tirelessly in and for the constituency. She was also heavily involved in voluntary work: for example, Crisis at Christmas. After my defeat, she worked full-time for voluntary organizations, particularly in the housing field, and then trained to be ordained in the Church of England. She became a parish priest in Birmingham working in a succession of parishes, most of them in socially disadvantaged areas.

son of Alastair.* She threw herself into it and found the insults of Liberal black propaganda on the doorstep about my allegedly inadequate performance difficult to sometimes take. One of the myths in politics is that the Liberals are always the nice guys. In reality they sometimes fight the dirtiest campaigns, much dirtier than Labour or my lot. I guess this is likely to be the end of my political career at Westminster, but I was buoyed up on my return to London in the early hours of this morning with a sort of Roman triumph in Smith Square. Lavender had none of that to ease the pain and disappointment. She is immensely brave and has dealt marvellously well with all the bitterness of defeat. She is incredibly resilient, but that shouldn't make one underestimate how rough it's been for her. I don't think that I could put her through anything like this again. Maybe I should have taken the advice to switch to another constituency like Westbury when it was suggested (even offered). But I couldn't face the prospect of confronting my party workers with what would seem like an admission of defeat. They have been so loyal to me and I think I owed it to them to be loyal in return. Even some of my friends seemed to suggest that this shows that I'm not really professional about my political career – 'career' that was, I suppose.

Anyway, since I got back to London at some God-forsaken hour yesterday evening, John has been immensely kind and generous. He kept on referring to his gloom at winning the election while I lost my own seat. No one could have been more considerate or more thoughtful. In among all the shouting and boozing and cheering, he took me into the little office next to my own in Smith Square where my political adviser used to work. He wanted straight away to run through some of the options for me. He mentioned the possibility of fighting a by-election, going to the House of Lords, continuing as party chairman without a seat in the Commons, or searching for a career in business and trying to get back into the Commons as soon as possible. But we agreed not to take things further that night. I slept on the options, insofar as I slept at all.

So on the morning of the unexpected (to some) Conservative victory and my own rather humiliating defeat, I walked over to Downing Street from our flat next to Westminster Cathedral. I went through St James's Park, which is always good for morale, and climbed the steps into Downing Street getting a very demonstrative salute from the policeman on duty.

* Alastair and I had been friends for years, first meeting when we were both at university. He entered the House of Commons six years before me and became a minister in a variety of departments, at this time in the Foreign Office. Magnus was the older of two brothers. We had gone on holiday with his family from time to time so knew him very well. After university he had become a successful organizer of venture capital businesses.

John and I met on our own in his study. We talked first of all about the Cabinet and ministerial appointments. He said that he had wanted to make me Chancellor of the Exchequer. I am at least spared that torture, especially given the difficult position that the economy is in. He then ran through all the options that faced me, adding the possibility of the governorship of Hong Kong. Almost the moment that he mentioned it, this seemed to me the best and most exciting of all the possible choices. We had briefly discussed candidates for this job before the election and I could remember thinking then that it would be a terrific challenge, and that in other circumstances I would have found it exceptionally attractive. Going through the other possibilities, he began with a ministerial job in the House of Lords, either departmental or as a sort of deputy and progress chaser for him. I don't think that it is possible to run a major department from the House of Lords – either, for example, the Ministry of Defence or possibly following Douglas Hurd* in due course at the Foreign Office. Having seen the difficulties that confronted my former boss, Peter Carrington,† during the Falklands affair, it seemed to me that it just wasn't possible to pursue a career in the long term at the centre of politics from the upper house. A by-election seems even more inappropriate. It would be both unseemly and reckless.

Saturday 11 and Sunday 12 April

Lots of speculation about my future, most of it well-meaning but without much reference to my own views. Some in the government, for example Tristan Garel-Jones,‡ are already suggesting that Nick Scott should resign from his seat in Chelsea and that I should be parachuted into the

* Douglas Hurd had been Secretary of State for Northern Ireland, where I worked for him as a junior minister, Home Secretary and since 1989 Foreign Secretary. I had supported his campaign to become leader of the Conservative Party in 1990, when John Major won.

† Lord Carrington was chairman of the Conservative party from 1972 to 1974 when I worked for him as his political secretary. He was Foreign Secretary from 1979 to 1982 and Secretary General of NATO from 1984 to 1988. He was the best man I ever worked for.

‡ Tristan Garel-Jones had been a friend ever since we were both parliamentary candidates. After school he had joined his parents in Spain, where he had helped to run their business in Madrid. He was married to a Spaniard, Catali, and they had five children; their youngest – Victoria, the only girl – was my goddaughter. Tristan became MP for Watford at the 1979 general election. He was a very successful member of the Conservative whips' office for many years and was minister of state for Europe from 1990 to 1993. He was my closest friend (though unlike me a teetotaller), widely read, a good linguist and a passionate pro-European. He was wise and full of guile but never duplicitous, and unlike most politicians devoid of most obvious ambition. There was hardly a week when I didn't speak to him, wherever I was in the world, on at least a couple of occasions. He became a member of the House of Lords in 1997, which for a variety of fairly mysterious reasons he loved. He sometimes seemed almost as happy in the precincts of Westminster as in his

constituency. This would be an exceptionally hazardous enterprise. What is a 'safe' constituency in these circumstances? I could easily be turned into the Patrick Gordon Walker* of Conservative politics. But above all I am wholly opposed to putting Lavender and the family through hell once again. As for trying to collect directorships and waiting for something to turn up, there is a real danger of me turning into a political wallflower – waiting for the next dance and then, when I'm finally made an offer, tripping over or treading on the constituency's toes.

These are many negative reasons for feeling positive about Hong Kong. But there are other far better arguments as well. Hong Kong seems to be a proper job, probably impossible to do to the applause of the world but nevertheless an honourable enterprise. Lavender said when we discussed it, 'if you don't do it, you will probably spend the rest of your life regretting it'. But if I were to do it, it would be Lavender who would have to make the biggest sacrifice.†

For myself, I am immensely excited by the prospect of being a hands-on mayor of Hong Kong, as well as dealing with the difficult diplomatic relationship with China in what would be a historic mission as Britain's last major colonial Governor. Add to that, I know from my work as Minister for Development that the Asian and Pacific rim is where so much of the action is going to be for the next generation and longer. It would be a difficult job, but I think it is important to show the world that we can handle this last imperial responsibility in a decent way and which doesn't betray the people of Hong Kong.

When I came out of No. 10 on Friday and Saturday mornings, John very generously steered me into the waiting crowd with him, trying to ensure that I shared in his huge personal success. And this is what it had been. He had not rushed to the polls at the end of the Gulf War to fight a jingoistic campaign, as he could have done and as many had advised him

home in Extremadura looking up at the mountains. He smoked himself to death, fully aware of what he was doing. He died in 2020. I still miss him.

* Gordon Walker was a Labour politician who lost his Smethwick parliamentary seat in 1964 in a nasty racial campaign at the time when he was his party's foreign affairs spokesman. He was nevertheless made Foreign Secretary by Harold Wilson, and then fought and lost a by-election in Leyton. He won Leyton in the following general election and became a Cabinet minister again.

† After reading law at Oxford, Lavender had qualified as a barrister but had not practised while bringing up our family. When our youngest, Alice, was almost into secondary school, she got a place in a Chambers where they principally practised family law. Lavender had been successfully building her practice, which she would have to walk away from if we were to go to Hong Kong. Nevertheless, she was prepared to make the sacrifice, recognizing what a big opportunity it was for me with quite a large role for her as well.

to do. He had actually gone to the country when we were still in recession with very few glimpses of light at the end of the tunnel. Conservative MPs owe him a great deal. What are the chances of them showing it?

Monday 13 April

Douglas and Judy Hurd invited us to supper after a weekend of Cabinet-making during which a number of my friends spent a good deal of time on the telephone worrying about what they might be offered and taking my advice on what they might accept. I began all these conversations saying politely that it might not be very helpful for me to talk about other people's jobs when I hadn't got one myself! Although he set out all the good reasons for going to Hong Kong, Douglas leaned over backwards to make clear that the Prime Minister obviously hoped I would stay in the UK. Douglas added that in ideal circumstances he would have liked me to follow him at the Foreign Office. But he also admitted that the governorship of Hong Kong was much more interesting than most of the jobs available in British politics.

Tuesday 14 April

News of the possibility of my going to Hong Kong has leaked, I suspect because one or two of my friends have been so noisily advocating my remaining in British politics. The story has rapidly turned into the suggestion that a short break that Lavender and I are planning to take with Alice in France over the Easter weekend is intended to be my time to reflect on whether or not to head east. Truth to tell, Lavender and I have pretty well made up our minds already.

Thursday 16 April

In the business class lounge at Gatwick airport on our way to Toulouse, we encountered Christopher Bland* and his wife. They were taking David Owen†, John Birt‡ and their wives for a weekend at the Blands' French home. It was an amusing encounter. David Owen's name has been mentioned in connection with the governorship of Hong Kong. In fact, in public and in private, he has been extremely positive about my suitability for the job. But at Gatwick we both fenced very courteously over the subject.

* Sir Christopher Bland was a British businessman perhaps best known for his period as chairman of the BBC from 1996 to 2001. He was also a good novelist.

† David Owen was the Foreign Secretary in Jim Callaghan's government from 1977 to 1979 and one of the founding members of the Social Democratic Party.

‡ John Birt was a television executive who became director-general of the BBC from 1992 to 2000.

Christopher and John thought that I should not take it. I would be bored. There was nothing left to do. Even David wondered whether I would get bored very quickly.

Friday 17–Tuesday 21 April
We had a marvellous Easter weekend in France, staying east of Albi. I wrote a letter to the Prime Minister to say that I would like to go to Hong Kong, which I sent immediately on my return, and then talked to him on the phone in Huntingdon. He was understanding. I felt a bit guilty about leaving him and the government. But, as Lavender said, I wasn't really to blame! The truth is that I am at the heart of a great irony in which the Governor of Hong Kong has been chosen by the electors of Bath, principally by Labour voters who decided for perhaps the first time in their lives – maybe the last – to vote Liberal.

The weeks until my departure for Hong Kong were crowded with meetings, lunches, dinners and briefings. At the end of June I summarized them and reflected on some of the main questions about the job ahead:

After I had spoken to John on my return from France, his private secretary, Andrew Turnbull, came on the phone to point out that I hadn't discussed with the Prime Minister what honour I wanted to take with me to Hong Kong. I told him that all I had been was a politician and I had what amounted to my house colours – that is, I had been made a privy counsellor. I didn't feel the need to take anything else but added that if anyone thought that there were likely to be riots in Hong Kong as the result of my not becoming a KCMG or something similar, I would of course be happy to reconsider the point. That was the last I heard of honours. I had to engage in some fancy footwork about not wearing the usual gubernatorial uniform, in which I was greatly helped when it came to this issue by the Foreign Office deputy secretary responsible among other matters for Hong Kong, John Coles.* He thought there was a case for not wearing the uniform, and the permanent secretary was happy to agree. The Palace – particularly Robert Fellowes† and Sue Hussey‡ – was

* John Coles had been ambassador in Jordan and High Commissioner in Australia and was to become from 1994 to 1997 the permanent secretary in the Foreign and Commonwealth Office.
† Robert Fellowes, later to become a member of the House of Lords, was the private secretary to Queen Elizabeth II from 1990 to 1999.
‡ Lady Susan Hussey has been for many years a woman of the bedchamber to Queen Elizabeth II. She is the widow of Marmaduke Hussey, who was for a time chairman of the

very understanding and so we disposed of the hat, plumes and all that nonsense. It must be more difficult to talk about openness and democracy if you're wearing feathers in your hat. I must also admit that this isn't just a consequence of a democratic instinct but plain vanity. Given my general shape I'd look pretty ridiculous in the sort of outfit which, to carry it off, needs rather more height and less bulk than I have.

There were 10 weeks between my appointment and departure for Singapore, and on from there to Hong Kong, to take up my duties on 5 July. I have still had to act as party chairman until Norman Fowler* takes over the job later in the summer. But I have spent most of my time in a small room at the Foreign Office crunching through briefing papers and meeting some of the diplomats who have been working on the Hong Kong handover to China. I have had an excellent temporary private secretary, John Morris, who confirmed with others all my views about the quality of our foreign service and about the populist nonsense which you often read in the tabloids about its disengagement from the realities of life in Britain. I am also extremely fortunate that the head of the Hong Kong department is a star called Peter Ricketts.† He is clever, sensible, amiable and extremely well informed. He has understood some of my initial instincts very quickly. He also never hesitates to tell me when he thinks I am wrong but is able to do it in a way which doesn't bruise my feelings.

All my briefings make me realize the conflicting pressures that I'm going to be under. First of all, in Hong Kong itself people both want a quiet life with China and at the same time a Governor who is prepared to stand up to China on their behalf. My predecessor, David Wilson,‡ was criticized, sometimes unfairly, for not being tough enough with Beijing, an attack which came not least from members of the business community. I suspect that the number of people in the former category (the quiet life) will increase the nearer we get to 1997 and the number in the latter will decline. Secondly, one group in Hong Kong will be pressing with the

---

BBC, and is the sister of my friend the former Conservative Cabinet minister William Waldegrave

* Norman Fowler had a long career as a minister in Margaret Thatcher's governments and became Conservative Party chairman under John Major. He was a particularly successful Secretary of State for Health and Social Services from 1981 to 1987. His last public office was as Lord Speaker from 2016 to 2021.

† There is a full note on Peter Ricketts and on the other FCO diplomats principally involved in work on Hong Kong and China in a note at the end of this diary.

‡ Lord Wilson of Tillyorn, as he was to become after he had retired as Governor, was a distinguished Sinologist who, as well as his career in the FCO, was also for a time the editor of the *China Quarterly*. He was Governor of Hong Kong from 1987 to 1992. In addition to other public positions, he became master of Peterhouse College, Cambridge, from 2002 to 2008.

enthusiastic encouragement of the world outside for greater democracy; they will get huge backing from the media everywhere, not least in North America. On the other hand, a more conservative and business-oriented group will argue (whatever they have said in the past) against anything which seems to annoy China. A lot of this group will have foreign passports in their back pockets. It is obviously perfectly possible to construct a wholly rational policy which will fall somewhere between the Bishop Muzorewa's and the Mr Mugabe's of Hong Kong, between those who will be happy to settle for anything provided it gives them a quiet life and those who are prepared to have a fight. But since we need a majority to get business through the Legislative Council, this will produce some problems for Hong Kong's executive. Thirdly, the business community while wanting to avoid any trouble with China will also look for continuing certainty that the rule of law and the conditions of stability for an effective market economy survive. Hong Kong's success depends not only on its free economy but also on freedom of speech and the rule of law. These are not things that you find where there is a communist dictatorship. Fourthly, there is the constituency at home to think about as well. On the whole people don't much care about what's happening in Hong Kong unless it goes wrong. They would like to feel a warm glow of satisfaction that we are doing the decent thing by Hong Kongers, but they feel somewhat constrained in their enthusiasm by dislike for the gerontocracy in Beijing, which doesn't give much of a damn about concepts like human rights. Meantime those old bruisers in Beijing want Hong Kong to go on being successful economically but certainly don't want it to appear as a focus for democratic dissent in mainland China. They plainly don't trust Britain at all. They think that we want to rip off Hong Kong, taking all the loot with us when we go, and to leave behind a political timebomb which will blow their autocratic regime to smithereens. It's extraordinary that given the effort we have put into the relationship with China – Sinophile experts in the Foreign Office, trade links and even Ted Heath* at his occasionally charming – that this degree of misunderstanding should continue.

There are a lot of circles to square. It may even be more difficult than coping with the poll tax or looking after the Conservative Party's interests during a recession. But it will certainly be more interesting.

* Edward Heath was Prime Minister of the United Kingdom from 1970 to 1974 and leader of the Conservative Party from 1965 to 1975. After he lost the leadership to Margaret Thatcher, he spent a good deal of time, during a period in his life known by others as 'the great sulk', working on his status as an old friend of China, not least to help sort out commercial problems. This sometimes led him to resile from what others would have imagined would be his commitment to democracy and human rights.

The Chinese have evidently decided to give me a rough time when I arrive. I am told that they are anxious about four things. First that the Prime Minister and I used the word freedom as well as stability and prosperity when my appointment was announced. Secondly Alastair Goodlad, a long-time friend and the Minister of State for Asia in the Foreign Office, on a recent visit to Hong Kong said that the Basic Law could be changed if the Chinese had the political will to act, in other words to increase the pace of democratization. (Alastair has a deserved reputation for being a wise owl; like other wise owls, part of this reputation is a result of knowing when to keep quiet, so his remark on this occasion was entirely correct if slightly out of character.) Thirdly they are concerned that the Prime Minister saw Martin Lee* when the latter was in London and they think that we are planning to put Martin and his Democrat colleagues on the Executive Council – something that they vehemently oppose. Fourthly they are said to be worried that we have referred again to the announcement that we made back in 1990 that we would return to them before the 1995 Legislative Council elections to talk about the pace of democratization. They are obviously going slow on the airport negotiations to try to use these as a lever on me politically. Indeed they have proposed both to the Prime Minister and less formally that I should go to Beijing to sort out the airport before I even arrive in Hong Kong. The linkage between politics and the airport is not something we can concede. If I agreed with them informally not, say, to appoint Martin Lee to Exco, they would inevitably leak the news, so that I would arrive in Hong Kong as a Governor who had kowtowed even before setting foot in the city.

Clearly building a new airport in Hong Kong will play a fairly prominent part in the politics of the territory over the next few years. Hong Kong has an international airport called Kai Tak, which has served the city for over 70 years but is now inadequate for its huge job as a growing international air hub. It is situated in the east of Kowloon with a single runway which stretches out into the bay. Landing at the airport involves a pretty exciting flight path over Hong Kong from the west with a large right turn down into the final descent over high-rise blocks of flats and – it sometimes seems – almost through the washing lines. Anyone who has taken this journey, not least those who have managed to do it while sitting on the flight deck, knows

* Martin Lee was a distinguished Hong Kong barrister who was the founding chairman of the United Democrats of Hong Kong. He was widely regarded as the principal political exponent of democracy in Hong Kong and reviled as a consequence by the Communist Party. They plainly found it difficult to understand why he was more popular than their United Front stooges.

that the excitement of this arrival is a guinea a minute. So Hong Kong has for years needed a new airport on environmental, noise and safety grounds – one which can accommodate night flights and with at least one more runway. There have been proposals on the table since the 1970s. Eventually a new and manageable scheme emerged from several consultants and planners in the 1980s. It involved flattening one small island (Chek Lap Kok) off the principal island to the west of Hong Kong called Lantau. This would involve a huge amount of reclamation, further development of the port (particularly the development of two additional container terminals) and a huge infrastructural network of bridges, roads, tunnels and rail links. The principal bridge, called Tsing Ma, would itself be a huge project. Along with the terminals, runways and concourses, this was going to be one of the largest construction projects of the century and of course very expensive. But the case for it was overwhelming, not just in terms of transport but also in expressing confidence in Hong Kong's future and building up the belief in the community in its own prospects. The decision to go ahead was taken bravely and imaginatively by David Wilson (with the enthusiastic and very competent support of his and now my Chief Secretary, David Ford).* This at around the time that the Tiananmen massacres in 1989 were undermining the city's confidence.

Noting the priority that the British were giving to this airport, the Chinese took the view that they could use building it as a way of trying to tweak British policy overall in Hong Kong to their own advantage. China's principal leverage was based on the fact that borrowing was likely to run beyond 1997, and so were many of the building contracts. So if they were so minded, they could throw large numbers of spanners in the works. While the costs were not insuperable for a community which had been growing its economy for almost 30 years and which had huge financial reserves and a superb credit rating, clearly some in China thought – or purported to think – that we were trying to leave Hong Kong with gigantic debts. Perhaps they also reckoned, in their most conspiratorial moments, that it was all a plot to get more business for British firms. I imagine that if the roles been reversed this would have been exactly what they would have been trying to do. Some of them also doubtless thought the priority should be given to developing the airport at Guangdong for the whole region. So my predecessor and the government had had great difficulty agreeing with China that the project should go ahead. Eventually and

* Sir David Ford joined the Hong Kong civil service on his retirement from the army in 1972 and was the last non-ethnic Chinese Chief Secretary of Hong Kong and Deputy Governor from 1987 to 1993. He was then Hong Kong commissioner in London until 1997. He died in 2017.

unwisely, his principal adviser at the time, Percy Cradock,* supported by David Wilson, persuaded John Major that he should visit Beijing in order to sign an agreement with the Chinese Prime Minister, Li Peng,† for the project to be given a green light. So it was that in September 1991 John Major was persuaded to become the first Western leader to visit Beijing since the murders in and around Tiananmen Square. The Chinese rubbed salt in the wounds, and added to John's humiliation and the criticism he received around the world, by getting him to inspect a guard of honour in the square where so many students had demonstrated and had been killed. John had tried to make up for some of this indignity by raising human rights issues with the Chinese leaders he saw, especially the Prime Minister, one of the most hardline of Chinese leaders implicated in the murder of students and others. At the same time Percy Cradock (whose terrible idea this trip had been) was telling the journalists in John's accompanying party that any references to human rights were just for show and didn't really amount to anything. So John signed an agreement with the awful Li Peng. Major took a lot of stick for going through the whole disobliging business. Needless to say, none of this made any difference to the way the Chinese behaved. They simply went on dragging their feet about the project and raising one objection after another. Inevitably this had a considerable effect on John's views on doing business with China and on the advice given by some of his senior officials, particularly the allegedly omniscient Cradock.

Thursday 2–Saturday 4 July – Last thoughts before departure

Ambassador Ma,‡ a more genial Chinese diplomat than most, gave a dinner for me just before we left London at which I explained the general outline of what I wanted to do pretty robustly, making it clear that I couldn't go to Beijing while the Chinese were stirring up controversy about

* Sir Percy Cradock was a Sinologist who was ambassador to China from 1978 to 1983 and a senior adviser to Margaret Thatcher during the Sino-British negotiations on the Joint Declaration. He was also for a time an adviser to John Major and chairman of the Cabinet's Joint Intelligence Committee. Major removed him from these jobs not long after his very difficult visit to Beijing. Cradock is alas a fairly regular visitor to the pages of this diary.

† Li Peng was Premier of the People's Republic of China from 1987 to 1998, and ranked as number 2 to party secretary Jiang Zemin for most of this period. He became the most prominent defender of the Tiananmen killings in 1989. We had a masseur in Hong Kong called Li Peng who changed his name to Li Justice, so appalled was he to share a name with a politician widely regarded as having so much blood on his hands.

‡ Ambassador Ma Yuzhen was China's ambassador to the United Kingdom from 1991 to 1995. After the handover in 1997 he became for a time the representative of China's Foreign Ministry in Hong Kong.

things that they wanted me not to do in Hong Kong. Their constant criticisms of any idea of appointing democrats like Martin Lee to any significant posts will make the issue harder to handle whatever I decide to do. I had rather liked Martin Lee when I had met him before my appointment as Governor. Reading about him he seems a decent and brave fellow. He is certainly no radical. I would reckon that in British politics he would count as a moderate conservative. His real crime as far as Beijing is concerned is to believe in the rule of law and democracy. I hope that Ambassador Ma passes on my comments, though I suspect that in the Chinese communist system it is far more difficult than in ours to tell the truth upward.

In any event it's clearly going to be difficult to untangle all these knots in a way which looks at all honourable to the rest of the world. To some extent our colonial history is going to be judged through the prism of the next five years. But, of course, the problems are very different to those we normally face in decolonization. A metaphor which I have found myself using is that our normal decolonizing job has been like firing a satellite into orbit. You put the rule of law, an independent civil service and the Westminster model on the launching pad, light the blue touch paper, and hope that the rocket takes off and puts the satellite into an independent orbit. With Hong Kong, we are talking about a docking in outer space – docking with a regime which, despite China's formidable economic achievements, a lot of people don't much care for. After all, a large proportion of Hong Kong's population are refugees from communism.

The actual system of government in Hong Kong puzzles me. The Governor and his colleagues seem to be trapped in a no man's land between executive-led government and some limited steps towards accountability. The existing Executive Council (Exco) is the top of the pyramid of surrogate democracy – lots of advisory panels in which good men (and women) and true from right across the community come together to participate in its administration. But perhaps they are not drawn from right across the community. Both those strongly in favour of democracy and the hard-line supporters of Beijing are usually overlooked. But with the arrival of greater democracy in the Legislative Council (Legco) as more of its members have been directly elected in recent years, the role of the executive and the relationship between the Executive Council (Exco) and Legco has ended up in a frightful muddle. What I'm inclined to do is to make a proper distinction between Exco and Legco and create some sort of hinge machinery between the two, which should probably turn out to be me. It would bypass the question of whether or not Martin Lee and other United Democrats of Hong Kong (UDHK) should be posted from the Legco onto Exco. I have explored this idea already with one or two people. I talked to my deputy, David Ford, about it. He's an amiable, competent and decent man with huge experience, not least on security. He is evidently also excellent at dealing with people and managing big projects. He clearly wants to go out of his way to help me as much as possible. I've also talked to Lydia Dunn,* the senior member of the Executive Council, and perhaps the most prominent member of the non-elective bits of political accountability in the colony. Lydia has also been a senior executive and director of Swire's for a number of years.

Dealing with this may take up an inordinate amount of time for a modest outcome. Of course, it will be particularly important in managing my life as, in effect, the city's mayor. I want to be able to tackle a lot of social and economic issues and to plan Hong Kong's infrastructure for the future so will need a political base to do those things. But the relationships I am talking about should not delay too much my work on other matters, even though it always takes a long time to deal with anything in politics, or I guess elsewhere, where egos are involved. The three issues that I am really bothered about are these:

First of all, I have to push through arrangements to secure Hong Kong's future judicial arrangements. These have focused recently on the establishment of a court of final appeal – the colony's senior judicial body – on which there is as yet no agreement with anyone. Indeed an attempt to put arrangements in place in 1991 failed in the face of condemnations by both the legal profession and Legco. Part of the argument adduced against these proposals was that they had been produced secretly after discussions with China virtually alone. The critics, and they were in a big majority, thought that everything was being rigged behind the community's back. This is a very strong argument for being as open as possible in handling big and consequential issues. It's terrible politics if it looks as though proposals have emerged only after discussions in Beijing, and, of course, the first knowledge of what's been agreed leaks very often out of Beijing itself.

The second issue is how we can bring Hong Kong's laws into line with the Bill of Rights that was introduced in 1991. This was partly done in order to try to steady morale after Tiananmen and partly to ensure that

* Lydia Dunn was born in Hong Kong to parents who were refugees from China. After university in California she returned to Hong Kong and pursued a business career, first in Swire's and later in HSBC. She was appointed to the Legislative Council in 1976 and the Executive Council in 1982. She was the senior member from 1988 to 1995. She was made a member of the House of Lords in 1989. She married the penultimate Attorney General of Hong Kong, Michael Thomas, in 1988. She moved with considerable guile and elegant agility through the minefields of Hong Kong politics.

the provisions of the International Covenant on Civil and Political Rights* are clearly understood and accepted as applicable to Hong Kong by Beijing before the handover. The Covenant itself is included in the Basic Law. This will involve getting rid of some colonial legislation (which no Governor these days could possibly use), much of it enacted in order to deal with the Cultural Revolution riots in the 1960s when over 50 people were killed. I guess that every effort to remove a bit of legislation which could be used to turn Hong Kong into something nearer to a police state will be opposed by China. Due process does not feature prominently there.

Thirdly, and most immediate, there is no agreement yet on how to conduct the 1994 elections for Hong Kong's local government and the Legco elections in 1995. We have got very little time, but there's no plan yet for what to do. The only clear agreement with Beijing is not to increase the number of directly elected seats unilaterally. I couldn't try to overturn this even if I wanted to do so. This ordains that there should be no more than 20 directly elected legislators from geographically based constituencies in the legislature after 1995; 30 members drawn from the so-called functional constituencies (which are supposed to represent the main interest groups in the city – like lawyers, teachers and agricultural workers); and 10 elected from a so-called election committee, the precise composition of which is unknown. I realize that I can't increase the number of directly elected legislators – the most obviously democratic part of the whole system. But I'm absolutely sure in my own mind that within the rather narrow confines which are left I can make the whole package more open, fair and obviously accountable. I expect Chinese apparatchiks will be unnerved by any attempts which seek to secure a fairer electoral process.

In all of these matters, while the Joint Declaration and Basic Law provide parameters, there is much more flexibility than some people seem to suppose. But we can't determine how much simply by waiting to see what the elderly bruisers in Beijing have to say. There are also very different views across the Foreign Office about how to deal with all this. Some of the differences are explicable in generational terms. There is a cadre at the top of the service of older Sinophiles who think that, at the end of the day, only people with their experience of dealing with the Chinese know quite how to behave. They pretty well take it for granted that ultimately you have to go along with Beijing rather than risk arguments. Beijing rules – UK. It may be that if you spend years of your life learning Mandarin, reading Chinese history and immersing yourself in the country's culture you inevitably fetch up taking this sort of view. Thus my predecessor in

* The treaty which codifies the UN Universal Declaration of Human Rights.

Hong Kong, David Wilson, a man of great integrity and a formidable China scholar, is certain to regard my political instincts with some distaste. There is a group in the middle of the foreign service about my own age who seem to be prepared to be rather more robust with the Chinese. They've spent a lot of time in the last 10 years engaged in hand-to-hand combat in the trenches with Chinese diplomats over the Joint Declaration and then over the airport. A younger group are much more ebullient in their views and think we should flex our own muscles occasionally. I'm bound to say that I've got increasingly cross about references to Chinese 'face' (by the older group in particular) and feel that we need to refer ourselves to British 'face' from time to time. I made this point to a glamorous Hong Kong United Front activist called Nellie Fong, an emissary allegedly sent to me by my opposite number in Beijing, Lu Ping.* She seemed rather shocked by what I had to say. Why did I not understand the honour of dealing with those who had the mandate of heaven? She didn't quite say the master race but it was what she implied. I suppose she could have noted that I didn't even have the mandate of Bath.

The permanent secretary in the Foreign Office, David Gillmore,† seems to take a view closer to my own about dealing with China, making clear that we care about what local citizens in Hong Kong think and have to say. He seems much more concerned than many others about the responsibility we have for their future. He certainly doesn't subscribe to the view that all the people in Hong Kong bother about is business and money and that they don't care anything about politics. He reminds me of the number of Hong Kong citizens who left mainland China because of the consequences of communist politics, and the number as well who have

* Lu Ping, who was born in Shanghai, was a Chinese diplomat who was head of the Hong Kong and Macau Affairs Office, which was part of the State Council of the People's Republic of China. He was the head of the office which was supposed to have responsibility for handling the handover to China of these two territories. It was never entirely clear how much authority he had to make policy in this area. He spoke beautiful English, loved classical music and was thought to be quite urbane. But he was under huge political pressure and this perhaps explained his occasional outbursts of temper. He did not appear to be in the best of health, which may also explain his irascibility. I have always thought it a pity that I couldn't form a closer personal relationship with him, while recognizing that part of his attitude to foreigners was almost certainly the result of the anti-Chinese racism he had experienced while growing up and being educated in Shanghai. He was removed from his post shortly after the handover in 1997 and died in 2015.

† Lord Gillmore, as he was to become, joined the FCO after being a teacher and rose rapidly to the top. He was High Commissioner in Malaysia and became permanent undersecretary in 1991. He helped John Major to get Britain out of a dead end in relation to apartheid South Africa. Not being a Sinophile, he approached issues involving China and Hong Kong with a great deal of common sense and commitment to our own values.

been to university and read as many books about what an open society is as he and I have.

I get John Morris to take a full note of my principal meeting with Gillmore and I do the same when I meet the high priest of all things Chinese in British policy, Sir Percy Cradock. He has been involved in every aspect of Chinese affairs since he worked in the embassy in Beijing during the Cultural Revolution, when a mob broke into the embassy where the ambassador and staff were playing bridge with very stiff upper lips and perhaps good cards. The last telegram before the embassy was burnt down allegedly began with the words, 'I had just bid three no trumps'. Cradock himself eventually became ambassador in Beijing and did every senior job in negotiations with China over the Hong Kong transfer of sovereignty. He became a principal adviser to Margaret Thatcher as well as to John Major, especially though not exclusively on China, and plainly regarded the Joint Declaration as very much his own work. He doesn't like politicians; it is our vulgarity I suppose. He is undoubtedly clever though intellectually spectacularly vain. When I say one or two things about dealing with China, he does everything except roll his eyes. He makes it clear to me that virtually every jot and tittle has been decided about the handover to China in five years' time. There is nothing else to do. We should just try to ensure that the train which he has constructed stays on the rails which he has laid down with a variety of Chinese partners. It may be a bit unfair but I'm not sure that the interests of people who live in Hong Kong are of very much concern to him, though he plainly thinks that they will be best off if nobody disagrees with him when it comes to planning their future. I normally like intelligent senior officials but this clever, conceited, acerbic man puts my back up. The feeling is obviously mutual. He gets particularly cross when I refer to debates about the Joint Declaration in the House of Commons when our commitments to democracy were referred to again and again by MPs and even (less robust) by ministers. He doesn't quite say, 'they don't know what they're talking about', but this is what he implies. During this meeting, which had quite an effect on me, Sir Percy uttered the lines which I am told he has often used before. Referring to his experiences during the Cultural Revolution and to subsequent events, not least the murders in 1989, he told me that the Chinese leaders may be thuggish dictators but that they were men of their word and would stick by what they had promised to do. I hope that is true.

I'm clearly going to have to do quite a bit to beef up the way that the Governor's job will be done in the last five years of British sovereignty. Douglas Hurd has suggested to me that I take what he rather charmingly calls a small 'équipe'. I've managed to persuade two of the best people who have ever worked for me to come to Hong Kong. Martin Dinham* was private secretary when I was Minister for Overseas Development. He is charming, very good company and hard-working, and everyone likes him. He jumps at the chance of coming to Hong Kong with his wife and two young children. I also ask Edward Llewellyn,† who helped me when I was party chairman, particularly with the international side of the job. He was very valuable when I was trying, successfully as it turned out, to negotiate the Conservative Party's membership of the European People's Party in the European Parliament. I want him to keep links with politicians back in London, not just John Major but Margaret Thatcher as well. He knows them both and they get on well with him, as does pretty much everyone else. Edward is unencumbered by family. He hardly ever stops working, is great fun, loyal and again clever. He's a good linguist but I doubt whether his abilities to speak French and German will enable even him to learn Cantonese in Hong Kong with all its difficult tones.

Much of the time during the summer is spent saying goodbye to our friends and above all to our daughters Kate and Laura. It is going to feel horribly like the break-up for the time being of a very close family. Kate is in Uruguay as part of a Latin American gap year between school and Newcastle University. Just as she heard about my defeat in Bath on the BBC World Service, she also learned about me going to Hong Kong in the same way. This was not ideal! But I think she's okay. Her main worry has been that I might have bullied Lavender into going to Asia. I hope we have reassured her about this. It's typical of Kate to be thinking about others rather than herself. She is a terrific young woman and it is not easy to have had to make big decisions which will affect her when she is so far away from home. She has a great deal of gumption and I think she will eventually enjoy the adventure. Laura has decided that she doesn't want to come to Hong Kong to work or study. She is not interested in trying for university but is set on going to the superb Prue Leith cookery school in

* Martin Dinham was my private secretary at the Overseas Development Administration in 1986–7. After working in Hong Kong he went back to what had become the UK's Department for International Development, where he was a director-general. After retirement from that job, he continued to work in the development field and became, for example, the chairman of the board of the Global Fund to Fight AIDS, Tuberculosis and Malaria. As a public servant, he was as good as they get.

† After Hong Kong, Edward Llewellyn came to work with me in Brussels when I was European Commissioner for External Relations. He then worked for Paddy Ashdown in Bosnia, and from there went to be David Cameron's chief of staff, first in opposition and then when Cameron became Prime Minister. When Cameron resigned, Edward was made ambassador in Paris and later ambassador in Rome. He became a member of the House of Lords in 2016.

London. Laura is far cleverer than she ever wants to demonstrate to her teachers, as they clearly recognize, somewhat to their annoyance! She is very close to both her sisters and I hope she won't mind too much the fact that one will be in Newcastle and the other in Hong Kong, because that is what Alice has decided she wants to do. We offer her the chance of staying in Britain and going to boarding school. Thank heavens she didn't want to do so. She is very bright, went to secondary school a year early and behaves with considerable maturity without being either precocious or a know-all. If she grows up like this, she will be a very lovely human being. We are obviously going to miss Kate and Laura very much and hope that Laura doesn't regret her decision. She is a lovable girl but at the moment very much a teenager – she knows what she wants to do and that's that. She will come out to Hong Kong with us for a few weeks' holiday before returning to become a cookery student. I think most parents sooner or later come to understand that as their children grow older they morph from colonial dependencies into rival sovereignties.

There is one other meeting I should mention with someone who is not a member of our family. (She has her own to cope with.) We had 40 minutes with the Queen at Windsor Castle in a beautiful room approached by a long corridor with corgis in its shadows waiting to leap out in ambush. She was in sparkling form, very knowledgeable, had read all the recent telegrams, and was full of stories about her recent state visit to France. She commands affection as well as respect, if it's not *lèse-majesté* to say this.

Sunday 5 July – off to Hong Kong

I went to mass in the cathedral* and then we left on our adventure. Five years ago, on a Sunday morning, I would probably have been sitting here doing my boxes as Minister for Overseas Development. When I'm back here in five years' time what on earth will I be preparing to do and what will Hong Kong have done to the Patten family? As Mother Julian of Norwich apparently said – though hardly anything else is known about her – 'all things shall be well, and all manner of things shall be well'. Leaving home was particularly emotional for Alice and Laura, above all Alice, who is coming for as long as her mother and I are there. She stood in the bedroom which has been the centre of her childhood in floods of tears. I said to her, 'I bet you cry in five years' time when you leave Hong Kong.'

* Westminster Cathedral is next to the block of flats where we had lived pretty well ever since I became an MP. Our daughters had been largely brought up there.

Monday 6 July
We flew on Singapore Airlines. I slept on the flight thanks to some sleeping pills which our neighbour next door, a doctor, had given us. We were met at Singapore airport by the High Commissioner, Gordon Duggan, and taken in his Daimler to his residence, Eden Hall. It's a handsome neo-colonial house, all verandas and whirling fans, and a garden with a swimming pool and lots of lush vegetation. The weather was of course sticky and the air conditioning in the bedrooms made them feel like refrigerators. But we were made very welcome and looked after rather as though we were being prepared for some great sporting competition.

Tuesday 7 July
Today I read a lot of telegrams, continued reading Jan Morris's brilliant book on Hong Kong, and looked again at my speech for my arrival in Hong Kong. I had meetings with the Prime Minister, Goh Chok Tong, and with the senior minister, Lee Kuan Yew,* with whom I had had conversations a couple of times before. The presidential palace is a handsome white stucco building in parkland with a golf course. With its skyscrapers and neat streets, I recalled again how much Singapore reminds me of Rex Warner's satirical novel from the 1930s *The Aerodrome*, just as the senior minister reminds me of the Air Vice-Marshal in the book. It gives a marvellous view of some of the social engineering consequences of mostly benevolent authoritarianism. Mr Goh is a perfectly friendly fellow, though rather low on charisma, and conversation was a bit of a struggle. On the other hand, talking with Lee is no problem at all. He hits a lot of shots and one doesn't often get much of a chance to hit the ball back. He is highly intelligent. He and his whole family are decorated with double firsts from Cambridge. He speaks very eloquently, using precise words to convey what he means, so for example he spoke of the danger of implosion in China rather than explosion. His main message was that he was pretty confident about the next 10 to 20 years in China and in Asia as a whole. Second, he thought the reforms in China were probably irreversible but it was a pity that both Deng's originally chosen successors had fallen by the wayside. He thought that Zhao Ziyang had shown weakness during the Tiananmen Square crisis. I didn't get the impression that Lee thought it should have

* Lee Kuan Yew was Prime Minister of Singapore between 1959 and 1990, after which he continued to keep a watchful eye on the city state's progress until his death in 2011. A clever Cambridge graduate, he had opinions on most international political subjects and very occasionally would listen to the views of others on the same subjects. He can properly take credit for much of the success of Singapore, though for many people it retains a 'Marmite' quality.

been handled with more delicacy! Third, he said that the job in Hong Kong was not the usual decolonization task. I would have to cope with a unique situation while sensitively ignoring pressure from Europe and North America. He was not wildly optimistic about being able to square all the circles, but thought that it would be right to set out clearly in my first speech to the Legislative Council in October what I wished to do and the criteria by which I believed we should be judged in Hong Kong. I should then stick to my guns. I should regard this as being like the Prime Minister with a new government in a new country setting out an agenda. Fourth, he believes that the iron parameters of our job in Hong Kong are the Joint Declaration and the Basic Law and that I should not try to push China too far beyond them. Fifth, he stressed that the Chinese were unlikely ever really to trust Britain. They would always think that we were attempting to make off with all the booty. He is impassive, shows little emotion, but delivers all these views with considerable force. To his credit he did listen a bit to what I had to say in reply, which is more than can be said for many world leaders.

I had a lunch with leading members of the British business community – Shell, ICI, Standard Chartered, Hong Kong and Shanghai Bank and so on – the general view was that Hong Kong and Singapore shouldn't be seen as competitors. (But, of course, they are.) Singapore was always likely to attract multinationals because it had no real local entrepreneurial base and was a comfortable place for executives to live. Hong Kong's great strength was its entrepreneurial vitality and growing links with southern China.

The Duggans took us out to a Singaporean family restaurant for supper. It was huge, throbbing with noisy and cheerful families, and with delicious food. I hope we can go out to eat in Hong Kong, but when I've suggested this to people from time to time they look as though I'm crazy. They honestly think that the Governor should be wrapped up in Government House and in oodles of protocol. I suppose that the ubiquitous press corps may make it more difficult to get out informally in Hong Kong; even in Singapore they are all over us.

Wednesday 8 July

This morning I met the finance minister, who told me an amusing story about a meeting he had with his Chinese opposite number in Guangdong where people seem to be showing increasing signs of independence from Beijing. The Chinese minister's Cantonese hosts had teased him that the waitresses in the restaurant were earning more than he did and were very patronizing about the central government. He thought the Chinese were coming to Singapore to try to learn about how to run a successful economy while keeping a reasonably tight grip on the population. He wasn't sure that Chinese communists really understood the means but thought they were very keen on achieving the end.

Edward Llewellyn rang from Hong Kong to say that he and Martin had already formed some fairly clear ideas about what needed to be done to change and improve things. They were very keen to see me as soon as possible after I arrived. They also wanted to have a go at my diary to get an early meeting with the secretaries – Hong Kong's cross between ministers and permanent secretaries – and with the political parties. They also think that I should get out and about around the territory without too much formality, seeing the bad things as well as the good.

Before dinner in the evening my private secretary from Hong Kong arrives. Richard Hoare* is a career civil servant in the Hong Kong government and a decent, sensible, hard-working guy passionately interested in tennis and the theatre. He came with my marching orders for the next day's inauguration and started to sound me out on how I want to run things in Government House. There is evidently a degree of apprehension about what my arrival is going to mean. More political mayor, less colonial Governor.

Lee Kuan Yew came to dinner with his wife, who is just as sharp as he is, a lawyer from Girton College, Cambridge, with, naturally, a first-class degree. He was again fascinating about the job ahead. He thinks I need to find an interlocutor in matters that have a bearing on China, an interlocutor with whom I can be candid and firm and whom the Chinese side will also trust. He also speaks of the importance of ensuring that we don't lose control of things before we leave in 1997 – so we need to make certain that the police, Special Branch, the anti-corruption squad and so on are in good order. He says that if the Chinese really want to make trouble, they will do it by subversion rather than by any more frontal attacks. But our period of responsibility ends in 1997, not earlier.

Thursday 9 July – the Big Day

We got up early in the High Commissioner's residence, repacked some of our nine suitcases, and said our goodbyes. We went to the airport with the Duggans and their nice 11-year-old son, Tom. He very much reminds me of Jim in *Empire of the Sun*, a marvellously old-fashioned bright spark. He gave us a spirited lecture at the airport on how to fill the holes in the ozone layer. I could have done with his advice when I was Secretary of

* Richard Hoare had been my predecessor's private secretary and he worked for me for more than a year. He then became director of administration before taking fairly early retirement to live near Chichester.

State for the Environment, a point with which he seemed to agree. He interrupted our conversation later on with a loud humming, which we assumed initially was coming from the air conditioning. It turned out that he was trying to discover whether humming made one's teeth rattle. Answer – probably not.

We travelled on Cathay Pacific, giving loads of interviews and being photographed most of the time – eating, blowing our noses, reading, going about our business, and in Alice's case going up to the cockpit for the final descent into Hong Kong through the washing lines. I talked to some of the accompanying press from the UK as well as to some of the locals. Jonathan Dimbleby is with us and his director, Francis Gerard. They are going to do fly-on-the-wall documentaries about my five years in Hong Kong. We will give them access with the promise that they'll try to give a pretty faithful record of how we spend five years in this last colony, how it treats us and how others behave in the run-up to 1997.

After we landed, we went straight to the main airport building, where our clothes were brought to us so we could make an appropriately well-dressed entry to the city. Lavender and the girls look terrific. I have a rather smart double-breasted grey suit which I bought just before we left from Aquascutum; later it was described by the appalling Nicholas Fairbairn as a Harry Lime outfit. At least it doesn't have broad chalk stripes and wasn't like most of my suits bought – off the peg on to the floor – at Marks & Spencer. I get my first insight into the marvellously competent way in which my life is going to be arranged from now on. My ADC, an immaculately dressed police superintendent, Felipe D'Oliveira, who is part Portuguese by background, has brought a couple of extra pairs of cufflinks and a belt just in case I forgot them myself. I'm to learn in due course that I'm not really trusted to dress myself any more. We drove from the airport to the quayside in Kowloon through cheering, waving crowds. They were very responsive when I practised my royal wave. They were probably more interested in the girls.

Then we embarked on the *Lady Maurine*. It is a spick and span little vessel, built originally I think before the Second World War to deal with fires and other emergencies. It was redesigned to provide occasional maritime relief for the Governor and has been performing that role for some decades. We crossed the harbour, one of the great journeys in the world. Fortunately, it had stopped raining and there were some occasional flashes of sunlight. Fire boats spray water; a 17-gun salute resounds from HMS *Tamar*, the onshore naval base; and there was a fly-past by planes and helicopters. I was never greeted like this in Bath.

We disembarked and shook a lot of hands and I saluted the guard of honour. Then we went into the City Hall for the swearing-in by the Chief Justice and for my inauguration speech. I had dictated what I wanted to say to Edward Llewellyn weeks before and then redrafted the whole thing myself. After that we had to telegram it to Beijing and Hong Kong for comments. We ignored most of them – particularly the suggestion from our Beijing embassy that it was wrong to talk about cooperation between two ancient civilizations since China was so much older than Britain. I am trying to be polite but I have never favoured pre-emptive cringes. I am certainly not going to accept the Chinese communist view of history. When Jiang Zemin* went to Cairo and Egypt, he was told as he looked out at the Nile and the pyramids that civilization there was more than 3000 years old. When he got back to Beijing the party line was quickly adapted to assert that China was 4000 years old, later adjusted to 5000.

I'm supposed to know about making speeches and this one seems to go perfectly reasonably. Naturally, I can't really tell whether people are just going to tell me (even more than is the case in other occupations) only what I want to hear. I try to project the image of being strong, calm and reasonable. Perhaps I really am! After the speech, there was a great bun-fight and we were introduced for an hour to various groups of leading citizens, and then we took off in the Daimler for Government House.

Nicholas Witchell from the BBC was at the gate of my new home to give me a smart salute. BBC's *Breakfast Time* apparently took the whole show live. We swept up to the entrance of Government House. Then took another salute from a guard of honour and went into the huge front hall. There was a horseshoe of GH staff, both domestic and private office. It was an awesome sight. There were private secretaries, valets, maids, cooks, gardeners, personal protection officers – the one on duty today is called Rocky, the other two are Wise and Alex. Along with their police colleagues in special protection, all are set to become friends. (Much the same thing happened when I was a Northern Ireland minister with my protection officers.) It was an overwhelmingly warm welcome.

We were then shown around the house. The great front hall is the cross-roads between my domain and Lavender's. As you enter, to the left are the housekeeper's office and the office of the social secretary. The housekeeper, Elspeth Collins-Taylor, a young Scottish woman who is tough, competent, charming and blessedly normal, is responsible to Lavender for the four

* Jiang Zemin was General Secretary of the Chinese Communist Party from 1989 to 2002 and President of the People's Republic of China. His generally 'bonhomous' nature made many underestimate his qualities as a politician. But I never believed that he could have survived for so long at the top of Chinese politics without formidable cunning and ruthlessness.

cooks, their staff, the stewards led by Ah Mo and Ah Chak, the cleaners, and the rest of the household and garden staff. We simply make over the household budget to Elspeth and she spends it as is necessary. Lavender leaves all that entirely to her. Also on this side of the hall are Lavender's social secretary, Louise Cox, and her PA, Candy. Louise is not only responsible for the invitations to all GH functions, such as receptions and dinners, but, more important, she looks after Lavender's myriad activities as the Governor's wife. In addition to accompanying me to many functions – we are told that we will go to more charity balls than ever before or again – Lavender has her own engagements which crowd her diary. There are, for instance, over seventy charities of which she is going to be patron or in which she has to take a particular interest. She is a core part of the team. She seems to have something to do outside every day.

On the other side of the hall is the private office under Richard Hoare, which looks after me and is the link with the rest of the government. Alongside the private secretaries, I have a press spokesman and of course Martin and Edward who have already taken up their jobs here. Between Lavender's domain and mine, the general office staff, for example Frankie and Johnny, rule the roost. We are told that Frankie knows everything you need to know in Hong Kong, where to get it and where to buy it at the best price. He turns out to be a superb wheeler-dealer who can also fix videos or hi-fi, type, do photo copying, deliver messages, meet Alice's occasional technical or retail requirements, and generally (with Johnny) keep the house running.

We had a delicious dinner in a small dining room off the main official one. I imagine we will eat here most of the time when we're on our own. If, that is, we are ever on our own. The food was superb – beginning with crispy duck pancakes. What another treat! We have a private flat on the first floor of the house and the girls have bedrooms in the tower, which was added by the Japanese during their occupation. It makes the whole house look a little like a Japanese railway station. We are all very happy with our accommodation, which is very much larger than the flat in Westminster. How could we possibly grumble? We look out at the view of the harbour which we can catch glimpses of in the gaps between the high-rise buildings that surround our gardens. The new Bank of China building by I. M. Pei is elegant and awesome. I'm not quite so keen on the Hong Kong and Shanghai Bank building. Princess Margaret is said to have remarked that it looked like the back of a fridge. To which the obvious response was – 'But how does Princess Margaret know what the back of a fridge looks like?'

Friday 10 July

After getting up this morning, I wandered into my dressing room and found my clothes for the day laid out neatly – boxers, socks, shirt, tie, suit, beautifully polished shoes. My very nice valet was hovering over them looking slightly nervous. I had to explain to him that I thought he had done brilliantly, but that in future I thought I would be able to dress myself in the morning. I hope I didn't hurt his feelings. Dressing is part of the job that I should be able to manage myself. I've cleaned my own shoes since my dad taught me when I was a small boy. As I have got older, I have taken less and less time over this sartorial task. From now on I can count on having the most shiny shoes in Asia.

My first Friday in the office began with a meeting with the Chief Secretary, David Ford, and the Financial Secretary, Hamish Macleod. We very briefly discussed some of my initial thoughts, then I had to go off for what amounted to a full day of interviews with the press. I also had half-hour chats with the Anglican Bishop Peter Kwong (I'm not sure that I'm going to like him very much) and with the Catholic Cardinal Wu, who seems both amiable and holy.

The press interviews didn't go too badly, though they began with a disaster. There was a great gang of journalists. I had thought it would be a good idea to attempt a cross between John Major's Downing Street briefings and an American president's rose garden media encounters. I suggested that we should get the media together in an easily recognizable place for something which wasn't quite a press conference but which enabled me to say a few words about what was going on. I thought – crazy fool – this would make it easier to avoid endless door-stepping. But what a mess. I had wanted to hold the conference in front of the house on the steps under the rather palatial pillared entrance. But our media specialists suggested that the back garden would be better. I walked down to the microphones and began speaking to a whole battery of them surrounded by a throng of radio, television and print journalists. Unfortunately, we discovered that the microphones didn't work! I then had an extremely uneasy 20 minutes with questions being thrown at me, which I would then repeat before attempting to answer without saying very much at all. It was not a happy experience. I feared that the press would be worse than it turned out to be. For example, it would have been reasonable to say that open and accessible government was obviously finding it difficult to get off the drawing board. I backed away from the microphones and headed back into the house as quickly as I could.

We then went through what a journalist subsequently described as a rather less restrained occasion than the campaigning that he had once covered with Rajiv Gandhi in Mumbai. I went to Mong Kok – not exactly the most salubrious area of Kowloon – and then on to Shatin and a squatters' encampment at Diamond Hill. We travelled to Mong Kok on the Metro surrounded by sweating, jostling radio, television and newspaper journalists, and lots of photographers. It was two hours of mayhem. I was worried that the old ladies and children whom we encountered would be trampled underfoot or beaten into submission by photographers and their large cameras as we heaved around the Metro and then the streets of this busy working-class area. Mong Kok is a district of fairly dilapidated small shops and flats with, not surprisingly, problems of crime and prostitution. I am told that it is the most densely populated place in the world; in the mid-1970s there were over 650,000 people per square mile. There were street markets everywhere, many of them selling obviously fake designer kit. It might have made good television but I'm not sure that I made as much impact with the public as I would have liked, although the people we saw seemed cheerful enough.

We went out to dinner with David Ford and his wife Gillian at their home, Victoria House, three quarters of the way up to the peak. The view from the terrace and garden in front of the house is absolutely stunning. We looked down on the mid-levels in the city from a position that was about the same height as the top of the Bank of China building. Hong Kong stretched glittering in front of us with the ships and the harbour, planes coming in low over Kowloon to make the final right-hand turn into Kai Tak, and high-rise flats in every direction. I wondered whether Britain really understood what had made Hong Kong – or what we had helped to make of it – or whether for that matter Beijing officials had the faintest notion of what Hong Kong was like these days. It's an astonishing mixture of Chinese hard work, entrepreneurialism, self-discipline and individual guts along with good old-fashioned British public administration. Where I've just come from there's not as much about of that as there used to be!

Sunday 12 July

Laura alas was taken ill over the weekend. She was rushed into hospital with appendicitis and had an operation today. Fortunately it went well, but it's not a very good introduction to Hong Kong for her. Of rather less importance during the intervals between everything else, I had some fittings for suits – one from a more expensive tailor and the other from a man everyone knows called Mr Sam. When it comes to his tailoring activities you could not regard him as a shrinking violet. I chose to go with the cheaper Mr Sam under the advice of my ADC, Felipe, himself immensely handsome and dapper; he gives sound advice about the right number of buttons on jackets and the seemly length of my trousers. If I don't look sufficiently gubernatorial, it won't be his fault. No more Harry Lime.

When I got back this afternoon from seeing Laura, whose operation went very well, there was a big mob outside Government House made up of illegal immigrants from mainland China. All of the men were without their wives and wanted an amnesty so that they could bring them into the colony. I was told that they would only hand over their petition to a member of the staff who wasn't a policeman. It was suggested that Elspeth, our marvellous housekeeper, should go out to collect it. I thought this was pretty daft and that I should do it myself. This was apparently regarded by some as a dangerous precedent and by others (Martin and Edward) as a sensible example of open government in action. It just seemed to me to be the right thing to do. When I walked out, the crowd who surrounded me looked quite rough. They were held back by policemen and were pushing children into the front line. As it turned out they were perfectly well-behaved. Try going to a political meeting in some parts of Britain. To my embarrassment a lot of them fell on their knees in gratitude after they'd handed over the petition. Then the crowd withdrew peacefully without any more genuflections and certainly without any bloodshed.

This encounter with the real world was followed by a meeting with some of my political officials, particularly those involved in the foreign policy area. My main political adviser from the Foreign Office, William Ehrman, is charming and clever with a sharp as mustard deputy called Stephen Bradley. The Governor has a Central Policy Unit whose head is Leo Goodstadt,* a serious economist and analyst of the local financial markets. He is a Catholic with a very strong sense of social responsibility. I made no decisions but sent everyone away to write papers.

Monday 13 July

I start every day with a routine office meeting at 9am with what is called by ministers in London 'morning prayers'. (I think it is rare for there to be any spiritual element to these occasions, though perhaps some ministers brought their beads along.) This is just an occasion to sit down with my private secretary, my spokesman, Martin and Edward, and any senior

* Leo Goodstadt was an Oxford-trained economist who arrived in Hong Kong in the 1960s, taught at the University of Hong Kong, wrote for a number of publications and was a prominent broadcaster and investment adviser. He was appointed by my predecessor Lord Wilson as head of the government's Central Policy Unit in 1989 and continued in that role when I was Governor. After the handover in 1997 he retired to Dublin and became a professor at the Trinity Business School there. He was a very serious believer in the obligations of Catholic social policy.

officials that we need to see urgently about my engagements for the coming day and to review the press. Whenever we have a big political issue to take, particularly anything involving China, we have what is called for rather obvious reasons an 'ad hoc' meeting. The core membership of these meetings are senior Hong Kong government officials, like the Chief Secretary and the Financial Secretary, other officials with line responsibilities, like the Secretary for Constitutional Affairs, my FCO political advisers, the leaders of our negotiations in the Joint Liaison Group, the head of the Central Policy Unit, Martin, Edward and my private secretary and spokesman. One of the most important reasons for these meetings is that they give us the opportunity to talk through the formidable range of issues which the JLG have to cover. The JLG had been established under the Joint Declaration and had to deal with all the details of changes affecting the transition, from infrastructure to civil liberties. The work here is incredibly tough, not least because the Chinese negotiators are usually programmed to be as unhelpful as possible unless they get their own way, and this changes sometimes with bewildering irrationality and speed.

I hope that my very clever advisers don't torpedo too many of my initial ideas. I have been knocking all these thoughts about with Martin and Edward; I'm so pleased they are here.

We are trying to sort out our information and communications. My main spokesman is a British civil servant, Mike Hanson; slightly improbably his home department is Customs and Excise. I like him. I would guess he is straight up and down, middle of the pack Labour (I have never asked people who work for me what their political views are), with a hefty dose of cynicism about what we are all trying to do. I don't think he trusts China's intentions an inch. Martin and Edward clearly rate him; if he gets on well with them, then there will be no problem about getting on with me. He doesn't give anyone any crap, including the Governor.

I talk to David Ford and Hamish MacLeod about the political agenda, how to embark on the budget process and the expenditure round, and what to do about my Executive Council. I consulted others on the same subject, including Lydia Dunn once again and Willie Purves,* the chairman of the Hong Kong and Shanghai Bank. He seems to me like a thousand other Scottish bank managers down the ages. He is as tough as old boots but doesn't appear to have any great perceptions about political issues. I've always thought that it is better that bank managers should be like

* Sir William Purves spent most of his life as a banker with the Hong Kong and Shanghai Bank and was appointed chairman of the group it controlled just before the purchase of the Midland Bank. He retired from HSBC in 1998.

this. The idea of a flashy bank manager should be a contradiction in terms. We finished the day with a big party and dinner for all the members of the existing Exco (inherited from my predecessor) and their spouses.

Tuesday 14 July

There is to be a meeting with Exco every Tuesday morning. It's like an informal Cabinet, a group of people from across the community chosen by the Governor to balance official advice. One of my first jobs will be to reconstitute Exco with people I have chosen myself. There were two tricky pieces of business on the agenda. First, I had to encourage members of the council to support our line on the airport negotiations. The Chinese have been suggesting that we should get on with the airport reclamation project – the airport is going to be built on reclaimed land – without settling the overall financial package. This is plainly daft and would leave us with very little negotiating room once we had built on and around the island of Chek Lap Kok with nothing connected to it. We had counter-offered with a deal on the overall financial package for the airport but no deal yet on the airport railway. Beijing plainly wants an armlock on Hong Kong whenever they wish to apply it. They have already used the airport issue to inveigle the British Prime Minister to go to Beijing on a pretty humiliating visit. He got damn all for his pains as he well knows. This is an issue on which we have to stick to what we think is right and there is very little wiggle room.

I managed to get Exco signed up behind this and then move on to another issue which is dear to the Liberal Party, as it has taken to calling itself (not a very accurate description). It's a group of rather pro-establishment characters which seems to have taken to defining the establishment as Beijing rather than Hong Kong and London. I like its leader, Allen Lee. He is a plainly decent man, though even his closest colleagues would not regard him as the sharpest pencil in the box. But I'm sure he does what he thinks is in the best interests of Hong Kong, which rather passes by the question of whether Beijing has in mind the best interests of Hong Kong. He is pressing us to support his group's proposals in Legco to quash the attempts being made by Martin Lee and the Democrats to get rid of an idea that they believe would amount to a rigged election system in 1995. The so-called 'rigging' would consist of establishing multimember constituencies with one vote per person in each one. I think we managed to avoid being drawn into supporting the Liberals on this, but it certainly demonstrates to me that if we tried to build our foundations on the support of Allen and his colleagues, we would discover very rapidly that we were building on sand.

Our ambassador in Beijing, Robin McLaren, and his wife, arrived in the afternoon for dinner and a talk. I'm not going to make life any easier for Robin, but he is a decent professional and will go along with any ideas which are supported by the government. I'm going to have to make a reasonably early visit to Beijing but not before I've announced in Hong Kong what I want to do. For him, that is the tricky bit.

Wednesday 15 July

I spent much of the day looking at the present airport – Kai Tak – and the proposed new airport and container terminals. Kai Tak is already one of the busiest airfields in the world. It has as many passengers as Gatwick and as much freight as anywhere in the United Kingdom. I am amazed at the scale of what is required to build the new airport and also at the confidence with which David Ford and others regard this massive enterprise. Can it really all be completed in five years? The general response implies that I would think like that having just come from Britain and Europe – impossible there but something which Hong Kong should be able to take in its stride. David said to me, 'You will probably be at the opening of this before you leave.' Not, I thought to myself, if the Chinese have anything to do with it.

I also met Li Ka-shing at one of his own container terminals. He is with his two sons. Li père is an exceptionally interesting man, probably the most famous of all Hong Kong's success stories. He is spoken of as a sort of financial genius and I rather believe it. He clearly regards the money he pours into charities as his third offspring. He speaks an amalgam of languages and it is not always easy to catch exactly what he means. But you know what he means when he laughs – a very engaging chuckle. I liked him a lot but probably shouldn't tell too many people this.

Thursday 16 July

After intelligence briefings, I had lunch at the Hong Kong and Shanghai Bank with Willie Purves and a group of local business leaders, including the taipans of Swire's and Jardine's. Apart from the guy from Jardine's, Nigel Rich, the conversation doesn't strike me as being terribly high-powered. They all seem rather naïve about politics and don't seem to understand that things just can't go on as they have been. If this is where political advice was coming from for the last quarter-century, no wonder we've got into the present difficulties. But there was one surprisingly liberal fellow there, called Joseph Hotung.* Apparently he funds pro-democratic political activities

* Sir Joseph Hotung was a successful businessman, a great collector of Chinese and French Impressionist art, and a very generous philanthropist donating to education, health and artistic causes. He has been a particularly substantial benefactor of the British Museum. He died in 2021.

and other good causes and is also a great collector of Chinese furniture and Impressionist paintings. The others, while being quite well-meaning, don't seem to comprehend that we can't just stand where we are. That is not an option. We have to convince the Americans and everyone else to go on investing in Hong Kong – not easy if the Chinese insist on trying to amputate most of its political structures and the attributes of a free society.

I didn't get much more sense of sophistication when I met Lord Young,* who is now the chairman of Cable & Wireless, which owns Hong Kong Telecom – a huge part of its revenue and profits. When he was in Margaret Thatcher's cabinet I always thought he had rather an inflated reputation; we'll see how good a businessman he is now that he is running Cable & Wireless. I'm not surprised to discover that the ministers he's talked to in Beijing want 20% of the shares in Hong Kong Telecoms. He seems to think that, provided he's nice to them, they will give him a reasonably free run in the telecoms sector in China. A likely story.

I almost forgot the most important event of the day – or, as Alice may argue, of most days. When she said she wanted to come with us to Hong Kong, she talked quite a lot about the desirability of having a dog, or maybe two. Lavender had a dog when we were first married and we are rather keen on canine company. We also thought that in a home as cavernous as Government House a dog or cat would have much to be said for it, though we are slightly more doggy people than cat lovers. I think cats can be very patronizing. After much discussion we settled on getting a couple of Norfolk terriers; they are the ones with ears that are flat to the head rather than standing. The first of our Norfolks, a male aged 10 months, who is to be called Whisky, arrived today. His companion, a bitch who is a bit younger, will arrive later. Whisky came via the hold on a BA plane and emerged from his temporary incarceration looking rather bemused on the lawn of our home. He is a very pretty little fellow and doesn't seem to bark. Perhaps it was just that he barked himself hoarse on the journey. I think everybody who works with us will take to him in a big way, though no doubt we may need recourse to sponges, mops and buckets for some time.

* David Young, who was ennobled by Margaret Thatcher in 1984, was a businessman brought into government as an adviser on training and employment by Thatcher and her economic soulmate Sir Keith Joseph after the 1979 election. He was later put in the Cabinet as Employment Minister and Secretary of State for Trade and Industry. He was regarded by Thatcher as a loyal 'can-do' supporter and was credited with helping deliver her enterprise agenda, though others were more sceptical about the actual scale of his achievements. Before Margaret Thatcher left office, he had resigned and gone back to business, becoming among other things executive chairman of Cable & Wireless. He was a strong leader of many important charities.

Friday 17 July

I spent much of the day with the police and got a very good briefing from some of the senior officers. Quite a few of them are expatriates heading towards retirement and a variety of occupations, including looking after an apartment in Andorra and breeding dogs in North Yorkshire. I was taken on a visit to the police tactical unit, where all the training is done for internal security and where Hong Kong's equivalent of the SAS train. They are very impressive and, like my own police protection officers, built like small wardrobes. I hope we don't need their services but, if we do, they certainly look up to the job. I was also taken up to the border to look over the barbed wire fence at the growing city of Shenzhen. The first time I came here, when I was a young backbencher in 1979, all you could see was a sleepy fishing village and paddy fields. Now the city is springing up complete with skyscrapers, and (the police say) with all the problems of raw capitalism – prostitution, Triad crime and so on. I am not sure whether Adam Smith would have been surprised by what is happening.

This week we have done several national day receptions and tonight we had a charity event – a concert by the Hong Kong Medical Association raising money for AIDS. This will clearly be the pattern for week after week. In the case of charitable functions, it's plainly the case that Hong Kong is a very generous community, which may have something to do with the low levels of tax but may also be the result of a real sense of community. I see more of Lavender than I used to do when I was a minister. She turns up at all these functions looking glamorous, well-dressed and cheerful. But she would concede that at the moment most people are mainly interested in Laura, who has happily emerged from hospital in good nick.

Saturday 18–Sunday 19 July

We went for the weekend to the Governor's country house at Fanling: it's in the New Territories, quite close to the border. It's a very nice, manageable villa, a bit like a 1930s Sunningdale or Wentworth home; and suitably surrounded by golf courses. There is a small but cheerful staff who have looked after the place for years, Ah Lam and his wife Ah Fong. Ah Lam got very excited on my first evening. Feeling rather exhausted after the week and wanting a serious pick-me-up I asked him whether he has any gin and vermouth so that I can make myself a dry martini. At the words dry martini his eyes sparkled. 'Dry martini', he enthused, 'I have not made one since Lord MacLehose was Governor. Lord MacLehose had one dry martini every day at six, second dry martini 6.15, if third dry martini big trouble.'

So no problem in that department. In the circumstances it seems appropriate that we watch *Dead Poets Society* after supper on the television. Dry martini? – 'Carpe diem.'

Last Sunday we went to the cathedral for mass and were mobbed by photographers. The parish priests made a great fuss of us and gave us a present when we left. Naturally we were asked to pose for lots of photos. This Sunday we went to mass in a little church in Taipo. It's quieter with some jolly American priests and a congregation full of Filipinos. There was lovely singing and again everyone wanted to be photographed with us. Getting photographed has become, as it were, consubstantial with going to mass. We went back to Hong Kong central by one of the helicopters which is always going to be available for longer trips around the territory. It landed on the front lawn at Fanling house and whirled us back across the countryside to Kowloon and the harbour, landing among the skyscrapers on Victoria Island. This is quite a lot easier than enduring a Sunday evening traffic jam on the M4.

Monday 20 July

A full day of meetings. There are three issues which we covered that will obviously come to dominate a good deal of my time over the coming months and maybe years. First we discussed the airport with the Chief Secretary, Financial Secretary and the head of the Joint Liaison Group, Tony Galsworthy, who does all the negotiating on detailed aspects of the handover with the Chinese. We agreed that we should be calm but firm, pointing out that sooner or later the airport will be built, but should keep to the position that we cannot do any more at the moment to allay alleged Chinese anxieties. We should also make plain that the Chinese should not be so naïve as to think that we would accept some linkage between political issues and agreement on the airport. If the airport is to be built, so be it. We can do it, and Hong Kong will be able to pay for it without much difficulty. But if the Chinese are determined to force us into a political row with the citizens of Hong Kong as the price for letting us build the airport with the territory's own money, then there is no game in town.

Second, I was also able to discuss with the CS, the FS and other senior officials how we can use our five-year spending horizon as the core of my first speech to Legco. I'm very keen to find easily identifiable targets for extra expenditure in areas like education and welfare without appearing to the business community to be getting too soft. Frankly, they're not going to be too upset about spending provided they don't have to pay more tax.

Third, as Martin and Edward have urged, I met some of the political parties, one by one. Martin Lee and his Democrats are much the most rational on political and constitutional issues. Unlike Allen Lee's so-called Liberals, who don't seem to know whether they're coming or going, the Democrats understand that one of the options in front of me is to make a complete break between the Executive Council and the Legislative Council. They also accept that one alternative to an increase in the number of directly elected members in Legco would be to change the election committee before 1995, for example by forming it out of the directly elected members of other local and district councils, and to increase the number of people who can vote in functional constituencies. Corporate voting in the functional constituencies leads to the creation of some really scandalous rotten pocket boroughs. It's much easier to see how you can do business with people provided you know what their price is likely to be and what their bottom line is.

John Major phoned to ask how Laura is getting on. I miss talking to him and some of my other friends. Tristan phoned the other day. I suppose this is the first week for years that I haven't had a really good natter with him about politics.

The dominating character today has of course been Whisky. He is starting to wander about the house; he came breezing into the private secretary's office and has found his way to the kitchen. He tends to sniff guests' trouser legs when they come in for meetings. One thing that has been resolved is the question of whether he has a bark. This morning he came into my dressing room, jumped up on a cushion, and started busily examining himself in the mirror. He found the sight of another dog rather exciting. He had a good bark at it and spent some time trying to get closer to the object of his animosity. I suspect that it won't take mirrors to set him off in future.

Tuesday 21 July

We spent a lot of time discussing the forthcoming meetings with Douglas Hurd and Richard Needham,* the trade minister, who are both arriving

* Richard Needham came into Parliament in the same intake as me in 1979 for the neighbouring constituency of North Wiltshire. He had beaten me for the selection as Conservative candidate there. An Irish peer, not entitled to take a seat in the House of Lords, he became a hugely successful minister in Northern Ireland from 1985 to 1992 responsible for pioneering much of the redevelopment in Belfast and Londonderry. He then became the trade minister from 1992 to 1995 after which he resumed a successful career in business and wrote entertainingly about the relationship between politics and business. He was and is one of my best friends, brave, principled and probably as funny a raconteur as anyone should wish to be. As a minister, he got things done which sometimes involved vigorous activity with omelettes and eggs.

later in the week in Hong Kong. At this morning's Exco meeting, the main subjects were pensions, on which we had a consultative document, and once again the airport.

In the afternoon the most interesting meeting was with Emily Lau. Emily has been for so many years one of the most outspoken and articulate of all the Democratics. She is generally thought by visiting British ministers to be a firebrand. This simply reflects the fact that what some ministers think to be an impossible and extreme position is a perfectly rational expression of legitimate aspirations in Hong Kong, which though difficult to deliver are wholly comprehensible. She is very articulate and plainly immune to my charm but I think recognizes that I am at least trying and that I have a good deal of sympathy with her general objectives. The fact that for a variety of reasons, some buried in history, you can't do what someone wants doesn't mean that you can't sympathize.

Wednesday 22 July

Two typhoons hit Hong Kong today. The meteorological office registered a warning at level 8, which is pretty severe. It rained very large cats and dogs, which means that I had to postpone a visit to housing estates. There was another blast from Lu Ping and Chinese officials about the airport. We decided to make it clear that we had published all the details of our position on the airport; we had been entirely open; and we thought the airport could easily be sorted out 'on its merits'. I suspect that people may be starting to see the linkage which Beijing is trying to make between the airport and other matters.

The second typhoon to arrive was the trade minister, my friend and former neighbour in his Chippenham constituency, Richard Needham. He was in wonderful form. When is he not? Richard makes things happen and gets things done. He did a fantastic job in Northern Ireland helping to develop Londonderry and Belfast after the bombing campaigns there. He gave us all a lecture within moments of arrival about how he was going to open up China and what we should all be doing. I had a late night drink with him and a long gossip about who's up and who's down at home, and about what I'm trying to do here. He wants to descend on us with about five score relatives at Christmas and the New Year. I love him to bits, though I know that for some less discerning people he may be a slightly acquired taste. I have always liked gin in my tonic. My dad claimed that in French West Africa during the war when he was there, you had to ask in the officers' mess for 'gin tonic avec gin'. Richard is a whole litre of the stuff.

A telegram came in today from Beijing commenting on our embassy's views on my ideas. The Foreign Office – this may mean the admirable Peter Ricketts – are bothered that I may find it too critical. The ambassador, Robin McLaren, who is in London at the moment, takes a similar view. I think that's a good sign. It suggests at least some officials want to be reasonably accommodating. We'll see how things go when Douglas Hurd comes at the weekend.

Thursday 23 July

Lots of meetings in the morning about security issues and illegal immigration. We've been dealing pretty successfully with smuggling by high-powered speedboats from Canton (Guangdong). The trouble is that they have now started using lorry containers too. I suggested during the meeting that we should purchase more x-ray equipment for looking at containers. I was told that very often the gangs cut up the cars which they have stolen into four pieces which makes them more difficult to spot. When I look back on some of our family vehicles down the years I think I must have purchased some of those with the parts put back in the wrong order. One issue which should affect the trade minister's agenda is that apparently the cars most frequently stolen and smuggled are Mercedes, BMWs and Lexuses. Nobody seems to care much about Jaguars.

Among the political groups that I saw in the afternoon, much the most interesting were the people from the Democratic Alliance for the Betterment of Hong Kong (DAB HK) – the long title for the pro-Beijing United Front lobby. This group was led by a couple of sharp fellows who delivered yet another message from Lu Ping, who they have just been up to the capital to see. I gave them a frank talk about my objectives in Hong Kong – Britain was not going to make off with all the treasure; we weren't trying to design a timebomb to blow the government of the PRC to smithereens, and so on. They responded rather well rhetorically to the points I made. The chairman, Tsang Yok-sing, is a middle school headmaster whose brother is the editor of one of the two principal communist newspapers. If he wasn't so obviously bound into the United Front, I think I could get on with him rather well. In his favour he plainly believes much of what he says; his main aim is to see the colonial power on its way, but within reason I think he wants to stick up for Hong Kong's interests. Presumably, he doesn't want to see one colonial power followed by another, far more brutal one.

People keep on asking me, maybe not as bluntly as this, what my game is. So what is it?

First, I don't want to be seen as Beijing's man in Hong Kong, nor as somebody whose principal concern is British commercial interests. I have to be seen as somebody who is prepared to stand up for Hong Kong both with Beijing and with London. I also want to talk to Hong Kong openly about the future and about my intentions.

Secondly, I don't want to lose control of what's happening in Hong Kong before we actually depart.

Thirdly, I obviously have to embed as far as possible the laws on human rights and freedoms in Hong Kong and to defend the independence of the judiciary, the whole question of due process and the cleanness as well as the openness of government. I suspect it's going to be more difficult as we get closer to 1997 to prevent corruption creeping in.

Fourthly, without breaking the Joint Declaration or the Basic Law I think we have to fill in some of the gaps in the present proposals for the 1995 elections to ensure that they are as fair and clean as possible. I think we can actually increase the number of people who are able to vote without breaking any agreements.

Fifthly, I want to use Hong Kong's spectacular economic success not only to build the airport and other important infrastructure projects, but to set in train some of the social changes and reforms which will help to close the huge gap between rich and poor. I don't want to increase taxation but I do want to do something about some of the really big social problems in education, health, welfare and pensions. Housing will be more difficult because of the relationship between the stock market and land supply. But we should be able to do rather more to give people decent accommodation.

That should keep me going. I don't know what Douglas Hurd will think about it this weekend. There will be a lot of criticism from both flanks about my ideas on elections, which are actually rather limited. In particular there will be loads of rubbishing of anything I suggest which annoys Beijing. Some people seem to take the view that the main measure of success in Hong Kong is to avoid being criticized by the communists up north. That certainly seemed to be the idea the other day of Lord Young (who will be here regularly since Hong Kong Telecom represents a huge chunk of the revenues and profits of Cable & Wireless). His enthusiasm for democracy seems to be pretty vestigial, partly perhaps because he's never stood for election to anything.

Friday 24 July

After the typhoon a lovely bright day on which I focused on education, making a number of visits accompanied by the secretary who covers education and manpower, John Chan. He is regarded as the front runner to be the first Chinese Chief Secretary.

We went first to the University Grants Commission, where we were briefed by the very bright chairman, a Cambridge-educated lawyer called Andrew Li, a successful barrister. We then went on to a teachers' in-service training centre and witnessed a display of martial arts by primary schoolchildren. They were led by a little bruiser aged 11 who hailed from Beijing and took no prisoners. There are a lot of educational projects funded by the Jockey Club, with whom I had lunch. Hong Kong has a very unusual arrangement – no betting tax but all the huge revenues from horseracing go to this autonomous body with the assumption that it will give loads of dosh to the charitable sector. This seems to work pretty well and there doesn't seem much point in changing it. People in Hong Kong are mad about gambling and bet almost as much in an evening at the races as would be gambled in a good part of the season in England.

After visiting the Chinese University (the Vice-Chancellor is a Chinese scientist who is regarded as one of the fathers of fibreoptics) I was greeted by a very polite students' demonstration about a Public Ordinance on the right of assembly. Are all students this polite? This was the first visit I've made to a university. There are seven or eight. I am required to be Chancellor of all of them, and since they all require different gowns my valet is going to have to pay attention when kitting me out for my visits. I tried to suggest that making the Governor Chancellor everywhere might not be a very good idea and suggested that perhaps universities could choose their own chancellors. No one seemed to think this was acceptable. I think in the universities themselves there is a nervousness that I might give up theirs and stick to one favoured institution.

Saturday 25 July

We took Richard Needham for a cruise on the *Lady Maurine*. It must be the smartest boat in the orient, admirably old-fashioned and neat as a pin. There is a small and well turned-out crew and we had a lovely little voyage along a coastline which looks magnificent, with rugged green hills falling down into the sea. We anchored off Lamma Island and the crew got the speedboat out so that Richard, Alice and her friend Kitty Dimbleby could waterski. While I was having a quiet swim, I suddenly found myself confronting a couple of large, battered-looking wooden freight vessels which came rather too close without (I think) noticing that I was in the water. The men driving our speedboat were rather alarmed. it's not in their terms of reference to have the Governor run over while on a voyage. When I got back to the *Lady Maurine*, we realized that the other ships were clearly smugglers – a Taiwanese vessel and a mainland Chinese ship offloading supplies onto it. My protection officer got on to the marine division of the police and as we sailed back towards Victoria Island we were passed by a police vessel with sirens blaring heading in the other direction.

We had a lovely supper anchored in Repulse Bay and – a reward for my efforts to stock the wine cellar – we drank a lot of very good Saint-Véran. We sailed back past Aberdeen and its floating restaurants with their glittering lights, and on round the west of Hong Kong island to come back into the main harbour between the mainland and the island itself. I suppose it's one of the greatest journeys you could take anywhere. I hope I manage to stay for the full five years!

Sunday 26 July

Richard left and Douglas flew into town. We had a good walk with him and his Hong Kong-based son and lots of staff on Lantau. We went to matins at the Anglican cathedral; I always have difficulty singing the psalms in the Church of England. After we had played tennis with Richard and Rosie Hoare (they beat us), Douglas got back from other meetings and we talked about some of my initial ideas. While there will have to be some consultation with the Chinese, we mustn't put them in a position where they can undermine the political impact of what we agree to do through selective leaking and general unhelpful noise. The other thing we agreed at dinner (with our respective officials) is that we can't commit ourselves to consultation for an indefinite period during which one idea after another is gradually sunk, as has too often happened in the past. Leo Goodstadt and Michael Sze* – who is responsible for constitutional affairs in the Hong Kong government – were particularly animated at dinner. The more I see of Goodstadt the more I like him. He is immensely knowledgeable about individual community figures and their foibles, and has a marvellous ability to think and jump laterally.

Douglas and I had a chat on our own after dinner. He is worried about the Prime Minister being tired, and the Prime Minister is worried about him being tired. Douglas obviously has a killing routine and is about to tell Judy that part of their holiday is going to be clobbered by the next Yugoslav peace conference. He encouraged me to go on thinking about domestic politics. Well okay, but even after a couple of months I feel rather

* Michael Sze was born in mainland China but his family moved to Hong Kong. After his education he joined the civil service and rose to become Secretary for Constitutional Affairs from 1991 to 1994 and then Secretary for the Civil Service from 1994 to 1996. He was appointed as executive director of the Trade Development Council from 1996 to 2004. A competent official of unquestionable integrity, Sze was the sort of public servant who helped to make Hong Kong such a success and so decent a society.

out of things and disengaged. But he says that I should go on phoning John from time to time. It seems to be perfectly obvious that John needs one or two friends with him on the spot. I suspect that when he is there solo, he spends too much time reading the newspapers and thinking of everything that can go wrong.

Monday 27 July

After visiting a Buddhist temple, Douglas and I had a walkabout in a housing estate. It was a bit like electioneering again. There was lots of well-managed enthusiasm, with a pack of journalists and cameramen forming a scrum around us. Douglas noted that the only thing we weren't saying was 'I hope I can count on your support.'

Wednesday 29 July

Today was a health day – I visited hospitals and clinics. I kissed my first baby or rather a baby kissed me. This will puzzle the old United Front lags at the New China News Agency, Beijing's main operational outfit in Hong Kong. We had a difficult meeting to discuss the awkward business of the forcible return of Vietnamese boat people, trying to ensure that we don't make too many rods for our back with the media and, to be fair, so that we handle the Vietnamese refugees themselves as well as is possible.* We went out with Felipe, Elspeth and some of the private office to dinner at Sai Kung. Again, there is a big enthusiastic crowd. One man pushed his daughter forward to get my autograph – or so I thought. What he really wanted to do was to announce that she was at Wycombe Abbey School and that his son was going to Prince Charles's old school, Cheam. It seems some distance from Sai Kung!

Friday 31 July–Monday 3 August

A succession of themed days. First one with briefings and visits about trade and industry. Our trade department is quite significant internationally. We have independent status as a full member of the WTO and have long been advocates for free trade across the board. The department is run by a neat, bright, bow-tied fellow, Donald Tsang, who has two sons at Ampleforth. I also visited the Industry Department, the Productivity Council and a number of individual businesses. One of the most impressive

* From the mid-1970s Vietnamese families had fled first the war and then the communist regime in their country. The great majority came by boat, a perilous journey. By the early 1990s there were well over 50,000 in Hong Kong. Some were classified as refugees and others, according to UN criteria, were put into a repatriation programme.

factories I visited makes plastic mouldings and is run by a genial patriarch who has given away all his shares, mostly to his staff. His workforce is well trained, committed and fit – all his apprentices have to go on a long hike every year in order to show they are fit enough to be technicians in the plant. Most of the managers I met turned out to be engineers with MBAs. I also met the boss of the Trade Development Council (promoting our exports), an entrepreneur called Victor Fung who runs a hugely successful import–export business.

I did another day on transport and discovered at the Mass Transit Railway Corporation that they not only make a profit but have a better credit rating than the People's Republic of China. Talking to some of the senior transport figures, I was told that there is a huge backlog of trucks waiting to go into China because officials on the Chinese side are conducting health checks. If these were necessary in either direction, they should be affecting Chinese vehicles coming into our territory. The suspicion of course is that backhanders have a part to play in all this.

Tuesday 4 August 1992

I had quite a big speech to the Hong Kong Chamber of Commerce with the biggest turnout ever – over 700 people. I suspect (which is often the case) that the most interest was not in what I said but the fact that I spoke with just a few notes. This professional politician's facility may wear thin after a bit, but for the time being I got a good response to what I say about the airport, political developments, stability and prosperity in the long term.

My most important visitor was Ambassador Ma from London, who was paying his first ever visit to the city. We spent a lot of time planning the logistics. We didn't want to take up valuable time besieged by the press and photographers. Felipe, my ADC, organized a spectacular decoy exercise so that we could get the ambassador, me, our wives and advisers onto a helicopter to one of the outlying islands, where we could pick up *Lady Maurine*, sail back to Lamma and stop there for dinner. Before this I had a long conversation with him and tried my usual act of being friendly but candid and firm. I told him that it would be useful if I had somebody in Hong Kong that I could talk to frankly. The head of the local New China News Agency, who is supposed to be China's man on the ground, is apparently a complete nightmare. He is an old communist hack and plainly believes in every conspiracy theory about the colonial power. I told the ambassador that so far I have done exactly what I said I would do when we last spoke in London. I want to go to Beijing after my speech at Legco; I'm postponing a visit to Canada (to speak to large meetings of the Hong Kong diaspora there) until I've been to Beijing. But I really can't go there before I've told people in Hong Kong what I would like to do over the next few years. I hope that I'll be able to develop a personal relationship with Lu Ping. I've decided to have a strong Executive Council separate from the Legislative Council. I can't be seen to be rigging the elections for 1995; it's not in anyone's interest that I should be regarded as Beijing's puppet. I will go to Washington in due course to lobby in favour of MFN status for China. MFN will mean that China will enjoy trade terms with the USA that are no worse than those of other countries given the same status.

I said that we have been making much too little progress in the Joint Liaison Group and add once again that any attempt to establish linkage between building the airport and political matters is not only clumsy but doomed to failure. Ambassador Ma is a courteous diplomat and gives the impression of being keen to convey the message that I've given him in the terms in which I delivered it. He seems to be a reliable and competent fellow, but quite what anyone will make of what I've said, heaven alone knows. Anyway, politics apart, or even politics included, it was a lovely evening which I think Ambassador Ma and his wife appreciated. We literally pushed the boat out for them and enjoyed it ourselves too.

Friday 14 August

We're starting to build a consensus within the team around the composition of the electorate for the functional constituencies, the composition of the election committee and the voting methods not only for 1995 but also for elections to the district boards the year before. At a meeting with the district councils on 5 August they were very critical of any idea that they should include a much larger elected element. I've thought that this should happen ever since I first came to Hong Kong in 1979. I don't think this is an argument which they are going to win. Flatteringly, after our really open discussion about all this with all my senior colleagues on 6 August, Leo Goodstadt and Mike Hanson said that they think it's the best meeting they've ever had in Government House. There is of course no point in having clever and well-informed people working for you if you don't give them their head a bit. While Margaret Thatcher was splendid in many ways, I don't think she got the best out of her team by announcing before the beginning of a discussion what its conclusions were going to be.

I'm getting fairly good press from most of the media, but the United Front papers are starting to run articles criticizing my political behaviour. They argue that I should be sorting out problems with China not appealing for public support. I suppose they must be a bit worried about me and don't really know how to cope with my approach at the moment.

Lavender had a good meeting yesterday about equal pay and job opportunities for women. There is no equal opportunities legislation in Hong Kong. She intends to visit both the women's centre and the legal advice centre and is clearly pleased to be able to pursue issues about which she knew a great deal as a barrister.

Felipe, Elspeth and Lavender's social secretary, Louise, have got lots of ideas about how we can give the house a bit of a facelift and start opening it up to the public for charitable events and concerts. On the downside Laura returned to London. She's going to stay with Tristan and Catali for a time. Talking to Tristan he says that the economic news at home is pretty bleak. The upturn in the economy seems not so much belated as non-existent. People are starting to get a bit frisky as Tristan puts it.

Saturday 15 August

We spent much of the day with our housekeeper, Elspeth, Lavender's social secretary, Louise, and my deputy private secretary, Anne Shepherd, looking at pictures and furniture that will make the house look rather better. The Museum of Art has promised that we can borrow some paintings, which will make a change from what we have at present – usually old copies or replicas of long dead British royals. I was particularly struck by one painting of a group of Chinese 19th-century men in the company of a few Western businessmen wearing top hats. It's a very dark, slightly eerie picture. I'd love to have it in Government House, but its size and gloomy quality probably make it impossible for us to take it. We found quite a bit of furniture in the back streets of Kowloon, where there's a lot of old stuff which has plainly been brought in from the mainland. We bought a wonderfully ornate altar table, a huge wickerwork dresser, and a big sideboard and one or two other pieces all for about £550. So far all this is for us personally, which we will use in GH. We also looked at some new furniture for the government to purchase for the house.

I'm still getting lots of messages from people who claim to be intermediaries from Lu Ping. But my main meeting this week – which is not going to be easy – is to be with the local head of the New China News Agency, Zhou Nan.

Monday 17 August

I spent a lot of time today with David Ford, Leo Goodstadt and a few others talking about the membership of Exco. I will obviously keep senior officials like the Chief Secretary, the Financial Secretary and the Attorney General on the council, but would like to bring in some other local Chinese officials – probably taking two from John Chan, Michael Sze and Anson

Chan. I also think that I should retain Lydia Dunn as senior member and Willie Purves, the boss of HSBC. But I want to drop all the rest, including the Commander British Forces, which I hope won't cause ructions with the Ministry of Defence. It would obviously be quite difficult to keep the PLA [People's Liberation Army] off the Executive Council after 1997 if we had had a British general on it until then. The people I'm keenest to have from the outside are Andrew Li* (barrister), Denis Chang (another barrister), Rosanna Tam Wong† (youth organizations), Professor Felice Lieh-Mak (a legislator at present and an academic), Edward Chen (an economist), Victor Fung (industry and trade), and C. H. Tung (business and shipping).‡ Tung's business used to be largely with Taiwan, but when all the main shipping operations got into trouble a few years ago his firm was largely bailed out by Beijing interests. Beijing plainly trusts him because of their commercial connections, but also because he's deeply conservative and knows America well. I think that most of his family have American passports. His conservatism runs deep. He's not a bad man at all, indeed I rather like him. But he plainly thinks that democracy is not something that flourishes in Asia, and indeed I suspect he reckons there's too much of it in America and Europe. It's just nice for his family to be able to live there if they want.

* Andrew Li Kwok-nang was born in Hong Kong and graduated from Cambridge University. He practised as a barrister back in his home city and was a member of the Executive Council from 1992 to 1996. He had already served as a deputy High Court judge and held a number of other public service appointments. He was appointed in 1997 as the first Chief Justice of the Court of Final Appeal by C. H. Tung. He stepped down from that post in 2010, subsequently receiving numerous honours and awards including an honorary degree at Oxford University.

† Rosanna Wong was a social work administrator mainly with young people before being appointed as a member of the Legislative Council from 1985 to 1991 and the Executive Council after that. I made her the convener of the council on Lydia Dunn's retirement in 1995 and she also served on the council for a time after the handover. She was chairperson of the housing authority from 1993 to 2000. She was awarded a DBE in 1997.

‡ C. H. Tung was born in Shanghai; he was the oldest son of the shipping magnate who owned the Orient Overseas Container Line and took over the firm in 1981. OOCL was bailed out by the Chinese government when in financial difficulties in 1986. He was a member of the Executive Committee from 1992 to 1996 and, after the handover, was appointed Hong Kong's Chief Executive from 1997 to 2005. In that year he became a member of the Chinese People's Political Consultative Committee. He was thought to be a useful spokesperson for Chinese viewpoints in the USA, though despite his affability, his hostility to democracy and the freedoms usually associated with an open society probably limited this value. He sold his shipping business to the Chinese state-owned Cosco shipping line for $6.3 billion in 2017.

Tuesday 18 August

I had three visitors today representing foreign interests. First I saw the Japanese consul (Masaki Orita). The Japanese invariably send first-class diplomats to Hong Kong, often I think to recover from more strenuous jobs they've had back home. The list includes my friends Yukio Satoh and Koichiro Matsuura, who is now the Vice Foreign Minister. He was my opposite number when I was aid minister. The Japanese have a very close economic relationship with Hong Kong and want it to go on working well. They seem to be quite good at getting messages through to Beijing without making the Chinese cross. Orita invited Lavender and me to Japan in November. I had to tell the Canadian consul who comes in next that I'm not going to be able to go to his country for the end of the Hong Kong festival in October, but will rearrange the visit for November so that I can visit Beijing first. He understood the point perfectly well. He thought it's very difficult to know who makes policy on Hong Kong in Beijing and reckoned that even good up-and-coming Chinese officials would try to keep well clear of policy on Hong Kong, regarding it rather as British politicians might think about Northern Ireland. He is obviously sympathetic to the Democrats' ideas about political issues and thinks one of my jobs is to try to find some centre ground for political activity between now and 1997. But he reckoned that the Chinese will be very suspicious of anything which looks as though it's increasing accountability in Hong Kong.

After this I had a meeting with an American senator from Montana, Max Baucus, and the local consul. He is one of the few Democrats who seems to be in favour of continuing MFN status for China, presumably on the grounds that he comes from a farm state and doesn't want to prejudice exports, principally of wheat. I noted that since Hong Kong at present represents about 19% of China's GDP (if you add in neighbouring Guangdong it must be almost 28%), any interruption to free trade would inevitably have a devastating effect on our local economy.

Wednesday 19 August

I've started having tennis lessons. I play early in the morning with a very amiable chap called Hans Franklin. Even playing at about 7.30, and taking both a cold shower and bath afterwards, I'm still sweating two or three hours later. I wish I'd played tennis earlier in my life. I'll never be better than the average club player now.

The head of the monetary authority, Joseph Yam, told me just how much we've got in the kitty supporting our strong currency. I'm very keen that we shouldn't run mindlessly large surpluses when we could be spending money on worthwhile social and infrastructure projects.

Thursday 20 August
A talk with my inner group of senior officials about functional constituencies (which we want to increase from 21 to 30 so as to cover most parts of the community). We also discussed how much I should say is unamendable when I make my speech to the Legislative Council before going off to Beijing. Plainly I won't want to set everything in concrete but will want to have a credible package. I suspect that whatever happens we will find ourselves falling somewhere between Martin Lee and Lu Ping. But the most important thing I have to do is to make sure that the majority of the community is supportive, and that, I guess, means that Martin Lee and his colleagues are the vital part of my audience. If I lose the community, and have no local political support, things will be pretty unstable in the run-up to 1997. I'm not sure that the Chinese will understand this, but they won't want to take over a city in which there is political turbulence. As we know, their idea for dealing with turbulence is to knock people over the head – and that's if they're lucky.

I had a meeting with Zhou Nan,* the local NCNA [National China New Agency] head. He's been a member of China's diplomatic corps for many years, is well known to our own Foreign Office people, and has a reputation for being some distance from amiable. He does speak beautiful English – and is not unreasonably rather proud of this – but he is cold and arrogant. He gave me some familiar warnings but seemed pleased that I was enthusiastic about paying a visit to Beijing. I stressed that I felt strongly that a smooth transition would not be possible if I had to sacrifice fair arrangements for the 1995 elections in order to get it. I'm sure this is going to be the point around which argument will revolve for the next few months. The Chinese continue to stress that what we must support is the concept of what they call a through train. What this means is that whatever is in place before 1997 can continue unchanged afterwards: but the underlying text is that they should determine what happens before 1997. We would have to take the blame for whatever we did on the ground and they would simply inherit it after the handover. I guess we

* Zhou Nan joined the Communist Party in 1946 and worked as a political commissar in Korea interrogating POWs. He joined the Chinese diplomatic service and rose to become ambassador to the UN in 1980. From 1983 he was engaged as a vice foreign minister and then head of the New China News Agency in Hong Kong during the negotiations for the transfer of the territory to China. The description of him on Wikipedia as 'a witty and urbane' man who 'liked to charm people' shows that political irony is not dead.

may have to contend with Chinese threats of disruption in 1997, which the local community would need a good deal of self-confidence to cope with. I don't want in any way to be seen to be reneging on the Joint Declaration or the Basic Law. That's part of my bottom line. But the way the Chinese communists define the through train makes it sound like a funeral hearse for British sovereignty, British honour and British competence in governing this great city.

Friday 21 August

The most important meetings during this week have been, first, to flesh out my Legco speech and, second, to get all my political proposals in reasonable shape. Lydia Dunn is very supportive when I talk to her. She argues that one has to be firm with China though not go too far. (I wonder what too far actually means.) She seemed to think that I've got it about right and I hope this continues to be her view.

I've had a lot of interviews with journalists, including a smart guy from the *Guardian* called Steve Vines and a group of what I'm told are children for the *South China Morning Post*. They are charming, bright and very interested in the environment. I asked the first one where she is at school. She is rather aggrieved and tells me she is not in school any more but is about to go to Magdalen College, Oxford, to read law! I told this to Lavender, who was just going off to cut a ribbon at a display ahead of the Hong Kong festival in Canada, in front of Alice. Alice is obviously cross with me for committing such an embarrassing solecism and I get a big thumbs down.

Tuesday 25 August

I saw the Commissioner of Police about Triad activity. The Triads are becoming a real menace as they try to put their roots down just over the border in Shenzhen and surrounding areas. They have a foothold in parts of the New Territories adjoining the border and are well-entrenched in some sectors, for example the film industry. We have to keep harassing them without transgressing the Bill of Rights.

Wednesday 26 August

The most terrifying event of the week, without question, was an afternoon with the CBF, General John Foley,* which begins with me firing a

* Lt Gen Sir John Foley had been director of the SAS in 1983. After being commander of British forces in Hong Kong from 1992 to 1994, he became Chief of Defence Intelligence. On retirement from the army he became Lieutenant Governor of Guernsey from 2000 to 2005.

machine gun during a routine military exercise and continuing with my piloting a landing craft rather erratically across Victoria Harbour. I was also flown in a Wessex helicopter around all the main defence sites in Hong Kong. We are haggling over their futures with the Chinese PLA. So I could see the military view rather better, the door of the helicopter was left open. As the helicopter circles the sites and banks sharply, I became more aware of the fact that the only thing between me and a long drop was my seatbelt. I pretended to be made of sterling stuff, but my stomach left me. But when you're the boss, you can't let on that you are scared witless.

Thursday 27 August

Peter Woo, who is married to one of the daughters of the late Y. K. Pao (the shipping billionaire), came to see me with the mayor of Wuhan, a city in which he is investing in the expectation that it will become one of the transport hubs of central China. I discover that Wuhan is at least the same size as London and is linked to Manchester. My family came originally from Manchester and I make a few jokes about the city's weather. Despite heroic attempts at translation, these are plainly not understood by the mayor, but at least are not regarded as discourteous or rude. Message to self – never tell jokes in your own language to people who don't understand a word of it.

Saturday 29 August

K day – which we've all been waiting for. Kate arrived in the evening on Cathay Pacific from her travels in South America. As her plane taxied into the stand, we could see her up on the flight deck with the crew. Hearts leapt. With the help of Felipe, we organized a helicopter to meet her, and she came down the aircraft steps looking blonder and even prettier than I remembered. Once in the helicopter (a great surprise for her) after lots of hugs we took her on a stunning flight over Hong Kong and then up to Fanling, where we landed on the golf course in the lights from two police vehicles. My godson Adam Codrington is also staying with us with a couple of friends from school, so we have a full house. The champagne corks flew. There is a sort of genial serenity about our lovely eldest daughter now she has grown up. So in a funny sort of way it's both a welcome home and in another sense a goodbye, farewell to the sixth former. I wish Laura was here as well. We miss her.

Wednesday 2 September

For our family the most important event this month was that Alice started at the Island school. It has a good reputation, like all the international schools in Hong Kong and genuinely comprehensive in terms of ability, social class, race and ethnicity. For a couple of days, she had to endure the press and television cameras when she went to school and even when she left in the afternoon. It made her a bit anxious but she seemed to take it all in her formidable little stride. She obviously likes the teachers (who all seem very good) and the other kids. The very sensible Welsh headmaster, David James, did a deal with the press which they stick to: photos and coverage twice a day for two days, and that's it.

I continued the visits to districts and to different aspects of Hong Kong's life and the government's administration of the city. Today, I went to Sham Shui Po, walked round the public housing estates there and up and down streets packed with hawkers. I was presented with bananas, melons, flowers and other assorted objects, and at the end, after a tea reception with the district board members, I had familiar questions from the accompanying press. My visit to the walled city in Kowloon before it was demolished was rather different. I'm glad it's being knocked down. It's an awful place and only when you're at the old courthouse in the middle can you actually get any view of the sky. In the middle of the day we moved in gloom down narrow alleys between high tenement walls. At least the rats seem to have been killed. The sooner it's blown up the better.

I have had the usual clutch of visitors, including Lord Irvine of Lairg, who will I suppose be Labour's Lord Chancellor one day. He was full of sense about the legal issues which I'm discussing with the Chief Justice, encouraging him to put in place rather better ways of administering the courts and the legal system as a whole. He also had great advice on purchasing Chinese antiques and demonstrated a good working knowledge of red wine.

Thursday 3 September

I spent the day with the discipline and rescue services – prisons, customs, fire services and the Royal Hong Kong Auxiliary Air Force. In the prison at Stanley even the people working in the factory shops seemed cheerful, energetic and committed. Can it really be the case that the entrepreneurial spirit thrives not just outside the prison walls but inside too? I have visited quite a few prisons in Britain and am aware that problems usually include not only drugs but also sexually transmitted diseases. When I asked the prison governor, who is showing me around, about that, he looks at me askance and says, 'That isn't a problem we have in Chinese societies.' Perhaps he has led a very sheltered life and never been into the showers.

I don't think that I would have got quite the same answer when I visited the aircraft carrier *Invincible*, which is paying a visit to Hong Kong. I stayed on the bridge while the captain took the ship out into the middle of the harbour. He was clearly an outstanding seaman who declined any help from tugs and took his vast carrier out into the water at the harbour's entrance himself. He dashed around on the bridge shouting instructions into a telephone and darkening his smart white shirt with sweat. His officers had that best of all British mixtures of competence, decency and good humour, and were obviously huge fans of their boss.

I got useful insights into China from Steve Tsang, an impressive academic at Oxford. He noted first that an indication of the political incompetence of the Chinese Communist Party in Hong Kong is that they'd allowed Martin Lee's Democrats to whip them so soundly electorally. Sooner or later, either Martin and Co. will be running the city or they'll all have been put in prison. Secondly, he pointed out that Taiwan provides a good answer to the usual proposition that democracy doesn't work in Chinese societies. Taiwan's democratic system actually seems to work rather well.

Sunday 6 September

A potentially awkward visitor was Margaret Thatcher, who came down to us from Beijing with her husband, Denis. We offered them lunch at Fanling and invited a group of their old acquaintances from the days of negotiating the Joint Declaration. Alastair Goodlad was with us, as the minister of state in the Foreign Office responsible for what we do. Edward Llewellyn was charged with getting the lady in and out of Hong Kong without any explosions. He did an excellent job, but that was partly because she knew the colony very well and had good instincts about our job here. Before lunch I had a chat with her and explained what we are trying to do. There was a bit of a frisson when I mentioned the functional constituencies – she thinks they smack of corporatism but seems to have forgotten that they were set up when she was Prime Minister. Anyway, she seemed to be onside. She had some rather strong views on China, which she thinks may break up. I politely disagree. She takes rather the conventional view that economic development is certain to have political consequences. Maybe that is what we all hope; it is rather a Marxist view. We managed to avoid talking about Europe, Maastricht and Yugoslavia for most of lunch. Just occasionally a little barb floated across the table about one of these issues like a paper dart.

Thursday 10 September

There was a drama involving two alleged Chinese dissidents who can't be kept in Hong Kong but have been denied entry to the UK. This had all the makings of a nasty political incident. I hoped the Canadians might be prepared to take the two women. What was absolutely clear was that we can't send them back to mainland China. But we seemed to be making progress on the issue of the new terminal, thanks to some very neat footwork by the senior civil servant involved, Anson Chan.* She found an ingenious formula which met some of my requirements about openness and competition while guarding against any lack of competitiveness in the running of the terminal and port as a whole. She has many of the things that I like about civil servants – she's decisive, smart, talks straight to me and is prepared to take on tough assignments. My team think she is terrific, together with Michael Sze, that she's the best of the local civil servants – and since most of them are very good that is high praise.

Friday 11–Monday 14 September

The main official discussions continued to revolve around the airport and the contents of my speech to the Legislative Council, particularly on political development. The importance of all this was heightened by the fact that John Major and Douglas Hurd think I should go back to London for a brief meeting of the appropriate Cabinet committee to get their approval for what I am proposing we do. It was important to manage this visit without giving the impression that something had gone wrong. If I can get a thumbs up from the Cabinet it will give me a lot of flexibility as we head into the future.

* Anson Chan was born in Shanghai to a family whose profound Chinese patriotism was unquestionable. Her maternal grandfather was a general who fought in the Sino-Japanese war. Her uncle was an orthopaedic surgeon who helped to care for Deng Xiaoping's son after he was defenestrated during the Cultural Revolution. Her mother, Fang Zhaoling, was probably the greatest female Chinese painter of the last half-century or more. (Her work can be seen in many galleries including the Ashmolean in Oxford.) After her father's death, Anson was brought up and educated in Hong Kong. She joined the civil service and rose to become Chief Secretary in 1993. She remained as the number two in the territory after the handover until 2001. Following her resignation from the civil service, she became more outspoken about the freedoms of Hong Kong and was elected to the Legislative Council from 2007 for one term after which she established a commission to monitor and comment on constitutional reform. She retired completely from public life after the passage of the National Security Law in 2020. Her husband Archie, after a business career, was Commandant of the Hong Kong Auxiliary Police. He died in 2010. Anson's many honours included an honorary GCMG from Queen Elizabeth II (the equivalent of the honour customarily given to governors), and the Hong Kong government's Grand Bauhinia Medal.

Tuesday 15 September
I returned to London overnight yesterday for a couple of days and had a good breakfast with the Prime Minister and Stephen Wall* this morning. John was obviously very worried about the position on sterling and the possibility of having to raise interest rates sharply. Even this, of course, may not do much to save sterling, and the economic forecasts still suggest that we have a long slog ahead of us before there is any improvement in the situation. They seemed pretty relaxed about my Hong Kong proposals. John wondered whether we are running too many risks in telling the Chinese much in advance; that we shouldn't give too extensive an outline of what I'm intending to say. I argued that we have to run some risk since we can't let the Chinese say that we haven't told them anything at all before my speech.

After talking to Peter Ricketts and John Morris, I made a presentation to the Cabinet committee. I warned them that I might just annoy everyone, but the proposals seem the best way of improving the government of Hong Kong and meeting at least some of the aspirations of the public for more democracy without disrupting the transition to 1997. After that we can't be entirely sure what the Chinese will do.

I then set out the plans we'd discussed in Hong Kong and with the Foreign Secretary and the FCO. We want to reduce the voting age from 21 to 18. As happened already in municipal council and district board elections, we will give each voter in the 20 geographical constituencies a single vote for a directly elected representative in a single seat constituency. We have to look at the existing 21 functional constituencies and the nine new ones which need to be created. The present system is indefensible. In the existing functional constituencies I want to see the replacement of corporate voting by election by individual voters. So, for example, all the directors of companies that were members of the General Chamber of Commerce would be able to vote instead of just the companies themselves as was presently the case. The simplest and fairest approach to creating the nine new constituencies would be to define them so that they include the entire working population broken down into the existing classification of our industrial and commercial sectors – from textiles and garments to community, social and personal services. In each of these constituencies every

* Sir Stephen Wall was private secretary to John Major from 1991 to 1993, responsible for foreign policy and defence. He became ambassador to Portugal in 1993 and Permanent Representative to the European Union in 1995. He was later EU adviser to Tony Blair. He is writing the official history of Britain's relationship with the European Union. What a fortunate chap.

worker would have a vote. These arrangements would extend the franchise of the 30 functional constituencies to a potential 2.7 million. All members of municipal council and district boards should be elected not appointed, and the election committee – which has to be established in 1995 under the BL – should be made up of all the directly elected members from these district boards. This indirectly elected committee would select 10 legislators. In order to ensure fairness, we would establish a boundary and election commission to supervise the new arrangements. The main constraint in the past had been that we felt that we could not increase the number of directly elected members set at 20 after a much disputed consultation in the community. What we are trying to do now is to make the agreed breakdown of the Legislative Council as fair and open as possible, bringing in more voters and making the maximum use of the flexibility that existed under the JD and the BL. We will incorporate these proposals in due course in legislation, and if it was amended or turned down by Legco we would have to accept this as the will of the community and live with the consequences.

No one seemed much disposed to criticize, though Michael Heseltine* wondered whether our last-ditch attempt to add a bit of democracy in Hong Kong was really very wise; it surely ran the risk of scuppering our national commercial interests. This has always been his position. I pointed out that we didn't seem to have done very well commercially in China while relations had moved forward smoothly on the political front. I suggested that there were other factors which would decide the market share that we got in China. Douglas, while being very happy about the proposals that we were advocating, was bothered – like John – about the amount of detail to give the Chinese in advance. Our discussion took about an hour and ten minutes, and the only real change made was that it was agreed that we should cut back a bit on what we proposed to tell the Chinese beforehand. Trusting them too much was likely to blow up.

* Michael Heseltine, a very successful businessman with his own publishing group, had served in senior positions in Margaret Thatcher's and John Major's governments. He had strong 'one nation' Conservative views believing both in the role of government in economic and social policy and in Britain's membership of the EU. This did not make him popular with right-wing conservatives, but even they had to accept that he was a formidably effective minister. He made things happen and they were usually sensible things. Heseltine was unashamedly broad-brush but the paintwork was visible and popular. We disagreed on China but this did not affect my huge admiration for his talents and likeability.

Wednesday 16 September

I returned to Hong Kong happy about how things had gone and had to go straight away to dinner with Zhou Nan and his wife with the whole family. We went to the NCNA bunker in Stanley, which was originally designed as a hotel. It now has a rather institutional feel about it. The food was delicious and Zhou Nan's wife is a sweet woman. I learned beforehand that Zhou learned his excellent English interrogating prisoners of war in Korea – he doesn't seem to have looked back since then. I wonder how he acquired such a very nice wife. But that probably applies to a lot of us. Zhou told me that I am to treat him as my main contact in Hong Kong. He is authorized to tell me this, he said, though there is obviously quite a bit of tension between him and Lu Ping. While I feasted in Hong Kong, the balloon was going up on the economy in London. Sterling crisis. Run on the pound. Speculators making a fortune betting against us. Interest rates soar. Departure from the exchange rate mechanism imminent. General disaster for the government. And to think, if it hadn't been for Bath voters, I could have been Chancellor of the Exchequer!

Thursday 17 September

Day after day we go round and round the wretched airport with the Chinese side buggering us about in increasingly imaginative ways. We put forward some new proposals reducing the amount of borrowing that is required and increasing the equity injection by using the money made from the sale of land along the new rail route to invest in the whole project. It's a perfectly reasonable approach – it builds on China's own proposals; it cuts the overall cost of the airport; it means that we will not have to channel resources from other public-spending programmes. But it didn't get a very good public reception, partly because some of the British press suggested that it is a kowtow and the pro-Beijing papers attacked us because it isn't exactly what the Chinese side have pressed for, whatever they may have been saying this morning. So much for the understanding which Li Peng signed with John Major.

Friday 18 September

I continued to talk to the people I would like to put on Exco. They have all been signing up, with the exception of Victor Fung. He said that he was too busy; we all suspect that he may feel that it would involve exposing himself too much. I also continued to take forward my proposals for the 1995 elections. One of the easier things for me to do is to stand down from the presidency of the council. To have the Governor as in effect the speaker of the legislature – something which apparently has happened for years – appears to me to be exceptionally foolish. How can you talk about the separation of powers if the head of the executive also has – presumably partly for ceremonial reasons – the chief position in the body which is supposed to hold him and his colleagues to account? Remember what happened to Charles I. When I told the existing president of Legco, John Swain, about my intention, he was naturally rather pleased.

Saturday 19 September

We celebrated Lavender's birthday by going out to dinner – the four of us – at the Italian restaurant Grissini's in the Grand Hyatt hotel. We had window seats looking out at the night-time harbour. I don't think I will ever tire of this view.

Sunday 20 September

Alas, today Lavender and Kate went back to London so that Lavender can help Kate go off to Newcastle University. She is going to read Spanish and Portuguese. I was left in charge of Alice and Whisky, and Her Majesty's colony.

Friday 25 September

There were a lot more meetings all week with party groups and with the four different sets of trade union representatives. They covered most of the waterfront – from Beijing to Taiwan to very democratic and less democratic. Afterwards one of the groups denounced me for having Tory views on labour market issues. This was because I noted in our discussions that with an unemployment rate of about 2%, there didn't seem to me to be a very strong argument for tough controls on immigrants who wanted to come and work in Hong Kong.

Saturday 26 September

Murray MacLehose came on a visit.* He was the Governor when I first came to Hong Kong as a young backbench MP in 1979. At the time I wrote an article for the *Guardian* proposing that members of district

* Lord Murray MacLehose was born in 1917, trained Chinese guerrillas behind Japanese lines in the Second World War, and afterwards joined the Foreign Office. He was ambassador in South Vietnam and was appointed the 25th Governor of Hong Kong in 1971. He held the post longer than anyone else for four successive terms until 1982. A British Labour Party supporter, he was responsible for a huge programme of social reform and infrastructure development. He was not much of a believer in political change in Hong Kong but a great colonial administrator. He died in 2000.

councils should be directly elected. He was not amused. He is a legendary figure, and was in many respects a great Governor in an interventionist, patriarchal way. At the time he was in Hong Kong, there was wave after wave of refugees from mainland China and MacLehose instigated the huge public-housing programme – partly based on what had happened in Singapore – which certainly made a major contribution to Hong Kong's stability and success. It is perhaps a pity that he didn't take the whole plan from Singapore's playbook and link public housing rentals with down payments on pensions. I don't think that Murray MacLehose thought much of ministers and indeed took some initiatives which skirted ministerial decision making almost entirely. For example, I am not convinced that he and Percy Cradock had full ministerial approval for the proposals they made in Beijing on a trip in 1979 (at about the same time as a general election in Britain) for handing over sovereignty in Hong Kong while retaining British administration. This idea was rejected out of hand by Deng Xiaoping,* who was surely never likely to sign up to such an obvious wheeze for keeping British control of what actually happened in the colony. We didn't have a very comfortable dinner together, though he did accept with enthusiasm a couple of dry martinis beforehand. Like many of the great colonial men of yesteryear, of which he is undoubtedly one, I don't think he much cares for democracy and probably regards it as an unnecessary provocation to China to even talk about it. He is in the House of Lords and I hope he doesn't cause problems for us from those red benches.

Sunday 27–Monday 28 September

We not only worked on the text of my big speech but also planned the public meetings that I want to have afterwards. What I really want is big question-and-answer sessions for the public. The difficulty is going to be getting a good translation so that all those members of audiences who don't speak much English can nevertheless follow what I am saying. It would certainly be pretty tiresome if something like this went off at half cock. I am told that my worries about attendance will prove to be groundless.

I have spent the last ten days trying to dispose of an awful plan, part of

* Deng Xiaoping emerged from the bloody turmoil of the Mao years as the paramount leader of China until his death in 1997. He was responsible more than any other Chinese communist leader for his country's boom years of spectacular growth, and for its opening to the West. During much of his time as the principal architect of China's success, Deng's only official post was chairman of the China Bridge Association. He certainly left China with a very good hand of trumps.

which has been leaked. The MoD have planned an exercise, Operation 'Winged Dragon', about how they could reinforce the garrison in case of trouble with China. There is of course an obvious point about this. Since the People's Liberation Army is rather large, and the only bunkers in Hong Kong are on golf courses, any military confrontation would be rather one-sided. As soon as I heard about this plan – with the exercise taking part about a fortnight after my visit to Beijing – I started ringing alarm bells. I can't imagine a more certain way of sending the Hang Seng Index into a nosedive in Hong Kong. I'm told that David Wilson had agreed it on condition that it was cleared with me. The present anticipation is that the airborne brigade will be brought in; Gurkhas are going to be placed on the border; and pretty well every general and brigadier who needs a new suit or shirts will be arriving in Hong Kong as well.

My informed hunch is that when someone in the garrison got wind of my substantial reservations, they leaked more and more details about the exercise, not least to the *South China Morning Post*, to try to make cancellation impossible.

On Monday, I had a meeting with the CBF British forces, John Foley (a man I much like), along with my political adviser, William Ehrman, and some others. Foley was very honestly shamefaced, apologized and said – which I believe – that it had nothing to do with him. But I don't want to be bounced into doing something really stupid. I came to the conclusion that we couldn't stop the exercise now but it must be in as low key a way as possible. What I am determined to do is to limit the tidal wave of generals and brigadiers. It's a rather typical bit of selfish, politically maladroit defence establishment nest feathering. It's probably lucky that I didn't become Minister of Defence myself. In any event scaling the whole thing down will be good for Hong Kong, with the exception, I suppose, of tailors like Mr Sam.

Tuesday 29 September

There was quite a lot of political tidying up to do before my speech to Legco. As well as fulfilling my parental duties looking after Alice, which are a joy, the highlight for me was a birthday dinner which I gave for her along with two of her school friends at a tasty Italian restaurant called Va Bene.

Wednesday 30 September

The evening before I took Alice and her friends out, I went to the China National Day reception at the NCNA. My expectations for the enjoyability of the occasion were not high, so I was not surprised by how it turned out. We attended a large reception hall owned by the mass caterers Maxims, and were conducted through a crowd of photographers, TV teams, journalists, United Front toadies and members of the diplomatic corps up to the stage. Zhou Nan read a speech which I was told afterwards is shorter and livelier than he customarily delivers, and I then made a few remarks myself on Hong Kong/China relations. I noted that what hurts China hurts Hong Kong, and that what is good for Hong Kong is also good for China. We were told subsequently that the NCNA staff were very cheerful that Zhou was upstaged because my speech was better. I bet they didn't say that to him, and to be honest I did not have to clear a very high bar.

Thursday 1 October

I completed my choice of Exco members. Everyone said yes apart from Victor Fung. I added to the list a very successful young businessman called Raymond Ch'ien, who has a degree from an American business school, and as an official I added Anson Chan. Martin Dinham has done one or two bits of work with her and is hugely impressed. On one quite complicated issue involving the airport and the terminal, she dealt with a mildly off-the-wall idea of his very firmly but courteously. I also had the task of what Richard Hoare calls kitten strangling. I had to say farewell to five former members of Exco whom I am proposing to remove.

Mostly we are still preparing for the big speech. While there is plenty to say about our spending priorities for the next few years, I want to give most attention to the 1994 district council election arrangements and the plans for Legco in 1995. As I told Ambassador Ma, I cannot afford to make the same mistake as was perpetrated over the plans for the Court of Final Appeal (CFA) which were negotiated in secret with the Chinese and then rejected by the Legislature in Hong Kong. I have to tell Hong Kong first what I propose while conceding that it may have to be changed. Having announced the separation of the Exco and Legco membership, I will then go on to set out the proposals for Legislative Council elections agreed by the Cabinet committee.

After my meetings in London, Douglas Hurd went off to the UN General Assembly and in the margins met his Chinese opposite number, Qian Qichen,* who is a sophisticated operator. Douglas set out for him in general

* After working as a journalist and an official in the Communist Youth League, Qian Qichen spent some time in Moscow and then joined China's foreign service. He held a number of senior diplomatic posts before becoming Foreign Minister, a member of the politburo and Vice Premier from 1993 to 2003. No other diplomat in China in recent years has held more senior positions for so long, a mark of his intelligence and skill. Qian died in 2017.

terms what we are proposing to do. Qian doesn't seem too fazed or cross about anything, especially when he learns that we are not proposing to increase the number of directly elected legislators, nor to give any role in the executive to Martin Lee. This may not mean very much. He may not be well sighted on Hong Kong issues and may leave them to other parts of the Beijing machine. There is a bit of a sense of so far so good, but the journey has only just begun.

Friday 2 October

There was a very different reaction when Robin McLaren in Beijing went in to see Lu Ping. The account of the meeting sent by the ambassador was confirmed in private messages passed to us through David Chu, a Hong Kong businessman and friend of Director Lu. The general view of the Foreign Office is that what Lu is saying is at the harder end of the spectrum. He complained that Beijing had not been properly consulted, that he and his colleagues were not being given any face, that we were bouncing them with these proposals, that they were out of step with the Basic Law, that they will be bad for our relations with China, that the Chinese side will attack them vigorously, and that he was planning to give me something when I went to see him (perhaps an agreement on the airport) but that I won't now receive any gift since I'm such a sinner. Finally, they want me to keep quiet about my ideas for the 1995 elections when I speak to Legco and not to announce anything at all until I have spoken to him and his colleagues and cleared it with them. This was my first experience, though not I suspect my last, of sabre rattling by Beijing.

We constructed a telegram for the ambassador when he goes back to see Lu just before my speech in order to hand it over. We went through the arguments one by one, particularly challenging the proposition that anything we are proposing is against the Basic Law. We also pointed out that the Chinese are always pressing us to be open about our proposals on the airport and it would be ridiculous for us not to be equally open about our proposals on the democratic future of Hong Kong. Nevertheless, we are clearly in for quite a fight, but I would prefer to be fighting Beijing than opinion in Hong Kong.

All the tickets for the first two public meetings to be held after my Legco speech in the City Hall and the Shatin town hall were apparently snapped up within half an hour. That's pretty well 3000 people. We've had to organize two more meetings and I'm also doing quite a lot on the local radio and television, including phone-ins. Several local politicians are getting a bit jumpy about this direct appeal to the public! They had better get used to it.

Wednesday 7 October

We set off at 2.20 for the Legco building with Lavender looking stunning in green. I am paraded through the debating chamber of the council, which is rather like the better sort of municipal auditorium. Lavender thinks it's more like a law court. Despite having looked through it several times, as I started speaking I realized that it is going to take a lot longer than the hour and a half that I had predicted. I also started to realize how much I have been talking in the last two or three days. I must've been nattering away for six, seven or eight hours a day, and my throat is raw despite Strepsils and Polo mints. Anyway, I plough on and eventually sit down after two hours.

I did the constitutional stuff at the end. Before that, I set out our broad proposals for Hong Kong over the coming five years. It has all turned into a sort of manifesto. I note that we are predicting annual growth of 5% a year up to 1997 and will continue to link the Hong Kong dollar's exchange rate to that of the US dollar. While we won't allow growth in public spending to exceed growth in the economy, that nevertheless gives us a great deal of scope for increases across the board, for example in retraining and research and development. We are also going to establish an efficiency unit to make certain that the money we spend is used wisely. I noted that recurrent spending on education will increase by 15.5% in real terms between the present and 1997. We will have more teachers, smaller classes, and all-day opening in our new primary schools. We intend to increase recurrent spending on welfare by 26% in real terms over the same period. There will be more nursery places, increases in Social Security and increases as well in health, especially for the elderly and our well women centres. We will also provide more beds for psychiatric patients. There will be a huge increase in housing, with the building of a hundred new flats a day between now and 1997. Home ownership is forecast to increase to just under 60%. We will spend more on water pollution and sewage. Relative to population size, we will have more police than Tokyo or London. Capital spending will increase by over 20% in real terms. In addition to all this we will of course be building the new airport. I added to this a number of ways in which we can be held to the pledges we have made and deal more effectively with complaints about administration.

After explaining my ideas for the relationship between Exco and Legco, I laid out the proposals agreed by the Cabinet committee at our meeting for the elections in 1994 and 1995. I also made the obvious point that while it is imperative to tell people in Hong Kong first what I would like to do, I then have to discuss it with Beijing and there may need to be changes. I said explicitly that I don't want to be forced into the same sort of calamitous reversal that we had over the Court of Final Appeal, on which we had reached a secret deal with the Chinese that was then rejected by the legislature. The citizens of Hong Kong have a right to know what is being proposed about their future. I think everyone was pretty stunned by the amount I had to say, not least about my social, welfare, education and economic priorities – three cheers for Hamish McLeod – as well as about the future government of the territory.

Then press conferences, broadcasts, phone-ins – the works. Coverage in all the papers was extensive and very positive, with the exception of course of the pro-Beijing press. The criticisms there were fairly predictable. First, can we really afford my social and educational programme, and second, why have I chosen to flout the Basic Law either in the letter or in the spirit? I spent quite a lot of time during the course of the day in interview after interview pointing out that we can afford our programme since we have a windfall this year of additional revenues. I also challenged my critics to say where the proposals on the legislature contravene the Basic Law and to put forward their own.

My first public meeting at the City Hall in the evening was packed. There must have been 1200 or 1300 people there. I made one or two introductory remarks, which were of course translated – very well as usual – about my surprise at the fact that holding public meetings was regarded as controversial. I said that my speech was about the future of the people of Hong Kong and it was right therefore that they should be able to question me about it. We then had an hour and a half with, alas, only 11 questions, because several of those who asked them made speeches or asked several at a time. I also invariably spend too long answering questions. There were a couple of obvious plants from the pro-Beijing lobby who asked almost identical questions about how dishonourably Britain had left its colonies and how important it was that we should get on with China. But, all in all, it was a terrific and cheerful occasion. We had a couple of headbangers, including one chap who asked me an involved question fetching up with a plea for a crackdown on pornographic literature. Afterwards my protection squad officer, Wise, said he had arrested the chap about a year ago for indecently assaulting a 60-year-old lady. Most of the questions were about bread-and-butter issues. The audience seemed to love the occasion, and without being able to deploy my normal rhetorical arts I nevertheless managed to get quite a few laughs and claps. The interpreters did a fantastic job. At the end I gave a little speech saying that when people doubted the ability of Hong Kong to run its own affairs, they should consider how responsibly and maturely the people of Hong Kong behaved on occasions like this one.

There was only one slightly awkward moment during the meeting which embarrasses the interpreters. I got a question from one member of the audience which is apparently – or so I'm told in my earphone – about policy for the deaf. I have to admit that my knowledge about the hard of hearing in Hong Kong is fairly limited, but I embark as politicians are often able to do on a rather rambling talk about disability in general. The audience begin to giggle. At which point the interpreter apologized at length and told me that he misinterpreted and that I was actually asked about agriculture and farming, the word for which in Cantonese apparently sounds like the word for the deaf. I made a joke about the whole thing and the audience genuinely seemed to think it was funny. Afterwards I have to make a fuss of the main interpreter so that he doesn't lose too much face.

Light relief after a big day:

I was then grilled on a television programme by a panel made up partly of political figures and partly of social welfare lobbyists. The programme overran by quite a bit. The producers told me that it was watched by 2 million people in Hong Kong and 10 million in Guandong. This must endear me even more to Beijing.

Back at Government House, I met Whisky's companion – called, guess what – Soda. She is a beautiful little ball of fur and is related in some pedigree way to Whisky. She arrived just this afternoon and her cousin (or whatever he is) is obsessed with her, trying to persuade her the whole time to give him a piggyback. Clearly we shall need recourse sooner or later to the vet's knife.

Friday 9 October

I had breakfast with George Shultz. He was very supportive and thought I was taking the right tack. He told me that when he was Secretary of State under President Reagan he had been told fairly early in his term that he could not do this or that because the Chinese would believe that it undermined the relationship with the US. He'd gone to Reagan and said that when he was a labour lawyer, in his experience firms started to get into difficulties when the management began saying that they couldn't possibly take a particular course of action because it might damage the relationship with the workforce. He had said to the president that a good relationship was the result of individual decisions that you took and agreements you made with the other partner. The relationship flowed from the decisions you took rather than the other way around. This makes a lot of sense to me. The view generally in the past has been that the UK and China have some great big relationship which we must safeguard at all costs and that Hong Kong is a tiresome aggravation. This agreement risks damaging the beautiful relationship whose contours seem to depend on the judgements made by the middle kingdom. Geoffrey Howe* has a ghastly metaphor about the relationship being like a priceless vase – or sometimes that is equated with Hong Kong – which you have to carry very carefully through the years without ever letting it slip. Truth to tell, I'm not sure that after 1997 we will have a terribly close relationship with China at all. We are a medium-sized European country albeit with a seat in the UN Security Council and with other global assets, and I wonder whether that represents for China nearly as much as Hong Kong with getting on for 20% of China's GDP. It's much the biggest part of our relationship at the moment and what will compare with it in the future? George Shultz was also very funny about the diplomacy of visits to Beijing. He thinks the Chinese will try to humiliate me and, if I try to stand up to them, will deliver what he calls the post-visit blast. That is, a great attack when I'm on the way to the airport or even in the aeroplane. Be prepared, he said.

Then I gave a lunchtime speech to all the Chambers of Commerce in the convention centre. There are about 1400 of Hong Kong's business leaders there. I have just named my Advisory Business Council, which seems to go down well. I hope I managed to demolish the criticism that my spending plans are reckless and unaffordable. I also dealt with the political arguments, saying that I want to get these out of the way early. It would have been much more destabilizing if I had been secretive about what I intended to do and much more hazardous still to resist any pressures for greater democracy rather than to accommodate some modest changes. But, of course, for some people the ultimate test is not what I am actually proposing but what China will accept. Who knows how much that will be?

We had another public meeting at Shatin town hall. Again, a very good

* Geoffrey Howe was a Conservative lawyer, MP and peer who played a hugely influential role in developing and implementing Conservative policy under both Edward Heath and Margaret Thatcher. In her administration, he served as Chancellor of the Exchequer, Foreign Secretary and Deputy Prime Minister until these two Conservative politicians fell out over the EU. His resignation from her government help to expedite her own departure from office. He was Foreign Secretary during much of the period when the Joint Declaration was being negotiated. In later years he tended to overlook the promises that had been made at the time of its negotiation by the British government about the development of democracy in Hong Kong, particularly whenever that issue threatened to increase tensions in relations with China.

turnout. There were more questions than last time, most of them on day-to-day issues – housing, education, social welfare and so on. A group of parents of disabled children gave me a very kind reception. I was told later that it's partly because when they were waiting for me recently outside a sheltered workshop, I went over to talk to them before climbing into my car. It's a surprise how small and rather straightforward human acts can make big impacts.

Saturday 10 October

Lee Kuan Yew came in to see me. He had just been in China and was interested in how difficult the Chinese find it to understand me. He seemed to have given them a fairly incisive description of what I am up to and my relationship with John Major and the rest of the British government. He then gave me an equally sharp pen picture of the Chinese leadership. He told me that he thinks that Li Peng was slightly distracted when he spoke to him. He suspects that Zhu Rongji* is going to be made an executive Vice Premier, in effect taking away much of Li Peng's power, especially on economic issues. This would leave Li Peng with the title of Premier in order to save his face. He suggested I should be rather cooler in my public handling of issues, firm but with no trace of impatience. He repeated what he had said to me on my way in, that I should try to find someone important with whom I can be frank. When I spoke after this to the editors and proprietors of some of the main Chinese-language papers – a rather elderly bunch – I found them rather nervous about China's reaction to my plans. I don't think any of them believe that we will actually stand up to China even if we think it's right to do so. They're very worried about the consequences if they prove to be wrong on this and we really do stand firm.

In the afternoon I interviewed candidates to take over the role of ADC from Felipe. The best candidate, not surprisingly, seems to be his best friend, Mike Ellis.

* Zhu Rongji was denounced as a 'rightist' after criticizing the economic policies of Mao but was brought back into the government as an extremely effective administrator, especially in the economic field, by Deng Xiaoping. As Mayor of Shanghai in the late 1980s he was known as a tough opponent of corruption. He was promoted to be Vice Premier with responsibility for economic affairs under President Jiang Zemin and clashed with the Premier Li Peng over economic reform. He was Premier of China from 1998 to 2003. I dealt with Zhu when I was European Commissioner for External Relations and thought him one of the cleverest public officials that I had ever met. He was prepared to engage in pretty open argument without ever departing from his Communist beliefs. He would almost certainly have got to the very top in any system of government.

Sunday 11 October

We went to mass at Tai Po. At the beginning, Peter Barry, our favourite priest at the cathedral, gave a little homily about my speech to the legislature, saying that it showed a political leader implementing Catholic social teaching. I can't imagine anything similar happening back home. Then we went on to Fanling to give a barbecue lunch for everybody who's been involved in putting my speech together. They brought partners and children. Alice is very good looking after the younger ones. The house itself is starting to feel more like a home; we've already brought here some of the things from our retail therapy expeditions. There is one unfortunate discovery. I bought for not very much a beautiful little Tang court lady a couple of weeks ago from an excellent dealer called Andy Ng, much recommended by Lord Irvine. She still had some of the original paint on her as well as centuries of dust and a bit of dirt. Ah Lam's jolly wife, Ah Fong, gave her a good clean so she is now sparkling white. I had to bite my lip. I suppose you could say – not that I said anything at all – that the court lady has been returned to her original state. I don't think that people around the house understand why we love these old things.

Until my departure later in the month for Beijing, my days are filled with talking to local politicians and interest groups, mainly about my political proposals, and also doing loads of interviews with the local and international media. The first meeting with the new Exco proved that we are certainly going to have livelier and more intelligent discussions. I have a third public meeting in Tsuen Wan with an audience of about 500. Similar questions.

Wednesday 14 October

Laura's birthday. We phoned her up. Her course has started well and she's enjoyed the first three days, but she's missing us and had a bit of a cry on the phone.

The barrage of criticism from Beijing and its supportive papers in Hong Kong continues. The abuse is pretty lame – surely they did better than this during the Cultural Revolution? One minute I am a dictator, the next a self-styled God of democracy. Public opinion seems to be holding up reasonably well. When I visited Aberdeen and the southern district, I got cheerfully mobbed on a housing estate. I visited some of the people who are living on boats in Aberdeen harbour. They live in appalling conditions and nothing happens to help them until the boats sink. I wonder whether I'll be able to do very much about housing while I'm here given the importance of the developers to the health of the Hang Seng Index. We can afford rows about politics but not economic turbulence which would affect people's everyday standard of living. The best meetings with political parties were once again with Martin Lee and the leaders of the Democrats on the one hand and the pro-Beijing Democratic Alliance for the Betterment of Hong Kong on the other. Martin Lee and his colleagues were enthusiastic about my package but worried that I'll retreat from it. They were also enthusiastic about holding a referendum. Martin went on to suggest that I should bring forward the 1995 elections by a year or so and then offer China the opportunity of halting the 'through train' and starting off with Beijing's own proposals after June 1997. Imaginative perhaps but far from wise. The pro-Beijing politicians are intellectually sharp (as before) and we had a good, if tough, exchange. They want me to agree to attend a seminar on the Basic Law, organized of course by them. I rejected the idea, arguing that it would be wrong to attend something organized by a political party, but it does give me an opportunity to demonstrate a rather more thorough knowledge of the BL than they seem to possess themselves.

Thursday 15 October

By this evening we have counted over 40 critical articles about me during the last week in the pro-Beijing press. In addition, Lu Ping has sent a private message asking that I should make sure that I respect his face when I go to Beijing and behave properly. Why are they so alarmed, especially when all the evidence suggests that they are preparing to give me as tough a time as they can?

We recover the day with our first concert in the ballroom of GH. It's given by the Academy for Performing Arts. The room is packed and the concert goes very well.

My natural caution makes me focus on the sort of criticisms that may be made when I get to Beijing. I keep on wondering – as barristers ask about their opponents – what their best point may be. I am all over the Joint Declaration and the Basic Law (I didn't learn the catechism at school for nothing). I'm also aware of the debates in the House of Commons and public statements by Beijing politicians. Is there anything I have overlooked?

Friday 16 October

I had a long meeting with David Ford, Tony Galsworthy, William Ehrman, Leo Goodstadt, Michael Sze and others to discuss the criticisms. I don't want all this to get tangled up in endless discussions in the JLG. We can't talk about the political package until 1997. Sometime there will have to be legislation to put my proposals in place. We also need to clarify once again our position on the airport. After the meeting Edward volunteered to go off and try to see if there anything about which I haven't been told.

Monday 19 October

I had a call from Edward over the weekend and fixed a meeting with him for early this morning. Looking through the principal telegrams about Hong Kong over the last three or four years, he had found an exchange of seven in 1990 between Douglas Hurd and Qian Qichen about the election arrangements in Hong Kong. A first look at them doesn't suggest that this is a real smoking gun loaded with any lead, though I should have been told about it. There was clearly an agreement that we wouldn't increase the number of directly elected legislators in 1995 (alongside a commitment on the Chinese part to increase the number in 2003), but there were also some rather ambiguous exchanges about the composition of the election committee. We suggested several criteria which should be met, though no agreement on what any of the arrangements might finally be. The general tone is that these are matters on which we need to go on talking, though there's nothing explicit which can be held against me as a breach of faith. Indeed, the criteria that Douglas covered for the election committee included the idea that I have presented. But it is all a little like the secret agreement on the Court of Final Appeal – done behind Hong Kong's back, the sort of secret diplomacy which always plays to Beijing's advantage. There is no point in having a witch hunt about why I didn't know about it. But it is extraordinary that no one mentioned the telegrams to me; nor were they ever included in my voluminous briefing. Douglas had presumably forgotten all about the exchange, and evidently Qian Qichen had as well. All those who must have been responsible for drafting the telegrams, seeing them and agreeing them, from Percy Cradock down, evidently didn't think that they needed to be mentioned to the new Governor. For very clever people to behave like this is not very clever, but now we had to cope with it. Or to be strictly accurate, I had to cope with it. Sometimes a political boss is responsible for his or her own egregious errors and officials fetch up taking the blame. This is rather the opposite to put it mildly. Anyway, it's done. The first thing to do now is to make sure that the lawyers are happy that we aren't in breach of anything explicit in setting out my own proposals; the lawyers in Hong Kong as well as London must have seen the telegrams already because they – or at least their main thrust – were known about apparently by Exco.

Tuesday 20 October

We set off for Beijing and were met at the airport by Robin and Sue McLaren and a low level Chinese official. No sign of Lu Ping. It's no skin off my nose but this is obviously the first snub to the wicked British Governor. I make a few remarks to the press and head off to the embassy to discuss how we are going to handle the next two or three days of talks. We went over the seven telegrams again with quite a bit of nervous shifting in seats by the diplomats. Sooner or later I suppose that I should have a bloody great row over this, which may make people more careful in the future. I've never liked shouting at officials, however.

Wednesday 21 October

We drove off at 8.30 to the state guest house for the first session with Lu Ping and his team. We passed through Tiananmen Square. The last time I was here, as Minister for Overseas Development, it was full of students. Because of my ministerial role, I was acting as vice chairman of the Asian Development Bank for its annual meeting. The meeting was held that year in Beijing just before Mr Gorbachev's famous visit to China. The Tiananmen 'incident' – as it was euphemistically called – started about a week after I left. For the week I was here, the city seemed much happier than it appeared now.

Lu Ping was waiting for me at the entrance of the guest house. Once again the press were there in huge numbers. I was greeted in Lu Ping's excellent English. He apologized not very believably for not being at the airport. The press will not of course take any notice of that. We then went into the sort of room that you see in the Russian parts of John le Carré films – heavy decor, rather bad paintings of mountains, waterfalls and lotus blossom. Since it's China there were also covered mugs of tea in front of everyone's place. The press were allowed in for a few moments. There were so many of them that they fetched up completely circling the table, shoving microphones under our noses. Lu Ping and I offered a few mild introductory comments, Lu dwelling on the friendship to China of my four predecessors while he has been director of the Hong Kong Macau office and of the previous ambassadors in Beijing, with whom he has worked so well. This was China-speak for 'you had better toe the line just like the rest of them'. It was also a not-so-subtle way of saying that this guy (unlike his predecessors) doesn't know what he's talking about. Eventually the press were pushed out but it was such a scrum and we learned afterwards that there had been a punch-up outside and at least one journalist was flattened.

With the room cleared, Lu Ping offered me the chance to take the floor. He had in front of him a written text which he left rather ominously until the end of the day. I set out my thoughts and responsibilities. I don't have a secret agenda; I want to do the job efficiently and honourably; I believe that making some honest accommodation to peoples' democratic ambitions is more rather than less likely to promote political stability; my bottom line for the 1995 elections is that they should be fair, open and accessible to the people of Hong Kong. The ambassador said afterwards that no Chinese official would ever have heard anything like this before. I think it's the style of what I said rather than the content that he is referring to. I don't think I've been remotely rude, at least I hope not. Then we got into exchanges for about an hour and a half on my constitutional proposals. This was all conducted through interpreters, though Lu Ping's English is good enough for him to understand what I'm saying. There were half a dozen chaps on his side of the table. None of them took any part in the discussions. The same is true on our side; I did all the talking.

At the end of the morning, we had a discussion about the airport. Lu Ping had some prepared remarks which appeared to be based on the assumption that we were going to tear up the memorandum of understanding between the Prime Ministers. The content of what he said was rather threatening; the delivery was both restrained and embarrassed. There were a number of threats about the Chinese blocking entry of Hong Kong aeroplanes into their airspace. It all sounded as though it came from the propaganda department of the politburo rather than from anyone who's been seriously involved in negotiations about the airport. I did the familiar routine. The airport will be built; it's of concern to Hong Kong and China; Britain will not depart with it in 1997; the best way forward would be on the basis of comprehensive agreements between China and Britain; but until we get such agreements we will proceed one step at a time in order to carry out the memorandum of understanding to the letter. We broke for lunch about 40 minutes late, just before 1pm. The gang of press and photographers had a sure sign that things are going badly wrong: my official car has developed a puncture. You would need to be a serious conspiracy theorist to believe that this had been deliberately organized by the Chinese propaganda department. But, of course, conspiracies are not unknown . . .

After a sandwich at the embassy – with comment from the ambassador and others that the tone is better than they've experienced at some other meetings – we returned to the state guest house for a private word with fewer officials present with Lu Ping, warned against demonizing Martin Lee and the Democrats. If Chinese officials go on like this, the Democrats will win every election there ever is. I also followed up some remarks I had made in the morning about a civil service training course in Beijing, which seemed to have gone down well. I would like a confidential dialogue with Lu about those civil servants whose careers are likely to span 1997. He appeared receptive to this. However, on the political development, even though his eyes occasionally flickered showing some comprehension of what I was saying, I got a straight 'down with Martin Lee' line. The more the talks go on over these two days, the more the Chinese obsession with Martin becomes apparent. How can this decent, mild-mannered daily communicant have become such a devilish hate figure for the Communist Party? In talking about Martin Lee I mentioned the rule of law. Lu said, but we have the rule of law too. No, I replied, you have rule by law. He asked me what I mean. I said that when I was a British minister, for example for the environment, I would very often be challenged legally in court, and sometimes overruled. I didn't always know whether I would win or not. The law applied to me just like everyone else even though I was a minister. I am not sure that he believed me, or perhaps he just thought, 'what a crazy system'.

We then go back to a plenary session and a long prepared tirade by Lu claiming that my proposals breach the Joint Declaration, the Basic Law and a secret agreement reached in 1990 by the Chinese Foreign Minister and Douglas Hurd. There were quotes from one or two telegrams. This was the first time that any of this came up. It's pretty curious to claim that there was an agreement; nothing was written into the Basic Law by the Chinese and they've been talking about the possible composition of the election committee to every visiting delegation from Hong Kong in recent months. But this was the first attack from China which came close to scoring any goals and I suspect that I will have to get used to being accused of three breaches.

I responded point by point at some length, and we then had a further exchange during the course of which he became rather emotional. He claimed bad faith. And that was that. No agreement and no very obvious way forward. I went back to the embassy and did a press conference on the steps saying not much more than that there's been no meeting of minds, which is the understatement of the month. Then we did a quick change and went off to an immensely long banquet at the top of the Swissotel. The mood wasn't too bad. I imagined that Lu is under immense pressure from above. He'll be told that he has let this perfidious foreigner out of what was assumed to be a locked cupboard. Since he was responsible for the Basic Law, I suspect that people are now saying to him – why did you get it wrong? The lightest relief of the evening was a visit to a room above our restaurant to place bets on the racing at Happy Valley and at Shatin. I chose a horse called 'Best of Luck'. I'm going to need it.

Thursday 22 October

We spent the whole morning at another state guest house with Jiang Enzhu, the diplomat at the Chinese Foreign Ministry who has oversight of relations with the UK and policy on Hong Kong. He did little more than smilingly repeat everything that's already been said by Lu Ping. He's obviously intelligent but a mouthpiece for others. I did manage to get the conversation onto security and smuggling and also onto Joint Liaison Group issues such as air service agreements, the future use of the defence lands in Hong Kong and right of abode. We had a rather dreary lunch with Jiang and lots more talk about the devil incarnate, Martin Lee, with whom I am clearly soon to share a co-starring role. After lunch we had a jolly meeting with the vice minister of trade which merely underlined that our biggest and most important economic relationship with China is extremely smooth. Finally, it was back to the state guest house for the meeting which represented my snub – at least the biggest snub this week. I was not going to see Li Peng let alone Deng Xiaoping, but the Chinese Foreign Minister, Qian. He had Lu Ping, Zhou Nan and a host of other now familiar apparatchiks with him.

We went through the familiar routines. He said that we have breached the Joint Declaration, the Basic Law and the agreements reached between Britain and China through his telegrams with Douglas Hurd. There was a good deal about my sincerity and the importance of cooperation and consultation. The Chinese had had great hopes of me after the Prime Minister had met Li Peng at a conference in Rio, but if issues couldn't be resolved with me, they may have to be taken to Foreign Secretary or prime ministerial level. In other words, the Chinese think that they should cut me down to size and bypass the uppity Governor of Hong Kong. It's all done with a pretence of amicability and a menacing air. Back to the embassy, another press conference, and then we gave a return dinner for Lu Ping. Before the meal we exchanged gifts. I gave him some CDs and he gave me some jade. There was one interesting incident before dinner: frantic telephone calls from London to tell me that the Prime Minister is so incensed by the way I'm being treated that he wants to cancel the visit which is going to be made shortly by Zhu Rongji, the up-and-coming Chinese Vice Premier. I talked to Jonathan Hill, John's political adviser, and Stephen Wall to tell them that this should not be done under any circumstances. People in Hong Kong (even the Democrats) would think we were crazy. It would lose a lot of middle ground and Zhu is precisely the sort of person we should want to do business with in the future. The exchange was more difficult because it's the middle of a Cabinet meeting in London and messages were plainly being passed in and out, to and from John and the Foreign Secretary. Anyway, eventually a cancellation of the visit was cancelled. I imagined that since we had to speak on open lines in order to get the decision made in time, some surprised Chinese spooks will have been listening to everything and relaying it to their masters. If there is one advantage to all this, it may be that the Chinese will now understand that I have rather a good relationship with the senior members of the British government.

Lavender meanwhile has been with Sue McLaren to the Great Wall, where she was amused first by the loudspeakers blaring Madonna songs with presumably lyrics which no one Chinese understood, and second by the slightly threatening-looking young men lounging around in mangy old soldiers' uniforms hoping to get paid for posing for a photograph. Of course, she thought it very impressive, as I did when I saw it during my visit just before the Tiananmen murders.

If I wasn't aware of the fact already that the Chinese communists didn't like my proposals, I was soon subjected to what George Shultz rightly called the post-visit blast. While we were in mid-air on the way back to Hong Kong, Lu Ping gave a press conference and delivered more or less the private text that he had read out at Wednesday's meeting. It was full of threats about changing everything in 1997 and refusals of cooperation if we try to go ahead with the airport on our own. Nothing was surprising but all was done with great verve. When I got back to Hong Kong, David Ford said that people remain pretty resilient but obviously we are in for a battering over the coming weeks. Will Hong Kong's nerve hold? I had to deliver a speech in the evening to an American Foundation dedicated to freedom of speech. I gave them my threepenny-worth on the subject; it seemed to go down quite well. Thinking about Lu in retrospect I found myself rather puzzled. He's obviously highly intelligent, sophisticated and charming with some civilized tastes – not least his love of classical music. But maybe because of ill-health and an unhappy family life, he obviously has a very short temper and a highly developed sense of amour propre. I guess one should also make allowance for the fact that he was brought up in Shanghai, subjected like so many other Chinese to overt racism by the dominant Europeans. I probably shouldn't underestimate either the amount of political pressure that he is under. He is plainly not an obvious communist stooge – unlike Zhou Nan – and this may mean that he has less political armoury than might be desirable in his position. I have dealt with far more dislikeable people in my life, but far more likeable Chinese ones as well, for example Xiao Xiyang, who is now languishing under house arrest somewhere in Beijing.

Saturday 24–Sunday 25 October

This morning I briefed the Executive Council, who were rather gloomy. There will be a lot of cold feet around over the next few weeks. Then I went down to Legco to answer questions and make a statement. I am asked straight away about secret deals. I put up what I hope is regarded as a fairly robust show. It's important to make people understand that I'm not backing off and that if enough people support me I'll still be there when it matters. 'Secret deals' was not the way I did business.

Much of the weekend is spent getting our lines straight on the seven letters. It helps that we have found an interview on the radio with Lu Ping back in April making it clear that the question of the formation of the election committee is still something on which he wants to hear the views of the people of Hong Kong and on which decisions still have to be made. I spoke to both Douglas and Alastair Goodlad, saying that I'm very keen to publish the letters as soon as possible. We have to be on the front foot on this issue, otherwise people will think we have something to hide. I wish we had known about that radio interview before we went to Beijing; even more I wish that I had known about those bloody telegrams before I left London.

Monday 26–Thursday 29 October

The last days this month bring the usual stream of visitors and interminable interviews with journalists. Alas, Alice and I are to be on our own again. Lavender had a telephone call from South Africa from her nieces and nephew to tell her that her stepsister, Jill, was dying of cancer. She decided to fly to Johannesburg and Cape Town straight away.

The politics is dominated by three issues. First of all, as (I hope not) ever, the airport. We agreed at Exco with good leadership by Lydia that – after giving Beijing due warning – we should try to get backing from the Legislative Council finance committee to provide the money to allow us to go ahead with the contract for site preparation. This would show our intention of implementing the wretched memorandum of understanding.

Second, we have to deal with the fallout from the secret telegrams issue. We got approval from London to publish them. Robin McLaren told them in Beijing that we are going to do it and we get in just ahead of them doing the same thing. The media reaction is wholly manageable, not least because the issue of the election committee on which Lu Ping had publicly opined is so complicated. No one has the wit to ask the killer question as to whether I had actually seen the telegrams myself before I put forward my proposals. I was able to go on repeating that of course my officials knew about the exchanges very well. I guess this will continue to be an issue with which the Chinese will beat us over the head and which they will try to use to peel off support in the civil service and in the business community. They are saying in their newspapers that civil servants are very nervous about what I have proposed and want a quiet life until 1997, when they will start working for a China-appointed administration. There isn't much sign of this so far.

Third, Beijing will obviously have more success with the business community. There was a meeting of my Business Council on 28 October at which Nigel Rich, the taipan of Jardine's, very helpfully pointed out all the reasons why business should support what we are doing. But others were flakier. For example, Vincent Lo – a successful youngish businessman who has a certain slightly creepy charm (whom I put on the Business Council to show that I wanted broad-based advice) – objected to Nigel and argued that at its next meeting the Council should talk about relations with China. He is one of Beijing's favourite sons and is said to be close to Lu Ping. We know that pro-Beijing cadres are really putting the squeeze on businessmen to criticize my proposals. This is a group that will get some comfort and support from a few of the old hands in Hong Kong who have been part of the establishment in the past. Sir David Akers-Jones,* the former Chief Secretary, is one of the leading members of this crew. Mind, he used to think that David Wilson was confrontational. People like this probably encourage Chinese apparatchiks to think that they will win if they press hard enough.

There will also be encouragement for the pro-Beijing lobby from occasional British visitors. David Young is back again. He has had a rather unsatisfactory meeting with Li Peng in Beijing, who didn't actually mention the Sino-British row. But clearly Young didn't get what he was hoping for. He wants an inside track for Cable & Wireless in the Chinese telecoms market. He won't get this if he thinks that the way of accomplishing it is by sucking up to senior leaders in Beijing and rubbishing what we are trying to do in Hong Kong. He will doubtless blame me for

* Sir David Akers-Jones was a career colonial civil servant who worked in Hong Kong from 1957. He rose to become Chief Secretary from 1985 to 1987 and stood in briefly as Acting Governor of Hong Kong in 1986/7 after the death of Sir Edward Youde. He was a critic of government policy in Hong Kong before the handover. He died in 2019.

failure and will give quiet encouragement – or maybe not so quiet – to the Vincent Lo's of Hong Kong. He should spend more time improving the management of Hong Kong Telecoms and appointing more local Chinese executives there.

Friday 30 October

I was invited by the Governor of Macau* to go on a weekend visit. Lavender is still in South Africa so I took Alice with me. We flew on the helicopter and were greeted by the amiable Portuguese Governor, a general whose rank went up and down with each tide of revolution or reaction in his country. Macau has a lot of charm – if you can avoid looking at buildings such as the casino – largely reflecting its Portuguese heritage. The Governor himself lives in a handsome colonial building, a pink house on a headland. Alice and I stayed at a little hotel in another smart colonial house, called the Bella Vista, and were invited to a performance of the *Barber of Seville* in gardens on a hill in the centre of town. Macau made me rather homesick for Europe. I had good conversations with the Governor about dealing with China; I think the Macanese have fewer problems than we do. There's an interesting Protestant cemetery where the painter Chinnery is buried. Alice is a perfectly charming companion.

Tuesday 3–Wednesday 4 November

Two snippets of information when I get back to Hong Kong. First, in a moment of role reversal, I learned that Beijing is now threatening to pull the plug on Zhu Rongji's visit to London unless he is guaranteed a meeting with John Major. Clare Hollingworth, who must be the oldest journalist in Hong Kong or perhaps anywhere (she is credited with being the first to report Germany's invasion of Poland in 1939), came in for a fascinating chat. She has lots of contacts in the Chinese military but also it seems in the British armed forces. She tells me that the NCNA were delighted to learn that we had postponed Operation 'Winged Dragon'. That's the first I've heard about the very welcome postponement – via the NCNA. Another triumph for the MoD. They obviously don't think it's worth talking to the Governor.

* Vasco Joaquim Rocha Vieira was a professional army officer who worked as Portugal's 138th and last Governor of Macau from 1991 to 1999. A thoroughly decent and friendly man, he was constrained in his role by Portugal's pervasive political embarrassment about whether it actually held any meaningful sovereignty over Macau.

Thursday 5 November
The Prince of Wales arrived to stay, leaving his wife on the plane, or perhaps it's more true to say she chose to stay on the plane. They have obviously had a wretched time being hounded by the press in South Korea, their last point port of call.

Friday 6 November
Lavender returned (after the sad death of her stepsister) to find a house full of courtiers. Rather gallantly she came straight from the airport to the house, did a quick change and came out with me to dinner for the Prince of Wales at the Hong Kong and Shanghai Bank with a lot of businessmen, several of whom are anxious to be presented to the Prince, but are obviously muttering in the background about the Governor.

Saturday 7 November
We have had quite a busy time with HRH in which Lavender had to do most of the work. She went with him to the official opening of the Bradbury Hospice run by some terrific nuns. We had dinners for him and the parade ceremony for Remembrance Sunday at the Cenotaph outside Legco. Lavender was amused that since I am the Queen's representative in the colony I took precedence at this event. I am, as it were, the Queen of Hong Kong. Prince Charles left for London tonight, by which time the most dramatic event of the week, or indeed of most weeks, had taken place.

From Lavender's diary:

'In need of some fresh air I went out with the dogs. At my driver Ronnie's suggestion we ended up at Aberdeen reservoir. He stayed with the car and I walked down to the water and then around it. It's very beautiful with all the soaring hills above. I'd walked nearly the whole way round when Soda suddenly bolted. Something or someone had scared her. At first I thought she was just exploring the undergrowth, but gradually I realized she must have gone further afield. By that time she must've been out of earshot. There were several paths she could have taken but there were no signs of her. I retraced my steps with Whisky, but after a while the light started to go, so I thought I'd better get back to the car and find help. The trouble was that I wasn't sure where I was or where the car was. I panicked a bit. I crossed over the dam where I was terrified that Whisky was going to hurl himself off (it has no guardrail at his height), just to complete the disaster. We made it to the other side and luckily I met a man who'd seen the car and could speak English. He very kindly showed me the way. It was a long way and all uphill.'

Tuesday 10 November

For several days search parties involving a large number of the staff at the house have started at the crack of dawn and gone on with torches in the evening. Lavender had to combine these worrying searches with official duties. She went to the Family Law Association and met a number of judges and lawyers and Tom Mulvey, the very competent and decent man who runs it, and then named a large container vessel for P and O. She organized a farewell lunch at the house for Felipe, who is standing down from his role as ADC after doing a terrific job for two governors. I went off to Canada this afternoon feeling miserable about losing our little dog, which was worrying me at least as much as the shells raining down on me from Beijing and the fifth column activity by some members of the business community in Hong Kong. The disappearance of Soda has made her the most famous terrier on the planet, though with a good deal of moderately racist tabloid stuff, particularly from the British press. Kate and Laura back home learnt about Soda's disappearance from the headlines with stories which suggest that she has probably been eaten. One headline runs, 'Chinese eat governor's dog'. The excellent Gareth Evans,* Australia's highly intelligent Foreign Minister, made a mistake quite common in public life with politicians who are genuinely witty, by telling a joke which he thought was private to a group of journalists in a bar. He said that Deng Xiaoping is well known for liking a couple of small dogs each day for breakfast. Questions are now asked in the Australian Parliament!

Wednesday 11th November

Back to Lavender's words –

'At about 7.25am this morning I was about to go out for another search when Elspeth telephoned. 'Soda's here, she's just been brought home.' I rushed downstairs with Whisky. Alice, unfortunately, had just gone off to school so missed the return of the wanderer. There was Soda in the private office, excited, pleased to see us all and totally fine. Whisky

* Gareth Evans is a barrister, politician, academic and international policy maker. Before becoming Australia's Foreign Minister from 1988 to 1996, he held a number of ministerial positions in the Hawke and Keating Labour governments. He was president of the conflict resolution organisation the International Crisis Group from 2000 to 2009, taught at the University of Melbourne and was Chancellor of the Australian National University from 2010 to 2020. He was a member of several international commissions and panels and was particularly active in campaigning for nuclear disarmament. He was a strong believer in standing up for human rights internationally and was a good friend of Hong Kong and its democratic aspirations. He is one of the best reasons for loving Australia, despite their cricket team.

was beside himself with joy. Apparently two joggers were in Aberdeen country park about a mile from the reservoir when they saw Soda trotting along in front of them and called out her name, which they had read about in the newspaper. She stopped, wagged her tail and then ran up the hill away from them. Fortunately, it was rocky and she couldn't avoid being caught. She seemed perfectly happy when they picked her up. Then they carried her back to Aberdeen, got in a taxi and brought her straight round to Government House.' As soon as the Prince of Wales saw the news in the papers he sweetly sent Lavender a telegram expressing his delight and relief. She went that evening to see the police beating the retreat with their Chinese pipe band, kilts and all. Perhaps there is a cheerful Chinese reel called the 'Return of the Terrier'.

I received the good news when I landed in Vancouver where I addressed a large lunch with hundreds of Hong Kong Chinese who now have Canadian passports. They seemed almost as interested in the happily terminated adventures of Soda as they were in the immediate future of Hong Kong.

Thursday 12–Saturday 14 November

I went on from Vancouver to Toronto and Ottawa. Ministers and everyone else were very supportive. While the Canadians have trade interests – and pretty substantial ones – in China, they have been extremely generous and helpful to Hong Kong, not just over passports but over other political issues too. I hope that Britain turns out to be as much on Hong Kong's side as Canada is. I came here quite often when I was Development Minister. Britain and Canada had some of the most professionally organized aid programmes in the world so talked together quite a lot. I still ask myself the question that I used to pose to my officials then: is there a nasty Canadian? This is probably taking a gamble and I may well discover one or two before my game is up. Now I had to see what the mood was like back home.

Sunday 15 November

I got into London early this morning bleary eyed, and went straight to the flat and then on to mass at noon in the cathedral. Laura was delighted about my brief visit and came with me to Tristan and Catali's for lunch. Tristan looked grey with fatigue. He has obviously taken a huge battering during the post-Maastricht ructions in the House of Commons. He has also been dragged into the rumpus about the sale of arms to Iraq, having been one of the signatories of an exemption certificate – simply because he was a duty minister that day. Some of the right-wing columnists are suspiciously nosing around what they regard as his ubiquitous insistence on throwing himself on any spears which point at the Prime Minister or Foreign Secretary. Once the Maastricht treaty is out of the way he wants to resign from the government. I hope he's allowed to do so. Laura cooked a delicious lasagne for supper.

Monday 16–Wednesday 18 November

I've had an absolutely crazy week in London. There were meetings with the Foreign Secretary and officials at the Foreign Office; lunch with the executive committee of the Hong Kong Association; a meeting with the Hong Kong parliamentary group; a dinner given by Douglas Hurd for Zhu Rongji, whose visit to London is taking place this week; a meeting with the chairman of the foreign affairs select committee, David Howell; another at the MoD with Malcolm Rifkind; breakfast with Jack Cunningham, the Labour Party's spokesman on foreign affairs; and a lunch with the Prime Minister. In addition, there were endless interviews, one of which at least annoys me, and is a reminder of what life is like in an open democracy. It's with Brian Redhead on the *Today* programme on BBC Radio Four. I was first of all played a package put together by Humphrey Hawksley, the BBC's man in Hong Kong, which quoted solely pro-Beijing critics, principally Elsie Tu, Vincent Lo and Selina Chow. Any idea that there is support in both Legco and in the community for what I am proposing was completely ignored. Needless to say, if I had adopted a different approach, the BBC would be taking me apart for not supporting democracy. Such is life – don't I love our public service broadcaster? Probably the most notable event of the week was that Zhu Rongji gave a speech at Chatham House, asked specifically to have a question at the end of his remarks on Hong Kong, and then delivered some fairly wintry arguments, going over all the old ground, which will have quite a bad impact. The Hang Seng Index plummeted as a result and there was a rather tough Exco meeting (without me) on the 16th with Willie Purves and C. H. Tung pretty hostile. Once again the dialogue (such as it is) with China was Kafkaesque. China told us to obey the BL. We pointed out that on the election committee and the functional constituencies for example it is silent. China then repeated that we must obey the Basic Law. And so we go on. Despite this I was not too unhappy about how things felt in London. Lunch at the Hong Kong Association was quite good, especially Jardine's. Murray MacLehose took me on one side and told me that he is sorry he is being miscast as a public critic of my proposals. He denied this and said he knows from personal experience how difficult the job is. He is an honourable man, probably disagrees with me, but is not going to do a Cradock. Most important, my support in the government and beyond seemed pretty strong. At a meeting of the Cabinet committee on Hong Kong with the Prime Minister in the chair, only Michael Heseltine and Michael Portillo* expressed any reservations. Ken Clarke† said very strongly that putting ourselves in the position in which Hong Kong opinion will finally decide how far to go is both sensible and honourable. Douglas Hurd noted that what China really wants is for us to do their dirty work for them – setting up institutions which will guarantee that they and their system are established in Hong Kong by the time we leave rather than allowing us to leave anything decent behind. This I refuse to do.

Thursday 19 November

I flew up to Newcastle to see Kate. She is living in what seems a very jolly hall of residence surrounded by loud and cheerful friends. She is having a wonderful time but I'd forgotten quite how squalid student life can be. The girl next door to her had been coping today with the consequences of a young man throwing up all over her floor the previous night. He sent some flowers but probably not enough! I took Kate out to a restaurant down on the wharf in the centre of Newcastle, Number 21. We had a terrific meal and she's really good company. I'd forgotten how much I miss her and indomitable Laura.

Friday 20 November

I got up with a huge black dog, not just because of the amount of red wine I drank last night. Seeing Kate has made me really gloomy. I don't want to leave Newcastle so quickly. I'm also rather fed up about spending the whole winter being rubbished by China, criticized by businessmen and

* I recruited Michael Portillo, who joined the Conservation Research Department in 1976 after Cambridge. He was an MP from 1984 to 1997 and held a number of ministerial posts, for some time as one of my junior ministers of the environment and finally rising to become Defence Minister in 1995. His father was a left-wing political opponent of General Franco who lived in exile until his death. Portillo moved to the right in Parliament as a Thatcherite, becoming rather unjustly a much-attacked political punchbag among *Guardian* readers. He subsequently pursued a career as a television presenter, successfully getting on and off trains around the world.

† Kenneth Clarke, who was an MP from 1970 to 2019, retiring then as father of the House of Commons, held many of the most important government positions during a career characterized by eloquent outspokenness, not least in favour of Britain's membership of the EU. He was one of Britain's three most successful post-war Chancellors of the Exchequer (alongside Rab Butler and Roy Jenkins) from 1993 to 1997. Having served as a senior minister under Thatcher, Major and Cameron, he was in effect thrown out of the party by Boris Johnson for opposing a 'no deal' departure from the EU. He had strong and well-informed opinions on most subjects from jazz to birdwatching and from sport to the condition of the Conservative Party. On the last subject he proved alas to be all too accurate.

perhaps watching public support drain away. I sometimes don't know what it is about me that seems to attract controversy. I don't mean to be anything other than an amiable fellow leading a life full of good intentions and with rather liberal views on things. How do I get into all this sort of thing?

Back in London I had lunch with Laura and my sister Angela and her husband Pete. Afterwards I had meetings with David Wilson and Ted Heath, which didn't exactly raise morale. David Wilson was politely unhappy about where things stand and worried about derailing the 'through train', which he thinks will leave Hong Kong in a terrible mess. Ted told me about a conversation that he had with Zhu Rongji in the car on the way to Oxford. Zhu had told him that China wouldn't budge in resisting my proposals, so naturally Ted thinks that we should go along with whatever China wants to do. This, from the man who when the Joint Declaration was debated in the House of Commons argued that the government weren't being sufficiently bold in pushing for greater democracy in Hong Kong. If you really want to find out what Ted Heath thinks these days, you ask what the government is doing and assume that he will want to do the opposite. This is even more so when his undoubted interests in China come into question.

Tuesday 24 November

While our meeting of Exco was on the whole supportive, when I reported my London discussions, there was a lot of hostility from C. H. Tung and expressions of nervousness from Willie Purves. I did some lobbying with Legco members to try to ensure that we get a favourable vote at the end of the week for funding the beginning of the work on the airport. It will be very damaging for our credibility and my political position if this doesn't happen.

Wednesday 25 November

Almost as soon as I got back I had to set off with Lavender to Tokyo to speak at the Hong Kong/Japan business cooperation committee. It's been a bit of a relief. Even a couple of days in Hong Kong was enough to raise my gloom level at the moment.

I learn more as time goes on about human behaviour. On the plane to Japan Lydia told me (she was coming to the business cooperation committee meeting) that the previous evening Murray MacLehose had phoned her up full of pessimism about events in Hong Kong and the controversy unleashed by my proposals. He was obviously trying to get me to think again, or get others to make me do so. He said I was behaving with China like a chairman of the Conservative Party dealing with Labour politicians. So much for his private word with me last week that anybody who said that he was trying to be unhelpful was wholly wrong.

The ministers I met in Japan, including the former Prime Minister, Mr Nakasone, gave discreet support. The most impressive political figure was the top official in the Japanese Ministry of Foreign Affairs, Owada, an immensely sophisticated official who speaks beautiful English. He was at Cambridge; apparently his daughter, who was at Balliol, now a diplomat, is spoken of as a possible bride for the Crown Prince. Our ambassador, John Boyd, and his wife Julia were extremely kind and knowledgeable hosts. Although John is now here, he was originally a China expert and spent some time in Hong Kong so understands very well the issues we are facing and the personalities involved. He managed to get together most of the friends that I have made over the years in Japanese politics for a very jolly dinner.

Friday 27 November

The Legco vote on agreeing funds for starting work on the airport went the right way. But it was close, we won by just two. Martin Barrow,* who had been with us for the meetings in Tokyo, went back specially to vote. David Ford and his team have done a fantastic lobbying job. It would have been a big blow if we had lost.

Saturday 28 November

This morning we went off to Kamakura to the Buddhist shrine there, which has been looked after for years by the grandfather and father of my first close Japanese friend, Yukio Satoh.

Monday 30 November

We have had a really bloody time since being back in Hong Kong. China's behaviour over the airport is bad enough, but they are also publicly threatening not to validate any contracts which are signed before 1997 but straddle that date. This evening, the Hong Kong Macau Affairs Office issued a statement implying that no new grants, leases or franchises awarded by the British government will be allowed to straddle 1997 unless they're specifically approved by Beijing. So it immediately looked as though

* Martin Barrow was an appointed member of Legco (from 1985 to 1995) and a company director of Jardine's Matheson. He had particular responsibility for their Japanese business and was vice-chairman of the Hong Kong General Chamber of Commerce. He was a strong supporter of the autonomy promised to Hong Kong.

the new container terminal is at risk, among much else. The legal position is perfectly clear. Under the Basic Law, contracts signed before 1997 should be honoured afterwards. We have been talking about franchises and so on with China in the Joint Liaison Group for some time. China's intention is plainly not to have an argument about the legality of contracts, but to shake confidence in the market, lower morale and spook investors.

Tuesday 1 December

In this at least they succeed for the time being. This morning, the market started to tremble and the Hang Seng Index fell. Tung and Purves were once again rattling the bars in Exco. We should drop our proposals straight away. Willie Purves unhelpfully dragged in comparisons with Britain's position in the ERM. Back home Percy Cradock, not denying himself the opportunity to put the boot in, wrote to *The Times* denouncing what we are doing. The tenor of his argument is that it may be unfortunate that China behaves in ways that we don't like but that's what happens with China. We all just have to lump it. I guess people used to make similar points during the 1930s about Germany. After questions in Legco I had a meeting with William Ehrman, who had received messages via an intermediary from the Chinese leadership. First of all, it confirmed what we knew already. Deng Xiaoping and other members of the leadership regard what is happening in Hong Kong as part of an international conspiracy against China. They put it together with the sale of F-16 aircraft to Taiwan, the visit of Carla Hills (George Bush's Trade Representative) to Taipei and the attitude of Germany, France and the Netherlands to Taiwan and to the issue of MFN status for China. It's all a Western attempt to subvert China and destroy the last great communist power. There are said to be some indications that they would be prepared to tolerate a democratically based election committee and more liberally defined functional constituencies, though not the ones that I have suggested – they're wondering whether proposals like this might come up from individual Legco members. Indeed they might. It's a point that William and I discussed with the Chief Secretary and the Financial Secretary. I also talked to Martin and Edward about it. We kept this very tight. The only compromise we could find politically tolerable would be one that came out of the Legislative Council.

Wednesday 2 December

The slide in the Hang Seng Index continued. We know that some of this is being triggered by China-based companies and the Bank of China itself buying and selling forward in the futures market. They are deliberately encouraging a mood of panic. I wonder how long they will keep this up before concluding that they are going to damage themselves – in particular the families of some of the senior leaders who have substantial investments (ill-gotten gains?) in Hong Kong. Do they really want to bring the roof down? When I had breakfast with the Beijing correspondent of the *New York Times*, Nicholas Kristof, he seemed to think we are being very brave. He reckoned, building on my metaphor, that the roof may indeed fall and that we will have to get out before we are hit by the debris. Kristof is an excellent journalist and knows a lot about China, so we should listen carefully to what he says.

Friday 4 December
So far the Hang Seng has gone down by over 400 points. Leo Goodstadt has written a clever paper showing how there have been much bigger falls in the past. In fact, the market is pretty well back to where it was earlier in the year, but there's not much comfort in that. There is a growing sense of panic and I'm taking all the blame rather than China. I'm not sleeping very well. That always happens when I'm politically worried.

Chinese officials are becoming increasingly imaginative in the names they call me: sinner for a thousand years, prostitute, triple violator and more. They have clearly been through the Cultural Revolution handbook to find the appropriate language to describe me. This is less unsettling than what is happening to the markets and the steady drip of criticism from members of the business community, invariably I suspect from the ones who have foreign passports. I am having regular meetings with civil servants as well as of course with the Secretaries of departments. Given the efforts that Beijing is making to undermine them it's important to do everything to keep them onside. So far so good. But at one meeting with David Ford today he passed me a note saying, 'You sound very low.' I perked up and tried to provide a bit more positive body language. Back in London Cradock continues to bitch away. I am helped in Exco by Robin McLaren, who comes down from Beijing to give a briefing. He puts on an excellent performance. He is realistically gloomy about attitudes in Beijing but supportive of my proposals. I am told that he has read the riot act to his embassy staff about any criticism of what we are doing.

Wednesday 9 December
My morale was lifted, curiously enough, by a meeting with an organization called the Business Professional Federation led by a pretty ghastly trio – Vincent Lo, David Akers-Jones and a retired taipan from Swire's called David Gledhill. The highlights of the meeting for me were, first,

Akers-Jones admitting that the sort of proposals he would like to see for the elections wouldn't stand a chance of being passed by Legco. Second, David Gledhill was forced to admit that the Chinese position on the container terminal was quite simply wrong. He began to refer to it by saying that the Chinese had made a statement about the subject 'rightly or wrongly'. I asked him directly, 'Well, was it rightly or wrongly?' Rather sheepishly he admitted the latter. It's quite comforting that they have nothing really to say and refuse, with a variety of spurious reasons, to put forward alternative proposals.

Saturday 12 December

I had a further sense that we had a very defensible position when at an informal Exco we went through all my proposals one by one. This had been Lydia's helpful idea. I think people are starting to understand the complexities of the issues. We can of course make adjustments but it would be useful if there was obvious support in Legco for any changes. As Ken Clarke said at the Cabinet committee meeting, we can't very well be a lot braver than the community is prepared to be. When C. H. Tung talked to me privately about having secret negotiations with China on all this, I pointed out that there isn't much to be said for trying to agree something with Lu Ping which can't then be delivered by Legco.

Monday 14 December

Definitely a day to remember. I spoke to the Hong Kong Exporters Association and made my usual pitch that MFN renewal on trade with the USA should be kept separate from the debate on Hong Kong's political development. After lunch Lydia Dunn told me that Allen Lee has been talking to the press assuring them that within three or four months I shall be on my knees to China. Then I saw three very sane Americans – Winston Lord, who used to be the US ambassador in Beijing, Morton Abramowitz, who was an ambassador and Asian expert, and Stephen Bosworth, an American academic and diplomat. They are all members of the Asia Society. Winston Lord has already said in public that it is astonishing that the Chinese are making so much fuss over so little. He believes they have really overreacted. The excellent Canadian consul in Hong Kong, John Higginbotham, has said much the same. They all think that what is really annoying China is that we are attempting to give substance to what is actually written in the JD and the BL.

Then came the big event of the day. Lee Kuan Yew was giving a lecture at Hong Kong University in the main hall and as Chancellor I agreed to preside. The hall was full and he delivered a rather dull speech – read word for word – comparing Singapore and Hong Kong as great Asian cities. As the audience were warming up to questions, I asked him one about the process of decolonization, which he uses to attack democracy in general and Britain in particular. He then received a question from a professor in the audience about the irony of the most autocratic leader in Asia sitting next to the most democratic Governor, and who went on to ask whether the prosperity of Hong Kong means that it now deserves democracy. Lee Kuan Yew had obviously prepared himself for a question like this and he delivered a real blast – his answer was longer than the lecture. He spoke for nearly 40 minutes with a wealth of cuttings, extracts from speeches in the House of Lords (rather rarely quoted in my experience) and transcripts of television interviews. He comprehensively rubbished the proposals I have put forward, and this from the man who not long ago was advising me to try to fill in the grey areas in the Joint Declaration and the Basic Law. Most damagingly, he asserted that the proposals were part of the plot directed at China to create havoc through democratization. Apparently we have planned all this with the Americans. This is exactly the sort of conspiracy theory which they believe in Beijing. There was also a lot of selective quotation from commentators as well as from Percy Cradock and Murray MacLehose.

Altogether, it was a seriously tiresome performance. At the end of it restraining myself from saying what I would like to have offered up, I thanked him and noted that I looked forward to the right of reply in Singapore after 1997. I got a burst of applause from the audience.

Tuesday 15 December

Lee cancelled his engagements today on the excuse that he was not feeling well – but well enough to fill his diary with interviews with television channels and newspapers in which he covered all this stuff once again. I guess part of his purpose was to damage Hong Kong while trying to improve Singapore's relationship with China. It is of course ironic that he used the freedom of speech in Hong Kong which is denied to critics of the government in Singapore. There is no doubt that he is clever, no question that he is interesting, nor that he has created in Singapore a considerable success story for a certain kind of social engineering in a fairly small community. As for the other qualities usually thought desirable in an amiable and courteous human being, it's a matter of taste, I suppose.

Saturday 19 December

There are a lot of other things which should keep me happy. I still get enthusiastic welcomes on all my district visits and even after the pounding we have taken. Mike Hanson showed me an opinion poll on the 13th that gives us a 2 to 1 lead for what we are trying to do and the way we are doing it. I was also greatly cheered by a dinner with a wonderful Italian priest, Father Lambertoni from the Pontifical Institute for Missions Overseas (PIME in the Italian). He had to leave Hong Kong a few years ago when he was campaigning against the Triads in his parish. The parish priest had been murdered, having been mistaken for Lambertoni himself. He had to be got out of the city, but after working for a bit in refugee camps in Thailand, he came back to Hong Kong. He rides a Harley-Davidson and has a very active parish in Kowloon. He is the best possible example of the social teaching of the Catholic Church in practice. He told me to 'Hang on in there' as a lot of churches have started petitions so that people can sign up to support what I've been trying to do. That is more or less what Peter Barry said in his homily in the cathedral last Sunday.

On top of all this I have Lavender and Alice, and Christmas, to look forward to. But alas I am losing my private secretary, Richard Hoare, who is moving on to another civil service post; Richard has been hugely supportive and he has got on very well with Martin and Edward. We gave him a farewell lunch and welcomed his Chinese successor, Bowen Leung. While the artillery fire has been raining down on us, I have a pretty comfortable bunker to go home to. I suppose that this might be a good time to describe Government House in a little more detail.

It truly does matter to have somewhere you love to live in when the going gets rough. It's probably best to describe it briefly in Lavender's own words from her own diary. She after all has to run it with a wonderful staff led by our housekeeper, Elspeth.

'GH – our home! – is amazing. It's up the hill from the central district, opposite the Botanical Gardens, and has been the residence of governors since it was built in 1855. It's huge – especially to someone used to a four-bedroomed flat in central London. From the outside the house doesn't really look like a typical British colonial building at all. It's much more oriental looking, and of course now it's dwarfed by all the skyscrapers and new building projects going up on all sides. Inside it's a handsome building, cool, light and spacious with beautiful rooms and balconies. But the decoration is all rather dreary . . .

'. . . The wallpaper and furnishings are faded and will need smartening up when we can get round to it. Our private rooms are on the first floor. We have a large sitting room and bedroom . . . We each have a bathroom and dressing room, though his is much more of a proper room than mine. The girls each have a room in the tower; Alice's has a kitchen. The tower is a Japanese addition to the house, which was rebuilt during the war when the Japanese occupied Hong Kong and the Japanese commander appropriated the house as his official residence. I think the housekeeper used to live up there before a bungalow was built for her in the grounds . . .

'There's plenty of space for visitors – and I envisage a steady stream – official guests and, I hope, friends too. There are three guest suites on the first floor consisting of a double and a single bedroom and a sitting room each.'

Back to me –

The house was surrounded by a sweeping garden falling away down the hill behind the house towards a wooded area at the bottom. There was a large lawn at the top of the hill and a swimming pool tucked in next to the house surrounded by shrubs and trees. There were also two tennis courts which in the past had been used frequently for car parking. Not any longer! We used the tennis courts a lot and allowed Hong Kong's junior tennis squad to train there too.

We were keen to cheer up the house, not least since we were intending to open it a lot more to the public for concerts and charity events. It needed a lot of repainting; the bathrooms needed redoing; the curtains and fabrics had to be cleaned or replaced; and in doing all this we wanted to try to ensure that the house showed off the best of Hong Kong design with both new and antique furniture. We also wanted to include some of our own things. We were told very firmly that before we began work, we should consult the feng shui master. I have a modest sympathy for geomancy; in building or decorating a home there is much to be said for taking account of the environment. But I find it difficult to believe that this is real science, let alone a set of almost spiritual beliefs, which should determine the decisions you take and the way you live. When our expert came to look around the house, presumably for a good fee, he told us that the house was oppressed by surrounding skyscrapers. He was particularly concerned that the sharp corner of the Bank of China pointed menacingly at the house. Before doing anything else he insisted on moving some of our furniture around, often almost imperceptibly. Having consulted his charts, he told us that we must not do any major works until next year.

Lavender talked to Thomas Chow, one of my assistant private secretaries, about all this. He is a Christian and told Lavender that as Christians we should have nothing to do with all this nonsense. Lavender was told that, when the feng shui man was leaving the house, he heard that we were disappointed about the delay in starting the work. He told Elspeth that he was sorry that he hadn't known this in advance. He could have fixed a date that suited us had he known we wanted to get on with things. This made Lavender very sympathetic to Thomas's point of view!

But the truth is that a large number of the staff actually believed in all this malarkey, as did a lot of senior Chinese business leaders, including C. H. Tung. When my predecessor but one, Sir Edward Youde, redesigned the garden with a trickle of water flowing down the steps from the pond away from the house, his subsequent visit to Beijing was thought to be doomed in advance. And indeed, when poor Youde – a really excellent man who stood up for Hong Kong – made this official visit north, he died of a heart attack and came back in a coffin. The critics of his redesign of the garden responded by making the point that this calamity was only to be expected since he had arranged for water to run away from his house, and life had followed water. So Thomas was right, but so was Lavender. We had to go through all this to get the staff to buy in to what we were proposing.

The staff rapidly became friends. They loved having Alice and our dogs around; daughter and terriers were all horribly spoiled. Inevitably, the dogs spent quite a lot of their time hovering around the kitchen hoping for scraps or sitting with the team responsible for telegram traffic in a basement room being fed too many biscuits. Lavender got on extremely well with all the staff – they worked very hard, were cheerful and conscientious. Our terrific chefs made sure that whatever was being said about me by Beijing, my morale was not entirely blown away. Inevitably I started to put on weight.

Thursday 24 December

The past 10 days have brought some further economic terrorism from Beijing. First of all, came a warning on 16 December from Ambassador Ma in London to ICI that they should lobby against my proposals if they wanted to benefit their business. To their credit they told him that there was a difference between economics and politics and that if the Chinese government did not like what we were doing in Hong Kong it was up to them to lobby against it. Second, far worse than this, as the Hang Seng Index continued to fall, was a blistering attack on 17 December by the New China News Agency on Jardine's, presumably because the firm has been quite supportive about what we have been doing. Peter Ricketts had a brief visit on the 17th to see what is going on in Hong Kong and noted not very surprisingly that things have got a lot more jittery, although he certainly hasn't.

I continued to get out and about as much as possible. There were large cheering crowds on a visit to the Kwai Tsing district. I'm still not sure whether this is the celebrity factor – that is, people turning out to see me because I'm well-known – or whether it represents something more political. I can hope.

I had an afternoon on the 17th looking at so-called 'black spots' with the Chief Secretary and a small team. We looked at unsafe structures which have been added onto buildings without planning consent, the building of commercial extensions in back alleys, the prostitutes in Sham Shui Po and so on. The nastiest thing we saw were the hostels for caged men. These are little bunks with cages round them which the most impoverished poor people in the community rent for tiny sums. They really are shockingly squalid in a city where there are so many very rich people.

The Jardine's affair rumbled on, but most of the press are very critical of what China has done. Then suddenly on the 22nd – the day when we were told we would get some sort of ultimatum – the noises out of China appeared to change, as our excellent spooks had predicted they would. Lu Ping gave all sorts of assurances at a meeting with a delegation of the principal United Front political party in Hong Kong – the DAB HK. He said that China doesn't want to appoint some kind of alternative government, that it's committed to the airport and the Joint Declaration, and it's certainly not going to walk away from that or the Basic Law. In addition, Foreign Minister Qian Qichen has made optimistic noises and said that Sino-UK relations will improve after he has seen Douglas Hurd in March. Whatever game Beijing is playing, I prefer this one to the last.

And then we were into Christmas. Kate and Laura arrived from London, as did my sister Angela and brother-in-law Pete and their daughter Lucy. We had a carol concert on the 22nd in the house with the choir from the Anglican cathedral and all went to the races at Happy Valley to the Governor's box yesterday. I know nothing at all about horses, got some tips from the stewards at the house and didn't win a penny. Kate looked wonderful when she handed over the prizes for the Ladies' Purse horse race.

Sunday 27 December

We spent Christmas Day and a short period afterwards at Fanling, went for terrific walks and ate lots of goose – apart from poor Lavender, who was ill on Christmas Day. Today we all went to mass at Father Lambertoni's parish in Kwai Chung. It's a working-class parish where we got a tremendous welcome. We had another walk in the afternoon in pouring rain, though I started to get out of breath a bit.

Friday 1 January 1993

The Needhams were all with us over the New Year, but New Year's Eve itself is awful. While we were all at a party I heard that there's been a terrible accident in Lan Kwai Fong, a very lively area just down the hill full of clubs, restaurants and bars. 20 youngsters were killed in the crush of a crowd celebrating the New Year. Lavender and I went back to Government House and changed out of black tie. Then we went to the police headquarters and the two hospitals that have been dealing with the victims and finally to the scene of the tragedy itself, not far from Government House. It was very grim indeed. Sleeping parents were woken in the middle of the night and brought into hospital to identify the bodies of their children. If we had not been at parties ourselves, Kate and Laura were planning to visit this area with some young friends. This is the sort of disaster which happens in life and I'm not sure that you can ever take precautions which make such horrible accidents absolutely impossible. However, this morning I set up an enquiry and asked for interim findings before the Chinese New Year. I have a strong feeling that if you're at the top when things like this happen you have to show your face. It may not do very much good but you have to try, and to show that you care which – unless you're made out of stone – you of course do.

Friday 8 January

We spent quite a bit of time after New Year trying to work out whether the Chinese line had really changed and if so why. The truth is we just didn't know what had happened. Anyway, it looked as though the Hong Kong Macau office was back in charge and that the NCNA bruisers were being pushed to the side. The press back in London still lean in the direction of reporting on the beleaguered Governor, exhausted by the battering he has taken, who is about to be eaten for breakfast by Deng Xiaoping as Hong Kong trembles. And so on. This is pretty much what Ann Leslie writes in the *Mail*. She's too good and intelligent to be churning out this sort of stuff by the yard. When I said in one interview with the London *Standard* that it is always possible there may be a compromise on political development, it's taken as a sure sign that we are in retreat.

Lydia Dunn says the rumour about town is that we are searching for an intermediary. I keep on saying to whoever is prepared to listen that we can't go any further than Legco wants, and that if there are going to be any changes they are most likely to come as a result of legislators making them. But wannabe intermediaries keep on popping up offering their services or claiming that we've already asked for help. It drives us all to distraction.

Sunday 10 January

Malcolm Rifkind* and his nice and articulate wife, Edith, came briefly to stay this weekend for discussions with the garrison. He sympathized about the intermediaries problem. Apparently, he used to get quite a bit of this when as a minister he was dealing with Eastern Europe. While he was with us he made a point of trying to talk to all shades of opinion. At a dinner I gave for the Rifkinds, Malcolm said to me that, whatever else happens, we should at least be able to leave Hong Kong with our heads held high. Let's hope so. He told Lavender that once he's made a decision on a big issue he doesn't spend a lot of time worrying about it afterwards. Fortunate and sensible chap! When he was talking as he does to a number of pro-democracy guests at a reception he was torn away from them by Willie Purves, who wanted him to know that the business community are very unhappy with me. Willie, who is not perhaps best known for his sense of humour, has just told Edward that he must stop me telling jokes. He says that the Chinese don't like it. I wonder how he explains all those Cantonese puns.

Saturday 16 January

This past week, the main questions about my political package have been when we should put it to the legislature, whether we should change it before we table it, what changes should we be prepared to accept, and how we should deal with China both about what is proposed and what is actually happening in the legislature. All these discussions took place against a background of suspicion on the part of the pro-democracy camp that we were trying to wriggle out of our original proposals. We had several extremely lengthy discussions in January in Exco accompanied by leaks and orchestrated lobbying from outside. Rightly or wrongly Swire's, for whom Lydia works, are thought to have a hand in some of this. Larry Yung, who is the head of the China mainland company Citic and who is believed to be not only influential but pretty moderate, has been talking to Adrian Swire in London. He told him and others that China expects my proposals to be knocked about a good deal in the Legislative Council, and that China's concessions to unblock things at the end will include amended but reasonably democratic proposals on the election committee. With, I

* Malcolm Rifkind was MP for an Edinburgh constituency who had ministerial posts under both Margaret Thatcher and John Major, in whose Cabinet he was first Secretary for Transport and then Secretary for Defence from 1992 until 1995, when he became Foreign Secretary. He lost his Scottish seat in 1997, but returned to Parliament as MP for Kensington and Chelsea from 2005 until 2015. He was a brilliant forensic speaker in Parliament.

suspect, some elbow nudging, several members of Exco wanted to go in detail through all the different ways of organizing the election committee, but no one came up with a better or more coherent idea than the one we have already proposed. Robin McLaren made efforts to see Lu Ping to clarify what we are doing and to try to disentangle us from intermediaries, the most recent of whom is Jeffrey Sterling, the boss of P and O, whose credentials for getting up to whatever he's getting up to remain unclear.

More agreeably we had interesting discussions with Hamish MacLeod about how to deal with our budgetary surplus – this is one of the problems of success to which I'm not terribly accustomed back home at Westminster.

I have also begun discussions with David Ford about how we can replace the expatriate heads of civil service departments with local Chinese appointments, so that by 1997 the entire team, with the exception of myself and the Attorney General, is local.

We got one piece of amusing gossip about the egregious Cradock. He was giving an interview to a journalist who works for a magazine owned and run by T. S. Lo, a local lawyer and bridge-playing politician who has become very close to Beijing. Cradock told the journalist that John Major was doing perfectly all right in relation to China, and doing what he was told, until suddenly he rejected a note that Cradock had passed to him during the course of a meeting in the summer with Martin Lee. In Cradock's view that is when all the problems seemed to start. He really can't understand what all this fuss is about since the Prime Minister – he claimed – was delighted with his trip to Beijing and had told him so. Now the Prime Minister is off the leash and there are problems all over the place. It is all absurd enough to be a true account of the Cradock view. I guess that Percy has spent too long working with and on the Chinese Communist Party to avoid being affected by their endless hunt for, and purported discovery of, conspiracies.

Thursday 21 January

We had lunch with John Foley and his wife on the 17th. I had two helpings of a delicious boeuf stroganoff and then we went out on a very cold afternoon to play tennis. We had barely begun when I started getting chest pains, which I assumed were the result of acute indigestion from which I used to suffer until I gave up smoking. When we got back to the house, Lavender sent for a doctor, who arrived with an ECG machine. This began days of discussions with, and examinations by, doctors, ECGs on treadmills, and all sorts of other tests for my blood pressure and much more. There was some dispute about whether I had actually had a heart attack; one of my tests showed large numbers of enzymes in the blood, which was apparently a bad sign. What there is no doubt about is that I am and have been suffering from fibrillation. Lavender supported my refusal to go straight into hospital but part of the price was that we had a permanent medical presence in the house for a few days. What I didn't want was headlines saying that I was about to conk out. One of the last things that Hong Kong needs is another Governor dead from a heart attack. All the doctors I saw, particularly three clever young cardiologists who looked as though they were barely out of school, were kind and plainly knew exactly what they were doing. Dr Yeoh, who runs the Hospital Authority, made sure that everything was well coordinated without any discernible sense of panic. This helped avoid media speculation about how ill I am.

One thing that cheered me up while this was going on was William Ehrman's account of a banquet which had been given for him after cross-border liaison talks in Guangdong. The authorities there seemed to go out of their way to tell him how sympathetic they are towards all of us in Hong Kong. Without too much subtlety they wanted to make it clear that they thought Beijing was behaving ridiculously in relation to political developments in the city. In return for this, William had to chomp his way through a great feast. He ate for Britain – peacock, half a dog (which he said looked exactly like what it was), a whole snake and a bowl of cockerel's testicles. 'Which was the nastiest of all these dishes?' I asked, 'The cocks' balls', he said with some feeling.

Friday 22 January

With a suitcase full of medicines and a promise to have an angiogram when I get home, we are heading off for a lovely week's holiday in Bali tomorrow, staying in a hotel on the beach. I plan to read more Hilary Mantel and John King Fairbanks' history of China.

Sunday 31 January

As soon as I got home, rather sunburned but much rested, I had another ECG and then a discussion with another young group of cardiologists, led by a doctor called Stephen Lee who was a bit more forceful than the others and didn't hesitate to tell me what he really thought. He wanted me to have an angiogram as soon as possible, so I went along to Queen Mary's Hospital today. It wasn't much fun. A catheter was inserted in my groin and ran up into the arteries around my heart. Then some sort of substance was injected and they started taking pictures. I watched all this on a screen in a state of controlled horror. But I should feel more sympathy for the young cardiologists, who had to do all this with a large team of the great and good in the Hong Kong medical profession watching them through the window. One reason why I like Stephen so much is his blunt honesty. He insists on giving me a real indication of the risks and shot down everybody who said that what was happening to me was 'a piece of cake'. The conclusion was that I have a badly blocked circumflex artery at the back of my heart and problems with another artery on the other side. Two out of three isn't good. They also concluded that the next stage should be angioplasty rather than a bypass, which pleased me a lot as I understand that with a bypass you sometimes have to face up to another one after 10 years.

Monday 1 February

Both John Major and Douglas Hurd phone up after they've heard about my problems. John wondered whether I'd like to come home to continue the procedure. I made the obvious point that it would be a terrible gesture of lack of confidence in the Hong Kong medical system if I were to do this, and that anyway I'm very pleased about the way that I'm being looked after by Stephen Lee and the others.

I have come back to a continuing dispute by Cathay Pacific stewardesses in which I am reluctant to intervene. Industrial relations are not really a problem in Hong Kong. We certainly don't need (as some legislators are suggesting) a change in the law. We have a good labour relations department and I don't want to interfere politically with how they are dealing with the dispute. Moreover the department is part of Anson Chan's economic affairs secretariat and she has plainly got a grip on what is happening. Indeed, the more I see of her, the more she seems very good at getting a grip on any problem which comes her way. As Martin says, she runs towards problems not away from them.

Tuesday 2 February

We had an pretty intelligent discussion in Exco about what to do with the election proposals. The line-up was fairly predictable. C. H. Tung was against doing anything that China doesn't like, though he expressed himself as usual both genially and with great courtesy. One issue that came up was whether Britain has simply changed its policy on China. In summing up I said that I wasn't sent out to alter British policy but that giving in to China self-evidently hasn't been in the interest of Hong Kong or Britain; that we are determined to take the Joint Declaration seriously; that China has greatly overreacted to our proposals; that we tried to satisfy them on direct elections and the composition of Exco; and that if there is a change the British government is proposing, it is to make absolutely clear (as I have said on several previous occasions) that it will only go as far as Hong Kong wishes. We agreed to go forward on the basis of the present plans and publish a first-stage set of proposals (covering issues such as the voting age and election to the municipal council and district boards) followed by a debate in the Legislative Council in a couple of weeks' time. We can continue with the rest later if we don't want to do everything together. We will ask our embassy in Beijing, and perhaps the Foreign Secretary as well, to tell Beijing what we are proposing to do, particularly laying out what gazetting of our proposals actually means – literally telling the legislature in broad terms what we are proposing to do in a bill. I don't want them to start banging on again about us not letting them know how we intend to proceed. (As though they would tell us what they are planning to do!)

I had dinner this evening with senior police officers in their mess. I made a little Eve-of-Waterloo-ball sort of speech, noting that one benefit of my illness is that the Chinese will no longer be able to argue that I don't have a heart. I got a standing ovation, which was good for morale, especially as I was not able to drink very much wine to cheer me up in a more traditional way.

Wednesday 3 February

Back to hospital and the catheter once again like last week. Stephen Lee was there with his hand-picked team; there is also apparently a standby team in case anything goes wrong and I need an urgent bypass. They started work just before 9 and went on till just after 12. It seemed a very long time indeed. They passed balloons up my arteries and inflated them for as long as I could bear the pain, which is a bit like having a heart attack. For the patient there is an obvious problem. You want them to inflate the balloons as much as possible to have the best effect, but on the other hand you don't want to be in pain for too long. I was delighted when the catheter was eventually removed and I have been sent off to Fanling for a few days' rest.

Friday 5–Sunday 14 February

I can put my feet up and David Ford can govern Hong Kong for a bit. Lydia Dunn and her husband, Michael Thomas (formerly the Attorney General and a distinguished barrister), have sent me a little CD player, so I've had a rather musical time, mostly listening to Mozart piano sonatas and Puccini in the garden. The heroes of all this are of course Stephen and his colleagues. Apparently, having saved the Governor, they are going to be in great demand even on the mainland. I suppose the villain is me for not taking enough exercise and having too much to eat.

There was one major political development during my week off. At the 11th hour Beijing suddenly warmed to the idea of talks. This came after Exco had agreed that we should go ahead and gazette the bill incorporating our constitutional proposals, with the idea of early debates in Legco. Have they just blinked? During the last week our ambassador in Beijing went to the Chinese explaining the proposals, handing them a copy of the bill and a letter from me saying how things will now proceed, with an additional letter from Douglas Hurd. This was couched in the usual terms, saying that we remained happy for a discussion at any stage. They then told Robin McLaren when he handed over the letters that they would like some time to consider them. So we agreed to delay gazetting our bill from 12 to 19 February. Today, Robin McLaren was summoned and given a reply from Qian Qichen to Douglas Hurd's letter proposing talks. There was a lot of noise and bluster in Qian's letter but no suggestion that we needed to drop my proposals formally before talks could take place. In other words, at the very last moment they have backed down, though this is not something we can say.

Tuesday 16 February

We do now face real difficulties. Previously, the position was absolutely straightforward. We withstood a barrage of abuse and attacks from China but proposed that Legco should take things forward. It's been a reasonably satisfactory few months (though it didn't feel like it at the time) because we haven't dropped anything; we've stood up to bullying; and the Chinese want to talk. The Hang Seng Index is higher now than it was when I made my Legco speech; the economy is in good shape; Hong Kong hasn't fallen; and Legco have started to behave in a rather more mature way. While the community will be greatly cheered and doubtless the Hang Seng will soar, actually handling the discussions with China will be enormously complicated. All the pressure will be on us to make concessions. We are already starting to see this a bit in some of the telegrams that we get from the Beijing embassy. The most pusillanimous members of the business and political community will claim credit for the talks, whereas in fact talks are a result of standing firm.

In my first discussions today about these developments I behaved in a rather Thatcher-like way and asked what you could euphemistically call challenging questions. I pressed very hard on William Ehrman and Tony Galsworthy about where the talks will actually get us. I'm very keen that we shouldn't drift into the usual Sinophile 'surrender and reparations' frame of mind. We agreed that there must be a strong Hong Kong presence on the negotiating team. I want Michael Sze, Peter Lai (an able Chinese official who is Michael's deputy) and William Ehrman perhaps, as well as Peter Ricketts from London, to join the ambassador. We want to start as soon as possible and there must also be an early announcement that talks are going to take place. This is imperative because the Chinese have started leaking already. I would like us to have a negotiating strategy which puts pressure on China to make its own proposals and an agenda of concessions on which we can press China. We can't just play the game on Chinese terms during the first round of talks and then cave in during the second and subsequent rounds. It was a spirited meeting and we fired off telegrams in all directions. Lydia Dunn is very pleased about the latest turn of events but concerned that we shouldn't allow the Chinese to drag the talks out. I think this is exactly what they will do. I talked to Martin Lee on what in Westminster one would call Privy Council terms. I don't want him to think that we are suddenly going to go weak at the knees. I think he trusts me on this but obviously his colleagues will not want to see any evidence of retreat.

There is one sign of disagreement in what we are hearing from China. The NCNA in Hong Kong is saying that I must withdraw my proposals before there are any talks. The Hong Kong Macau Office in Beijing is saying simply that I must withdraw my proposals. The significance of this distinction would not be clear to anybody who wasn't already well-versed in the arcana of Sino-British Hong Kong politics.

Wednesday 17 February

I've started playing tennis again and did so before a meeting with Rupert Murdoch and the chairman of the *South China Morning Post*. They have just changed the editor, Phillip Crawley, whom they don't appear to think is sufficiently pro-Beijing at a time when Murdoch himself is trying to get more deeply into China. It's sad for Crawley. He's a fine journalist and a very competent editor. The *Post* has not been mindlessly supportive of me. Indeed, it has sometimes been quite critical. If I was the proprietor I would think it had struck rather a good balance. I found Murdoch himself slightly more charming than I had expected but I'm not sure that you would take much notice of him in a crowd. This evening, I had dinner with Jim Prior,* now the chairman of GEC, who is with some of the

* Jim Prior was a Conservative MP from 1959 to 1987, until he retired from the Commons and became a member of the House of Lords. He was close to Edward Heath and was Minister of Agriculture and Leader of the Commons in the Heath administration before 1974. He later served as Employment Secretary and Secretary of State for Northern Ireland under Margaret Thatcher. They did not get on; she regarded him as too soft on the Union and general economic policy. I had worked for him when he was Peter Carrington's deputy as chairman of

company's fixers and would-be customers. Jim had recently seen Zhou Nan, who tried to put the frighteners on him saying that in the light of my disgraceful behaviour China would not be buying anything from Britain. Mafia tactics again. We also hear several rumours that the NCNA is pushing companies for kickbacks in return for not having projects or commercial sales blocked.

Thursday 18 February

We had a telegram late last night from Douglas asking us to set out our bottom line so that he can let the Prime Minister know what it is. I dictated a telegram first thing this morning, saying we would be prepared to give a bit on the election committee and functional constituencies, but would need something in return to make a reality of convergence (between the political system before and after the handover) and the through train. For example, if we make any concessions, those who were elected in 1995 should be allowed to travel right through to 1999 provided they accept the BL. If we are going to find ourselves making concessions during the talks, we will want something in exchange. At a stand-up with the press after I opened an expo on education and careers, I was asked whether the reason that I can't say anything about talks is because nobody has told me about them. There are rumours around that I am being cut out. I guess that this will be a story that I will have to deal with a lot over the coming weeks. 'Patten being bypassed'.

Thursday 25 February

This past week has been filled with 'will they, won't they' talk. This is pretty tiresome and part of me wants simply to get on with things, to let Legco start to debate the election plans. This would clearly put us in a position where we could say that the community, or to be strictly accurate its representatives, was determining where to draw the line. For a time Exco, or at least a majority, seems to have come to this view itself. We've had some good meetings, including an unofficial one today, at which Exco eventually came down on the side of not putting the bill into the legislature in the next few days. The two barristers on Exco continue to be both eloquent and sensible. Andrew Li usually leans in a slightly more cautious direction; Denis Chang pushes for us to be more open, robust and democratic. He is a spirited Catholic with pronounced liberal values. He can be very funny and is both very likeable and clever. Even C. H. Tung seems to

the Conservative Party before the 1974 election, and also as one of his ministerial team in Northern Ireland. After politics he had many directorships and was chair of GEC.

accept that if Beijing doesn't commit itself to talks soon, we will have to press on. But for the time being, I was persuaded (against my instincts) that we should 'go the extra mile'. As Edward reminded me, in the past this has come second in my lexicon of how not to conduct decision making only to 'the doctrine of unripe time'. I suppose that if we simply pushed ahead the moderate centre in Hong Kong would think we were being unnecessarily bold or rash, and the business community would have yet another grenade to toss over our fence.

Senior officials representing the Chinese government seem rather reluctant to see anyone from London or Hong Kong who is asking for a decision about whether we talk or don't talk. Maybe they just don't know. In London, Alastair Goodlad summoned Ambassador Ma to ask what is going on. But the ambassador was not 'available' and sent along an underling from the embassy. To his credit the person to come closest to getting some action out of Beijing is Willie Purves. He has been there on Hong Kong Bank business, but spent most of an hour-long meeting with Lu Ping arguing the importance of coming to an early decision about talks, unless, that is, the Chinese side is really happy to give the initiative to the legislature in Hong Kong. He seems to have spoken very well for Hong Kong, and C. H. Tung tells me that he has said the same sort of thing in a telephone call with Lu. There is obviously a struggle in Beijing and people are waiting to get a decision from higher up about what to do. The Foreign Ministry and the Hong Kong Macau Office seem to be briefing along a moderate line, explaining how if talks take place it won't really represent any backing down by China, since when they use the word ' withdraw' all that they mean is that my proposals should not be the basis for the talks; they don't mean that we have to withdraw the proposals in order to have talks in the first place. On the other hand, the NCNA is briefing fiercely that there will be tough conditions for any talks. These appear to include cutting the legislature out of any part in deciding the future of political development in Hong Kong. We sent some ideas to London today about how we should respond if we are offered ridiculous conditions by the Chinese, and I don't want to be caught off balance.

Friday 26 February

We are getting into difficulties about the defence costs agreement under which the Hong Kong government, that is the Hong Kong taxpayer, pays for 70% of the costs of the garrison in the territory. Some sort of garrison is plainly required, though not to deter Chinese aggression. What on earth would we be expected to do if the Chinese army came over the border?

What I suspect has been happening is that the scale of the garrison costs has in practice enabled MOD to postpone taking tough decisions about the future of the Gurkhas, who are present in the territory in quite large numbers. They are very welcome but Hong Kong taxpayers can't be expected to fork out so that London doesn't have to decide on their future. About 50% of the garrison costs are what is called 'tail'. Moreover, we have paid for 700 MOD visits to Hong Kong in the last year (what a lot of suits and shirts) and have just been required to purchase 117 new cars. When Sir Christopher France, the chief civil servant at Defence, came to Hong Kong on 23 February, I pointed out that this problem is an indication of how we are trapped these days between old-fashioned colonial government and the beginnings of democracy. As Governor I have very few reserve powers over a matter like this. It is surprising that some of my predecessors who weren't so keen on democracy still managed to give away many of the reserve powers which governors had previously had in the locker. This is a particular bore when it comes to expenditure issues. You can't expect Hong Kong politicians to behave responsibly or sensibly about paying for the costs of the Ministry of Defence.

I have continued to get warm receptions from large crowds. There is not much sign of mute apathy, let alone antipathy, which I suppose counts for something. The most difficult point about these visits tends to be the press call at the end. After a visit to Shatin on 24 February – it's a wonderful new city with a population of over half a million – where the reception was particularly enthusiastic, I faced the press, who had lots of questions about talks. I can't say, which would probably be the only honest response, that there are not even talks about talks, just talks about talks about talks. When pressed to say what Michael Sze meant when, asked by legislators when we would make a statement on this subject, replied, 'imminently', I replied that 'imminently' was an adverb which meant 'fairly soon'. We can't go on much longer like this.

Saturday 27 February

The Hang Seng Index continues to rise and there's lots of suspicion about insider trading by Chinese mainland companies, who are clearly betting on the start of talks leading to a consequent spike in the market. Hamish Macleod is making good progress constructing a budget which will be full of the sort of goodies made perfectly respectable by the size of our burgeoning surplus.

There has also been lots of coming and going about Washington and MFN. John Major saw the recently elected President Clinton earlier this week and it has been agreed that I should visit him in the spring. We are working on a date in early May. I can do a lot of other lobbying in the Senate and House of Representatives at the same time.

The most difficult afternoon I have spent for ages involved a group of parents of haemophiliac children who are now suffering from AIDS because of pre-1985 blood transfusions. They want government help, perfectly reasonably, and we have agreed to provide some assistance in Hamish's budget. But it was a pretty harrowing meeting. A couple of the mothers are sisters and between them have three haemophiliac sons. Two of them are already suffering from AIDS and the other is HIV positive. There were a lot of tears and much anguish. The sort of heroism that people like this show day by day puts the rest of us to shame. In my position you can offer financial support and you can offer sympathy but you can't really do much more to help people who have to live in such dark places.

Monday 1 March

We have heard from China at last. They want the basis of the talks to be the JD, convergence with the BL and the relevant agreements and understandings between Britain and China. There was also a lot of nonsense about keeping the talks secret and cutting Hong Kong representatives out of them. But at least it has given Robin McLaren something to get his teeth into and it may enable us to announce a date for talks reasonably soon. In telegrams to London and Beijing on what to do next, I said that we don't mind about the proposed basis for the talks but can't accept China's position on secrecy or keeping Hong Kong away from them. I feel passionately about both these points, particularly the latter. Lu Ping has made clear to a delegation led by Allen Lee and also to a group from the General Chamber of Commerce that what happens next must have nothing to do with the legislature or Hong Kong civil servants. The Chinese clearly want the talks to be seen to be between the sovereign powers and don't want Hong Kong to have a look in. They have a metaphor to cover this point which is either meaningless or daft – they talk about not having a three-legged stool. But I wonder whether whoever thought of this ridiculous metaphor has ever tried to sit on a two-legged stool. Of course, for Hong Kong to be cut out of any say on its own future by the present and future sovereign powers would lead to considerable instability – and for the British government, around the world, a good deal of obloquy.

Wednesday 3 March

We've had some very jolly visitors recently – first Jossie Dimbleby, the famous food writer, and later Caroline Waldegrave, who runs Leith's cookery school, where Laura is studying. To the great delight of our cooks, they both spent some time in the kitchen teaching them dishes which they don't normally tackle, including bread, curries and some pasta dishes. Jung Chang and her husband, Jon Halliday, came to lunch yesterday. They were travelling through Hong Kong before going on to China. After writing the wonderful *Wild Swans* she is now tackling a biography of Mao and is going to interview some of his surviving colleagues. I was surprised that they are letting her into the country when *Wild Swans* demonstrated among other things the terrible inhumanity of Chinese communism. I think it's fair to say that Mao got worse and more wicked as he got older. Jung Chang reminded me that he coped with the news of mass starvation during the great famine by going on a diet. On the same day, Mother Teresa came to call with a group of her nuns. She radiated holiness, laughed a lot and asked for quite a bit of help (mostly a land grant for building a new hostel). She noted rather charmingly that she always gets what she asks the Almighty to give her. So what can I say!? As she left, she scattered holy medals and prayer cards around the office and asked me to pray for her. In response, I said, 'But you are supposed to pray for me.' She headed off with her giggling colleagues in the general direction of Macau. Of course, we handed over the land. It shows the power of prayer.

Friday 5–Saturday 6 March

I had a brief weekend visit to Japan for the UK–Japan 2000 conference, which I have regularly attended since I first went to Japan as a young backbencher to meet other young politicians, civil servants and business leaders. Their idea of who is young made me better understand one of the differences between our countries. Our meetings took place in a hotel with lovely views over a bay to Mount Fuji. I had to talk quite a lot about Hong Kong and China. I made one rather obvious point, that the rest of the world will regard China's treatment of Hong Kong as one of the touchstones in determining the sort of relationship it is going to have with the international community in the century ahead. In responding to one crackpot businessman who compared what I am doing with Tiananmen Square, our ambassador, John Boyd, said that you cannot put the values that are increasingly being applied elsewhere in the region into the moral refrigerator when it comes to Hong Kong.

I got a pretty good reception in the Japanese media, and though in Hong Kong the papers are more mixed, they have been largely supportive back in London. There was a hefty leader in *The Times* urging everyone to rally behind me and stand up to the FCO. At the same time the *Guardian* is arguing that the backsliding has begun and that the Foreign Office is trying to get me to dilute my democratic proposals. It even suggested that I have threatened to resign if this happens. I have been telling everyone who wants to listen for some time that while there may be some pockets of Cradockian resistance around the place, and though there is a growing amount of criticism from business lobbies, overall I couldn't look for stronger support where it really matters – No. 10, Douglas Hurd and the Cabinet, Ricketts and McLaren. In addition, the support seems to be cross-party.

Wednesday 10 March

We went out for a meal with Alice's excellent headmaster (David James) and her history teachers with their spouses. They asked me how I'm enjoying Hong Kong and I said that I like everything about it except dealing with China. (But, of course, I couldn't be here if I wasn't dealing with China.) I've also just had a letter from John Major's Foreign Office private secretary, Stephen Wall, who is off to Lisbon as ambassador. He describes negotiating with China by referring to the Catholic priest – I think it was Ronald Knox– who retired as chaplain to a convent. He was asked what it was like hearing nuns' confessions and replied that it was like being pecked to death by ducks.

Friday 12 March

I had to tell Legco today what we were intending to do and I cannot go on saying 'imminently' (or various formulations more or less equivalent to 'watch this space') until the crack of doom. In my statement I said that we have been talking since early February, that our position on the basis of the talks and on the representation at them is perfectly reasonable, that even after all this time we don't have a date for talks or even when we can announce them, and that the Chinese are trying to establish second-class status for Hong Kong at any talks as a deliberate attempt to humiliate and sideline Hong Kong officials. One indication of the absurdity of the Chinese position is that at one time Qian suggested that the talks could take place in the Joint Liaison Group, where of course several Hong Kong officials are part of our team.

The resulting rhetorical bombardment was more limited than I had expected. There is a clear distinction between what China's Foreign Ministry says – it issues a careful statement which doesn't completely pull the plug on talks – and the remarks of the NCNA, which revert to the language of the Cultural Revolution. I reckon this will be quite useful for us in future political arguments.

Sunday 14 March

We had drinks and a meal for among others Henry Keswick,* who said that it was the first time he had been to dinner in GH for a decade. He is still in favour of what we are doing.

Saturday 20 March

Elton John came to town for a concert. Alice got to sit next to him at lunch. He was great company and is grateful to us because he and one of his travelling companions, who just happens to be his tennis coach, played on our courts. His concert was fantastic, every number a knockout.

Friday 26 March

Lavender's old law tutor from Oxford, Lenny Hoffmann, and his wife arrived for a meal. He is now a Lord Justice of Appeal, has admirably liberal views and is about as clever as it's possible to get.

These weeks have been dominated by arguments with Beijing about the nature of talks, the basis for them, the starting date and the participants. For much of the time it wasn't clear who was actually making policy on the Chinese side. By the end it seemed relatively clear that something positive was more likely to happen when Foreign Minister Qian was around to give political cover to officials at the level below him. Most of the talks, undertaken in Beijing by Robin McLaren and the Vice Foreign Minister, Jiang Enzhu, turned into what seems like an unending game of pass the parcel – every time we thought that the last piece of wrapping paper had been removed, another piece was whipped from under the table by Jiang. Meanwhile I've had to cope with restless media, rumblings in Legco and a slightly febrile atmosphere in Exco, with one group wanting me to gazette proposals sooner rather than later, another (rather smaller) group wanting to find out exactly what Beijing wants and then to do it. Everyone is anxious to know more, from us and from Beijing, about exactly what is happening. As though we really knew . . .

* Henry Keswick is a senior member of the family of the same name which has built up and run the Jardine Matheson company. He has been a director, managing director and chairman of the company. A right-wing Conservative, he owned the *Spectator* magazine from 1975 to 1980. He was also chairman of the National Portrait Gallery. Jardine Matheson was one of the original Hong Kong Hong trading houses. Its very successful business is mostly in Asia. Keswick himself, perhaps inevitably, has tended to see Britain's imperial role as largely about safeguarding the company's interests. He was usually hostile to governors who did not share this view of the world. Keswick once told me that having reached the age of 70 he had decided to forgive me for my sins. Without questioning his Catholic virtues, I have my doubts about whether this has actually happened.

The exact nature of China's demands changes with some regularity. In the beginning, they pressed for the discussions to be based on 'convergence with' the Basic Law rather than just on the basis of the Basic Law. Some in our embassy in Beijing and in the Foreign Office as a whole seemed to think that this matters. It didn't seem to me to be a very substantive point, and I was happy to concede it in order to make progress on what I thought was the more important issue, that is the nature of the delegation at the talks. China is still determined to keep out anyone from Hong Kong, or at least any Hong Kong officials that are simply advisers in the delegation to us, the sovereign power. Beijing plainly wants to humiliate Hong Kong and sideline the territory by distinguishing between British and Chinese officials, and they have tried umpteen different ways of varying complexity to do this. As we wandered round and round this point, telegrams whizzing backwards and forwards to the eternally patient Robin McLaren, there were occasions when one started to lose the will to live. The question of secrecy is no longer being raised.

Hamish Macleod has produced an excellent budget, smart and balanced, in which he announced more spending, particularly on housing and welfare, lower taxes and larger reserves. In Britain this would be the moment to call an election. I have continued to explore with David Ford and Hamish the departure of expatriate senior officials and their replacement by locals. I am pretty clear in my own mind that David should be followed by Anson Chan, with Michael Sze as *proxime accessit*. In my experience it's far easier to delegate when you have civil servants like her. But I am warned by both David and Hamish that the fact of her gender will not be well received by some of her senior male colleagues. There is not much she can do about that! On the British side the Foreign Office have managed a real cock-up. They wanted to move my three senior diplomatic advisers – Tony Galsworthy, William Ehrman and Stephen Bradley – all at the same time; they apparently arrived together and should leave the same way. Excellent personnel management, which does not suggest giving Hong Kong policy the priority it deserves.

We have seen more of Simon Murray and his wife, Jennifer; he was once in the Foreign Legion, is a very successful member of Li Ka-shing's team, and is publicly very supportive of our stance. He is obviously well paid but I'm told that he pays more tax than anyone else in Hong Kong – not because he is the richest guy in town but one of the most honourable and honest. It's probably true. It is extraordinary how in almost every society the very rich spend a lot of money finding ways of avoiding paying tax for the services on which they like their community depend. Recently, we had an enjoyable evening with Peter and Nancy Thompson. He provided much of the funding for the Hong Kong jazz club and has a terrific collection of Chinnery paintings. On top of everything we also had the Hong Kong rugby sevens at the end of the month, an annual sporting pleasure, which is not meant for teetotallers. We gave a big reception at GH for many of those involved. It's lucky that we refreshed the drinks cellar. This is not an atypical list of guests and events; even though we are not having a very pleasant few months in political terms, life continues to be fun for a lot of the time.

But the onslaught from the north continued partly because the National People's Congress, China's sham Parliament, was meeting in Beijing. Lu Ping gave a press conference and several interviews to the media during the course of which no cliché of vitriolic abuse goes unused. The markets weren't particularly unsettled and appeared to take the view that they were expecting things to be worse. Whether or not British business leaders will be quite as relaxed is another matter. Exco wasn't too bad; predictably one or two members don't really seem to know what we should do except avoid a row with China. C. H. Tung wrung his hands but continued to speak with great courtesy. We are rather confused about where China's bottom line may actually be; it wanders about like the border in Northern Ireland. We thought that Beijing would be happy on the point of representation if Robin McLaren led our team, whose membership would be a matter for him in consultation with us. This would enable us to get round the point about whether Hong Kong should be anywhere near the table. Sometimes Chinese officials seem to get themselves on hooks, aren't sure whether they should be hanging there at all, and then want us to help them get down.

Tuesday 30 March

I travelled with my new private secretary, Bowen Leung, my spokesman, Mike Hanson, and Edward Llewellyn to Brussels. One of my tests of whether or not I want someone as a personal secretary or close adviser is whether or not I think it would be agreeable to spend a lot of time with them in international airports, waiting for flights, or travelling long distance on planes. Bowen, Mike and Edward pass this test with flying colours. I stayed for two days in Brussels with our ambassador to the EU, John Kerr. From having sat next to him in council meetings when I was a minister, I already knew just how clever and smart he is. He is also very wise about the way that the EU works and the way that the British government works (or sort of works). He pointed out that widening the European Union isn't an alternative to deepening. Every time the bounds of the community have been broadened there's also been institutional change in order to make decision making at the centre easier when there are more members. This is inevitable. On the working habits of Number 10, he argued that while Margaret Thatcher was Prime Minister, the staff in Downing Street assumed many of the powers that had previously been exercised by the Cabinet Office. Among other things this destroyed the traditional relationship between the Cabinet Secretary and the Prime Minister, so the Prime Minister no longer had a senior mandarin to look after his or her interests around Whitehall. Today, John Major finds himself without, as it were, either a Willie Whitelaw or a Burke Trend. He thought that the institutionally avuncular role of the Cabinet Secretary should be reinvented.

I met all the top dogs in Brussels, including Jacques Delors, an extremely engaging interlocutor, and Leon Brittan, who was probably the second most significant figure in the commission after Delors, largely as a result of his sheer hard work and intellectual grasp. Leon looks after the community's external economic relations and obviously enjoys the job hugely. I guess that the timing of my governorship will rule out me ever getting to Brussels to work. I addressed a big meeting of Belgium's equivalent of Chatham House and met several figures from the Parliament. Politically we had a thumbs up all round.

Thursday 1 April

Bowen, Mike, Edward and I arrived in London, where I met up with Lavender and Alice. It's great to see Laura and Kate, fresh back from a skiing holiday. I had a dinner for some of my journalist friends at our favourite local Italian in Pimlico, the Gran Paradiso, where I was greeted with much kissing and hugging. I think it is only because of their politeness that they refer to Hong Kong. It clearly doesn't register very much on their radar screens in comparison with (say) Yugoslavia or the turbulence in British politics. When asked about what's happening in London, I didn't feel that I had anything particularly interesting to say.

Friday 2 April

I saw John Major for lunch. He's clearly having a pretty cheerless time. He's working very hard and is immensely resilient, but if you get to the top you should surely enjoy it more than he is able to, mostly because the Conservative Party seems to be developing a nervous breakdown over Europe. He worries that even as we start to get the economy right, we won't get much credit for it. I hope he understands that without him the Conservative Party really could fall apart.

Foreign Office officials are mostly on the same page as the Prime Minister and Douglas as far as Hong Kong is concerned, which is of course as it should be. Peter Ricketts is terrific but I get a slight sense that the under-secretary responsible for Asia, Christopher Hum, is the card-carrying representative of the Cradock faction. He subjected me at one of our meetings to a long and sceptical series of questions about where we are going.

Friday 9 April

I have done lots of media in London, including *Newsnight*, *The Frost Programme* and a Good Friday *Any Questions?* with Gerald Kaufman, Roy Jenkins and Ann Leslie. I had a courteous argument with Roy Jenkins about Hong Kong, which appears to have been well received. He is sceptical about the wisdom of standing up to China so late in the day. I wonder what he would have done if he had become Governor, a job which he has said publicly he once turned down in a Paris lavatory. The highlights of the visit were of course seeing all our friends and above all Kate and Laura. Long-range parenting can be a hazardous business but so far so good.

Sunday 11 April

We have had a glorious weekend over the Easter holiday in Dorset with my former colleague in the House of Commons Robert Cecil and his wife, Hannah. And then Easter Saturday – we are going to have talks! Douglas Hurd had sent a message to his opposite number confirming that we were happy to engage on the basis that we had almost agreed in March (choosing our own team from the foreign office and the Hong Kong civil service under the British ambassador), with the addition of a sentence saying that the British government representative in talks would be our ambassador in Beijing, who would deal principally with Jiang Enzhu. This is what the vice minister had himself suggested at a much earlier meeting; it then appeared to be an abandoned position. The Chinese have now said yes, suggested that talks should start on the 22 April and merely enquired rather plaintively whether we were intending to say anything more about Hong Kong government representation. They obviously don't want us dancing up and down saying that they have backed down. Fair enough, but they have. Heaven knows exactly why.

Tuesday 13 April

We announced the start of the talks yesterday, noting that, as far as we were concerned, the position of Hong Kong representatives was the same as ever; we didn't crow about the Chinese having backed away from one of their preconditions. Some in the press assumed of course that it must be the British who have backed down. But overall we came out of things pretty well. It rather confirmed my existing view that things are always rather better when Qian is in Beijing and is able to overrule hardliners. I guess it's also true that the Chinese obviously didn't believe that we actually had a bottom line. They now seem to have recognized that we are serious. Qian had replied so quickly to Douglas Hurd that I rather wonder whether the NCNA in Hong Kong even knew what was happening at the end. Wrapping up all this, we had a long meeting with Douglas at which we agreed our negotiating position and opening statement. Douglas is as robust as anyone in the Foreign Office about where we stand. He doesn't think the Chinese position is as strong as others appear to believe. The Chinese can't behave too badly in the eyes of the rest of the world. I sometimes think he is one of the few people who has served as a diplomat in China who hasn't become rather overwhelmed by its size, strength and the aesthetic charms of its irrationality. As a man, a minister and a politician, I find him hugely impressive – calm, unflappable and authoritative. Wally Hammond on a good day.

It is just about a year since I was defeated in Bath. It has been a great adventure, and one that matters, working with and for people about whom I have come to care inordinately.

Round and Round the Mulberry Bush: April 1993–April 1994

Thursday 15 April

While we've been away, the house has been getting its redecoration and refurbishment. The work isn't quite finished (the whole house is still full of tins of paint, planks, unlaid tiles and dust) but by the standards back home they have so far done everything both well and quickly. We won't be able to use it for meetings or putting up guests for a week or so. We found a lovely red lacquer cupboard for the hall today with beautiful Chinese calligraphy telling the world that books make you happy.

We're going to have to continue to talk about the wretched airport, our negotiations in Beijing and preparations for my trip to the USA to discuss MFN for China. This will secure more or less tariff-free entry for Chinese exports into the American market. There is a lot of opposition in the American political system and in the media to this because of China's continuing abuse of human rights, but it's an important issue for us in Hong Kong. An interruption of US–China trade would be bad for our economy.

Tuesday 20 April

Robin McLaren arrived from Beijing today and sat down with the team from Hong Kong who will accompany him in the talks. We considered the terms of the opening statement and a number of rather more prosaic administrative matters. Most of the younger Sinologists are pretty sceptical about whether we can make very much progress. Robin and Tony Galsworthy are like old war horses – their nostrils are twitching a bit at the scent of battle to come. Tony seems to think that the Chinese may actually be prepared to do business. I hope so, but am not so sure.

Normally I hate making speeches which other people have written for me, but for an American Chamber of Commerce lunch (attended by about 700 people) Stephen Bradley wrote a corker. I was very happy to use his words to put the case for largely unfettered trade between the US and China.

Monday 26 April

We've had several round and round the mulberry bush discussions in Exco on all this. C. H. Tung continued to bat for a deal whatever it is. Maybe he would stop just short of the slaughter of the first born. By Saturday the 24th we were able to review the first round of talks. There has been heavy concentration on principles. There was no progress at all on any substantive issue. Tiresomely, the Chinese didn't want to have the second round for almost a month after the first. We want to get on – if there is too long a lag between rounds, each one will just start off with one exchange after another of the same alleged principles which have been excavated and put on show before. This will inevitably mean heightened acrimony. People will also start to think – the very idea! – that the Chinese are trying to string us along. Eventually Beijing agreed to a second round before the end of the month.

I've had a disagreeable time just before our team goes off to Beijing. Tony Galswothy let it drop that Percy Cradock is coming to Hong Kong in late May and then going on to China. Tony has apparently known this for two months and has invited Cradock to dinner. Cradock has now moved from being a critic on the sidelines to working actively to scupper what we are trying to do. His presence in China while talks are going on would be seen by the outside world as though it represented the arrival of a secret emissary or else as a general attempt to undercut us. Certainly, the Chinese – who (I now learn) told William Ehrman at the banquet at the end of the recent round of talks that they were looking forward to Cradock's arrival – will make the most of it. My suspicion is that Cradock finds out from officials who used to work for him what we are doing and then tells the Chinese. I didn't quite pound the table but I did make a bit of a scene when I heard this news. I said that I've constantly ignored reports that the Foreign Office is working against us in Hong Kong but that this piece of news is pretty intolerable. I really should have been told about this. Tony has made at best a serious error of judgement. William and Peter Ricketts have nothing to reproach themselves for. I phoned Alastair Goodlad to say that Cradock should be asked not to go to China and should certainly not be briefed on what is happening. The Foreign Office have so far taken the view that it's better to brief him on progress in the hope that he'll then behave better. Since he behaves badly whatever happens, I see no point in briefing him. When he has dinner with Tony Galsworthy, who used to work for him and who I'm sure has a reasonable professional relationship with his former boss, are they simply going to talk about moths? There is a tendency to treat Cradock as though, like David Wilson, he is an honourable man. David is but I wouldn't say the same thing about Cradock.

I had a dinner with the American ambassador from Beijing, Stapleton Roy, and America's consul in Hong Kong, Dick Wilson, to go over some of the most important messages about MFN in Washington, which the ambassador thinks may be difficult. He knows how important a good relationship between the US and China is for the future of Hong Kong.

Tuesday 27 April

Lavender visited International Social Services [ISS], where she met the legendary Anthony Lawrence who used to be the BBC's Far East correspondent during the Vietnam war. The ISS are providing educational services in the Vietnamese camps which Lavender has visited before. Lavender told me that the ISS staff are concerned because the UN High Commissioner for Refugees is reducing the funds for adult education services in the camps. Like the volunteers there, she thinks this is pretty misguided. The idea seems to be that if the inmates are not being educated they're more likely to go back to Vietnam. This is just going to make the camps more difficult to run. I'll see what I can do about it.

The greatest pleasure of the week was a dinner with Simon Murray and his wife, Jennifer, at their beautiful house in Mount Cameron Road looking south through trees towards the sea. It could be an unspoiled part of the south of France. (I wonder if there is one these days.) They are a remarkable couple, brave and funny. Simon told one anecdote after another, some of them (which may even be true) about his days in the French Foreign Legion, on which he has written a very good book. He loves Hong Kong and wants it to stay free under the rule of law.

Less cheerful was another meeting with a jet-lagged Jim Prior, who came to see me with GEC's principal fixer, John Lippitt, whom I have never much cared for; I suspect that he gives fixers a bad name. Jim is full of foreboding about what will happen to the glittering prospects for GEC if the row over Hong Kong's political development continues. Both he and Lord Young have recently seen Li Peng, who told them without very much delicacy that if the political row continues British firms won't do as well as they should in China. It doesn't seem much like China's application form for the WTO but I doubt whether they told him this.

Thursday 29 April

The next round of talks in Beijing don't produce very much progress. Without changing our position fundamentally, we have given Robin McLaren's team slightly different words on the election committee, the continuing limit on the number of directly elected seats and the functional constituencies. If the Chinese want to do so, they will have an excuse for accepting that we've dealt with all the eight original points on principles that they raised at the beginning. They seemed to imply at the close of the last round that the details on four or five of these points were satisfactory: for example, surprise surprise, we still accept the LJD and the BL. But plainly round and round the bush is continuing. The next round is to be over the weekend of 21 to 23 May. This will be after Jiang Enzhou has returned from a visit to Europe. The Chinese have produced a piece of paper which they want to negotiate with us before moving on from the debate about principles. If pressed I am not sure that even so soon after the talks I can remember what these principles are, but they probably can't either. We think this is the time for Douglas Hurd to send a message to his opposite number saying we should really get on now to talk about detail. We can't go on forever like this. We're starting to get more and more questions about whether we will table legislation for the 1994 and 1995 elections in time for it to be considered before the end of July.

Friday 30 April

We've reached America, by way of Los Angeles. We have stopped here for a night with our friend Mike Medavoy* and his wife, Patricia. Mike is a political junkie whom we first met at an Aspen conference for alleged would-be future leaders. (There's a kiss of death if ever there was one.) I was there with Ken Clarke from Europe; the Americans included Gary Hart and Chris Dodds, both then up and coming Senators. We had a lovely dinner in the garden. At my table everyone talked about health reform and medical bills; Lavender tells me that at hers everyone said they have had some experience of being mugged. Health costs and crime: America in 1993.

Saturday 1 May

The Medavoys flew off before us this morning for Washington, where they are doing some political rounds themselves, and we went later in the day to stay with the ambassador, Robin Renwick, and his delightful French wife, Annie. I last saw them when I was Development Minister and Robin was our man in South Africa.

* Mike Medavoy is a successful film producer who co-founded Orion Pictures and Phoenix Pictures and was charman of Tristar Pictures. He has overseen the production of many notable films, including *Amadeus*, *The Silence of the Lambs*, *Sleepless in Seattle* and *The People v Larry Flynn*. He is keen on politics; we first met at a conference organized by the Aspen Institute when I was a back-bencher. He has been a major West Coast supporter of Bill Clinton and Barack Obama.

Sunday 2 May
Tonight we met John Newhouse* and his wife, Simmie, for a drink at their home in Georgetown. I correspond with John a bit. He is a very good journalist, which I might say in a more qualified way had he not written an extremely nice piece about me in the *New Yorker*. Lloyd Cutler† joined us for a bit. He is a Democratic Party elder statesman, brought into the White House to help Jimmy Carter. John thinks that if he had been brought into the White House straight away under Clinton it might have avoided some of the problems which seem to be assailing the new president. Most of the people I've talked to clearly want Clinton to do well, but feel that his operation is a bit shambolic.

Monday 3 May
A meeting first thing with our lobbyist and our trade consultants. The most impressive is Stuart Eizenstat, who was the domestic affairs adviser under Carter. Alas we are going to lose him soon since he is tapped to become the US ambassador to Europe. Then it was off to the White House with Robin, Bowen, and the competent Mike Hanson to look after the press. As ever it took an age to get into the White House through the usual security bureaucracy. ('You're from where?') In the White House itself, which is elegant but not particularly grand, Clifton Wharton and Winston Lord were waiting for us along with the deputy to the National Security Advisor, Sandy Berger. Clifford is the Deputy Secretary of State and Winston his senior official dealing with Asia. We waited for a bit in the Cabinet Room for our meeting with the president – people say he is always late – and then were ushered into the Oval Office to meet him, the Vice President, Al Gore, and the communications director, George Stephanopoulos. I'm always surprised that some of the political leaders I meet ever went into politics since they don't seem to like people very much. Bill Clinton is exactly the opposite. Articulate and very bright, he would obviously be keen to work the room even if there was only one other person in it. Both the president and Al Gore are big chaps and they radiated geniality. ('So what did you think of them?' Lavender asked. 'They were very big', I said. 'Well that's very profound', she replied.) There was a press call for

* John Newhouse was a distinguished American journalist, mostly at the *New Yorker*. He also worked as a government official and was a negotiator at the Strategic Arms Limitation Talks. With a grant from the Ford Foundation he lived and wrote in Paris for some time about European affairs; for example, his book *Europe Adrift*. He died in 2016.

† Lloyd Cutler was an American lawyer who worked as White House Counsel for both Jimmy Carter and Bill Clinton. He died in 2005.

American journalists, most of whom shouted questions at the president about Bosnia, and then the Hong Kong and British press came in asking questions about my proposals on elections, which Clinton supported with a few elegantly turned sentences. Once they were out of the room we got down to business.

I said there are three background points to what I will be saying all week about MFN. First, a good relationship between China and the US is important to Hong Kong's prosperity and stability in the long term. Second, it would be bad for the region and the world if China's economic opening was not carried through successfully. Third, the consequences if China's economic changes are put in place and locked into the global system will be good for all of us. And, of course, if these things don't happen the reverse is true. I said that I recognize that the new administration's policy is unlikely to be the same as its predecessor's. I know that the new administration and Congress are likely to be looking for a new policy on MFN which will involve some attempt to nudge the Chinese in directions on trade, weapons proliferation and human rights of which we would all approve. But if there is to be conditionality on MFN we would prefer the lead to be taken by the executive rather than the conditions being written into the bill by Congress. Any condition should be as general as possible. I would also hope that the position of Hong Kong could be taken into account, but that it would not be very helpful at the moment to mention political developments in Hong Kong in any list of conditions. We spent about 40 minutes talking through these points. I was quite surprised by the amount of time that President Clinton devoted to weapons proliferation. It's obviously a real concern to the administration. Both he and the VP were embarrassingly flattering. Al Gore said that I'm an example of the way that individuals can change history – so there! I suppose that cuts both ways. I can think of lots of people who changed history in rather disagreeable ways. Gore knows about my background in environmental issues. It's all very cheerful and I don't think it could have gone any better.

I then had a lunch with the Asia Society and after that a meeting with the Secretary of the Treasury, Lloyd Bentsen, a courtly and silvery Southern gentleman who noted that there are a lot of trade issues worrying Americans about China. He would like to resolve them without too much trouble, but China will have to give some ground if this is going to happen. Then we met Wharton and Lord again at the State Department. They said that the administration is looking for a policy which won't involve them in a fight with Congress but will push the Chinese along the road without provoking them to dig in their heels and react truculently. Winston said that the Chinese are trying to put pressure on the Clinton administration by producing as many orders for American goods and equipment as they possibly can during the coming weeks. He also noted that there is quite often a big difference between what the Chinese say they will order and what eventually they buy.

I gave them a pretty frank account of where we stand so far in our talks with Beijing. The community wants a settlement, though not at any price; Legco will probably back whatever we agree with Beijing; and this really means that we have got to get the best possible deal we can out of the talks. After a meeting with Senator George Mitchell, who has been an advocate of a strong conditionality for MFN, we had a dinner at the embassy with lots of senators, congressmen and journalists. There were four Balliol men in the crowd; I knew two of them a bit: Christopher Hitchens, who is chubbier than I remember but as ever good company (and for the first time I can recall he seemed to agree with what I'm doing), and David Boren, who is now a senator; we overlapped at Balliol and shortly after Oxford he became Governor of Oklahoma. We agreed that he's fortunate he doesn't have to give Oklahoma back to China in 1997.

Tuesday 4 May

This morning began with an early meeting with Senator Mitch McConnell, who drafted the US Hong Kong Act which allows the US to treat Hong Kong separately from China in trade and economic matters after 1997. He said all the right things in the meeting and to the press afterwards. Then it was on to the National Press Club for a speech which is being covered by Jonathan Dimbleby and Francis Gerard for their BBC documentary. More difficult was a long session with the editorial board of the *Washington Post*, tough but not unreasonable questions, then more meetings on the hill with mostly Democrat Senators and Congressmen. I got the impression that while they want to be as helpful as possible to the Clinton presidency – after all they have been in the wilderness for some time – they are worried that it doesn't seem to be as focused or as professionally run as they would like. A couple of Congressmen told me how hard Nancy Pelosi has been working on her bill to condition MFN. I sat next to her at dinner last night. She is interesting and knows a lot about China. She has a San Francisco congressional district which includes the headquarters of Levi Strauss and quite a large Chinese diaspora community. Whenever she talks to the press about China and Hong Kong – and she was doing it again today – she tells them how persuasive I am but that I haven't changed her mind about putting conditions like human rights improvements on trade with China. So clearly I haven't been all that persuasive. Lastly, a dinner for a lot of experts on China given by the Carnegie

Endowment. The most difficult question was from an ex-ambassador who asked me exactly what I think I have achieved during the past year. And what do you want on your gravestone, Governor? I'd better think about that.

Wednesday 5 May

After a long press conference early this morning I had a meeting with Speaker Tom Foley. He is tall, handsome, very charming and extremely Irish. Robin tells me that the corpse of the special representative to Ireland is buried under Tom Foley's carpet. From others whom I met later in the day, including Robert Rubin, the president's main national economic adviser, and Lee Hamilton, chairman of the House foreign affairs committee, I heard a great deal about Nancy Pelosi's lobbying skills. Then lunch at Brookings and an afternoon giving evidence to the House and Senate foreign relations committees. At an hour-long meeting with my old friend Bill Bradley* I got much the same tune, though what seemed to be worrying him most is the possibility of America being sucked into the Bosnia quicksand. He would have been a very cerebral president but (as he would himself recognize) doesn't have the Clinton charisma.

Thursday 6 May

We went by train to New York, to stay at the Hong Kong-owned Peninsula Hotel with wonderful views from our suite up and down Fifth Avenue. A big lunch at the Waldorf Astoria with well over 600 people, a visit to the New York Stock Exchange, where its incomprehensible operations were explained to me, and an hour with the editorial board of the *Wall Street Journal* followed by TV interviews. Best of all I had a long talk with Henry Kissinger,† who is just off to China. He agrees with what I am saying about MFN and seemed to support the political package as well – he even said so to the press afterwards. When a journalist asked him what advice he gave me, he replied amusingly, 'He didn't ask me for any.' By the time we got to dinner with the British consul-general, Alistair Hunter, I was completely knackered. Lavender said that my speech was getting slower and slower.

* Bill Bradley was Democratic Senator for New Jersey from 1979 to 1997. He lost to Al Gore in the nomination race for presidency in 2000. He had been a basketball star and played professionally in Europe while an Oxford student.

† Henry Kissinger's fame, not least his role in building contacts between the United States of America and communist China, overwhelms any description. Volumes of biography, the size of telephone directories, weigh down library shelves. I have always found him interesting and friendly and he seems especially good at dealing openly with students of international affairs of all ages. His views on China however are not mine.

Friday 7 May
I started the morning with David Hannay, our ambassador to the UN, with whom I used to work a lot when he was ambassador to the European Community. He is wonderfully sharp and tells me lots of stories about the UN which are not dripping with charitable assessments about his colleagues there. I have never had a conversation with him from which I haven't learned a lot. He is pretty withering about policy everywhere on the Balkans. He was accompanied for part of the time by Bob Peirce, who is going to be my new political adviser now that William Ehrman is off. I think I'm going to get on well with him – very smart, funny, direct and constructively cynical. Afterwards, meetings with the Council on Foreign Relations chaired by Dick Holbrooke, and the editorial board of the *New York Times*, and then a press conference and an interview with CNN. In the evening Lavender and I had a drink and dinner with my old mentor Sherwin Goldman. When I was in New York on a travelling scholarship from Balliol back in 1965, I worked on the mayoral campaign for John Lindsay, and Sherwin (a bit older than me, a Texan from Yale and Balliol) was my boss. He taught me a great deal about politics as well as about America. I think he was as responsible as anyone for the most important career choices that I have made. He was also someone with wide cultural interests and for a time even made me interested in ballet, not actually difficult when the American Theatre Ballet was at its peak.

Sunday 9 May
We got back to Hong Kong on Saturday evening after a very long flight and a 2½ hour changeover in Tokyo. The work on the house has been finished and it looks terrific, more cheerful and elegant. Alice was happy to see us, and Whisky and Soda too, though the staff, particularly Ah Chak, spoil them rotten.

Tuesday 11 May
It's straight back for more discussions about the talks with Beijing. Do we simply accept endless arguments about principles and do we think it would be a good idea to move the talks into the JLG? Some Exco members are being a bit tricky. They want more information (as though they haven't already had it) on fallback positions. A lot of the grumpiness is driven by Willie Purves. The truth is that we've talked about all this a lot before, that the position we are now in is one which Exco explicitly approved, and that if we start talking about fallback positions, they will all be leaked. Lydia told me that Exco does not want to be regarded as

being there just to give me political cover. I should be so lucky. They tend to keep their heads down when it comes to saying anything supportive about decisions in which they have shared. One of my new political advisers, who will be the main deputy to Bob Peirce, John Ashton, has until recently been the principal Mafia expert at our embassy in Rome, which is an excellent background for his work on China and the United Front in Hong Kong. He is completely charming with (rather surprisingly for a diplomat) a good science education.

We are having a bit of difficulty explaining to Legco about the new British National Overseas passport which they regard, not unreasonably, as a second-class cousin to a real British passport. They are particularly concerned about how you get one of these passports and the entitlements under it. I am not able to give very precise answers, only to offer general assurances. I'm sure that I'm going to get much more about citizenship rights the closer we get to 1997. It's a long time since living in a British colony made you a British citizen. The Romans were rather clearer about these things.

Wednesday 12 May

We're starting to make some progress on economic issues with Beijing. They are being a little more positive about the airport though rather noisy about the defence estate, at least in private. Obviously, the PLA don't want to be cut out of any share of the spoils after 1997. Rather more serious discussions are also starting on the rundown of the present garrison, which in due course should help in dealing with the legislature about funding defence costs.

Lord Callaghan (Jim, as was) had a brief stay on his way into China as, I imagine, an old friend of the communist regime who will get a red carpet and the sort of treatment he would have had when Prime Minister. In other words, the usual lushing up. He has a lot of bluff charm but he doesn't really believe that we should do anything at all about democracy or the rule of law before 1997. He says that I mustn't think that I have to martyr myself for the future of Hong Kong and the British interest is to make sure that our businessmen can do a lot of trade with China. Since we can't do anything to affect what the Chinese do to Hong Kong after the handover, there's not much point in making a fuss before. In effect I should keep my head down and get out in due course without any controversy. At least he said all this to my face rather than like some businessmen, including former Conservative politicians, behind my back. It's difficult to dislike him, but as Edward reminds me, when he was in British politics he usually ducked the big issues like trade union reform. He was a suitable political leader for a time of national decline and makes one see the value of Margaret Thatcher. To borrow Al Gore's remark, politicians can make a difference to history. Anyway, it's clearly his view that the Joint Declaration was flimflam and – while speaking as a former leader of the Labour Party – any guff about human rights should be composted and put in the wastepaper basket.

Callaghan headed for Beijing today, my birthday. 49 today. As he departed, Margaret Thatcher arrived. She has been addressing a conference on international tourism in Hawaii, which she pronounces – 'High Wye'. She is clearly in fighting form. We had a very jolly birthday dinner with most of my private office plus Jonathan Dimbleby, who is here to interview me again. Margaret joined us for a drink after supper. Jonathan got her going on Bosnia. She hasn't lost any of her pizzazz.

Thursday 13 May

We gave a dinner for Margaret with some of the livelier younger business leaders, including Dickson Poon (who owns – among other things – Harvey Nichols), Simon Murray and Martin Barrow. She emphasized how she had always stood up against aggression from the Gulf to the Falklands. During her stay with us, she's received a lot of lobbying from the business community to rein me in.

Friday 14 May

C. H. Tung organized a dinner this evening at which Margaret handed out vigorous lectures on the rule of law and the relationship between political and economic freedom. She can't have done any more to support me, in public and in private.

Saturday 15 May

Today I invited her to accompany me on a visit to Eastern district. There were huge cheering crowds, a scrum of photographers and cameramen and a trip on an open-top tram through packed streets. She obviously gets the point and compared what she has seen for herself with the stuff she gets from some of the business leaders. She said slightly acidly that she assumes that most of the people who have been getting at her have foreign passports.

Monday 17 May

John Coles is here from London and was told by Willie Purves that there is a danger of a crisis of confidence in Exco. And Lydia obviously thinks there is some British conspiracy afoot, that we are not keeping Exco sufficiently informed about what is happening in the talks. I wish there was something to be secretive about. I'm afraid that years of intrigue and secret diplomacy have left their mark on even the sanest people in Hong Kong. When we checked around, we find that at their private meeting to prepare for the official one the members of Exco didn't even talk about our negotiations with Beijing.

At the Hong Kong Journalists Association ball, Lavender drew the prizes for the lottery and I won the first, which is worth HK$20,000. Naturally, I had to give it back. This is the prelude to two pieces of embarrassment. First, to raise money Lavender and I agreed to dance a tango. This relates to a local joke. When asked on one occasion about when talks with Beijing would begin, I said that it took two to tango. So now, I am not only a whore (a recent insult) but widely described in the pro- Beijing papers as a tango dancer. And I've only been to Argentina once. I soon demonstrated on the dance floor that I certainly could not earn my living doing this particular shuffle. The second embarrassment was when a pro-China delegate to one of the communist consultative committees in Beijing got up to do a karaoke turn and instead made a speech in Cantonese which was apparently very rude about me. Everybody seemed rather ashamed of this and the poor woman was booed off the stage. To complete the evening another guest who got up to do a karaoke turn had a heart attack and died. So a strange and rather grim evening.

Thursday 20 May

Robin McLaren has come back to Hong Kong to discuss our preparations for the next round of talks. At a very calm Exco meeting today, I made it clear that as we move from principles to detail – if that is we do! – we will need to get a broad steer from them, and eventually precise agreement on the bottom lines which we can then get endorsed by London. This approach seems to satisfy the council, even Purves.

Saturday 22 May

I've just been told by Charles Powell* that Willie Purves is telling anyone who will listen that I am the worst Governor there has ever been. Anyway, he is off before long to some grander job back in London with the bank. It is seeking to base itself there, which may be thought in Beijing to be a less than helpful sign of confidence in the future.

* Charles Powell was Margaret Thatcher's main foreign policy adviser in Downing Street. He left the Foreign Office in 1991 and pursued a business career with seats on several boards including Jardine Matheson. He was clever and ubiquitous. He became a peer in 2000.

Willie talked to me yesterday about his successor on Exco. I rather like his number two at the bank, John Gray, and will be happy to appoint him. There is obviously some row going on between the bank and Jardine's about whether their taipan in Hong Kong can remain on the Hong Kong Bank board now that Jardine Fleming has been accepted as a bank in the colony.

We have had several meetings this week about the future of the defence estate over which we have been wrangling for years. How much of it should go to the People's Liberation Army? How much should we be able to develop now in the interests of the citizens and taxpayers of Hong Kong? Should the defence estate which is picked up by the PLA remain in the ownership of Hong Kong or will the PLA be able to develop it, doubtless with multiple opportunities for rake-offs? There is also the incidental question of whether the public will be worried about the prospect of a Chinese garrison in downtown Hong Kong. On this last point, I don't myself believe – Martin makes this point strongly to me – that this is as neuralgic an issue as it would have been at one time. The other day there was a report that 10,000 PLA troops were going to come into Hong Kong rather than the original 4000 proposed by Deng Xiaoping years ago. In the event this bit of news went off perfectly quietly. Anyway, it doesn't seem to me that our hand on these matters is going to get any stronger the longer we leave them. Unless we reach an agreement with the Chinese soon, they will block any development on the land that we want to carry out and will get the whole lot in 1997 without the question of title being resolved. I therefore proposed a new push on this subject based on us offering the Chinese the Tamar site (the main defence plot in the middle of downtown Hong Kong) as a step forward from our previous rather negative position.

Monday 24 May

Robin and the Hong Kong team returned from their latest round in Beijing, saying that the body language of the Chinese delegation was rather better than their verbal assaults might have suggested. We appear to have got them to agree to discuss district boards and municipal councils at the next meeting. But this may not be the breakthrough into detail which we need. First of all, they obviously want to salami slice the political proposals and will only agree on movement each time they get a change from us on a particular agenda item. Secondly, they will doubtless return to their bloody 'principles' whenever they find themselves under too much pressure on detail. We have started to consider fall-backs on both the election committee and the functional constituencies. We are not going to float anything yet, but we need to know where we should go if we do find ourselves obliged to move.

Tuesday 25 May

Today's Exco meeting went pretty smoothly. Indeed, when I asked for views on how things should be taken forward, there was initially complete silence. But we got the outcome we want. There was an endorsement of our approach in the next round of talks and agreement on the line I have proposed on defence lands involving offering Tamar to China. Now we are starting to look at alternatives to the original proposals, Exco seemed to be starting to realize why we came to the conclusions we did about both the election committee and the functional constituencies all those months ago. Any other options are difficult. I suppose this is one reason why some members of Exco find it easier to grumble about not being consulted rather than offering coherent adjustments to what is already on the table. Given that we have had to make as much as we could out of a tricky starting point – not being able to increase the number of directly elected Legco members – any backing away from our 1992 plans is inevitably going to be less obviously fair and democratic. Moreover, I'm not sure whether a watered-down version could actually get through Legco. It would be very difficult to make a case for it that had any intellectual or political integrity. When I game-played all this with Edward and Martin, we found it very difficult to convince one another.

Wednesday 26 May

We had another of our public concerts in the ballroom at GH, given by the Academy of Performing Arts. Everyone was very complimentary about how much better the house looks. Three cheers for Lavender and Elspeth, and for the fact that all the spending decisions on this (which are not very great) were made by the Hong Kong government and not back in London. I don't think that anyone in Legco has raised a single question about the refurbishment, not least because we've taken the opportunity to show off the best of what can be made in Hong Kong.

Friday 28 May

The fourth round of talks, which opened today, seems to have been a no score draw. Robin McLaren told me on the secure line that he thinks the Chinese are getting a bit grumpy at our insistence that they should put forward proposals of their own. They have now started to take a tough line about our proceeding with legislation to establish the boundary and election commission. They have had a copy of this bill since January and it doesn't seem to be unreasonable to think that they might have said something about it over the last four months. Leaving their squeaks of rage until we are about to complete all its legislative council stages is plainly daft.

Sunday 30 May

At the end of getting nowhere for a couple of days, the Chinese side said that the next round can't take place before the middle of June or thereabouts. We don't think there's anything sinister about this, it appears to be because Qian Qichen is going to be out of Beijing, but since we are getting nowhere it's pretty frustrating. We have no choice for the time being except to plod on with as much patience and firmness as we can muster. We can't be pushed into precipitate action merely because the Chinese are not prepared to say anything substantive. There will of course be some in the community who will press us to do exactly this, which I assume is what the Chinese are counting on. I wish we had a fifth column in Beijing working for us.

The wretched Cradock is now in town, having arrived allegedly on Kleinwort's business; he apparently has a job with them. In an interview for television he is asked the perfectly reasonable question, 'If you're in Hong Kong and China as a private person on a private visit, why are you giving this television interview?' He asked for the cameras to be switched off while he thought of an answer.

Monday 31 May

Best bit of the day on the last day of the month was that Lavender gave a superb speech to the Rotary Club. She let me suggest one or two jokes and told me that they went down well. I don't suppose she would tell me if they didn't.

We have so many guests staying with us, including Alastair Goodlad and his officials, that Lavender tells me every bed in the house bar one is occupied. I wish that included Kate, who phoned up this morning to tell us she's had a car crash on the A1 near Darlington. Thank heavens she's fine, but clearly very shaken. We are pretty shaken ourselves. She took my 32-year-old classic Morris Minor to Newcastle and driving back with three friends to the city in terrible rain crashed into the barrier when the car in front braked suddenly. They were then hit from behind by another car. She reckons that the Morris is a write-off but mercifully she and her friends are unharmed. This is the sort of occasion when separation is painful. She is a brave and resourceful girl and a good driver. She will be mortified about the fate of my lovely old car but what the hell. It was quite a famous old thing in Bath. So this really does seem like the end of part of my life. 424 MAE RIP.

Tuesday 1 June

At a working breakfast with my principal China experts, including most of the team who have been in Beijing and Alastair Goodlad, who arrived on 29 May, we agreed that it may be time for another letter from Douglas Hurd to Qian Qichen proposing that some of the secondary matters should be cut back at their meeting in June in order to prepare the way for a meeting between Foreign Secretaries in July. We have got to try to do something to give the talks some impetus. We also talked about our line at the next meeting on airport construction and funding. We are getting hints that the Chinese are likely to propose a ludicrously large injection of new capital into the project. Frankly, if we can restrict the argument to talking about cash it will be quite a move forward. Afterwards, at Exco with Alastair in attendance, nobody seemed too upset by the need for patience in the Beijing discussions. There was general agreement that we should hang on and get the Chinese to make a first move, though Willie Purves is starting to press for us to shift our ground.

Wednesday 2 June

We had a supper yesterday evening with Legco members and there was the usual problem with leaks afterwards about what was allegedly said by the visiting minister in private conversations. None of this is Alastair's fault. One story suggested that we intend to put what we agree with China into a memorandum of understanding which will then be debated and amended by Legco. The result of that process would then be taken back to Beijing for approval. This is exactly the sort of thing which will make our friends in the north rather cross.

Lavender found herself at dinner sitting next to Elsie Tu. They had a perfectly civil conversation, but, as Lavender said, she is a seasoned campaigner whose political interests began with reasonable attacks on police corruption in Hong Kong. She is now basically a real old-style lefty, anti-American and anti-British, who reads political tracts in her spare time. When Britain was resisting proposals for democracy, she opposed the colonial establishment; now we are meeting our promises on democracy, or at least trying to do so, she is against that as well. Her motivation seems to be to oppose the colonial government rather than to support democracy. She is about 80, in terrific fighting form, and is in many respects a rather admirable creation of the British Empire. We have left a scattering of Elsie Tus all around the world. If the Chinese Communist Party had been in our shoes, she would have been in prison or shot years ago.

Thursday 3 June

My most interesting interview of the week was with William Rees-Mogg for the *Independent*. When I say interview, I am not sure that that is quite the right noun. I felt more as though I was having an audience with the great man. I like William and his wife, Gillian, a great deal; they were very kind to us when we were in Bath, inviting us to rent for a tiny sum a cottage on their estate when I was first a parliamentary candidate with not much money and the need for a roof. We only did this for a few months but long enough to learn to like them for their kindness and charming battiness. You don't have to always agree with people to like them. Anyway, William has clearly made up his mind about the future of the world and our audience took place in that context. He thinks that Europe is finished and that China in particular and Asia in general represent the future of mankind. He doesn't think there's anything much that we should be arguing about in Hong Kong. I'm not sure that anything I say will have much of an impact on these *ex cathedra* statements. I guess it's a useful starting position for someone who is a director of GEC and looks elsewhere – I mean outside its own manufacturing and research capacity – for its salvation. After the Rees-Moggs were so kind to us, it would be nice if we could return their hospitality sometime. I tell William that we would always be happy to welcome any of their children to stay; after all, we've already had lots of the children of friends to spend time with us.

Friday 4 June

I have started to focus, with a sense of unease, about what we can do to resurrect proposals on the Court of Final Appeal. At a meeting today (with the demonstrators assembling again in Victoria Park for the vigil to recall Tiananmen) I learned that since Legco kiboshed the plans we had agreed in secret with China over a year ago, no further work has taken place on what to do instead. I had assumed that there would be a draft bill waiting in the locker. No such luck as Martin has discovered. It's really ridiculous. Anyway, we will now have to get ahead with this sort of work at the same time as we try to strengthen the bench itself. I plan to keep on talking to the Chief Justice about this. Once we've got more proposals we will have to go back to the Chinese and for another big row.

Before going off for the weekend at Fanling, we had what Lavender calls a typical Friday evening for the Governor and his Mrs. It was the Auxiliary Police ball. Anson Chan's husband, Archie, is the Commandant and they are amazing ballroom dancers. It's interesting how many smart and well-off women in Hong Kong have ballroom dancing lessons; I guess it's good exercise. More surprising perhaps is how good some of the men are when it comes to quicksteps and tangos, in contrast to my own desperate performance at the journalists' ball.

Monday 7 June

My ad hoc group discussed a meeting Alastair Goodlad had with Ambassador Ma back in London. Alastair made clear to the ambassador the sort of progress we would like to make over the rest of the summer in our talks. We have said that we would like to have a substantive discussion on functional constituencies and the election committee at our next two meetings. If we could manage this, I would then be able to go back to London for a meeting of the Cabinet committee on 1 July and get amendments to my marching orders. I rather doubt whether we will get any movement from China yet. Their officials are now being grumpy over what they allege are our little tricks, for instance over airport funding.

Tuesday 8 June

David Ford is away and Anson Chan is acting in his place. I have made my mind up that she should get the job permanently when he retires to the post of Hong Kong representative in London. Promoting Anson has undoubtedly annoyed some of her male peers; whether it has led to the retirement of one or two ahead of time is a reasonable source of conjecture. With Anson and Hamish McLeod I discussed corruption and the civil service pay settlement. I want to put more resources into the Independent Commission Against Corruption. I think we need to do more to fight corruption as we get closer to 1997 and I also think we should add to the inflation-proofing settlement for this year in civil service pay. Some civil servants are grumbling that we need to make up for what was forgone because of overall fiscal prudence in previous years, but I don't want us to get the reputation of being profligate and risking a resurgence of inflation. The private sector would certainly bash us if we were to go as far over this pay demand as the civil service unions would like.

Wednesday 9 June

We started discussing a draft paper largely produced in London for the Cabinet committee, which prompted further discussion on possible fallback positions for both the functional constituencies and the election committee. I questioned whether we should really be showing any movement to the Chinese at the moment. I don't necessarily disagree with what is being suggested, though I think it's some distance from anything that the Chinese would be likely to accept. I'm also reluctant to go along with what

I think was a strategic error made back in the mid-1980s when we seemed to concede the point that everything we did before 1997 had to converge with whatever the Chinese wanted to do afterwards. This in effect gave us power but no responsibility for our last period of sovereignty.

Lavender told me a story which confirms my feeling that we are now having to make up for some awful mistakes made in the past. Lydia Dunn took her out to lunch today and was rather gloomy about how much Hong Kong will be able to protect its values and way of life after the handover. Lydia said that she was one of those who was involved in the campaign after the Tiananmen Square murders to get half the seats in the legislature directly elected. This was a policy which, despite attracting huge public support right across the community, was blocked by David Wilson, the British government and of course Cradock. There seems to have been some fairly murky work to try to prove that the community opposed this idea, a dodgy poll for example. Lavender reckons that we shouldn't be critical when some community leaders fail to stand up for us today when we have let them down so badly and regularly in the past. Alas, I think she is right about this.

Thursday 10 June

We gave a dinner for Peter Barry, the American priest who says the English-language mass in the cathedral every week. It's the 28th anniversary of his priesthood. Peter has spent quite a lot of time visiting the underground church in China (not least on his hiking holidays) and also, I think, the recognized (the communists would call it the patriotic) church as well. He told us that, looking for a local Bishop of the underground church, he was directed to a small house, knocked loudly on the door and heard someone shuffling down a corridor to open it. It opened a fraction and there was a little fellow in a T-shirt and flip-flops peering nervously at him. Peter said that he was looking for the local Bishop. The little guy closed the door saying he'd be back in a moment. He shuffled back a couple of minutes later and offered Peter his episcopal ring to kiss. He had gone away to put it on.

Friday 11 June

We had the first Queen's Birthday reception since I've been here. It's been pouring with rain all day (it even stopped my tennis this morning). To avoid everyone getting drenched we moved the ceremonial Beating the Retreat into the ballroom. The excellent police pipe band marched up and down making a terrific noise and closed the performance with my favourite pipe tune 'Highland Cathedral'. I think I will ask for it to be played when I leave in just over four years' time. Lavender suggested that the staff and our friends should bring their children along; they all seemed to enjoy it a lot.

Rupert Murdoch came to see me again. He is trying to buy part of Sir Run Run Shaw's television empire, clearly with the intention of using Hong Kong as the base for jumping off into the Chinese market. We may have some legal problems accommodating Murdoch, which would be bad news since his media would doubtless then go into overdrive to rubbish us. His world view and his business interests don't just overlap, they seem to match perfectly.

Saturday 12–Sunday 13 June

At the weekend we went to David Tang's* beautiful little house at Sai Kung with its wonderful garden and marvellous views out to sea. Sai Kung is a charming peninsula close to two country parks and with very good walking, beaches and little fishing villages. It must be a lovely place to live and David has made the most of it. He is one of the most memorable Hong Kong characters, indeed he would stand out anywhere. He is the grandson of a famous and very traditional Chinese comprador who made a fortune, including running one of the bus companies. Having fallen out with David's father, the old boy largely brought up David himself. David was sent off to a school in England aged 12 speaking hardly any English. He speaks and writes beautiful English now and is a fine pianist. He is himself a successful showman entrepreneur with shops and clubs which enable him to demonstrate just how stylish he is. On top of all this, he is hugely generous, has a wide circle of friends and acquaintances, does a great deal for the arts and for promoting the teaching of English in Hong Kong, and seems to include a large number of members of the royal family among his connections.

Rosa and Dominic Lawson were also invited to lunch. Dominic is writing some articles about Hong Kong and about me. I tried to avoid saying anything too interesting about politics back home, where Norman Lamont has been sacked and is, perhaps understandably, making a fuss. I don't always agree with Dominic but he is a fine journalist. David Tang said during lunch that he is struck by the extent to which the rich in Hong Kong have already sold out to China.

* Sir David Tang was an extravagantly generous, highly intelligent and civilized entrepreneurial businessman. He was as well known in Britain as in Hong Kong. He strongly supported democracy and the promised autonomy in his own city. Tang died of liver cancer in 2017.

Monday 14 June

The fifth round of talks is taking place. We thought that the Chinese had decided to make a bit of progress this week but they must have decided instead to attack us for our so-called 'little tricks', and to insist that we agree with them on the district board and municipal council elections before moving on to other matters. My more experienced officials in these pretty awful encounters say that there is a world of difference between how we are being treated at the moment and the way the discussions on the airport were conducted back in 1991. Then, Chinese officials shouted abuse and held a press conference after discussions to continue the slagging off which they had begun inside the meetings. Some suggest that they may be being a little more careful about their behaviour now because they aren't sure whether I will suddenly pull the plug on the talks. If only. Inevitably our Beijing team is starting to get rather weary.

I spoke in the evening to the Hong Kong College of Physicians. The dinner was full of the doctors who have been looking after me. They clearly regard me as their prize, slimmed-down, exhibit. My newish ADC, Mike Ellis, can I suppose take some credit for this (alongside our housekeeper, Elspeth, who keeps an eye on my diet). Mike has had a rowing machine installed in the rather gloomy basement of the house close to where the bodyguards crash out. I am obliged to go on this wretched thing frequently with Mike, who is himself very fit, shouting at me to 'dig deep'. I get very bored on this machine; apparently some people row for fun! Dig bloody deep, indeed. Dig deep and die of boredom.

Tuesday 15 June

With our team back from Beijing we now have to decide what to say about progress to the Cabinet committee in London. I don't want to be too defeatist. I think we still need to say that we will be very reasonable in negotiations if the Chinese will only put forward their own proposals. Why should we shift before they say anything? The general opinion is that the absolute deadline for ending the talks is early December. This would be late and difficult but possible. I'm not sure we can go beyond this.

At my main interview with Dominic Lawson, he reported on some of the criticisms that he's heard from the business community. One imaginative fellow has threatened both to shoot me and has also promised to raise £5 million for the Conservative Party if I am recalled to London. The party could obviously do with the money but I think this might be pushing fundraising a tad too far.

Friday 18 June

We had a meeting to discuss further Rupert Murdoch's ambitions to take over the TVB TV channel. The established wisdom, which I am not sure is very wise, is that we should block this purchase. I am not so certain. Murdoch is of course a foreign owner but it's just possible that he may be rather more resilient in standing up for broadcasting freedom than, say, one of the local Chinese entrepreneurs would be. Can this be a case where the public interest may equal Rupert Murdoch? One or two of my advisers think I am being more than naïve. Martin thinks that Murdoch simply wants to have a base for getting into the main China market, and that at the point where this becomes a possibility he will lean over backwards to accommodate communist officials.

I gave a lunch to say farewell to William Ehrman. He has been four years in Hong Kong and will be replaced by Bob Peirce, whom I met in New York. William tells me that a rather limp Cabinet committee paper which I disliked on Hong Kong and our talks with China was written by Christopher Hum not Peter Ricketts. I am not surprised. I will miss William, not least his sense of humour. We now have a busy week ahead of us – a three-day meeting of the JLG, the next round of political talks in Beijing, and preparations for the Cabinet committee meeting before the end of the month. We are starting to get some movement from China on economic issues. On the airport they have agreed to beginning the Western harbour crossing and have been engaged quite positively in haggling over airport money, only asking us to put up an extra HK$20 billion. I'm not sure myself that I regard China easing up on its politicization of economic issues as a great sign of magnanimity. The Western harbour crossing will not be a straightforward issue when we put it to Legco. In the past Hong Kong has been very good at using private investment to meet public goods, but this depends on not mucking about with the financial returns for the investors. So we want to remove the legislature's ability to set toll levels which would undermine any chance of getting reasonable rates of return for the private investors. Populism is rarely on the side of sensible financing arrangements.

Sunday 20 June

We had a group of British journalists and their wives for a drink. Lavender did an interview recently with the *Daily Mail*. Their man in Hong Kong apologized for the fact that it hadn't been printed in the paper. 'You didn't say anything sensational', he explained.

Monday 21 June
We had an instructive meeting about the Chinese nuclear power station at Daya Bay just along the coast from Shenzhen. Clearly in the event of an accident or emergency of any sort at the station there could be considerable consequences for Hong Kong and the public would be extremely worried. The Chinese are insisting that they should have in effect a veto over any information that we want to give to the public about an accident or emergency there. This would be completely unacceptable. The matter hasn't yet been resolved but I took the view that we may be better off not having any agreement with China, and explaining why this is the case, rather than settling for an agreement that we simply could not defend to the public.

Wednesday 23 June
Despite an admirable display of pyrotechnics by Tony Galsworthy in the JLG talks nothing much shifted, which presumably encouraged Moody's credit rating agency to take rather a dim view of Hong Kong's prospects after 1997. I doubt whether even this will have much of an effect on the pro-Beijing members of the business community or those who think that safety lies in keeping quiet and their heads down.

Thursday 24 June
Just before an enjoyable day at the dragon boat races in Aberdeen, I did another district visit, which proved useful for reasons other than keeping in touch with the public. I want to see what is not going well in Hong Kong as well as the good side. I'm aware of what could be called the official visit paint pot syndrome. Before you go out on an inspection, things are tidied up as much as possible. On this occasion, visiting a temporary housing area, the local residents made sure that I didn't just see what the housing authority officials would like me to be aware of. Much to the concern of officials and the police I was dragged off by residents to look at some truly dire housing. With the connivance of Martin and Edward I am now starting to organize snap visits with as little notice as possible.

Friday 25 June
Robin managed to put the Chinese on the back foot by criticizing their announcement that they are appointing a group of advisers to help prepare for 1997. They had said about three years ago that they were going to establish a working committee to clear the decks for governing after 1997. There was of course no cover in the BL for this. This committee is to be called preliminary rather than preparatory. It will presumably prepare the

ground for the main committee and give Beijing the chance to undermine the government in Hong Kong. They've chosen the usual sort of suspects, whom I imagine will simply tell them what they want to hear, so there isn't really much chance of us being sidelined.

Saturday 26 June

The sixth round of talks in Beijing suggests that China may be happy to tell us what they would like on functional constituencies and the election committee. Plainly they want the numbers voting in the functional constituencies to be as small as possible and we want them on the contrary to be as large as seems reasonable. Any fool can tell very easily whether an election is rigged or not. The vestigial shift in Beijing's position may be the result of the Chinese knowing about the forthcoming Cabinet committee meeting and their fear of what I call 'the mad Governor factor'. They probably really worry about us imposing our own deadline on the talks. We have dangled just above their heads the carrot of a possible visit by Douglas Hurd in early July to Beijing on his way back from a summit in Tokyo. Douglas is slightly worried that this may look as though he is undercutting Robin and me, but I think it would be a good idea.

Tuesday 29 June

Before setting off for the Cabinet committee meeting in London, we had quite a long discussion in Exco about airport funding. So far we have proposed injecting HK$22½ billion as an initial equity investment in the project, which we are prepared to increase to 25 billion. The Chinese have asked for 40 billion. Some of our members simply think that we should hand over the whole lot, which I suspect would surprise even the Chinese. I have a majority for 25 billion. The Chinese are playing games, partly I reckon because they are used to winning them.

Lavender is off to Korea to launch a ship which rather unhappily is called *Soro*. I don't know what it means in Korean, but it seems rather an unfortunate name for a ship.

Wednesday 30 June

I got back to London early in the morning. It's a beautiful summer day. I realized in the car on the way to our Victoria flat that four years from now I'll be returning to London more permanently, provided no one has claimed their 5 million for shooting me.

It's great to see Laura again. I went off to have lunch with Tristan and Catali. Tristan is full of schemes. He wants John to appoint John Kerr as his chief of staff and is clearly lobbying John and Douglas to bring me back in some Whitelaw-ish role to take pressure off the Prime Minister. I told him that this isn't on; much as I love him, I tell him to bugger off. The more I think about it, the less attractive is the idea of being the government's sweeper and spokesman. I've done that sort of thing before. Look where it got me – Hong Kong! A proper job which I want to see through to the end. Tristan has bought a new Spanish painting. I think the polite word for it is 'interesting'.

We had lots of meetings in the Foreign Office in the afternoon to prepare for the Cabinet committee meeting and then I took Laura, my sister, and her husband and daughter to a local Italian restaurant for dinner.

Thursday 1 July

Up early this morning for radio and TV interviews, including another one with Brian Redhead, who this time was positively benign. The Cabinet committee meeting went well enough. To be honest the discussion is rather desultory. There was a senior group of ministers, including the PM in the chair, Douglas, Ken Clarke, Michael Howard and the Chief Whip, Richard Ryder. Robin McLaren and I reported on what's been happening. Looking around the table I doubted whether Hong Kong features in the first half-dozen of anyone's list of priorities. I think they are all pretty happy to leave it to me with Douglas looking over my shoulder. We agreed that he should go to Beijing. If the talks continue to go badly and we don't get any sort of deal, we must be able to show that we did everything we possibly could to secure one. Equally, since Qian Qichen seems to be in the driving seat on Hong Kong, it's important that he and Douglas should have as good a relationship as is possible in the circumstances. We could perhaps have arrived at the same conclusions with an exchange of telegrams, but there is something to be said for me coming back and it's probably jogged the Chinese to some extent. Later in the day I had a pleasant talk to Jack Cunningham, Labour's foreign affairs spokesman, who has been helpful and very civil.

Kate got back from Newcastle and in the evening I took her and Laura to Clarke's in Notting Hill. They are great company and we saw lots of friends in the restaurant.

Friday 2 July

I had breakfast with John this morning. He doesn't seem to need my attempts to cheer him up. He pointed out that things are much worse in some other OECD countries, that economic growth is starting up again, that the Maastricht rumpus is virtually over, and that he has been proved right over Europe. But he seems to be carrying too many heavy bags, a lot of which are full of rather disagreeable right-wing MPs. I only have to read about them; he has to meet them. Once again, I feel a little bit guilty that I'm not around to help. In practice I'm not sure that there's anything much I could do. At least now he's got a very good Chancellor of the Exchequer in Ken Clarke, much better and more resilient than I would have been. Ken listens to experts but has enough self-confidence to follow his own instincts as well. They usually seem to be right.

Saturday 3 July
I got back from London just after Lavender's return from Korea. When she launched the ship, the bottle broke against its side at the first effort. This was taken, she was told, as a particularly propitious sign – good news given the name of the vessel. The newspapers are full of stories about peasants getting angry in China, capital flooding out of the country, and Zhu Rongji being given more and more authority over the economy. Zhu appears to be the most economically literate leader with a serious knowledge of how markets work, much respected abroad, and a reputation for not taking crap from anyone. We also heard that Larry Yung, the head of the big Chinese firm Citic, has just bought Birch Grove, Harold Macmillan's old home. I'm not sure that the family silver went with it but it certainly has lovely grounds around, which I once wandered with the old boy; perhaps they will be turned into a golf course. Anyway, it is perhaps an indication that relations between China and Britain have not been entirely cut off. Money has a language all its own.

Monday 5 July
I gave a farewell lunch for Anne Shepherd who has been my deputy private secretary. She has had the unenviable task of writing the speeches that I don't much want to do myself for things like the international plumbers' conference or the anniversary celebrations of the society of funeral directors. (I've made up those titles but only just.) These sorts of events go with the job and you have to do them as well as possible, evincing the greatest possible knowledge and enthusiasm for taps and coffins. Anne has done it all fantastically well; she radiates amusing charm but now has to return home to the West Country to join her husband, who is a well-known cameraman for natural history programmes. Anne is being replaced by another expat member of the Hong Kong civil service, originally from Wiltshire, called Kim Salkeld. I have not before met a Kim outside Korea. In addition to the private secretary and deputy in my office, there are always two or three younger local Chinese civil servants as well, hotshots on the way up.

Tuesday 6 July

Facing a further month of doubtless getting nowhere in the Beijing talks, I clocked up our successes so far with Martin, Edward and Mike Hanson. We stood firm over the talks taking place without a blanket of secrecy and to having officials from Hong Kong as part of our delegation. Some apparently think that that represents a triumph. I guess we have to calculate even the smallest examples of sanity as real progress when dealing with these 'speak your weight machine' Chinese officials. Douglas is to meet Qian in Beijing this week for dinner on Thursday 8 July and will then come on to Hong Kong afterwards to talk to Exco and to Legco members. If the leaks to the pro-Beijing newspapers are correct, the Chinese side is going to suggest separating whatever is decided for the district board and municipal council elections from the arrangements for the elections to the legislature. This is argued as a way of avoiding getting into deadline problems. We are not keen on the idea; we would prefer to deal with things as a package and avoid the beginning of salami slicing.

We are now having serious talks about when David Ford will step down from the job of Chief Secretary and Anson Chan take over. It looks as though this should happen in November, though I am supposed to be doing quite a lot of travelling then, and there may be problems with the talks in Beijing either ending or reaching – we should be so lucky – some sort of climax. If nothing much has happened by then I shall probably want to put my original package in a bill to Legco.

Wednesday 7 July

I went to look at the progress being made at Chek Lap Kok. It's really remarkable. The reclamation work moves remorselessly across the South China Sea in the general direction of Macau. When, or if, we get the job done, it will be one of the wonders of the world, if an airport can qualify for that prize. I also established a personal first this week. After visiting the Prince Philip Dental Hospital, I got a question from the press afterwards about ... dentistry. Thanks to Anne Shepherd I now know a lot about it. Actually, I've always thought myself that modern dentistry is one of the principal reasons for living in the 20th century.

Thursday 8 July

Willie Purves came to see me again about his successor on the Executive Council; he is keen on his number two, John Gray, getting the job and for once we see eye to eye. I think it is right to have someone on Exco from the banking sector. It will also be agreeable not to have to spend quite so much time removing a Scottish banker's dirks from between my shoulder blades. I've been wondering how much Willie's Eeyorish behaviour is explained by the fact that he is having to spend a good deal of diplomatic capital talking in Beijing about relocating the headquarters and more of the operations of the bank to London, now that HSBC has taken over or merged with the Midland. I guess that he will want things to be as politically tilted in Beijing's direction as possible on the assumption that this will curry favour with the northern communists. This would be understandable if it were true though not terribly honourable. Nor I think would it represent particularly sound calculations. Most of HSBC's employees don't have foreign passports. But when I said all this to Lavender, she replied philosophically, 'It is what it is.' You run a business in Sicily and like it or not you pay off the Mafia.

Friday 9 July

Douglas had his dinner with Qian yesterday and came on to Hong Kong today, arriving on a Chinese Airlines plane 90 minutes late, so he was very busy when he was with us. But he was cheerful and up for everything that is thrown at him. The discussions with the Chinese Foreign Minister were pretty calm and mostly about issues other than Hong Kong. So far as we were concerned, the most bankable point was Qian's observation that while it would be desirable to have a through train in order to make the transition as smooth as possible, if this was not possible then we would have to do what we wanted before 1997 and the Chinese would do their own thing afterwards. He also accepted that the talks should concentrate on the functional constituencies and the election committee. We would be prepared to make some compromises on these matters if the Chinese showed a similar willingness. I think this is what is called 'a Spartan if'. What the Chinese would regard as a concession would simply be to make the arrangements in these areas as loaded in favour of Beijing as possible. At the end of the day we have to get whatever emerges from the talks through the legislature in a bill. During his brief stay in Hong Kong before catching the late plane back to London, Douglas managed to fit in informal meetings with members of both Exco and Legco. We faced one crowd of pro-democracy demonstrators, led by Emily Lau, who presented us with a petition while chanting fairly amiably in favour of a wholly directly elected Legco in 1995. This is clearly a year in which cows alongside pigs are likely to take to the air. How many of those demonstrating actually think this is possible is a nice point. They would doubtless counter with the argument of this might have been so if we'd started down this track some time ago.

After seeing Douglas off at the airport, I changed out of my suit to spend half the night on patrol with the police, both land and sea, on the border. We played with thermal images while belting up and down the coast at high speed in small boats, but didn't of course catch anyone. I flew back to Fanling at about 3.30 in the morning by helicopter.

Monday 12 July

In Ad Hoc, we talked about how we could change our proposals on the functional constituencies and the election committee, adding additional voters to those who would at present get to take part in the election without going as far as my original ideas. The truth is that everything becomes immensely complicated once you move away from my own proposals, which were at the very least both simple and clear – and pretty fair. Finding new ways of making this part of the election process work in a fashion which would both satisfy those who want a reasonably clean election and Beijing is quite a puzzle. The present functional constituencies are completely indefensible and should never have been accepted by my predecessors or by the British government. The electorates are in most cases tiny and easily manipulated by the Chinese. The man who represents the regional council functional constituency is at present serving time in Stanley Prison for having bribed some of the small number of electors. In the constituency (which mostly represents the bosses of the Chinese Chamber of Commerce and not much more) the legislator called Ho stepped down very suddenly just before the last Legco elections because his business interests were threatened by China after he had expressed some opinions about the airport which they didn't like. And so it goes on. There isn't actually a functional constituency called 'rotten borough' but that must have been an oversight.

We also started to focus on what we think is the Home Office's attempt to narrow the pledges made in the past to members of the ethnic minorities (mostly Indian) in Hong Kong about their status after 1997, and in particular whether they qualify for any sort of British passport and for visa-free access to the UK. A lot of the Indians worked for the garrison or for the colonial administration in the past and now risk facing a loss of any citizenship rights, since for China citizenship is a question of ethnicity, an explicitly racist policy. These issues around citizenship and UK entry are going to become stickier and stickier as we approach the handover. As has happened in other parts of the British Empire, a lot of the people involved have worked for the colonial power over the years, not least in the uniformed services. We have not had a very good record in looking after people like this.

Wednesday 14 July
I joined some training sessions for the Black Watch and had lunch with them. They are an impressive lot with some very polished officers, one of whom talks about the tough little blokes (though he isn't quite as polite as that) in the other ranks. From what they say to me, many of them in the broadest Glaswegian, the single soldiers don't much care for being in Hong Kong. They find it difficult to pick up girls. But it's nice for those with families, not least because most of the wives find it easy to get jobs.

Monday 19 July
We're getting close to summer holidays. Alice and Lavender flew back to London, leaving me in charge of the dogs, who seem surprised to discover that I too am capable of going for walks. We are making some progress on reducing the costs of the garrison and are pleased to have got 84 bills through Legco in this session, including most of our spending plans, not least on infrastructure.

Tuesday 20 July
The eighth round of talks have begun in Beijing. We get nowhere on China's plans for the so-called through train, and our willingness to try to find some modifications to our plans on the election committee and functional constituencies doesn't appear to buy us any favours.

Ah Liu, my excellent young valet, has enquired about whether I need any more clothes from Mr Sam. This rather suggests that my tailor has been phoning up either him or Mike Ellis, my ADC. Anyway, I agreed to go off and see Mr Sam at his shop in Kowloon and, being on my own, have accepted his invitation for a private meal. After the usual business with my measurements and the choice of some material for a jacket and some shirts, we headed off for the Indian restaurant where I was to be entertained. I should not have been surprised when I got there to find that not only is his entire extended family at the table and several others, but in addition half the Indian community in Hong Kong seemed to have turned up. All this said, it is I suppose an understandable consequence of getting a suit made in Kowloon. The suits and shirts are very good, a cut above what I used to buy and wear. This is not a Governor who is knowingly underdressed, except for the lack of feathers.

Friday 23 July
There is to be yet another round of talks in the middle of August. I can't believe that it's going to be possible to find an agreement, but we are

scrambling about now trying to put together some new proposals on functional constituencies. These will involve a substantial reduction in the number of people who can vote in them down to below 1 million. But I'm sure that this will still be too many for Beijing, and, even if they were to agree with us, it would be too few for Legco and the community – not to mention the media. At least Exco agrees with the new ideas and, rather more relevant to the future, Anson Chan is delighted that she will be taking over from David Ford in November. She is very sensible about this. She talks about her husband's view; he has evidently been very supportive, which may not be easy for a Chinese husband with a successful wife. (I'm not sure that this is only a problem in China.) Anson also says that she can't guarantee to stay on after 1997, nor even to stay on right up until then if she finds she is constantly having to look over her shoulder at what China thinks about this or that decision she takes. I gave her a little speech, which I think represents the truth, that I like delegating provided I have good people like her to whom I can delegate major and difficult decisions. I obviously want to focus on the biggest issues, with her advice all the time, and will be happy to have her running much of what happens in Hong Kong without me second-guessing her.

Saturday 24 July

I had a cheerful dinner with David Tang and Simon Murray at the French restaurant in the Mandarin hotel. I tell them in confidence about Anson. They both think she is terrific, as is the meal I am delighted not to be paying for.

Monday 26 July

I took David and Gillian Ford to dinner at the Café de Paris to talk about Anson and the Fords' move to London. He has been fantastically loyal and supportive and I owe him a great deal. I hope he realizes how happy I have been working with him. David and Gillian have become real friends.

Thursday 29 July

I arrived in London yesterday before I head to Italy for a holiday with the whole family and some friends. I continued to ward off suggestions that I don't really have to spend five years in Hong Kong. I saw Douglas and John Major yesterday, both on their own; John for lunch today, the same day as the Christchurch by-election. (The MP who died, Robert Adley, was one of the relatively few critics of our Hong Kong policy in the House of Commons; no black spot, honestly.) I admire Douglas as much as anyone.

Inevitably he is looking for ways in which he can manage his exit from the Foreign Office as decorously as possible. I'm sure that John will put a lot of pressure on him not to depart. I wish I could stop John ringing up newspaper proprietors and editors, and above all reading what some of their more disagreeable and patronizing right-wing columnists have to say. It won't have any effect save to make them think that they're taken more seriously than they deserve. John is himself much cleverer than most of them. Of course, I know that it's easier to make these points than to act in that way. I can often myself become obsessed with criticism and have to avoid 'Patten against the world' fixations. John doesn't drink (well, not much), so his only addiction is reading the unfair and often brutal things which people write about him. I really don't think that anyone could do better than him, given the present state of our wretched party.

Saturday 28 August
The house where we stayed in Italy is in Umbria just north of Spoleto and not far south of Spello and Assisi. It's near some famous springs much visited by the Romans and written about by Byron. The house itself was charming in a rundown sort of way. Some rather grand Italian family owns it and apparently is letting it for the first time. The very nice cook who looked after us, and them when they're there, said rather philosophically that the family hasn't worked for several centuries so it's not surprising that they now have to let foreigners rent the house in order to pay the bills. Looking for wine glasses one day in a cupboard, we came across some framed photographs which had plainly been put away before we arrived. One of them showed a group – presumably the parents of the count – wearing fascist insignia and looking very pleased about it. We all have our family histories and some of them are much better locked up in the cupboard.

Wednesday 1 September
Back in Hong Kong we had to start preparing for yet another round of talks in Beijing; this will be the 10th, shortly to be followed by the 11th and then nothing for about three weeks until the end of September. Our general expectation is that China won't budge at the next two rounds but may give a few inches at the end of September just before a meeting between the foreign ministers. The intention is, I suppose, to put more pressure on us. Sooner or later there will be no point in going on like this. We will have to manage a breakdown. So much of our effort this autumn will be trying to ensure that this happens in a way that gives us as soft a landing as possible. And, of course, we don't want to get stuck with all the

blame. But tick-tock goes the proverbial clock. We have to put in place the pretty complicated sets of arrangements for three lots of election starting next year. This is going to require quite a bit of both primary and subsidiary legislation. There's also a lot of complex work for the Boundaries and Election Commission to do. We have from time to time to take a cold bath of reality. I really find it difficult to believe that the Chinese will accept a first past the post voting system since this sort of plurality voting favours Democrat candidates. Second, while they might accept a through train for civil servants and judges, do they really accept the case for one covering legislators? At bottom, they don't want Hong Kong people to run Hong Kong if they disagree with Beijing's view of what constitutes good governance.

Thursday 2 September

We have had to start work already on my next annual speech to Legco. It doesn't seem very long since the last one. Until recently the Treasury was predicting that we would be running a deficit this year. But this is Hong Kong. Further calculations now suggest that we will be running a large surplus, so that should give me quite a bit of room for more social initiatives.

We rounded off our first week back by going to a play starring Derek Nimmo. We had a drink with him and his wife, Pat, who are both completely charming. The play, by William Douglas Home, is a very average English drawing-room comedy. Derek does his considerable best, but it is uphill work.

Monday 6 September

Most of the bigwigs in the Securities and Futures Commission have had meetings to brief me on a tricky issue involving Jardine's. The commission's responsibilities include policing the takeover code. That naturally begins with the question of its reach. Jardine's have managed to change their listing as a company from Hong Kong to Bermuda. This obviously reflects their nervousness about possible events after 1997, above all a repeat of the difficulties they had in the past when they were almost taken over by a local company. Their argument is that since they are now listed in Bermuda (though they plainly don't do much business in the Caribbean), they should not be subject to a takeover code in Hong Kong. There is no doubt about the commission's jurisdiction and there is equally no doubt that it can be challenged in court. But it would obviously be extremely legally and politically damaging for me to intervene personally to try to overturn an independent and legal commission decision. I could myself face a legal challenge, and the politics of a British Governor intervening to protect a British company from the consequences of the rule of law don't bear thinking about. What would China think about this, even while pocketing it as a precedent for the future. So if Henry Keswick and Co don't like what is coming down the track, they can always go to court about it. I'm told now that Jardine's were raising this issue in London well before I became Governor. There is no reason why they should not make a legal challenge.

Senator Dianne Feinstein had dinner with Lydia and her husband, Michael Thomas. She too came to see me. She has just been in Beijing and thinks that all the members of the leadership there are obsessed with stability, which is presumably in part a result of some of the economic issues China is facing that we hear so much about.

Wednesday 8 September

We are starting to get into a bit more detail when thinking about my Legco speech. I had a lively discussion with David Ford, Hamish McLeod, Leo Goodstadt and others, including of course Martin and Edward. How many of the pledges that I want to make on health, education, welfare and infrastructure are already government policy or should be? How many of them can we afford? Can we reallocate money from our surplus this year without running up unaffordable current spending consequences in the future? How can we put some of our long-term capital allocation decisions into the speech? I'm going to start writing something myself which is sometimes the best way of bouncing people into decisions. I am starting to get more relaxed about the Beijing talks now that I know that they cannot be infinite. I'm sure that the Chinese are pretty resigned now to a breakdown. While they are battling against their own economic problems, I don't think that they are going to be prepared to take too many risks about Hong Kong. It is probably true that they understand that any settlement to which we could agree might be potentially destabilizing in Chinese domestic politics. When Robin came down to talk to me about all this he was correctly keen to spell out what he believes might be the results of a breakdown. He suggests that we might have a rough few months, a worsening of Sino-British relations, no further dialogue between Chinese officials and me, and attempts to build up pro-Beijing provisional bodies (including the threatened provisional legislature). He is not trying to suggest that I should simply cave in (with the support presumably of the British government) but that I should not be too gung ho about what lies ahead. In other words he is doing exactly what a good official should do.

Murdoch is selling the *South China Morning Post* to a Malaysian group. I imagine that he wants to remove any possibility of his television ambitions in China being affected by having a newspaper in Hong Kong.

The bid for the paper has been bankrolled by the Bank of China. I had been told in the past that it is strapped for cash, but I suppose that Beijing would want to turn it into a Hong Kong version of the *Straits Times*. Pity.

Friday 10 September

We don't really have any work to do to prepare for the next – 11th – round of talks in Beijing. Robin McLaren had an awful incident on his flight back to Beijing. The plane's windscreen shattered in an electric storm when they had almost got to the end of the journey and they had to fly back all the way to Hong Kong on autopilot because they weren't allowed to make an automatic landing in the capital. Lavender reminded me that Robin has a very bad back and must have been in awful pain. Sitting through all the negotiations must be agony too, physical even more than intellectual for him. He is a very brave man.

After this round of talks, there will be a gap until October while the leader of the Beijing team goes off for a trip round Europe with China's Vice President. It's clear that the Chinese side have been tipped the wink that our deadline isn't October but December. I'm pretty certain that some officials who used to work for Cradock are still happy to treat him as someone on our side. I don't for one moment believe that on issues like our approach to the talks he misses any opportunity to tell Beijing what we are up to. But I'm sure that there are other channels of communication as well. In any event I mustn't get too obsessed about deadlines.

Saturday 11 September

We had an informal Exco meeting at GH with Robin McLaren to discuss tactics and strategy for the coming months. We think that we should probably make a very small concession during the 12th round of talks, beginning on 14 September, probably reducing the number of people who can vote in the functional constituencies. We also need to draft a message which Douglas can send before he meets his opposite number about the through train, and we have to think about what I can say on the talks in my Legco speech. Peter Ricketts has prepared the draft of a White Paper in the case of either success or more likely a breakdown. This is not easy to do given the number of audiences to whom we would be appealing. In continuing JLG talks, we should now be able to reach a deal on the defence lands, not least since we are giving away almost everything. But we are trying to insist that the Chinese should make a verbal commitment to use the defence lands as they have been used in the past, handing them back to the Hong Kong government for social and economic development if they are not needed for purely military purposes. Everyone will assume that the main reason why the PLA wants so many defence sites is so that they can then develop them commercially for themselves. However, there is obviously some difficulty in trying to refuse sites to the PLA which our garrison has gone on saying for so long that it needs.

Sunday 12 September

Father Lambertoni has been pressing me for some time to go for a hike with him and a few friends from his Italian missionary order. After our wedding anniversary on the 11th (which I remembered and bought Lavender a very nice candelabra, plus a good dinner with Kate and Alice), we set off with Kate to meet Father Lambertoni on a hiking trail in Sai Kung. Kate was prepared to be bored, obviously expecting to meet a lot of old farts in long cassocks, but when we got to the meeting place, there was a group of fit-looking young and middle-aged Italians wearing trainers, shorts and bright T-shirts. They are making lots of noise and doing a lot of singing. We had a great morning with them, though it is very hot and sweaty. There were about 12 of them and when we got to the highest point in our walk, they sang us a lovely Italian folk song. We then went off to their mother house nearby to have an Italian meal with all the members of the order present in Hong Kong, including a lot of the older ones. There used to be over 70 of them here; now they are down to just over 40. We had prosciutto, lasagne, osso bucco and a huge gateau. There was lots of Chianti and Asti Spumante. We must do it again. I'm not sure whether this is the church triumphant but it is certainly the church molto frizzante.

Monday 13 September

I had a good discussion with Lydia Dunn. She is a great one for picking up rumours and has heard a lot of talk in London that I am going to go back there to help John Major in some senior job or other. One of the rumours she's heard is that I will be made Leader of the House of Lords with general sweeping up responsibilities across the whole of government. I assured her that almost regardless of what happens in London or Hong Kong, I intend to stay and do the job until 1997. The only thing that would change my mind would be if all my plans were thrown overboard, or if the community turned against what we had been attempting to achieve. She also seemed to think that we could have agreement to disagree with the Chinese on political affairs and just get on with running Hong Kong as best we can. She feels that the business community has largely written off the prospect of any agreement on politics. If they are right, this would mean of course writing off all the stuff about the through train. But as I go on saying to people, if we are expected to do China's dirty business for them before 1997, then it is simply not a bargain we could accept.

I also had a useful conversation with John Gray, who will be the new boss of the Hong Kong Bank here when Willie Purves goes back to London, and I invited him to join Exco when Willie departs. He is a fine man and we had an open talk. He pointed out that some people would criticize his appointment because he is an expat and that on political issues he takes the same views as many other businessmen in the territory. At least, however, I will know where we stand with him. I think he will disagree with me, when he does, to my face.

Tuesday 14 September

John Redwood arrived. He is now in the Cabinet as Welsh Secretary. Martin asked whether this is the first time we have had a Dalek to stay. It must be difficult for John Redwood, who is probably the most right-wing member of the Cabinet, to be responsible for one of the most interventionist bits of government, which he has brought with him, namely the Welsh Development Agency. They want to know whether they should invest here, or on the mainland or in Vietnam. I met the Australian trade minister, who is attempting to find a middle path between his Prime Minister, Paul Keating, who is trying to drum up as much business as possible with China (no questions asked), and Gareth Evans, Foreign Minister, who is happy to do more business with the Chinese but doesn't think that Australia can avoid raising human rights issues. Most of the conversation, however, was about European protectionism. He has been told about the piece I wrote in the *Economist* about free trade which apparently came out the previous week. When I met at lunch the senior team from Jardine's, several had read it, including Nigel Rich, who told me that he started reading it but fell asleep. There's honesty for you.

Wednesday 15 September

We took Kate and Alice to William and Caroline Courtauld's home for dinner this evening. Caroline had lots of young people there for Kate and Alice to meet. The Courtaulds are wonderful company and very generous. William is Rab Butler's stepson (he works for Jardine's) and Caroline knows lots about both China and Burma, on which she writes good books. She is a friend of Aung San Suu Kyi. Edward will be interested, he is very keen to visit Burma. I would like to do so as well but don't think I can while the generals are in charge. I should add a confession about William's mother, Molly Butler, who is Rab's widow. She is getting on, but sharp as a tack and wonderful looking. She continues at every opportunity to fight

Rab's corner, in particular laying into Harold Macmillan whenever the chance arises. I am a huge fan despite the fact that she can't stand the European Union. I think she has sort of forgiven me for being a supporter. She wrote an extremely good memoir, and the passages about the death of her two husbands, a Courtauld and a Butler, made me cry. The book was by the bedside when I stayed once with Francis and Valerie Pym before making a speech in his constituency. I love it when hosts have obviously taken some care about choosing the right books to tempt a guest at bedtime. Books of collected obituaries are usually welcome, but perhaps they make it more likely that you will die in your sleep.

Friday 17–Saturday 18 September

Over the weekend we had political guests from London, first Virginia Bottomley, who is now the Health Secretary, and then David Hunt, who was my number two when I was Environment Secretary and is now the Secretary of State for Employment. David is one of the best House of Commons speakers that I know. We were almost hit by a typhoon; at least, a typhoon passed quite close by. It's the third of the season and there was a storm warning eight. The rain lashed down. The house shuddered under the gale. Lots of meetings were cancelled, the good side of the bad weather. When it was over, I went off to play tennis with David Ford and the two senior members of the Hong Kong Davis Cup squad, Colin Grant and Mike Walker. They are becoming an important part of my life support team, extremely nice chaps and of course very good tennis players. They don't try to knock me off the court (they couldn't do that with David, who is himself an excellent player) but keep the ball in play so we have long rallies. I have to start playing rather better because I've accepted a challenge to play in a charity game with, among others, Roscoe Tanner, who serves at the speed of light. My serve is more readily comparable with the speed of my alas now dead Morris Minor.

Monday 20 September

Douglas has, a little surprisingly, torn into the Chinese bid to hold the Olympic Games, which I imagine will cause a bit of a stir when he next sees his opposite number from Beijing, and we started trying to work through the various scenarios for dealing with the end of the talks. The nightmare scenario is one in which we can't get a majority in Legco for anything at all, not for anything we manage to agree up north, and not for going forward with our own original plans. That's the charm of democracy for you. After Exco I announced Anson's appointment as the new Chief Secretary. When we finished answering questions in English from the journalists, Anson went back to do the whole thing again in Cantonese. I guess that is part of the point.

Tuesday 21 September
After doing an interview for *Panorama* at No. 10's request about John (Douglas and Ken Clarke are the other two people they are interviewing), we had a lovely evening at a charity performance in our ballroom of *The Magic Flute* by a visiting chamber opera. The acoustics were terrific.

Wednesday 22 September
We gave a farewell dinner for Willie Purves and his wife before they go back to London. This seemed to be one of a string of such evenings. He is having more farewells than Frank Sinatra. I've been told about some of the things he has said about me at other dinners; he must presumably know that people will all report them back to me. I have a moderately thick skin but thought I could respond (with a degree of subtlety) in the speech that I gave for him. I noted that Exco's role has changed, that it does not any more have the responsibility of providing a sort of representational legitimacy for the colonial government (that has changed with the development of Legco), but that it does help the Governor to make political judgements. I went on to say that whether the Governor is a wise and urbane diplomat or a vulgar and cackhanded politician, these judgements are difficult. I then did a little turn on politics and principle, the importance of loyalty, and finally flashed a few emaciated compliments in Willie's direction. He is an old bruiser with a very thick hide and I rather doubt whether he got the points I was making. But others clearly did. As I've noted before, he is presumably a good bank manager.

Thursday 23 September
A sadder occasion was the farewell lunch that I gave for Tony Galsworthy. He is a very clever diplomat and it cannot have been easy for him to work for me after so many years as part of the Cradock team. As the chairman of our side in the JLG he has been as effective as is possible in coping with some pretty dreadful diplomats on the other side of the table. I hope that sooner or later he will become our ambassador in Beijing. He would obviously like it. It's a good job the offer will never be made to me. Now Tony can spend a bit more time with his moths. He is to be succeeded by Hugh Davies, who was a long-term China hand and gets very good reviews from all his colleagues as an excellent and sensible team builder.

Speaking of Craddock, the *South China Morning Post* have run a story saying that at my insistence his memoirs are being suppressed by the government. He has apparently been phoning up journalists to tell them this. It's a complete lie. I actually wrote to Robin Butler, the Cabinet Sec, saying I didn't want to have anything to do with looking at Percy's memoirs. I think the truth is that the FCO and the Cabinet Office have been trying to get him to take one or two things out of the book he is writing. They are exactly the sort of things that he wouldn't have tolerated a civil servant saying in his days in office. He is such a vain old thing. I was about to describe him as a bore. But he's not really that. It's what he's doing that is boring; it takes up too much time having to think about it and deal with it.

Saturday 25 September

The Waldegraves came to stay with us yesterday. William has to fly on to Tokyo for a few days, but Caroline stayed and hugely helpfully spent a lot of time in the kitchen teaching our chefs all sorts of useful and delicious new tricks. It's been raining very hard and I had to go off to the New Territories to inspect flood defences. We are working up on the border and it's been difficult getting agreement with the Chinese authorities for some of what needs to be done.

Wednesday 29 September

After another good district visit, this one to Mong Kok, Lavender and I had to go to our second Chinese National Day reception. Bob Peirce wrote a first-rate little speech for me which I more or less knew off by heart. He included some lines from an eighth-century Chinese poet about the need to climb higher in order to get the long-term view. I'm not sure that I really knew what I was supposed to be getting at but it went down well. Zhou Nan and I toasted one another at the end in feigned good humour. Jonathan Mirsky, a really excellent journalist who is now working here for *The Times*, told Edward that the photographers were instructed not to photograph us when we did the toasts – no signs of Entente are to be allowed. Jonathan is a great addition to our social life in Hong Kong, not least because he knows so much about China and has admirably clear views on the usual behaviour of the Communist Party.

Thursday 30 September

We had a bit of time with William and Caroline when William returned from his ministerial trip to Tokyo. Any time with them is a bonus, and Caroline and Lavender went on quite a few walks together. William is having a tough time because of the wretched Scott Inquiry into the alleged ministerial complicity in the sale of arms to Iraq. Scott himself is a judge whose knowledge of the law must be a great deal stronger than his ability to tell honest people from charlatans. In having to decide whether William and Nick Lyell are telling the truth or whether he should believe Alan Clark, he seems to have some difficulty arriving at a judgement which most people who know them all would have reached in a nanosecond.

Friday 1 October

Today, after the Waldegraves left, was a public holiday. I worked at Fanling while Lavender went to visit the Down's Syndrome Centre at Tung Tau. Back in August there were some awful demonstrations by a few local residents against its establishment. This small group of neighbours didn't want to live next door to a few kids with Down's. Lavender (who is patron of the charity that helps look after people with Down's) thought very properly that she should visit the centre with one or two others, including David Tang, who has himself done a lot for them, to show support. It is sometimes argued, though I am not sure that I wholly believe this, that there is a cultural Chinese hostility to facing up to disability or death, for example the existence of AIDS or the establishment of hospices. Lavender's gesture of support was very well received – except by the protesting neighbours. She was told in advance that there would be a big and noisy demonstration and that some of the protesters were planning to throw bags of urine at her. 'I suppose there is a first time for everything', she said. In fact, it all went off very peacefully and with good humour. Lavender was told that the majority of residents were fed up with the small band of protesters and were isolating them. It amused Lavender that only a few days ago our friend Mike Medavoy, who is looking after Laura in Hollywood while she is there on holiday, telephoned to announce Laura's arrival. She was apparently asked at Immigration where her mother was. She replied, 'I'm sure that she is playing golf and walking her dogs in Hong Kong.' Lavender said, 'I hope that she doesn't think that that is all I do all day.'

Saturday 2 October

Douglas had a meeting with Qian again yesterday. As we anticipated, it was a pretty barren discussion. After the meeting Douglas and Christopher Hum, who was with him at the UN in New York, discussed whether we could perhaps separate the issue of the elections to the district boards and the municipal council from the rest of the political package, giving us more time to talk to the Chinese about Legco. There are a lot of technical reasons why this is difficult, but there's also a solid political case that we need to consider. The Chinese will only move when they really believe that we have got a deadline. If we keep on changing the ones we have already specified, they won't believe that we have a deadline at all and will refuse to budge from their existing positions. We sent off a telegram to this effect. We also discussed whether in the event of a breakdown we should put to Legco my original package or an amended one taking account of the moderate changes we have suggested both to the election committee and to the size of the functional constituencies. I'm not sure myself that this will take any tricks. It will probably lose support on both sides in the legislature, meaning that we finish up with no one agreeing to what we suggest.

Tuesday 5 October

Tony O'Reilly (the Irish businessman and former international rugby player) is in Hong Kong. When I was a schoolboy, I once saw him play rugby: a big, strapping, handsome Irish lad. He still is. As well as running Heinz he also owns several newspapers. He is in town for a world press freedom conference. Despite all my usual bluster about doing my own speeches, I made one opening the conference written by Edward, which is a real cracker and went down very well. When I had a drink with Tony and his wife today, he invited me to go to Dublin to give what has become a very prestigious lecture organized by his newspaper group. It's not until next March and it looks as though I can manage the date. Putting cream on the cake, he says that there is a fee of about £20,000. Very nice but I told him that I can't really receive it; I'm already paid for doing my job. I don't think he really understood my ethical problem and replied, 'We could make it a bit more.'

Wednesday 6 October

And so, after a lot of work in recent weeks I came to my annual Legco speech today. When I got to the building, there was a pro-democracy demonstration outside with lots of familiar faces. They were obviously expecting me to run up the white flag. This is odd really because the NCNA and quite a lot of the pro-Beijing business community think I'm going to pull the plug on the talks and table my bill straight away. I was rather worried that the speech was going to take most of the rest of the month to deliver but I got through it all in just over two hours. Lavender advised me to go faster than normal. After setting out all my views on economic and social policy (with several new proposals on welfare), I turned at the end of the speech to politics in Hong Kong. I'm quite pleased with what I wrote in the peroration. 'We now have only weeks rather than months to conclude these talks . . . We are not prepared to give away our principles in order to sign a piece of paper. What would that be worth?' I finished by going a bit over the top, 'We cannot be bolder than you, because liberty stands in the heart. When it shrivels there, nothing can save it.' Then came the press conferences, interviews with local and foreign press, radio and television broadcasts and once again public meetings, the first of them once more in Shatin tomorrow.

Friday 8 October

The worst part of the week was a meeting today with two ghastly blokes from the bank Robert Fleming – the one from London is called John Manser and the even worse one, who looks after the bank's interests in Hong Kong, is called Alan Smith. A lot of what they've been saying in private has been played back to me already. People might be surprised to discover how much the Governor gets to hear. They have spent a good deal of the week kowtowing to the NCNA. If they only knew how much derision this causes in the ranks of even the most hard-boiled of Chinese apparatchiks. Apparently, they have even told the Chinese that of course the UK demonstrates some of the inadequacies of democracy and that nobody in Hong Kong agrees with me about elections. What creeps.

Sunday 10 October

There was an important poll this weekend in the *South China Morning Post* suggesting that quite a good majority think it's important to stand up for democracy. Alastair came for one of his regular ministerial visits, but this time he had other things that he wanted to say. He asked for a private word during which he set out in some detail one or two quite specific suggestions about the notion that I should go back to a big job at Westminster. It's probably the only job that I'd be really keen to do. But I went through all the reasons why it would be impossible and pretty dishonourable. I've promised again and again that I would be in Hong Kong for five years provided enough people here want me to stay. I guess if Legco threw out my plans I'd probably have to leave with my tail between my legs, but that might not be the best recommendation for a post in the government. We have to go back to London in a few days for a Cabinet committee meeting to agree on the way forward and I guess that I'll get a lot more of all this stuff about returning when I'm there.

Monday 11 October

We spend a lot of time thinking through what modest concessions we can make in order to secure at least some progress in the talks which are now heading for the 14th and 15th rounds. We also have to get the Cabinet committee meeting and the paper for it prepared. Allen Lee and some of his colleagues came to see me yet again. They want us to split the discussion of district board and municipal council elections from the arguments about the bigger matters involving Legco. I explained to them that this would be a red herring and that we need to get all our legislation in place by July 1994. If the Chinese are prepared to agree with us on the voting age, on the local elections and on the voting method for the geographical elections – none of which raise Basic Law or Joint Declaration points – we would be very happy for them to make this clear at the outset of the next round of talks. I said this myself in stand-ups with the press after a degree congregation at Chinese University. The real problem is what it has always been: the Chinese side won't agree to anything which would make the elections even moderately fair and acceptable, and we won't put anything forward which will leave us looking like a pathetic transmission mechanism for Beijing two or three years before 1997. In a way the Chinese cat is let out of the bag when David Akers-Jones gave evidence to the Foreign Affairs committee of the House of Commons on Hong Kong. He told the committee during the course of one of their sessions, 'The Chinese style is not to rig elections, but they do like to know the results before they are held.' Quite so.

Sunday 17 October

Today, we started a sponsored walk by 10,000 civil servants at Shatin and then Lavender went off with Caroline Courtauld and Millie Yung, an old friend of Caroline who is very smart and knowledgeable about China, on a visit to Yunnan in the far south-west of China.

Wednesday 20 October

At the beginning of the 14th round of talks today, the Chinese offered the prospect of vestigial progress. They said that they will take note of our view that they should recommend objective criteria to the committee that will be set up before 1997 to prepare for the transition and to vet the legislators who will be allowed to travel on that clattering through train. They have also said that if we will agree not to press for completely elected district boards and municipal councils, they will consider sympathetically our ideas about the voting age and the voting method for the local elections. As concessions go this takes very few biscuits. It wouldn't even satisfy Allen Lee and his pals.

Friday 22 October

Nothing happened on the second day in Beijing to compare remotely with the excitements I had to face in Hong Kong on the 21st. This was the day when I took part in a charity challenge tennis match in front of a large crowd in the stadium at Victoria Park. I played with Vijay Amritraj against David Ford and Roscoe Tanner. My increasingly good friend Colin Grant, along with his tennis pals Hans Franklin and Mike Walker, have spent a lot of time trying to get me into shape for this game. I more or less survived, though I was so nervous that I found it very difficult to toss the ball over my head when serving. I did have one or two quite long rallies and eventually Vijay and I won a tiebreak with a backhand volley off the frame of my racket. John Barrett, the former tennis player and correspondent for the *FT*, wrote a report about the match which was modestly flattering but which did include a count of my unforced errors.

In Beijing, Chinese officials boasted about the huge concessions they have made. We think again about how we should handle a breakdown and what package to put subsequently to Legco. I really don't think we are going to be able to make up our mind on this until the event, but I would be surprised if we don't table the 1992 package. I keep on coming back to the same mixture of the practical and the honourable. There isn't much point in us changing our plans if they then satisfy neither Legco nor Beijing.

Sunday 24 October

Lavender got back this weekend from Yunnan, where she had a terrific time, and I managed to talk to Laura in Los Angeles. I have also started writing the lecture which I have to deliver in Newcastle when I visit Kate there on our next home visit. Pretty much every visitor who comes in to see me here thinks that the economy in China is in some trouble or, if not actually in trouble, is defying the laws of gravity. In my experience people say this when they don't really know what is going on. James McGregor from the Asian *Wall Street Journal* makes the most interesting good sense. He says that it is not surprising that no one knows what is happening in China. It is in effect run by a secret society. What launched the recent economic frenzy? It was one old man (Deng) going to Guangzhou. Li Peng, the Prime Minister, disappeared for four months this year; no one knew where he had gone or what was happening while he was away. He then suddenly reappeared in his bathing trunks. Hu Jintao is said to be a great figure in the leadership. He has come from nowhere. He was party secretary in Tibet but couldn't go there very much because he suffered from altitude sickness. What's the secret of his success? Altitude sickness? Meanwhile, with the politics entirely inscrutable, the economy is probably booming away in a way which baffles traditional economists. Or perhaps it isn't!

Thursday 28 October

The 15th round of talks started yesterday. Paint drying on wall. Will to live disappearing fast. On the second day today, however, the Chinese made quite a clever move which suggests they don't want the talks to break off. At the beginning of the round, out of the blue, they suggested that we should record an interim understanding on five points that we have been discussing and which they think we have come close to agreeing. They will accept a reduction in the voting age to 18, pocket the right of Hong Kong citizens who are members of the National People's Congress to stand in local and Legco elections in Hong Kong, go along with a single-vote, single-member system for local but not for Legco elections, accept the nature and function of district board and municipal councils elections though not the size of the electorates, and recognize that while we can replace appointed members of these bodies before 1997, they may be put back by China after that date. In other words there would be the return of appointed members. Whether or not there is any chance in the future of an agreement on contentious issues such as the voting system for Legco and the possibility of duly elected legislators travelling on the through train was to be put to one side. On the through train, I suppose that we could accept a reasonably drafted oath in order to qualify for the post-1997 Legco, after all, MPs at Westminster take an oath. But there could be no question of retrospection. This would have to be explicitly ruled out. Clearly (insofar as anything is clear) the Chinese side seems to be keen on avoiding a breakdown, but we haven't really got into a serious discussion about the membership of the electorate in the functional constituencies and their delineation, nor about the other fundamental matters.

Friday 29 October

After discussing all this we worked on a paper for the Cabinet committee and on a message which the Prime Minister could send to his opposite number, focusing on the many issues that remain outstanding and calling for a speeding up of discussions. This will be sent after the Cabinet committee have agreed on the way forward through any future talks.

Monday 1 November

I began the month with a deeply depressing lunch with the board of Standard Chartered Bank. They are critical of what we are doing in Hong Kong – no, not critical, really hostile. They don't think we should be doing or saying anything which annoys Beijing. Their advice and knowledge of what is happening in Hong Kong and China seems remarkably limited and deeply and uninterestingly small-'c' conservative. No wonder that despite the fact that a few years ago they were the top bank in Hong Kong, they have been knocked far off this perch by HSBC, who were much more prepared to lend money to up and coming local Chinese businessmen.

Wednesday 3 November

Nancy Thompson has lent Lavender the catalogue of the old Chater collection of works of art which used to belong to GH and was lost during the war. The pictures were buried in the garden of GH, but the two men who knew the spot died during the Japanese occupation and the paintings were never discovered. It's a tragedy because the collection contained some beautiful works by Chinnery.

Lavender and I had a quick trip to Macau today. The Governor invited us to a performance of *Turandot* at the music festival. We get on very well with him and his wife. Lavender suggests that this is clearly in part the result of the fact that we are in a similar position in relation to China. Macau is of course very different, much smaller, and the Portuguese half threw in the towel in 1967 during the Cultural Revolution, and then threw it in again after it had in effect been handed back into their safekeeping during one of their own Portuguese revolutions. But whatever the differences in our respective colonies, the Chinese Communist Party and its behaviour remain the same. On the way home we just miss a big storm.

The general mood of foreign journalists is captured by the great Jonathan Mirsky, whom I much like even when he is annoying the hell out of me. But he is brave, knows a lot about China and is very lively company. Apparently he tends to storm out of dinners from time to time but the people he treats like this are normally people who deserve it. Anyway, when he interviewed me, he plainly couldn't make up his mind whether we are heading for a sell-out or a complete and utter ceiling falling down disaster.

Friday 5 November

I had a drink this evening with Eric Anderson and his wife. He is stepping down as head of Eton and is off to be Rector of Lincoln College in Oxford. A more regular visitor is the formidable Jessica Rawson, who has been running the Asia department in the British Museum, and is going to Merton College. I wonder what those jobs are like? We had a few good rambles with Jessica through the back streets of Hong Kong looking for antiques. There couldn't be a better guide on this hunt for bits of old China.

Sunday 7 November

We got back to London at dawn on 6 November and after clocking in at Morpeth Terrace I went off for a Turkish bath at the RAC Club. Apart from talking about Hong Kong to Douglas over the weekend, I also checked where we stand on a difficult civil service pensions issue in the territory. It's all about sterling safeguards, with the Treasury trying to avoid setting the figure at today's Hong Kong dollar price against the pound. It's not about who we pay in Hong Kong but what the retired civil servants get in sterling. The Treasury are being as mean as they have been with most colonial civil servants' pensions, but they are obviously dug in. There will be one not very high-ranking official in the Treasury who has made it his life's work to screw colonial pensions, thinking every evening as he waits on the platform in the cold and wet for a train to Guildford about all those allegedly living it up in warm climates, with servants at a snap of their fingers, being taught a bit of reality by the man in the Treasury. The problem is that these are the sort of relatively small issues, except for those who are personally affected, which ministers rarely think are worth trying to understand or deal with in a way which contradicts official advice. In my experience the best ministers, like Tristan, George Young and Richard Needham, take the trouble to understand and deal with the sort of questions which will only appear in lengthy submissions at the bottom of their ministerial boxes. Douglas also wants me to encourage the Prime Minister, when I see him, to keep up his interest in Northern Ireland.

Monday 8 November

I saw John for breakfast this morning. He seemed much more cheerful than I had been led to expect. He is fine about what we are doing in Hong Kong and thinks that on most domestic policy issues, and even maybe on Europe, the worst is behind the government. Others have appeared a little more doubtful on this, given that for a small number on the right of the party Europe is now an issue pursued with religious fervour. On Northern Ireland, which I raised dutifully, John thinks there may be what they endlessly call in Northern Ireland 'a window of opportunity'. He obviously gets on very well with his Irish opposite number, Albert Reynolds. They met first when they were finance ministers; in my experience former holders of this office remain very clubby even when they go on to other things.

Later in the day I met Sir Philip Haddon-Cave, who is often spoken of as one of the architects of Hong Kong's economic success alongside the brilliant economist John Cowperthwaite. It is said that Cowperthwaite was sceptical of government playing any role in the economy at all. He

1. Greeted by the Chief Secretary, Sir David Ford, on our arrival on 9 July 1992. Lavender, Alice and Laura follow down the steps.

2. Hong Kongers get their priorities right – but what about Kate?

3. Getting out into the crowds was one of my favourite activities as Governor. This was mine and Lavender's first visit to Mong Kok soon after our arrival.

4. Meeting Lu Ping, head of the Hong Kong and Macau Affairs Office, in Beijing, 21 October 1992. It was not a meeting of minds.

5. Lee Kuan Yew trying to be unhelpful, Hong Kong University, December 1992.

6. The annual address to the Legislative Council (Legco) was always an important date in my calendar. In October 1993 it was focused on welfare provisions and democracy.

7. Whisky and Soda outside their kennel, Government House.

8. 'Lavender Patten speaks her mind' – not for first time, 1993.

9. My tennis partner Colin Grant always won of course.

10. With my press spokesman Mike Hanson in the Radio Television Hong Kong studios during my first year. Presumably I'd just made a good point.

11. Louise Law (née Cox), Lavender's Social Secretary and Tommy Chow, one of my Private Secretaries.

12. The Home Team (*L-R*): Elspeth Collins-Taylor, Housekeeper, Martin Dinham, Political Advisor, Steve Law, police inspector and Louise's husband, and Edward Llewellyn, political advisor.

13. Formidable allies – Peter Ricketts and Michael Sze on the Great Wall during a break from endless negotiations on constitutional issues, 1993.

14. And formidable rivals – Zhou Nan, head of the New China News Agency, straining the limits of politeness at a China National Day reception in 1993.

15. Gathering support for my plans to improve transport for those with disabilities.

16. Announcing the appointment of Donald Tsang (*second right*) to follow Sir Hamish McLeod (*right*) as Financial Secretary in March 1995. Anson Chan (*left*) and Kerry McGlynn (*back left*) look on.

17. Where's our driver?

18. The *Lady Maurine* went with the job – thanks be.

even harboured doubts about collecting economic statistics. Haddon-Cave did not go this far but there's no question of his important role in rejecting any idea of Hong Kong pursuing a Singapore style model of government intervention in economic matters. He was plainly a considerable admirer of Teddy Youde and believes – more and more people have been saying this to me – that it is a great tragedy that he died since it allowed the 'don't at any cost have a row with China' school to prevail in determining policy in the colony.

Tuesday 9 November

I went to see John Smith and Jack Cunningham in the Commons. They were extremely amiable. John Smith asked intelligent questions and was interested in whether the Chinese seem particularly interested in what would happen in the event of a Labour government. He has obviously twigged the fact that the next election is likely to come just before the end of our time in Hong Kong. He looks rather overweight but he's sharp and likeable. Come the next election I imagine he will be a terrific asset to his party. He has always appeared to me to be a very identifiable form of politician, a decent, radical Scottish socialist lawyer. He is also a brilliant public speaker, especially in the Commons, rather like Malcolm Rifkind, also from Scotland.

Wednesday 10 November

For the Cabinet committee meeting today we produced a rather complicated paper on the way forward. I had a chance of going through it yesterday with John Coles, the new permanent secretary at the FCO who has taken over from David Gillmore. We suggested aiming for a first-stage agreement in the next couple of rounds of talks, dealing with local elections in the district boards and the municipal council, the voting age and other more technical matters. We can also have a go at drafting and tabling the sort of oath which members of Legco might be able to take in order to guarantee a place on the through train. If we don't make progress on these questions in the next few weeks, we will go ahead and legislate on some of them anyway, giving ourselves some breathing space to decide what to do about the more complicated and controversial issues like the functional constituencies. But eventually Legco will have to decide. We will not be able to go any further than they are prepared to travel.

The meeting went pretty much to plan. The PM had (as ever) read the paper carefully. Ken Clarke and Tony Newton were very supportive. Ken said, 'We must trust the Governor's judgement on these matters.' Michael Heseltine asked some reasonable, searching questions about the impact of a row with China on our economy and on British business. I was able to point out that during the last few years, when we were leaning over backwards to avoid any fuss with China, the economic consequence was not just minimal; our exports were actually doing quite badly. Any British business which did not now get a contract in China would blame our policy in Hong Kong whatever the real circumstances. The Chinese of course fed this suspicion. Other than these questions we had an easy and helpful ride. The bad news this week was that we are going to have to work for a while without Robin McLaren. For some months he has been suffering terrible back pain and has been taken into hospital for an operation. He is a brave, phlegmatic and thoroughly decent man. For the next few rounds of talks, we tried to secure Tony Galsworthy to lead our team, but the FCO tells us that he can't be spared. So Christopher Hum is to do the job. I doubt this will be greeted in Hong Kong with delirious enthusiasm.

I had the usual round of interviews, including the *Today* programme and John Humphrys for a TV show called *On the Record*. It's much easier to do these interviews nowadays since (though I try not to be too cocky) I know a lot more about the subject than the interviewers, and in addition China has not been playing its hand very well. After a good dinner with Douglas and Judy Hurd, we watched the last episode of a series on Margaret Thatcher's years in Downing Street, which dealt with her fall. She wasn't critical of me but observed quite gently that I hadn't used any beautiful words when I spoke to her explaining why I thought she should step down. Perhaps I should have been more elegiac; but they weren't very elegiac times.

Thursday 11 November

We went up to Newcastle to see Kate and for me to give the Earl Grey memorial lecture on human rights. We stayed in a pub on the way to Hexham. Kate is living in a rented house with a few friends. It is the usual sort of student pit; they have obviously tried to clear it up before our arrival, but it is still fairly grotty in a friendly way. Lavender got me to admit that at least it's more salubrious than my small flat in Oxford when I was in my third year there. There was a packed audience for the lecture with an overspill. There aren't really any pickings for the Hong Kong press who have travelled all the way to the north-east to hear me. Beforehand we had tea with the Chancellor, Matthew Ridley, who is far nicer than his brother Nick. There was then a dinner given by the Vice Chancellor, James Wright, who is a classicist from Scotland and Cambridge. Slightly to my surprise he turned out to be a serious foodie and a collector of modern Scottish art. He and his wife were delightful company. I also met John

Ashton's mother, who is a professor at the University, and quite properly proud of her clever son.

Friday 12 November
On this crisp autumn day, we took Kate and a friend for a bracing walk along Hadrian's Wall and then out to dinner at the restaurant Number 21 Quayside, where we had a meal together last year. She brought along a very nice young man called Mark. Rather against her advice, he had on a tie and jacket for dinner. I doubt whether he has worn either for some time. He told us that his mother had asked him to cut his hair but he declined to go that far.

Sunday 14 November
Back on a plane to Hong Kong on Saturday night. While I've been away there has been a storm about the sacking of one of the senior staff of the Independent Commission Against Corruption. This has involved the use of the fairly draconian powers that we have to use in cases like this. Some people understandably get a bit nervous about this and I can see that it could all be abused after 1997. But there is really no other effective way of dealing with creeping corruption, and in order for us to use the powers it is always necessary to get judicial approval.

Monday 15 November
We still can't make up our minds about whether the Chinese are serious about wanting a deal of some acceptable sort. We occasionally get messages leaning in a positive direction through intermediaries like C. H. Tung. But whatever Lu Ping says in Beijing, the NCNA continue to give very hard-line briefings in Hong Kong. We spend a lot of time at meetings looking at possible draft oaths for would-be through train legislators. Quite how to describe subversion in such oaths, in a way which Chinese communists would find acceptable, seems some way on the road to intractable.

I had a meeting and dinner with President George Bush and his wife, Barbara. They are very fond of John Major. The former president shares John's concern about the press, arguing for example that they downplayed the economic statistics in America which had shown the beginnings of economic recovery. The statistics have now been revised upwards and he says that he thinks that this economic story torpedoed his campaign. All this said, he is remarkably un-bitter and very gentlemanly. He has near-perfect manners, rather like my old boss Peter Carrington. He is just about the only visiting political leader who has thanked me for all the help he has got from the police and others while he has been in Hong Kong. I do reckon that he was a very unlucky loser and a good example of a Conservative internationalist. I am not surprised that he got such good people to work for him. The Princess Royal also arrived, and is staying with us. She is here for some sort of international meeting involving horses. I'm sure that it's important; but I have not the faintest idea what it is all about.

I am becoming more preoccupied with the number of Vietnamese migrants who are still in Hong Kong and have a useful meeting with the new UNHCR [UN High Commissioner for Refugees] head about encouraging returns to Vietnam. I doubt whether there are any refugees, or rather illegal migrants, around the world who are being offered a better deal to go home than the one we are prepared to subsidize. We have still got about 30,000 in Hong Kong's camps and I fear we are likely to be left with an institutionalized hard core to deal with. Unfortunately, while the presence of these migrants and camps is a live issue in Hong Kong, this would be the same story anywhere. Perhaps the fact that so many Hong Kong citizens were themselves migrants makes it a less toxic issue than would otherwise have been the case. But we have to find some civilized way of making it more manageable. Lavender has paid more visits to the camps than I have and had more meetings with the voluntary organizations which are trying to help them.

Thursday 18 November

The day began with the doctor telling me that I have to lose more weight, but continued more satisfactorily, not least because I spent an hour with Henry Kissinger. He is never boring. He thinks that America has got to sort out its relationship with China and reckons that Bill Clinton will pay far more regard to jobs and prosperity in the run-up to the 1996 election than to human rights. American business wants access to the China market, though it is possible that some investors may find over the coming months they have done the equivalent of buying the Eiffel Tower, in other words put their money into dud investments. He talked quite a bit about Lee Kuan Yew, whom he describes as being in effect the mayor of a medium-sized city between Malaysia and Indonesia. (Harry, as he calls him, would love that.) This is one reason why the connection to China is so important to Lee. He told a very funny story about a visit made by the Singaporean leader to Harvard in the late 1960s. Lee had a discussion on Vietnam with a group of members of the faculty, who all gave him their views, which were highly critical of American policy. At the end they asked him what he thought and he just replied, 'I think you are a bunch of traitors.' He told me that Lee does not speak disdainfully of my intellect even though he strongly criticizes my views on life and politics. Henry

Kissinger, as he was departing, returns to this theme. 'At least he doesn't think you're stupid.'

We had dinner in the evening for the Princess Royal and her lady-in-waiting. It was just Lavender, Alice and me. As usual, she was intelligent and interesting company. When she takes on honorary responsibilities, she finds out a lot about the issues involved. So, for example, she is more knowledgeable than many of the ministers I used to deal with at Overseas Development on international aid. But I fear that I can't do horses.

Today, for reasons that no one can quite fathom, unless the Chinese have been selling on the basis of a pessimistic assessment of our talks, the Hang Seng Index plummeted. There have also been some pessimistic stories about the China economy. Barton Biggs, who works for Morgan Stanley, and who was puffing China's economic prospects back in September, has now said that it is a bubble and he has advised people to sell Chinese stocks. I sometimes think the extraordinary thing is not that stockbrokers are so highly paid but that they are paid at all.

Friday 19 November

When will this all end? The 16th round of talks began today with the Chinese side back-pedalling fast and with no apparent embarrassment on what they promised in the last round about making progress on some less important issues. How are we supposed to know what their game is? The rules seem to be written by Lewis Carroll. Perhaps this is all a sophisticated negotiating tactic or, on the other hand, maybe they were just stringing us along. They aren't prepared to do the sort of first-stage deal that we could manage, and even appear to be going back on what they said about the local elections, namely to agree to disagree, with the possibility of different situations before and after 1997. They now refuse to accept that we can abolish appointed seats. I hope they are not miscalculating and misreading any signals from us or being badly advised by some of our home critics. We may just have to tell them that if nothing is accomplished in the next round we shall pull the plug. Chinese Vice Foreign Minister Jiang Enzhu is said to have come close at one point to frothing at the mouth in denouncing our infamy.

Saturday 20 November

To cheer me up, we had a visit from Chancellor Kohl* on his way back from Beijing. I have got to know him a bit over the years and we get on

* Helmut Kohl became leader of the CDU in Germany in 1973 and was the Chancellor for 16 years from 1982 to 1998. He shared with Bill Clinton the ability to draw principles and

very well. I saw him when I used to do exchange visits with the Konrad Adenauer Stiftung when I was director of the Conservative Research Department, and again more frequently when I was chairman of the Conservative Party and attempting to negotiate the party's membership in the European Parliament of the centre-right grouping – the European People's Party. Surprisingly, before my time as chairman, Margaret had been keen on the idea and John Major gave it a big push. Kohl suggested that we should talk together on our own with just his interpreter as we had done in the past. She often seems to know exactly how he's going to end a sentence when he begins it. We had a cheerful but rather meandering discussion. He obviously sees China through the prism of what has happened in the Soviet Union and central and eastern Europe. He doesn't think that the opening up of the market will do other than erode the structure of Marxism/Leninism. He larded discussion about China with lots of references to Prussia, Bismarck and the Stasi. He is particularly interested in the activities of the intelligence community in Hong Kong, seeing similarities between our city and Berlin, but nevertheless expressed scepticism about the product of intelligence. He wasn't a bit surprised that the business community is not supporting our efforts to put in place fair elections. He doesn't think that they are likely to look further ahead than the following day and the profits they can make. Elections don't have a place on balance sheets. He said that Hong Kong came up during his discussions and that he was promised by the Chinese that they would go for a smooth transfer. It's not unfair of course to wonder how different his own attitude is to that of the businessmen he criticizes when he himself is talking to Chinese leaders. We had just over an hour together. Before leaving he expressed once again great enthusiasm about John Major and some understanding about Britain's problems over Maastricht. He invited me to go and see him next time I'm in Germany. I wish he had worked to help us revalue sterling within the European exchange rate mechanism before we crashed out of it. Much as I like him, I doubt whether he lost very much sleep over that.

Back from Beijing, Michael Sze (who as the new Secretary for Constitutional Affairs has been part of our team there) told me how appallingly badly the Chinese side had treated Christopher Hum in particular and indeed all of them by the end of the meetings. This behaviour continued during the end of talks banquet (if that is the right word for a meal with

quite profound lessons from simple anecdotes. I enjoyed his company and so did John Major. But experience does not suggest that he ever did as much to meet British positions in the EU as we thought he would.

these bullying and reckless hacks). Jiang Enzhu refused to talk to Christopher for the first three courses. He was subsequently rude and didn't see our negotiators off the premises. And they tell us that this is the greatest civilization in the world. I have to go on believing, which is I hope and trust true, that there is a difference between China and the Communist Party. Michael for example is Chinese, courteous, kind and intelligent. It's the party which is the awful problem. I rely on Michael, like Anson, a great deal. They are both very honest with me and tell me when they think I am wrong.

Sunday 21 November

William and Gillian Rees-Mogg came to dinner during a visit to the city; their son Jacob is staying with us while preparing for a job here. We have known him since he was a titch – five going on 45. He's a kind and amusing young man who has decided to embark on life dressed and behaving as though he was playing the part of an English upper-class twit in an Ealing Studios film. He comes on hikes as though dressed for the City, though he does take his tie off when he goes swimming. He is kind to Alice and helps her with her maths homework.

Monday 22 November

We began work with a discussion on the 16th round. I'm not sure how many people outside could believe the way the Chinese behaved. I wish that everything had been recorded for the TV. One of their more surreal tactics is to decline to explain what something means unless we offer a concession on our side. In other words, openness, accuracy and transparency are themselves regarded as Chinese concessions. This is a long way from the Confucius Analect in which the master says that the first thing a ruler should do is to rectify the names, by which he means that what you say should represent what the word is actually meant to signify. The bad good news is that this can't go on very much longer. We will need to carry Exco with us in sorting out the best way of concluding this purgatorial episode. I made a speech at the Foreign Correspondents' Club at lunchtime (the club made famous in a John le Carré novel) about the universality of values. It was an abbreviation of the lecture I gave in Newcastle and dealt with the relationship between human rights, the rule of law, democracy and economic progress.

I had afterwards one of those curious discussions with Lydia, a result I think (as I've said before) of the extent to which in the past leading members of the community, and I suppose everyone else, were kept in the dark about so much of what the British government was up to. It led to a rather unhealthy search for conspiracies fed by the most improbable rumours. Lydia has heard – from whom? – that I didn't go to Newcastle at all. Apparently, I was either being interviewed for the job of president of the European Commission or attending a special secret Cabinet meeting. It is said that I gave my lecture in Newcastle via a television link. When I probed gently on the basis for this, what it amounted to was that the daughter of Philip Crawley, the very nice former editor of the *South China Morning Post*, who is at Newcastle University, tried to go to my lecture but couldn't get into the main theatre. She went to the overspill instead, where they had to watch me on television. Of such things are conspiracies constructed.

Tuesday 23 November

C. H. Tung came to see me twice before Exco. He has been talking to Lu Ping, who wants to assure him of Chinese sincerity, claims that the Chinese haven't changed their position at all, and that he cannot understand why we are making so much fuss about the voting method in Legco elections. At a long Exco meeting there was general agreement that we should go ahead with what is described as a part one bill dealing with the easier issues without too much delay.

Wednesday 24 November

A highlight of the week was a lunch with the American Chamber of Commerce. They are incomparably more sophisticated than most other groups of business leaders. They said just the right things to and about China. Maybe it helps to have the American economy behind you.

Thursday 25 November

During a discussion on trade, Hamish MacLeod gave an interesting readout on the Apec meeting which he has just attended. He said that Jiang Zemin – all those present at these meetings are national leaders or their substitutes – only contributed what he was able to read out, but one rather bizarre result of this was that what he said invariably had very little relationship to what others had just been saying during the discussion.

Friday 26 November

The first day of the 17th round of talks – yes, 17th – went entirely as predicted. The Chinese went back to what they seemed to be saying a couple of rounds ago. There was no give at all on the voting method for Legco elections and a reaffirmation that after 1997 members of district boards and municipal councils will be appointed with the Hong Kong government able to decide the appropriate numbers. Any idea that the Hong Kong government or Legco should have any autonomy in this matter is for the birds. So much for the Joint Declaration. Predictions about an imminent breakdown in talks come thick and fast, partly a result of some judicious leaking on our part. Mike Hanson did this very well. Understandably maybe, the embassy in Beijing and Christopher Hum are trying to find ways in which we can keep things ticking over. Most of us take the view that it's once again a case of 'Carpe diem'. If Horace meant by that that we should enjoy ourselves then it's certainly true that nothing could be much more miserable than allowing Chinese apparatchiks to continue stringing us along with no regard for the best interests of people in Hong Kong.

Sunday 28 November

We had an informal Exco discussion in GH in the evening. Andrew Li and Denis Chang were particularly strong in pointing out that the latest proposal about appointments after 1997 to the local government institutions is a serious erosion of the autonomy of the Hong Kong Special Administration Region government and would be a flat contravention of the JD and the BL. There's no sign of Exco going soggy and general acceptance that we should go ahead as we agreed with London – splitting our proposals and tabling legislation on the first part of them – and that if we were to go back on this we wouldn't have any serious position in any future negotiations.

Monday 29 November

I had an investiture this evening. We do these in the ballroom with a police band at the end of a large room with the doors behind open to the main corridor of the building. About halfway through the ceremony I looked over the heads of those who had come to see their relations honoured and caught sight of four or five of Alice's schoolfriends creeping down the stairs in their Doc Martens from the tower where she has her bedroom and out into the main part of the house to make their escape. It's fun seeing normal life carrying on while I'm doing these duties. I doubt anything happens like this in Buckingham Palace.

Tuesday 30 November

The formal Exco meeting today was a continuation of Sunday's discussion. Almost everyone favoured gazetting our proposals this Friday and introducing legislation in Legco next week. My first instincts are on the same side. But the Foreign Secretary wanted to give it another week largely because his timetable over the next few days is impossible. We spent some time afterwards looking at drafts of my statement on all this, the press briefing, the draft of the White Paper and so on.

Wednesday 1 December

Before making a statement on Thursday in Legco, I had discussions with lots of legislators, including Allen Lee. He has just been up to Beijing, where he was given a rough time with officials bending his arm while he was trying to persuade them not to be provocative and stupid. He was annoyed by the way they tried to beat him up. He is fundamentally a decent man who occasionally falls among rotters and the faint of heart. Even when I have disagreed with him I still find him very likeable.

Thursday 2 December

I made my statement to Legco about our intentions on handling the electoral proposals: we will put our original plans to Legco if we cannot reach an acceptable agreement with Beijing. It seemed to go pretty well and the press was fine. The only comment so far from Beijing is that if we introduce any legislation at all on our own, that will end the talks.

Saturday 4 December

There was a sort of mini blast from Beijing this morning. They claimed that they made what is a very good offer and that we have behaved wholly unreasonably, not least by claiming that Legco should have more than an advisory role. So far the polls suggest that opinion is running in our favour by a margin of about two to one. According to our friend from Northern Ireland, Hugh O'Neill, Peter Sutch of Swire's told him and others at a briefing for businessmen that Hong Kong was being run by 'a politician from Somerset'. Sutch's brother is a monk at Downside, but I still don't think that this was meant as a compliment.

Monday 6 December

Before having a talk to Francis Cornish,* our consul-general and the main focus for British trade efforts in the territory, I had a look at the British trade figures. Francis gets a huge amount of flak for our policies allegedly screwing British industry's prospects in the China market. The official

* Francis Cornish had been the Foreign Office spokesman for Douglas Hurd and deputy private secretary to the Prince of Wales. He was senior Trade Commissioner in Hong Kong from 1993 to 1997 and British consul-general after that date until 1998. He then became British ambassador to Israel from 1998 to 2001. After retirement from the diplomatic service, he was chairman of South West tourism and had a smallholding in the Quantocks. Magnificently unflappable as some British businessmen flapped all around him.

figures confirm that our exports to China actually fell during the high days of genuflecting to China from 1985 to 1992. Amazingly at the beginning of this period we had a surplus with China, but by the end the surplus was two to one in China's favour. We will see in due course what is happening while I have been behaving like a Somerset politician. Douglas Hurd's statement in the House of Commons went very well. Every intervention on our proposals for the way forward has been supportive. The House of Lords has been more negative. I suppose it is best described these days as Westminster's version of a functional constituency.

Tuesday 7 December

We came back after Exco from a very successful housing visit with big and enthusiastic crowds to learn that the Hang Seng Index has started to rise very steeply. Can this be Chinese mainland buyers putting their cash on the table before the megaphones are turned up in Beijing? A group of pro-Beijing advisers have gone there to – surely not give advice – receive their instructions. Nothing is emerging from the latest JLG discussions. No surprise there.

Thursday 9 December

We woke up and turned on the radio to the pinched tones of Percy Cradock giving his very critical evidence to the foreign affairs committee. I guess he'll make a bit of a stir at home, but it really doesn't matter much here since (to put it charitably) he would never win a popularity contest. It's interesting that we have produced a generation of Sovietologists who thought that it was right to stand up to the Soviet Union alongside a generation of Sinologists who thought we should cave in to China.

Friday 10 December

Lavender and I went off to a ball organized by the Black Watch at Stanley Fort. We always get someone to give us a short tutorial on Highland dancing before events like this, which helps to avoid too much embarrassment. We did rather a good reel together and I got to dance as well with the colonel's wife, who was perfectly charming and told me without any self-pity a harrowing story about what all parents fear above all else, the loss of a child. Dancing went on far too late, and, as Margaret Thatcher's parliamentary private secretary, Ian Gow, used to say, wine was taken.

Saturday 11 December

The noises from Beijing have gone up several notches. Both Qian Qichen and Li Peng talked ominously about the damage done to British trade and the economic relationship with China. This was in marked contrast with Ambassador Ma in London, who spent part of this week going around advising British firms to invest in China despite the row.

Tuesday 14 December

Apart from endless talks this week about how to handle China in the New Year, the most interesting discussions have been about pensions and whether we should introduce a comprehensive pay-as-you-go scheme with an iron link between money paid in and pension withdrawn. This is a big issue for Hong Kong. Until now the government's policy has been to make private schemes mandatory, but this has become more and more nonsensical as the government had to accept contingent liability for any schemes which go wrong. Neither Anson nor I are wholly happy about introducing a new scheme, but we concluded that this is the only way we can meet the community's demands for better care for the elderly.

Wednesday 15 December

Michael Sze introduced the first-stage bill in Legco today. We had the private office Christmas lunch and Lavender's brother and his wife – Malcolm and Jenny – arrived for Christmas. My sister, her husband, Pete, and their daughter, Lucy, arrived as well, and Kate and Laura flew in too. Up and up went the Hang Sang Index, maybe a reaction to Laura's arrival. I had a long meeting with Anson and the officials involved about housing, sewage strategy and land use planning in the New Territories. I am rather an expert on sewage, much to officials' surprise, a consequence of my ministerial responsibilities a few years ago. I always seemed to be dealing with sewage plumes and outfalls during European meetings. I've also had lots of interviews with foreign press and politicians this week; I suppose many of them are having Christmas breaks with better weather than back home. In London the *Sun* had a go at me. I bet that's the first time they have ever had an article about Hong Kong. Various old foes are said to have had a hand in this. Do they really want me to return to British politics?

Wednesday 22 December

The weather is gorgeous and the stock market is going through the roof. We had a lovely carol concert yesterday. With the stock market still roaring ahead, we visited the school in Father Lambertoni's parish for the end-of-term celebrations today. It was great fun and Cardinal Wu brought me a Christmas message from the Pope (how nice of him to think of me!).

Thursday 23 December

Sir S. Y. Chung came to see me. He was a stalwart of past colonial administrations, serving both on Exco and Legco. During the 1980s he tried to play a more assertive role on behalf of Hong Kong public opinion in the discussions on the handover – being tougher with China – but was rebuffed rather rudely by the British government and MPs. Perhaps inevitably, having failed to influence the departing colonial power, he eventually went over to the other side and is now one of Beijing's advisers. I rather admired him and thought he had been badly used in the past. He didn't believe much in democracy but felt passionately about Hong Kong. He gave me a long explanation about China's position. At the end of it I'm not sure that I understood it any better but felt I should keep in touch with him. I wished I'd seen more of him earlier.

Thursday 30 December

I played some tennis with Colin on Christmas Eve. He is wonderful to play with because he just keeps hitting the ball back until eventually I make an error, as of course I always do, and is thoroughly good company. He runs a small business at the moment renting videos mostly to expats. After tennis I did some late Christmas shopping and after a delicious dinner we went to midnight mass at St John's Anglican cathedral. The house was absolutely full for Christmas Day and the days after. Lots of friends from Hong Kong, relations and our American friend Mike Medavoy with his son Brian. We played lots of games – carpet bowls, Chinese checkers, table tennis, charades and so on – and after Christmas made several expeditions and had an evening at the jazz club.

By this time, Ken Clarke and Gillian were staying with us (on the way to meetings in Seoul), including some officials and a brilliant young private secretary called Jeremy Heywood who looked far too young to be carrying so much responsibility. Ken said that he was superb. As well as taking the Clarkes to the jazz club (about which Ken was very complimentary, partly I guess because Guy Barker was playing), we also went bird spotting in the Mai Po marshes. Ken claimed to have spotted 50 different sorts of bird. We also had a good hike on Lantau, finding all sorts of wild flowers. The Clarkes and the Treasury team left us for South Korea. One game in which we did not involve them was our extremely noisy version of sardines around the house. I won by cheating, taking a bottle of wine out onto the veranda next to my dressing room and enjoying a quiet glass while everyone ran around looking for me.

There was one drama. On Christmas night, the stewards forgot to put the candles out after dinner. Mike woke up early on Boxing Day morning and came to knock on our door at about 7.15 a.m. to say that he could smell smoke. I went down and there was a blaze over the fireplace in the dining room; flames were leaping out of the wall, so it seemed. Anyway, I got lots of water and put it out with a couple of stewards who had woken by that time. Meanwhile (as Lavender noted) the cooks next door in the kitchen were happily making breakfast unaware, but it caused considerable damage in the dining room which we have only just redecorated. It really could have been much nastier. Elspeth has gone home for Christmas. It just shows what happens when she's not around. I hope she'll forgive us. I assured the stewards that it wasn't really their fault. At the end of dinner we had all rushed away from the table to start playing a noisy game in the sitting room, and I think it distracted the staff, who were probably slightly mystified by why and how we were having so much fun. The dog that didn't bark was of course the fire alarm – a room full of smoke but not a sound from the alarm.

Between Christmas and the New Year there was a steady drumbeat of criticism from Beijing and indeed quite a lot of activity in London, part of it apparently resulting from Lord Young's efforts to persuade the business and political communities that I was ruining Britain's prospects in China. The word has it that Tim Bell, the ubiquitous PR man, is helping him out, for example with the *Sun*.

We had one more direct confrontation in Hong Kong. Before our enjoyable walk on Lantau I had to go first to the inaugural ceremony for the Tian Tan Buddha statue at Po Lin Monastery on the island. It's a large, indeed colossal, bronze statue of the seated Buddha situated on a hill above the monastery. The monks were lined up on the steps leading to the statue wearing saffron robes and carrying gold and orange parasols. Zhou Nan and I both had to make speeches. He greeted me with a Buddhist gesture rather than a handshake, which the press all took as an insult. In his speech Zhou said that China had always respected people's religious opinions and beliefs. You couldn't make it up.

Monday 3 January 1994

There is clearly growing interest in Anson among the senior communist officials. They seem to be particularly concerned about the civil service transition and economic issues. Maybe it indicates a little nervousness on their part about their ability to cope competently with Hong Kong. I hope they will trust her. She would cope very competently with Hong Kong without a lot of political fuss. She comes from such a distinguished patriotic background, never communist but a greatly respected Chinese family.

I have made Rosanna Wong chairman of the housing authority and we had a good discussion with Anson and Hamish about housing policy. The authority needless to say is flush with money and the main question is what to do with it. Rosanna is handling the job with considerable political skill.

Tuesday 4 January

In Exco there seemed to be an emerging consensus for sticking to my original '92 proposals in the second stage bill that we will put to Legco in the next few months. One of the principal considerations with everyone is of course what will actually get through the legislature. But we don't have to make our minds up finally until nearer the time. The Preliminary Work Committee met in Beijing. It seems that about one third of the members have foreign passports – a vote of confidence in the future I suppose. There was a poll showing that people don't regard this group as representing their interests, about two to one against. They are pressing us to send civil servants to brief them in Beijing and accuse us of not being cooperative because we decline to do so. They just want us to give them credibility as what they call a second stove. I'm perfectly happy that the first stove should talk to them in Hong Kong as we would to any other group, but we are not going to cut across existing means of communication such as the JLG and the committee that deals with airport issues.

Thursday 6 January

Among my guests in the first week back was Senator Mitch McConnell and his fairly new wife, Elaine Chao, who was born in Taiwan. At the end of a long conversation, she asked me whether we are not in the same position as the recently defeated Mayor of New York who has been making appointments just before his Republican opponent takes office. I replied politely, noting among other things that we still have three and a half years before we leave. But I don't give the reply that I should have offered, which is that, if we had been in the position of the incumbent mayor, I doubt whether we would have been defeated. There can't be many other examples of colonial situations where the local citizens want the colonial power to stay on.

Friday 7 January

Alastair Goodlad and Peter Ricketts are with us to talk about what we should say in a White Paper and in the preparations for the next Cabinet committee meeting. Do we stick to the 1992 plans or amend them, particularly to reduce the number of voters in functional constituencies and to make the election committee less democratic? My own view is that there is not much to be said for abandoning our original proposals and that we should press ahead with the second bill as soon as the first is out of the way. We also have to take account of the fact that drafting a bill based on the putative compromises looks tricky; we can't really disguise the fact that they would be an obvious second best. A further complicating factor is the timing of the National People's Congress meeting in March, though I really wonder whether we should bother much about this since its noises about Hong Kong are entirely predictable even now.

Monday 10 January
We had a stimulating meeting and dinner with Rod and Emily MacFarquhar. He is probably the most respected commentator in the academic world on Chinese politics. He thinks that after the death of Deng, there will be a three-way split and perhaps a fight between a group rather on the left around Li Peng, a more centrist crowd behind Jiang Zemin, and a competent and conceivably reformist faction behind Zhu Rongji. He seems to expect the balance to be held between the second and third groups, though whether that will lead to real reform is another matter. The centrist group are pretty useless but they are great political survivors.

I saw Sir S. Y. Chung again. He has fallen hook, line and sinker for the Chinese version of the end of the talks. It's sad and surprising. He used to argue that we should hold on to Victoria island and bring in water by tanker if necessary. After taking Jack Cunningham on a visit to some of our public housing with Rosanna Wong, I had dinner with the Australian consul-general to discuss my forthcoming visit. The Australian papers are writing up a clash between Paul Keating and Gareth Evans, with the former not wanting to support what we are doing in Hong Kong but the latter doing so vigorously. Keating doesn't want to do anything which might upset China and its economic and trade relationship with Australia – his view of it anyway.

Wednesday 12 January
Jack Cunningham, the Labour Party's foreign affairs spokesman, came to lunch with his wife. They are in Hong Kong for a few days. I gave him a full briefing and he is overwhelmingly helpful.

Thursday 13 January
I had to answer questions in Legco after Lavender and I had too good a lunch at the Ritz Carlton with the Duchess of York and David Tang. While sipping my wine carefully, I looked enviously at the two unfinished bottles

of Château Pétrus on the table. The Duchess was charming and very much on best behaviour, though I don't know what bad behaviour would have been like.

Friday 14 January

Hugo Young has been in Hong Kong and has written a thoughtful piece for the *Guardian*. To put it mildly he doesn't think that the rich are behaving well, though at the 25th anniversary ball for the Community Chest, held in our ballroom at GH this evening, they coughed up huge amounts of money for good causes – HK$7 million in all – 2 million is raised in an auction for a Ferrari. I think that if we were able to aggregate the value of the jewellery on show we would have raised a lot more than that. When I think back to charity functions, for example for the Conservative Party back home, I recall coronation chicken and auctions conducted by Jeffrey Archer. The main point that Hugo makes is that when he was last in Hong Kong four years ago the rich were all in a panic and criticizing the Governor for being too weak. Now they say the Governor is too tough. This also appears to be Geoffrey Howe's line. He is starting to give interviews in London criticizing our stance just before I have to give evidence to the Foreign Affairs select committee.

Monday 17 January

At a conference on press freedom organized by the Freedom Forum, I made the usual points but got one or two difficult questions about how far we have come in Hong Kong in reviewing our laws on the press, introducing freedom of information laws and tabling more legislation to protect rights in general. The truth is that we have done a bit but we should probably have gone further, and I hope still can do so. The main reason for caution so far is that there is quite a conservative feeling in the political establishment, both Exco and the administration, as well as back in London, about human rights protections. The argument is that we shouldn't go out of our way to antagonize the Chinese on too many things. We may need to review this rather more before we leave. As William Shawcross said to me when he was here, and has subsequently written, it is important for us to put lots of panes of glass in the windows in Hong Kong before we leave. It will be vital for people to be able to see when the protections for human rights are being broken.

Tuesday 18 January

Lavender opened a new centre for the charity Against Child Abuse. For reasons deep in the social culture it is very difficult for the government to intervene in tough family situations in order to move and safeguard abused children. Lavender says that most children in institutions in Hong Kong are orphans or have been rejected by their parents for some reason. Very few have been removed from the family home against the wishes of their parents. But it does appear that more cases of abuse are being reported by neighbours. It shows that public awareness of children having rights is starting to increase. This is the sort of area that Lavender used to work in as a barrister.

I talked to the CS and the FS about the draft budget statement. Our latest figures for the predicted fiscal surplus in 1997–98 have almost doubled from HK$78 billion to over 130 billion. This puts our proposals on the airport and container terminal in a slightly new context. We can certainly afford to be more generous in making offers on the airport, and could perhaps embarrass the Chinese by meeting the whole of their demands on funding. We can also look at other ways of funding the container terminal if, that is, we really need more container terminals.

Before taking the night plane back to London, I saw the heads of our overseas offices who give lots of evidence about the French and Germans sucking up to China. The rather shameless way in which the French have just done this makes one wonder whether the word perfidious was attached to the right side of the Channel.

Wednesday 19 January

I arrived home at the flat at the crack of dawn, took Laura on a spending spree ('don't tell your mother'), and then went off for a very dreary meeting with Geoffrey Howe. He kept on falling asleep during my attempts to explain what we are doing. His most substantive point was that we have done something fundamentally wrong on functional constituencies, but he doesn't quite say what it is. I hope that any criticisms will be conveyed in his customary code. He is a decent man who has done great service to the Conservative Party and the country. I saw him having to take far too many brickbats from Margaret. I think the problem today is that he feels that his baby – the Joint Declaration – will grow up into a difficult teenager. Some of those who were involved in negotiating the JD now have some reluctance to accept that English words should mean what they say, even when expressed to a Chinese communist. You cannot live indefinitely with concepts which mean one thing to Parliament in Britain and the citizens of Hong Kong and something completely different in negotiations in Beijing. Is the rule of law, and is democracy, to have one meaning in Hong Kong and another in the capital of China?

I saw Robin McLaren before a number of meetings in the FCO. Even though he doesn't look awfully well, he is about to return to his post in Beijing. He is rather worried about the upcoming National People's Congress and what will be said there about Britain and Hong Kong. I think this is another argument for introducing the second stage of our proposals as soon as possible after we have got the first-stage bill through Legco towards the end of February. Delay until after Easter, for example, would give the rats an awful lot of time to gnaw away at everything.

Thursday 20 January

I gave evidence to the select committee, supported by David Ford, a welcome face, and Michael Sze, who are holding things together for us in London. The main points I made in my evidence are fairly familiar. First, it may be true to say that as a politician I probably do take more account of public accessibility and accountability than some others might. Second, I don't regard Hong Kong as an unnecessary irritant in the Sino-British relationship. There is no element in our relationship with China which is as important as Hong Kong; it's natural that I should see things through the prism of our last major colonial responsibility. Third, I don't regard it as acceptable to try to cover up matters of substance with forms of words packed with strong nouns and weak verbs. Finally, I'm not persuaded that, because the Chinese may behave in a thuggish way, we should always give in to them.

Monday 24 January

After the *Today* programme, I had a meeting in the FCO with Douglas and senior officials. He is completely on my side on the way forward. The 1992 proposals are the ones most likely to win majority support in Legco. We should introduce the bill as soon as the first one is out of the way and show the minimum excitement over the threats that China makes on trade. The subsequent Cabinet committee meeting goes well with everyone very supportive, as they were apparently last week during a full Cabinet discussion. At present, government backing at home is the least of my problems. I had a City lunch with business and banking leaders. Jim Prior was there and in a very gentlemanly way expressed understanding of our position but nervousness about the threats to our trade prospects in such a rapidly growing market. I don't think that the financial services people there are too worried. China needs them and I don't think they will suffer from any discrimination against the UK, but Ambassador Ma can still make knees knock elsewhere. The figures of course still tell a rather different story, but the Chinese get away with their often repeated threats to British exports and investment.

Wednesday 26 January

We arrived back in Hong Kong on a glorious clear day. The Chinese have just put out a ridiculous statement on the airport, obviously angered by the vote in favour of new funding for it by 38 to 2 in Legco on the previous Friday. We are going to put them on the spot now by making a new offer which will meet all their financial demands. I guess that will simply encourage them to redefine what the demands are or just to say that those were never their demands at all. Sicilian threats.

Just to lower my spirits, I saw Willie Purves after lunch, who is at his most sanctimoniously thuggish. He told me that many business leaders are talking to him about the difficulties of our present policy and its implications for British trade with China. (No figures or examples given of course.) He is sure that they will want to call on the Prime Minister to change tack. This will be very awkward for John Major at a time when he is under a lot of political pressure. But they will want a U-turn in government policy, otherwise they will be reluctant to support the government in general or the Conservative Party in particular. All this was said with a lot of sad shaking of the head. I can't wait for him to go back to London. He also told me that he is going to address the Conservative foreign affairs backbench committee on 22 February. Of course, he would like to talk just about banking, but he fears they may want him to talk about China and Hong Kong. Not being a politician, he added, he might find it difficult to give adroit answers. I doubt whether in fact he will have any difficulty at all in saying that I'm completely off my rocker. How much I prefer dealing with old-fashioned pro-Beijing hardliners such as Tsang Yok-sing* and Elsie Tu.

We have started to prepare for my visit to Australia. I had several interviews with the Australian press and CNN. Lavender and I went to southern district near Stanley accompanied by Australian journalists. We started in a squatter area which is apparently about to be cleared and were mobbed at a children's club by lots of excited kids. Lavender insisted on seeing some of the toilets and kitchens, which looked pretty primitive. We went on from there to see some of the massive rebuilding programme with impressive new blocks of flats which have been splendidly landscaped. Big crowds of cheering and excited residents should make a statement on Australian TV about whether people in Hong Kong think we are trying to do the right sort of things.

* Tsang Yok-sing was born in Guangdong and moved with his family to Hong Kong as a child. He was a founding member of the pro-Beijing party.

Thursday 27 January

Two lots of goodbyes. First Lavender and I said farewell to Sgt Lo, who has been looking after the gates and the security at GH for several years, and I also had a last discussion with David Gillmore, who is making a farewell visit before retiring as permanent secretary. He is far from convinced that China's emergence as a superpower will go smoothly. He thinks that at the moment people are treating China a bit like they treated Germany in the 1930s. He doubts whether many Chinese businessmen understand at present what we are saying about the rule of law. I pointed out that the more cynical among them make it clear when pressed that they don't really expect the rule of law to survive 1997. They shrug their shoulders, accepting that Hong Kong will then be a Chinese city much like any other.

Charles Powell (who since he sadly left the FCO has been an adviser to Jardine's among other things) called in for a chat. He doesn't think the business criticism at home is yet too severe, not least since nobody can actually point to real examples of discriminatory treatment by the Chinese. We also discussed the wretched takeover code again. Martin Dinham is having to spend an inordinate amount of time on it and it's driving us both mad. If Jardine's want to try their arm in court so be it. But there's no way I can simply ride roughshod over what the SFC [Securities and Futures Commission] has argued.

Friday 28 January

Lu Ping tore into us over the airport, making totally fabricated claims that we had agreed with Beijing levels of borrowing for the airport and railway which we are now exceeding. Apparently even Percy Cradock says this isn't true. Wow! We have no idea what game the Chinese are playing. It may be they are getting nervous that we will make an offer which they would have difficulty refusing. On the other hand, they may just want any offer we put on the table, and which they accept, to look like a Chinese victory rather than a triumph of common sense. Anyway, we are putting the final touches to a new offer, which, in view of their allegations about secret deals, we will make public before the Chinese New Year.

Tuesday 1 February

Before heading off to Australia, we clarified the details of our airport funding plans which will be passed to Chinese officials before they are published, and also the arrangements we need to make for Legco debates on our first stage political proposals at the end of the month and for the subsequent White Paper and the gazetting of our second stage bill. I continued to urge that the review of legislation on press freedom produces sustainable and defensible answers. Among the several more interviews that I do with business leaders, the one with the geologist, Sir John Jenkins, who is now chairman of Shell, took the first prize for ghastliness. (I wasn't in the best of spirits, because I had just been speaking for 2½ hours.) He was keen to tell me that everyone in London wants my guts for garters, that Ambassador Ma was an excellent fellow and had made no threats to British interests, and that Hong Kong's success at the moment was a sign that everybody was happily waiting for 1997 and Britain's departure. I learned afterwards that Shell was trying to start a US$4 billion refinery and petrochemical project in China alongside PowerGen who would be required to pick up responsibility for most of the financial exposure. I could not help wondering how what I had heard would square with the commitments made by Shell in their annual reports to confront the world's social concerns.

Saturday 5 – Tuesday 22 February
We arrived in Australia on the 5th, had a few days holiday north of Sydney at a small resort, and then embarked on a round of Sydney, Melbourne and Canberra. I made speeches and had multiple meetings in each place. Two in Sydney were particularly interesting. I met the distinguished Australian jurist, Justice Michael Kirby, who has been very active internationally in support of human rights. He follows closely what is happening in Hong Kong. Before my trip, there had been much speculation about whether Paul Keating would see me and how the Australian government would balance the difference between the Prime Minister's and Foreign Minister's views on China. In the event, and I think slightly to his surprise, I got on rather well with Keating when we met at his official Sydney residence looking out across the harbour. I noted at the outset that we were both the offspring of Irish immigrants. I don't think he was expecting this. He had obviously anticipated meeting what Gareth subsequently described to me in his words as 'a Tory weasel' and a be-feathered colonial Governor. He was highly intelligent, listened more than I'd expected to what I had to say and gave me a lot more time than the press had been led to expect. Everyone says that he has a chip on the shoulder of pretty substantial proportions being both clever yet not formally educated. He clearly resents the fact that some, because of other advantages, get to the top in what is called a meritocracy without having much discernible merit at all. When I met Gareth in Canberra he told me that he had teased the Prime Minister about the fact that we seemed to have got on so well.

Everywhere we went the boat was pushed out. We saw state governors and stayed with the Governor in Melbourne in his magnificent mansion. In Canberra we had good discussions with Gareth and his impressive foreign ministry officials. I enjoyed an engagement with the Australian Asia Institute. In remarks after my speech, one of Australia's leading sinologists who had been ambassador in Beijing noted the tendency of the old school of diplomacy to accept negotiations with China entirely on that country's terms. He said that I was doing the rest of Asia a favour by focusing attention on China's treatment of Hong Kong since this would be a paradigm of China's treatment of other countries in the region. Throughout our visit I had loads of telegrams from London and Hong Kong about the publication of our White Paper and the other arrangements concerning the next phase of our political agenda. Everything seemed to be going smoothly.

We both loved Australia. But Lavender noticed that state governors are treated differently here. When we paid a call on the Governor of New South Wales, the butler walked out backwards after serving us tea, bowing as he went, and the Governor was served his tea and biscuits first before the guests. Lavender's conclusion was that Australia wasn't ready quite yet to become a republic. I'm glad that nobody has to walk backwards when leaving the presence of the Governor of Hong Kong.

Wednesday 23 February

The bill that Legco considered today dealt with what should have been – at least if one wasn't dealing with Beijing – the less contentious part of our plans. In the geographically-based constituencies in Legco and the municipal councils and district boards, elections would be on the basis of a single seat, single vote system. Appointments to the local government bodies would be abolished, and the voting age would be reduced to 18. We would allow Hong Kong residents who were also members of the Chinese People's Congress to stand for elections in Hong Kong. The beginning of debate had to wait for the rejection of an attempt by Elsie Tu, giving a vitriolic speech, to defer discussion. We won this vote by 36 to 23, and then went on to win the second reading vote by 48 to 2. In the light of her performance, I have decided to rename her, Elsie Vous.

Thursday 24 February

We published the White Paper, following which I made clear at one of my regular question and answer sessions in Legco that in early March we would proceed to legislate on my 1992 proposals. The questions homed in on whether or not I would block any bill which gave Hong Kong more democracy than I had proposed, and whether I was prepared to contemplate any amendments to the legislation. I tried to tread the line between on the one hand saying that we wanted to get the bill through Legco and on the other hand seeming inflexible in responding to majority feeling in the council. Needless to say, all this increased Martin Lee's anxieties that we were going to conspire with some members in the centre of opinion in Legco to water the bill down. I suppose he is entitled to want to have it all ways. He intends to vote against the bill to try to make it more democratic while at the same time we are supposed to defend it at every stage. I hope on reflection he will give support. The White Paper itself got a bit of a mauling at a press conference which Bob Peirce and Peter Lai rather heroically give. It isn't their fault. We are in the usual position. If we had offered the London A-Z, the press would have asked for the telephone directory as well. The journalists want to know about every splutter and hiccough in the talks.

Friday 25 February

The Chinese reaction is fairly muted by their standards. It's as though they don't think there's much point any more in going through the motions of an issue which has been resolved on our side. It may have helped that the government in London has made clear that the White Paper and the decision about further legislation have the complete backing of the Cabinet. Nevertheless, I'm sure that we will have further blasts down the line. In Beijing they brought out their answer to our White Paper which is published too late in the evening to get much coverage and, perhaps above all, serves to underline that when it comes to understandings of the JD and of Hong Kong's promised autonomy London and Beijing are streets apart. We were also helped by an excellent statement that Leon Brittan (the European Union's Trade Commissioner) made in Beijing giving the Chinese trade minister a dressing down about discrimination on trade and investment issues. He put the point very strongly that in the European Union, discrimination against one member would be regarded as discrimination against them all. He said that he has been given assurances 'at the highest level' that there won't be any discrimination. We shall see whether this amounts to very much, but at least it's on the record. Christopher Hum said there appears to be no sign of discrimination against British trade in either Shanghai or Guangzhou despite all the noise. He quoted a British official in Shanghai saying that he had heard a conversation between Shanghai municipal bureaucrats saying that they should keep trade and politics separate and that all the stuff about British exports was Beijing rhetoric. Whether it will actually turn out like this, we shall in due course see. Lavender and I went with Alice and Martin and Janny Dinham to a Bob Dylan concert. Alice seemed to enjoy this treat for the oldies.

Tuesday 1 March
We had a quiet Exco meeting to start the month. I suggested that the best line to take after the Legco success, the publication of the White Paper and the announcement about the next stage of legislation, is to draw a line under the whole issue, and move on to areas where we should be able to cooperate with Beijing. I repeated all this to the press after the meeting. I reckon it is probably the mood of the community.

Thursday 3 March
We had the budget, which is another success for Hong Kong's economic management. Taxes were cut for individuals and corporations, expenditure was increased in priority areas, and we announced bigger reserves every year from now through to 1997. Time once more to call an election? It would certainly be a reasonable conclusion to reach after Lavender and I went on another district visit to Tai Po. There were big enthusiastic crowds. We visited a Taoist temple and the cleanest factory I have ever set foot in.

We heard that Rupert Murdoch is going to drop the BBC from Star, the satellite channel which he has bought and which he wants to use as a jumping-off point into China. My own suspicion is that however much he grovels in Beijing, the Communist Party is never going to allow a foreigner to control much of the media in their own country. They leave that sort of thing to us in Britain.

Bob Peirce has been in Vancouver with Peter Ricketts and Peter Lai talking to their opposite numbers from Canada, Australia, the US, Japan and New Zealand. It's clear that these countries, while hoping for the best in Hong Kong, are making plans in case the worst materializes. For example, they're considering how (or if) they would cope with a lot of emigration from Hong Kong before and after 1997. I am told that we are having trouble at one of the camps for Vietnamese immigrants. The numbers have now fallen to 26,000 but we are starting to hit difficulties in shifting the hard core and persuading them to return to Vietnam.

Friday 4 March
The news out of China is that the leadership has been vigorously locking up dissidents, including Wei Jinsheng. This may be related to what Robin Munro of Asia Watch tells Edward, namely that there is at present a lot of social and industrial unrest in China, which is worrying the authorities. Or maybe it is simply that they are trying to shut critics up before the next meeting of the National People's Congress. For this to be happening

just before the visit to Beijing by Warren Christopher [the US Secretary of State] is clearly far from ideal and it will complicate the resolution of MFN.

On the home front the Jardine's issue continues to bubble away: the Securities and Futures Commission [SFC] is resolute on the importance of making it clear that if you're largely based in Hong Kong, you can't avoid the provisions of the takeover code. The Hang Seng Index has been falling. This does not seem to be related to any local politics; but part of a wider fall in equities and bond markets. That doesn't mean that we won't be blamed for it. The worst news is that we are to lose Peter Ricketts. He is off to another posting in Paris. We will miss him hugely. He has protected our backs in London and acted as a perfect conduit with the Foreign Secretary and other senior members of the government and of the FCO. I admire him and hope that he can remain a friend whom I see from time to time.

Sunday 6 March

The Princess Royal is here once again and we also had a visit from the new head of Asian affairs in the FCO, David Wright. I filled him in on where I think we are – the United Front attacking us, Martin Lee and the Democrats suspecting that we are about to abandon them, Beijing firing occasional broadsides, and the community, on the whole, seeming to support us and give us the benefit of the doubt. Despite the row with China, I reckon that we can govern Hong Kong perfectly adequately until 1997 and lock in as many of its liberties as possible. But ultimately, after the handover, much will depend on whether the Chinese Communist Party can actually be trusted to honour 'one country, two systems'. There may be worries on the Sino-British trade side, but the statistics just don't bear out the fears which are sedulously encouraged by Beijing for political purposes. Robin McLaren is also with us for medical reasons. His back continues to give him a lot of pain. He gives us all a pretty deadpan assessment of what is happening in Beijing. He must be as well informed as anyone but no one really knows exactly what is happening behind the walls of the Zhongnanhai.

Monday 7 March

This is going to be the sort of week in which I'm given huge numbers of assessments of what's happening in China from businessmen, diplomats, academic experts and politicians and will finish discussions conceivably better informed but not much wiser. Something which I don't normally record here is that some days I must spend literally four or five hours talking. There is hardly an American politician, British politician, business leader, European politician – this week's visitors include a former Italian Foreign Minister, lobbyist, fixer and so on – who doesn't get in to see me. I could make a celebrity list of all those who appear to be interested in the fate of the last (or pretty well the last) outpost of the British Empire. I think I do have to see them all, and of course they get the same sort of messages. Mike Hanson, my excellent and preternaturally gloomy press chief, sits in on quite a few meetings and I watch him glaze over as he hears the same messages repeated over and again. 'Hong Kong is probably the only example in the world of a society which is liberal but not wholly democratic. Its route to full democracy has been curtailed by the imminence of the handover to China. It is and has been an extraordinary example of the successful relationship between economic and political freedom. The Chinese communists have promised to allow that to continue after 1997, a pledge which is contained in the Joint Declaration. We have no choice but to try to trust them and assume that they will be as good as their word. For Hong Kong to do well is good for China; and the reverse is true. But we have to give Hong Kong and its way of life the best chance of continuing as a free city after the handover. Most of the people who live here in Hong Kong are themselves refugees from events in mainland China. They know the difference between communism and freedom. I am determined to give them as much of a chance as possible of deciding how strongly to build the defences of Hong Kong's sense of its own citizenship. I don't believe that there is really a cost to the British economy in doing this. There are threats but no statistics.' And on, and on, and on. This doesn't mean that I don't believe it, but I do get a bit bored saying it and certainly feel sorry for Mike. The visitors will continue to pour in and I think I have an obligation to see as many as possible.

There's a story in the papers about Jardine's delisting from Hong Kong. From their point of view the story doesn't look good. Charles Powell came up from Malaysia incandescent with rage. Poor Martin had to take an earful. The truth is that Jardine's have brought this down on their own heads. Martin discovered that the initial leak came from Jardine's themselves, and when it was checked out by the newspapers the SFC leaked back rather more effectively. What's more, there's nobody in the market who has much sympathy with Jardine's. But it will probably confirm Henry Keswick's view that we are not going to provide a proper payback for their initial support for me over the first year or 18 months. David Wilson was regularly rubbished by this great figure of British imperial might. And I assume that it's my turn next, not least since Keswick apparently already regards me as a socialist.

Tuesday 8 March

Lavender and Edward have written an excellent speech for her to deliver on International Women's Day to an audience of almost 400 business and professional women. She had to be careful to skirt around one or two live political issues like whether we should join the international convention which seeks to eliminate all forms of discrimination against women, and whether we should also create a women's commission. But she still managed to say a lot of interesting and important things about equal opportunity and pay, about discrimination on promotion and about sexual harassment. The subjects are much the same here as elsewhere around the world and as ever men have dragged their feet. Lavender told me that there was one man in the audience. I suppose it should have been me.

The changing of the FCO guard continues here. Hugh Davies took over some time ago from Tony Galsworthy. He is not a moths man but I don't regard that as a terrible defect. He knows a lot about China, has a lovely wife and is polite, funny, charming and competent. His skills as a tolerant negotiator and indeed as a charitable human being are going to be tested by his chairmanship of our side of the JLG. It continues to be a horribly demanding job, which he and his team do with great intelligence and competence. Indeed one of Hugh's great strengths is the way he manages those who work for him sensitively. He has an excellent team with a very clever deputy, Alan Paul. They do much of the grinding ground work that will make the handover possible, even given the fairly dire quality of those they have to deal with. It's difficult for an outsider to know whether the Chinese officials in the JLG cannot help how they behave because their instructions are to be obstructive, or whether they are appointed because they fit naturally into these roles.

Wednesday 9 March

Peter Ricketts is to be followed by Sherard Cowper-Coles. I would not say that his appointment has been greeted with universal enthusiasm by his FCO colleagues; they are able to contain their joy within polite bounds. He is said to be clever. When I met him today, he was clearly keen to make the best sort of impression. Why should I disagree with those who have slightly reluctantly suggested the appointment? They presumably know what they are doing, though they say that I can decline.

On the same day, I had dinner with the Federation of Hong Kong Industries. I noted some statistics in my off-the-cuff remarks after dinner. Twenty years ago the per capita GDP in Hong Kong was about US$1800, the Hang Seng Index stood at 400 and there were about 5000 students.

Today, the respective figures are US$18,000, the Hang Seng now stands at just over 10,000 and there are 35,000 students in tertiary education.

Thursday 10 March

I went to breakfast with Vincent Cheng,* a decent man, and some of his fellow independent members of Legco. They mostly supported us on the first bill and are now looking around to see what amendments they can make for the next piece of legislation on the elections. They are very keen to get some sort of steer from us suggesting that we would be happy to see the '92 bill turned into an outcome closer to the sort of compromises we were prepared to make during the negotiations. But we have to play an absolutely straight bat. One of the members present, Eric Lee, asked us to provide the possible '93 compromise proposals in legislative form. But if we give any impression at all that we are not rock solid on the '92 plans, Martin Lee and the real liberals in Legco will argue that we have been involved in a cynical manoeuvre, and there would be some truth in that. It's going to be a tricky summer. My reckoning is that there is a 50–50 chance of us getting the '92 bill through as it is. If we don't achieve this we will probably get some of the '93 proposals instead. That wouldn't be a bad outcome for Hong Kong but not a particularly good one for me and the government. But we have to make sure our hands are absolutely clean as the process develops.

I then saw Anson Chan and Bob Peirce about the Independent Commission Against Corruption. We are checking out some allegations made by the ICAC in intelligence reports about corruption and the discipline services. We can't quite make the reports stand up but we have to be on our guard as we run up to 1997. The last thing we can afford is an insidious growth in corrupt behaviour.

The Princess Royal left in the evening. She always works very hard when she is here. Royal visits continue apace. They take quite a lot of time and effort. But when the visitor works hard, it makes it all worthwhile.

Friday 11 March

Li Peng made his big speech yesterday at the beginning of the National People's Congress, called here the mother-in-law of parliaments. He was remarkably moderate about Hong Kong, certainly more moderate than

* Vincent Cheng was an economist who spent most of his commercial career with the Hong Kong and Shanghai Bank rising to a number of senior positions in it. He was an appointed member of both Legco and Exco, and in 2008 was appointed a member of the National Committee of the Chinese People's Political Consultative Conference.

expected, though his remarks were enlivened by a marvellous Freudian slip in which he initially blamed the Chinese side for the breakdown in talks before hurriedly correcting himself. Lord MacLehose has given rather a tiresome interview to the *South China Morning Post* rotting me off. George Walden did much the same the other day in a British paper. I used to be a colleague of his in government, in the same department. I wonder what they think the point of these contributions may be. Exactly whom do they think they are helping?

We had a rather difficult meeting with officials to discuss private members' bills. Several senior officials simply want us to announce that we won't allow private members' legislation to proceed if it has financial implications. This would put us in a very difficult position politically when, for example, Christine Loh introduces proposed legislation on freedom of information and when Anna Wu introduces her own bills on anti-discrimination and the appointment of a human rights commission. We have to try and get involved in a dialogue with Christine and Anna, both independent-minded and moderate appointed members of Legco, and make at least some commitment to taking over parts of their bills. It won't be easy. Anson and Hamish are very alive to the full political horrors of slapping down these private members' bills and not allowing them to be discussed. It's all made more difficult by the fact that the constitutional arrangements in Hong Kong are pretty ridiculous. While the government may be executive led, there is no governing party and the executive doesn't have the sort of fallback powers which, for example, an American president would have. The constitution has certainly not been designed by a politician used to political activity. But, of course, we can't start rewriting it now.

Sunday 13 March

We had a cheerful day playing golf and tennis in Macau against the Governor and his wife. Just to make sure that I won, I asked Colin Grant to play with me. Mind, the Macau Governor's political adviser from the Portuguese Foreign Ministry was the University champion in Portugal so we needed to confront fire with fire. The Triad problem in Macau is difficult; it's one of the main reasons why I am resolutely opposed to allowing the building of any casinos in Hong Kong. Much better to let the Hong Kong Jockey Club take the money from betting on horses and spend it on good works.

Wednesday 16 March

We are now having what I hope will be a fairly quiet week in Hong Kong, though it did begin with a meeting with Henry Keswick and Charles Powell on the 14th. On the delisting issue and the takeover code they seemed to be trying to prove that the Hong Kong Bank has the same problems as them. This is a point which the Hong Kong Bank and the Bank of England vigorously resist.

Monday 21 March

After another good district visit to Wong Tai Sin, I was asked about remarks that Qian Qichen made at the end of the NPC [National People's Congress] about Hong Kong. He seemed to have suggested that while there can't be any cooperation on politics, we would all have to cooperate on other things in the interests of the territory. If there is an agreement to disagree in the offing that seems to me no bad thing. After spending 10 days with us, and even going to the races in our box at Happy Valley, Sherard seemed to think that we are doing the right thing though he is gloomy about the prospects for Hong Kong after the handover. After I talked to the Premier of Tasmania, he said to me, 'There's one thing that you haven't said.' 'What's that?' I asked. 'What you are doing is right.'

Tuesday 22 March

London is suggesting that Alastair Goodlad should go to Beijing at Whitsun to 'thicken up' our relationship. The argument appears to be that since the Chinese haven't kneecapped us, we should go and visit them to see if they still like us. In Hong Kong we all think this is barmy. There is a terrible tendency on the part of the Foreign Office to keep on wanting to take the cake out of the oven to see if it is cooked. We think there is very little upside in a visit and a lot of potential downside. Among other things it would concentrate Chinese attention on Hong Kong, and they could hardly admit they were prepared to go on doing business. This is a situation in which what we should want is a general drift in the right direction. The Chinese are very unlikely to be explicit about this. Obviously, Alastair and the FCO aren't happy that we are so hostile. I guess we might have to give in but a visit at about the same time as our second bill on the elections is going through Legco will undoubtedly increase conspiracy theories there about what we are doing – especially if the bill is amended in any way.

I'm spending quite a lot of time preparing speeches for the period between Easter and Whitsun and receiving lots of messages that the Chinese want to put the political row on one side and carry on with other business, provided that we don't get up to any of our 'tricks'. The visit to Beijing by Warren Christopher has clearly not gone very well and may make MFN negotiations rather more difficult. We have continued to have difficult discussions about Jardine's, including at Exco today (someone suggested that the company has folk memories of what happened in Shanghai in the 1940s), but overall it's interesting that there appears to be a more normal political discourse in all the meetings I attend.

Is there anything much that we can do about soaring property prices? Both Anson and Hamish warn that the only thing worse than prices going up would be a collapse in prices and in the market. If you try to prick the bubble you may fetch up pricking it far too much. If we had longer to deal with the issue than the period between now and the handover we might be able to approach this more resolutely. I don't want to see a stock market collapse in the next year or two. When I was asked by a visiting British MP, Terry Dicks (who, given his generally right-wing views, is surprisingly supportive of John Major), what worried me most about the next three years, I thought of referring to the stock market and property, but instead I said – which would indeed be a bigger, a far bigger, problem – 'Another Tiananmen Square massacre.'

While Michael Sze, in his relatively new job as Secretary of the Civil Service, is pressing ahead in dealing with some of the complicated issues involved in localization, we are aware of a characteristically heavy-handed effort by the NCNA to make lots of contacts with civil servants. After a dinner or a meeting, they are handing out three documents – the collected works of Deng Xiaoping on Hong Kong, a copy of the Basic Law and a copy of an essay from one of the newspapers in Hong Kong about how Britain always leaves its colonies in a frightful mess in order to extend British influence. They then offer a private telephone number in case the civil servants want to 'come over'. The results are predictably dire, with civil servants increasingly worried about having to do business with this lot of gangsters.

Thursday 24 March

The Jardine's row goes on and on with more attention in the press, which is particularly bad for the firm. They really haven't handled this at all well even though I bet they have had very expensive PR advice. I doubt whether Charles Powell has been allowed to steer this issue. We are also deeply embroiled in discussions about the private members' bills especially Anna Wu's on the human rights commission and anti-discrimination legislation. Lavender made another visit to a Vietnamese migrant detention centre, this time the one at Whitehead, where there have been strikes and demonstrations in protest against the UNHCR-forced returns to Vietnam. She has taken a particular interest in the position of the children; increasingly she also wonders how families can think it's worth continuing to live in these camps, given their conditions, when the position in Vietnam of the returnees seems to be getting so much better.

Friday 25 March

Jane Fonda and Ted Turner came to breakfast. Jane is much more interesting and articulate than her partner, though I suppose he must be a very good businessman. He expressed views on human rights in China (very different from his wife's) which suggest that he is hoping for the chance of getting his television channel accepted there. I think that is very unlikely. The corpse of this ambition will doubtless be found on a battlefield which contains so many other similar corpses.

And then it was the rugby sevens! Bowen Leung had to do some fancy footwork in advance to prevent a catastrophe because the liquor licensing board failed until the last moment to give the stadium a licence, and the temporary licence allowed by the police prescribed an amount which would clearly be regarded as Lenten teetotalism by most of the 40,000 fans. Bowen got people to see sense. We gave a reception for the organizers of the sevens and some of the players, for which happily no liquor licence was required. David Cameron, who is a friend of Edward Llewellyn and worked in the Conservative Research Department before becoming a special adviser in the Treasury and the Home Office, is also in Hong Kong, presumably for the sevens. He has charm and intelligence and Edward is not the only one who told me he is on a fast upward trajectory in politics. He seemed likeable and was easier to get on with than the principal guest at the sevens, the King of Tonga. To describe him as vast is an entirely insufficient adjective. The organizers found a seat which was sufficiently large to accommodate him wrapped in his enormous raincoat. He is perfectly amiable with a sweet smile but is no great talker. The chairman of the Hong Kong RFU struggled for half an hour but secured no response until eventually the king turned to him and said, 'Did you know there are twelve nations here that have red, white and blue in their flags?'

Saturday 26 March

Simon Holberton of the *FT* is just about the first journalist who is starting to write stories suggesting that we have come through the worst in Hong Kong and that life is returning to something which can pass as normal.

The French are being bloody about the fact that Hong Kong has observer status at the OECD. They have been trying to make us change Hamish

MacLeod's alterations in his budget statement to excise duties which increase the price of expensive French wines even while they lower the price of cheaper wines from elsewhere. The French are claiming that this is in some way against the spirit of the GATT [General Agreement on Tariffs and Trade]. It's no such thing but it just happens to be unpopular with France, whose officials regularly make it more difficult for me to remain a Francophile. This is a reminder of how little support we have got from the European Union. All our support comes from Australia, Canada, America, Japan and New Zealand. The European Union, except for Leon Brittan, has done damn all. French ministers are pretty well the only ones from anywhere who come through Hong Kong on the way into China while studiously avoiding seeing me or any other members of the government. They must think we don't notice. Europe's aspirations to have a world view and reputation based on values is regularly shredded by corporate sales departments.

Tuesday 29 March

At Exco we discussed Europe and also the beginning of discussions with Beijing on the public order legislation. This has previously been subject to my least favourite doctrine. Every time we have been about to start discussions on the subject there have been a number of people around who have argued that the time is not quite appropriate. We have to do it sometime and this seems as good a time as any. Gareth Evans passed through Hong Kong today on his way into China. We can depend on him to speak up for us. After a quick chat with him I took the night plane back to Dublin.

Thursday 31 March

I had a meeting yesterday with the Taoiseach, Albert Reynolds. There was some confusion back in Hong Kong about this meeting before I set out. I kept on looking at drafts of my programme and, despite the invitations from the Irish government, could see no reference to it; one of my local private secretaries asked Martin eventually why the Governor was so insistent on going to a teashop. Reynolds is a genial fellow but I guess he has to carry a club behind his back. Then I went on to give the lecture organized by Tony O'Reilly and the Independent group of newspapers. I was introduced by my old friend Maurice Hayes, who was one of my permanent secretaries when I was a junior minister in Northern Ireland, and the lecture seemed to go well. It was on freedom of the press. Lavender noted that despite everything I seem to be in favour of it. Beforehand, there was a reception in the library at Trinity College and then after the lecture a dinner in the panelled room of the Bank of Ireland where the Irish House of Lords used to meet. On either side of the narrow room there were big tapestries featuring King Billy, which led Tony O'Reilly to describe it rather happily as 'the ravine of the ascendancy'. We slept last night at Castlemartin, Tony O'Reilly's splendid house full of great Irish paintings, several by Jack Butler Yeats, brother of the poet.

Friday 1–Saturday 9 April

Back in London, Douglas told me the whole story of a humiliating climb-down over the voting method in the European Council (it seemed to be about qualified majority voting) and that it had been the worst week in his political career. The government had been all over the place and nobody had behaved particularly well. I made what will probably not be very helpful remarks telling everybody to get a grip and behave properly. It's much easier to say that when you've just flown in from Hong Kong. I explained to John once again why I can't leave Hong Kong until I've completed the job. Anyway, it's all a shambles and the government is making a very good fist of tearing itself apart. I had dinner with Carl Bildt, the Prime Minister of Sweden, who is an old friend from way before we both got into Parliament. He has obviously been extremely upset by our balls-up over qualified majority voting in Europe and finds it inexplicable that we got into this scrape.

While I had some disagreeable meetings with businessmen and fund managers (a group who have just cheered Ambassador Ma when he addressed them on China's policy on Hong Kong), I sense that the political support in London remains pretty solid. The rumour is that the Select Committee report on Hong Kong, which will be out soon, will be supportive.

Lavender, Alice and I had a great time with Kate and Laura, celebrating Kate's 21st birthday with some of her friends. We have sold our small cottage outside Bath and did a little desultory house-hunting in London thinking about our return in due course. We spent Easter with Robert and Hannah Cranborne in Dorset again and went to see the Dimblebys just outside Bath. Returning to Hong Kong was not too difficult – except for leaving the two girls. But I have been told that I have to get more fit and take more exercise than the regular games of tennis.

Winning the Big Vote: April 1994–April 1995

Monday 11 April

We got back from the UK to a familiar agenda. One new issue is that a journalist from *Ming Pao*, Xi Jang, has been arrested in Beijing for allegedly stealing state secrets; what he has actually done is to produce some excellent and accurate reporting on the management of the Chinese economy. There is bound to be a chilling effect among journalists in Hong Kong. He will undoubtedly be locked up after the usual Chinese trial with a preordained verdict. The pity of it is that there isn't much we can do about it apart from harrumph.

Other than this, we are going to have to focus on possible legislation on human rights, the actual legislation we are bringing forward on Legco elections, and the consequences of Lu Ping visiting Hong Kong, with his quisling groupies doing as much as possible to undermine the present government and the properly elected Legco.

Robin McLaren is with us for a short visit, and before we had discussions about human rights he told us that there is no real sign so far of discrimination against British trade, though he is given rather a frosty time by the Chinese Ministry of Foreign Affairs. Amnesty are going to publish a report during the week advocating the establishment of a human rights commission, but nobody seems very clear about what exactly such a commission would actually do. The things that have to be addressed – awareness of human rights, affordability of pursuing human rights cases and accessibility – could all be done without a commission. The main argument against setting one up is that it could endanger the Bill of Rights itself. It isn't going to be easy to hold the line on this even though we are certainly intending to do more on freedom of speech and on human rights protections.

Monday 18 April

I met a brave Chinese writer, Professor Wu, who was locked up for years by the communists. He is pretty pessimistic about China and told me that in his view it will take many years for it to change. He also reckons that Hong Kong will have a tough time after 1997, though whether it will be wrecked will depend on how much people are prepared to fight for it. But what, I asked, will the communists do if people do fight for it? We both have an uneasy feeling that we know the answer.

Wednesday 20 April

We have been offering Lu Ping a meeting when he comes to Hong Kong, but no replies are forthcoming. When I saw the Portuguese Prime Minister, Cavaco Silva, after a visit he has made to China, he continued in private as in public to avoid saying anything about our rather different approach in Hong Kong to what is being done in Macau. Nevertheless, he is quite explicit that whether or not Macau succeeds will depend above all on what happens in Hong Kong.

Friday 22 April

I got to speak at the American Chamber of Commerce, once again on MFN, and Anson has flown to Washington to lobby on the same subject. Sir Michael Palliser, one of the FCO's now retired master diplomats, who has just been in Beijing, agreed with Robin that there is no real sign of discrimination against British trade. But he thinks the economy there looks as though it is in danger of getting out of control. Most of the argument about British trade now involves an unprovable negative.

Saturday 23 April

I had a gubernatorial 'first' when I made a speech at an exhibition held by the Confederation of Trade Unions.

Sunday 24 April

It was announced that President Nixon has died. I hope they are wearing black armbands in Beijing.

The Prince of Wales is to come and address an environment conference in November. Patrick Jenkin, for whom I worked for a brief period as parliamentary private secretary, is one of the organizers. Initially he was enthusiastically pressing me to take part. But today I received a letter from him saying it might make a difference to Chinese participation if I were to do so, so maybe I will understand if I am stood down on this occasion. Of course, he still wants to stay with us!

Monday 25 April

Patrick Gillam, the chairman of Standard Chartered Bank, came in for a meeting and wanted to explain to me why Percy Cradock has been taken on as an adviser. He said that this is no sort of political statement, to which I responded that the Hong Kong government and the British government may take a rather different view. I then suggested that perhaps his recruitment is a result of his being so clever about derivatives trading. Percy has just made yet another speech rotting us off. I'm not sure that it makes much difference these days, though maybe it encourages Beijing to behave badly. Someone who has behaved very well is Jimmy McGregor, who as a result has been thrown off the General Chamber of Commerce executive committee by a huge margin. His opponents had organized all the proxy votes against him. This is another reason why we need to have decently organized functional constituencies.

Tuesday 26 April

Today, I said farewell to a clever and decent woman, Mrs Chiu, who was my interpreter when I went to Beijing. She is the Hong Kong government's main Mandarin interpreter and did all the talks for us last year. Her family has gone off to Vancouver, even though her husband doesn't yet have a job, and she is going to join them. She says that she can't face the prospect of Hong Kong after 1997. She is a first-class interpreter and an extraordinarily nice woman. We shall miss her. I suspect that we gave her too much exposure to Beijing communist officials, which must have given her all too accurate an idea of what the future might have to offer. The worst person for whom she has ever had to interpret? Zhou Nan, she replies.

I then saw the very kind and smart Canadian journalist John Fraser. John has worked for the Toronto *Globe and Mail* in Beijing. He is negative about the prospects for anything resembling freedom in China and worried about the position of some of today's dissidents. He is another addition to my tally of good Canadians; the other side of the balance sheet is pretty bare.

We got the widely forecast 'big snub' from Lu Ping with a letter saying that unfortunately he can't meet me when he is in Hong Kong owing to his busy schedule. One of the things he is doing is attending celebrations in the Bank of China, to which I am not of course invited. I suppose that is kind of them.

Monday 2 May
Lu Ping week. My tone is going to be sanctimonious energy, but not too frenetic. I began with what was a fairly normal day: a discussion on lobbying in Legco on our election proposals, a parade by the police to mark their 150th anniversary followed by a reception and speech, the inspection of a ceremonial guard at GH, lunch at the Canadian Chamber of Commerce with Canada's Governor-General, followed by a meeting with the New Zealand opposition leader, Helen Clark (bright and feisty), and then off to open a Chagall exhibition for the French at the Cultural Centre. Lu got off to a bad start on Sunday by declining to answer journalists' questions when he arrived at the station in Hong Kong, after which he was slipped out of the building through a back door to avoid demonstrations about the Xi Jang case. For the whole of today he has been holed up with his brethren on the Preliminary Working Committee, presumably telling them what they should be doing.

Tuesday 3 May
I had a thoroughly enjoyable visit to a housing estate where quite by accident I met the mother of one of our stewards and the father of one of my private secretaries, Clement Leung. How's that for a coincidental double? Clement's dad, who is a refugee from the mainland, is rightly proud of his son. Clement is an example of how, unlike so many other places, Hong Kong really has been a great place for social mobility. His parents speak very little English, if any at all, and his dad is a lorry driver. Clement went to university and passed through exams into the fast stream of the civil service. You would like him in your private office if you were a minister anywhere. He is both cheerful and serious and works flat out the whole time. There were big crowds around the public housing blocks, and at a press conference at the end I was able to say, looking as cheerful as possible, that my door is always open for Lu Ping.

Thursday 5 May
Lu Ping has had rather a difficult week on the whole trying to do the double of avoiding the press while getting publicity. His training has not surprisingly failed to furnish him with the talent or experience to bring this off. Tsang Yok-sing has told some journalists that the reason why Lu Ping hasn't seen me is that Percy Cradock advised Zhou Nan and other Chinese officials that nobody should give me face by meeting me. After all, he had apparently said, if they were to meet me it would suggest that you could stand up to China and get away with it. But how would he know?

Monday 9 May
There's lots of polling in the press, and since some of what it tells us is good news I read it very carefully. (When I was party chairman I was so used to getting bad polls that I find the contrary experience one in which I can enthusiastically paddle.) Lavender thinks that this may be bad for me. She will always, thank heavens, be ready with correctives to any signs of vanity or megalomania. Anyway, the general readout of the polls is that Lu Ping's visit has lowered people's confidence in the transition, that I seem to have become more popular, and that confidence in the future is at its lowest ebb. That is not something that can cheer any of us up.

Thursday 12 May
My birthday, and no ordinary one. I am 50 today. Lavender gave me a really beautiful Tang horse. Just because I am 50, I hope that I don't have to regard this as the beginning of the home stretch. After an extremely interesting discussion with senior officials in the Education Department about the appropriate language instruction in schools – how much should we do in Cantonese? And how much value would young people get from better spoken and written English? – I went off for the wonderful evening treat which Lavender organized, a surprise party on Lamma at the Pigeon restaurant. We travelled in the *Lady Maurine*, which has some difficulty in berthing at the right place, so we then arrived pretty late. I am not sure why so many of our staff find it impossible to map-read and equally impossible to admit that they can't. But we had a smashing evening – the Murrays, the Courtaulds, the Thompsons, the Holbertons, the Mirskys, Peter Barry, David Tang, Lavender and Alice. I like receiving presents and got an especially nice painting from David Tang.

But in the midst of life ... When we got home to GH we heard that John Smith died today of a heart attack. It is very bad news for Britain. He was a fine man and would almost certainly have made an excellent reforming Prime Minister. Scotland would have been thrilled, and the rest of the kingdom would have found him an authentic radical with whom they could identify even if they disagreed with some of his views. A sad day for our country.

Friday 13 May
We're starting to be a little concerned about manoeuvring in Legco to find support for amendments to our election bill. These suggested changes (for example, specifying what we were prepared to talk to Beijing about during our endless rounds of discussions) could in effect destroy the whole

bill, or at least undermine the integrity of our proposals. In the course of some general lobbying at a lunch given regularly for members of what Hong Kong regards as its establishment, one ghastly old stockbroker at my table told me that Martin Lee should be shot or at the very least told to go back to China where he came from. If we applied this to Hong Kong as a whole, of course, there would be hardly anyone here. I just about manage to button my lip and avoid telling the ludicrous old bore that maybe he should go back to Hampshire or wherever he came from.

Just before going off to Fanling for the weekend, we attended the Auxiliary Police ball, where Anson is of course the consort accompanying her husband, Archie, the Commandant. Anson and I had a good talk about her recent trip to Washington, which has been very successful, partly lobbying for MFN. She has had great access and has terrific credibility there. If only the Beijing bruisers understood that this is good news for them as well as for Hong Kong.

Sunday 15 May

I finished writing my Rab lecture (for delivery when I am next in London). He was a great man and of course it is a political cliché to say that he was one of the very greatest prime ministers that we never had, with a remarkable ability to turn sensible policies into workable legislation. It is sad that he and Macmillan had such an awful relationship, divided by their attitudes to Hitler and appeasement.

Monday 16 May

I saw Henry Kissinger. He has been in China and had pretty routine meetings with most leaders except Zhu Rongji, who gave him the impression of being rather nervous about things and who spoke extensively in the first person singular. He said that he had never heard this before from any Chinese leaders, including Mao. He recounted all the things that Zhu was trying to do to save the economy and how he seemed to be thwarted at every turn. In the evening I spoke to a full meeting of Amnesty International on human rights. At the end somebody asked me about the case of a boy going back to China. I hadn't heard of it and say so. I scent trouble.

Tuesday 17 May

The trouble comes in big time. The story has hit the front pages. The little boy in question was born in China and smuggled into Hong Kong by his mother, who has residence here. She left his sisters, one at the time aged six, with their grandparents and the rest of their family in China. For the last three years the mother and her husband have apparently been fighting a decision in the courts to remove the child to China. It's been through all the normal legal channels, including the Court of Appeal, and been handled in exactly the normal way. Since 1980 petitions haven't been dealt with by governors but have been the responsibility of the Secretary of Security on the Governor's behalf. However, in this case, it's particularly embarrassing in view of the question asked last night and the fact that the security branch didn't give me or any of us at GH any warning about it, despite the fact that it's a pretty sensitive matter. I've reviewed the papers and come to the conclusion that the branch actually made the right decision, though it is the sort of outcome which will be impossible to defend to part of the community. I'm thinking in particular of those with liberal sympathies and expatriates. We get huge numbers of faxes and letters about it. 'How could you be so hard-hearted as to send this little boy back?' The truth is that it was his mother who abandoned him in China not the government that is separating the family. Going through all the legal processes, how can we justify making one decision for this little boy while we have apparently sent back 2200 other children in the last three years? What, moreover, do we do the next time there is a case like this? While a lot of people with liberal opinions are bashing us, we are not being criticized by any elected politician.

These sorts of issues normally come at least in pairs, so we find another case has been raised involving two illegal immigrants, young women who have been held in prison for over seven months as witnesses in a trial. It seems to me a pretty intolerable way of behaving but I'm told that it has been standard practice for some time. We let the young women out straight away into the care of the Social Welfare Department and set up a review of the whole practice. It's obviously an area where one can act reasonably without facing awful repercussions elsewhere.

Wednesday 18–Thursday 19 May

We had visits from Lord Young, who seems rather downbeat now about what is happening to the economy in China, and Geoffrey and Elspeth Howe, who have just been in Beijing. Geoffrey has now abandoned his metaphor about Hong Kong being like a Ming vase and now compares it to a rhubarb tree. I'm not really sure what he's talking about, but even though we disagree about Hong Kong he clearly doesn't intend to be publicly embarrassing. There is also a House of Lords debate in which there continues to be a front bench consensus, but there are one or two predictable speeches attacking us. Is it simply a coincidence that the main critics all have commercial interests in China or Hong Kong which they think are threatened by being in favour of keeping our word here? Lord Cromer, who is a director of Inchcape, is very noisy in his criticisms; no surprise here since the senior executive, Charles Mackay, who was initially very supportive when we told him what we were planning to do, is now particularly outspoken. It's a pity that he doesn't spend more time running a better company given all the advantages it has here. Richard Marsh also has a go at us; he just happens to be a director of an investment company in China. Rather like Jim Callaghan he doesn't seem to give great priority to human rights. Perhaps this is socialism with British characteristics.

Monday 30 May

We flew back to London on Friday night 20th May, and saw daughters, relations and friends. The political atmosphere does not suggest that the government is brimming with self-confidence. I had lots of meetings at the Foreign Office, mostly about human rights, and supper at No. 10 with the Prime Minister, who is in pretty good form given the poisonous political mood. I gave a speech to the Thirty Club on Hong Kong, my lecture on Rab at the Carlton Club, and a lecture in Manchester to the splendidly called Literary and Philosophical Society in the great hall of the town hall after visiting Chinatown. I did a bit of my usual stuff about the returning son of Manchester, or at least grandson.

But the highlight or maybe lowlight of the Patten week is that, back in Hong Kong, Whisky has been arrested for nipping a labourer who was doing some repairs and decoration in GH. The rule of law applies to all, including the Governor's terrier. He has been taken off looking very sorry for himself to government kennels for a week in quarantine. The press are hugely excited. It's a big story and even makes the English papers. Some people think that our dogs are better known than Lavender and the Governor. Perhaps this is because neither of us has ever bitten a builder.

Public debate is going to be dominated for a bit this summer by the question of whether or not we decide to set up a human rights commission and what we will do about private members' bills both on this and about statutory rights to information and equal opportunities. This whole tangle of issues will need very careful examination. We haven't even got the political reform bill through yet, but we are already being denounced for being feeble about human rights. There are always two major stories here: either you are kowtowing to Beijing or you are looking for a fight. People sometimes move from one position to the other in the space of the same paragraph, or even sentence. I just wish that those who are pressing us to go further now on human rights (with no very obvious community support or political gain at present) would stand up and support us when we do something which is really important like making the electoral system reasonable. In due course, we will have to make small changes on issues like public order.

Tuesday 31 May

I told Lydia a few days ago that we had heard from London that the Hong Kong Bank had briefed members of the House of Lords before the recent debates to give them ammunition to fire at us. She wrote immediately to Willie Purves and within days I received a personal letter from him saying that the Bank was entirely innocent of this. Things are looking more hopeful on one or two fronts, for example the airport and defence lands, on the last of which it is suggested that the Chinese have overplayed their hand because of intervention by the military, but that they really do want a settlement. We just have to keep calm and maintain a firm line. We are putting together some ideas for cooling down property prices and are planning the final proposals for an old-age pension. We want to sell this hard in July. We intend to put HK$10 billion into the scheme as the government's contribution, which would mean that employers and employees would only need to contribute about 1/3 themselves. This should give us a chance to open up a new agenda. Better care for the elderly at an affordable cost.

Saturday 4 June

The 1989 Tiananmen killings vigil went off peacefully in Hong Kong; at least 30,000 people turned out in Victoria Park. Edward went with the Courtaulds and the Labour MP Mark Fisher, who is visiting. They were snapped by a *Ming Pao* photographer. I wish I could go myself but I guess that would be regarded as more than injudicious. Our political discussions are still dominated by the management of our election bill. It looks as though there are two main hurdles to clear. First we have to see off the Allen Lee party amendment, which may have attracted some middle ground support on the argument that it represents some sort of consensus by making all the adjustments which we'd tentatively discussed during the endless rounds of talks; and secondly, we have to get the majority for our own bill. There are all sorts of awkward problems. How will the pro-Beijing legislators vote? Will they be abstaining on the Allen Lee amendment on the grounds that they shouldn't do anything to try to 'improve' the bill and then vote against us? How will the independent group vote? We are doing all the lobbying we can. There is also some suggestion that Allen Lee's lot, if they lose their amendment, will then vote for Emily Lau's bill, which is being taken after ours and which would allow for a completely directly elected Legco. I can't believe that they would actually be so daft, although some of them are saying that they will do this to embarrass me.

Wednesday 8 June

Emily Lau came in for a meeting. She wanted to check on whether I have lost my nerve and am about to kowtow to China. I patiently went through everything we have been doing. She even nodded in agreement from time to time. But, of course, she left my office to go out and denounce me. I sometimes think that for many of the politicians who come to see me, the main objective is to be able to have a stand-up with the press afterwards and to rot me off. To her credit, Emily, like others, has good reason for being suspicious of the British and for speaking out about it. This point is rubbed home when David Ford, who is in town, confirms that three peers told our office in London that the Hong Kong Bank had offered to brief them for the recent House of Lords debate. I can now write back to Willie Purves and say that three peers obviously got the wrong end of the stick. Emily, Martin Lee and their political colleagues don't stab in the back and are not hypocrites. Talking of hypocrisy, Charles Mackay comes in to grovel and to apologize about Lord Cromer's remarks in that almost entirely ignored Lords debate. Why do they bother? I am also told that Mackay's wife is complaining that I snubbed her at Glyndebourne the other day on our trip back to Britain. I'm sure she is a very nice person, and perhaps I should know her, but I don't think I would recognize her unless she landed by parachute singing an aria on GH lawn.

Friday 10 June

Lavender and I went again to the Bradbury Hospice at Shatin. She, Caroline Courtauld and a few others have – with the help of some of our favourite nuns – really helped to get the hospice movement off the ground. I don't think there's much willingness to face the prospect of death in any society, but there seems to be particular resistance in some Chinese communities. Giving people the chance to die in dignity with as little pain as possible is a terrific cause, and there is no reason at all why it shouldn't become much more widely supported in Hong Kong. In the evening, we had the Queen's Birthday reception at GH and it stopped raining in time for us to be able to hold Beating the Retreat in the garden rather than the ballroom.

Sunday 12 June

Richard Needham is staying with us. He has supported what we are doing but gives me a lecture about not allowing a bunker mentality to develop. He says that I've got to be nicer to businessmen; who he claims are feeling hard done by. Well, it can't be because of anything happening in the Hong

Kong economy, which is still blasting away at full throttle. Maybe this rankles with some who have been proved wrong; we stood up to China and the roof didn't fall in. But he is right that without loving them all to bits, I should at least love those who don't constantly claim – usually behind our backs – that we've done a disastrous job. And he concedes that the hypocrisy is quite difficult to take.

Monday 13 June

It's a public holiday so we went off to the dragon boat races in Tsuen Wan. Thomas Chow, who used to work in my private office, is now the district officer. He helped to give us a great day despite the murky weather. We got a friendly reception from the oarsmen and from the crowds, and afterwards went to have lunch at one of the Greasy Goose restaurants. There was a wonderful view of the new bridge; it's starting to look terrific.

We're trying to work out how we should handle the launch of new proposals on open government, but our principal discussions at the moment are about vote counting for our election bill. I see individuals and groups to try to persuade them not to scupper it, in some cases by being too clever about how some amendments may (or more likely may not) please Beijing. At the same time, we're detecting an improvement in the atmosphere of our relations with them. This is affecting discussions on the airport, the container terminal and defence lands. Why should this be happening? I think there are three reasons. First of all, China's relations with Taiwan are going very badly; they may be reluctant to see things deteriorating in other areas too. Secondly, domestic policy in China, especially in relation to the economy, is beset with difficulties; they may want Hong Kong to be a more positive element not least because of its economic importance. Thirdly, time is starting to run out for them to muck us about without it affecting their own interests. They are also realists. I don't think they want to keep a row going on indefinitely, and maybe our restraint over the human rights commission and one or two other matters has marginalized those who continue to pretend that we are part of an international plot, trying to turn Hong Kong into a community which is going to subvert Chinese communist rule. They may also have observed that our successful lobbying in Washington about MFN is a rather unlikely element in any anti-China plot. But as ever, who knows? To my surprise I even see a banker from Barclays who thinks that the fact that they have been handed back a bit of business which they had previously lost is a sign of a warming in the political climate.

Friday 17 June
We had a very good discussion of the details of the deal on defence lands with Alan Paul and his excellent JLG team. All the sticking points remain much the same – exclusive use of the lands for defence purposes, our refusal to give financial guarantees about re-provisioning which could land the UK with contingent liabilities since we can't be sure that this Legco would vote the funds at the moment, and the size of the naval base. But all in all, it looks as though we are very close to an agreement. We know that China wants one and that Alan is an extremely skilful negotiator.

From now until the end of the month is probably the most important week or so in my time as Governor. Can we make progress on defence lands and the airport while at the same time getting our election proposals through Legco? Kevin Murphy, from the *Herald Tribune*, is suggesting that the story should be 'Patten is getting away with it'. No one was saying this would be possible, but in his view it provides an opportunity for establishing politics in Hong Kong in a way that won't disappear. I am not so sure about this but it is certainly true that we would be making rather a substantial point about dealing with Beijing. Doubtless the result in some quarters in Hong Kong will be that we've done some sort of secret deal with China. Who said you could ever win? There is a huge amount of lobbying to do over the coming days. Lydia has arranged to be on holiday, not the best timing for the senior member of Exco.

Wednesday 22 June
We haven't made much progress in the JLG, though the atmosphere is said to be better. They are obviously having some difficulty making up their minds about defence lands but are proposing a meeting on the airport in the next few days. Our pension plans are going forward very well. The Chinese side are suspicious about welfare state spending, which is odd really from a communist regime – and even odder since they are pressing us to increase the amount of money put aside for civil service pensions.

This afternoon, after I opened the Pamela Youde Eastern Hospital, I returned to learn that the Chinese side weren't ready to reach an agreement at the JLG today on defence lands. So what we hope will be the final discussion is postponed until next week. This may also mean going slow on an airport agreement. Just to help things along, the Treasury in London, having agreed a form of words on defence lands a couple of weeks ago that limits any obligations in the future on British funds, is now making objections that we haven't gone far enough in ensuring that there won't be a contingent guarantee by the United Kingdom to cover any necessary expenditure on the defence estate in the future. We have responded that we haven't landed the UK with future obligations, but the Treasury insist that we shouldn't reach an agreement until the matter has been sorted out. I sent a telegram back to London saying that we just can't wait and that we are going to go ahead with our present proposals. If anybody wants to take the matter up, I continued, I will discuss it with the Prime Minister and the Foreign Secretary. I hope this rather grand gesture will have its effect.

Saturday 25 June

I've heard from Alan Paul that the defence lands talks appear to have made a final breakthrough and agreed a form of words on guarantees which the Chinese can accept. It's not yet in the bag. But we seem to have shut up the Treasury in London. Alan has been doing a wonderful job.

Sunday 26 June

We spend a lovely day at Fanling. Lavender and I have had our longest talk yet on what happens if our election bill is sunk without trace during the next few days. We agreed that it would be very difficult for me to hang on, politically wounded and not capable of getting much done. It might be better to go home, tail between legs, and try to find something else to do in life. I'm not sure that the community would find a really lame duck Governor much inspiration between now and 1997. I think I would be finished in politics. Lavender and I would both be extremely sad. But I don't think I'd leave regretting what we've tried to do.

Tuesday 28 June

We seem to spend most of the week beginning on 27 June lobbying about our electoral proposals. Allen Lee's group of alleged liberals (most of them appointed by the government) are trying to force through amendments that they suggest would take things back to where we were prepared to compromise during our talks in Beijing. This isn't actually true but it sounds like a sufficient compromise to convince one or two more centrist members of Legco that it would satisfy the CCP without looking as though any democratic ambitions had been abandoned. These more centrist figures (who call themselves the breakfast group) are under huge pressure from employers like HSBC and the Hang Seng Bank. In addition solicitors seem to be lobbying for this sort of bill-wrecking compromise, and the barristers are pressing the other way. I feel sorry for those in the middle who are on the whole decent in their opinions but are all too easily persuaded that what they are being asked to do is really helpful to us and the rest of humanity. The arguments they use tend to be too clever by half. In my experience this has always been a recipe in politics for disaster. We've also had a crazy sideshow which went nowhere about whether a couple of representatives from the New Territories, at least one of whom is an adviser to Beijing, will involve themselves in an elaborate manoeuvre of abstentions on the Allen Lee amendment in return for cutting a deal on their (as usual) pretty Neanderthal plans for the New Territories with Martin Lee's Democrats. And so it goes on. There have been phone calls from Lu Ping during the debate to Legco members who are said to be wobbling, and it is also alleged that Willie Purves has been making calls from Beijing. If true it's convenient that the CCP will know through intercepts that he's been a good boy. I guess that the whole thing would have been immediately comprehensible to LBJ in Texas.

Wednesday 29 June

This had been the crucial day and evening some of our officials and one or two Exco members, notably Denis Chang, talked and lobbied heroically throughout. I waited for the result in GH with my private office, Martin and Edward. Whether or not the Almighty intervenes, as the night wears on towards dawn, we win across the board. We saw off the Allen Lee amendment by a single vote, with a majority of eight – 32 to 24 – on our bill, and then saw off Emily Lau's bill for a completely directly elected Legco by 21 votes to 20. How nice if this could have been our attainable objective; a few years earlier it might well have been, but the dubious consultation with the community on the number of directly elected seats in the late 1980s closed off this option. In any event the overall result is terrific. After nearly two years of ups and downs, we have made it. The result has been achieved in the face of the Chinese Communist Party, a good part of the Hong Kong establishment, the Hong Kong and Shanghai Bank, quite a large part of the Anglo-Hong Kong commercial aristocracy, several of our most distinguished FCO former mandarins, and almost everyone who has been honoured by the Crown or who has profited most materially from Hong Kong. Needless to say, if you had stripped out of the voting figures those who were appointed rather than elected, the results would have been very much better for us. I suspect as well that those who do not have foreign passports would have given us a big majority.

Thursday 30 June

Up at 6.15 and thought I should go and pay my respects. I went to early mass; Edward came with me. He didn't go to bed at all. It was a beautiful morning. Leo Goodstadt was there in his pew. My head felt as though it is made of cotton wool and I couldn't quite bring myself to recognize what has happened. There is a big headline in one of the English-language papers – 'Patten Triumphs'.

Once again, Lavender had helped to keep me sane and to manage my nerves. It's worth looking at this rather dramatic day from the perspective of her diary:

'I don't want to have to endure another day like today too often. There were rumours and reports all morning of wobbles and backsliding, of cock-ups and cackhanded behaviour. Later on, we heard that Lu Ping had rung up two of the independents to try to persuade them to support the Allen Lee group amendment. So far they had resisted ... If that isn't political interference, I don't know what is.

'Chris spent the morning prowling from room to room trying to occupy himself. I had a meeting with the Community Chest people, then had a chat with Caroline Courtauld and did an interview with Francis Gerard for the programme he is doing with Jonathan Dimbleby. Chris had a district visit to keep him busy in the afternoon and later I had the AGM of the Community Chest. Afterwards there was tea and I met some of the people the Chest gives money to. Then there was a board meeting. I thought it was significant that not a single one of the business people said they hoped it would go all right for Chris, but they may just have been being tactful. My heart was in my mouth as we got back to Government House at 7pm, but in fact the results of the first important amendment, the one by Allen Lee's lot, didn't come until nearly 8pm. Chris and I had been watching a repeat of Wimbledon in a desultory way when Edward came rushing up to the flat and said that we had defeated the amendment by 29 votes to 28. The narrowest of margins but enough. The relief was huge. We went down to private office, where everyone had gathered ... And we had a lot of champagne and then supper. There was much hilarity. Afterwards, the chaps stayed in the office to hear the rest of the debate on the main vote, but the feeling is that it's fairly plain sailing from here on.

'Chris came up at 3.45am to tell me that the vote was 32 to 24. It's all over and it's all been worth it. How wonderful that it's out of the way. Good for Hong Kong to have taken such a big responsibility and come up with the right result. Of course, there was a lot of the 'we was robbed' and 'it was only a tiny majority' quotes from the opposition, but a majority is a majority. Chris got up at 6.15 to go to church. Then a big breakfast to celebrate. The first time he has had bacon and eggs for months!'

At our first meeting back in the office there are many tales from the trenches. Who said what to whom and with what effects? It's the last day of this round of the JLG. The general wisdom, except from Hugh Davies and Alan Paul, is that the Chinese couldn't possibly let us have the defence lands deal the day after the bill has passed. In the event, that is exactly what they did. So much for General Wisdom, who quite often gets things wrong, not least when he is based in London. In the evening we went to David Tang's China Club to celebrate the Club's third anniversary. Gossiping, we conclude that those we expected to behave well have done so, and the reverse is true. One or two people have already been putting themselves forward to the Foreign Secretary as possible successors, and alas I'm told that Jim Prior has been berating Jardine's in London for 'letting' Martin Barrow go his own decent way.

Friday 1 July

The British press has been very good, with supportive leading articles from the *FT*, *The Times*, the *Telegraph*, *Independent* and *Guardian*.

I spent much of the day phoning people or writing to them to say thank you and I did quite a few interviews for newspapers and television. It's the Canadian National Day and the excellent, though alas departing, consul, John Higginbotham, described in his usually sharp way what has happened – that instead of being told we're dead, we have just got notice that we are simply terminally ill. I got his point straight away. He does not have much trust in the CCP. So, as he is suggesting, it's important to keep one day's votes for decency in perspective. I also went to visit the registration electoral office, where our voter registration drive has just ended with very good results. Registration has gone up about 50% or more during this last campaign. We went to a concert in the evening with Richard and Rosie Hoare. Verdi's *Te Deum* on the programme. When they decided (presumably weeks ago) what to perform today, did the Hong Kong Philharmonic know something that we didn't know?

Saturday 2–Sunday 3 July

Over the weekend I've ticked off the week's successes: the election bill, defence lands and agreement from Legco only yesterday for HK$15 billion to continue work on the airport. And we seem to have survived a moderate row over deciding to stay where we are for the present on human rights legislation and not to set up a separate commission. The agreement on money for the airport means that it doesn't really matter very much now whether we get an early deal with the Chinese or not; we can still carry on with the work.

I'm reading a book which the *FT* want me to review by my old permanent secretary in Northern Ireland and my good friend, Maurice Hayes. It's called *Sweet Killough Let Go Your Anchor* and is about his life growing up a Catholic in the Province. It is beautifully written and I always enjoy writing things for this paper. They don't muck your copy about too much and your articles are read by people you want to read them.

Monday 4 July

Discussion about senior appointments. I think the sensible thing to do is just go ahead and make them, telling the Chinese in advance rather than trying to make each one the subject of a haggle. We would never get anywhere in those circumstances. Those officials given the thumbs down by the Chinese would be put in an impossible position.

Lydia Dunn came in for a meeting back from holiday and full of praise for the result of the vote. Many thanks; sad you couldn't be with us. I have a definite feeling that in London the vultures have been circling. Jim Prior evidently had a very bad meeting recently with Li Peng, who put the frighteners on him, and David Young has also been getting at Margaret. She remains stalwart, to use one of her own words. She has written me a very nice letter, as has Paddy Ashdown. I have dinner out with Michael Sze and a group of middle-ranking civil servants. They seem pretty relaxed about the future. Michael has lined up a good guy called John Tsang to be my next private secretary when Bowen moves on.

Tuesday 5 July

We had a farewell dinner at GH for John and Diane Foley; he has been a very good CBF. He is what, I believe, the army call a thinking soldier. Alice has left for the UK for the summer holidays. The tower in GH will be very quiet and the dogs will be sad for a couple of days.

We seem to be having some success with our attempts to control the rise in property prices rather than flatten the whole market. The top prices have fallen by between 5 and 20%. I've had a fairly argumentative interview for the papers with Margaret Ng. She is a clever, brave and articulate barrister who takes the traditional anti-colonialist view. Nothing we ever do is right. I understand why people got into this situation; only 10 or 15 years ago they were treated as enemies of the state for wanting a modest amount of democracy. But in any argument about fundamentals I think I would always find myself on the same side as people like her. Then I took Lavender out for a quiet dinner at Grissini's to say thank you. We are approaching our halfway mark here. As my mum would have said, Lavender has been a real brick. She does about twice as many engagements as people were expecting. I have started calling her 'Central', like the politburo. Martin doesn't think this is very romantic. But she is certainly central for me.

Thursday 7 July
At a Legco Q and A this afternoon I tried to be courteous, charming and uncontroversial. This is what Jonathan Mirsky calls my 'Confucian mode'. I saw Gerry Segal and Nicholas Colchester, who runs the Economist Intelligence Unit. He is concerned about the rule of law in Hong Kong and I pointed out some of the difficulties confronting us. Good barristers are paid so much that they are disinclined to go on the bench and solicitors are always ready to compromise with China given the amount of business involving mainland companies and investors. After that Lavender and I then went to the community English-language lab organized by the Anglo-Hong Kong Trust, a David Tang and Simon Murray initiative. There were lots of people there and six children reciting rather difficult poems in English. It would be difficult to find six English children reciting English poems back home. Inevitably one of them (given David Tang's sense of humour) recited Cavafy's poem on a Greek colony: 'That things in the colony aren't what they should be / no one can doubt any longer, / and though in spite of everything we do move forward / maybe – as more than a few believe – the time has come / to bring in a political reformer'.

Friday 8 July
I went to the police special duties unit at Fanling – it is our equivalent of the SAS. I fire machine-guns and pistols at targets. When the unit do this they get their colleagues to stand next to the targets. I make the suggestion to Martin and Edward when surprisingly they decline to do the same. I wrote this week to Lu Ping about our pension proposals; he told his Preliminary Working Committee, and they passed all the details to the press. We will remind Lu of this next time he asks to be briefed on everything.

Kim and Edward came up to Fanling. We all went out to dinner at the Pigeon restaurant at Shatin and the following day we took them and the Dinhams out on the boat, though I had to spend much of the time working in the cabin. In the evening we gave Robin and Sue McLaren a dinner with some of their old Hong Kong friends. There is a story in the papers about signs of cholera being detected at a couple of restaurants: we will have to follow this up quickly next week.

Thursday 14 July
At my Business Council meeting this morning we discussed the Consumer Council report on banking. This has proposed getting rid of the interest rate agreement under which the banks in effect coordinate a view on not paying any interest on people's deposit accounts. There is a good competition

policy argument in favour of removing this, but on the other hand I don't want to put the banks in any difficulties between now and 1997. We got a general endorsement for our land proposals, which seem to have taken the heat out of the market. At the end someone asks whether the Business Council can help with the job that I have referred to from time to time of building bridges between the business community and the pro-democracy politicians. I've spoken only recently to Martin Lee and the Democrats about this. I gave the council my oft-repeated line (which I can now do in my sleep) about the importance of the business community recognizing that more democracy isn't bad for business, and the pro-democracy politicians recognizing the importance of the business agenda. So they should all now sit around the campfire and sing 'Kumbaya'.

It turns out that the worrying cholera story, promulgated by the *Sunday South China Morning Post*, was based on water samples from the fish tanks of two restaurants. Apparently, the newspaper knew that the surveys were inconclusive when it printed the story. The latest checks have shown that the water samples were fine. I hope the newspaper gets taken to the cleaners by the restaurants concerned.

Friday 15–Saturday 16 July

Alastair Goodlad is in Beijing on the visit which we strongly advised against making and it is obviously very difficult for him. I hope it doesn't set things back too much. The telegrams about his meetings at the weekend, on 16 July, make pretty grisly reading. He saw Jiang Enzhu and Qian Qichen and received stern and unbending responses to his efforts to move everything onto a friendlier plain. It's not his fault. What were we expecting? It was a bloody silly decision by the FCO to send him. After the talks Qian denies in reply to a question from a journalist that he had ever said it was possible to separate political from economic issues. So far from moving things forward we've been pushed backwards. It's the point that the press are most excited about until that is they learn that Alastair is not going to see Lu Ping. (Actually he never was.) They regard this as a huge snub. The one thing that we can't say, much as we would like to do so, is 'we told you so', although we did. The press afterwards is ghastly. It's so ridiculous to be chasing after the Chinese in this way. We really should just have sat under the tree and waited for things to warm up in their own time.

Monday 18 July

We've started discussing the arrangements for functional constituencies (which should not be too complicated) and also decided that with only a couple of years to go we have to make a fuss in the autumn about slow progress in the JLG, where we face a combination of Chinese obduracy and incompetence. We have such a good team there but they are trying to push boulders uphill. I want Douglas to raise this when he sees Qian at the UNGA [United Nations General Assembly].

I had my first one-on-one meeting with the new police commissioner, Eddie Hui. He is a bit concerned about his first trip to Beijing in mid-August. We've had a couple of difficult cases of Chinese dissidents slipping into Hong Kong whom Chinese security would like to see returned to their embrace. They are starting to make all sorts of threatening noises about not allowing us to send any illegal immigrants back over the border unless we also send them the people they want to lock up. During an interview with a journalist he tells me that he went to Yunnan shortly after Lavender had been there. One of the people she had spoken to there, a musician who had once been in prison for allegedly dissident activities, was interrogated by the secret police a couple of days after she had met him.

Thursday 21 July

Discussion with FCO advisers and our security officials on how we can take forward the forced repatriation of Vietnamese migrants in September. This is going to be very tricky to organize, particularly as we get closer to the deadline over the next two years. Pushing people in handcuffs onto planes is never going to be comfortable, and it's not just the most fainthearted liberals who feel queasy about it.

I had my last talk in Hong Kong with the Canadian consul, John Higginbotham, who is off to be number two in the Canadian embassy in Washington. As ever he was full of good sense. He pointed out how the Chinese have failed over the last three years. They polarize the community and yet we have won the argument. Their only support, and that's pretty rickety, is from the business community, and there the greater backing comes from those with foreign passports. Thanks to their efforts, the airport will cost more than it would have done. They also got rid of David Wilson and got me instead. They have lots of warring groups on their side, all hoping to get their snouts in the trough in Hong Kong. He believes that we have been successful in getting Hong Kong accustomed to the software of a free, open and plural society, that policy previously was a matter of just keeping our fingers crossed about the Joint Declaration and the Chinese commitment to it. We weren't telling people the truth or making them face up to the reality that they would have to want Hong Kong to succeed if it were to have any chance of doing so after the handover. He thinks that this was in many ways a dreadful hoax. At least we have given Hong Kong citizens the chance to make some of their own decisions about the future. I wish this man had been working in our own foreign service for the last 20 years.

Friday 29nd July

The Cabinet was reshuffled in London on the 22nd. I wonder whether it will make any difference. The last polls before I leave for London, and a holiday in France with Lavender, Alice and a succession of friends, show that here in Hong Kong we have growing, indeed huge, support for our proposals on pensions.

In meetings in the last week of July with the Prime Minister, the Foreign Secretary, Alastair and officials I've been arguing that we have less than three years to go; we have had a struggle and there will be some tough pounding to come but I hope we are through the worst. I hope that 'events' don't make it even tougher. At a meeting in the FCO Alastair suggests that one way of putting some more vitality into the JLG would be for ministers occasionally to chair meetings. Needless to say, this sends officials into a tailspin. But it might show that we are prepared to push the Chinese harder to make progress.

The Prime Minister was more cheerful than I've seen him for some time. There is a very odd disjuncture at the moment between the economic news, which gets ever better, and the political news, which is ever bleaker. John is happy about the way the reshuffle has gone. Douglas is going to retire from the scene next year. He still doesn't seem convinced that I can't conceivably give up in Hong Kong and take over from him. But I suspect that I had the decisive conversation on the subject with John just before the reshuffle, when he phoned up for my views on one or two of the ministers who were going to be involved in the musical chairs and I said once again that I should stay in Hong Kong until the handover.

Sunday 28 August

A big bonus from our holiday in France is that we've found and bought a holiday house – at a ridiculously bad exchange rate, but there it is. We were recommended to Stella Wright by John Fraser. Stella knows the property market for foreigners in and around Najac, where we used to have family holidays. We drove across from the Dordogne, where we were staying to see her. She showed us two or three perfectly nice houses. We went back with her to her own house to talk about them; and I said truthfully that much as we had liked them we didn't care for them as much as we liked her own – to which she replied that she and her husband were selling it. We walked around the garden and made an offer on the spot. Stella and her husband, George, left Britain for New Zealand, found it too quiet even for them, so they upped sticks and came to live in the depths of the French countryside. There is a guest cottage which will need a lot doing to it, but George runs a small building business and his deputy will do the work for us. We have been incredibly lucky.

The only downside of our holiday is that Laura and Kate haven't been with us. Laura has been working for the *Mail on Sunday* getting some experience of fashion journalism, and Kate has been travelling not without incident in Asia. In Thailand, the friend with whom she was travelling lost her passport and Vietnamese visa so they weren't able to get into Vietnam, which had been the principal object of the trip. Anyway, we will see them in September for Lavender's birthday.

Monday 29 August

We've got back and I've been in a gloom. It seems to have been raining here ever since we left for our holiday. The house has been leaking and there are signs of mould in one of the guest bedrooms. I find myself answering the same old questions and having to give the same old answers. We don't seem to be making progress on anything; the JLG is stuck again. It's never quite clear whether the Chinese are trying to make a point, or whether they simply don't know what to do, or whether no one in Beijing has the political clout to take any initiatives. But the girls are now with us and David Frost has come to stay and is as ever an amiable parody of himself. Archbishop George Carey and his wife passed through Hong Kong on their way into China to check up on their beleaguered flock there.

Friday 2 September

The National People's Congress in Beijing has announced that it intends to dissolve the elected legislature in Hong Kong after 1997. I don't suppose that this should surprise us too much but it's very depressing, for us, but much more importantly for the community as a whole. I see Ron Brown, the American Commerce Secretary, who has just been in China himself. He is pleased as punch that the Chinese have signed some trade deals with Washington, but the *Wall Street Journal* is sniffing around to see whether they amount to real business or simply memoranda of understanding with not much follow-through. They also appear to have made threats both before and during his visit that if they don't get membership of the GATT, they will break international rules on trade and investment whenever it seems to suit them. I think they'll break the rules even if they are members of the GATT. At least Washington denounces the decision by the NPC.

The best bit of scandal, or maybe it's just an embarrassment, is that Tsang Yok-sing apparently applied for a Canadian passport after the Tiananmen murders in 1989, although he subsequently withdrew the application. This doesn't look good for the leader of the pro-Beijing party. His family went ahead with their application and are now settled in Canada.

Monday 5 September

We held a reception for all the families who had received us into their own homes on our district or public housing visits. Most of them had never been to Government House before. We gave them a tour as well as drinks and had a good chat. They seemed delighted. It was well worth the rather modest effort.

Thursday 15 September

We're spending quite a lot of time considering how we may be able to energize the JLG process. Despite all his problems with Bosnia, Douglas Hurd has agreed that he can break into a longer trip and make a short visit. While he is with us he will go to the JLG. The day before he arrived (15 September) China had another bash at Jardine's and its involvement in the proposed container terminal nine. There is no particular agenda for Douglas's brief call, but it's felt – probably correctly – that it will put him into a stronger position when he meets Qian at the UNGA.

Douglas has met Hugh Davies's opposite number, Guo Fengmin, and they had a rather inconsequential discussion, which presumably gives Guo himself a certain amount of face. Afterwards, Douglas indicated that he now has a better feel for the problems confronting our JLG team, who continue to try to plant seeds in exceedingly stony ground. We had a delightful dinner for Douglas and FCO officials with a few locals like Martin Lee and Rosanna Wong. Looking for good news wherever one can, Rosanna is extremely complimentary about the improvement in GH food. She says that in the old days she always ate before coming here!

Friday 16 September

We had a really excellent dinner with Raymond Chi'en and his wife at their wonderful house full of fine Chinese antiques in Deep Water Bay overlooking the sea. One of Raymond's guests is a lawyer who had spent three years in jail in China for alleged spying. He worked for the Chinese politburo and had then gone to work in the USA for an American law firm. The next time he went to China he was arrested. He refused to confess to being a spy, and it took three years to get him out of prison, even longer to get himself rehabilitated. Now, he is back with his own company doing business in China. He takes it as a matter of course that he was wrongly accused by people he knew, who did it to save their own position.

His attitude seems to be – 'that's what China is like'. This is not a way of life for the fainthearted.

Monday 19 September

Lavender's 50th birthday. I arranged for her to be woken up by a piper playing 'Happy Birthday to You'. To be honest it sounded rather odd on the pipes, but it certainly got everybody up. The girls took her out to lunch and then in the evening we have the big treat. After supper, we blindfolded her and took her into the hall, where we had arranged three portraits of the girls that I got a Northern Ireland painter, Tom Hallifax, to do secretly. Blindfold removed, Lavender was thrilled to bits and a little tearful.

Tuesday 20 September

We had held the district board elections today, and after our registration drive we got a record number of people voting – over 600,000. The Democrats have won the majority of seats; Allen Lee's lot have done badly; and the pro-Beijing DAB have performed reasonably well, which might perhaps constrain just a little Beijing's hostility to fair elections. But all our sucking up on the JLG seems to have got us nowhere. Hugh Davies and his colleagues have gone to Beijing for meetings and nothing much has emerged, though we have reached a triumphant deal on postage stamps. At a side meeting with Lu Ping, Hugh raised the question of the reporting obligations under the UN covenants and Lu lost his rag for reasons which nobody can quite fathom. Hugh, who is unfailingly polite and courteous, is really quite shocked by the outburst. We will see whether Douglas's meeting with his opposite number in New York helps to get things moving faster.

Friday 23 September

We have a difficult corner to turn, moving from being thought to be too confrontational with China to offering in a sensible way cooperation without abandoning any of our principles. I am worried about being manoeuvred into no-man's-land with some people attacking us for kowtowing and others hitting us over the head for still not getting on with China. And whatever we do, how will China respond? My former PA in Parliament, Freda Evans, has arrived for a visit and so have Bob Alexander and his Irish barrister wife, Marie. We saw them in France in the summer. Bob is now chairman of the NatWest Bank and has been in China with a trade delegation. They were given assurances by Vice Premier Li Lanqing that trade and politics would not be mixed up. The truth is that we just don't know. Exports continue to be very good and British direct investment and joint ventures are also running at a high level.

Sunday 25–Monday 26 September

I arranged a two-day meeting for all my political advisers and the JLG team plus Hong Kong government officials, partly to do a bit of bonding and partly to discuss how to get on better with Beijing, the outlines of what Douglas Hurd should say to Qian and what I should say in my Legco speech on 5 October. We had a barbecue for everybody on Sunday night with open and free-flowing discussion for the best part of two days. We have good ideas on how we can cooperate with Lu Ping's working committee without compromising the Hong Kong government. Lu has been pressing us to allow somebody from the Hong Kong Monetary Authority to attend a seminar on the link between the US dollar and the Hong Kong dollar. It seems to me to be a harmless gesture to let somebody go along, and the Trade Development Council have already been involved in a similar seminar. We will let Len Appleyard, our new ambassador in Beijing, take this back as a pressie for Lu. I think Len is going to be much happier about talking to his opposite numbers whenever there is nothing difficult on the table. We will miss Robin McLaren, but someone has heard that Sherard Cowper-Coles reckons it's time for cringe mode. We covered a number of other subjects from the JLG agenda, to the civil service transition, to nationality, and finally the sort of ceremony that we will want at the end when the handover actually takes place. Sherard and I agree that we don't really need to go plugging away at a comprehensive adaptation of laws. If the Chinese don't like some of our laws they will doubtless adopt them after the handover. Why should we be obliged to do it all for them beforehand in the interests of 'convergence'? I hope we can clear problems like this away rather than march them in phalanx up to the conference table.

Tuesday 27 September

At Exco we talked about the pitiful results from the JLG and had a long discussion about the reporting obligations under the International Covenant [on Civil and Political Rights]. Denis Chang is very strong on the principles involved. Andrew Li thinks that the issue is rather more nuanced. He has just been in Beijing, where he was presumably being inspected for future reference. My guess is that he would be reluctant to get involved in the competition to be the next chief executive. The better people there seem to be interested still in Anson among others. Later in the day I see the US Air Force chief of staff and the commander of the

Seventh Fleet, who came in with Richard Mueller.* He said that Donald Rumsfeld and a group of Republicans who were in Beijing recently saw Qiao Shi, the chairman of the standing committee on the NPC and a member of the standing committee of the politburo. He told them that there were differences about how to handle Hong Kong that they were trying to resolve. This seems a surprisingly honest admission. Richard also said that he has had a rather bleak meeting with Li Chuwen,† who senior leaders use to try to find out what is happening in Hong Kong. He seemed to be gloomy about any improvements in relations with Hong Kong. He blamed the deterioration on the fact that, after saying that I would leave decisions to Legco, I then lobbied for my own bill on electoral arrangements. This of course overlooks the extremely hard Chinese lobbying, with phone calls from Lu Ping and others to legislators during the debate itself. Li Chuwen spent some time in Hong Kong in the 1980s as the deputy head of the NCNA and has a rather shady past on the fringes of the security services – it is even suggested that his one-time vocation as a pastor was simply a cover.

Douglas seems to have had a productive meeting with Qian Qichen in New York. Qian appears to be reasonably interested in and impressed by what Douglas had to say. Basically, this was that we were very happy to work constructively with the committees established to support Lu Ping, for example we could help them to understand the budgetary process, the way the Hong Kong Monetary Authority worked and our system of immigration controls. But plainly we would not be able to do anything which undermined the existing government and its officials before the change of sovereignty. When there was a designated chief executive we would also want to give him or her support, including staff. Qian put away his speaking notes and there was an unusual role reversal, Douglas delivering a long speaking note and the Chinese Foreign Minister chipping in from time to time. The body language was pretty good, and nothing was said afterwards which detracted from the atmosphere.

Friday 30 September

We celebrated Alice's birthday by going out for dinner. Before that not part of any sentient human being's idea of celebration, we had to attend the China National Day reception held this year in the convention centre.

* Richard Mueller was the US consul-general who retired from Hong Kong to become a school principal, first in Massachusetts and then back in Hong Kong.

† Li Chuwen was deputy director of the New Chinese News Agency in Hong Kong from 1983 to 1988. He died in Shanghai aged 100, in 2018.

There was a large police presence for a rather small crowd of demonstrators outside. The evening was as ghastly as ever, but Zhou Nan was on best behaviour – all smiles and courtesy – and his wife is a genuinely nice woman. It's the usual combination of forced bonhomie, Chinese communist diplo-speak, a gathering of the quislings and a gauntlet run through the press. I hope that I managed to get away with it; it helped to have Lavender with me. Perhaps Zhou Nan feels the same about the two of us as I do about him and his wife.

Len Appleyard saw Lu Ping today to hand over a copy of the speaking note which Douglas had delivered to Qian. Lu was amiable and read the note with apparent interest and care. However, there is always a piece of grit in the sandwich – Lu gave a warning on the Taiwanese National Day celebrations called 'Double 10', because they're held on 10th October. This is real Murphy's Law nonsense. A Taiwanese cultural organization has booked a room in the cultural centre for the commemorations. The Chinese are making a huge fuss about this, claiming that it shows we have changed our policy on Taiwan. 'We have to accept responsibility for the consequences of our actions', and all the rest of the garbage. It is all part of Beijing's general upping the ante on Taiwan. They have recently bashed the Japanese and said very tough things to the Americans, probably a response to Taiwan's increasing assertiveness. Just at the moment when we are trying to improve relations, this is quite likely to derail things again. Predictably we're getting lots of sound and fury from the local NCNA.

Monday 3 October

I had a very interesting talk with two of our young women researchers from Beijing and Hong Kong, who decided to focus their professional careers on China, and are now starting to discover that they can't stand it. While they are downbeat about the immediate future, they both reckon that China will muddle through the next few years. After them I had tea with the former Canadian Prime Minister Brian Mulroney and his wife. I like him whenever I see him and can't understand why the Canadians chucked him out. He says that Hong Kong is the only place where he thinks some people have been prepared to give up freedom for money. A lot of business leaders appear to have done a Faustian deal with the Chinese; you give us the capitalist part of the Joint Declaration and you can do what you want with the rest. But, sooner or later, the law for Martin Lee is the same as the law for the big corporate bosses.

Tuesday 4 October
At Exco I went through the main points in the Legco speech that I've been working on for Wednesday. A lot of it will be showing the progress we've made in our social commitments since last year thanks to our healthy economy. But there will be some comments on trying to improve our relationship with Beijing and to move things along in the JLG. We of course discussed the Double 10 row. Virtually everyone is resigned to Chinese explosions, hoping they don't blow too much apart. Only C. H. Tung thinks in his usual agonizing way that 'something must be done', but he is rather less clear about what exactly that is. During a brief talk to Martin Lee, I made the point very gently that during his trip later in the month to the Conservatives' conference he would be wise not to spend too much time attacking the government. I need to keep the Conservative Party on side as well as Labour.

Wednesday 5 October
My Legco speech seemed to go perfectly well, though you never know that in the chamber since there is barely any reaction at all. It is a bit like speaking to yourself in the bathroom. I gave updates on all our social and educational programmes and explained once again the nature of the cooperation we are very happy to have with Beijing and with the Preparatory and Preliminary Working Committees established by the Hong Kong and Macau Affairs Office (HK MAO). I also looked forward to the Legco elections next year and to working with the new legislature. People seem to be scratching their heads about whether we have changed our policy about dealing with Beijing and about the nature of our conversations with them over the next three years. Are we really offering olive branches? If we are, will the Chinese just turn them down? It is really quite simple. If we just give in to all they want us to do with and for their Preliminary Working Committee we might as well cave in now and go home. We would in effect be accepting the same sort of status as Macau. We have got through the last year without having our authority eroded and we have to continue governing Hong Kong ourselves while being as helpful as is reasonable about the future. The thing I worry about most is the establishment of the Court of Final Appeal, where nothing has been done since we came a cropper in Legco in 1991, being defeated over a bill that reflected a secret deal with China on the replacement of the Privy Council as Hong Kong's top judicial authority. My hunch is that this is going to take up a lot of our energy and political credit over the coming year. I keep on saying this to people and they smile benignly.

During the media phone-ins and interviews and a Legco Q and A session, I hammer away at the same points, that there is a difference between the Preparatory (to be set up) and Preliminary Working Committee set up by Beijing, which are not part of the government of Hong Kong, and the Joint Liaison Group established as part of Sino-British agreements. We are quite prepared to have more cooperation now. We have put forward precise proposals for speeding up the work of the JLG – greater frequency of meetings, and more expert groups with (if China wants) members of its Preliminary Working Committee on these groups. It would be wrong for civil servants to be members of this committee themselves or to attend its official meetings, but we are being as flexible as possible about contacts with individual PWC members. We are not going to put Hong Kong government officials in situations which could compromise them, nor are we going to cede authority to Beijing-appointed committees before 1997.

Thursday 6 October

Richard Mueller gave me a readout of Qian Qichen's recent meeting with Warren Christopher. Qian spoke fairly warmly about his meetings with Douglas Hurd, remarked on the more positive British approach, but said that he thought we had always recognized that constitutional arrangements without the approval of China would be a second-best and we would have to accept that a consequence was that there would be changes in Hong Kong after 1997. We are picking up now from this full reporting telegram that there was some indication during the Hurd meeting that Qian was concerned that we shouldn't spend all the money in Hong Kong before we left, nor change all the laws.

The Taiwanese National Day is approaching and the embassy in Beijing, in their maximum cringe mode, are getting very nervous about the Double 10 issue. They want a 'something must be done' solution. Perhaps one will arrive by first class post, though this may be too reliant on the deal we've done on postage stamps in the JLG. They are behaving as though the Chinese were acting perfectly reasonably. Somehow we should have stopped it all happening, though exactly how is unclear. We go through all the legal arguments about the booking at the Centre, which seem watertight when I talk to senior officials. They are happy with the position that we've taken on the Preliminary Working Committee, but one or two are upset by the fact that China has started to target them, telling the media for example that they weren't invited to the NCNA reception. While one response might be 'Lucky them', the intention is obviously to unsettle them about their futures. So we have Mafia behaviour in Hong Kong and cringe in our Beijing embassy. Len phones and says that the Double 10 row is going to wreck all our initiatives. Isn't there something we can do about it? I politely tell him that there isn't. I suspect all this is a sign of things to come. As luck would have it, the Anglo-Taiwanese Parliamentary group called to see me today. They are a bunch of mostly right-wing mavericks – Nicholas Winterton, Richard Shepherd, Jerry Wiggin and more similar. At least they support what we are doing in Hong Kong. I hope no one notices they've been here, because it will all be regarded as part of a plot – not least by our own side!

Monday 10 October

In the event, the Taiwanese celebrations at the Civic Centre all went off quite quietly, not least thanks to our encouragement behind the scenes. For example, there was no display of flags. My own hunch is that Chinese outrage over this has been pretty routine, but with them who knows?

Lydia Dunn has been in Japan for a week. She expresses Swire's nervousness that there are indications of people starting to opt to leave Hong Kong before 1997 and concern about rumours that the Chinese Civil Aviation Authority is planning to set up its own airline in Hong Kong after the handover. This would demolish the assurances it has given in the past and would pose a real threat to Cathay. I am not at all sure what the market rate of CCP assurances is.

Friday 14 October

There are more rumours at the end of the week about Deng's state of health. I guess we must get used to lots more stories about this until the last chapter is actually written. Francis Cornish says that he and the DTI [Department of Trade and Industry] are getting more pessimistic about China trade, rather more because of China's worrying attitudes to foreign businesses than because of anything we are doing in Hong Kong. There has been a lot of unease about the suggestions that China will set up a provisional legislature (which I think is quite likely) and that all professional qualifications in China will have to be recognized in Hong Kong. I gave a speech for the Hong Kong General Chamber of Commerce and the Federation of Hong Kong Industries (an audience of about 500) pointing out that we are not a socialist administration and that we believe in the importance of the rule of law. We want to get on with China but not at the expense of destroying Hong Kong's autonomy. It all went quite well in the room, despite a hostile put-up question which I bashed over the boundary, so I don't believe there will be much publicity. Adrian Swire and Peter Sutch* talked to me about the same problems that Lydia mentioned at the beginning of the week.

Monday 17 October

We face a busy week though politically there's a slight feeling we are in limbo. It's as though we're waiting for something to happen, maybe something dramatic in Beijing or perhaps just an indication of movement on some of our business. For example, it feels as though we are very close to an agreement on the airport and that it is now only a question of when the Chinese decide that face allows them to sign up. If all this stuff about 'face' is a mark of an ancient and sophisticated civilization, then bring on the barbarians. Sir Richard Evans, who used to be our ambassador in Beijing, is rather dismissive of Jiang Zemin, saying that he used to see him at the embassy when Richard was the number two there and thought him a rather silly fellow; perhaps this was because of his singing and regular quotation of chunks of Shakespeare. He doesn't think that Jiang will last very long after Deng's death. This is a rather conventional view of Jiang, which I am not sure is right. He's got to the top in that cut-throat system; and has already stayed there for five years. He must have something going for him apart from the ability to remember bits of English poetry and the names of British film stars.

Tuesday 18 October

Richard Needham is in town with a group of 25 businessmen, going elsewhere in Asia rather than China. He wants me to talk to this group and set out our side of what is happening. They were surprisingly understanding. The general view is that doing business in China is never easy and they don't seem to think that they have actually lost any business recently, even though it may not be politically correct to trade with Britain. One of the businessmen said he is on his 87th visit in China, that it is always ghastly and that rows over Hong Kong don't seem to make much difference. The feedback from the meeting was very positive; meantime, alas, Jim Prior is still going around London denouncing our policy in Hong Kong and telling anyone who will listen that as a result GEC is doing very badly in China. There is no evidence for this but it doesn't seem to stop Jim saying it. The truth is that GEC is just not doing very well. Like some other badly performing corporates, they hunt everywhere for a reason that doesn't point any fingers back at them.

* Peter Sutch was a popular chairman of the Swire Group in Hong Kong from 1992 to 1999. He died in March 2002.

The present Secretary General of the French RPR [Rassemblement pour la République] (who was last here with Mme Pompidou) rather surprisingly endorsed this general view when he called. He is both intelligent and cynical (not at all unusual in my experience in France) and doubts whether being nice to the Chinese actually makes very much difference to doing business with them. He is very reluctant to take China at its own assessment.

Wednesday 19 October

Dinner this evening with Tony Howard* and his wife, Carol. He doesn't sound so starstruck by Blair as many others. I suspect this is partly because he can't stand Peter Mandelson. There are quite a lot in that camp but it won't stop the ascent of this clever and able schemer. Tony thinks that John Smith was far more soundly rooted than Blair and much more part of an authentic British Labour tradition.

Tony Galsworthy is briefly passing through and told us one interesting piece of gossip which he thinks has come from the head of Swiss intelligence. (I imagine this service is good because its members must have the details of all the bank accounts the Chinese leaders have – they have to put their money somewhere as well as Hong Kong.) The story is that Deng's family are busy looking for a cosmetic expert, and not the sort that you need when you are alive. This is thought to have some significance because when Mao died he apparently went green, which caused all sorts of problems when it came to embalming him.

Friday 21 October

Margaret Thatcher is here and so is Princess Alexandra, once again doing things for the police. We gave them dinner but before that I took Margaret on a district visit to Sai Kung, where she was in indomitable form despite having been obviously knocked about by an operation on her teeth under general anaesthetic during the summer. She charged into crowds and generally behaved as though she was in an election campaign. She has been laying about her with her handbag in meetings with some businessmen, trying to knock them into something approximating to decent shape and criticizing them for crawling to Beijing.

As part of our attempts to do some more serious work with the CCP,

* Anthony Howard was a distinguished left-wing journalist who was editor of *New Statesman*, deputy editor of the *Observer* and obituary editor of *The Times*. As a *Sunday Times* journalist covering Whitehall, he annoyed the Prime Minister, Harold Wilson, in the 1960s by campaigning for greater government transparency.

we have been trying to find ways in which we can coordinate our activities on cross-border infrastructure projects. What we are looking for is genuine liaison, not things which would give them an armlock on our investment decisions at the moment in Hong Kong. We are autonomous before 1997 and the SAR [Hong Kong Special Administrative Region] government is the same under the JB and BL after that date. We're trying to agree on some reasonable terms of reference and understand from Lu Ping that at the moment he would like discussions to proceed at a more junior level rather than through someone more senior like Anson Chan. Len Appleyard is having discussions about this with him today.

Sunday 23 October

I've been making speeches and going to dinners all week. Gareth Evans and William Rees-Mogg had supper with us on Sunday. Gareth says that when he was last in Beijing, he asked Li Peng about the imprisoned human rights activist Wei Jingsheng. Li responded by saying, ' You have come here to visit our country. If you want to have an enjoyable visit, you won't mention that man again.' Gareth identifies Li Peng as a complete bruiser, which is not difficult. William Rees-Mogg tells us that he doesn't think the Conservative Party is heading for a wipe-out on 1906 lines. He thinks that Blair will suck away much of the Liberal strength and that the election will be a bit like 1964, with the Labour Party just sneaking home. These ex-cathedra statements by William are (how can one put it courteously?) not always correct. He is not infallible. This is Somerset speaking not Rome.

Anson has just got back from a terrific trip to Canada and the US. She said there was general support in Canada and only a few queries in America about whether we were handling China correctly. She gave typically robust replies to these questions and warned about the avoidance of self-censorship and the importance of freedom of speech, so some of the United Front papers and rent-a-quote politicians are attacking her. We are spending a lot of time talking about the arrangements for infrastructure liaison and on a variety of infrastructure projects, including the airport and my own speciality, sewage strategy.

Tuesday 25 October

Just before we headed off for a rather crowded visit to London, I met the Chief Secretary, the Attorney General, the CJ [Chief Justice] and Michael Sze to talk once again about appointments to the bench, trying to get as many good judges there as possible. The CJ appeared optimistic that he will be able to replace senior judges as they retire with adequate successors. The rest of us were less confident. The real trouble is that there is still a big financial disincentive if you are a successful QC in becoming a judge in Hong Kong. We suggested to the CJ that he should look more widely for candidates, and consider doing a bit of headhunting in Britain and other common law jurisdictions.

Wednesday 26–Monday 31 October

London. I spoke at the Trade Development Council dinner with the Governor of the Bank of England, gave a lecture attacking protectionism for a Swiss bank, had lunch with the Hong Kong Association and another that Alastair Goodlad has organized with Arnold Weinstock, whose only suggestion was that we should withdraw from Hong Kong early since obviously we were going to annoy China until we had abandoned our responsibilities in the territory.

The Prime Minister is in good form, perhaps one of the fruits of the outbreak of peace with the IRA. We went for a walk around the park. I haven't known him in such high spirits since the last election. All in all, I got the impression (fingers crossed) that the business community was slightly calmer and that nobody much was interested in Hong Kong. I should concede that some of the reactions after my Swiss bank lecture, in which I had called into question the suggestion that human rights were not universal, belonged to the 'stuff democracy, three cheers for Lee Kuan Yew' saloon bar school of geopolitical wisdom.

I have refused to see the Conservative Party treasurer, who asked for a meeting, and one or two individual MPs who are keen to lobby on behalf of individual businesses or individuals in Hong Kong. I told the Prime Minister and he is wholly supportive.

At the end of a couple of extremely busy days, Lavender and I flew to Toulouse with Laura and drove up to stay in Cordes for a night while we completed the purchase of our house at Monbretal, did lots of measuring, talked to a builder and started to make some plans for next summer. The thought of having this beautiful French bolthole is certainly going to help me survive whatever the next year or two have to throw at us.

We flew back to Hong Kong on 31 October in time to present awards to industry. I've already had a talk to Anson, who came out to see me at the airport full of beans. She had made a fighting speech in Legco defending us against the criticisms of my address there and had then made another commanding speech at the Foreign Correspondents' Club about the importance of people in Hong Kong standing up for themselves. I think feisty is a word that was specially created for her.

While we seem to be getting close to an agreement on the airport, there is nevertheless concern (expressed very well by David Ford, who is visiting to receive an honorary degree) that we should avoid looking beleaguered and should be aware of some low spirits just below the surface among the civil service, many of whom may depart in the next year or two.

Tuesday 1 November

Jung Chang and her husband, Jon Halliday, had dinner with us. I asked her to rate monsters from 1 to 10. She gave Mao, whose biography she is now writing, 10+.

As we approach the end game over the airport, the Chinese are naturally trying to screw us, going back on things they had accepted even in the press release on the actual text of the agreement. We are digging in. One of the little tricks we are having to cope with is their effort to replace the word 'monitor' in the text of the agreement with 'supervise' in relation to expenditure. But it's only a word, they say. A word that makes rather a lot of difference.

Wednesday 2 November

I've seen Lord Limerick, the chairman of De La Rue. The Chinese are trying to push the company into a joint venture on the mainland which would in effect transfer technology plus profits in the banknote printing business. A familiar story. You wonder why so many fall for it. He certainly does not. Also, a jolly farewell lunch for Christine Chow, the regional secretary for Hong Kong in Kowloon. She has invited a lot of her female contemporaries, outstandingly good public servants. It seems quite obvious that the public sector has been a much better employer for women than the private; that's probably the same back home. They had a great gossip about corruption in the '70s and the Cultural Revolution riots before that. The present dramas seem rather slight by comparison.

Robin Cook has not only become shadow Foreign Secretary but intends to look after Hong Kong himself and wants a lot of briefing about it. I am not sure whether he will try to end the cross-party consensus on our policy here. This would be unhelpful but also unwise.

Amazingly, it seems that we may well get an agreement on the airport by the end of the week. I'm now keen to know where we stand on the Court of Final Appeal [CFA]. Consultations have begun with the legal profession, so we can't avoid coming to some decisions soon on whether we could set up a credible court to replace the judicial authority of the Privy Council. In Beijing, Len Appleyard is continuing his efforts at bonding. I am not sure how they will withstand the first bad news that he has to pass on to anyone, but I suppose it's a worthwhile exercise.

Friday 4 November

We signed a minute about the airport at 9.30am. Yet while all this wrangling has been going on, we have been actually building the airport. 11,000 people turn up each day to do the job. Some of the best of it is that the Chinese weren't able to use the airport as a lever against us. The downside is that the final agreement certainly doesn't represent the most sensible financing package, but that is for the Special Administrative Region to deal with after 1997 – we are in effect going to fund the airport out of our revenues as we go along, which will be more expensive (given our credit rating) than borrowing the larger part of the costs. But Beijing got obsessed with the idea that we were trying to leave them with huge debts after 1997 on a project which would be a pork barrel for British business. It is always going to be difficult to persuade them that we wouldn't behave as they would have done.

I gave a farewell lunch to Mike Hanson, who has done such a great job while retaining a remarkable equilibrium as well as his sanity, perhaps helped by the fact that he strongly suspects that it will all end after we've gone in tears. To replace him we have an Australian called Kerry McGlynn, who reminds me of why I like Australians (despite cricket) almost as much as Canadians.

Saturday 5 November

In an early test for Kerry, rather than a commemoration of Guy Fawkes's activities, we had to deal with what the journalists and newspapers concerned think is a wonderful and important stunt. A journalist from the *Sunday Times* and another from the *South China Morning Post* broke into Fanling as a demonstration that the security there is awful. Frankly, it is; we tend to apply it only at midday a few hours before someone like the Prince of Wales is due to arrive. I have deliberately turned down suggestions that we should have lights, barbed wire and lots more police at Fanling. What would be the point or justification for this sort of expenditure? But the whole thing is unpleasant. Lavender doesn't much care for the idea of journalists poking around in our bedroom. The press became very sanctimonious when we quite properly pointed out the costs of police time and so on of this little prank. I am delighted that the police had ensured that the two journalists concerned are still 'helping the police with their enquiries' after midnight.

Sunday 6 November

This evening the Prince of Wales did actually arrive for a visit and I'm pleased to say that the security was in place. He's here in the first place to speak at a conference on the urban environment, and does so much better than most of the others I hear. His officials are keen that I should do an interview for *Panorama* on the monarchy. They spend rather longer trying to brief me than the interview will take and, while perfectly amiable, behave rather as though I've never been on television before. When I actually do the interview the *Panorama* team think it is pretty boring because, as they say, I play a very straight bat. The truth is that I like and admire Prince Charles and his mother, think that the most important quality in a royal family is a sense of duty, and only get a bit critical when they agree to turn themselves into public celebrities. That's when they get all the stick. There are also too many of them.

Tony Eason, our senior civil servant responsible for cross-border infrastructure, has returned from China after the first meeting on the subject. It all went very well. Can I say, improbably, that the Chinese behaved very reasonably? If only life was more generally like this. Tony's interlocutors agreed that the new liaison machinery should not undermine Hong Kong's autonomy, should speed up rather than delay projects, and that the agenda for meetings should be by mutual agreement. Well, fancy that. We will follow all this up rapidly.

Tuesday 8 November

The editor of the *Sunday Times* has phoned up to say sorry, not something which editors often do, and so has the journalist concerned. It was all rather daft. I've never been very bothered about security, taking the view on the whole that if 'they' are going to get you, 'they' probably will. I hope that isn't regarded by the gods is as an excessively simple challenge, like my friend Gary Hart's challenge to journalists to catch him with his pants down. Alas, good man that he is, that didn't take them very long.

Wednesday 9 November

I headed out with the Prince of Wales to visit a housing estate. It all went perfectly well with big, well-ordered crowds – a bit too well ordered for my liking. Everybody was behind barriers and Edward discovered afterwards that the Housing Authority had rather foolishly repainted a lot of what the Prince of Wales was going to see. I talk to Rosanna Wong about this and give instructions that it mustn't happen again. The Prince obviously doesn't approve of all the high-rise flats and wants us to try something, in his own words, more 'holistic'. I wonder what this actually means – I don't dislike all his views on modern architecture but sometimes, like most enthusiasts, he goes over the top. How were we supposed to rehouse all those refugees from mainland China into Hong Kong given its size and topography? But he is miles ahead of most people in public life over the environment and gets criticized for it as though he were off his trolley.

Leon Brittan came for a meeting mostly on trade and I had a good private talk with him about the position the party is getting into over Europe. We are starting to minimize the influence we could have in the Union. We also discussed how foolishly Norman Lamont is behaving. Does he want to get into the government again or does he just want to ruin John Major? The latter seems to make the former impossible, not least since there won't be a Conservative government if he and others go on behaving the way they are.

Thursday 10 November

We are going to have problems with Legco and parts of the business community about our pension plans. We may have to strike a compromise and in the meantime fetch up paying higher allowances for the elderly. Many businessmen have been arguing for this though it smacks of welfarism and would be a pale copy, or not even that, of our own original proposals. Hong Kong is not a poor community, to put it mildly. If we can't have the sort of pension scheme that exists in so many Western countries, I will focus on a provident fund – with mandatory contributions from employers and their staff – like the one in Singapore.

Lavender has been making a lot of speeches – on family welfare, on AIDS and even on diarrhoea (don't ask me). I have also done loads of 'say it again Guv' interviews and a prize-giving at the excellent King George V School speech day in Kowloon. 'Success is not enough . . .' and all that: a very well-travelled speech.

Saturday 12–Sunday 20 November

We've had a short visit to the West Coast of America (starting on 12th November) with loads of speeches from Orange County to Los Angeles, to San Francisco and finally Seattle. They are mostly organized by World Affairs Councils. There are very good audiences of 600 to 700 and an excellent atmosphere with none of those 'so what's your next trick?' contributions that you get quite a lot in Hong Kong. I've met political leaders from the Governor, Pete Wilson, down to most of the mayors. I've also seen businessmen and do a seminar with a group of rather congratulatory

Sinologists at Berkeley for our friend Nelson Polsby. The political atmosphere is pretty excitable since only last week the American electorate gave the Republicans a majority in Congress for the first time in years. Newt Gingrich is dominating the news; there is a sour populist mood in the American working (they call it middle) class, not least because living standards go on being squeezed. The trip started off with an enjoyable if rather surreal visit to Hollywood to see Mike Medavoy and his beautiful new partner, Irena. We had a lunch with Barbra Streisand which makes me wonder why the word diva is normally associated with Italian sopranos, and a dinner with a group including Gregory Peck. If I had to look like anyone else, he would be my first choice; the choice that many other blokes would make too I expect. He was also charming and interesting with mainstream Democratic opinions.

Monday 21 November

There seems to have been a gentle thaw in our relations with Beijing, but the last thing we can do is claim that things are getting any better. However, they probably are. The Chinese have been mostly positive on infrastructure coordination, but are still intent nevertheless on making trouble over the sewage scheme. The puns are obvious. They clearly think this is yet another attempt to spend all Hong Kong's money and to give the project to British companies. In fact, so far only one contract has involved a British company and the two big contracts to come are unlikely to be won by Brits. At the same time, they obviously recognize that they are unlikely to win a public relations battle over sewage. I suspect we will also see a bit of progress on the JLG agenda, though not on any political issues. And they won't give us any help on the Court of Final Appeal where they are being tiresome. They are in effect trying to second-guess the legal judgments of the law officers in London and the Attorney General in Hong Kong. This will not be allowed to happen, not least by the lawyers concerned.

What would the lawyers make of a case close to recidivism in the GH dog community? Soda has followed her partner's earlier crime and nipped a labourer who was working in the house. She too has been carted off for a week in clink. Will the rules apply to dogs as well after 1997?

We are having some difficulties returning Vietnamese migrants. The government in Vietnam has just refused to take back 125 people because they were of Chinese ethnic origin. But when they are returned to us, it's impossible to keep them locked up in a camp; we would understandably lose cases on habeas corpus grounds. This is going to affect our ability to get most of the Vietnamese home before 1997. The Chinese and the United

Front in Hong Kong are stirring things up as much as they can, suggesting that any Vietnamese who are left at the time of the handover should be taken to Britain. Tell that to the Home Office! The Chinese of course discount the fact that most of the Vietnamese who got here came by way of China where they at least had a refuelling stop.

Louise is getting married to a very nice police officer in the commercial crime squad. At their engagement party, one or two of Steve's bosses there tell me about the difficulties they are having in persuading people to give evidence in one particularly high-profile case involving Macau and Portugal, even though they have a good deal of documentary proof of wrongdoing. When we raise this case with the Portuguese they tend to look the other way or shift the conversation.

Tuesday 22 November

Opening one of the latest urban-renewal projects in Wan Chai, I got a real insight into the problems of property prices. The flats are well done but small; probably suitable for yuppies. They will apparently cost about HK$3 million. Having to make a down payment of HK$1 million and then spend about HK$20,000 a month on the mortgage payments does give an idea of what those with aspirations to purchase are going to have to face.

Later on we went to Alice's school parents' evening. Alice is starting to talk to her teachers about her A-level options. They all love her (quite right too) but they note that while she is really 'A star', without being pushed she wouldn't mind settling for 'A/B'. No blame attached; it's quite a natural sentiment. We will just have to give a little push from time to time.

Thursday 24 November

At a thanksgiving lunch with the American Chamber of Commerce, a very nice crowd, I heard what is becoming an old, old story. Several people point out the dreadful problems of trying to do business in China but go on to say that they've more or less signed up to doing this as a sort of act of faith, believing that everything must be all right eventually and that China will somehow muddle through without the economy imploding. By and large, this is probably my position too. But the bridge between reason and acts of faith becomes ever more rickety and sometimes quite difficult to detect. There has been recently a string of cases involving Chinese companies ratting on their debts and wriggling out of contractual obligations. And so, I suspect, the story will continue.

Anson has been making some splendid speeches in London this week, saying that it is imperative that I stay until 1997 and that it is extremely unfair for British businessmen, who have passports and will leave in 1997, to be less than supportive about the rule of law and related issues. She doesn't allow anybody to slip a piece of tissue paper between the two of us.

Saturday 26 November

We went out to the USS *Kitty hawk*, a huge American aircraft carrier. A spectacular day. The senior officers – Admiral Blair is commander – are very impressive and the young pilots have our stomachs turning with stories about the horrors of landing, particularly at night, with the sense that you're dropping down a black hole with only your instruments guiding you to about 1200 feet and then simply going for it. Act of faith again I suppose. I also find the whole naval technology of catapulting planes from the deck and landing them with their trailing hooks catching at the wires which are there to halt them almost literally incredible. They were doing much the same thing in the Second World War and it's still the method that is used. I should record that Lavender probably saved my life when we were taking off, or at least prevented me being injured. She noticed just before the plane whizzed off down the deck that I hadn't put on my seatbelt properly and was not in the correct position to take off. She just about sorted me out but I still got quite a nasty bump from the seat in front. I am so maladroit doing anything that involves opening, shutting, clipping in, getting out. No wonder my valet had such difficulty believing that I could dress myself.

We gave a dinner for the Duke and Duchess of Kent (seventh or maybe eighth royal visitors of the year); the Duchess talks a lot about Northern Ireland and the Catholic Church.

Thursday 1 December

Lavender went with the Duchess of Kent to the paediatric ward at the Queen Elizabeth Hospital. Lavender had opened the play areas there three months ago. The Duchess was very good with the children, some of whom had been in hospital for all too long. Lavender agreed with the hospital administrator that she would return soon and see some of the AIDS patients. If he agrees, she wants to be photographed with Mike Sinclair, a Scottish dentist who went public about a year ago about being HIV positive and has been a tireless educator about AIDS ever since. He is now getting very weak and Lavender wants to help with the educational programme and demonstrate that nobody is going to get AIDS simply by shaking hands with someone who is suffering from it.

While Lavender was at the hospital, I was doing a degree ceremony at the Chinese University. Once again, I was overwhelmed by the sense of social revolution that you get on these occasions, with more than half the graduating students coming from public housing. Ordinary working-class families – some dads wearing a suit probably for the first time in their lives – were seeing their children graduate. It was a cheering spectacle and I hope the best for them. When you go into their homes, lots of them have a photograph on a sideboard or on top of the television of a son or daughter in a graduating cap and gown. I had a great hour or so afterwards with Anwar Ibrahim, who is now the Deputy Prime Minister of Malaysia and Finance Minister. He made a good speech at the Foreign Correspondents' Club [FCC] saying that no one should use the argument about Asian values as a justification for autocracy or for setting back progress towards a representative government.

Sunday 4 December

After playing tennis with them Lavender and I had dinner with Lothar and Christina Wesemann and a group of friends, including Charles Brown (an American architect), his wife, Rosamond (an excellent painter, we've bought two of her paintings), and some others, including Edgar Cheng (who is married to the fourth of the Pao – shipping empire – daughters, Doreen). Edgar, who seems to be well educated and quite sophisticated, generally takes the view that cooperation is doing whatever China wants. It is not for China, he tells everyone, to make people in Hong Kong feel comfortable about the handover; all the accommodating towards a smooth transition must come from Hong Kong and its citizens. Everyone present likes Edgar and was obviously disappointed that he feels the necessity of defending Beijing over Hong Kong on just abut everything. He doesn't seem to understand it when I say that there are some things I couldn't possibly do, like agreeing to China's recent demand that we should hand over all the personnel files of civil servants to Beijing, which would completely undermine the confidence of the civil service. It's said that a benign consequence of being educated in open societies, or working in them, is that some of our values rub off on people, but I keep on seeing examples where that simply hasn't happened.

Monday 5 December

I made a speech at an international conference on drug abuse outlining new proposals we are intending to make to step up our campaign on drugs in the city. By the standards of many other communities our figures are still low, but they are starting to rise. I'm going to call a summit next year to deal in particular with the question of public education and the role of schools in this. In the afternoon we had an investiture. These occasions still appear to be very popular with those receiving an honour and their families and friends. I wonder if the recipients will still be wearing their Orders of the British Empire after 1997. Jenny Best* organizes these events and my ADC calls out the names of those who are going to be honoured, while another honorary ADC hands me the medals on a red velvet cushion. The ADCs look very smart in their white uniforms with silver and navy tassels and epaulettes. In times past, the Governor would have worn uniform and a hat himself to conduct the ceremony.

Tuesday 6 December

There has been a last-minute hitch before we can conclude the negotiations on cross-border infrastructure. The late Chinese trick is related to 'three legged stoolism', that is, the attempt to ensure that there is a member of the political adviser's office (that is, someone who works for the British government) as part of our team; in other words they don't want it to look as though they have done a deal with a Hong Kong delegation. After a lot of ridiculous argument, we add someone to our side who is actually a Hong Kong civil servant though he works for the political adviser's office.

Lavender and I then went to an exhibition at the Museum of Art featuring the work of Anson's 80-year-old and very distinguished mother, Mme Fang. She is a traditionally trained Chinese painter, using lots of calligraphic strokes, and probably the most famous female artist in China for many years. All four of her sons went to Oxford or Cambridge; two daughters went to university in Hong Kong. She is clearly very forceful and strong-minded. It is not surprising that she has a daughter like Anson – indeed, Anson says that if people think that she herself is tough, they should meet her mother.

At Legco questions I've started to get some tough interventions on the CFA. I have bad vibes about what lies ahead on this still to be agreed proposal and subsequent legislation. No one in London and our embassy in Beijing is going to want another row with China. Lawyers in Hong Kong will want us to deliver everything that they criticized us for failing to get when the last proposal was defeated in 1991. Beijing will be difficult over both the extent of the court's jurisdiction and the presence of foreign judges from common law jurisdiction on the court. Business will want the court to be on parade after the handover but will not lift a finger to help us secure it. Hard pounding ahead. Just to make it harder still, Lu Ping has

* Jenny Best was my private secretary throughout my years in Hong Kong. She was outstandingly competent and an important member of the Government House team.

appeared to suggest that CFA judges won't travel through 1997. He is not going to make it any easier for me to square the lawyers in Legco and the Bar Council.

Sunday 11 December

A visit to South Korea, staying in Seoul with the ambassador, Tom Harris, and his Taiwanese wife. The weather was freezing. I saw the President, the Deputy Prime Minister and the Minister for Trade; two out of three were called Kim. I spoke at a business conference and had lots of other meetings with business leaders. They seem keen on both Britain and Hong Kong and we should obviously do more in their big and growing market. They are rather ambivalent about China, but their museum on the war with the North, which we visited, seems to downplay China's role. They obviously recognize that they are moving economically into the big time. They were rather more cheerful than I expected them to be, mostly tall and good-looking. Lavender took me along to the local market, where I bought (out of the many available there) a rather good fake Rolex. It will probably stop tomorrow. Lavender bought leather jackets for the girls. Lavender was rather disappointed that we don't have any Korean meals; since I can't stand the smell of kimji I don't mind this a bit. (No kimji when we ate with the Foreign Minister.) An American senator who has just visited Pyongyang tells us that when he was shown the Metro system, it was obviously a bomb shelter rather than a transport network, but to make it look more authentic, a ceremonial train was produced which arrived at the platform empty; twenty would-be passengers had been lined up on the platform to embark.

Wednesday 14–Tuesday 15 December

A remarkable three days in Japan. I was given even better access than I receive in London. It's difficult to know the reasons for this. While some of the Sinologists in the Japanese Foreign Ministry are reluctant to do anything which will cross China, I do now have many friends in the Japanese bureaucracy and Japan is doubtless happy to send one or two messages to China in view of a recent fracas over Taiwan. The Japanese will not want Beijing to think that their views can be taken for granted. This sentiment may be enhanced by knowing perfectly well that they're likely to get a bashing over the next year from China, given that it will be the 50th anniversary of the end of the Second World War. Hong Kong also has a very close trading and economic relationship with Japan, which sends excellent diplomats to us as consuls-general. Our friend

Orita* was followed by Nogami, another real star. He is rather improbably a Japanese rugby player with a ponytail and an Irish wife. And, of course, in John Boyd and his wife, Julia, we have a formidable duo in Tokyo who have worked and lived in Hong Kong and have many friends there.

At the end of the week we were given an audience with the Emperor and Empress. We went to the Imperial Palace, a modern Japanese building in spectacular grounds, and were immediately cocooned in the bureaucracy of the imperial court, being told how to begin the meeting, how to end it, how to behave and how to bow. The Emperor and his wife were completely charming, like trapped butterflies. I was sat with the Emperor and had to make the pace a bit. On the other side of the room Lavender talked to the Empress, who is obviously rather easier going. She has the face of a saint, full of courage and suffering and pity. You can't help but get the impression that they are prisoners in this court. When the Empress was criticized in the Japanese media last year on some absurd grounds, she lost her voice for three months. Was that a breakdown or was it (as some suggest) a strike? Anyway, they leave the same impression as former Premier Miyazawa, who was one of the many senior politicians we met – the gentle, porcelain side of Japanese society and culture.

At the end of the audience (and we were under strict instructions that it was up to us to terminate the conversations, of course with great politeness), we withdrew from the large, bare, modern Japanese room and descended the stairs outside. When we got to the bottom, we turned to bow and curtsey to the Emperor and his wife. They were framed in the doorway above us, he in his double-breasted suit and she in her traditional Japanese dress. I think it will be my most abiding memory of Japan. Heaven knows what the Crown Prince's wife will make of it when her time comes. She is a Balliol graduate and daughter of Owada, who has been the Japanese ambassador to almost everywhere and who is certainly one of the most impressive civil servants I have ever met.

While I was doing a television interview late one night, Edward chose instead to watch one of those dreadful Japanese television programmes on another channel in which people (most particularly nubile young ladies) do unspeakable things to one another, eating creepy crawlies or throwing mud. In those sorts of Japanese television programme, pain and humiliation are never far from what people laugh about. What a contrast – from lotus blossom and exquisitely presented Japanese food to sumo wrestling and popular Japanese TV. But I suppose that if I had to choose between

* Masaki Orita later became Japanese ambassador in Denmark and the United Kingdom.

watching an interview on television with me or one of those popular TV shows I would probably choose the latter every night of the week.

Monday 19 December
Discussing the scant pickings in the JLG recently, I start to wonder whether we don't get anywhere because the Chinese aren't capable of getting anywhere at the moment. Maybe, as some alleged China experts suggest, they are in a long-drawn-out slow-moving series of economic problems with political implications. Then at a routine meeting with the Commissioner of Police I expressed my concern about the number of officers who are currently being investigated by the ICAC [Independent Commission Against Corruption]. The Commissioner doesn't seem to think that the number is exceptional, nor that this is producing a morale problem in the force.

Tuesday 20 December
Just before we start closing down for Christmas, I went out for a private 'black spots' visit to three temporary housing areas and to a really unpleasant housing estate in Eastern. It's a good idea making these visits without telling anyone in advance, surprising people in their own communities, and not being surrounded by huge numbers of press. I should do it more often. It also tells me things that I should know but that officials may not be too keen on me knowing.

Thursday 22 December
Kate and Laura have come for Christmas and Matthew Parris is here to write a few pieces about Hong Kong. He used to work for me in the Conservative Research Department before going into Margaret's private office, getting into the House of Commons and becoming a media star. We have our first turkey of the season at a Christmas lunch for our private office.

Friday 23 December
We had a talk with my FCO officials about some of the difficult questions which we will be facing in the New Year in negotiations with the Chinese. We have to discuss – which will be a nightmare – rendition (that is, the return of fugitive offenders). We will doubtless provoke Chinese outrage when we deal with the draconian emergency powers legislation which sits unused on the statute book and has been there ever since the Cultural Revolution riots. Most awkward though will be the return to legislation on the Court of Final Appeal. This has been a dark cloud hanging over us ever since I got here.

The Hong Kong government did a secret deal with China and lost the legislation based on it under huge assault from every lawyer in town and Legco. It was one of the lessons from the past which encouraged me to avoid any secret dealing over the voting method. I don't imagine that we'll be able to get anything agreed with China unless we are able to make some compromises. But what is important is to get an agreement before our departure, to avoid any attempt to introduce a mechanism for second-guessing it if Beijing doesn't like its decisions, and to secure the appointment to the court of foreign judges. I imagine that the business community is likely to support us provided we avoid compromising the integrity of the system. Insofar as the necessary thumbs up from Beijing is likely to involve some sort of adjustment from the ideal, we will doubtless get a drubbing from every lawyer, and of course the Democrats have many lawyers in their ranks. And on top of all that, London and the embassy in Beijing in their new mode of operation will be second-, third-, fourth- and fifth-guessing us. It will be welcome to a New Year of fun and frivolity.

Lavender went off to the North District flower, bird, insect and fish show, and bravely put her hand into a beehive, which is more than I would do.

Friday 30 December

We had a very happy time over Christmas with the girls and a houseful of unattached youngsters. Lots to eat and drink, lots of good walks, lots of tennis. But I end the year rather fed up. It feels as though the walls are closing in. As far as international investors are concerned, the shine seems to have gone off the Chinese economy, as the Hang Seng Index is reflecting. Qian Qichen has pronounced that he is going to visit the UK, which some people see as a sign of improving relations. But you don't have to be the Delphic Oracle to see some of our FCO friends girding up to write all the telegrams about not rocking the boat and threatening a promised improvement in the atmosphere. We will get the usual attacks because we haven't got on better with Beijing, because we haven't done more for human rights, and because the closer we get to 1997 the more our authority will drain away. But I must try to keep cheerful. We are still running Hong Kong. There is still plenty to do and the public are still supportive.

Monday 2–Wednesday 4 January 1995

Perhaps the background mood has helped to put me in bed for a couple of days feeling ill with a nasty bug. Just to lower morale further, Kate and Laura have gone back to London. Lavender thinks that the last year has been the most stressful so far. There is a remorselessness about China's pursuit of its goals; the arguments go on and on. Talking to senior officials from the Hong Kong government plus the JLG team and my political advisers, we've concluded that the best way forward, without being provocative, is simply to do what we think is going to be best for Hong Kong wherever we can. The only way we can really warm up the relationship with Beijing is by doing whatever the CCP wants on Hong Kong, which is extremely *un*likely to be in Hong Kong's best interests. There are lots of rumours about Chinese determination to remove all department secretaries appointed by us; I don't believe they could be so stupid. There are also rumours about Deng being near death, and the stock market is still affected by general nervousness about China and by what looks like an impending US/China trade war.

Lavender has been again to see Mike Sinclair, the dentist who has been a powerful spokesman about AIDS and HIV, trying to ensure that people know how to protect themselves and to show compassion to those who have the disease. They give a press conference together at Queen Elizabeth Hospital and have lots of photographs taken shaking hands.

Sunday 8 January

Alastair Goodlad came to see us on one of his regular parish visits, checking out the ground before Qian goes to London and Michael Heseltine to Beijing with a big party of businessmen. Alastair was accompanied by Sherard, who at dinner with my senior team worked himself up into a great state about the dangers of us going unilateral with legislation on the Court of Final Appeal, which we will have to do if there is no movement from the Chinese side. There is plainly some anxiety on the part of London officials that Douglas leaves things to me, provided I can convince him, and doesn't listen enough to them. Since the Chinese know very well how we behave, they will play cat and mouse with us over the visits and hope that we return to our past way of doing business with them. But in Hong Kong, we are all too aware that we are going to have to legislate on the CFA come hell or high water by the summer holiday. We have to convince London that while we can delay on the bill for two or three months, we can't do so indefinitely. Anson feels very strongly about this. It's an issue which goes right to the heart of the government's credibility and authority.

Alastair will pick up the growing sense of economic jitters here, mostly related to China, with which the world is rapidly falling out of love. Francis Cornish, noting the herd instinct among bankers and businessmen, suggests that people are moving on China and Hong Kong from ridiculous optimism to the reverse.

Tuesday 10 January

After a meeting with a pretty downbeat Exco – C. H. Tung is away, so there's no one to tell us that everything will be fine come 1997 – I saw the heads of overseas offices. One surprise. Our man in Ottawa says that the relatively new Canadian government under Jean Chrétien is much less likely to be openly supportive of what we're doing in Hong Kong than the previous one was. Brian Mulroney was extrovertly on our side. The new-ish government gives the impression of wanting to do the opposite of Mulroney on every possible occasion, and in addition seems to have a crush at the moment on China. They see – here we go again – treasures beyond human craving just over the horizon.

Alastair left on the evening plane just as David Wright (the senior FCO official responsible overall for Asia) called in en route to Beijing. His mission seems to be to lay the foundations for future meetings and visits by ministers. He is anxious to minimize any suggestion of differences between London and us. How to make me suspicious! I go the following day to Happy Valley for the Governor's Cup. I place a few bets and don't win a thing. Once again, I have been advised by the stewards at GH. I shall have to accuse them of trying to bankrupt me.

Thursday 12 January

Photographs have appeared of Deng taken last October looking barely alive. Presumably Beijing officials are trying to prepare the public for him not to appear at the spring festival, or perhaps not appearing again at all. Deng's daughter more or less confirms in an interview with *The New York Times* that the old boy is on his last legs. The head honcho of the CIA on China makes the shrewd point, when Mao was no longer really on the scene the Chinese had difficulty in reaching an agreement about GATT trade negotiations. So perhaps at the moment there is no one around to bang heads together and to take decisions.

Friday 13 January

Beijing has begun lambasting me for not agreeing to hand over secret information about civil servants – their private human resources documents, for example – and for suggesting that it was in everyone's interest to ensure that government had authority before as well as after 1997. They claim that the government after the handover will be an entirely different entity. Telegrams on David Wright's visit to Beijing demonstrate that absolutely nothing has been achieved except to confirm to the Chinese that we are extremely anxious about the forthcoming visits. Len Appleyard in the embassy beats up the dangers of unilateralism on the CFA. While this is an important issue, I can't help thinking that FCO officials have lost any sense of perspective about it.

Monday 16 January

The papers preparing the way for my meeting with Douglas Hurd and others at the end of the month more than bear this out: Sherard – or is it London officials as a whole? – has – or have – convinced themselves that the CFA is going to be a defining issue in our relationship with China. They begin from the assumption that there is the possibility of a state of genial harmony in Sino-British relations. This would be exemplified by a successful visit to London by Qian and by a good trade-boosting visit to China by Michael Heseltine. In the wake of this, so the argument seems to go, we might be able to persuade the Chinese to behave more sensibly over issues such as the right of abode for expatriates in Hong Kong. They believe that for us to go ahead on our own on the CFA would provoke a row rather like the one on the election arrangements, so we must avoid this at all costs. All the other issues that could provoke an argument, such as scrapping the draconian measures under the emergency powers legislation, queue up in the margins for a look-in. The real issue of course is whether we now settle for as quiet a life as we can get with China and whether this produces beneficial results for Hong Kong. London wants us not to commit ourselves now to going ahead with the CFA but to try to win Chinese agreement to proceeding over the next few months. Naturally, whenever we decide the time is ripe to go ahead, London officials will be against us doing so unless we have the imprimatur of the CCP. The argument is pitched in exactly this way to offer British ministers what may seem like an acceptable cop-out. But Anson and I feel very strongly that if we don't go ahead with the CFA before the summer, this will fatally undermine the government's credibility. More than that, it will make a mockery of all our arguments about the rule of law. We are not going to get very much from China in any event, so there is no point in simply giving in on everything. We also don't believe that the CFA is the sort of defining argument which London is suggesting. Anson thinks they are exaggerating the importance of the Chinese reaction, but I am afraid it may be a sign of things to come in the next few months. So the week is dominated by telegrams going backwards and forwards on this issue. I end up sending a personal telegram setting out my views for the Secretary of State.

I've given an interview to a local Chinese newspaper in which I refer to remarks from Beijing's Preliminary Working Committee – the advisers to Lu Ping – about handing over secret information on civil servants and on bringing the Monetary Authority under greater political control. This is not a very sensible time for them to float this idea, just as the Monetary Authority has been distinguishing itself by fighting off speculators who have been attacking the link between our currency and the US dollar.

Tuesday 17 January

We have started to get a bit more clarity (principally from well-briefed but unnamed sources) about what the Chinese actually want to know about civil servants. They are looking for details of people's passports and of our integrity vetting. Needless to say, we won't (and couldn't) provide either. We destroy the integrity-vetting material once it has been established whether or not someone can be promoted, and it would be illegal for us to hand over (for instance) details about people's nationality under the British Nationality Scheme. We have hacked out a statement in which we made clear that all archives will be handed over in 1997 and that there isn't any question of sovereignty involved in our concern about precisely how much and what information to give the Chinese now about individual civil servants. We also agree that I should send a letter to Lu Ping, who is having dinner with Len Appleyard later in the week, suggesting that we should stop the megaphone exchanges on the civil service and try to take things forward in the JLG. The media in Hong Kong are starting to get the impression that Lu Ping's outspoken and occasionally out-of-control performance is a result of ill-health. My own assumption is that he must be under a lot of pressure, from the political uncertainty that presumably has Beijing in its grip as Deng's final hours or days or even weeks tick past. Given our customary ignorance of what is happening at the top of the CCP, I wouldn't be surprised if we were in exactly the same position come the handover.

I saw Henry Keswick and Charles Powell in the afternoon. As ever, the conversation gets round to Jardine's being driven out of Hong Kong. I don't mind the sort of bullying tirades that one gets from Henry. I half understand his ways. He has spent his life behaving like this and he's not going to change now. But it must be rather demeaning for intelligent Charles having to try to turn Henry's prejudices into some sort of effective lobbying. It was an enormous relief afterwards to have a meeting with Jackie Charlton and his wife.

Monday 23 January

A big week for Whisky and Soda. Lavender has arranged for them to have their first training session with the police dog training unit. Actually, it is really an assessment to see if they were trainable. Lavender is more optimistic than I am and later says that the assessor regarded them as pretty good after only one session. On this subject I belong to the 'ye of little faith' brigade.

I am variously reported this week as (a) too hawkish in the *FT*, (b) giving up any attempt to retain authority and influence in the *Independent*, and (c) offering olive branches in *The Times* and the *Daily Telegraph*. These rather varying views on my approach seem to have been based on a speech on economic policy that I made to the FCC in which I mentioned the need for China to give some reassurance about the future.

Tuesday 24 January

We had a good discussion at Exco about the CFA. No one thinks the Chinese will make a really big fuss about it but that we should go ahead whether or not we have their endorsement of everything we are proposing. C. H. Tung is associated with both points of view. That will disturb the FCO. It will doubtless be regarded as an unfair last-minute attempt to destabilize the view they are trying to set up for Douglas Hurd. I will doubtless be accused of browbeating Exco's members.

Our journey back to London was dreadful. We were not allowed to fly directly over Afghanistan and were rerouted over India. As a result of strong headwinds there, we had to put down in Munich and we were held up by snow. So I didn't get into London until lunchtime and had to rearrange things frantically. I missed my lunch meeting with the UBS bank which I agreed to do for Tristan, who is now advising the Swiss gnomes there. I am pretty mortified. I hate missing things I've promised to do for friends.

Wednesday 25 January

It was only when we got to the Secretary of State's office at the FCO after lunch that I realized just how much officials had tried to stitch things up in advance of my meetings. Fortunately, Douglas's political adviser, Maurice Fraser (who had talked to his friend Edward Llewellyn) had been at the pre-briefing meeting with Douglas and had put our case against all comers very vigorously. It really was an attempt at a hijack and included a draft minute to the Prime Minister which none of them had told us about. Officials have convinced themselves that the only reason why everyone agrees with me in my Hong Kong team is because I have a strong personality and nobody dares disagree with me. This is pretty insulting to people like Anson. Anyway, they haven't won what they wanted, but they are still capable of pulling the pins from under us.

Douglas had a private word with me and with Alastair before officials came in. Basically, his view is that there will be a row if we go ahead without the Chinese on the CFA, but we should nevertheless set up the court if we possibly can, having consulted the relevant Cabinet committee if necessary by correspondence. If there is going to be a big row, Cabinet colleagues will then have endorsed our strategy. This will make life a tad more awkward, not least because of Michael Heseltine's forthcoming visit to China in May. His eyes are already starting to glint with enthusiasm. I doubt whether that will actually change anything. I imagine FCO officials will now be racing around to the DTI and trying to stir them up to make a fuss. Ditto the Treasury. Anyway, it could have been worse. It is just rather a bore not being able to trust people who are supposed to be on our side.

I had a meeting with the Prime Minister and Douglas along similar lines. Obviously John and Douglas have been told I feel very strongly about this. Foreign Office officials have ludicrously convinced themselves that I was going to threaten to resign. As a result John treats me with kid gloves. He agrees that we should go ahead and set up the CFA, but says that we need to take the Cabinet committee's mind. He thinks that Ken Clarke and Michael Heseltine will need working on, and that there may be a fuss among right-wing members of the Cabinet. I've got what I wanted but it was touch and go. We will need to watch the FCO officials in London like hawks. I do a press conference in Downing Street and after that I go to a dinner at No. 10 for Sarah Hogg,* who is going to write a book about the 1992 election. Brave woman.

Thursday 26 January

A full day of engagements with lots of interviews and two speeches – a lecture for Atlantic College on protectionism and a speech to the Marketing Group of Britain on China and Hong Kong. Ambassador Ma has apparently spoken to them recently and had much impressed them. Throughout my speech, I was aware that Lord Chalfont† was demonstrating through lots of body language how much he disagrees with me! This is particularly embarrassing since he is sitting next to me. He is one of

* Sarah Hogg was an outstanding economic journalist who was appointed by John Major as head of his Policy Unit. As chairman of the Conservative Party, I worked closely with her and formed the highest opinion of her wisdom and good sense. She married the Conservative politician Douglas Hogg, pursued a successful career in business after his retirement from government, and was made a member of the House of Lords in 1995.

† Lord Chalfont, who died in 2020, was a retired army officer and military historian who was made a Foreign Office minister and member of the House of Lords by Harold Wilson. He left the Labour Party to no one's great surprise in the early 1970s and supported Margaret Thatcher's election in 1979.

those people whose political rise to a modest and temporary degree of prominence is completely unfathomable. The speech seems to go down reasonably well with others. I get lots of 'we need you back here' comments from, for example, Maurice Saatchi, Peter Gummer, Sue Timpson and Nick Lloyd. All flattering but they don't represent a strategy or even a tactic. After the lecture, with lots of ex-permanent secretaries in the audience, there was a question from a young man from Africa who wants to know whether it's really worth him trying to go back to his home country to change things. A good and difficult question: I hope that my reply was more than rhetorical.

Friday 27 January
I went up to Manchester to open a new building at St Bede's School, where my dad was educated in the 1930s, and to hold a reception for the Chinese community. I saw Laura for a couple of meals. We got back to Hong Kong on Sunday evening, in time for the Lunar New Year holiday, which we've spent at Fanling for a whole week, the longest amount of time we have ever been here. Lots of reading (including an excellent book on the French by Theodore Zeldin), a bit of tennis, bad golf and loads of videos.

Monday 6 February
Back to work. The NCNA owned up to the fact that they are coordinating the campaigns of pro-Beijing candidates in the forthcoming elections. Imagine the fuss if we owned up to doing the opposite, or if the British Consulate-General said that they were organizing pro-British campaigns after 1997. David Wright and Christopher Hum took Ambassador Ma out to lunch. No prizes for guessing how much butter was spread. We are still discussing pensions (exploring the option of a provident fund) and the brief for a visit by a team from our immigration department to Beijing. Meanwhile the figures on applications for foreign passports are rising steadily and we are getting worried about civil service morale.

Tuesday 7 February
I told Donald Tsang that when Hamish goes soon, I am going to ask him to take the post of Financial Secretary. He makes a moving little speech about his commitment to Hong Kong before and after 1997. Francis Cornish came in with lots of news about British firms winning business.

I'm told by one of the most generous funders of the Conservative Party that Lord Hambro – the present party treasurer – has been going around Hong Kong all week telling people that I am about to be got rid of and trying to get money out of them. I say to Edward that I simply can't believe this; surely no one could be so stupid. He gave me an old-fashioned look.

Wednesday 8 February

We seem to be meeting more and more people who are planning to move elsewhere after 1997, and localization is picking up pace. In one area this creates particular challenges. One of my bodyguards, Tony Chow, is going off to run bomb disposal. I am pleased for his sake that we haven't had a bomb in Hong Kong for a long time, my guess not since the Cultural Revolution riots. I like Tony and hope this state of affairs continues.

Thursday 16 February

I had one of the best meetings yet with the Business Council. We discussed among other things reclamation of the harbour; all the property developers are against too much reclamation at the moment, except of course when more roads are to be opened up and services for existing developments. But there are obviously real aesthetic problems about the harbour. You can't go on with reclamation forever or you fetch up with a canal rather than a harbour.

Friday 17 February

We discussed in Ad Hoc the options on the CFA when the legislative process begins. Having had to argue so strongly with London for going ahead has meant that I need to be much clearer about the downside if we fail when it actually comes to legislating. We are also examining whether we can try to meet Chinese concerns about the number and type of judges who would be on the CFA, but this is very difficult because the executive doesn't appoint judges under our system. The most important issues are whether the court can actually be set up, whether the question of what constitutes an act of state should be taken beyond what the Basic Law says (in other words should we explicitly define acts of state as simply applying to foreign affairs and defence?), and how we can best reject the monitoring of judicial decisions with Beijing able to overturn the ones it doesn't like.

Saturday 18 February

A long meeting with the Governor of Macau, Vasco Vieira, at Fanling. The Portuguese are very concerned about what happens in Hong Kong and the impact on Macau, for which they will continue to be responsible until 1999. They obviously think that our own experience will be decisive for them. I had some very candid exchanges with the Governor, who is a thoroughly decent man. Macau is having particular civil service issues but they are also worried about Triads and organized crime. We had open day in the gardens again at GH this weekend. Alice overslept and just got away to Fanling before the crowds poured in. Wouldn't it be nice to be able to oversleep?

Monday 20 February

A new element is starting to push its way into the whole discussion about contacts between us and Beijing's Preliminary Working Committee [PWC]. Now that we are talking about briefing the PWC on positions that we have taken in the JLG, Beijing is getting a bit 'iffy' about the whole thing. In other words, they don't really want the PWC involved in anything very much; they obviously don't have a particularly high regard for the quality of its members or their opinions, a point on which we could find a rapid consensus. They just want to use it as a way of battering away at us and our continuing authority.

Thursday 23 February

Quite a cheerful Q and A session in Legco today in which I knocked members about a bit on pensions. I noted that when our last pension scheme was debated in Legco, only one member supported it in an unqualified way. Now they are all lining up to say they are in favour of it provided it is hung about with Christmas decorations. The week is enlivened by two very good concerts held in our ballroom, one of harpsichord music and the second with the King's Consort, James Bowman and a stunning young English soprano. Why do we have such great countertenors in Britain?

Mike Sinclair has alas died. Louise and Lavender have been to his memorial service. The music was apparently lovely and three of Mike's friends talked about him. It came out once again that he wanted to set up an AIDS hospice. Lavender is determined to make sure that happens. Fortunately, Lavender says that her friend Sister Maureen and the Keswick foundation are moving ahead with this.

Friday 24 February

I saw the German Deputy Foreign Minister to try to persuade him to use his influence to get Anson in to see Kohl and his own boss, Kinkel, when she visits Germany. Somebody says that he couldn't even get in to see Kohl himself so is unlikely to be able to get Anson in. In the evening we took the Husseys (who have been staying with us again) out to dinner before they went off to Australia. Coming out of the restaurant we are mobbed – not staged, so good for morale.

Sunday 26 February

I had a personal telegram from the Foreign Secretary. Michael Heseltine is clearly expressing his concern about anything which might impede the success of his visit to China. No one should be surprised. It's now very apparent that the political cost of going ahead immediately on the CFA is too great. I will have to postpone putting a bill into Legco and find a way of doing so without destroying morale in Hong Kong, particularly among our senior officials, who have been following this saga with considerable attention. The last message we want to give is that we think that a few business deals in China (such as they may be) are worth more to us than Hong Kong's future.

Barings Bank is going bust, which will have more repercussions in my judgement than the conclusion of a deal between America and China on intellectual property. It looks as though the Americans think they have pushed the Chinese into taking some tougher measures against intellectual piracy. Beijing is going to close down some factories where this issue has been notoriously obvious. At least, this is what is said.

Monday 27 February

Peter Lai, the new Secretary for Security, came in for a talk with Anson and me about the proposed bill on public order. The Democrats and others are pressing for the establishment of an appeal committee to consider decisions made by the Commissioner of Police about public order events. If they don't like what he has decided they want to be able to second-guess him. I am not keen on putting the Commissioner in this position but he would probably buy it if a judge is chairman of the appeal board. But the Chief Justice is reluctant to have the judiciary pulled into yet another function like this in order to bail out the executive. We need to find a way through this mess.

Saying farewell to one of our senior expatriate officials, I learned that he is intending to do the pilgrimage to Santiago de Compostela when he gets home. He told me that this is for tax reasons so that he doesn't have to stay in Britain for too long before going elsewhere for his retirement. I'm sure that St James would approve of this argument for a pilgrimage.

Wednesday 1 March

Ash Wednesday. We went to St Joseph's for mass and to have our foreheads smeared with ash. I have given up alcohol for Lent. The priest wished me a cheerful preparation for Easter. That'll be the day. In the afternoon I made an unpublicized visit to Castle Peak Hospital, which looks after the mentally ill. It is very grim – most of the patients are locked up with fences around the grass strips next to their wards. I must come here again before I leave Hong Kong and see what improvements have been made.

Hamish has delivered his last budget. It seems to have gone down pretty well. It's prudent, a bit boring and there isn't much to attack. If anything, people are criticizing us for running up too large reserves. Richard Needham phones. His boss, who likes to be known as the president of the Board of Trade, is still very concerned about whether we are going to screw up his visit to Beijing by pressing ahead with our CFA bill. I give Richard the assurance that we will try to find some way around this. I don't seem to have much choice. Officials in London have so upped the ante that if we go ahead there will be a row, and if we don't get the bill through either sooner or later it will look like a spectacular pratfall. If there is no agreement on the CFA by 1 July 1997, it won't be the president of the Board of Trade who gets the blame. Moreover, we all know that on his trip to Beijing he will be given lots of face but the actual trade benefits will be negligible.

Thursday 2 March

We gave a farewell lunch for my private secretary, Bowen Leung – a really sweet-natured man who is loved by the dogs and rather more importantly by the rest of us. He is decent, full of common sense and well plugged in to Hong Kong's gossip. He is also amusing and a very good boss of his staff. Afterwards I chaired a seminar on employment for the disabled. It's the second one I have done and I think it is starting to prod things forward, though not without a lot of effort.

Friday 3 March

We work out our position on right of abode and emigration, look at the residence qualifications for candidates in elections, and have a good go on the CFA. I am having to start nudging people towards the very disagreeable option of doing a deal with London in which we don't introduce the bill until late May (after Hezza's trip to Beijing) and in return have London's support for trying to get the bill through in this session when he has returned from Beijing, victor ludorum. My best Hong Kong officials are starting to give me rather beady-eyed looks on this. We now hope that we can get Legco support for a motion on pensions backing our latest changed proposal for a mandatory provident fund, but I'm sure there will be amendments tacked on increasing social security rates.

Saturday 4 March
Lavender whisked Alice and me off for the opening of the extension to David Tang's new shop; it's full of wonderful kit and we are witness to a spectacular Lion Dance which is supposed to bring luck to the opening of a new building.

Sunday 5 March
A personal telegram from Douglas arrived giving us a bit of time to try to sort out an arrangement on the CFA which will more or less satisfy us as well as Michael Heseltine. He assured me that the civil servants haven't been ganging up on us; I guess he was bound to say this. It shows that the arrows that I have been firing have hit some sort of target, although have probably only convinced officials that we are isolated and paranoid in Hong Kong. We shall see soon enough whether we are just being humoured. I visited polling stations for the municipal council elections. There was a significant fight between the veteran Democrat Szeto Wah and Elsie Tu.

Monday 6 March
Very pleasing results in local council elections. Szeto Wah has beaten Elsie Tu handsomely. This was the contest that all the experts were looking at and the unequivocal result is definitely very positive for us. All in all, the Democrats have done pretty well and the pro-Beijing parties have done respectably enough for them not to take their bat and ball home. So another corner turned though I doubt whether we will get much credit for it. It looks as though we may soon get financial agreements on the airport and the airport railway. But there is still nothing on the CFA except Chinese warnings not to take unilateral action and the suggestion that sooner or later they're going to ask for expert talks again.

I met the chairman of the Vietnamese National Assembly. After a lot of buttering him up with talk about trade and commerce, I came in quite hard on the importance of getting all the Vietnamese migrants back home before 1997 and in particular the allegedly non-Vietnamese migrants. He plays a straight bat (if, that is, the Vietnamese know anything at all about cricket and straight bats).

Then it's off to Hong Kong University for a seminar on drugs. 250 people turned up. Initially there seemed to be a certain amount of cynicism as to whether the seminar would amount to anything, but the audience was surprised by our commitment and by the action programme at the end covering principally education and public health measures. The important thing now is to keep the pressure up. There will be quite a lot of foot dragging in some parts of the administration and from the outside a search for examples of us falling down on the job. But I think people do recognize that this is something both Lavender (with all her work with voluntary bodies) and I feel strongly about. It's not a problem which you can tackle just by increasing punishments and sending in more police if you can find them, not least in an Asian city.

Tuesday 7 March

Donald Tsang's appointment as Financial Secretary succeeding Hamish has been announced and gone down well. It must have been the worst-kept secret in Hong Kong and that is saying something. I gave a small drinks party for Donald and the other local Hong Kong civil servants whose appointments have been announced as secretaries of the main departments. We have almost transformed the senior ranks of the civil service since I arrived, but the whole process should have been started earlier. Their calibre is extremely high and I can't think of more than one or two who wouldn't have got to the top in any public service anywhere. It is a rather under-celebrated aspect of our colonial administration, which has been politically neutral and very well paid. The remuneration at least is something we have in common with Singapore.

Wednesday 8 March

Off to Singapore for a couple of days leaving Lavender behind. Tom Hallifax is making a few changes to the portrait he has done of us and Lavender has encouraged him to paint more portraits of the stewards. He has already done Ah Mo and Charlie, which pleased them no end, and now we hope he will paint Lavender's maid, Janet, and Ah Chak, who is a particular friend of the dogs. My main purpose in Singapore is to take up an invitation to make a speech on the rule of law. Everybody has assumed that they will hear a response to the exceptionally unhelpful remarks that Lee Kuan Yew made shortly after our arrival in Hong Kong, and this is more or less what I am going to do, though couched in very courteous terms. When asked if I am criticizing Singapore, I say that I understand that some people think there are different values in Asia. Perhaps one of these is the feeling some people have that you can go to another person's country and criticize it even though you're a guest. I add that this isn't one of my own values so I wouldn't do this myself. When asked about disagreements with LKY, I note, 'There are of course differences between us; for example, I have never been a member of the Socialist International.' The High Commissioner is clearly rather nervous about what I am intending to say but he doesn't actually protest. I admire a lot about this city state but I think I would need a lobotomy to live here.

I had lots of interviews in the afternoon and a dinner given by the High Commissioner with, among others, the Finance Minister and several other ministers and businessmen. They were extremely downbeat about China – corruption, hard landing, ruin ahead for Hong Kong et cetera et cetera. It is not exactly LKY's tune.

Thursday 9 March

My speech after breakfast seemed to go very well. I gave a press conference afterwards. I learn from the journalists about yesterday's Legco voting on pensions. Our proposed scheme got a comfortable majority, then Allen Lee's lot went home, and there was another vote in favour both of our scheme and the addition of lots of increases in Social Security payments for the elderly. In other words a pretty good farce, but since we got the biggest vote for our own scheme we will go ahead with it. I had a long meeting with the Prime Minister and another with LKY's rather charming and clearly very clever son, though he is fairly obviously not someone who is likely to suffer other people's opinions very gladly. The words chip, old and block come to mind. After lunch with the PM at Raffles, I went for a meeting with LKY. He is amiability itself: a big smile and Chris this, Chris that. The High Commissioner thinks that LKY was on 'receive' more than he has ever seen him before. I gave him a full and accurate briefing on what is going on. His view is that the Chinese will bugger it all up. He doesn't think that they are really capable of doing anything else. After we talked about possible chief executives, he said that there only seem to him to be two positions that people could take up. First they shrug their shoulders and decide to get on with China as best they can (he takes this to be the position of S. Y. Chung, who used to be in the other camp). The second option is what he describes as the existentialist position. This is the one he says he would take up himself. He couldn't bear the prospect of working for communists so he would only do so for a price and he would set that price as high as he could. I avoid the temptation of noting that I've been trying to give everyone in Hong Kong a similar opportunity. But his mood is very different from my previous encounters with him. He doesn't of course say that in view of his fears for Hong Kong's future, it is right to try and stand up to China a bit. I suspect he would say that this is a hopeless task. As ever he is very sure of his opinions, changed though they may be today. I was told afterwards that my meeting with him went on so long that the Cabinet was kept waiting.

The *FT* man here says that when he and one of his editors were receiving background briefing from LKY recently, they asked him about Tiananmen. What would he have done? He said it was quite simple. He would have turned the lights out in all the main hotels. He would have kept the foreign press at bay. He would have ringed the square. And then he would have released a bit of cholera into the crowd. Once there were a few victims, he would tell their families. Panic would have set in, shifting everyone from the square very rapidly. Job done, no tanks, no killing.

Friday 10 March

Peter Lai as Secretary of Security has been in Vietnam and thinks we are starting to make a bit of progress about returns. Next week there is a conference in Geneva which he reckons has a good chance of reaching decisions about speeding them up. At a later meeting with Anson and the Chief Justice the CJ clearly supports our overall position on the CFA. He is also now prepared to accept the appointment of a judge to chair the board which may need to be set up to consider appeals against decisions made by the Police Commissioner under the Public Order Ordinance. This should help us get the bill through.

Saturday 18 March

I spent a lot of time this week in lobbying Legco members about pensions but there are a few other highlights (or at least medium lights). First an excellent meeting with the French president of the Senate foreign affairs committee, who seems sympathetic to what we are trying to do. I reminded him of the book by Alain Peyrefitte on Macartney's mission to China in 1792 on behalf of King George III. What the Chinese used to say then, and their attitude to the world outside the Middle Kingdom, is remarkably similar to their approach today.

Second, a meeting with Jimmy Lai, the Giordano chief whose brave criticisms of Li Peng have led to retaliation against his company in China. He told me that he is going to start a newspaper which will have the aim of cheering people up and making them realize that they can affect their own destiny. He came to Hong Kong as a 12-year-old stowaway, has made a fortune here and thinks that he and others like him are walking examples of the relationships between economic success, the rule of law and political freedom. I think he is a Catholic. I tell him that I find it extremely difficult to understand what is happening in Beijing, even with all the advice I get from people who claim to know. But one thing for sure is that it is only pretence that everything is going smoothly. I think it is as though one was a Martian looking down on a yachting regatta. The boats would move this way and that. Had the race started? Was there a race at all? If there was who was in the lead? And finally who had won? I would clearly be a pretty hopeless spectator in Beijing, and indeed in Cowes.

Third, Lavender and I had a good visit to Central and Western district including spending some time at a boys' primary school. Lavender pointed out that some of the older boys are looking both taller and plumper than the typical Cantonese. She thinks, probably correctly, that it marks a new age of affluence and the fact that Chinese children are eating more and more Western food. One of the teachers tells us that she doesn't think they take enough exercise and spend too much time playing with their computers. Now that does sound like teenagers back home. We have had to say goodbye to Ah Ho, our senior driver, this week and had tea with him in our private quarters. He is a sweet man who has been putting his son through an American university. Heaven knows what it must have cost him and his wife.

The week ended with another telegram from Douglas Hurd about the CFA, which we are told his office toned down in its original draft by officials. The telegram asks all the usual questions about whether we will get the bill through and what the impact or row would be on British trade with China. Qian is proposing to meet Douglas at the UN for a working lunch in April. This will presumably further complicate the CFA business. We discuss China's demands to hand over more information about civil servants. We have a wholly defensible position on this but, since it will continue to be the source of a row, presumably we will be leaned on by London sooner or later.

There have been one or two reports, for example in the *Daily Telegraph*, that Lord Hambro came to Hong Kong to raise money for the Conservative Party and went away empty-handed. This is a result, so the papers say, of the government's troubles and of criticism of our Hong Kong policy. But imagine what the reactions would have been if the reverse had been happening.

Monday 20 March

We had a round-up of JLG progress. It looks as though we will start to get somewhere on immigration and nationality and we may get a satisfactory conclusion on financial services agreements for the airport and railway. We will be under lots of pressure from the Chinese on the budget, on defence lands and on civil service files. So we expect them to be very active on all the matters that interest them, and on anything that we want they will continue to drag their feet. Hamish MacLeod is rightly pleased that we have got around several difficult bends in the last few weeks. The economy has survived some doubts about its stability, largely related to external factors; his budget has gone down pretty well; and we seem to be moving from a proper pension scheme to a provident fund without too much fuss about benefit levels. It's still only a second-best horse but we may be able to ride it to the finishing line.

Tuesday 21 March

I am fuming over an appalling white flag telegram from the Beijing embassy on the CFA which could surely not have been drafted without the imprimatur of officials in London. It is an essay in pusillanimity. We responded vigorously. Our senior Hong Kong civil servants are getting very angry about this sort of craven behaviour. They make the point that it is inevitably difficult this close to the handover to get civil servants to do the right thing for Hong Kong rather than just roll over like poodles, but far more of a problem when they feel that London and the Beijing embassy are in surrender mode.

Wednesday 22 March

I got a similar sense of London's feebleness when I saw our man in Taiwan. He reckons that we are being much weedier about Taiwan than any of our European partners for fear of annoying China. Our trade ministers are declining to see a Taiwanese trade minister when he visits London, even though several other European ministers are prepared to have meetings with him. It will be interesting to see how much real additional business comes out of Hezza's trip to China. In the afternoon, I wrote another 'Letter to Hong Kong' for Radio Television Hong Kong (RTHK) on the theme of the importance of people in Hong Kong believing that they can make a difference and that if they stand by the values that have created this great city it will help those values to survive. Near the end of the letter I wrote: 'Hong Kong will change in 1997. It's bound to change in some respects. It's a largely Chinese city with an international outlook which the chance of history made a British colony ... And come 1997 it's a Chinese city in China albeit with its special qualities preserved and guaranteed ... So when I'm asked after 1997 to write a letter to Hong Kong, still with its freedom of speech and still able to entertain every point of view, I believe that I'll still be addressing a free, prosperous, decent society, living with the rule of law – under a Chinese flag. If the people of Hong Kong believe that, too, and want it to happen, it will. Because Hong Kong is a taste of the future not left over from the past. That is Hong Kong's achievement; no one can take it away.' I do not add, God willing.

Saturday 25 March

Last night, I had to go to another alcohol-free ball. Roll on the rolling back of the tombstone! Lu Ping is visiting America and trotting out reassurances about the rule of law, the CFA and so on. Some of his travelling colleagues from the PWC appear to be making mildly racist comments about colonialism. I'm surprised there isn't more of this. Most Chinese of a certain age probably have stories of Western condescension if not worse. We're discussing the possibility of putting down a motion on the CFA in Legco in order to smoke out positions there, but I don't think we would get very much information from the exercise and it would probably be regarded by the Chinese as being almost as provocative as actually tabling legislation. We gave a farewell lunch for Clement in my private office, the end of the Leung dynasty. He is a fine young man and makes a very moving speech. What lovely people have worked for us here. Then we have a reception for the rugby sevens. The tournament itself is won by the New Zealand team. No surprise there. The Pope is a Catholic; New Zealand wins rugby games.

Monday 27 March

I've had a long chat with Nigel Rich, who went back to London for Jardine's to run Trafalgar House for them. Not surprisingly he is finding London at the moment pretty punishing after Hong Kong. He was on his customary good form and is still very robust about this community. Lavender and I miss him and his wife, Cynthia. He told me how bad he felt when he left here and said goodbye to his driver, who had been a friend for years. He agreed that we can't just sneak away from Hong Kong hoping to avoid any arguments with China and to pick up whatever crumbs they offer us from the table. We have to leave people in Hong Kong the chance of continuing to lead a decent life.

We had a blessedly normal evening with the Cornishes and a couple who have come relatively recently to Hong Kong, Jeremy and Angela Palmer. Jeremy has run Barings in Hong Kong and Angela has been a journalist on several of the big London papers, and is a great friend of Tim Heald, who was at college with me. They are much younger than us, interesting and fun.

Tuesday 28 March

Long discussion at Exco about the CFA. All the unofficial members, including C. H. Tung, John Gray and Raymond Chi'en, agreed that we should go ahead and try to set up the court as soon as possible. Anson spoke particularly well about it. We have telegrammed the results of the discussions in London, though I dare say that it won't make much of a dent. The noise of the attempted stitch-up is now becoming deafening. Clearly what happens is that through the commercial counsellor the Beijing embassy get in touch with FCO officials who then spring into action to supercharge the DTI and its ministers. Sherard and Tony Galsworthy, who has written a paper for the Joint Intelligence Committee, can be depended upon to make sure that the worst possible gloss gets put on whatever we are trying to do. Sherard has produced a draft Cabinet committee paper which has allegedly been cleared already with the Foreign Secretary. I don't believe a word of it. It would be unheard of for this to happen without us saying what we think. Much of the analysis in the paper is fine but the judgements at the end are completely loaded. Apparently, we must prepare for the end of the British Empire and any trade prospects in Asia if we go ahead with the CFA. I exaggerate, but only a bit.

There's been an incursion into Hong Kong waters by a Chinese gunboat and the abduction of two Hong Kong boats and their crews to China. They were obviously involved in smuggling. We have taken the mildest action, which has clearly made some of our police cross and also the garrison who weren't told what was going on. The incident wasn't very well handled; I have tried to ensure at a meeting that the rules of engagement are got right and that in future the police recognize that they have to tell the Navy what is going on. But we are in real difficulties. The Chinese are unlikely to give back the vessels or the men. The truth is that the number of such incursions has fallen dramatically over the last few years, so the Chinese have been trying to behave better. But in this sort of rogue incident they are not likely to back off.

Wednesday 29 March

We are having discussions in Beijing over the next few days on the budget and we are keen to make it clear before they start that we make a distinction between the procedures for determining the budget in 1996 and the content of the budget in 1997. This is what the Chinese agreed last year. Now they are trying to change their tune. We refuse to cave in and won't start the talks until this is accepted as the basis of them, a point they eventually concede with a bad grace. Meanwhile the FCO talk about 'a gradual restoration' of relations with China. Yet the Chinese are behaving just as badly as ever. They have discourteously turned down an invitation to have dinner during the next JLG meeting next week with Anson.

I've been interviewing future ADCs to take over from Mike. I choose a very tough guy called Lance Brown, who is at present running the special duties unit, our equivalent in the police service of the SAS. He is a very grown-up fellow and you would want him on your side if things ever got sticky. Lance clearly understands that my main requirement for my ADCs and bodyguards is competence and geniality, certainly not formality.

A cheerful former American diplomat, Mort Abramowitz, has given me a readout of Lu Ping's visit to the States, which he thinks has been pretty much of a disaster. Lu comes across as a typical Chinese bureaucrat repeating over and over again that everything will be all right in Hong Kong because the Chinese will stick to the Basic Law. Mort says that hardly anyone believes this nonsense. Bob Peirce is back from a visit he has made to America at the end of the week. He doesn't wholly agree with Mort – he doesn't think that Lu's visit was a complete disaster. But he plainly hasn't reassured anyone and he came across as very wooden. How could he be expected to be anything else? Bob also feels that it's a pity that the FCO isn't as supportive of us as the State Department.

Friday 31 March

Margaret Thatcher has arrived in cracking form; and kept us up until 1am. In Beijing she socked it to Li Peng but was impressed by Qiao Shi. Most Westerners are, which perhaps is a problem for him. She has a good lunch with Anson and is all fired up about the CFA. She seems to me to be one of the few people who ever actually stands up to the Chinese. It must have been very alarming for Len Appleyard to have her staying in the embassy. Needless to say, he kept her in the dark about some of the nuances of what is happening and put loads of downside into her briefing.

Saturday 1 April

Lavender has gone to Mexico with Alice to see Kate, who is there as part of her Spanish course. Her presence might have helped to calm me down. It's becoming clear that we will be pressed not only to postpone action on the CFA until after Michael's visit to China, but also not to do anything afterwards to poison the atmosphere that will doubtless have been created by it. At some stage I am going to have to go back for a Cabinet committee meeting and perhaps even put my own position on the line. I am furious with officials for putting ministers and me in this position. As far as people like Anson and her senior colleagues are concerned, it is a clear sign that Britain puts alleged commercial interests – I stress the word 'alleged' – above any concern for Hong Kong.

Monday 3 April
Douglas had a 40-minute talk with me on the phone. He has had a meeting already with officials. They have taken the usual line about the CFA. He wanted to be walked through all the arguments as I saw them. Michael Heseltine is obviously being difficult. He is very flattering about me, Douglas says, but goes on to argue that I've got all this wrong. China trade glitters. Anyway, I go through the arguments about timing, the position in Legco and so on. Douglas is very realistic about the likelihood of any 'gradual restoration' of relations with China over the next couple of years or so. He doesn't think we should expect anything other than continuing struggle diplomacy – a bleak but realistic outlook. Anyway, whatever some of his officials may be saying, he himself remains wholly supportive. He says he will speak to the Prime Minister and Ken Clarke later in the week. I don't want to put my friends in a difficult position, or the government for that matter, but I do want to do the best for Hong Kong. I am more and more struck by what this looks like to the best people in the Hong Kong government.

Tuesday 4 April
The JLG has begun dourly. I had a discussion with Francis Cornish about whether we should offer a British gift for Hong Kong when we leave. I suggest that we could provide a work of sculpture or another sort of memorial incorporating the text of the Joint Declaration. Francis responds, with a wry smile, that this may be a bit confrontational.

Thursday 6 April
Last night I had a very nice supper with Martin and Janny Dinham, after which we went to see *Pulp Fiction*. It puts me in the right frame of mind for seeing Sherard this morning. He has come for the second part of the JLG meeting. He bangs on (with a straight face) about restoring the relationship between GH and the Hong Kong Department. It was of course perfectly fine when Peter Ricketts was running the department and when Robin McLaren was in Beijing. He doesn't know whether we will need to have a Cabinet committee meeting on the CFA. It does rather depend on whether Hezza will accept the suggestion that we should postpone introducing the CFA bill for two weeks after his visit to China, which is a compromise which I suppose we could just about sell, or whether he wants a much longer postponement, which would really jeopardize the legislation and the establishment of the court.

Friday 7 April

The last day of the JLG has told us much that we need to know about 'gradual restoration'. The Chinese have saved up the worst to the last. They tell us that they have decided which firm is going to print the SAR passport – nothing like an open tender involved here – and also announced that they want to interview senior civil servants in Beijing over the next few months. They can get stuffed. If (or when) this gets out, it will have an awful effect on civil service morale. This is one of the worst JLGs that anyone can remember.

I finished my Lenten abstinence a bit early in order to attend the wines of the Pacific Rim festival. I am sure that St Vincent, who I seem to recall is the patron saint of winemakers, will put in a good word for me. Afterwards, I had a very long sleep.

Tuesday 11 April

At a meeting held to sweep up after the JLG, we agreed that it is becoming more and more apparent that in the name of sovereignty the CCP is prepared to erode Hong Kong's autonomy – civil servant appointments, the budget and public procurement are the best examples of this. The company they have chosen to print the SAR passports is of course Chinese owned and so far as we know has no previous experience of security printing.

The Commissioner of Police is concerned about morale and thinks that the figures for departing officers, particularly expatriates, are going to be very high. Lydia Dunn told me that Swire's are worried that the Chinese proposal to run an airline out of Hong Kong has been a complete burial of all the assurances that the company got from Chinese leaders. I was a little cheered by a meeting with Hilary Armstrong, even though she is full of confidence as a Labour MP about politics back home. She is a nice woman who used to be John Smith's parliamentary private secretary. She passes on the best wishes of her father, Ernest, who used to be the Deputy Speaker and brought to that office all the skills he had acquired as a headmaster. She now represents what used to be his seat in Durham. He was a lovely man and the two of them represent the best of the Labour Party and a very good reason why we should never be too bothered in Britain by the prospect of a moderate Labour government.

Thursday 13 April

Lavender and Alice have come back from Mexico. The most significant event this week is the death of Chen Yun, who was one of Deng's closest and most important advisers. There has been lots of speculation about what is meant by the decision not to give him a public funeral. The general consensus is that there is always official nervousness about the security implications of gatherings of large numbers of people. So much of the trouble in China stems from demonstrations at funerals or in the margins of them.

Saturday 15 April

The Chinese have decided to hand over the two Hong Kong residents they picked up during their incursion into our territorial waters. The NCNA phoned up first of all to make it perfectly clear that this has nothing to do with our protest but everything to do with the Chinese legal process. But of course. Anyway, it's a success for handling things as we did, reasonably (but not too) firmly. Beijing officials are discreetly circling Anson to find out more about her. Since she comes from such a distinguished patriotic family, with a grandfather who was a general killed by the Nationalists, an uncle who looked after Deng's son after he was thrown out of a tall building in the Cultural Revolution, and a mother who is probably the greatest female painter from China over the last century, and who herself has a record of public service which is an open book, it is difficult to know what else they need to be sure about. We shall need to be discreet in anything we say about this to London and the Beijing embassy for very obvious reasons.

Sunday 23 April

There are four things in particular worth noting about the week after Easter. First we had a visit from Ted Heath, who comes straight from what he tells us is his 19th official visit to China. As usual, according to him there is nothing wrong with China. While here he was restrained in what he said in public about me but he made it abundantly clear in private that he thinks we should simply have spent our time in Hong Kong trying to teach China about the community. He has two very good private secretaries with him (Batey and Burn), one of whom tells us that most of his meetings with Chinese leaders consisted, as always, of mutual flattery. Len Appleyard talked him through his alternative approach on the Court of Final Appeal which Ted was inclined to raise with Lu Ping, though in the event he found Lu so slippery that he could see there wasn't any point in pressing him on whether there would be Chinese acquiescence if there was a slower timetable on the CFA. Li Peng evidently told Ted that our policy on Hong Kong had changed in 1992, that we had come to the conclusion then that China was going to fall apart, and that we would therefore be able to hold on to Hong Kong after 1997. Yes, he really said this.

Second, the Princess of Wales came to stay, or rather she came to Hong Kong but stayed at the Mandarin. We got to do lots of charity things with her, mostly it seems organized by David Tang. She looks beautiful and smiles a lot. She is a great celebrity star. What more do I know? And what more can I say? I must ask Jonathan Dimbleby next time he is here filming. He has after all written a book about Prince Charles.

Third, we started to think about the visit which Lu Ping is planning to make here in May. It obviously makes sense for me to write to him in advance saying that even if he doesn't see me, I hope he will have meetings with Anson Chan and some of our senior officials, just as he saw David Ford in the past. There is a political downside to this – people will say that I have finally made myself a lame duck, that the Chinese can pick and choose who they deal with, and that I am completely sidelined by Anson. There is a bit of this around at the moment anyway. But it seems to me on balance better to take the initiative in what will be seen by some at least as a reasonably statesmanlike gesture. It would be far worse to find ourselves in the position in which we are losing authority in the civil service in a rather slippery and underhand way. Our local civil servants support this line; Kerry and one or two others are less sure.

Fourth, we are still going through the tortures of the damned over the CFA. Douglas had a meeting with Michael Heseltine and the Prime Minister after the Thursday Cabinet and they are keen to see if there is any way in which we can put more time between Michael's visit and introducing the CFA bill. Michael is asking all sorts of questions about it, as though he was actually interested in any other issue than having a trouble-free troop through China with a lot of pipedream trade announcements to make at the end. This is all pretty annoying and I may still have to go back and argue my corner in the Cabinet committee.

Richard Needham is giving me lots of his thoughts on the CFA and on how to govern Hong Kong. I know that he is trying hard to be supportive but has also to show that he is a vigorous trade minister. Just at the moment it may be rather a difficult circle to square. But after talking to a number of local businessmen, he told me with his usual robust honesty that none of them thought going ahead with the CFA would make a huge impact on British trade. Of course, his officials are saying the reverse having latched on to the stuff that FCO London officials are saying and writing. Nor is Michael Heseltine likely to change his view. He is second-guessing all our own opinions on timing. The whole situation is becoming ludicrous. The trade visit to China is being allowed to drag Hong Kong policy by the nose.

Tuesday 25 April
Continuing my campaign on drugs, I visited a gospel-based drugs rehabilitation centre in Sai Kung. It's rather impressive, but the fact that its appeal is partly based on religion means that it isn't getting any government subsidy. I think this is daft, a prejudice-based policy, and want to review it. The centre seems to be doing a great job. If you save abusers from drugs by changing their whole personality, what's wrong with that?

Wednesday 26 April
I got a personal telegram from Douglas. Reading between the lines, he is saying that the Prime Minister and he will support me on the timing of the CFA if they have to and that I will probably win against Michael. But he also asks whether it's really too difficult to put the whole thing off until October, rather longer after Michael's visit. The whole row is putting my relationship with John and Douglas into the scales on one side, and my relationship with Anson and senior officials onto the other. I find this extremely difficult, but in the circumstances the only thing I can do is think about Hong Kong and Anson. There is to be a debate thanks to the admirable Jimmy McGregor next week in Legco on the CFA, which should give us some idea of how opinion is forming there.

Thursday 27 April
There has been a debate back home in the Commons about Hong Kong. It went well, mostly supportive with the exception of a dreadful speech from Ted Heath and another which is almost as bad from the resident Commons pseudo-Victorian, Rhodes Boyson. Robin Cook is excellent and we still have lots of cross-party support.

There have been lots more rumours this week about the death of Deng. One day soon I imagine he really will. Meanwhile the Beijing party boss has been purged so, even if the president of the all China Bridge Federation is still with us, something pretty dramatic is going on in the CCP.

Friday 28 April
I have sent a fairly robust response to Douglas pointing out why we can't leave things until October. But I note that we can perhaps come to a final conclusion on this after the debate in Legco. We may, I suppose, be able to combine a shorter delay than Hezza has been demanding with some minor amendments to our proposed bill provided we hold on to the most important bits. Judging by the discussion of the CFA in the JLG today this may not be easy. They have started to raise some of the real Chinese

objections to the court. First, they don't like the fact that there is no remedial machinery for overturning CFA verdicts that the executive doesn't like. If there were, that would be the rule of law Chinese style. Second, they want to be explicit about those acts of state which are excluded from the CFA's ambit. I don't think we can go further than referencing the Basic Law, and even that will bring down criticisms on our heads from a lot of the Hong Kong lawyers and some of Martin Lee's Democrats. But we obviously can't change the Basic Law now, and Martin after all was one of those who helped to draft it. Third, the CFA shouldn't be able to pronounce on the constitutionality of laws. I imagine that if there was yet another trade visit in the offing, the DTI, Len Appleyard and a good number of FCO officials in London would urge us to accept this agenda. I wish the Chinese position was better known publicly. At least most businessmen are hanging in there, saying that we have got to get the court set up. We also have a lot of international support for this.

Hold the front pages. Deng still lives. Vivat.

Starting the Countdown: May 1995–May 1996

Monday 1 May

Lavender has accepted the post of patron of the AIDS trust fund. With Sister Maureen and others they are searching for possible members of the Board of Trustees and a suitable building for a hospice itself. The hospital authority says they will have difficulty in supplying the hospice with appropriate services until prejudice in the community has lessened, but Lavender is pretty confident that in due course they will give as much support as they can with money and a building.

Tuesday 2 May

One or two of my senior colleagues are worried about how we will handle Legco after the elections in September. They are fussed about issues like private members' bills, but I am not too bothered. We simply have to make it clear that the present rules regarding the financial implications of these bills will still stand. A private bill involving financial costs has to be approved by the execution. I will be able to veto a bill if I don't like it, but I don't believe this will happen too frequently. I reckon that an elected Legco will behave responsibly and won't try to put in place all sorts of things before 1997 just to provoke Beijing.

I saw Sérgio Vieira de Mello from the UNHCR [UN High Commissioner for Refugees], who is trying hard to help us with a more rapid return of Vietnamese migrants to their own country. He is exceptionally impressive – very frank, not remotely servile, and makes good sense. How wonderful it would be if every UN representative was like this.

Wednesday 3 May

The Legco debate on the CFA. Handling the issue in the legislature has not been made easier by a leak in the newspapers this morning setting out the Chinese position on the CFA in all its gory detail. We didn't really get very much of a steer about the proposed legislation from the discussion; the motion passed simply states that the court should be set up in accordance with the Basic Law and the Joint Declaration. There is no reference to the secret 1991 agreement which caused so much anxiety – not least because of China's efforts, which continue, only to allow one non-local judge on the court. Doubtless, in its present mood London will think that the 1991 deal was fine. My only conclusion is that we will get a real caning if we don't try to legislate at all, from lawyers, politicians and business leaders. Much of the trouble in the weeks and months ahead will be the usual favourite Hong Kong sport of trying to find ladders for people to climb down. I don't want our own to be too steep.

Thursday 4 May

I had a quiet dinner with Geoffrey Howe, who is staying for a night. He was a bit preoccupied with the dreadful Scott Inquiry, but we talked mostly about Britain and Europe. He wants me to go back to UK politics and thinks that it would be fun particularly to be part of a Ken Clarke team after the election. I point out that it might not be so much fun if we got a complete drubbing in the election (which seems quite likely) or if Michael Portillo is party leader. He noted rather wryly that life isn't too bad, now that he has a bit of money. He has been a very considerable public servant; it's a pity we don't agree about Hong Kong and China.

The local election results in England have been awful. I'm not sure whether this will affect the internal dynamics of the government. I rather doubt it. So I don't think that it will make very much difference to the debate, such as it is, about Hong Kong, China and trade pipedreams. A good thing about Michael Heseltine is that he fights clean and doesn't allow differences about policy to affect his personal relations. I wish I could say the same about all the officials who stir him up.

The NCNA are inviting senior Hong Kong officials to go and talk to them about the future. This does cause a certain amount of unease. I don't think that I can or should stop anybody having these sorts of discussions in Hong Kong. But I can certainly stop them being summoned from Hong Kong for meetings elsewhere. More trouble at the weekend from Ted Heath and an interview in the Sunday morning *Post*. But does he really matter anyway any more? It's sad that he has spent so long in such a mega sulk. He could have run NATO or the European Commission or had another international job. What is the point of a life devoted to rotting off other people, particularly, of course, Margaret Thatcher?

Lu Ping is going to be here for 7½ days on his forthcoming visit but doesn't appear to have any time to see Anson, who has offered lunch or a meeting. She is being asked to go to Beijing if she wants to see him. The dates he has offered happen to be ones when she is likely to be in London both for a business meeting and on leave. Prime ministers, foreign ministers and finance ministers all round the world have time to meet Anson when she is in their countries, but the director of the HKMAO [Hong Kong and Macau Affairs Office] is here for almost 180 hours and over 20 meals and can't find time. Meantime, Beijing endlessly criticizes us for not sharing enough information with them about how Hong Kong is run. All crazy. What a bunch to have to deal with.

We spent some time discussing a Legco question from Emily Lau on Britain's responsibilities for Hong Kong after 1997. We have produced a robust draft and the FCO are spending their time trying to strip all the legal and moral toughness out of it. I don't think they can have any idea of the impact of this on our officials, who seem at one and the same time to be both flabbergasted and not terribly surprised about this further evidence of Britain's lack of interest and concern. I can imagine the conversations without too much difficulty. 'We really mustn't dig ourselves in too deep on Hong Kong because, after all, once we've got 1997 out of the way we will be wanting to restore our relationship with China.' I'm not sure that China will actually give a toss about us after 1997.

I gave a lunch for the Hong Kong–United States Economic Cooperation Committee. Paul Volcker is the head of the American team. When Willie Purves was chairman of the Hong Kong side, Volcker apparently told him he really must understand that in the USA the sort of remarks that Purves made about China's human rights record simply wouldn't play. Some of the Americans are clearly sceptical about all the assurances they are getting in Hong Kong that everything is going to be all right. I have to be rather careful what I say since C. H. Tung is sitting next to me. I am told the Americans have been advised by Tung and others that it may be a good idea not to mention the rule of law when they go on to Beijing, and they shouldn't lobby on the CFA since this might be counter-productive!

Tuesday 9 May

Francis Cornish doesn't think that Hezza's visit to China later this month is attracting very high-quality business leaders. Francis is also extremely sceptical about this sort of trip as well as the likelihood of it producing any really big business breakthroughs. There are the usual problems in organizing details with the Chinese, including getting permission for the aircraft to fly around China. The Beijing embassy has written to our JLG team questioning their judgement that the Chinese don't want to make progress on the CFA and taking up their cause on issues like post-verdict remedial mechanisms. After all, they say, perhaps the Chinese are worried – I'm not making this up – about recent miscarriages of justice in

Britain and don't want the same thing to happen in the SAR after 1997. I'm not sure that the Chinese would know a miscarriage of justice if one got up and hit them over the head with a rolled Whitehall umbrella.

Meetings about the container terminals conclude that, while we must carry on with the port development, we must at the same time open it up to greater competition. We must also retain our reputation for clean public procurement. It does look as though we will complete work on the airport in 1997 but won't be able to open it until the first part of 1999 because of the delays caused by China's negotiating tactics. This is probably more or less what people are expecting. So we will do the work and Beijing will get to open the result.

Edward has found a wonderful photograph of John Major and myself being clapped outside No. 10 by the Prime Minister's staff after the election of 1992. Percy Cradock is in the front of the picture helping to lead the applause. Now that must find a place in a book some time. Perhaps he was silent clapping.

Douglas has sent a good letter round colleagues endorsing the way we want to handle the CFA, taking the legislation through a couple of weeks after Hezza's visit, and asking for replies by the week of 22nd May, that is, after Michael returns from his triumph. Len Appleyard has sent the inevitable telegram promising support if ministers take this courageous decision to go ahead with the bill, but predicting serious trouble in these circumstances and noting that this will come shortly after so many businessmen have been trooped around China.

Friday 12 May

High points of my 51st birthday: Kate called in the morning; I opened a Methodist shelter for Filipinos at Stanley; I'm given a wonderful birthday tea by the private office with a Black Forest gateau and the gift of a splendid wooden Chinese God; and the Courtaulds and Cheung Man Yee take us out to dinner with other friends to a Shanghainese restaurant. On top of that Alastair phoned up from London having already sent a very funny telegram full of appropriate Chinese poems. Hezza's armada has set sail – or at least taken off.

Discussing the functional constituencies, we found that registration is already beyond 900,000. We still have about a fortnight to go to push the tally higher. I had an interesting discussion with Pam Youde. She is being pressed to see Lu Ping while she is in Hong Kong. She was advised by the FCO that this might be embarrassing and she wants to get my view. Why did she check? She says that she remembers that in Teddy's day he very often disagreed with the FCO and she just wanted to check what the score was now. I was not surprised to learn from her how difficult relations were between Teddy and Cradock.

Lydia came to see me and confirmed that Swire's are getting increasingly nervous about the state-owned China National Aviation Corporation and the pledges they have had in the past from Chinese officials about Cathay's position in Hong Kong. People outside are bound to compare the strategies towards Beijing of Jardine's and Swire's. The first has to some extent repositioned itself and been slagged off; the second has tried to cosy up to the Chinese and doesn't seem to be doing any better.

The press have got quite excited because it turns out that one of the senior members of Lu's Preliminary Working Committee has a dodgy past with criminal convictions before he became a company director which were not notified to the stock exchange. 'Are we surprised?' asks Martin Dinham and goes on to question whether we should stop counting the dodgy pasts of PWC members on the fingers of one hand.

Monday 15 May

The unemployment figures have risen to 3%. There will be pressure on us to do something about the Labour Importation Scheme; in other words, stop people coming in to work here. There has been a poll today in which 75% of those asked think that Lu Ping should have met Anson.

I did a long interview for the London *Spectator*. The journalist used to live here. His former bank colleagues don't like what I'm doing but his tailor is a supporter. I guess the tailor at least will still be living here after the handover.

Friday 19 May

A drink with the charming and chatty Duchess of York and then out to dinner to celebrate Jannie Dinham's birthday. Before those I had a perfectly awful meeting with Sir Alan Walters, Margaret Thatcher's former economic adviser, who was just as bad as I thought he would be. He has been here to talk at a seminar organized by the PWC on Hong Kong's role as an international financial centre. I was bombarded by vain stuff about how he himself is responsible for the link between the Hong Kong and the US dollars and a disgraceful suggestion (he is going off to visit Argentina) that we should pay the Falklanders to vote for the Argentinian embrace. Margaret would love that! I was told that within half an hour of seeing me, he denounced me and democracy in his speech. Why do I bother?

Saturday 20 May

We are trying to clear some of the migrants from one part of the camp at Whitehead, a difficult exercise. We keep in touch with events from Fanling. There have already been quite a few police casualties. Later I visited police and correctional services staff, as well as a few fire brigade members, who took part with the others in the operations. An independent monitors' report has commended the police and their colleagues for their restraint. This seems all the more admirable when I see some of the weapons used by the migrants.

We had two telegrams today which raised eyebrows. First, there was Len Appleyard's description of Michael Heseltine's visit to China. It reads a bit like a spoof. 'Outstanding . . . Brilliant leadership . . . Billions of business to be done . . . The only problem is Hong Kong.' Inevitably we also get a telegram from London about a conversation between the Foreign Secretary and Michael over the weekend. Hezza has really dug in over the CFA. He wants to send a message to Li Peng, with whom he thinks he has established a great relationship. (Presumably they did not discuss Tiananmen.) He wants to put off any question of legislating on the CFA for the rest of the present session of the legislature. It's worse than we were anticipating, or at least as bad as it could have been. Bob Peirce and I had a talk, and I sketched out a few notes, then Bob produced a brilliant telegram setting out our case pretty comprehensively in his customarily pellucid prose. This is a British diplomat's drafting at its best.

Sunday 21 May

Another Len Appleyard telegram has arrived in which, while being about as unhelpful as he possibly could be, he includes the ridiculous proposition that our policy should be neither to confront China nor to back down. I am not sure what this means – if anything at all. Well, actually, I am sure it's white flag time. Oh for the days of Robin McLaren.

During a barbecue that Lavender and I gave for her tennis team and their spouses, we hear that the Prime Minister's meeting with senior colleagues has endorsed our timing for the CFA bill, so that it can be considered before the end of this legislative session. But presumably in order to save Michael Heseltine's face, there is to be a message from the Prime Minister to Li Peng. It's a small price but a barking idea. It will ensure that the Chinese reaction is noisier than it otherwise would be, but I guess we had to make some sort of payment for being able to go ahead. Ken Clarke apparently let the Treasury know before the meeting that he was backing us and this must have been pretty decisive. Anyway, the meeting appears to have blocked off any subsequent room for manoeuvring away from the decision to introduce the bill. What is so annoying about the whole saga is that it has put a strain on our relations with London, raised the political price for me of failure, and made it very difficult to fight an issue as hard as this again. I don't like having a fight with somebody I like as much as Hezza, though I don't any longer give a monkey's for having arguments with some of the FCO crew back home. They won't get any easier as we get closer to the election.

Thursday 25 May

Len Appleyard telephoned with his congratulations. Martin spoke to him – I hope briskly. Len is now into his 'tin hat' routine: we must all fight together rather than fight each other, etc. After what has gone on so far it is all rather ludicrous. We know perfectly well that he and Hezza were planning how to dish us while they were staying in a luxury hotel in Guangzhou. This is where they cooked up the idea of a message to Li Peng about which Len is now having second thoughts. The hotel is presumably bugged by the Chinese security forces (who probably own it), so unless they are totally incompetent the Chinese will know exactly what the split is on the British side.

I talked to Martin and Bob about some of the problems that we've been having both from London and Beijing since Peter Ricketts and Robin McLaren left. We plainly have to go on fighting our corner, but maybe we shouldn't take too tragic a view of it all. First, governors of Hong Kong have invariably been regarded as tedious distractions from improving Sino-UK relations by the chaps at home: just think about how unpopular Murray MacLehose was in London. Second, again it's inevitable that a lot of officials will be looking ever more enthusiastically to the end of our colonial responsibilities in Hong Kong and not having to bother too much about what is left over from the almost extinct British Empire. Third, they have never thought very much about the impact of their behaviour on the morale and attitudes of those who work for us so diligently and often bravely in Hong Kong. Fourth, the caricature of the Foreign Office, namely that a few of its officials regard diplomacy as, principally, getting on well with foreigners, is not always unfair. George Schultz used to say this as well about the State Department. Finally, so long as we have ministers on our side – and we have been extremely lucky in that regard – we can and should go on standing up for ourselves knowing that we will usually, if we go on long enough, win the day. Ever more scraps will doubtless take place as we get closer to handover day. One country, two systems under the present custodianship of one country, two lots of interests.

There is an energy-sapping row because a senior official in the recreation and culture branch in the absence of his boss has suggested to Legco that we are intending to drop our proposed bill on broadcasting because it may annoy the Chinese. It's complete rubbish, but the more he tries to explain away what he said, the deeper the hole becomes. I suppose it will add to the suggestion that we are putting off difficult decisions just to please the Chinese. But I don't think that is going to be the idea over the coming weeks as the CFA argument comes to a head. There's a rather chilling reminder of the influence that the Triads still have in Hong Kong. In a trial in which the boss is accused of violence against some of his former employees, he gets off scot-free as they all develop amnesia when called into the witness box.

Friday 26 May

Lavender has left for London and France. She is going to see Kate (returning from her studies in Mexico) and Laura, and is then off to sign the final contract for Monbretal and to organize the builders, decorators and plumber.

We are having a tough time in the JLG over the financing of the airport and the railway to it. The Chinese have really convinced themselves that our financial arguments are unsound. They are presumably being put up to this by the Bank of China.

Tuesday 30 May

A really serious discussion has started in the JLG on the CFA. The important point for us is to have the court set up with its judicial integrity in place. We can't possibly allow Hong Kong's Supreme Court, with much the same jurisdictional role as the Privy Council, to be subject to second-guessing or having its remit constrained by a definition of 'acts of state' which allows Beijing to add whatever they want to the explicit reference to foreign affairs and defence contained in the BL.

Alan Paul, the outstandingly able and dryly witty FCO official who normally leads for us on this issue in the JLG, has had to go back to Britain for the funeral of his brother, so for this final stage – at least I hope it's final – of the CFA talks our team is being led by Richard Hoare, my former private secretary who is now the Hong Kong head of administration. In the first session the Chinese have been stressing two things. First, whatever happens, there will be a CFA on 1st July 1997. They want it to be set up with our participation, which indeed they will encourage. Second, there are lots of hints and nudges that if we will only accept some of what they are saying, they will give in on the court being debarred from adjudicating on the constitutionality of laws and on the post-verdict remedial mechanism: in other words they will no longer insist that the executive should be able to change judicial conclusions after they've been made.

They will also accept having more judges from outside on the court for individual cases.

After a discussion with members of the Ad Hoc group, and with their total agreement, I authorized Richard to say at dinner with the Chinese side that for us there is no question of face involved in setting up the court. What we are concerned about is the nature of the court that is actually established. We prefer a decent court set up in 1997 on agreed lines to no agreement and a row. Since we can keep the Privy Council's role going until 1997, the point about a judicial vacuum is less important to us than the argument about the jurisdiction of the court. It will be interesting to see whether we have smoked out their real problems: first removing the ability to second-guess judgments, and second limiting the ability of judges appointed from abroad to try particular cases . In the evening, I had dinner with two *FT* journalists who were sceptical about how much people in Hong Kong want another fight, even over the CFA. I suspect they are right, though it won't come out like that if we actually do a deal which the Chinese can accept and which will therefore be regarded with suspicion by lawyers in Hong Kong and by the Democrats. At least on this, the business community seems to be onside and I think may have been putting pressure on Beijing, insofar as anyone can.

Wednesday 31 May

We agreed with Richard Hoare five points that we can put to China on the CFA. First, we are prepared to amend the bill we put to Legco to take account of some presentational points proposed by the HKMAO Preliminary Working Committee. Second, the Chinese must drop the demands for a post-remedial mechanism and on the court being barred from any jurisdiction on the constitutionality of laws. Third, while the legislation should go ahead now, and preparations for the court should be made, it won't actually sit before 1 July 1997. Fourth, they will support our bill. Fifth, we're happy that the preparatory team for the future Chief Executive and SAR government should work with us in arranging the establishment of the court. We worked out a precise form of words to put to London and the embassy in Beijing. It seems clear that they are both now in practice letting us conduct the negotiations much as we like. London officials are presumably sighing with relief that there is at least a chance of a settlement and no row. Even if this does not happen, and there is no settlement along these lines, we will look decent when everything comes out into the open.

Thursday 1 June

After Exco, which endorsed our approach to the CFA talks, I did a Legco session mostly on registration in the functional constituencies. We have done pretty well, registering about a million people in all, which is 14 times as many as voted in functional constituencies last time round. In the new constituencies that we have created there are getting on for 900,000, and I think this number is likely to climb over the years. For the moment we are likely to be criticized by some because it isn't even higher and by others for such a disgraceful increase in the number of people who have the right to vote for Legco. We have managed to get rid of most of the worst examples of rotten borough constituencies too.

Richard Hoare tells us that his Chinese interlocutors have taken delivery of our proposals and have left us dangling in the usual way. They tell us that they will give their views in due course. We have gone through all this pain because the 1991 agreement was made in secret and then, partly as a result, torn up by Legco.

Tuesday 6 June

A summit on employment. I was expecting almost anything, including a union walkout. There was a crowd of trade unionists outside shouting, and a bit of a political show inside. I was presented with a bitter melon by one trade union representative for the benefit of the cameras. I reminded some of the press afterwards that this fruit was one of Chairman Mao's favourites. When the meeting actually got underway, it went well. There was a lot of agreement about labour market issues with the exception of the importation scheme, and everyone was fairly constructive. Naturally, there was the usual posturing afterwards and there are allegations from the unions that this has just been a political show. But I think we've accomplished the first objective, which is to get people talking in a helpful way.

Alan Paul is now back from London and leading our team again alongside Richard Hoare. They have established an expert group with the Chinese to look at the details of the CFA bill. We seem to be some way from agreement, though it appears clear that the Chinese do want to deal. They are already hinting to Len Appleyard in Beijing that Qian will now be able to make his visit to London. They will of course still try to get everything they can from us and will battle right down to the wire, and indeed even beyond it.

Wednesday 7 June

I went to open the Joseph Conrad Library at the French International School. I began with a few words in French and after the first sentence everyone present burst into thunderous applause, as if it is amazing that an Englishman can manage even a few words in their language. I then surprised them again by saying quite a lot more in French. But I had to think of it all rather carefully beforehand.

Hard pounding continues in the JLG on the CFA. Francis Cornish says (perfectly reasonably) that there will be a lot of dashed hopes if we don't get an agreement, though he doesn't think that this result would be calamitous. On the other hand, there will be a huge sigh of relief if agreement is possible.

Friday 9 June

Lavender got back last night and had to come with me almost straight away to a charity dinner in the ballroom for the Liver Foundation. I was dragged in and out of the dinner by our CFA negotiating team. There are a couple of points left outstanding which are still dividing the two sides. In my judgement, if we conceded both of them it would make it more difficult to sell the deal. Our team are keen to settle because they think the Chinese might kick over the traces on other matters if we dig in. My own hunch, however, is that if we hold firm the Chinese will back down because they plainly want a deal and know that we will simply go ahead with the bill in a couple of days if there is no agreement. We send our slightly reluctant team back into battle and at 11.45pm we got the news that we have won the points that we wanted. The text is all we needed.

The agreement says, first, that we will accept the presentational points suggested by the PWC; they are fairly technical. Second, the Chinese will drop their arguments to limit the CFA's jurisdiction on the constitutionality of laws and they will also drop the idea that alongside the CFA there should be a post-remedial verdict mechanism. Third, we accept that how matters can be raised in the court should be as it was set out in the Basic Law. Fourth, the Chinese assure us that if Legco deals with the bill this summer, they will be positive about it. Finally, the Chief Executive designate and his team will be responsible in partnership with us for setting up the court in 1996–7 on the basis of the legislation that we pass now. It will actually start work on 1 July that year.

This morning we began with a an Exco meeting at which the agreement was enthusiastically endorsed. I saw the Chief Justice just afterwards, who is supportive. Allen Lee is all over the place and is being got at by some of his colleagues on heaven knows what grounds; mainly I suspect the fact that we are putting it forward at all. Martin Lee came in to GH to denounce what I am proposing, saying the whole thing is a sell-out. He is particularly critical of the fact that we have used the language from the Basic Law about acts of state, though he was of course on the committee which drafted this mini constitution. He's obviously quite pleased that he's got a stick to beat us with but says that he hopes that our disagreement won't affect our relationship.

At a Legco question and answer session on the agreement, none of the questions was particularly difficult. The Democrats were hostile and others sat on the fence. Even Emily Lau said to me (as I'm leaving the chamber) that, while she doesn't support what we have done, she thinks I did well in dealing with questions. In talking to the press, we seem to do better with the locals than with the foreign media, who are in British kowtow mode. I don't think I've ever worked with so many officials who could do the sort of sophisticated briefing that is required as well as these ones do it. Kerry of course conducts the band. Nelson Polsby once said to him flatteringly, 'It is an impossible job which you and Chris make seem possible.'

Saturday 10 June

The local press is pretty good; the foreign press is pretty bad. There is a very critical editorial in *The Times*. I had to go in the evening to a football match between an Italian team and a hopeless local side. I avoid yawning too much. The crowd was very friendly. Over the weekend, local business organizations are coming out with supportive statements (makes a change) and so are the local consulates-general.

Monday 12 June

Lydia Dunn, eyes demurely cast down, told me that she has been offered a post on the Swire's parent board and would be leaving Hong Kong at the end of the year. She thought she should step down from Exco at the end of July and wishes to announce it this week. She is going for 10 days in London after that to do whatever she does in London apart from the season. I thought this would happen sooner or later and that she would simply glide away from Hong Kong like a beautiful swan without anybody really noticing, but it has all come rather sooner than I was anticipating. It will make a few waves (though not many more than swans normally cause) but she is a skilful operator and can certainly ride any swell. I'm sure she will also manage to explain away some of the things she has said in the past about the future of Hong Kong.

We have all been out and about doing interviews and talking to the press, radio and television. Martin Lee has been particularly busy with the clichés. Apparently, Percy Cradock is now living in Government House cohabiting with Neville Chamberlain. One of the senior members of the embassy staff in Beijing stops off in Hong Kong on his way back from five weeks' leave and tells some of our FCO officials that he and other members of the embassy are very disturbed about the way that their ambassador has been behaving. Ever since ministers took a decision in January on the CFA, he has been manoeuvring to overturn it. They don't much care for this. Apparently when this chap was in London he spoke to the personnel department about the appalling relations between Beijing and Hong Kong and London, but was told that no one knew what he was talking about. Who knows? Maybe true, maybe not. What does it matter now? Anyway, the pro-Hezza faction back home are all saying that the deal is a result of his thickening up of relations with Beijing. So there you go.

Tuesday 13 June

We hosted a concert by the Academy for Performing Arts and gave a dinner afterwards for some of the sponsors. Anna Sohmen tells me that her family is locating its shipping business to Singapore, not of course because of 1997 but because of the larger size of the Singapore port. Ho ho.

One of Hong Kong Telecom's main external advisers has talked to me about the mess the company is in. It provides getting on for 70% of the profits of Cable and Wireless but its management here is now in hopeless hands. David Young, who is chairman of the parent company, seems to think that the answer to the relationship with China is to have meetings with prime ministers and the like. In order to head their operations in China, they have appointed the son of a senior Beijing official. The problem is that, while he has a title and lots of money, he is – to say the least – not very highly regarded by his own staff.

Thursday 15 June

Our CFA bill was introduced in Legco today.

I've spoken to Sarah Hogg on the phone about a book she is writing on the 1992 election and today I talked with the Prime Minister. Like Sarah, he is pretty low. He had a very bad meeting with fifty or so Euro rebels this week. I've written to him pointing out that there's a nasty precedent about allowing a small minority in the party to tell a leader in effect that unless they get their own way they will kick over the stall.

At a meeting with Peregrine Worsthorne, who is going into China with Clare Hollingworth, he was obviously rather sceptical about democracy in Hong Kong, or anywhere else for that matter. He sounded very enthusiastic about China. We had a perfectly civil conversation and he was very courteous afterwards in a patronizing sort of way – he said that I have come on a lot since I left Britain and turned into a statesman. So there!

Lydia has done a press conference announcing her departure. I think she will get away with it. It was a class act which I would love to have seen her deploy more frequently. Hidden agendas are the subject of much speculation, but, as Lavender points out, she is not criticized for abandoning ship. People wish her well. Lavender notes wisely that it really is a refugee community with a refugee culture.

Friday 16 June

The usual Queen's official birthday reception. Despite grey clouds we were able to hold the Beating the Retreat outdoors. In two years time it will be our retreat.

Over the weekend I've been reflecting further on Lydia while recovering from a golf lesson at Fanling. She said some loyal things at her press conference which made it more difficult for the press to write that she and I had fallen out. I guess that her view on loyalty is inevitably different from mine, given what she has experienced from the colonial power in the past. She has never actually been disloyal; on the other hand, she doesn't exactly put her head over the parapet with any enthusiasm. But how much could we legitimately expect her to do? She was let down by Britain before and particularly after 1989, when there was a consensus on electoral arrangements which she had helped to push through. Like others in Hong Kong, she has found herself marching up the hill with the Union Jack in her hand only to find that the British are not there when she gets to the top. I don't think that history will be at all harsh on her or others like her. I'm not sure how significant a political player she has actually been, but she has operated as a skilled establishment colonial public servant. She has done quite well out of Britain and I guess you could say the reverse is probably even more true.

We got agreement at Exco, after a slightly difficult discussion, to go ahead with scrapping regulations under the emergency powers ordinance. These are the sort of rules that we would never use ourselves nowadays but which might be conveniently to hand in any crackdown after the handover.

Alice finished her exams today. Big sigh of relief.

Lavender had a pretty depressing visit to the psychiatric hospital at Castle Peak, which we have had squarely in our sights for improvement. The high point of her visit was to meet a man who she said looked perfectly normal but announced that he was King George V. My dad used to visit a similar hospital in West London with the St Vincent de Paul Society every Sunday afternoon before benediction and spent a lot of time talking to someone who thought he was Napoleon. Dad used to say that he regularly advised him not to march on Moscow.

Steve Vines has said to Edward that he is very grateful to us because now all he has to do is to touch the keys on his word processor and all the old stories about kowtow pop up again. Martin Lee is over the top and all over the place on the CFA. The Canadian Commissioner says that he is in his martyr mode, but it is losing him some support among the mainstream foreign observers. Nevertheless, he will still get the first paragraph in any 200- or 300-word article on Hong Kong.

Friday 23 June

We heard yesterday that John Major has resigned as leader of the Conservative Party and is intending to put himself up for re-election in early July. Today Douglas Hurd has announced that he is resigning: he is a man whom I admire as much as anyone, for his intellectual depth, wisdom and generosity. With all this going on, our scrapping of the emergency powers regulations has hardly got any attention, surprising when you think how much thought and effort went into what we are doing, though I suppose there would have been a big fuss if we hadn't done it. There will also be no coverage of the fact that Standard and Poor's have just given us a very good rating, higher than the one for China – one country, two ratings.

Saturday 24 June

I spoke to the Prime Minister and he seems quite buoyant believing that he has done the right thing for himself, the party and the country. The fact that John Redwood is evidently going to stand against him in the leadership contest may have contributed to this.

Tuesday 27 June

We gave a dinner for Legco which went surprisingly well given that some of them are intending to support a vote of no confidence in our CFA deal. Martin Lee made a rather heavy joke about at least having confidence in Lavender's cooking. Lavender got through the evening heroically. She is on crutches because she has just twisted her ankle walking down the stairs with the dogs. She reckons that on our large table she and I are the only parents having a child educated in Hong Kong! The intelligence during the evening is that everyone we talk to seems to think we will get the CFA bill through Legco. In some cases they seem to be a bit sheepish about voting against it. Anson has a trip to Beijing next weekend, organized by her uncle, the distinguished doctor Harry Fang. All the arrangements seem to have gone ahead very smoothly.

Thursday 29 June

Another meeting with Henry Kissinger, who is rather waspish about the American administration's handling of its relations with China. He told me wryly about his recent visit to Windsor to get his honorary knighthood from the Queen: he was driven from there to Ascot in her open carriage, which he says must finally have destroyed any reputation he had left with the New York Jewish liberal community.

I visited some of the blackspots in the New Territories (container dump on agricultural land, bad housing) and was shown what our officials are doing to deal with them.

Monday 3 July

Good news this week: it looks as though we may get an agreement on airport funding and acceptance of our legislation on the Mutual Provident Fund. The negotiations on the financial support agreements for the airport authority and the mass transit railway company have suddenly moved rather rapidly towards a settlement that was well above our bottom line. The newspapers are full of the airport deal, which will cheer people up in the community. They may even make some of our people in London and Beijing recognize that standing firm against tough Chinese bullying from defensible positions has much to be said for it.

I talked to the Prime Minister on the phone, who seemed dangerously elegiac. I said to him (and to Tristan and others to whom I've spoken) that he mustn't set himself an impossible target in terms of the number of votes he secures. The fact is that no other candidate would get as many votes as he is going to get. I also spoke to Anson, who saw Lu Ping today. Remarkably he came out of hospital to see her. She thought he looked rather drawn. She didn't go into detail about the conversation but he was positive about wanting to work with her. She is going to see Qian Qichen tomorrow. Our conversation was discreetly phrased; we both assumed that it is being intercepted. We agreed that she will have to tell Exco about her meeting on Tuesday morning and the media afterwards. The wonder is that no one has got on to it yet. We went out to dinner with the Maryknoll fathers and sisters at Stanley. Very nice people and I'm clearly able to count on the aggregate of their prayers! The only bad news is that Alice went off to France this weekend. We are going to miss her lively company and that of her friends around the house for the next few weeks.

I told some senior colleagues this morning that Anson has been in Beijing for the weekend, to general enthusiasm. It will add to the feeling around the place that at last we are making a bit of progress – though inevitably there will also be shouts of betrayal just because the atmosphere has improved. But that has not happened because of any white flags on our side of Hong Kong harbour. During dinner with the French consul-general, I was interrupted by the news that the story of Anson's visit seems to have leaked from London. She is understandably furious. What morons. This will confirm Anson's views about not being able to trust British officials in London or Beijing. At least I think she still trusts me and my team here, including the really great guys on the JLG who have notched up some great successes recently.

Tuesday 4 July

Anson came in early and gave a few of us a readout of her visit to Beijing. She was treated with great courtesy and got all the reassuring messages she could have asked for on the civil service from Lu and Qian. The latter apparently said that it was important that the people running Hong Kong should love China but even more important that they should love Hong Kong. No real business was done but the atmospherics were good; telephone numbers were exchanged but no invective. They were obviously looking for a way out over the container terminal development. Qian said that it was unrealistic for us to expect that all the transitional business would have been completed by 1997. Anson went on to tell Exco what had happened, who were delighted. Then she told the media. There was a bit of stuff about secret deals and the Governor being sidelined, but on the whole it all went well. It is ironic that the Chinese, who only recently were still refusing to talk directly to Hong Kong government officials on the grounds that this would represent a manifestation of the three-legged stool, are now saying that they want to talk to Hong Kong government officials but not to me. I remind people that I've been saying for a couple of years that as we get closer to 1997, I would try to take more of a back seat and delegate more to local officials. I don't think people necessarily understand that if you have been a Cabinet minister who loses his seat, you develop a fairly thick skin about what others believe to be political slights. If this bit of the adventure all ends with Beijing thinking even half as well of Anson as I do it will be a triumph.

I did long interviews with Steve Vines for the *Independent* and Jonathan Dimbleby for his documentary. They are both quite sharp about kowtows. Jonathan in particular banged on about acts of state; he has bought Martin Lee's line. I forbear to mention that the last time he was here, Margaret Ng told him that we shouldn't make such a fuss about the CFA but leave it until 1997.

Wednesday 5 July

We got the result of the Conservative leadership ballot yesterday. John has won by a clear majority. As the Maryknoll fathers reminded me the other evening, there is a God in heaven. I hope John will now be decisive about the reshuffle and get rid of one or two unreliable and disloyal jerks. He has made Michael Heseltine Deputy Lord of Hosts and Malcolm Rifkind

Foreign Secretary, which he will do very well. There's a slight tilt to the centre-left. Alastair Goodlad is to become – oh thankless task – Chief Whip. I will miss him a lot. He is much more than a safe and steady pair of hands, but that alone counts for quite a lot.

We had a discussion in Ad Hoc about the Vietnamese boat people. If we are to keep up the pace of returns there have to be some mandatory repatriation flights. These are not much fun to do, to put it mildly; there's another planned for August. I've agreed that we should have independent monitors for these flights, so I don't think that there is any more reason to give the press the right to film everything that goes on at the airport. There are no human rights arguments for it but there is a lot of downside. The cameras encourage some of the Vietnamese to behave badly, and the more this happens the more the media love it, and the more we get pressed to stop the flights.

Thursday 6 July

A long private meeting with Anson this morning. She is really fed up with the Foreign Office. She was particularly cross that when she went to see Douglas at the beginning of June, she wasn't able to see him on her own. We had asked that this should happen, but Christopher Hum sat in on the meeting. Francis Cornish has an idea about which I'm not at all enthusiastic, to get some of the leading figures in the Hong Kong British business world to come together to raise funds for the handover ceremony in 1997. I'm told that Charles Mackay, Willie Purves and Adrian Swire have already turned down the handsome offer of leading such an effort – they are pretty terrified of being seen to be British. I guess that in Mackay's case the very poor Inchcape results may have been an added complication. Anyway, I think we should go ahead without any of that and the British government will have to pay. Later in the day Malcolm Rifkind phones me after Cabinet, which was very civil of him, to ask who should be minister of state now that Alastair has moved to be Chief Whip. The choice is between Jeremy Hanley, who used to be my PPS, and Nicholas Bonsor. I go straight away for Hanley, though I know that he will get a drubbing in the Hong Kong press, who are cruel to junior ministers. He also tells very good jokes.

I afterwards did a speech day at the Sacred Heart Canossian College, where Anson went to school. There are lots of lovely nuns and nice jolly girls. All the sixth formers go to university. In the evening we went out for our third anniversary dinner with about 40 past and present members of the private office. We have been so lucky to have had so many excellent people around us.

The local papers predictably have a go at Jeremy Hanley, who apparently is not Aristotle or Winston Churchill. It is suggested that his appointment is a demotion from having been party chairman and therefore an insult to Hong Kong. Sometimes I think that we suffer from too much intellectual Womble journalism, but that's the price of freedom – even when you think that some of the people writing the stuff need therapy. It hasn't been very different at home with the treatment dished out to the Prime Minister.

Michael Heseltine has invited me to lunch when I'm back in London for a couple of days in mid-July. He's a proper person. We disagree about China but that doesn't mean that we have to stop being friends. Meanwhile, the careers of David Wright and Christopher Hum are taking them to new posts – Wright as ambassador to Tokyo and Hum as ambassador to Warsaw. Congratulations all round, particularly from all my colleagues in Hong Kong.

Saturday 8 July

We've come over to Macau as guests of the Vieiras and are having a very good time with competitive tennis and some nice Portuguese meals. Coming to Macau always feels like taking a trip to an odd bit of Europe for a cheerful weekend. The Governor is obviously all too aware that he has two more years in Macau even after we leave in 1997; he has already been there for five years, and is wondering what more he can do. He obviously regards dealing with the Chinese as an increasingly frustrating occupation. He is particularly concerned about signs of growing lawlessness in Macau and also that the civil and security services are clearing things more and more with the NCNA. His frustrations in dealing with the Chinese are made greater because he has a much weaker hand to play than me. I hope he doesn't go before we do. Lavender is departing on 11 July for France and the summer. She will have to miss Louise and Steve's wedding. But I'm going to be able to be there and the reception is being held in the ballroom. When I go off as well, the dogs are going up to Fanling to stay with Ah Fong; after all the spoiling they get in GH they are to be put on a strict diet.

Tuesday 11 July

We had a no-confidence debate in Legco on the CFA agreement. Both Anson and Jeremy Mathews* make strong speeches. We win the vote by just over 2 to 1 – 35 to 17. Another corner turned.

* Jeremy Mathews joined the legal service of the Hong Kong government in 1968 and became a competent and reliable Attorney General in 1988, serving in that post until 1997.

Thursday 13 July
A Q and A session in Legco, but unfortunately Martin Lee isn't there so misses some of my better barbs about the best way of standing up for the rule of law. His colleagues look a bit shifty. But now I will have to rebuild bridges that I didn't actually knock down myself. Peter Stothard from *The Times* came for a talk. I've always liked him since he used to edit some of my opinion pieces for the newspaper when I was a young backbencher. He has an original line which begins with flattery: he says that Hong Kong has one of Britain's best politicians, but since I am not sufficiently appreciated here I might as well go home and help sort things out there, leaving a year early so that Anson can take over. I explained the importance of trying to preserve Anson for the future and of my role as a sort of buffer or lightning conductor for the Hong Kong administration and an expert team of senior civil servants. I've arranged for him to go and see Anson, which I hope will put him off this particular argument. I then gave a farewell dinner for Hamish and Fiona McLeod. He has been an excellent Financial Secretary. He never makes a fuss but just gets things done very competently. They are returning to Edinburgh but not, I hope, retiring.

Friday 14 July
In Ad Hoc we discuss our review of legislation regarding freedom of the press. We are a bit worried about the localization of the Official Secrets Act. Our conclusion is that we will have to set out in public the rudiments of what we are proposing to discuss with the Chinese. If we don't do this, we will put ourselves in the impossible position of refusing to talk about the localization of the Official Secrets Act on the grounds that it's too secret. We also need to talk about the future relationship between a more democratic Legco and the appointed Exco. I'm not in favour of changing the membership of Exco in any significant way, and I'm also rather wary about the argument we should change the Letters Patent, bringing the situation regarding private members' bills into line with what it would be under the Basic Law. I think we should wait and see whether we have the existing authority to choke off unwelcome private members' bills if they start to appear incontinently.

Gerald Segal tells me that after he wrote a piece for the *International Herald Tribune* saying that Beijing's authority over its regions was fracturing, he was visited by a couple of diplomats from the Chinese embassy

---

After that date he retired to England and became chairman of the Overseas Service Pensioners Association.

in London to say that either he should write a retraction of the article or he would have his visa to enter China permanently withdrawn. The Chinese try to terrorize scholars with this sort of threat. The sad thing is that most people seem to go along with it. Segal believes that the rest of the world should take a firmer line with the Chinese over their bullying tactics. Needless to say, I agree with him.

Anson has offered Zhou Nan dinner in order to give him some face. The pretence was that he had helped organize her visit to Beijing. In truth, he probably didn't know anything at all about it and would have tried to block it if he had.

Saturday 15 July

I am in London for a short visit. It all seems much calmer than on recent trips. The Prime Minister thinks that the outcome of the leadership contest has given him at least a chance of pulling the party into some sort of re-electable shape. The prospect of returning to British politics if we lose is not exactly enticing. There are one or two safe constituencies, one in particular as a result of boundary reorganization, which are being dangled in front of me.

Monday 17 July

A very enjoyable lunch with Michael Heseltine. He said that he hoped there weren't any hard feelings between us because of our disagreements on the CFA. There are not: I said and meant that a disagreement about China was not going to disrupt a friendship, based in part on my admiration for his views on so many subjects, from the role of government in the economy and in promoting social harmony to the country's relationship with Europe. He is thinking of going to China again, or rather he is being pressed to go. He thinks that his meeting with the awful Li Peng was a breakthrough. I didn't try to put him off this view and it may conceivably be that he did help a bit to convince the Chinese that we were not out to ruin Hong Kong or to leave it behind when we left as an explosive device aimed at the CCP. We agree that it will be very difficult for the government to get re-elected if most of the press is against us. He has tried to win Rothermere round, but apparently the proprietor and his *Mail* editors do not think that John Major is a winner. Scarcely surprisingly, Hezza is making a lot of waves in Whitehall.

Malcolm Rifkind was very well briefed. I went through everything with him. I argued that we were at a turning point. Relations with China have improved largely because, in the spring, the Chinese seemed to have come to the conclusion that unless they were more cooperative with us, it would damage their own interests since we were only two years away from the transition. They were also probably rather concerned about hearts and minds, and the momentum for an improvement had been increased by their dispute with America over Taiwan. Secondly, I ran a largely Chinese administration and people are inevitably looking to the future. They want me to act as a buffer, taking the tough decisions in relation to China, which would be more difficult for them to take. Third, I said that having been assaulted for being confrontational for the last three years, we were doubtless going to spend the next couple being criticized for kowtowing. There was something inherently unappetizing about what we were bound by history to do – hand back a free society to China – and inevitably public opinion will focus on this and on our inability to give complete reassurance about the future. We discussed the importance of trying to ensure that some solid achievements come out of his meeting with Qian in the autumn. I'm going to write to Lu Ping about cooperating with the Preparatory Committee and in due course the Chief Executive's team designate.

Tuesday 18 July

Jeremy Hanley and his officials were also helpful and I subsequently had a long session with Sir John Coles, the permanent undersecretary. I told him that Anson now trusted Foreign Office diplomats in London about as much as she trusted the NCNA. He understands the point and is coming to Hong Kong in September. He wants to talk to Anson personally. He said that he has just talked to Len Appleyard and raised his failure to retain the confidence of even FCO officials in Hong Kong. When I saw Len in London he said that he hoped that now that the wretched CFA business was behind us, we could work successfully together.

David Steel* was helpful and said that he thought that Martin Lee, whom he had been trying to calm down, had been wrong in his criticisms of the CFA. Robin Cook† noted, presumably jokingly, that after Hong Kong, and assuming that Labour won the election, he would have to send

* David Steel was leader of the Liberal Party, and briefly of the merged Liberal and Social Democrats before Paddy Ashdown, and later became a member of the Scottish Assembly and its Presiding Officer.

† Robin Cook was a Scottish MP who became Foreign Secretary in the Blair government from 1997 until 2001 and then Leader of the House of Commons from 2001 until 2003. His speech after his resignation from the government because of his opposition to the Iraq war was a tour de force. I greatly admired his rhetorical skills and was nervous on the few occasions that I had to debate him. Apparently, despite his republican views he got on well with the Queen because of their shared enthusiasm for horseracing. He died of a heart attack while walking in the Scottish Highlands in 2005.

me off as a special envoy to Bosnia. The friends that I'm seeing all seem in better shape, not least William Waldegrave, who is fighting back against Scott with his own legal submission. Edward has picked up a lot of gossip, not least about attempts over the last year to get me to return to the government.

Wednesday 19 July

Lavender, Laura and two of Nicholas Dimbleby's sons (Nicholas is a sculptor) set off for France at the crack of dawn with an estate car full of bits and pieces. It's a heroic mission to start to knock our house into shape.

Thursday 20 July

Back to Hong Kong. I've got Martin Dinham to write an article for the *South China Morning Post* in effect responding to a piece I read on the plane in *Le Monde* saying that after 1997 the rule of law in Hong Kong would be flattened by the use that China would make of its definition of acts of state. This is really damaging and is a direct consequence of the exaggerated criticisms by Martin Lee. He has not been very sensible about this and there are these international consequences.

Friday 21 July

My main meetings were about the prospects for the Provident Fund and CFA bills and the best way forward on freedom of speech and the Official Secrets Act. Exco are very nervous about saying much about official secrets at the moment lest we have to back off in the face of a strong Chinese reaction. In fact their response so far to our proposals has been mild; perhaps they will get noisier when they have a chance of studying them. I also had a follow-up meeting to my visit in March to Tuen Mun. I didn't tell anyone in advance and when I got there discovered all sorts of problems and less sign of progress than I would have hoped for. I fired off a couple of rockets. At the weekend Steve and Louise get married: a good-looking and charming couple.

This week has inevitably been dominated by the Legco debates and votes on the CFA and the Mandatory Provident Fund. Hamish and Lydia attend their last Exco and we had a discussion about Sino-US relations, which appear to be in free fall, particularly since the PLA have just been firing missiles – only tests, of course – north of Taiwan. In the debate on the CFA on Wednesday we won hands down by 38 to 17. The closest vote was a majority of seven on the composition of the court. The local press will be pretty positive about this, but not the foreign press. The following day we got the MPF bill almost unscathed through Legco. I had lunch with John Tsang and Martin Dinham before packing for my holiday. John has fitted in brilliantly – clever, amusing and a good manager. He hits it off very well with Martin and Edward; come to think of it everyone here does.

I would certainly have settled for going off on holiday with agreement to set up the CFA and with a new pension scheme under our belt.

Saturday 26 August

Monbretal is one of the best things we've ever done. Lavender and her gang have done an amazing job in getting it into shape and preparing it for some quite big building works and decoration next year. It is as Lavender says a perfect holiday home, not grand but immensely comfortable, big enough to fill with family and friends, and in a beautiful part of the country with a lovely garden that I can start to have fun with. Thinking about it will cheer me up on the grey days.

Sunday 27 August

I came back to Hong Kong ahead of Lavender but with Alice, who is wearing with her usual modesty her battle ribbons from GCSEs – five A stars and four A's. I am now on active parental duty. With Alice, this is no burden. I sometimes think that she largely runs the household herself through the exercise of huge charm. Her friends from school come in and out all the time. We have one or two serious conversations. We disagree about Conrad, whom I always think is a bit clunky.

Monday 28 August

The main reason for coming back early is that this is the week we are celebrating the 50th anniversary of the liberation of Hong Kong. It's also the week when the Hong Kong Volunteers Regiment – the so-called 99 – are disbanded. There's a real feel of the beginning of the end, which I guess will exist for the whole week. There was a commemorative parade at the Cenotaph this morning. The weather is filthy with very high winds but at least it didn't rain. There was a fun band and much clapping of the veterans as they marched around the square in front of the Hong Kong Club next to the Cenotaph. Then a lunch for the British Legion and the veterans at which I had to speak; Edward had written a good draft. After this an evening reception for the British Legion and a dinner with the CBF and an admiral. We were supposed to be having dinner on a nuclear submarine but the choppy water in Hong Kong has obliged it to leave early because it kept on breaking its moorings.

After dinner I sat around in my dressing room having rather black thoughts about the next 18 months. Liberals worldwide will give us a kicking for doing the job which history has given us. On the other side, there will be all sorts of parades of pretty dubious Chinese patriotism. And we've got horrid issues like visas to get right. It can't be fun all the time.

Tuesday 29 August

There is pressure from some of my senior officials to change the Royal Instructions and Letters Patent to bring them into line with the position on private members' bills in Legco after 1997. The worry is that that after the elections legislators will cut loose irresponsibly. I just don't think that it's very good politics to change the constitution immediately after elections for whose integrity we fought so hard. I would much prefer to use my existing powers if necessary. If we still have arguments then we should focus them on the particular issue of the legislation concerned. Anyway, we have to sort this out without a division opening up.

Anson has made another visit to China while I've been away to see her grandfather's grave in Anhui. He was a heroic figure and she has also seen an official film about him. She doesn't have to prove her patriotism to anyone, not least to any of the United Front activists in Hong Kong. The president of the US Heritage Foundation, passing through the city, told me that we have once again won the poll for the freest economy in the world.

Thursday 31 August

There was more military stuff on Wednesday at Stonecutters: a tattoo by the Volunteers and Beating the Retreat. We will be beating it a lot. As the pipes wail there was a bright moon on a lovely evening. But today we had a nearly-typhoon. We managed to avoid a direct hit but there was still a number 8 signal and the usual havoc with the roads shut. Lavender managed to get home after a bumpy landing. Len Appleyard phoned in the afternoon. When Anson was in Beijing she talked about civil service matters to officials there. Len seems to want a bit of the action on this, but, of course, I'm going to leave it all in Anson's hands.

A US Congressman called Chris Smith came in for a meeting. He is one of the authors of a bit of legislation in the House of Representatives which is likely to cause us a lot of difficulty with Vietnamese migrants. Smith is urging the rescreening of all migrants – in effect checking that they're all wholly voluntary and political not economic refugees – which will delay the return programme since they all think that if this happens they will be given the right to go to America or elsewhere as political refugees. This is not of course going to be the outcome, as the US has made clear. It's going to lead to a lot of bitter disappointment for the refugees and more trouble for us. But I don't think we will get through to him; he has that driven look in his eye.

Saturday 2 September
Jeremy Hanley and his wife have arrived. We all went to the Gallipoli lines for the disbandment parade of the Royal Hong Kong Regiment, more beginnings of the same end.

Monday 4 September
We discussed with Jeremy the visit that Qian will make shortly to London. I hope that we can get some sort of deal on the cooperation we could reasonably have with the Preparatory Committee, and how to arrange contacts with senior civil servants. It would be a nice bonus if we can also get an agreement on the container terminal.

In the afternoon there is yet another meeting about how to deal with private members' bills in the new Legco. I repeat that I want us to examine the real scale of the problem. We obviously need to strengthen our position about the sort of financial hurdles which any private member's bill would need to clear. At present the Attorney General's chambers seem to take a very relaxed view about what may or may not constitute the financial effect of a piece of private member's legislation. I pointed out that if we try to make some big constitutional change in Legco about this issue there will be a lot of opposition. It is not only on livelihood issues that we can then expect a majority against us. I made it pretty clear where I stand but remain determined as far as possible to avoid a gap opening up between GH and the rest of the administration on this.

The president of the Chelsea Conservative Association phoned. Do I want to put my name forward for the new Chelsea seat? I went through all the familiar arguments once again. He seems disappointed but resigned.

Tuesday 5 September
After Exco with Jeremy and a light agenda (though one or two members argue that China is making a rod for its own back by still refusing to speak to the Democrats), Jeremy and I went off for a district visit to Shatin, which was as cheerful and enthusiastic as ever. Jeremy survived his first encounter at the post-visit press stand-up with the Hong Kong media. We gave a farewell lunch to my ADC, Mike Ellis, who is off to Bristol University before becoming a solicitor as soon as he can manage it. He has been very competent and next in line is his friend Lance Brown.

Thursday 7 September

We are starting to have discussions about the handover ceremony, which gives me pause for thought – not long to go – and are also preparing my next big Legco speech. This evening one of my doctors came for a talk not about my heart but about his pension. He told me that he is going to resign this year. Why won't he stay on after he is 55? Because, he replied, he doesn't trust the Chinese to pay his pension. I tried hard, but there's a limit to how much reassurance I can give.

Saturday 9 September

It's the traditional Chinese mid-autumn festival. We are at Fanling, where I'm reading and reviewing a book by Andrew Marr. Jonathan Dimbleby came for supper. He detects a growing mood among liberal opinion in Hong Kong. It goes something like this. All the argument about democracy in Hong Kong really didn't matter. It was only an attempt by the British to look good before we quit. We are not really bothered about anything else. We've now given up and are trying to get out without any further rows with China. The only thing that really interests us is our commercial prospects.

Short memories. For myself, I shan't forget our first two years here or indeed the arguments that preceded my arrival. As for the real thing, there's been a lot of campaigning for two months for the Legco elections next weekend. There are noisy public meetings and street canvassing, and while we have a restful weekend there are lots of people knocking on doors all across the city. Lavender points out that there is hardly an inch of spare space along the roads that is not covered with photographs of candidates trying with more or less success to look appealing to the public.

Monday 11 September

Our wedding anniversary: 24 years. Lavender and I agree we are as happy as if not happier than ever. Corny, but also true. Before going out to a celebration dinner, I had one of my regular meetings with the Police Commissioner. There has been a small increase in crime in the first half of the year, but the Commissioner seems to think that this is easing off. Like me, his real worry is the chance, which admittedly seems remote, of a breakdown in social order over the next couple of years. After the recent typhoon, the road at Tuen Mun was blocked, producing chaos in the New Territories. The police handled it and their relations with angry local residents extremely well. The Commissioner thinks this is indicative of high police morale.

Tuesday 12 September

John Coles has come for a short visit and accompanied me to Exco. He asked about the relationship between China's recent row over Taiwan and Hong Kong and got a variety of responses. C. H. Tung made the point very strongly that if Taiwan were to move towards independence, there is no doubt that China would fight. But I don't myself think that Taiwan would dream at the moment of testing China like this. As far as Beijing is concerned, Taiwan is an issue which it has to make a fuss about from time to time in order to appeal to nationalist sentiment.

I visited the registration and electoral office, where a hugely complicated operation is being handled with competence and enthusiasm, and attended part of a briefing for 1600 civil servants who will be helping as election agents at polling stations next Sunday. I'm told that 14,000 civil servants volunteered for this sort of work. A long talk with John Coles, mostly about visas and how we handle the next 18 months. I think the main reason he is here is to repair bridges with Anson and other senior Hong Kong civil servants.

I think senior officials are now resigned to the fact that I don't want to make any constitutional changes to cope with private members' legislation in the new Legco: they just want to be assured that I will take a firm line with any bills that we don't like. We also talk about how to handle the election results at the weekend.

Sunday 17 September

Lavender and I went to a polling station near Fanling. Everything seems to be going very smoothly. It's great for morale to see the people of Hong Kong exercising their freedom to vote for their own legislature, I hope not for the last time. They have been promised by China that democratization will continue steadily. We shall see.

I went down to the central count after supper. 1.4 million people have voted, 170,000 more than ever before. The vote in the functional constituencies has totalled well over 400,000. The exit polls suggest that the Democrats have done much better than expected.

Monday 18 September

I woke up to the first results of the elections, which confirm what the exit polls were saying last night. Very good results for the Democrats. The leading pro-Beijing figures have all been beaten. So has Elsie Tu. I doubt whether any of them were helped by a statement from the NCNA yesterday morning saying that it didn't matter what happened in the elections since this elected Legco would be wound up in 1997. The allies of the Democrats have done well also, for example Margaret Ng has won the legal constituency against the odds. Other independent-minded candidates who support openness and democratic accountability have also won, such as Christine Loh, Emily Lau and the former Secretary for Health and Welfare, Elizabeth Wong. Some people are suggesting that Beijing will have to take account of the results. I wouldn't bet on it, though of course it would be the sensible thing for them to do – sensible in every political sense.

Tuesday 19 September

After singing happy birthday to Lavender, I had breakfast with Winston Lord. We agreed first that I mustn't allow a gap to open up between the Hong Kong government and Legco, and second that the Democrats should be encouraged to behave responsibly and cooperate with the government when it's in everyone's interest to do so. No one will be helped if they cut loose and appear to be acting in a reckless and populist way. He says that Washington is keen to put its relationship with China back on a more even keel but that this is not going to be easy because of uncertainty in Beijing about the direction of policy and next year's elections in the US. I gave Lavender a birthday dinner with friends on the *Lady Maurine*.

Wednesday 20 September

I've started to talk to Legco parties and winning candidates, telling Martin Lee that he should be making as many contacts as possible with business and with civil servants. I am making clear to members of the administration that we need to realize the necessity of boxing much more cleverly with Legco than we sometimes have in the past. In the evening we gave a farewell dinner for James Blake and his wife. James has been responsible for the government works programme. He is the last expatriate senior official left in the administration, apart from the Attorney General, Jeremy Mathews. It has been a remarkably swift and comprehensive process of localization, and the competence of government in Hong Kong has not suffered an iota. His departure is a significant day for Hong Kong.

Thursday 21 September

Len Appleyard has come for 24 hours and joined Crispin Tickell (who used to be my permanent secretary when I was aid minister) for dinner and, in Len's case, a bonding session with me. As diplomats, Len and Crispin are about as different as it is possible to be. I doubt whether they like one another much. One of Crispin's greatest successes was to advise

Margaret Thatcher about climate change. He is quite grand but very good company and, that rare thing, an English intellectual.

Friday 22 September

A big and dangerous occasion tonight. We agreed some time ago to do an *Any Questions?* BBC broadcast from the ballroom in GH with a panel consisting of Emily Lau, Jonathan Mirsky, David Tang and myself. There was of course a live and very lively audience. I didn't realize when I was doing it what a storm I'm about to create. I had rehearsed beforehand with Edward and Bob Peirce what I should say if asked about the holders of dependent-territory passports being given right of abode in the UK. I told Edward and Bob what I thought and they didn't tell me to belt up. How could I? And what was it that I thought?

I said I believed that the formal policy of the Hong Kong government was as it had been ever since the 1990 British Nationalities (Hong Kong) Act was passed after the killings in Tiananmen Square. This had slightly opened up Britain's strict immigration controls by offering up to 50,000 selected British subjects in Hong Kong the right of abode in Britain. This had been a modest attempt to calm the community at a time when people were very worried about the prospect of the arrival of communist China and the PLA only eight years after the bloodshed in Beijing. Ever since then the formal policy of the Hong Kong government had been that all the existing dependent-territory passport holders in Hong Kong should be offered right of abode in the UK. David Wilson had always said this, and if I had said anything different I would have been not only out of line with an existing policy (carefully agreed with this UK government) but would also have created an enormous row in Hong Kong itself. I would also have been saying something that I didn't believe. In my reply to the question, which came from the veteran BBC journalist Anthony Lawrence, I said that I thought that a British passport shouldn't just be about helping people to hop on and off an aeroplane nor that this would mean that everyone with one of the dependent-territory passports would get on a plane and head for the United Kingdom.

Sunday 24 September

It turned out to be a slow news weekend, and my reply that the passport should give the right of abode has dominated the news in Britain and on the World Service. There were of course time lags between the recording and the broadcast, but Lord Tebbit, lots of right-wing Conservative MPs and the tabloid press went nuclear as soon as the programme was aired. The gunfire sounds as the passport war rages. I am accused of grandstanding and of raising expectations. Maybe I should have nuanced the issue a little, but I said what I thought and we should probably have this argument now rather than wait for a year or two. Michael Howard* slapped the idea down very smartly and has said that the government is not going to change its policy. No surprises there. Jack Straw says the same – if anything he goes rather further and says that there are Indians and Africans in the queue for British nationality who would have pride of place over Hong Kongers any day. There is of course a moral case for us to give British citizens a proper passport rather than simply a travel document. In any event they are exceptionally unlikely to take up the chance of living in Britain at the moment. There are hundreds of millions of Europeans who could theoretically live in Britain tomorrow but they won't do so. It is quite revealing that from 1990 to 1994, 140,000 Hong Kongers went to live in Canada, 70,000 to the US, 56,000 to Australia, 17,500 to New Zealand and only just over 5,000 to the United Kingdom.

Monday 25 September

The tabloids are in full cry. They are after my blood. Too long in the sun. Flunkies and all that grand living have gone to his head. Out of touch with reality. Well, at least no one now will think that I'm hunting for a Conservative seat.

I am going to ask Jimmy McGregor† to join Exco. He will be a good representative of the better parts of the business community and will be useful in building bridges to Martin Lee and the other Democrats in Legco. After Edward's birthday tea we had dinner with Paul Bryan and his wife, Cynthia. Paul was the leader of the small delegation of MPs when I first came to Hong Kong as a young backbencher in 1979, and he

* Michael Howard was a Conservative lawyer and MP who held cabinet jobs under both Margaret Thatcher and John Major. He was briefly one of my junior ministers when I was Environment Secretary and a very good and hard-working one. I saw him most frequently when he was Home Secretary from 1993 to 1997 and we clashed a good deal over the rights of people who lived in Hong Kong to settle in Britain. Once a strong proponent of British membership of what was then the European common market, he later became an articulate Brexit campaigner. He was fairly right-wing in most of his views (which was probably the main reason why he was elected leader of the Conservative Party in the run-up to the predictably unsuccessful 2005 general election) and politely inflexible in expressing them. Nevertheless, he was personally courteous, and the fact that he had an extremely nice wife and children always rather disposed me towards him. He became a member of the House of Lords in 2010.

† Sir Jimmy McGregor, after service in the RAF, joined the Commerce and Industry Department of the Hong Kong government and later became the director of the Hong Kong General Chamber of Commerce from 1975 to 1988. He represented a functional constituency covering commerce in Legco until 1995 and was a member of Exco from 1995 to 1997. After 1997 he retired to Vancouver where he died in 2014. Jimmy was a brave and consistent supporter of democracy in Hong Kong.

told rather a charming story. They have had dinner with an elderly Chinese businessman, a refugee from the mainland and an old friend. He couldn't stop talking about the vote he had cast in the Legco elections. It was the first time he had ever voted and he was obviously extremely excited about it.

Tuesday 26 September

The media storm over passports has abated a bit. Both William Shawcross and Hugo Young have now written supportive articles and there is a good leader in *The Times*. After Exco I had a perfectly calm and intelligent discussion with Tsang Yok-sing and colleagues from the pro-Beijing Democratic Alliance for the Betterment of Hong Kong (DAB HK), who didn't cry foul over losing to the Democrats in the elections. After that, a talk to John Gray, who is leaving HSBC next summer. I suggested that, if he leaves a bit earlier, I can put Vincent Cheng onto Exco. Vincent works for the Hang Seng Bank, which is largely owned by HSBC. He has been an appointed member of Legco and is a moderate centrist. I obviously couldn't have two members from the bank at the same time. John was wholly amenable to this idea and very supportive on passports. Exco will soon be a bit different. With Lydia going, I'm going to make Rosanna Wong the senior member, and Jimmy McGregor and Vincent Cheng will join us.

A telephone conversation with Jeremy Hanley in which he was perfectly friendly but wanted to check that I'm not launching some great campaign on passports. He gives the impression that he thinks that what I said was a gaffe. He seemed rather surprised when I told him it has been the Hong Kong government's policy for over five years.

Wednesday 27 September

I talked to Vincent. He wants to build bridges with the Democrats and is delighted by the offer of a seat on Exco.

Thursday 28 September

A very unpleasant visit to three temporary housing areas, which turns into a bit of a disaster. I have seen a few of these areas before – about half a dozen – sometimes on my own and sometimes with the press. This time, we learned just before we went that there was probably going to be trouble, and there certainly was. The first stop was pretty straightforward, just some peaceful petitioners. But things had really been stirred up at the second and third temporary housing areas. There were accusations that we have broken our word about clearing them, which is actually untrue, though that obviously doesn't win any points. We are retaining some, which we need to do to have somewhere to put new immigrants from China and people who were cleared from squatter areas. Anyway, we are surrounded by demonstrators who are egged on by some of the social workers who – allegedly – work in the camps developing the community. They've certainly developed it in at least one sense. I completed the programme but we were surrounded by yelling crowds, people wanting to present me with rats, people sitting down in front of us, and others trying to push children and old people into the firing line. It all ended with an attempt to block the departure of my car. The television pictures are awful and I was worried about the safety of my bodyguards and the officials who were with me. What is true is that the housing in these places is awful and the fact that we've been steadily getting rid of them doesn't really count if you're still having to live there. *Sangfroid* is much diminished, but the only real response is to go somewhere else that is a real black spot as soon as possible.

Saturday 30 September

Cheering news from Laura yesterday, who has been promoted at her magazine. She is going to be assistant to the beauty editor, a very suitable post as far as the subject is concerned, says her father. Lowering my spirits, I had to go again through the annual routine of the NCNA China National Day reception. This morning the papers were full of an attack by the vice director of the NCNA on what I said at this reception. I had mentioned the successful Legco elections and referred to the fact that neither the vice director nor myself would be around 50 years after 1997 to celebrate the 50th anniversary of the Hong Kong Special Administration Region (SAR). I'm not sure whether the problem is that he thinks he will be here in 2047 and that I have been rude about his prospects of longevity.

It's Alice's birthday and we've come up to Fanling with lots of her friends. We are preparing for a potentially difficult week with Qian's visit to London. In Hong Kong we are on the edge of another typhoon, which means that Exco is cancelled. After lunch I had a call from the Prime Minister, who wanted to talk about his meeting with Qian. I went through what I think he might say and underline the importance of flagging up our concern about Legco.

Tuesday 3 October

Apparently Qian's visit to London started well yesterday when he met Michael Heseltine, and his meeting with the Secretary of State also went extremely well. We got agreement on our own proposals for contacts with the civil service and with the Preparatory Committee, and they have also agreed to set up an expert group under the two ambassadors who run our respective teams in the JLG to discuss the final departure ceremony. There seems to be broad acceptance of the need to resolve problems about the container terminal. Malcolm didn't raise the future of Legco, nor did the Prime Minister. But apparently when they came out of the Foreign Office for a stand-up with the press, there were a couple of questions to Qian about Legco and he said bluntly that it wouldn't have a role after 1997. Malcolm was standing next to him and said nothing as if he implicitly accepted it, which was clearly a mistake. But Malcolm didn't have an interpreter so he didn't know what Qian was saying. I sense trouble and have phoned Sherard to say that somebody must say something about Legco and the sooner the better.

Wednesday 4 October

The trouble has come pouring out just about as badly as is possible. Whether or not it was inadvertent, FCO officials aren't helping. The papers in Hong Kong are full of how we didn't raise Legco and there are also stories of Foreign Office officials in effect saying that I've been sidelined and that things don't have to be seen 'through the prism' of the Governor of Hong Kong. So instead of the story being that, within 2½ weeks of the Legco elections, we have got all these deals with China, which shows that you can stand up to them and still do business, it is that we have done business with China because we have sidelined the Governor and Legco. One reason why this is annoying is because it removes the chance of building up people's confidence here in their ability to stand up for themselves. Another is that it's going to make it more difficult to handle Martin and the Democrats. Martin Lee inevitably goes off the deep end. He says that the Foreign Office is up to its old tricks. Cradock rules, OK. (Or as self-styled wits claiming to be dyslexic scrawl on lavatory walls, Cradock rules, KO.) The Governor is ignored. While there is always a tendency to put the worst construction on things, there is no question that the Foreign Office have cocked up quite seriously, both explicitly through briefings and doubtless through their body language. All the pro-Beijing press here is of course delighted. Meanwhile Anson and Michael Sze are explaining the sensible arrangements for civil servants seeing representatives of the future SAR government. At least everyone is happy about that.

Sidelining stories are continuing and we have gone into damage control, pointing out that Jeremy Hanley had set out our position on Legco last Friday, that Qian had set out China's position over the weekend, and that after that plainly both sides had nothing to gain in a meeting of just over an hour by a further sterile exchange. I have to say that this isn't very convincing. We are always trying to get other countries to raise Legco and related matters with the Chinese, but why should they do so when we don't? Somebody has pointed out, all too accurately, that the State Department seems to be rather more supportive of Hong Kong than the Foreign & Commonwealth Office. The Foreign Office are doing a bit of damage control too, claiming that Nigel Sheinwald (the head of the news department), who was the most damaging source of the story about sidelining, was quoted out of context. But the main journalist who wrote the story for Hong Kong – David Wallen, a very trustworthy journalist for the *SCMP* [*South China Morning Post*] in London – is a reliable man and stands by his story. I know who I believe.

Thursday 5 October

The FCO has eventually put out a statement on Legco and the Foreign Secretary has agreed to write an article for the Hong Kong papers. He is also going to say something in his speech to the party conference about Hong Kong. He phoned this evening to give a quasi-apology, saying that his brief had only said he was to raise Legco if it was raised with him. Well, up to a point, Lord Copper! The trouble is it was actually raised with him in front of the cameras although he didn't know it at the time. There's no point in me having a row with Malcolm, who is a good man. On the other hand, his officials have behaved in a rather sneaky way. So the story is all about good old FCO rescuing Sino-British relations and getting deals that Hong Kong couldn't get. Don't ask me this week whether I trust the Foreign Office in London. We predicted that China would start doing business in the second half of the year. That is what they have done. But so far they have been doing business on our terms because we have been tough and shown that we have got a bottom line. That is not how it now looks.

Friday 6 October

Even worse today is an awful piece in the *Economist*: Patten sidelined to get deal with China. It's by an excellent journalist, Dominic Ziegler, who phones to apologize and to say that he realizes he got it wrong. He says the main reason is that he had several steers from officials in London. He is not the sort of man I disbelieve. Another consequence of the sidelining story is that we have lost an initiative which we were about to launch. We have invited Zhou Nan to come in for a briefing on my Legco speech. His officials were plainly gobsmacked. They still haven't come back to us. My guess is that they are trying to clear it with Qian. They won't want to come. It would have been a good ploy as well as a sensible thing to do had the week not turned out as it has. Now if it happens it will doubtless be read as 'Rifkind orders governor to see Zhou Nan'.

Monday 9 October

To kick off the week of my big policy speech to Legco, Percy Craddock has given a long interview to RTHK calling me the 'incredible shrinking governor'. When I said to Edward that it's rather a good phrase and I'm surprised that he didn't go into politics, Edward replied, 'But he did.' Just to fill my cup, I'm told that his life was made complete when he was invited by the FCO to the dinner in London for Qian.

Julian Seymour, Margaret Thatcher's private secretary, came in to talk about the plans for her visit in January. She is coming here on her way from Taiwan. I've been invited to her 70th birthday party at Claridge's but alas can't make it. I'm sure that Ted Heath will be sad for me.

Wednesday 11 October

Going down to the Legco building to make my speech, there was the usual line of petitioners outside, but this year there were some new faces. Several of the old faces are now actually inside, in the case of one of the best-known campaigners in Hong Kong (known as 'the bull') wearing a tie for the occasion. As ever my speech was long. I went through all the figures which show that we've started a real revolution in social welfare in the last three years. Spending has gone up by 40% in real terms. Spending on the elderly alone has increased by over half in real terms. I think there's a chance that during my five years here we will move from second-world provision to first-world provision for the needy. Last year I was accused of not saying enough about bread-and-butter issues. I didn't make the same mistake this time which is one of the reasons for the length of my oration. I not only pointed out where we have made progress but also touched on some of the things that we haven't managed to achieve. I made a big deal of the balanced changes that we are intending to make to the Labour Importation Scheme, reducing the number of people covered from 25,000 to 5,000, and setting out how much better targeted it is going to be in future. I also said quite a bit about the success of the Legco elections, expressed the hope that the new Legco will recognize its responsibilities, and said that were anything to be done which appeared to damage Hong Kong's prospects or economic solvency I would have to turn it down with the powers that I already have.

Thursday 12 October

This morning I went to RTHK for a phone-in programme, which lasted for an hour and a half. At the end there were still calls stacked up by the dozen. At a Legco Q and A session I was expecting questions about what one or two papers have called my threat of a veto to Legco (i.e. my suggestion that I don't have to accept everything Legco proposes whatever its consequences), but no question came.

Emily Lau and Christine Loh are off to Geneva next week for the UN hearings on Hong Kong's position under the International Covenant on Civil and Political Rights [ICCPR]. More trouble, I dare say. But Emily has told some Labour MPs this week (just before denouncing me, that is) that I'm the best Governor there has ever been. I'm not sure she would think that others had set the bar very high! I did get rather soft questions in Legco from the DAB HK. That will probably change, but I keep on surprising my staff by saying that I find them largely painless to deal with.

We are starting to get a little whiff of nervousness in London, where some officials are becoming alarmed at reports that Britain has given up caring about Hong Kong in return for trade deals in China. They are apparently trying to persuade Michael Heseltine to address the issue in his speech to the Trade Development Council. I rather doubt that he will do this in the terms they would want, but they've only got themselves to blame for getting into this trouble – and particularly for getting us into this trouble.

This afternoon I saw a group of Labour MPs led by Paul Murphy, their Hong Kong spokesman. They are decent, helpful and interested. I told them the sort of problems that they could expect to face if they were to come into government in the spring of 1997 – passports for the ethnic minorities here, the Vietnamese migrants left in the camps, the extent to which Britain would stand up for Hong Kong over the Joint Declaration after 1997, the pressure from some business lobbies to wash our hands of any sense of responsibility for the territory, last-minute problems about the handover ceremonies and so on. They obviously realize that we have got quite a lot of support in the community, though the critics are out and about as well. I then had a briefing from Joseph Yam (who runs the monetary authority) before my meeting with the Governor of the Bank of England next week. The Governor wants to talk about our economic prospects and the long-term position here of our major British banks.

Friday 13 October

Before I went off for a public meeting on my Legco speech at City Hall, we had the official launch at GH of the Society for AIDS Care. Lavender has put a lot of work into this and the government has now given the charity a house in the New Territories for a residential centre for AIDS patients. The AIDS home care nursing service is also about to begin work.

I'm going to have a grim week preparing loads of speeches for our short trip to London, which begins on Friday. At a meeting with the CBF (Bryan Dutton) we looked at Chinese requests to move in a substantial shadow garrison well ahead of June 1997. As far as I'm concerned it is absolutely no deal. The CBF has also worked out some pretty good ideas for the handover ceremonies, though I'm not sure that the Chinese will warm to the idea of one of our royal visitors inspecting a Chinese guard of honour alongside me. The most difficult thing I have to write is a lecture for the Conservative Political Centre on Britain, China and Asia, and what we can all learn from one another. I'll do my usual stuff about 'Asian values' (values are not localized but universal) and something on the importance in Britain of following Asian countries and not allowing the state's take of national income to rise too high. I want finally to say something positive about Europe.

Tuesday 17 October

This week's Exco is Vincent Cheng's first and John Gray's last. Jimmy McGregor won't arrive until next week. We had a discussion on student fees and the unit costs of higher education. The costs of tertiary education have gone up too much and we have to take this into account in any proposals on the proper level of fees. The expansion of tertiary education in Hong Kong has been a terrific success story, but the long-term financial bill is going to be too much both for the taxpayer and for students and their families.

Wednesday 18 October

Graham Fry is staying with us. He has taken over from Christopher Hum with responsibility for China, our own affairs and those of much of Asia. He brings to the job the great advantage of being a Japanologist who isn't carrying all the baggage of having been a Cradock acolyte for years. He is obviously bothered that the Qian visit went so badly for us and appears to have a fairly clear-headed view of British interests being at least related in some ways to behaving decently in Hong Kong. Lord Elgin* looks in for a meeting. Three people can't help themselves and ask me afterwards whether he has lost his marbles. The old and familiar ones are the best. An ancestor was responsible for giving the order to burn down the Summer Palace in Beijing so I hope nobody tells the NCNA that he has spent some time with me.

* This 11th Earl of Elgin was a former soldier who after his retirement from the army held a number of business posts.

Thursday 19 October
A legal subcommittee of the PWC have advised that the Bill of Rights should be gutted and so should other bills that we have changed in order to make sure that they are consistent with the ICCPR. They say that the changes we have made will weaken the forces of law and order and therefore the executive. This makes quite a few people in the community wonder what they have in mind which might provoke disorder.

Friday 20–Sunday 29 October
With Lavender to London. I've had a very full programme seeing the Prime Minister, the Deputy Prime Minister, the Foreign Secretary, the Home Secretary, senior officials, Robin Cook, Paddy Ashdown* and Menzies Campbell†. I also spoke at the universities of Oxford and Buckingham, the Institute of Directors business conference on Hong Kong, the Conservative Political Centre [CPC] and the Trade Development Council annual dinner. All the speeches went well but there was a surprisingly large controversy about my CPC speech, which was full of qualifications but basically said that the state in much of western Europe takes a share of national incomes well beyond what individual countries are earning. The press line is – Patten moves to the right. At the end of the week, Tony Blair claims that the speech demonstrates a general rightward lurch by Tories, which I guess has much to do with party management and the general assault on us. Just for good measure Denis MacShane, (a Labour MP who happened to be at school with me) and is a perfectly amiable cove, says that I have abused my position as a public servant to help the party and should resign. Other comments include one description of my speech as being like driving a Formula One car through a wood without hitting any of the trees. What I said was, however, factually correct – and, interestingly, Chancellor Kohl said much the same thing at his CDU party conference this week. So has he lurched to the right as well? It's also of course pretty much what John Major and Kenneth Clarke have been saying for months if not years. I have not suddenly morphed into John Redwood (as he would be the first to admit).

The most important and difficult meeting of the week was with Michael Howard on visa-free access for Hong Kong passport holders. He refused

* Paddy Ashdown was the leader of the Liberal Democrats from 1988 to 1999. He was High Representative for Bosnia from 2002 to 2006 and later a member of the House of Lords. He died in 2018.

† A British Olympic sprinter, Menzies Campbell was leader of the Liberal Democrats from 2006 to 2007. He became a member of the House of Lords in 2015.

to accept that in political terms there is a distinction between right of abode and immigration on the one hand and visa-free access, that is easier travel, on the other. He has always had the annoying habit of simply repeating his own arguments and not listening to other people's. His case is that certificate of identity holders today need a visa and that their successors, SAR passport holders, will need a visa after 1997. So we are not changing anything. I deployed all the obvious arguments in response. The rest of the world will follow suit if we don't give these passport holders free access and blame Britain for their own decisions. The Chinese will be able to make it look as though Britain doesn't give a toss about Hong Kong and that we are motivated by racism, and the community will agree with this. It will also look as though we are undermining Hong Kong's future commercial importance by making it more difficult for people to travel in and out of Hong Kong. Britain's long-term commercial interests in Asia will suffer, and it will make governing Hong Kong much more difficult over the next year or so. But I got nowhere with him. He is dug in, and even though the Prime Minister, his deputy, the Foreign Secretary and many MPs are on our side (and even some of his own officials), he reckons that he has the tabloid papers in his corner so he won't budge. Tabloids – even more than Percy Cradock – Rule on this.

John Major was in the best form I have seen him in for a long time. Everyone agrees that the economy is in good shape with net disposable income now rising. But none of this seems to make a scrap of difference to the government's chances. The Labour lead in the opinion polls seems set in concrete. This defies most of the usual laws of politics. Economy up, politics still down – discuss. There was the usual conversation about returning to British politics, but it doesn't seem a very appetizing prospect. What I would really like is an interesting international job, but you can't campaign for those and you certainly can't plan for them either.

It was great to see Kate and Laura and Laura's new black and white cocker spaniel, which was given to her by her friends for her birthday. It's clearly a barmy gift but it's a lovely little dog. While on the subject of dogs, at a dinner with some friends Lavender has a go at Douglas Hogg* about pet quarantine and rabies. He obviously gave her a fairly dusty answer and does not, she thinks, seem to know much about the subject. If she has anything to do with it, he will soon. Whisky and Soda and their owner don't give up easily.

* Douglas Hogg, son of Viscount Hailsham, was a Conservative MP from 1979 to 2010 and Minister of Agriculture from 1995 to 1997. He joined the House of Lords in 2018. A barrister, he was decent, brave, combative and a good parliamentary speaker.

Monday 30 October
The argument about the Bill of Rights continues to rage. Beijing is more or less saying that it backs the PWC position but the public mood has been very hostile. I made a little speech this evening to a dinner organized by the management committee and board of Bank of America, noting that not everyone seems to agree with me that the future lies with those communities that can offer both economic freedom and human freedom as well, but everyone seems to want to live in such places themselves. I am going to have to go on making the distinction between what so many rich people think is all right for Hong Kong and what they want for their own families.

Tuesday 31 October
We had a long discussion at Exco about the forthcoming Geneva UN Human Rights Committee report. It seems likely to be positive on some things but critical on the treatment of Vietnamese migrants, the police complaints machinery, the independence of the legal aid service and the existence of functional constituencies.

Wednesday 1 November
A public holiday – the day when everyone goes and sweeps their ancestors' graves. This has always seemed to me to be rather an admirable way of remembering one's own family. It is far too long since I visited my own parents' graves. My parents lie side by side, and close to my stepfather, in a rather cheerless cemetery in Greenford. Perhaps that shouldn't matter, but I like the idea of an old churchyard, a decent view and a few trees somewhere that encourages the living to visit. It's interesting that despite this annual family event, so many of the Chinese seem reluctant to talk about death or even to use the word.

Thursday 2 November
Boris Johnson,* who used to be a correspondent in Brussels, has written a piece about me for the *Daily Telegraph* which is surprisingly kind. I'm quite pleased that the only person who is rude about me in the article is David Chu,† whose name Johnson spells very satisfactorily as though he was a

* Boris Johnson was a successful journalist who blagged his way into politics, the mayoralty of London, the leadership of the Brexit campaign and then of the Conservative Party, and thus became Prime Minister in 2019. He was correctly described by a former Conservative Attorney General as a 'moral vacuum'.
† David Chu is a United Front Hong Kong member of Legco and of the National People's Congress of the PRC. He cancelled his US passport in 1994.

character out of *Thomas the Tank Engine*. That is how I will remember him from now on, Choo Choo. (He claims to be a close friend of Lu Ping; but when I sat next to him at a dinner he was unpleasantly bitchy about him.) Peter Woo* will get into some difficulties as he is quoted as saying that the British have had the Chinese under their thumb for 150 years but 'we are the masters now'. Letters of apology arrive from him every few moments but this may not have been the best way of securing a knighthood.

Friday 3 November

So far it's the Democrats who are behaving pretty well in Legco and Allen Lee's lot, who insist on calling themselves Liberals, who are looking for populist issues on which to bash the government. They have led the efforts to block increases in fees and charges and voted against my Legco Address whereas the Democrats voted for it. We are continuing to defend our sensible package of proposals on labour importation.

A group of senior expatriate civil servants has just been to Beijing. They are in a real difficulty. They can't now get to the top of the service because of the requirements of the Basic Law (reserving top jobs to those who are ethnically Chinese), but they want to stay in it. Many of them are real Hong Kongers married to local girls. I hope they don't believe that all this democracy business has screwed things up for them.

In a discussion about our last Honours List I mused with Martin and Edward about who will actually want to take them. Answer: no problems there, and we're actually trying to get an increase in the number of awards that we usually hand out. I had my most interesting meeting for some time with the two trade unionist legislators (Lau and Lee, who both spring from the Christian Socialist movement) and an international trade unionist delegation. They mostly wanted to talk about the state of our labour laws and their relationship to the Bill of Rights. They were very well briefed and made their points cogently and courteously.

Saturday 4 November

The UN Human Rights Commission report has been published saying more or less what we anticipated. I'm pleased they have made it abundantly clear that China will have an obligation after 1997 to report on compliance with the International Covenant. That is an obligation both under the Joint Declaration and under case law, which has been built up

* Peter Woo is a billionaire businessman in Hong Kong who is married to the second daughter – Bessie – of the late Hong Kong shipping tycoon Sir Y. K. Pao. Politically ambitious, but unsuccessful garnering public support.

since the breakup of the Soviet Union and Yugoslavia. I spoke later in the day to a reasonably supportive delegation from the US Council on Foreign Relations, and was delighted that one of their members is Richard Solomon, whose excellent book on negotiating with the Chinese I recommend to everyone. They have of course been told by some of the businessmen they've met not to make a fuss if China steamrollers human rights in Hong Kong after the handover.

Sunday 5 November

No fireworks, but we did attend the Scout rally for an hour and a half. I am the Chief Scout, but since I don't wear ceremonial uniform elsewhere, I don't have to wear shorts when I'm doing my scouting business. Fortunately, no knots or toggles are involved. But, as the Chief Justice (who is the president of the Scouts) observes, I would march better than they do. 'No sense of rhythm,' he kept on muttering.

Monday 6 November

The JLG team are still away bonding, so they say, though there isn't much sign of it just at the moment, particularly given the promises made at the Qian meeting in London, and the row over the Bill of Rights and associated legislation resonates. All the media are being taken up to Beijing at the moment for struggle sessions. According to the NCNA, one by one the papers are told that they should be more positive in their coverage of China.

I had a talk to Donald Tsang about the economic outlook. He is rather more confident about the future than I am. Unemployment is largely the result of a huge increase in the workforce over the last couple of years. It hasn't been matched by an equivalent increase in the number of jobs that we create. We have actually increased jobs by about 2½% but the workforce has increased by almost 4½% – returning emigrants from Canada, Australia and so on, and an increase in the number of legal Chinese immigrants. In 1993 and 1994 it increased by 180,000; in the previous five years, it had increased by only 60,000, and in three years out of these five years it actually fell. At the same time consumer confidence remains flat, with some impact on the retail sector and restaurants. I hope that confidence will start to go up over the next year, though it certainly won't happen if China continues to sound off as has happened in the last few days over the Bill of Rights.

The Police Commissioner told me again about his concern that crime in China may be spilling over into Hong Kong. We have got a range of difficult security issues just ahead of us, all of them with human rights aspects such as telephone interceptions, official secrets, sedition and treason. Happy days will be here again.

Tuesday 7 November

After a reception in the evening at Government House for the Duke of Edinburgh's Award Scheme, we went off for what I was told would be 'a quiet dinner' for my tailor, Sam, otherwise known as Manu Melwani. It had been turned into a great banquet for most of the Indian community, including all the Harilelas, who are Hong Kong's South Asian royalty. The women were dressed up to the nines in fabulous saris and covered in jewels. There was wonderful Indian food, dancing and lots of speeches. During the course of the evening Manu was decorated by the Belgian Consul-General with an award he has received for making suits for the Crown Prince. The Order of the Inside Leg Measurement First Class. I made a speech towards the end and we then left the party in full Indian swing. I think Sam deserves the 'face' he got tonight. He is a Hong Kong institution, has given us and our guests excellent and quick results, and he has the best intelligence network in Hong Kong. Lance Brown told me that he often seems to know who is coming to stay with us before we do.

Wednesday 8 November

I discussed the discouraging lack of progress in the JLG with Hugh Davies and Alan Paul, focussing on the blocking of awards of franchises for new mobile phone operators in a way which is plainly an intervention in the affairs of the Hong Kong government. It may be that the Chinese are being lobbied by existing telecommunications companies in the city who don't want any more competition (it has to be noted that Lu Ping's son works for Hong Kong Telecoms), or perhaps the Chinese think that it will be just too difficult to tap a larger number of new lines. Whatever the reasons, it's rather threatening for the future.

Thursday 9 November

The unemployment summit, which has been looming over me, actually went rather well, not least because of the advice of my really excellent private secretary, John Tsang, and our outstanding departmental secretary, Joseph Wong. Of course, we didn't get agreement on labour importation, but there was a positive atmosphere and we can certainly say that there has been a constructive effort at cooperation on other issues such as training and retraining. Joseph has done well in avoiding anything coming to a crunch on labour importation and it may be that we can put off the evil day indefinitely.

Friday 10 November

The employment summit doesn't seem to have played too badly in the press, though the Chinese-language papers still expect us to produce rabbits from hats (actually, I received a tortoise from a union representative in a box which is now browsing in the garden). We are more worried by the mobile phones issue. Where it is clear that some interested business lobbies are trying to get Beijing to intervene in decisions that the Hong Kong government is taking on the future of this technology. This is dangerous because, first, it would suggest to the Chinese that we think they could go on intervening in issues like this after 1997. Second, it would encourage members of the business community to politicize every issue which they don't like, and to go up to Beijing to lobby against decisions made by the government here which they believe don't favour their own commercial interests. It's interesting that it's a few business leaders that are causing us the most problems, not Democrat legislators. Anson is adamant that the whole community has to be as one on issues like this if Hong Kong's autonomy is to survive 1997.

Members of the government information service are back from their struggle session in Beijing along with representatives of the rest of the media. The director is putting a brave face on it all, but when questioned it became perfectly clear that anybody intelligent would have regarded the whole thing as an appalling disaster. Apparently everyone in the media will have to behave more patriotically after 1997. When I saw David Rockefeller from Chase Manhattan he asked me whether I would still give the same answer as I gave to him in October 1992, when he asked me if everybody was right to be so euphoric about China. I said much the same this time – namely that the right position is to be caught somewhere between euphoria and deep gloom.

I've had my first meeting with Rosanna Wong in her role, following Lydia, as convenor of Exco. She is a nice, intelligent woman who has done wonders at the Housing Authority, where she has been chairman and where there have been some real horrors in the in-tray – for example, how to deal with better-off tenants and with some of the incompetence in the management of the authority.

I'm told that last night we lost a vote at the Oxford Union saying that the British government had let Hong Kong down. Denis MacShane (him again) proposed the motion and Tim Renton gallantly argued on the other side. The criticism mostly seems to have been about pre-Patten governors and I daresay that the issue will get a bit of a run in the Hong Kong papers. I think I have only set foot once in the Oxford Union, the experience of a lifetime.

The Commonwealth Heads of Government Meeting is taking place in New Zealand and we're anxious to get some suitable reference to Hong Kong in the communiqué. Christine Loh, Margaret Ng and Libby Wong are all in Auckland arguing away. I hope people listen to them. They certainly know as much or more about what democracy means as most people there.

Sunday 12 November

We had balls to attend on both Friday and Saturday nights. Today the Cenotaph service. Will these services continue after 1997? In the evening we went to eat hairy crabs with Anson and some of her family and Shanghainese friends. The hairy crabs are not all that easy to eat but delicious. Anson tells me that the CJ has emerged into the limelight on the Bill of Rights, which safely places Hong Kong's freedoms under the rule of law.

Monday 13 November

I see what Anson means. The spokesman of the NCNA has made a statement saying that at a private dinner the Chief Justice had expressed reservations about the Bill of Rights, mainly arguing that it did override other legislation and that we would have been better off to have followed a different model such as the one in New Zealand. I wonder how much he knows about it. As I understand it, the New Zealand Bill is not entrenched above all because New Zealand is governed by parliamentary sovereignty. I wonder whether he gets the point or perhaps thinks that our legislature should be supreme. That might not be the view of the NCNA. I suggested that the Chief Secretary should get a written statement of his views. It would be nice to know what they are on anything really. He has now been spotted going in to see the Chief Secretary, so of course the story will be that he has been hauled in to explain himself and that the government is interfering with the judiciary. At best the CJ has been injudicious (not good for a judge) and it should remind people that in dealing with Beijing you are dealing with a mincing machine, or, as I have put it from time to time, trying to shake hands with a bacon slicer.

In the evening we went off to Jennifer Murray's art exhibition opening at the China Club. I bought rather a nice painting for France. There is hardly anything that this couple don't do except kowtow.

Thursday 16 November

While the CJ is apparently putting together a document setting out his views on the Bill of Rights, I had a question session in Legco. Most questions were about the bill, so I set out just why it isn't in contravention of the Joint Declaration and the Basic Law. It hasn't led to chaos in Hong Kong, but the laws that China says she wants to see put back on the statute book would lead to several contraventions of the Basic Law, which entrenches the International Covenant on Civil and Political Rights. I also mentioned several times the reporting conventions clearly set out in the Covenant. While one can only speculate about the reasons for the CJ jumping into this issue with the sharks of the NCNA, the sharks plainly thought that by quoting him they could swing the argument over the bill but they are being proved embarrassingly wrong. His published views the next day were as lame as we had expected. Someone, I am sure unfairly, said that it sounds as though he learnt his law off the back of a Corn Flakes packet.

In the afternoon we have a long meeting in Ad Hoc on the handover ceremony. I think it is going to be extremely difficult to reach agreement with China on a ceremony which meets our requirements as well as theirs. What I am determined to avoid is anything which would have us sneaking out of Hong Kong with our tail between our legs.

Tuesday 21 November

We talk in some detail at Exco about a response to the CJ. Andrew Li and Denis Chang suggest improvements to what is at present a rather legalistic draft. The points which we want to get upfront in our statement are clear: the Bill of Rights is entirely consistent with the Basic Law; its implementation has been very measured and does not lead to chaos; it has preserved a sensible balance between the individual and the state; and it reflects well on our society, including the judiciary.

I spent a lot of time in the afternoon discussing Vietnamese migrants. The truth is that there aren't any alternatives to the course on which we are at present launched, trying to encourage the Vietnamese government to welcome as many migrants back as possible and, within the terms of the UNHCR agreement, to conduct mandatory returns in some circumstances of those who are plainly economic migrants, not political refugees. We operate within implacable but extraordinarily tight realities which close in on us the whole time. Altogether getting on for 200,000 Vietnamese – who mostly of course arrived by perilous sea voyages – have passed through Hong Kong in about 20 years; the greater part of them have settled abroad and the others have returned home. No one gets thanked for the work of looking after them in camps as humanely as possible and trying to move them on under the watchful eyes of civil liberties lawyers. The number still here has been steadily falling. We need to get the figure as close to zero as possible by the time we leave, but the problems don't get any easier. First, the Vietnamese government drags its feet about the speed of return of migrants because of the costs involved, despite the financial assistance the migrants receive from the UN and us. Second, civil liberties groups continue to attack us for holding the Vietnamese migrants in camps and they challenge our policy in the courts. There is a particularly tricky issue facing us regarding the so-called pending cases, those that the Vietnamese government hasn't yet cleared to return to the country. These cases are at present with the Privy Council. Third, American congressional opinion continues to give the Vietnamese the impression that if they hang on long enough and decline to return home, they will be allowed to go to the United States – which is totally untrue. Fourth, China and most populist opinion in Hong Kong, including Allen Lee's lot in Legco, are totally opposed to the Vietnamese presence in Hong Kong and will use the issue to whip up resentment against Britain (for example, arguing that any migrants not returned by 1997 should go back to the United Kingdom with me). Fifth, the correctional services department and the police have an awful job coping with the migrants and they don't much care for this part of their responsibilities. (Nor would I if I was in their position.) At the end of a very long meeting, we come to the conclusion that all we can do is to continue what we are already doing. I suppose that life is often like that, not always a bowl of cherries.

Wednesday 22 November

Sir S. Y. Chung, who in the view of cartoonists has gone from polishing Britain's shoes to polishing Beijing's, has made a pretty daffy speech suggesting that China should set up a shadow government during the last year of British sovereignty. When he was the senior member of Exco and arguing that the Joint Declaration did not go far enough, he was one of those who argued that they would only accept the Joint Declaration on the understanding that nothing was done which would undermine the effectiveness of government in Hong Kong before 30 June 1997, and that any erosion of governmental authority would have effects long after the transfer of sovereignty. *Autres temps, autres mœurs* as no one says here. In the afternoon I visited a methadone clinic as part of my anti-drugs campaign. The figures are actually showing some improvement. I think it helps to treat the problem principally as a public health issue, as we are doing, while of course continuing to go after the big traffickers.

Thursday 23 November

Lavender's wonderful elderly friends Phyllis and Esme Wren (who have stayed with us before) arrive as well as Lady MacLehose, the widow of the former Governor. In addition, Len Appleyard has come down from Beijing and Graham Fry and Sherard Cowper-Coles from London for a meeting with my senior team to review policy on every front. They are useful meetings and may even have resulted in some greater mutual understanding. Graham Fry is extremely good to deal with and plainly gets on well with the FCO diplomats here and also the senior Hong Kong government officials. We seem to agree on most things in these meetings, though there is a bit of space between us on how much we should try to prioritize JLG work and how we can best carry forward issues on the nationality and visa agenda. After seeing Graham, my private office take down notices on our democracy wall which lists (as a sort of parody of the usual CCP-speak) the three FCO preservations – preserve the gradual restoration of relations; preserve the channel to Qian; preserve the warm afterglow. In a side meeting Len assures me that he has never worked against our policy and is a loyal member of the team.

Saturday 25 November

We have continued our bonding and strategy session and cover the handover ceremony and the discussions between our civil servants and Beijing officials. There was good news from Legco, where we won a vote to begin paying for the Provident Fund. This has been a long but ultimately successful struggle for the elderly. We've also got agreement from the Chinese side on issues related to the airport, particularly around appointments where they had wanted to go back on the original wording of the memorandum of understanding. We got the result because we stood firm.

Sunday 26 November

We have made two discoveries this weekend. First, Lady MacLehose, who is a little stiff to begin with, soon unbends, particularly after Lavender has taken her to a charming display of riding by disabled children. She founded the admirable association which promotes this back in the '70s. We also discover that like her husband she enjoys a dry martini or even two. Second, between them in 1971 they saved the 135-year-old magnolia tree which stands in the middle of the lawn at the back of the house. They spent three years sedulously feeding the roots. She gets on famously with Phyllis, who paints away with her usual productivity. We are now encouraged by her to call her by her nickname, 'Squeak'. My sister and her husband are also staying with us and have found her rather endearing.

Monday 27 November

Anson is away in France and Italy. We learnt today that she has had difficulty in Italy in seeing any political leader. Perhaps there aren't any this week or maybe they are nervous about China. But the Pope gave her an audience, which was only marred by the fact that after giving her a rosary he said how much he looked forward to Hong Kong becoming independent in 1997. Perhaps he has had a message on the celestial grapevine.

It appears that we are likely to have both Malcolm Rifkind and Douglas Hurd in Hong Kong not long after Christmas at more or less the same time. At the JLG talks in Beijing, at which we are proposing (at their request) to tell the Chinese about our budget plans, one of their representatives has accused me of introducing welfarism and policies which would smash up the economy as a result. You might have thought that an official who represents an allegedly communist regime would be in favour of spending on welfare. Apparently not. Anyway, our own officials reacted courteously and firmly and in Putonghua.

Wednesday 29 November

Much of the local press today is very critical of the welfarism attack, but the pro-Beijing papers continue the assault and go on to describe me as a 'big dictator'. Being such a diplomatic fellow there is an obvious rejoinder which I refrain from making. In London the Foreign Office have summoned a representative from the Chinese embassy and given him a ticking off about this attack on Hong Kong's autonomy. The JLG team tell me the best of the metaphors used to attack our welfare spending. I am the driver of a Formula One racing car hurtling out of control and liable to crash and kill all 6 million Hong Kong people.

Friday 1 December

The argument has rumbled on through the week while Beijing practises what I think they call 'splittism', trying to drive a wedge between GH and our civil servants. We have had the first of our get-together sessions between the HKMAO and Hong Kong government officials. It's gone pretty well. Not least because it's a long way from where the Chinese wanted things to be – the handing over of personal files and senior officials being summoned to Beijing for interviews.

Sunday 3 December

I talked to Kim Salkeld about his extraordinary negotiations with the chief of staff of the Archbishop of Canterbury about whether the Archbishop should stay in GH when he is here. Apparently, the Archbishop himself is rather embarrassed about it since the local bishop has said that he shouldn't come near GH because it will be bad for relations with China. It all seems a long way from the delegation of Anglican bishops who came to see me before I left for Hong Kong, led by the Archbishop of York, urging me to stand up for Hong Kong's democracy and civil liberties. Last night we went to a play at Island School in which Alice is taking part, an excellent performance of *The Crucible*. Plainly the Anglican Bishop of Hong Kong should go along to see it. Taking rather a different line, Peter Barry preached at 9.30 mass in the cathedral this morning about an upcoming meeting between the local Catholic church and the Patriotic Church of China, which completely excludes the underground church. So I suppose we can welcome the fact that both the main Christian communities here are 'broad' churches.

Monday 4 December

Beijing has started rowing back on the idea of appointing a shadow government and on its attack on welfare spending. They must recognize that they have kicked several balls into their own net. The following day after Exco, C. H. Tung told me that he has been invited to go on the HKMAO's Preparatory committee and after a great deal of wrestling with himself has decided to accept. I bet this contest did not go the full 15 rounds. I don't really mind Exco members going on this committee, though I dare say that in due course there may be conflicts of interest. But we are bound to have lots of fuzzy edges over the next year to 18 months.

A meeting with the diplomat, Alan Collins, who runs our operations in Taipei. The last time I saw him he was the number two in Addis Ababa. He tells me that the Taiwanese are obsessed with what is happening in Hong Kong. Beijing seems to think that sabre rattling during the recent local elections in Taiwan helped to produce a stand-off in the results with a prize for everyone, and that this will encourage them to step things up in terms of threats between now and the presidential elections next spring.

In what has been quite a light week the most consequential meeting was over intellectual property theft. The Americans are starting to get critical of us for not doing more about this, and I think we should. One of the problems is that factories in China which are involved in for example CD-ROM piracy are owned by Hong Kongers, and Hong Kong is seen as the conduit for much of the trade in stolen intellectual property.

There have been lots of talks about how Malcolm Rifkind's visits to Hong Kong and Beijing should be managed. He is kindly concerned to use his visit to make it clear that I'm not being sidelined, but I don't think we should tie ourselves into knots about this. I am rather more worried about getting ministers back in London to make a decision about the visa-free access issue before Michael Howard goes solo and turns down the idea completely in evidence to the foreign affairs select committee, as he seems keen to do.

Wednesday 6 December

At my Business Council I did a bit of table thumping about how damaging it is when businessmen go up to China and lobby about decisions made in good faith by the government. This is of course exactly what has happened on reclamation, mobile phones and the container terminal. I made the same point to the new chairman of Cable & Wireless, Brian Smith, who gets it very quickly. He is a great improvement on his predecessor.

Thursday 7 December

The funniest moment of the week has been our visit to Macau for the opening of the new international airport there. Elaborate precautions were taken to ensure that we are not snubbed by the Chinese. Our friends, the Governor and his wife, are charming and as it turns out very resourceful. The plan involves getting Lavender and me to the airport before the Vice President of China, Rong Yiren, which involved our car overtaking his cavalcade on the way to the terminal. We managed it and got our handshakes in the terminal building and then went out onto the tarmac with hundreds of others to the coldest day I have known since we've been out here. There is a bitterly cold wind and two hours of speeches and ribbon-cutting by President Soares and others. It's a bit shambolic but it goes off very well, and Lavender doesn't think that anyone has actually died of hypothermia. When we left I got the usual stuff from the press about whether or not I am jealous of Portugal's good relations with China. The fact of the matter is that Portugal gave up about 30 years ago and look at Macau now. Portugal has only stayed on as a favour to China. That's one of the reasons why the Governor is such a hero.

Sunday 17 December

Lavender and I are on a short official visit to the Philippines. Manila is a chaotic place with all too many signs of poverty. It's going to take them a long time to turn things around. They do seem to have started to open up their economy and are trying to reform the bureaucracy and the administration of justice, but there is a wild atmosphere about the place. (While we were there a distinguished Filipino Chinese businessman was assassinated.)

We had breakfast with President Ramos and his wife separately. Lavender thinks that she is a great character, interested in social issues and has had lots of rows with Cardinal Sin about contraception. She was also a world-class badminton player, so presumably has more trainers and fewer high heels than her predecessor. My own breakfast with President Ramos was predictably dominated by discussions about what is likely to happen to the 129,000 domestic helpers in Hong Kong after 1997. I could only give limited reassurance, but there is of course a worry that after 1997 the Filippinas will be sent home to make way for mainland Chinese. We have one niggling legal issue concerning a couple of Hong Kong citizens who are being held for drug offences of which it seems that they are probably innocent. The local justice system is taking a very long time to wend its way towards a conclusion, a point which I had to put rather delicately to the president.

The other memorable meeting is with Cardinal Sin himself. He told wonderful stories with scant regard for political correctness about his role in overthrowing Marcos. When I visited the old American base at Subic Bay, which has now been turned into a sort of enterprise zone attracting lots of investment from Taiwan and Hong Kong, I talked to some of the girls in the factories and discover they are paid about a third of what they would get as domestic helpers in Hong Kong.

Because of an accident which has put part of the runway in Manila out of operation, we had to go back in a private jet. It became apparent that the pilot has never landed at Kai Tak before. We had to give him directions about the final approach while wishing that Cardinal Sin had given us some rosary beads.

Discussing some polling figures on the transition, it's interesting to see the extent to which Hong Kong people identified themselves as Hong Kong Chinese, or simply as Hong Kongers, or Hong Kong British, rather than as Chinese. If pressed by interviewers it seems that they would prefer some other future than the one they are going to get; in other words they would prefer to remain a British colony or to become an independent country or a member of the Commonwealth. It doesn't bode well for the future that the Chinese have lost the hearts and minds battle hands down. Moreover, when people are asked an open-ended question about corruption in China the interviewers can't get them to stop talking.

Monday 18 December

We are continuing to talk about the preparations for Malcolm Rifkind's visit after Christmas. This is producing the usual crop of telegrams from the embassy in Beijing advising the Secretary of State against raising anything awkward with China. What that of course means is that they are advising him not to stand up for Hong Kong on anything. So what has changed after all the bonding?

We are starting to see names of the HKMAO Preparatory Committee which are beginning to dribble out; all the usual suspects and of course no sign of a Democrat. The CJ came in for a brief talk, as he does from time to time. He was rather contrite about the fuss over the Bill of Rights and thinks that this has hurt him and hurt the office. He is planning on retirement in the middle of next year. He says that Zhou Nan had invited him to a kiss-and-make-up dinner and asked him for his thoughts about a number of candidates for CJ. All the names Zhou suggested would have been ghastly. In the evening we gave a farewell dinner for Lydia Dunn and Michael Thomas. Lydia is cheerfully full of pessimism about the future.

Tuesday 19 December

After the GH Christmas lunch, I had a meeting with Martin Lee and his inner core of Democrats. They had announced that they were coming to see me to press the government on human rights. I spent most of the time giving them an amiable bashing over their unhelpfulness to the administration, stressing the extent to which civil servants are increasingly unable to do business with them. They look a little sheepish and, I think, take the point. But afterwards they went out and spoke to the press as though none of this has happened, and announced to the world that they had indeed bashed me over the head on human rights. Well, I want the administration of Hong Kong to go on moving forward reasonably effectively, and being bashed over civil rights by the Democrats is a reasonable price to be exacted for this.

Wednesday 20 December

I talked to Peter Sutch about Cathay's problems. Larry Yung, the boss of Citic, has been speaking up for Hong Kong. It is ironic that it has taken a mainland businessman to do this. It may be because of CNAC's [Chinese airline] attempts to screw Dragon and Cathay in Hong Kong – Citic have a big stake in Dragonair. Lavender took me on a tour of the staff quarters at GH, something she does fairly frequently with Elspeth. They compare pretty favourably with most housing authority flats. We gave a farewell dinner for the Nogamis, the Japanese consul-general and his wife. He is pessimistic about Hong Kong's future and says that this is the view of the Japanese business community as well. They think that China will interfere in quite a big way, if not immediately then soon enough, and that corruption will take off.

Friday 22 December
Last night we had carols at Government House as ever. Today I opened the new park at what used to be the Kowloon walled city. It's a great improvement: I used to find the walled city quite spooky. Kate and Laura arrived.

Saturday 23 December
I crashed what is normally Lavender's personal treat and helped her open the flower, bird, fish and insects show at Fanling. All the girls came with us and enjoyed it as much as we do.

While of course I don't care a toss about these things – oh, really? – there is an opinion poll out today which gives my approval rating as 74%, up on last year. Maybe Jiang Zemin will ask me to stay on.

Friday 5 January 1996
We had a tiptop Christmas. Lots of people in the house, almost every bed occupied. Good walks, especially a lovely hike out in Sai Kung followed by a delicious lunch at the restaurant belonging to our Chinese friend from Blackpool. It's beautiful, quiet countryside and you wouldn't know that you are so close to the heart of the city. One evening there was a very smart party at the Grand Hyatt organized by Lydia and Michael Thomas to say goodbye to all their friends. There was a slight feeling of *Come Dancing* about it because Lydia had invited all her ballroom dancing partners, including her teachers. There was a photographic and video show about Lydia and Michael which didn't quite claim that they had built the pyramids or discovered penicillin. No one is surprised to see them go but it's still sad. At the end of Christmas week we went off with all the girls and some friends to stay on an island in the Philippines. We had our own small house on the beach; the weather was hot with a strong breeze; I laid about and read three novels for the first time in ages. Kate and Alice did a scuba-diving course and qualified. Blissful.

Sunday 7 January
Not only is Malcolm Rifkind in town with his wife, Edith, but Douglas Hurd is here as well. It was only by the skin of our teeth that we avoided having Robin Cook in the same week. I had breakfast with Douglas, who is full of supportive wisdom and so laid back that he is virtually horizontal. He is much enjoying being relieved of the burdens of the Foreign Secretaryship. Malcolm is clearly greatly excited by his responsibilities and seems wholly on top of everything quickly. We all went for a long walk and picnic on Lantau guided by Kim, starting at the Buddha, where the crowds

were very enthusiastic about me, which had some effect on Malcolm. He is being lobbied by Jardine's on the takeover code and by Swire's on the activities of CNAC (with British Airways pulling the other way and undertaking to help CNAC with the latter's application to become a carrier in Hong Kong). He said that he wants to speak up on the Bill of Rights and Legco while sounding a realistic note about the prospects ahead.

I tried to brief him on the gracelessness of the reactions that he may get in Hong Kong. Sometimes people come here and are so overwhelmed by the extreme lack of generosity in the reactions they get that they start to wonder whether it's worthwhile making much of an effort about Hong Kong. I think this is at least partly a result of years of colonial patronizing and even from time to time duplicity – or at least failure to tell the whole truth. My FCO officials here and senior Hong Kong advisers briefed him over dinner in the evening. He asked intelligent questions and received bright replies. I think that he is genuinely impressed by the quality of our team here. I used to say that about London officials too when Peter Ricketts was there. Still, Graham Fry is a great improvement on the recent past.

Monday 8 January

After he presided at a topping-out ceremony for the new consulate general, visited Eastern District with me, where there was a good reception, and spoke at a lunch with the British Chamber of Commerce, Malcom went down to Legco for a question-and-answer session. Inevitably, since it is my trade too, I observed his performance with considerable interest. He was very good indeed – on top of his material, probably more direct than I would be, and unlike me answers hypothetical questions with very brisk replies. One result was that some Legco members and some of the press didn't like the answers, mostly because they are true. For example, he stated bluntly that we will not take any Vietnamese migrants back with us if they are left in 1997. They will not be our responsibility. He was clear about all the human rights issues and about Britain's responsibilities to stand up for them under the Joint Declaration after the handover. There is something which is terrific for my morale as a politician about seeing another politician at the top of his game. Over dinner he said to me that, even though people like Martin Lee and Emily Lau are a bit aggravating, he identifies with their values and wholly understands why they take the point of view that they do. Exactly.

Tuesday 9 January

An intelligent discussion at Exco at which our lawyers were on cracking form talking about the rule of law and local autonomy, with just the right audience in Malcolm. It was a successful visit insofar as it is possible these days for a British minister to come, be subjected to the politics of Hong Kong, and escape unscathed. I hope that it demonstrates to people from time to time what a difficult job we all have here. We saw Malcolm and Edith off on the plane to Beijing with arguments about the importance of securing visa-free access for SAR passport holders ringing in their ears.

Wednesday 10 January

In Beijing, Malcolm had a long meeting with Qian in which he was given lots of assurances about the container terminal and the continuing rights of permanent residents to stay in Hong Kong after the handover. He also made progress on air service agreements and on the SAR passport, and over and again delivers the same sermon in public and private on confidence, relating it to Legco, the Bill of Rights and dialogue with the Democrats. Nobody could accuse him of not talking up Hong Kong. Just to show how much he likes Britain, Li Peng tells him how enthusiastic he is about Wall's ice cream. I think that it is actually made in Italy but we should take any praise we can.

Thursday 11 January

The Chinese have started trying to claw back what have been taken to be helpful concessions on their part. At a meeting with Lu Ping, he began putting in all sorts of qualifications on right of abode after 1997 and the container terminal. It does make one wonder what is the point of negotiating with the CCP. They only give you what they want to give you; a visit is regarded as successful if they are not downright rude. Reiterating what they have already promised to do in a treaty, for example, ensuring that Hong Kong enjoys a high degree of autonomy, is taken by parts of the press as a great breakthrough.

Friday 12 January

Legco has agreed to some ferry fare increases and the unions have accepted our revised proposals on labour importation about which we have done so much negotiating. We have decided to drop a bill on broadcasting dealing with issues like balance and public service principles. If we try to push it through before July next year, China will get stuck into it. This is the sort of issue which should be entirely a matter for an autonomous SAR. There's just a chance that after 1997 the SAR government may be able to get away with it if they wish.

Discussing the future of the judiciary with Anson and others, it was clear that if the present CJ can be persuaded to hang on until the end of this year, the Chief Executive designate could make the new appointment, which we all hope would be Andrew Li, who would be far and away the most qualified candidate.

Monday 15 January

We are starting to think about the next big visit, which should be by the Prime Minister in early March. But I don't think it will make sense unless we've got the right decision on visa-free access by then. We're starting to plan what I hope will be the last stage of our campaign on this.

Tuesday 16 January

Bob Peirce and I had a meeting with Francis Cornish, Adrian Swire, Peter Sutch and Rod Eddington of Cathay about the company's position in regard to the Chinese airline CNAC. I am not sure that Cathay has a strategy on this. Obviously, from our point of view, we need to do everything we can to push any decisions back beyond 1997. I think it will be more difficult for CNAC to muscle their way into Hong Kong immediately after the transition. As for the longer term, who knows? The government team seems much clearer about what Cathay should be up to than they are themselves. Adrian Swire still appears to repose a great deal of faith in past assurances that he has had from Chinese leaders. But who on earth would believe any of them, not least if money is involved?

After this I had a talk with Martin Lee and gave him a readout on the Foreign Secretary's visit to Beijing. The conventional view is that the Chinese reached the conclusion last year that they should warm up their bilateral relationship with Britain and that they should do business on strictly economic issues, but that they didn't intend to budge on the big political matters. There are rumours that Martin Lee and the Democrats have been approached by the Chinese side. Martin doesn't give any indication of this. As for myself, I don't believe a word of it.

Thursday 18 January

David and Natasha Wilson arrived yesterday and today Margaret Thatcher came. She is full of beans, between Taiwan and the Philippines, and as supportive as ever. I had an hour with David Wilson, who was polite but sceptical. I then gave him an honorary degree at the Chinese University along with Jonathan Spence, one of the greatest historians of China and a professor at Yale. I have read most of his books. We gave a dinner for David and Natasha. Natasha (who sits next to me) has been going around town telling everybody she meets that I've screwed everything up, that she agrees with Percy Cradock, and that Lavender and I have been incredibly extravagant in smartening up the house and in particular that it was awful that we got rid of the (ancient) Laura Ashley curtains. She must presumably know that it all comes back to us like a squash ball off the wall. But Lavender had an agreeable evening sitting between David, who was pleasant and easy, and the previous Archbishop of Canterbury, Robert Runcie. After dinner, when we were seeing the guests off, Jonathan Spence told me how much he supports everything I've been trying to do. That rather makes up for my own difficult evening.

Friday 19 October

Charles Powell told me that he thinks relations with China are improving; Zhou Nan went to lunch at Jardine's the other day and – though it's difficult to believe – was positively cheerful. After a discussion on the budget, I had a very long session with two American senators, Dianne Feinstein and John Glenn. Their general worthiness is not matched by brightness and they were very under-briefed on Hong Kong. Senator Feinstein seems to think that she has a personal relationship with Jiang Zemin dating back to the days when they were respectively mayors of San Francisco and Shanghai. She thinks that he is a decent fellow, and if only we could prevail on him to be constructive, everything in Hong Kong would be all right. I gave them a hard hour and a half. Perhaps it will do some good. I then set off on a district visit with Margaret and we went to the Tsing Yi Technical College, where she did a Q and A with the students. We then took her to have a look at the magnificent bridge, which we hope she will open in due course.

Monday 22 January

I had breakfast with Winston Lord, who has been in Hong Kong again over the weekend. He knows the place well. Unlike the American senators, he thinks that Martin Lee is sounding more moderate than in the past but finds some of the members of the Preparatory Committee expressing absolutely appalling views. He remarked on the great difficulty of dealing with China at the moment, when the country is in a state which combines arrogance, self-confidence, scratchiness, nervousness and nationalism all at the same time. He believes that those who ask why we have done this modest amount about democracy late in the day should recognize that we are reacting to the development of a middle class and middle-class values in Hong Kong. Not to have taken the action we have, particularly after Tiananmen, would have been destabilizing. He is obviously worried about stability after 1997, particularly if the Chinese scrap Legco and refuse to talk to the Democrats.

Tuesday 23 January

A first discussion in Exco on the handover ceremony, and later the JLG had an expert meeting on the same subject. The Chinese have clearly dug in. They are still insisting on a small, diplomatic occasion in City Hall and raising all sorts of absurd objections to our own plans for doing something bigger. It's clear that they want us to leave with the minimum fuss, taking our washing with us, and to organize splendid festivities for themselves on 1 July. I think it is going to be a long slog before we either reach an agreement or go our separate ways. David Wilson has returned to London and Natasha Wilson gone on to see their son in Beijing. We very much look forward to the next visit by Pamela Youde. We have a good discussion about the possibility of a prime ministerial visit, preferably in early March, and the progress we are making on visa-free access. Malcolm is going to see Ken Clarke and Michael Howard this week. If we can get the progress we want, we can ensure that it's announced at the time of a visit.

In the afternoon I went to see how the strategic sewage disposal programme is getting on. After my years at the Environment Department in London and negotiations on sewage plumes with the European Commission I regard myself as something of an expert on the subject. My officials seem surprised and impressed by my interest in and knowledge about the subject, and Martin Dinham thinks it's all put on. But it's for real. It's the Victorian coming out in me. So no sneering. The work done so far is very impressive. We have ignored Chinese criticisms and ploughed ahead with the work, which really will be completed by the middle of 1997. Perhaps it can be named after me. No bridge, no airport, no tunnel, but a sewage treatment plant. I went back to GH to have a quick drink with the very nice young New York stockbroker who bought me a CD a few years ago when we were in the same shop in Central, to say that not all stockbrokers think I am the devil incarnate.

Thursday 25 January

A productive discussion about our plans for improving temporary housing areas. We are converting some older blocks and trying to spruce up the existing THAs. There will continue to be a need for this sort of housing for the indefinite future, largely because of the number of people still flooding in from China. I talked later with the head of the policy planning department in the German Foreign Ministry. He is very understanding about our position and deeply sceptical about China's intentions and ability to continue with its mixture of Leninism and unbridled capitalism.

Monday 29 January

Talked to Donald Tsang about his budget. Before announcing it, he is off to Davos to tell them how sound the Hong Kong economy is. We will have budget talks with the Chinese this week. Our aim is to try to delay the next 1997/98 phase of the budget discussion so that as much as possible takes place with the Chief Executive designate. Once the Chinese have got their foot in the door on the budget, we will never get them out of the room.

I met the new *Financial Times* man, John Ridding, along with the existing correspondent, who's a friend, Simon Holberton. Simon has become more and more gloomy about Hong Kong as he comes nearer to the end of his posting and thinks there is a great conspiracy to hide what is likely to happen here. The *FT* is one of the few papers that I take seriously these days.

There were incursions into our waters by Chinese boats over the weekend, which in the end were handled well. But we are a little alarmed, first by what seems to be a tendency to feebleness among the police who had to deal with the Chinese, and second by the fact that at the centre we were kept in the dark for so long about what was happening. The Commissioner gets the point. Overall, we are lucky to have him.

The Preparatory Committee met over the weekend. Nothing much seems to have happened. They got their marching orders and were told to keep quiet. They then went to lots of exercises by the PLA future garrison in Guangdong. The TVB Chinese language television channel ran endless propaganda pictures of the PLA and the English Channel merely referred to 'anxieties' over Tiananmen. Perhaps censorship really has arrived in Hong Kong already. The PLA boasted about how well trained the soldiers were, all of them speaking Cantonese and so on. In practice it seemed rather difficult to find one of them who could speak Cantonese and certainly they spoke no English. The exception was one of the two deputy commanders, who was once at the Royal College of Defence Studies in London; the other apparently has connections to one of the regiments that 'dealt with' the students in Tiananmen Square. So they seem to have got most angles covered.

Tuesday 30 January

Discussion at Exco about the way that the mechanism for dealing with police complaints operates. We are going to set up the independent complaints body on a statutory basis. The Democrats will probably want us to go a lot further than the police would like. With the exception of C. H. Tung,

Exco is in favour of giving the body as much credibility as possible with an independent outsider as chairman.

After lunch I went to the Convention and Exhibition Centre. It really is a spectacular building, and work there is going ahead pretty well, but I have to keep cracking the whip to make sure that it's finished before 30 June next year. It looks as though the Prime Minister will be coming in early March and I hope he will lay a foundation stone at the centre. It will be one of the greatest modern buildings in the world and certainly most dramatically placed, jutting out into the harbour.

Friday 2 February

The stock market and property markets are beginning to look better with American interest rates having been cut and a lot of money starting to pour into Hong Kong again. In the JLG, Chinese negotiators are trying to bounce us into accepting that once the budget for this year is agreed, cooperation should start on the 1997/98 budget. We are stalling because we don't want any real discussions on that one until there is a Chief Executive designate. If we let Beijing into the budgetary process in the way they want for 1997/98, the SAR government will never get them out.

I talked to Bob Peirce and Edward Llewellyn about plans for the Prime Minister's visit. Michael Howard still hasn't thrown in the towel on visa-free access, but it looks more and more likely that the PM will be coming for a day and a bit at the beginning of March. We have to do a speech for him. Things seem to be going a bit better for him at home.

I'm told that C. H. Tung is desperate to avoid what is being called rather oddly 'the chalice', in other words becoming Chief Executive. He is also bothered about how to put over an optimistic message to the Americans when he leads a team of businessmen over to the US shortly. The trouble is that these groups of Hong Kong businessmen talk to American audiences as though there weren't any problems at all in Hong Kong. At a time when Sino-US relations are starting to get very scratchy, with worries about arms proliferation, human rights, trade, intellectual property and Taiwan, the suggestion that all is well doesn't go down frightfully convincingly.

Tuesday 6 February

Lavender went to a women's prison at Tuen Mun, and while she says there is a great deal of overcrowding, she was impressed by the staff and by the job they are doing. About one third of the inmates have drug problems. Meanwhile I went to a Q and A session, organized by RTHK, with about 200 secondary school students. It was very enjoyable, not least because I got questions on a rather wider range of issues than normal,

19. As Chancellor of all the universities in Hong Kong, I had to rely on my valet to remember the right robes.

20. At the House of Sin, in the Philippines, December 1995, with Edward Llewellyn, Kerry McGlynn and the Cardinal of the same name.

21. Kate, Laura and Alice can't have been laughing at one of my jokes.

22. Superintendent Lance Brown, who became my ADC in 1995, looked after me with and without feathers.

23. Fanling – our weekend retreat whenever we could make it.

24. Discussing the Court of Final appeal in Legco, 1996. Anson Chan and Jeremy Matthews lend support in the front row.

25. Garland's cartoon shows John Major and Douglas Hurd nervously watching while take the Hong Kong High Wire.

26. Hezza, almost as tall as the Tsing Ma bridge, 1996.

27. With C.H. Tung outside Government House, 23 December 1996. Feng shui persuaded him to live elsewhere.

28. The Executive Council (Exco) in 1997. Front row (*L-R*): Denis Chang, Jeremy Matthews, Anson Chan, self, Rosanna Wong, Donald Tsang and Felice Lieh-Mak. Back row (*L-R*): Nicholas Ng, Bob Peirce, Andrew Li, Raymond Chi'en, Vincent Cheng, Jimmy McGregor, Edward Chen, Simon Lord (Clerk of the Council) and Kerry McGlynn.

29. Fireworks over the opening of the Tsing Ma bridge, 1997.

30. Wong Po-Yan, Chairman of the Hong Kong Airport Authority, *sedet ad dexteram matris* Mrs Thatcher. Anson, as always, is by my side.

31. Chek Lap Kok, the new airport, rises from the sea.

2. President Jiang Zemin with British Foreign Secretary Malcolm Rifkind, 1997.

33. Leaving GH, 30 June 1997.

34. Boarding *Britannia* with the Prince of Wales.

35. The empire goes home.

from sex education to euthanasia. A long interview with Graham Hutchings for the *Daily Telegraph* during which I don't say anything particularly new but probably say rather too much. I note that the Chinese seem to have some difficulty in comprehending the nature of a free society and that they shouldn't just listen in Hong Kong to billionaires, who are principally interested in remaining billionaires. Also the tendency of businessmen in Hong Kong, who want passports to a free society for themselves, and yet don't seem to bother about Hong Kong remaining a free society itself. Hutchings asks good questions and perhaps foolishly I say what I think.

David Wright has just been staying here with his wife on his way through to Tokyo and he has been followed today by Andrew Burns, the new deputy secretary covering Hong Kong, who has just taken over from him. Edward Oakden is also here with a team from No. 10, looking at the Prime Minister's itinerary for his Hong Kong visit. He wants to spend a day with me at Fanling.

Thursday 8 February

The Hutchings interview makes waves in Hong Kong among my normal critics but – a reminder that we have to play to several audiences – there is a very helpful and supportive editorial in the *Telegraph*. Following my question session with students the other day, I made a speech today at Shatin College, once again with excellent questions.

Saturday 10 February

The Governor of Macau and his wife are paying a weekend visit but Lavender and I had to dash to the Prince of Wales Hospital when we heard about an awful tragedy involving schoolchildren who were out on a Duke of Edinburgh's Award trek in the Pat Sin Leng hills when they were engulfed by a hill fire. Three schoolchildren and one teacher have been burnt to death and there are a lot of awful burns injuries and smoke inhalation problems. Once again it is difficult to know what you can say to parents and other relations when the prognosis for so many of their children is so bad. There's more bad news in London as well. There has been a bomb in the city which will presumably halt the Northern Irish peace process for a time.

Sunday 11 February

Lunch with the French Foreign Minister and a group of his officials. They have just been in Beijing. From what they say it doesn't appear that they have been much help over Hong Kong, which is the usual European story. I also asked him if France could take more of the asylum seekers from

China that we have got at present in Hong Kong. Since Tiananmen we have dealt with over 190. Most have gone on to the US, quite a few to the UK, and (to be fair) to France too, which comes next on the list.

Friday 16 February

We have had to spend all too much time this week lobbying Legco members to support us in a vote on the Labour Importation Scheme. We eventually won it with a reasonably comfortable majority. We have also won a vote on the Provident Fund. Hard work all round but good results. Also lots more meetings on the Prime Minister's visit and a visit to Island School to find out how to complete UCAS forms. At another meeting on the handover we have agreed to put Stephen Lam* in charge of arrangements.

Saturday 17 February

A week's holiday for the Chinese New Year has begun. It is bitterly cold, the coldest Chinese New Year for 46 years in Hong Kong. A few old people, some living on the street and some living on their own, have allegedly died of hypothermia. We have increased spending on services for the elderly a great deal in the last three or four years and have been denounced for welfarism for doing so. But there is still much more to do, even assuming that Hong Kong will not be as cold as this every year.

Sunday 18–Tuesday 20 February

The Husseys are visiting us again which reminds us that back home there is an approaching debate on the Scott report, with a few Conservatives threatening to vote against clearing Lady Sue Hussey's brother, William Waldegrave, and Nick Lyell. This is deranged troublemaking, but is plainly very worrying for William and Nick. Lavender and I returned to the hospital to visit the children who were burnt in the fire and their families. Shelley Lau, who is the regional secretary looking after community relations, has done a great job helping to care for them. She is a cheerful, energetic woman and what she has done goes well beyond what might have been expected. Lavender has now gone back for a few days to London to see Kate and Laura.

* Stephen Lam, a Hong Kong career civil servant, was the director of the handover ceremony in 1997. As the rain bucketed down, he asked me whether the ceremony should be curtailed. I replied firmly in the negative and like many others got very wet. After 1997, Lam became Secretary for Constitutional and Mainland Affairs and Chief Secretary for Administration. After retiring from the civil service, he studied theology at the University of Oxford.

Monday 26 February

A terrible own goal by the NCNA, who have announced – though it should have nothing to do with them – that it is not suitable for the Lutheran Federation to have its conference (world jamboree) in Hong Kong in the middle of July 1997. Freedom of religion? High degree of autonomy? Et cetera et cetera. The media stuck it to them – the NCNA that is, not the Lutherans.

It looks as though we are making good progress in London towards acceptance of visa-free access for SAR passport holders, and having read his briefing on ethnic minorities and war widows the Prime Minister is keen to do something about them too. Naturally the Home Secretary is digging in and even trying to hedge the visa-free decision with lots of qualifications. The idea is that John should announce this decision when he is in Hong Kong. We are trying to keep it all under wraps until then.

We have now received post-mortems on the elderly who allegedly died of hypothermia during the cold spell over the Chinese New Year. It appears that nobody at all died of hypothermia and that the number of deaths for the week was about average for this time of year. We actually have quite a good story to tell about improving services for the elderly but we need to get it across better in a more coordinated way. I wouldn't dream of mentioning it, but there doesn't seem much sign of Confucian values in the lack of neighbourly help for old people living on their own. What we do of course get is a lot of 'something must be done' noise about the government recruiting more social workers.

Tuesday 27 February

There is no Exco because of the holiday, but I had a very good discussion with Rosanna Wong about the Prime Minister's visit, housing policy and on how we can deal better and with greater sensitivity with the Democrats and other legislators.

Wednesday 28 February

A visit to the new airport site. It's mind-blowing how much has been achieved over the past three years despite all the sniping from the Chinese. If we had less obstruction from them, we could of course open it before the handover. They would hate that, so instead it will be opened in 1998 by some aged communist hack who will take all the credit.

Thursday 29 February

We've been told that the Prime Minister, who has now arrived in Bangkok for the ASEM [Asia–Europe Meeting], has added an excellent paragraph to the Hong Kong speech draft we sent him (mostly written by Bob and Edward) saying that the UK will continue to have a moral commitment to Hong Kong after 1997, and that if China breaches the Joint Declaration, Britain will not only take it up on its own but also raise it with the rest of the international community. Bravo!

I saw the Luxembourg Prime Minister, Claude Juncker, who has been in Beijing, again on his way to the ASEM. When talking to Chinese leaders he was very vigorous on Hong Kong's behalf, arguing against the abolition of Legco. This matters because Luxembourg will have the presidency of the EU in the second half of 1997, so he is taking a particular interest in our affairs. Back in London this week, two or three delegations of Legco members are seeing British ministers who have just about managed to keep the lid on the visa-free access decision. There has also been a visit to London by the Chinese trade minister with claims that it will result in £2 billion of trade for Britain. We shall see.

Martin Lee has had a *predictable* 'ships passing in the night' sort of meeting with Michael Heseltine. Martin came out denouncing Britain for selling Hong Kong down the river for better trade with China. Michael must have been understandably a bit galled by this. It may be in a sense what he would *like* to have done and he certainly feels we have missed commercial opportunities in China because of Hong Kong. Anyway, I hope he can take some satisfaction from the trade minister's visit if it really does produce what has been promised (unlikely though that may be). The Prime Minister has seen Li Peng in the margins of the Bangkok meeting. Nothing much seems to have emerged. It was perfectly civil. He raised Legco and the Bill of Rights and got nowhere. Li said that he wouldn't send civil servants to run Hong Kong or raise taxes here. Of course not. He also said that he recognized the importance of the appointment of the right person as Chief Executive.

Friday 1 March

There is a very United Front organization called the Better Hong Kong Tomorrow Foundation. It is close to C. H. Tung. Its director has just given an interview to *USA Today* saying that all that people in Hong Kong care about is making money and that nobody had heard about democracy until I came along. The article notes of course that all the tycoons who sounded off with similar sentiments during the interview had foreign passports.

This is not going to be very helpful just before C. H. goes off with other local businessmen for the annual US–Hong Kong business conference.

At a meeting on the handover, we decide that we will move ahead gently and quietly with our own arrangements, hoping that the Chinese will come in at some stage and that we can avoid a row. I doubt whether this will be possible but we've obviously got to start thinking about how to manage the handover sooner rather than later.

Saturday 2 March

Lavender has come home. I telephoned Martin Lee to take him to task for denouncing the Prime Minister for saying a number of things which have been made up, perhaps by Martin's research assistant. I also take him to task for apparently advocating to the Foreign Secretary what sounded very much like secret deals with China rather than 'Patten-style' politics. I pointed out to him that it will start to look a bit odd if people can claim that I am being more democratic than the Democratic Party. He is a brave man and on the right side of the biggest events, but I do very often question his political judgement.

Sunday 3 March

The Prime Minister arrived last night. He is extremely tired, which is not surprising. He has had a hell of a week, including the Anglo-Irish summit and the debate on the Scott Report, which, thank God, went just about all right, though the vote was narrow. After all that he had the flight to Bangkok and the summit there with lots of side meetings. He must have the constitution of an ox. He was so tired that he had difficulty going off to bed. We are at Fanling and Lavender rustles up a cheese sandwich which he devours with a glass of whisky before tottering off to bed at about 2am.

After breakfast and a long chat on the terrace, including his very nice Foreign Office private secretary, John Holmes (the only other person with him is his private detective), we talked a bit about the current issues in Hong Kong before he went off to read his briefs. After lunch we took him to see the new bridge and the airport. He was as impressed by both these projects as everybody else is. It really is a great tribute to Hong Kong that we have been able to do so much against a background of trouble-making from China. He is up to speed on all our issues, as I would have expected. He went to a reception organized by Francis Cornish for businessmen in the evening and I agreed to do a lobby briefing for the journalists who are travelling with him. I give them a good talk about Hong Kong and then they asked to go on the record on my own prospects. I give them the usual routine – I don't think about a future job while I am still doing a present one. For example, when I was Environment Secretary I didn't think about what I would be doing afterwards. I have got my hands full until 30 June 1997. I'm not ruling anything out and – cliché coming up – I'm not ruling anything in. It would be ridiculous for me to be going around saying that I wanted to be a European Commissioner or to do some other international jobs (though I would). I'm still interested in political issues. I have been in politics since I was 21. They also asked me off the record about Europe and I repeated my familiar line about enlargement mattering more than the single European currency. Kerry said that they went away quite cheerfully but that there was a lot of muttering that I should be back in British politics.

We gave a big dinner for John tonight. There were over 170 people, a piper outside and Chinese musicians in the room. John and I both made substance-free speeches, though he emphatically underlined his own commitment and that of the government to Hong Kong. Everyone seemed to enjoy it and to behave pretty well, though there are some funny stories that I heard later in the evening. Jonathan Mirsky was at the same table as the pro-Beijing businessman Paul Cheng, who spent most of the evening denouncing democracy. Jonathan had to leave at one point in order to avoid throwing a fit or a punch!

Monday 4 March

A killer of a day for the Prime Minister but throughout he overwhelmed the scepticism about his visit, about what he can do or say about the future, with a bravura display of competence and decency. He started by laying a foundation stone at the magnificent extension to the Hong Kong Convention and Exhibition Centre and then came back for an excellent meeting with Exco. He clearly impressed them with his conviction and his sincerity. More surprisingly, it was the same with about 40 Legco members who had a meeting with him in our dining room. He answered questions on Vietnamese migrants, breaches of the Joint Declaration, the Preparatory Committee, the Bill of Rights and Hong Kong residents detained in other countries. Emily was very forceful but extremely courteous as well. Martin Lee was very polite and hands over the bet that he lost with Malcolm Rifkind over visa-free access which John tells them about. All in all it's an excellent session. On Vietnamese migrants he explained that he had a meeting with the Vietnamese Prime Minister in Bangkok and that officials are going to Vietnam in April to prepare the way for a visit by Jeremy Hanley the following month so that we can try to expedite matters. He surprised with the announcement on visa-free access, ditto on the ethnic minorities – we are giving them a guarantee that if they come under pressure to leave they will be allowed into Britain – and passports for war widows. He also surprised with the strength of his commitment to Hong Kong and to taking whatever action is required if the Chinese breach the Joint Declaration.

After seeing an old veteran, Jack Edwards, who was thrilled by the announcement on war widows (on which he has been campaigning for years), he went off to make a speech to the Chambers of Commerce which went extremely well and was interrupted by applause several times. A lot of the best bits, underlining our continuing commitment to Hong Kong and our determination to stand up for the Joint Declaration, have been added by him and his staff, which makes it all the more satisfactory. After this, we visited Shatin, where we were mobbed at a school and in a shopping centre. Some of the British press were there and are obviously impressed. People in the crowd are shouting out, 'thanks for the visas' – yet another demonstration that we are not entirely regarded as colonial oppressors here.

He came back to the Government Secretariat and after a briefing in GH we had the last press conference. This is of course the sort of occasion when all the gains can be frittered away. But he didn't put a foot wrong. I'm reminded why I like and admire him so much . He just doesn't have as much self-confidence as he should have and asks too often how he is doing. The answer is 'bloody well'. He is a terrifically likeable man, genuinely good if given half a chance, and he has that huge ability – he wouldn't be flattered by the comparison with Bill Clinton – to radiate sympathy. I took him off to the airport for his next flight to Seoul and went home for an early night. It has been one of my happiest days in Hong Kong, indeed in politics.

Tuesday 5 March

There's a very good press for the Prime Minister, which is almost unheard of in Hong Kong. There is a general recognition, first, that he has gone as far as or further than people thought possible on nationality issues, and second, that his commitment to Hong Kong is rock solid. Given how difficult it is for a British minister to get in and out of Hong Kong without disastrous trouble, he really has done exceptionally well. The other press story which is played back from the British press is that I am going back to UK politics. It's crazy but I suppose inevitable and conceivably even mildly flattering. I couldn't have completely ruled out a return to British politics, but it's difficult to get the balance right.

Exco was brief; everyone seems very pleased about John's visit. There was a short discussion about the Chinese threats to Taiwan, which have started to cause anxiety. C. H. Tung kept very quiet. We talked about

Donald Tsang's budget. I think it will get a good reception, not least because it's the first budget presented by a local official. My former private secretary, Bowen Leung, is going off to run a liaison office for us in Beijing. Anson and I discuss how he can best do this job using his huge charm. I am starting to plan programmes for North America and London in the autumn. The CBI have asked me to talk to them. I think I should do this. But it will probably prompt more 'Patten bombshell' headlines.

Wednesday 6 March

In the afternoon I went to Wong Tai Sin and got a tremendous reception, which is, once again, good for morale. If it had been an election and we had won Shatin by 25,000, we would have won Wong Tai Sin by at least 50,000! On the way back to GH, we heard in the car from Kerry that the Prime Minister has given an interview to Robin Oakley on the plane back from Seoul for the *Today* programme. He said how much he hopes I will go back to British politics, how sad it was that I was defeated in Bath, and how I am one of those who would be among possible successors if I were to return. By the time we get back to the office the lines were red-hot – 'Major sees Patten as heir', et cetera. One snag is that I don't think anybody has convinced the 1922 Committee of this! We went to a parents' evening at Island School. No surprise that Alice is doing very well.

Thursday 7 March

A long meeting with Lee Wing-tat, a Democrat in Legco who is certainly on the more responsible wing of the party. He has some interesting thoughts on reforming the Housing Authority. It's very important that his colleagues listen to his particular brand of sensible politics and I don't only say that because he told me that he has read my book *The Tory Case*. I'm picking up that quite a few who claim to be close to Beijing – and even a few in the civil service – are going around saying how important it is that we don't start criticizing China if Legco is dismantled and the Bill of Rights is gutted.

There is apparently a right-wing reaction in some papers back home to all the speculation about my return to British politics. I've taken the opportunity of an interview with the *Guardian* to bash all this guff over the head and at the same time to bash the right wing of the Conservative Party. After Lee Wing-tat, I saw Frederick Fung, who is another legislator close to the Democrats and who has chosen to join the Preparatory Committee. He told me that their next task will be to endorse the proposals for a provisional Legco. He is obviously finding his first experience of working with Chinese officials rather daunting. Any idea that the Preparatory

Committee can reach its own conclusions is for the birds. I guess this will also be true of the selection committee for the Chief Executive designate when it is chosen. We really shouldn't allow ourselves to get sucked into a process which will be anything but democratic.

Monday 11 March

We have had some tidying up to do after the Prime Minister's visit and Donald's budget, which everyone appears to agree was a very clever one – cautious but generous. China seems to be stepping up the pressure on Taiwan and the Hang Seng Index is sliding. Taiwan trouble will make our lobbying for MFN in Washington more difficult. I discussed our next big visit with Francis Cornish; Michael Heseltine is going to China again in May and coming to stay with us afterwards. I imagine there will be lots of comparisons drawn between his positions and the Prime Minister's. At Exco Bob gave an assessment of the situation in Taiwan. He said that all the evidence suggests the Chinese action is substantially reducing support for unification. C. H. Tung says that everyone should recognize the strength of nationalist feeling in China. We need to sort these things out peacefully, and the fact that Taiwan is being intimidated by China is neither here nor there for a lot of the business community. It is American action in sending carriers to the area which is regarded as the provocation. You do wonder sometimes why his family ever got American passports.

Wednesday 13 March

I have a morning preparing speeches for my visit to the UK in April. I'm doing one at the Bank of England on the Asian miracle (or lack of same) and another on 'Asian values'. Wise George Shultz came in again and articulated the view that when you mix up trade and politics or human rights issues, you finish by achieving nothing on any of them. It's only the Chinese who effectively tangle trade and politics and get the rest of the world dancing to their tune. The French and the Germans are trying to do a deal with China to avoid Paris and Berlin supporting the UN resolution on human rights in Geneva. There's lots of rubbish being talked about better ways of securing human rights improvements being possible – this in the week that Amnesty International has produced a devastating report on Chinese human rights. The French are concerned about Li Peng's visit to France in April and the Germans are as ever only bothered about trade. They tried to hijack the Prime Minister in Bangkok but to no avail. Now they are pressing for talks with China but the Chinese, thank heavens, aren't giving an inch.

Friday 15 March

In the talks about next year's budget, the Chinese are trying to hold out as long as possible rather than accept that the negotiations will be with the Chief Executive designate. They want a foot in the door so badly. We have accepted that there should be a through budget; it wouldn't make much sense to have a budget for three months and then another for nine. But I do want us to be negotiating with the Chief Executive designate not with Beijing.

Monday 18 March

Taiwan continues to dominate the news. I saw Peter Tarnoff, the US Under Secretary of State for political affairs, who was understandably gloomy about MFN given Chinese behaviour. Tom Phillips, the UK's political counsellor at our embassy in Washington, who does a lot of our legwork on Hong Kong there, also thinks that this year the hill on MFN is going to be more difficult to climb. Another American visitor, Robert Rubin, reckons it doesn't help that the Chinese leaders seem to have convinced themselves that the MFN argument is simply a regular Washington ceremony. He also thinks that the markets would take a pretty dim view of restrictions on human rights or democratic accountability in Hong Kong. It would eventually affect confidence and would certainly have some influence on the attitudes of the potential employees of multinationals in the city. After my meeting with Rubin, Richard Muller told me that C.H. and other businessmen who have just been in Washington have been begging the Americans not to get too interested or interfere in Hong Kong's affairs before or after 1997. Paul Volcker has pressed hard on this. Did they really mean that they didn't want the Americans to take an interest in their well-being after 1997? That appeared to be the message.

Thursday 21 March

It seems as though Jardine's think they have achieved some sort of modus vivendi with the regulator, thanks to a legal opinion they have which says that they are in effect clear of the Security and Futures Commission's jurisdiction. If this stops Henry Keswick wandering around saying that I've failed to defend British interests in Hong Kong (in other words I haven't done whatever he wants), and if it means that we no longer have to spend so much time on this issue, then so be it. At least we haven't put ourselves in the embarrassing position of intervening in the regulator's business on behalf of Keswick. I have never understood why he has thought this would be good for him, his firm or Hong Kong.

I've added to my remarks on a provisional Legco, challenging existing legislators who are on the Preparatory Committee to make it clear that they wouldn't serve on a provisional body unless all their fellow Legco members could do so as well. There is a cut-off date for people getting BNO [British National Overseas] passports by the end of the month and huge queues have been forming outside the immigration department. We're going to try to find some ways of speeding things up.

Sunday 24 March
Over the weekend Lavender and I went on a lovely two-day walk on Lantau with Francis and Jane Cornish. It is a hard hike through beautiful scenery. We came back this evening to the news of the Preparatory Committee work. They voted 148 to 1 in favour of winding up Legco and setting up a provisional legislature. The one dissenting vote was Frederick Fung. He has been told that for voting against, he will be excluded from the selection committee and the provisional Legco itself. The community gets the message! What a mess: democracy with Chinese communist characteristics.

Monday 25 March
At a meeting with Donald and Anson, she made clear that she thinks that the best thing a new Chief Executive could do will be to confirm that everyone in the civil service would transit 1997. We had a delicious dinner with Donald and his wife, Selina, almost entirely beautifully cooked fish.

Tuesday 26 March
I saw the director general of the Commonwealth War Graves Commission who wants us to raise with the Chinese the position of the cemeteries after 1997. I also talked to Yeung Sum* in my quest to encourage the Democrats to behave as responsibly as possible, which is in their own interests. He is supportive on the budget, though he wants us to make some promises about social security rates for the elderly next year. There are rumours, sourced to a briefing that Li Peng is said to have given to journalists on an unattributable basis, saying that all civil servants will have to agree to

* Yeung Sum was a lecturer at the University of Hong Kong who in 1990 became the founding vice-chairman of the first pro-democracy party in Hong Kong and was elected to Legco during the 1990s and again from 1998 until 2008. A moderate member of the Democrats, he was briefly Martin Lee's successor as chairman of the party 2002–4. He was arrested for taking part in the protests against the extradition bill in 2019. Courageous and genial, the fact that he was targeted as an enemy by communist hacks says most of what one needs to know about them.

support the provisional Legco once it is established. He is also said to be very cross that the Prime Minister's visit and his comments while he was here demonstrate that I'm not going to simply roll over and die. Rosanna Wong is concerned about the threats to the civil service which she suggests show the Chinese determination to try to isolate me – again. Anson is about to make a second speech within a week criticizing the closing down of the existing Legco and the establishment of a provisional legislature. She has not consulted me about either of these speeches. The idea that I force her or anybody else to speak out on these matters is completely absurd. I cannot imagine obliging Anson to do anything she didn't want to do. She feels particularly passionately about the integrity of the civil service, which she rightly thinks is one of the mainstays of Hong Kong's success and values.

Thursday 28 March

Jan Morris is in town preparing the final edition of her terrific book on Hong Kong. She came to talk to me and I have the impression that her last chapter now will suggest that the British tried near the very end to do something about democracy, for which some thanks are in order, but this should have been done much earlier. A wise woman, she's right about that as about so much else.

Back home the mad cow row with Britain and Europe has been rumbling away. There is an assumption that I will be ordered not to do anything about British beef. But since there is now a global ban on its sale by the EU, I shoot the media's cow and stop its purchase here while pointing out that there shouldn't be any real health worries.

Friday 29 March

Looking back on the previous few days, it seems to me that this has been a very bad week for Hong Kong. After the Taiwanese elections last weekend, when President Lee Teng-hui did extremely well partly because of the threats from Beijing, the CCP seemed to harden its line right across the board. The sight of democracy flowering in Taiwan while Chinese officials announced its imminent demise in Hong Kong left a nasty taste in many mouths. The same has been true of the pressure put on civil servants. Anson is going to see all senior officials on Sunday morning. The press is very supportive of her. She goes on speaking out, even though lots of her friends are telling her to keep her head down. ('If only you would keep quiet you could carry on being Chief Secretary after 1997, or even perhaps Chief Executive.') She thinks that C.H. is now a shoo-in. There is also some sort of deal in the offing under which Cathay will sign up to selling off a big stake in Dragonair to CNAC for a sweetheart price in the hope that they will then be allowed to carry on without any interference. I wonder. There doesn't seem to have been any agreement with CNAC to drop their application to operate an airline from Hong Kong, challenging Cathay themselves on their main routes The words salami slicing come to mind. There's also been a terrible meeting in the JLG about the handover ceremony, with the Chinese, among other things, denying that there was any reason for inviting foreign visitors and insisting on having joint vetting of journalists. Bad, bad, bad. At the rugby Sevens at the weekend, the Governor of Macau tells me that he and his colleagues there are getting rather depressed about the hardening of Chinese positions on their front too. Jung Chang and her husband, Jon Halliday, are staying with us. They tell me that at least 50% of the costs of the Communist Party in the Yan'an years came from the sale of opium.

The *South China Morning Post* is now trying a new tack editorially. Their argument used to be that we weren't standing up for Hong Kong. Now they have started to say that maybe John Major and I did try at the last moment to stand up for the territory but all it has demonstrated is that there's nothing really we can do. We should apparently just hope that China doesn't insist on British influence being stamped out even before 1997.

Monday 1 April

Huge numbers of people have been queuing up for their passports. We dealt with about 100,000 over the weekend, which makes 180,000 in the last week. There was a small punch-up over queue jumping. This immediately resulted in pictures being flashed around the world about riots and the queues for British passports. This is just an example of the sort of thing that Hong Kong can expect as it receives more sceptical public attention over the coming 15 months.

This morning we looked at the lists that we've had so far from Beijing about what they want us to do to help the Preparatory Committee. Some of the proposals are pretty blameless. Others are quite impossible – for example, providing facilities for the provisional legislature. One immediate conclusion is that since it's taken since last October for the Preparatory Committee to come forward with any ideas, there is no need for us to rush our response. We will let them have it sometime after Easter. In the meantime, we will speed up plans to help the officials from China who are coming to the Preparatory Committee meetings in Hong Kong after Easter, which are allegedly going to take soundings about membership of the Selection Committee and related matters.

It looks as though we will have no real difficulty getting Legco to agree the budget this week. How people used to worry that we wouldn't get the budget through this close to the handover! I talked to Martin Lee about the importance of him speaking up for unconditional MFN renewal when he is in Washington next, and that it will be used against the Democrats if it looks as though they are advocating measures which would harm Hong Kong jobs and prosperity.

Wednesday 3–Tuesday 9 April

Alice has already gone off to Nepal with the school, so when Lavender and I set off for London for Easter and lots of speeches back home, we had only the dogs to bid farewell to. We flew to London overnight and then dashed to Gatwick to meet Kate and Laura there and catch a plane to Toulouse. We had a wonderful week over Easter at Monbretal. The weather was as warm as late May or early June in England. Everything looks fine, particularly our new gates, shutters and outdoor stone table. We walked, bought bicycles, cycled, shopped, ate, gardened, read and thoroughly enjoy our time together; the house, the garden and the surrounding countryside all live up to my fantasies about them.

Wednesday 10 April

Back to London. I had a meeting with the Prime Minister in the afternoon. He was as supportive as ever and wonders what more we can do to underline Britain's continuing commitment to Hong Kong. He was a little concerned in case Michael Heseltine's trade jamboree in May in China, his second effort to drum up business, should lead to an increase in worries that we are really going to sell Hong Kong out for Britain's commercial interests. I made a speech in the City of London on the Asian miracle, such as it is, and the following day spoke at the Royal Society of Arts on Asian values. I had two talks to Eddie George, the Governor of the Bank of England, about Hong Kong risk, and was assured by him that the Bank is handling the issue very sensitively. Jeremy Hanley has had a good visit to Vietnam following the Prime Minister's discussions with his opposite number at the Bangkok summit.

Saturday 13 April

A brief visit to Northern Ireland to support an umbrella organization for charities there. I spoke at the Institute of Directors annual dinner in the evening. It was encouraging to see the progress Northern Ireland has made, particularly the developments in Belfast. All rather nostalgic for us both. Lavender used to come regularly when I was a junior minister there. We said goodbye to Kate and Laura and left for Hong Kong tonight.

Monday 15 April

There has been quite a fuss while I've been away about some slightly rum remarks made by Raymond Chi'en. He opined for no very good reason that there was a legal base for a provisional legislature. The media have of course raised questions about collective responsibility in Exco, and Dennis Chang has written a couple of excellent pieces in the papers raising serious question marks about the legitimacy of the provisional Legco. Jimmy McGregor wants a discussion about collective responsibility and there is a general wish for a discussion about the sort of interim Legco which the Chinese want to appoint.

As luck would have it, Lu Ping is in town this week to work with the Preparatory Committee. They are all behaving worse and worse during what is supposed to be a week taking soundings in Hong Kong and have been completely put off their stride by a few demonstrators who have got a lot of attention. They have also refused to see some teachers because the delegation included pro-democracy legislators. They shuffle in and out of meetings by the back door. Clearly, they encourage people's worst fears and appear to confirm that consultation is a farce. They are being obliged to take the consequences for what they want us to do, namely to fix the legislature.

While I was away Peter Mandelson came to Hong Kong and has written me a letter which, while charming on the surface, bristles with his own political agenda. He talks about sympathizing with me for being beleaguered and about my need to have an intermediary. Presumably he doesn't mean like him. I must say I don't feel particularly beleaguered, but if Lu Ping felt anything I imagine that he might.

The Garel-Joneses are staying for a week (Tristan is here with UBS [bank], to whom I'm going to speak later in the week) and Richard Needham came to dinner with his wife, Sissie. Quite like old times. Tristan and I even have an argument about Napoleon . . . again. He is a Bonapartist at heart.

Tuesday 16 April

At Exco this morning I went through the arguments about the legislature and the provisional one. There is only one Legco in Hong Kong; that remains the case until June 1997. A provisional Legco isn't mentioned in the Joint Declaration or the Basic Law and can't have any constitutional position before June 1997. Whether or not it has any position after that is for the Chinese to justify. I note that we have applied the rule of collective responsibility with some generosity over the last years (so didn't for example take too tyrannical a view of Raymond Ch'ien's recent remarks), and I intend to do so until the handover, since I regard it as important to have a broadly based Exco. After a long discussion, everyone seems to go along with what I have said. I think there is a general feeling of relief that we have got the issue out of the way.

We invited to GH the two Hong Kong Chinese men whose case I raised when I was in the Philippines. They spent 4½ years in prison before their conviction for drug trafficking was overturned. They were part of a tour party in which some Malaysians were caught carrying drugs and were wrongly accused by association. We are trying to ensure that they get the right help after this dreadful experience.

Thursday 18 April

At a Q+A session with Legco I took much the same line that I did in Exco with lots of questions about the work of the Preparatory Committee, the provisional Legco and the exclusion of some people from any pretence of consultation. Anson has had dinner with Lu Ping and with Zhou Nan. It was perfectly cordial apparently, but the Beijing duo didn't give any ground at all. Lu Ping still seems determined to set up the provisional Legco before the handover even though it's clearly not needed in practice. I suspect that they want to get it established, hopefully with our connivance, so as to avoid the rumpus that will be caused after 30 June. They are obviously nervous about losing control, which is probably what motivates many of their actions. Anson has been invited to Beijing next week. We hope she will see some other senior officials. The CJ has also been invited.

Saturday 20 April

Suffering from flu, I had a call from Malcolm Rifkind. He is about to have a meeting with Qian. Some of his officials want him to start haggling about the membership of the provisional Legco and the date – as late as possible – when it might start work. I think this would be very unwise. We have a very clear line at the moment and have to stick to it. Once we start to fudge things, the Chinese will leak what we are up to and anyway won't take any notice of what we are saying. I feel strongly that we mustn't have our fingerprints all over the establishment of the provisional body. Malcolm doesn't need much persuasion. At his meeting he speaks up very well for us and bluntly denies Qian's claim that I encouraged the demonstrations against the Preparatory Committee. Qian gives lots of assurances about Britain being sovereign until 30 June 1997, about the civil service being politically neutral, and about being keen to make progress on the handover ceremony. Maybe they have absorbed the suggestions that I have been making that if there isn't any agreement on a handover ceremony, we shall go our own way.

Monday 22 April

We are starting to help prepare for Anson's visit to Beijing, when she will talk about the sort of cooperation we are ready to provide to the Preparatory Committee and the Chief Executive designate, and the unnecessary and damaging establishment of a provisional Legco. I'm also starting to get ready for my forthcoming visit to America and Canada. Kerry has wisely noted that unless I continue to speak out fairly clearly about Beijing's behaviour, the community will become very nervous and be in danger of falling apart. He thinks that what is required is a continuing show of strong leadership.

Tuesday 23 April

I talked to the American Chamber of Commerce about lobbying on MFN. Martin Lee is at present in the United States and being pursued everywhere he goes by representatives of the Better Hong Kong Tomorrow Foundation, doubtless doing Hong Kong's image huge damage. They do no favours to Hong Kong businessmen in the USA. Martin on the other hand is saying just the right things about MFN and is getting a very good response.

Friday 26 April

After discussing whether or not the Chinese are going to try to bully civil servants into 'coming over', the Ad Hoc group briefly reviewed the debate yesterday in the House of Lords. It didn't go too badly. Margaret Thatcher made a strong speech and there were a number of other supportive ones. On the other hand, David Wilson made a surprisingly feline attack – the importance of quiet diplomacy, of not shooting from the hip, of working closely with China, of being pragmatic not least in relation to the provisional Legco. Who on earth could he have been thinking about? I resolve even more strongly not to say anything publicly about him.

At lunchtime, I gave a speech to the General Chamber of Commerce about MFN. I say what an excellent job Martin Lee has been doing in arguing for unconditional MFN renewal, and that it is particularly important he has been saying this because of his high credibility in the US. You could, as they say, hear a pin drop. Anson's meetings with leaders in Beijing seem to have gone well, only becoming frosty when she set out our position on the provisional Legco. She got lots of assurances about China's determination not to create a second power centre.

Monday 29 April

Robin Cook arrived today. He seemed a bit user-unfriendly when he arrived but certainly thawed out during the day. We had a good working lunch and he asked all the right questions. In the afternoon we went together to Wan Chai and were mobbed in a teahouse where we had dim sum. It was quite good for him to have the opportunity of seeing the colonial oppressor going about oppressing. I also did an interview with Dominic Ziegler for the *Economist*. They are going to do an editorial on the importance of international support for Hong Kong. At dinner in the evening we had a passionate and lively discussion with lots of different political figures which was also very well behaved.

Tuesday 30 April

Robin Cook had breakfast with Martin Barrow and the executive committee of the General Chamber of Commerce, including Paul Cheng. Apparently Cheng said that if Britain will sort out 'this Emily Lau business', then China will give us a decent handover. I bet that went down big with Robin Cook. He asked me whether I think that Tony Blair should come to Hong Kong and China at a reasonably early date. I said that I could understand why he might want to do this – Hong Kong is going to be an early item on Labour's agenda if they win the election. But it seems to me that it would be pretty high-risk stuff. He would get asked endless 'what if?' questions. As Govenor of Hong Kong I would love to see him, but if I were his political adviser, I would suggest that he should go to India or somewhere where the downside and the risks were rather less obvious.

Wednesday 1–Saturday 11 May

Canada and the United States. I did big lunches and dinners with speeches, 1200 people in Vancouver and 600 in Toronto. I saw the Prime Minister, the Foreign Minister and other ministers. They were all sympathetic but obviously conscious of the potential impact of 100,000 Canadian citizens in Hong Kong suddenly arriving on their doorstep in 1997. I pressed them on visa-free access for SAR passport holders. They seemed to concede the point in principle while recognizing that some of the details would have to be worked out. Axworthy [Foreign Minister] is more interested in human rights than Chrétien [Prime Minister]. With both of them, and indeed more generally, it isn't always easy to tread the narrow line between optimism and pessimism.

We then went on to New York, Washington and Seattle. Just to remind myself in future of how hard I worked and what access a retiring colonial Governor could get, I will record most of those that I saw and most of my speaking and interview engagements. In New York I spoke to the Council on Foreign Relations, the US China Trade Committee, *The New York Times*, the *Wall Street Journal*, *Time* and *Newsweek*. In Washington I spoke to the Heritage Foundation, the National Press Club, the Oxford and Cambridge annual dinner (at the latter, to Lavender's relief, some new jokes). And I saw the President, the Vice President, the Secretary of State, Secretary of the Treasury, Secretary of Commerce, chairman of the National Security Council, chairman of the National Economic Council, and most of the leaders in the Senate and the House of Representatives. I also spoke to the *Washington Post* and *Washington Times* and the Freedom Forum. Lavender and I had a dinner at the embassy, where the Kerrs were marvellous hosts. So there! A confession: there were one or two other highlights, a fantastic concert by Jessye Norman in New York and a visit to an exhibition of treasures from the Palace Museum in Taipei, including some fantastic bronzes.

A few thoughts:

1. There is huge antipathy to China, much greater than last time I was here in America. It's a result of Taiwan, the treatment of dissidents, Tibet, intellectual property theft, threats to Hong Kong, weapons proliferation and so on. This spills over into views about Hong Kong. Everyone is very pessimistic about the prospect of democracy and human rights. People routinely ask what will be the outcome when Beijing controls the Chief Executive, the Legco and the courts. Many assume that Martin Lee and his colleagues will fetch up in the jug.

2. We had astonishing access, very big turnouts at meetings and there was great interest in the message. Last time I was in Washington I recorded that I didn't think that we would ever be able to pull off a trip like that again. But this time we did even better.

3. On MFN, I made clear that I wasn't there as a representative of China. I was speaking for Hong Kong. Ending MFN would hurt Hong Kong at a sensitive time. It was more credible because of the fact that I am not seen as a spokesman for China and because Martin Lee was saying exactly the same thing only a few weeks ago.

4. Everyone seems to be thrashing about trying to find some way to deal with China. I think there is a general recognition that removing MFN would be a very crude weapon, so crude that nobody will ever really use it. It's the unwieldy focus for every resentment about China. There is a lot of feeling that if America takes a strong line on anything with China, Europe will try to undercut it to get trade benefits. But I was told that, despite

the rows and the rhetoric, US exports to China had increased in 1995 faster than the volume of imports for the first time in years.

5. I said that America should show its interest in Hong Kong by speaking up in private and in public and by not allowing the territory to be swallowed up in general China issues. I repeated over and over that Hong Kong has been a bridge between communist China and the rest of the world and that the way Beijing handled the territory in the next few years will go right to the heart of the sort of issues which would determine what sort of country China was and would become.

6. President Clinton made it perfectly clear that if or when he got a second term, he would give priority to trying to establish a better relationship with China, but not by giving up the assertion of the importance of human rights and liberal values.

It was a really punishing schedule. If anything like this happens again I need to be a bit fitter. Presumably (down vanity!) some of the access and the turnouts were a result of people knowing that I'm not a complete pudding. We returned via Seattle, taking an inaugural Cathay flight on a Boeing 777. It was nice to have a morning in Seattle shopping, not least at my favourite bookshop, Elliott Bay.

Sunday 12 May

Back to Hong Kong in time for my birthday and a magnificently confected row. From the time I arrived at the airport, where there was a demonstration organized by the NCNA, it was alleged that I had been internationalizing Hong Kong and badmouthing it. Being accused of internationalizing Hong Kong is a bit like being accused of localizing a parish council. Moreover, it's interesting that when you are dealing with the consequences of China's behaviour over Hong Kong, you are accused of doing the damage which Chinese actions have actually done. The stick which is most regularly used to beat me is an article in *Newsweek*. The magazine interviewed a lot of businessmen and then talked to me. They then produced an article featuring the word 'betrayal' all over the front cover arguing that the tycoons had betrayed Hong Kong's move for democracy and much else besides. Needless to say, I didn't actually use the word 'betray' myself; the trouble is, it focuses the attention of some of my critics on what they know I think even if I say that I didn't say it. Still, I've long known that politics and journalism are not in thrall to the truth fairy.

Monday 13 May

James Tien, who is a not very bright weathervane of a politician and is now also the chairman of the Hong Kong Chamber of Commerce, has written an article denouncing me on the grounds that I have called businessmen in Hong Kong traitors. Anson and I both address the Commonwealth Parliamentary seminar and both say that the people in Hong Kong should speak up for the territory. Anson added that if Hong Kong prizes its autonomy and way of life then its citizens will have to say so; she called on the international community to reassure Hong Kong if things seem to be going wrong after 1997. How could I have put it any better? A reasonable Exco yesterday. Apart from C. H. Tung, people were pretty supportive about my visit to and speeches in the USA. I tried to be firm but emollient, far from easy. I rather gave up on the emollient bit when I saw James Tien and Henry Tang.* They are shifty and James even says when challenged that he hadn't actually read the *Newsweek* article before he signed his own newspaper piece. I made it clear to them that while I would like to end the row, if it's going to be stoked up they will find me slogging away in the trenches but none of it will do Hong Kong any good. They departed in a cloud of geniality saying how much they want me to come to dinner with a group of their friends. At least if Henry Tang is in charge of the wine, that will be no disappointment. He seems not to travel beyond first-growth clarets. I once served Château Musar, a very well-regarded Lebanese wine, at a dinner that he attended and he was rather sniffy about it. Some people tend to judge wines almost entirely by the price. I also like thinking of the Château gallantly hauling the grapes across Beirut, as the bombs and rockets fall around them, on their way to making their marvellous vintages.

Tuesday 14 May

I've had rather a low week as we wait expectantly for Michael Heseltine and his lions' tour of business leaders to make their way once again across the Middle Kingdom in the general direction of Hong Kong, which Michael will reach on 24 May. I am not feeling very well, which is the result, I think, of the flu that I never really got over and the fact that I am stupidly once again doing the cabbage soup diet. Elspeth persuaded me that it was a quick fix which would please my cardiologists. More cheerfully, Yvonne Hawker has an exhibition of paintings at the Fringe club in Lan Kwai Fong which I opened. We bought a wonderful luminous painting of a yellow plastic bowl sitting on a table with fish tanks behind it. She had several paintings of fish, which made me rather hungry. We were told

* Henry Tang was a member of a very rich mainland family who had close ties with some Chinese communist leaders and became Financial Secretary of Hong Kong for 2003–7 and Chief Secretary from 2007 to 2011. He was defeated for the post of chief executive by C. Y. Leung in 2012, which took some doing, but he was equal to the task.

at dinner that Nellie Fong, who is (to be charitable) rather close to Lu Ping and is a lustrous long-term member of the United Front, has been responsible for organizing much of the quite effective stirring of the row over my American trip and the *Newsweek* headline. She was herself part of the group from the Better Hong Kong crowd that visited the USA recently flying a lead balloon in their efforts to convince Americans of China's good intentions. My diet came to a climactic end with bananas and skimmed milk, which tasted wonderfully exotic.

Wednesday 15–Thursday 16 May

My businessmen critics have sent an open letter to John Major expressing 'profound disappointment' with my comments about them; that is, the comments which I didn't actually make. John has fired back a corker of a letter pointing out what I had actually said in the USA while doing such a good job to promote Hong Kong. He added that they should be very grateful to me, which of course is not a sentiment that comes easily to them.

Thursday 23 May

I have eaten my last bowl of soup and consumed my last baked potato for some time. The trade triumph is now approaching. We have waited, like the Ephesians in church a couple of weeks ago, with humility, gentleness and patience. Whatever else happens, Nellie Fong or no Nellie Fong, we shall have an exciting time with the president of the Board of Trade.

The Empire Goes Home: May 1996–June 1997

Friday 24–Saturday 25 May
The Lord of the Jungle roars into town. Hezza arrived just before Friday lunchtime after a week in China with nearly 300 British businessmen. He's seen Li Peng, Li Lanqing (who has held senior economic and trade posts) and – this morning – Jiang Zemin, who is in Zhuhai for a bit of 'R and R' and a meeting of the Preparatory Committee. I like Michael, who has always been kind to me and loyal – though my views on China and my record here have tested that. He is brazenly broad brush and sometimes hams things up pretty outrageously. But he's one of the few 'big beasts' in British politics: the PM himself, Ken Clarke and possibly Malcolm Rifkind. A Hezza premiership would certainly have had a lot of flash, bang and sometimes wallop, but on most of the big things he is absolutely right – for example Europe, improving the management of government and dealing with urban deprivation, not least in the north.

Yet I'm deeply sceptical of the sort of show business trip that he's just completed. It's not real business. You get glad-handed by the Chinese. El Dorado is glimpsed. Promises are made of untold commercial benefits if only political relations can improve. Middle Kingdom leaders smile and offer platitudes. Memorandums of understanding are signed. But what about the actual business? The Chinese never really budge from any positions which matter to them unless it suits their game. No progress at all for example on Hong Kong was either expected or made, but I'm sure that the trip confirmed Beijing's view that we will always put Hong Kong's interests behind that of British business. And, of course, they play one country off against another. As I keep on arguing, the figures don't actually suggest that that there is any real relationship between trade and kowtowing. The American trade representative, Mickey Kantor, was saying exactly this to me the other day in Washington.

Anyway, Michael's happy, especially since his meeting with Jiang lasted 45 minutes longer than the expected 30. So the president would have had more time to talk about Vivien Leigh and to deliver his selection of

Shakespearean quotes – the normal routine. It's reported that Michael gave Jiang a tear-jerking account of the sort of handover ceremony we wanted. There is invariably a tear in the Lion's eye as he talks of the end of Empire. The Chinese don't think that their own empire is ending at all – think of Tibet, Xinjiang and Taiwan.

Anson Chan, Hugh Davies, Bob Peirce and I gave Michael lunch and talked him through the usual Hong Kong issues. Then he went out to face the whole press pack on the steps of the house. It was relentlessly hot and sticky and everyone was in a bit of a bad temper. Michael wielded the big brush in a chirpily incoherent way. The difference between his position and mine yawned as he expressed his huge confidence in China's good intentions and declined to answer questions about the relationship between freedom and democracy on the one hand and Hong Kong's success on the other. The press smelled blood, got crosser and crosser, and in return got a blast from Michael about the fact that they are to blame for talking Hong Kong down. He was a tad under-briefed – 'One country, two systems' turned into 'one nation, two regimes', not quite what Deng had in mind. I suppose that all this will do, though none of it is actually out of line, is to confirm the cynics in the view that Hong Kong is being sold out for British business and that beleaguered Patten is now not only attacked by China and the business community but abandoned by Britain. *Plus ça change.* Mirsky phoned Kerry McGlynn afterwards to express outrage at the press conference. 'Sedition,' he says. I said to Kerry that Mirsky knows better than anyone that sedition is what happens in China. In an odd way I feel quite comforted by the whole show. If I'd taken a different tack while I was here, I'd have had four years of press conferences like that myself. I was told afterwards that, though I think I behaved impeccably at the press conference, my body language was horribly revealing.

Later in the afternoon we showed Michael all the new infrastructure we're building around the airport, which much impressed him, and then gave a dinner in the evening for him and his terrific wife, Anne. There were about 40 guests at two tables. Mischievously, I put Hezza next to Margaret Ng, a relentlessly forensic Legco Democrat, who pursued him on China. In his speech, he did his new version of the old mantra. 'One nation, two states,' he said. 'Was that okay?' he asks afterwards. 'They all looked a bit stony-faced.' He was probably very tired but we can't help comparing Michael's show with John Major's superb performance here a few months ago.

Otherwise we had a great weekend with them. We did some retail therapy in the Hollywood Road, where they bought some seriously good Chinese antiques, and then some goodies in David Tang's shop, before we all lunched with him at the China Club. We also fitted in a visit to the bird sanctuary at Mai Po. Michael seems to know as much about birds as Ken Clarke, and he is also very knowledgeable about trees and shrubs – he and Anne have what Denis Healey called hinterlands, which is one of the things that makes them so interesting and so much fun. And politics is not everything as far as Michael is concerned. I was told that he wanted to have a private word during the weekend and assumed that this would be to set out some of his disagreements with me about Hong Kong and China. Nothing happened. Then, after our last meal together, he said, 'Do you think we could have a private word?' Of course I agreed, expecting a short lecture on the wonders of China. He took me on one side and said, 'I hope you won't take this personally. As you know I regard you as a friend. But I just wanted to say to you that I don't think you're pruning your bonsais properly.' We had been lent the bonsais by a local monastery and we were told afterwards that the abbot had pruned them personally. Michael and Anne flew off with a van full of boxed purchases following behind their car to the airport.

Sunday 26 May

Pentecost. Impressed by how jolly the cathedral looks at 9.30 mass, with red and white silk streamers, banners and flowers everywhere, I reflected over my prayer book that the place where I worship does to some extent affect my devotions. Are other people like this? Does it suggest a lack of seriousness on my part? When I was growing up, our parish church looked like an aircraft hangar. Why should a church look as though it's been built for the Holy Ghost rather than an Airbus? Moreover, in both the Anglican and Catholic cathedrals here, the English hymns they sing are proper ones about 'death's dead moments' rather than 'Kumbaya'. I assume it's also true of the Cantonese hymns, which are beautifully sung by excellent choirs.

Monday 27 May

At a dinner Simon Murray played back one of my own favourite anecdotes but with a twist. When I was coming here and visited Singapore, I asked Lee Kuan Yew at one of our meetings how his government had dealt with the Triads. 'We used one of your colonial ordinances,' he said. 'We locked them all up at Changi. They're still there.' 'How many?' I asked. 'About 1000,' he replied. 'All Triads?' I wondered. 'Probably,' he replied. Simon said that he's recently heard my Exco colleague Raymond Ch'ien, an American-educated businessman in his 40s, tell the story to a Japanese audience as an example of how much better is the Singaporean way to my wishy-washy liberalism. Raymond is a kind and decent man with a lovely wife, but this sort of implied defence of Asian values is unconvincing and not based on facts. According to Interpol, Hong Kong's crime statistics are even lower than Singapore's. The other day the *Straits Times* said so too. So it must be true!

Much of the week will be spent in bilateral discussions between C. H. Tung, me and various members of Exco. He wants to resign from our ranks, saying that it's become increasingly difficult for him to be both on the Preparatory Committee and on Exco. I do understand this, not least because I think it also suggests that he is thinking of his own chances of becoming the Chief Executive after 1997. T. S. Lo, a tough and unscrupulous bully, has started to campaign openly for the job, an outcome that would horrify the majority in Hong Kong. C.H. probably feels that he has a duty to go for the job himself but needs first to slip out from under my rafters. He would be much better than some of those who are talked about but not nearly as good as Anson. I suspect that he is one of those businessmen who isn't actually capable of running things, and while he speaks well to conservative audiences outside Hong Kong, his political touch seems fairly hopeless.

We also have to sort out in the next few days exactly what the relationship between the Hong Kong government, the legally elected Legco and the Chinese provisional Legco (which they now seem determined to establish) is going to be. Should we also press Beijing to ensure that the provisional body has as democratic a basis as possible? This all requires quite a lot of political delicacy. We can't give the impression that we are either undermining the credibility of the existing Legco or endorsing the credibility of China's provisional body. We also need to show the community that we want the transfer of power to go as smoothly as possible.

Tuesday 28 May

This comes up at a dinner with Francis Cornish, the British Trade Commissioner. I suggested a few months ago that we should have a meeting of our FCO team to discuss the UK's national interests in Hong Kong before and after 1997. The senior officials in the political adviser's office, some of the JLG team, and Martin Dinham and Edward Llewellyn are all there. The main points to emerge are, first, the flak that Francis and his team in the Trade Commission have to take from the business community about the government's policy, or rather – this is how they put it – about me. We are told again and again that I have made life much harder for them. They will of course want us to cooperate with the provisional Legco – 'face reality, old boy'. Second, we are all pleasantly surprised by the extent to which the civil service is continuing to behave with integrity and loyalty despite huge pressure from the Chinese side, partly a result of Anson's leadership. Third, we've still got some nasty issues to resolve; for instance, do we try to tackle the question of the privileged position of British workers here (no work permits required) before 1997 or leave things until after the handover? I rather favour raising the issue with the Chief Executive designate and asking him or her to clear up the situation after 1997. I don't want to start throwing Brits out myself. Fourth, after some months of hardball, we all think we can now expect rather more cooperation from the Chinese They're clearly going to say 'yes' to our proposals to start a second runway at the new airport this week and they will, I suspect, agree more franchises for other products like mobile phones. Yet for the time being I'm going to have to hold the line on one tiresome issue after another. For instance, how do we handle the budget which straddles 1997 without conceding to Chinese officials the question of whether or not the existing Legco can approve or reject it? We can't fudge this indefinitely and we must try to get the sort of solution which the Chinese accepted over the future Court of Final Appeal, where they allowed the present Legco to place it on the statute book.

Wednesday 29 May

Bryan Dutton (who is doing an outstanding job in a very unshowy way) has just been on a fraternal visit to the Chinese general in Shenzhen. He was shown the future garrison and, perhaps maladroitly, lots of pictures of the soldiers in anti-riot gear. They are plainly training hard for that eventuality, just in case. Bryan says that they all (officers included) live in pretty austere conditions. Just wait until they see the barracks at Stanley and the officers' villas. They are apparently very keen to have a substantial military presence here from next January, about 250 strong. Sorry, chaps, I'm not prepared to be Governor with two garrisons; two systems yes, two garrisons no. Bryan had to drink gallons of Mao Tai. He thinks that the Chinese have hand-picked their military team for Hong Kong, including an alumnus of the Royal College of Defence Studies. I wonder if they've included one or two property developers.

Thursday 30 May

Leon Brittan is with us. First of all he had to endure a dinner organized by the European Commission office in Hong Kong which appeared to be loaded with a slightly odd bunch of trusties. There were two former judges there including Simon Li, who was a sort of Chinese Mr Justice Cocklecarrot. Leon wondered how many of the party would have held foreign passports. One of those present, Leonie Ki, who is from the Better Hong

Kong Foundation, has made himself well-known by claiming that I invented democracy in Hong Kong but that no one is really interested in it.

Friday 31 May

Before dinner at GH, Leon asked me whether I will return to British politics. I told him that I'm still undecided, but that whatever else I will certainly want to get stuck into the European debate when I get home. We talked a lot at dinner about a fairly disastrous interview that Lu Ping has given to CNN. Having declared that beyond 1997 the press in Hong Kong would remain free, Lu admitted under questioning that of course there are some things that journalists won't be able to write about, such as Taiwanese independence. Storm clouds gather. I suspect that this may be the end of the present charm offensive.

Saturday 1–Sunday 2 June

The Chinese-language press take Lu Ping to task on Saturday morning. We say nothing.

Tim and Sally Kitson are staying at Fanling for the weekend. He used to be Ted Heath's PPS and the chairman of the defence select committee when I was on it. It has been a magical weekend, which reminds me how lucky we are to have this very comfortable house. It is definitely 1930s Sunningdale. There is a long drawing room with a terrace looking out onto a two-tier garden. Lavender and I both have nice studies and there are big cool bedrooms. We keep a lot of our own things here, including the huge Dutch-Indonesian desk on which I'm writing this. There is a garden bright with bougainvillea, a fine pergola with a view of distant mountains, and the whole estate is ringed with tall trees and golf fairways beyond. It's only a couple of miles from the border, maybe less, and is surrounded by encroaching motorways, scrapyards and urban development, which, of course, you can't see. But here with the golf courses all around it's a real oasis. A couple of years ago we were asked about putting in heavy security all around the garden, but I gave this a big thumbs down.

Tim tells me that he recently had a conversation in London with Willie Purves, who told him that I was doing my best in a very difficult job. Perhaps he has seen the light. I must remember him in my prayers.

Monday 3 June

After about 40 of us had given blood in the ballroom at GH, organized by the Red Cross, C. H. Tung came to see me again with a letter jutting out of his pocket. We had a perfectly amicable chat for 20 minutes. He had talked to Anson and others, had reflected on what they had to say, but thought he should retire now from Exco. Indeed, he thought he should probably have gone at the beginning of the year since he didn't believe it was possible to straddle the Preparatory Committee and Exco. His letter was fine and we agreed that we'd release it to the press together with my reply – no mention of disagreements in either draft. I told him, first, that I greatly respected him as a fair and intelligent exponent of a point of view with which many agreed, though not me. Second, I knew that if fate tapped him on the shoulder it was a decision which the administration and civil servants would be happy about, as would many others in the community. But I added that it appeared to me that Anson's role was crucial to the smoothness of the transition and to international confidence. Third, sooner or later those who shared his views would have to reach an accommodation with the Democrats, otherwise there was bound to be trouble. Moreover, the number who would support the Democrats was bound to increase given sentiment among younger people in Hong Kong. I said I would certainly ensure that – while respecting our legitimate institutions – nothing was said or done by anyone in the administration which would make it more difficult for us to work together in the future, or easier for the press to say that we couldn't.

Kerry McGlynn's phone glowed all evening as he spun away assuring the world that there is no terrible split between C.H. and me.

Tuesday 4 June

After Exco (when we toned down a rather aggressive paper on health education), I saw Charles Powell, who has started to become my buffer from Henry Keswick. The conversation strayed onto Europe. He mused about an alternative European agenda which he believes is what the Bruges speech was supposed to provide. But unfortunately Bernard Ingham apparently gave it a populist, nationalist spin. 'Things might have been different,' he muses. Norman Lamont is currently apparently casting himself in the role as leader of the 'quit Europe' campaign. Poor Norman, once so brightly ambitious, now driven to distraction by anguish at losing his position on the greasy pole.

I learned today that Michael DeGolyer, who runs a widely respected transition-tracking project at Baptist University, has been scolded by the Vice Chancellor, Daniel Tse, for having made some critical comments about China to a journalist from *Newsweek*. He has been told to be more circumspect in future. Tse is on the Preparatory Committee. How's that for *trahison des clercs*? He and Professor Woo, the Vice Chancellor at the University of Science and Technology, don't seem to be very strong supporters of the liberal values of universities but rather enthusiastic about totalitarian governments. Lavender tells me that when Woo had talked to her he seemed to be principally interested in whether I had a prostate problem like him, because I always pee before and after university congregations. Well, they are rather long, but it's good of him to be bothered.

Wednesday 5 June

There was a big turnout at the candlelit vigil last night to commemorate the killings in Tiananmen Square. Police say 16,000; organizers 40,000. Edward was there and says that there is general agreement that the figure has been going up over the last two or three years.

Police behaviour was intrusive and unnecessary – they videoed everyone there with big cameras and bright lights, which had an unpleasant and intimidating impact. The official line is that this is always done in any case of disturbances during a demonstration. The film is said to be destroyed soon after the demo. I hope this is true and I'll check it with the Police Commissioner. But if even I feel a trifle nervous about the whole business, what do the protesters think?

A boisterous police chief superintendent has been on the early radio justifying the videoing and criticizing youngsters who have been shining bright lights at the cameras to prevent them working. He doesn't sound like an enthusiast for the Bill of Rights. I have to play these civil liberties issues with great care. I don't want to see a gap opening up between the administration and the police, nor find the police semi-publicly looking forward to tougher tactics in 1997. On the other hand, I don't intend to give an inch on the fundamentals. In a press conference after another district visit, this time to Tai Po, I was asked about the vigil and about remarks by Lu Ping who has been tying himself in knots during a 'visit of reassurance' to Japan (which seems to have been far from reassuring). He appeared in the speech to be saying that after the handover demonstrations would be for the Chinese chop. The trouble is that the Chinese communists don't really understand what happens in a free society. How could they? But on no account should we allow them to get away with redefining what liberties in Hong Kong really mean. I lay it on the line that if people want to exercise their right to peaceful demonstration even close to the handover next year, they will be able to do so in any suitable venue. I'm not having any suspicion of connivance that there will be a pre-emptive clampdown on freedom before then.

Thursday 6 June

As luck would have it, I had one of my regular meetings with the Commissioner of Police. He is an honest man, Eddie Hui ('steady Eddie' as he's known to his force), who is deservedly widely respected in the community. I asked him about videoing demonstrations and he says that he'll look at the justification and report back on the destruction of tapes once they are clearly not going to be required for court action. Eddie has just been in Beijing, where he had a good meeting with the Minister for Security. The Minister gave him – in Eddie's words – 'lots of blah blah' about the Basic Law and made it clear that Eddie would go on reporting to the Chief Executive. It would have been amazing if he'd said anything else.

The minister raised two important issues. First, he pressed for the extradition of an ex-party secretary whom the Chinese wanted to get hold of. On this, there is nothing we can do to help, above all because we don't know the whereabouts of the official the Chinese are seeking, doubtless to shoot. Second, the minister is worried about the security arrangements for the handover ceremony. He is obviously nervous about looking after senior Chinese officials. But where on earth is safer than here? Is there even now some crazed Democrat in a Kowloon bedsit oiling a rifle to aim at a member of the politburo next year? I rather doubt it. How would you recognize a politburo member anyway? I suppose that the giveaway would be the dyed hair.

Friday 7 June

Kerry told me a grim little story when we were in the car on the way to the RTHK studios to record my monthly 'Letter to Hong Kong'. A young expatriate friend of his wife, Jenny, had been travelling in a lift, the only Westerner with a group of Cantonese. One had said to her rudely, 'why don't you go home?' 'I am home,' she replied. 'This isn't your home,' he went on. 'Go home.' They had continued down in the lift with the Westerner feeling besieged by hostility. She was telling this to some scriptwriter friends and one of them said that a similar thing had happened to her recently. Another of Kerry's friends, who ran corporate affairs for the Hong Kong and Shanghai Bank, is married to a Chinese woman. When Kerry told him the story, he said that he thought there was a definite increase in hostility and that this was sometimes followed by the recollection of old humiliations and slights. His wife is a professional woman who still fumed over the patronizing way she'd often been treated by third-rate expat businessmen, some of whom seemed to regard Hong Kong as an extension of Guildford. She'd also been discriminated against from time to time. It looks as though as colonialism unravels we will inevitably have visited on us some of the bitterness felt against past racial disadvantages. The sins of blimps in blazers at the Hong Kong Club, now retired to Gloucestershire or Scotland with their millions, are going to rebound on us. Were we so bad? I bet some people were really awful, although it was probably a minority. And there must've been a lot of Chinese biting of tongues as they watched many third-raters make so much money. It's not surprising that the communist papers have latched on to the campaign to make the British apply for work permits here in the future like everyone else. At the heart of all this too is the fact that the Chinese are just as racist as other ethnic groups, maybe more so, at least that's the general perception. It's even more difficult to be black in China than it is in most other places. I do hope we leave behind some moral decency when we go. The jury is out on how much.

Saturday 8 June

At the JLG meeting this week the Chinese have agreed with our position on the budget talks, accepting our form of words to describe the legislative procedures. So we have been right to stand firm. I hope that local officials notice. Beijing blinked first over the budget: they will not control the spending plans for 1996/97. It's another big success for Hugh Davies, Alan Paul and their colleagues in the JLG team who make progress in interminable meetings inch by inch.

Wednesday 12 June

A mild difference between Anson and me on the provisional Legislative Council has become apparent. In her speeches in America and elsewhere, she has said that while it would be wrong to scrap the present Legco which was fairly elected, clearly attention is going to switch to how representative its successor will be. This is taken as a softening of our position. The cartoonists make much of it all – with one strip in *Apple Daily* showing me tied to a railway line going nowhere while Anson speeds past on a parallel line trying to catch up with the 'through train' just ahead of her. Cartoons invariably get to the heart of what people are thinking. It's unsurprising and I suppose reasonable that Anson should open up some daylight between us. I am sure we can make certain that it doesn't become a question of substantive policy rather than simply one of presentation. I talked to her about this when she was about to go to Washington to lobby Congress and the administration on MFN. We agreed that it is largely a semantic point. The provisional body won't include any Democrats and therefore can hardly be said to be representative, a point that I make as forcefully as I can in the afternoon at a press call after a housing tour with Rosanna Wong.

We gave a farewell dinner for Haider Barma, the Secretary for Transport. His family, originally from India, have been in Hong Kong for over a century. But he's not ethnically Chinese and therefore can't hold a senior policy secretary post after 1997. This explicitly racist policy was just accepted in discussions on the Basic Law as China's right. People like Haider are trapped between Chinese racism and the British Home Office, which is reluctant to give the South Asian community in Hong Kong, about 7000 strong, the right of abode in Britain. Haider is a charming and very competent man, and we've found him a job as chairman of our public service commission, policing the integrity of our public service arrangements which have ironically been so unfair to him.

There's a growing amount of gossip about the jockeying for position post-1997, with C. H. Tung clearly the front-runner for Chief Executive. There are rumours about some of his rivals, particularly T. S. Lo, trying to do the dirty on him. Henry Keswick, who has had some sort of feud with C.H. over the years, is now trying to put that in the past. He has invited Tung to dinner: the Field of the Cloth of Gold, Hong Kong style.

Friday 14 June

This year we've been able to hold the reception for the Queen's Birthday outside on the lawn with the police band once again beating the retreat. The director of music, a north countryman from Bridlington, Frank Parkinson, retires this year, so I said a few words about him and presented him with a signed photo. (Why do we always give people signed photos? Are they proudly displayed on Bridlington sideboards or shoved in a bottom drawer?) Frank has a big smile and a shining bald head which always glitters with beads of perspiration. He is a man for whom the expression 'salt of the earth' could have been coined. Next year, the captains and kings will depart; this year it's the bandmasters. As the band march off, they play 'Happy Birthday'. The woman next to me in the crowd, president of St David's Welsh Society I note by her chain, asks me, 'Is it your birthday?' The old Queen of Hong Kong.

Saturday 15–Sunday 16 June

James and Jane Loudon are staying with us. He used to work with me when I was Lord Carrington's political secretary during his stint as party chairman (a job he cordially loathed), and Jane was our PA. We took them out on the boat and I'm reminded of a story which Peter Bottomley told us about a trip on the same boat which he once took with Julian Amery. As they swam around the boat during the hot afternoon, Julian said to him, 'Just think. When I started in politics we had about a hundred of these around the world.' That's one way of looking at the history of the British Empire. The following day we show them the Chinese frontier city, Shenzhen. No one quite believes me when I describe the transformation that I've witnessed since I was first brought up to this frontier post in 1979: then, a winding river, fields of vegetables, a sleepy village – now, an explosion of raw capitalist development, the law of the jungle, Chinese socialist style.

Edward has got back safe and sound from a weekend in Burma. He went there at Easter and met Aung San Suu Kyi. He's just met her again and took her some videos for her to watch with her staff. She likes to sit with them at weekends and do a bit of bonding while watching a suitably cheerful film. Her choice was interesting – nothing too sexy. She was expecting to be arrested this weekend but thank heavens she wasn't. Lee Kuan Yew has given an interview this week on Burma, naturally taking the generals' side.

Monday 17 June

Anson is back as well after her successful trip to the US. The Americans liked and respected her. While she was in New York she was contacted by relatives of one of the senior leaders in Beijing, who wanted copies of some of her American speeches and to find out her intentions for the future. He indicated that senior leaders wanted to meet her. I hope it's true and that it happens. She loves and knows Hong Kong better than most; and she is a Chinese patriot, which she would not think was the same as being a Chinese communist. (That may turn out to be her problem.) On top of all that she is competent and decisive. I sent her some flowers to welcome her home and had a positive talk with her on the phone. I said I quite understood that the closer we got to the handover, the more she and others would have to position themselves discreetly and prepare for the future. We just have to know what we are all doing and try to avoid opening up gaps over issues of substance.

Tuesday 18 June

We are having trouble with London about the way we handle legislation on telephone interceptions. We want to get something on the statute book which reflects the views of the Law Reform Commission. If we don't take action and produce a sensibly balanced piece of legislation with judicial oversight of what we do, there is a danger of a private member's bill succeeding which we would not be able to veto. Officials in London seem to want to second-guess and micromanage every inch of the way on this and one or two other matters. Letters and phone calls from the Hong Kong department rain down on poor Martin. Ministers are regularly referred to as being 'interested' in the issue. I don't believe they are for a moment. It's another case of a group of officials in London trying to run us from behind ministerial skirts (or trousers), which doesn't make governing Hong Kong any easier. We look back to the days of Peter Ricketts with profound nostalgia.

Wednesday 19 June

The doctor who supervises my treadmill test at the hospital thinks that my weight is greater than is suggested by the scales at GH. I dispute his finding! He is retiring in September even though he's only 55, and said that he wants to collect his pension before 1997. I tried to persuade him that his pension would be quite safe after the handover. He told me that his wife had said this is what I would say, but they both thought that what he was proposing was the safe thing to do. His nurse tells me that she is going to England in August to put her 12-year-old son into school before the handover. So I am in denial about my weight, but Hong Kong's professional middle class is not in denial about their fears of 1997.

Back at GH I saw Michael Yahuda, an academic who has just finished a book on the Joint Declaration. He says that the Chinese gave us the JD because they thought that a clapped-out nation like us needed it for face but wouldn't make a fuss about its terms since all we could conceivably be interested in was commerce. After all, we'd taken Hong Kong for money, and we'd want to go on making money when we left. Then we turned round after Tiananmen and started making a fuss about the JD's provisions. He thought that Tiananmen had been the crucial event in the transition. After that we seemed not to care as much about a 'through train'. The Bill of Rights, the British nationality scheme and the decision to build the airport had all annoyed the Chinese. The scene had been set for my arrival and demonizing. Unlike my doctor and his nurse, he reckons that most people in Hong Kong will 'wait and see' and hope for the best after the handover.

Friday 21 June

Bob Peirce and I discussed a telegram for me to send to London before my return next month. We have to try to persuade them to accept that we will all have to stand back from Hong Kong from now on and allow local officials to manage things for themselves rather more, not least their relationship with China. London's attempts to micromanage everything will have to end. The Hong Kong department is always these days tiresomely at our elbow. FCO officials here, and Hong Kong government officials, find this meddling from a distance even more annoying than I do.

Everyone has been hearing stories about Anson being invited to Beijing to see Jiang Zemin, Qiao Shi and Li Peng. It's not inconceivable that the NCNA is leaking all this in order to try to stop it happening.

Saturday 22–Sunday 23 June

A weekend at Fanling as the rain crashes down. When it rains here, it really rains. I have boxes of speeches, telegrams, Exco papers, briefs and submissions. I've always been pretty good at doing my boxes; one result is that I've always got more of them. But I'm slightly better these days at knowing when to skim and when to concentrate hard. The real trick is to be able to hone in on the things that could blow up, and the decisions which are going to count. I find nowadays that I'm deliberately standing aside from some issues and letting other people – like Anson, Donald and the JLG team – handle them. I'm doing this with the current row over the Western Corridor Railway, the next large infrastructure project on our agenda.

Kerry has lined up getting on for 20 interviews this week – one year to go and all that. Nearly all of them were from a rather sceptical direction – but how will Hong Kong get on after 1997? That was the question to which everyone came back. There's very little criticism that I've cocked things up by being too confrontational with China.

Monday 24 June

David Ford is over from London this week for a meeting with all the heads of our overseas offices. He's always the best thermometer for the political temperature in Hong Kong. He's a bit dubious about whether we will hit our growth target this year, but Donald Tsang gives me the same bright and breezy answer when I ask him about this. David says that all his rich Chinese friends are most worried about their security; some of them are asking him if they should hire bodyguards. There is a story about kidnapping and ransoms for large amounts of money. The view is that the Triads are targeting local big shots, bringing in mainlanders for the hits, and working their way steadily through the social pages of Hong Kong's *Tatler*. When I raise this with the Commissioner of Police, he says he's been looking into the stories and can't find any corroborating evidence.

David also has insightful analysis of what a Labour government would mean for (a) me and (b) Hong Kong. First, he says that Mandelson and Co. won't want me to return from Hong Kong looking like a hero. Second, some of them probably do believe (naïvely) that they could get on better with China. Third, Robin Cook doesn't like Tories and will want to distance himself from responsibility for post-'97 problems in Hong Kong, such as the dismantling of Legco. He'll say that we started democratization too late and then I bungled the job. The script for next year?

Wednesday 26 June
Michael Jones is here from the *Sunday Times*. He came with me three years ago to see the dragon boat races when I was mobbed. He wants to come on another district visit so we took him to Aberdeen, and got the same public reaction. It makes a point to which he is decently receptive. His instincts on Hong Kong are as good as they invariably are on British politics. After that we had our annual bash for everyone in the private office, past or present, plus our bodyguards, which was great fun. Mike Hanson was cheerfully gloomy. He's going back to the UK at the end of the year and can't wait. My first ADC, Felipe, is leaving the police and joining Michael Sze's Trade Development Council. He sees no long-term future for an expat officer. I hope that we don't see the departure of some of our best people right across the public service.

Friday 28 June
I've had a quasi summit on employment opportunities for people with disability, the sixth meeting I've had like this on disability. We've had three meetings on transport and three on jobs. We get representatives of disability and rehabilitation groups, employers' organizations and government to discuss the issues, to agree on a programme for the coming year and at the following meeting we review progress and set new goals. These meetings have been extremely successful and we have really helped to improve conditions for those with a disability. That's been one of my priorities here, but of course there's also an economic spin-off. I figured that unless we change things before 1997, and establish some momentum, nothing much would be done afterwards; to put it mildly, Chinese attitudes to disability are not very enlightened. Those present want a further meeting next year with me and the Chief Executive designate. A through train for the disabled? We shall see.

Monday 1 July
On the first day of our last year, Hugh Davies has had quite a good meeting with Zhao Jihua, his opposite number in the JLG, about the handover ceremony. The Chinese are now obviously prepared to accept the convention centre as the venue, but will refuse anything outside. We've still got a long way to go – for example, we need to establish that there will be no separate vetting of the media – but it looks as though we should be able to get everything more or less in place for agreement at the foreign ministers' meeting at the UNGA [United Nations General Assembly] in the autumn. The next question is whether we should hold a farewell ceremony in the

open at Tamar next to the harbour before the joint handover. I'm in favour but we need to get UK money to fund it, about £2 to 3 million, and I can see the government getting shirty. But it's out of the question to arrange anything unless Britain will put its hand in its pocket. It's got a lot out of Hong Kong down the years; it shouldn't hold back on a small gesture of generosity at the end.

Francis Cornish has just been to Macau, on which he is eloquent. Tarts, pimps, thugs, Chinese security officials from Zhuhai, Stanley Ho, 90,000 empty flats which no one wants to buy, two McDonald's bombed because of a commercial row. The German manager of the Holiday Inn has just been chopped and almost killed because of an argument with the owner of the nightclub in his hotel about his pricing for prostitutes, which was luring them away from those in the club. The head of the judiciary police said to Francis, when asked why he wasn't arresting the gangsters whose photographs were displayed in profusion on his office walls, 'Why bother cutting down a few trees in the forest?' Macau is a great warning to us – what Hong Kong could be like if things went wrong. The rot gives it a certain piquant charm, and the Governor is a decent figure, but it's not a great tribute to Portugal, any more than were Angola and Mozambique.

Kate phoned up from Newcastle pleased as Punch. She's got a 2.1 in her exams. I listened afterwards to Handel's *Dettingen Te Deum*.

Tuesday 2 July

Unusually for me I went to early mass (7:45 at St Joseph's) trying to make good the *Te Deum*. Martin Lee was serving and Donald Tsang was in the front pew. Apparently they are there almost every day.

At Exco, we began with a report of yesterday's trip to Beijing by a group of pro-democracy legislators. They wanted to present a petition in favour of keeping the existing Legco. Despite the fact that they all had valid travel documents, they weren't allowed to leave the plane and their documents were confiscated. The press who were covering the trip were given a dressing down by Chinese officials. Then the legislators were flown back to Hong Kong in the same plane. Thus does China trust those who will be its citizens after 1997. What will happen to dissenters then?

We then got on to the bill which will set up the police complaints body on a statutory basis. The police are strongly opposed to having a civilian in the top job. I think Legco will take a different position. More difficult still is the draft bill that we have to present on sedition, treason, subversion and secession. All these matters are covered in article 23 of the Basic Law and we are being pressed to draft legislation to cover them. Legco wants us to have something on the statute book before 1997, of course, since the Chinese are unlikely to put forward anything acceptable after that date. It's inevitable that we will have a horrible row with the Chinese about whatever we propose and then another row with Legco, who won't like whatever can be agreed. They need no telling that there is some difference between our view on an issue like sedition and what the law will be when there is enlightened Chinese rule!

After lunch there was a meeting of my Business Council – tycoons and taipans – at which our international image was on the agenda following the confected row about the *Newsweek* article earlier in the year. I went through all the critical articles in the international press one by one, and pointed out some of the criticisms that are being made about the playing field being tilted for business in China's direction as we get closer to 1997, about the threats of loss of autonomy and increasing corruption and so on. I say that we're going to prepare 'song sheets' on all these issues from which we hope business as well as government leaders will sing. I doubt whether we will get much support from the real quislings on the council like Paul Cheng, the American Chinese head of Inchcape. He spent the whole of the dinner we organized for business leaders with John Major telling all those on his table how disastrous democracy is. The other day he responded to criticism of commercial favouritism towards Chinese companies by saying that there is nothing wrong with this because British companies had been favoured for years. Well, that certainly is not true of recent years (which has been Jardine's complaint) and it's a bit odd coming from the head of Inchcape, though it's probably true to say that they are performing so badly they could do with a bit of favouritism.

Wednesday 3 July

The new Australian Foreign Affairs Minister, Alexander Downer, is in town. I briefed him and gave him a dinner. He is a long-time politician, educated in Britain when his father was High Commissioner, and was briefly Leader of the Opposition. He arrives as 'walking wounded' having recently been accused of a sackful of gaffes. Once the press think you're a gaffer, an eagle-eyed gaffewatch begins in earnest. You tend to find that even otherwise blameless statements of policy or reiteration of what you and others have said a hundred times before are hit with the 'G' word. It's difficult to shake off save by staying out of the news for long enough for someone else to catch the disease. But poor Downer has arrived with a whole comet's tail of journalists on gaffe patrol. Will he be as supportive of Hong Kong's democracy and civil liberties as his predecessor, Gareth Evans, was? Martin Lee doesn't help by giving an interview before he meets Downer saying that the Australians will sell Hong Kong's freedoms down the river for more trade with China. Sometimes Martin has quite a large political sense deficit. He should be stroking people like the Australian Foreign Minister. In the event Downer, whom I rather like but who doesn't give the impression of being entirely on top of matters here, sounds positive about what we are doing, if less openly so than Evans. The gaffe watchers are disappointed and head off in different directions – some say he has spoken out for Hong Kong and is heading for a row with China and some say the opposite.

Thursday 4 July

At a meeting the following day C. H. Leong, the thoroughly decent chairman of the main business committee in Legco and the representative of the medical profession there, talked to me about the continuing lobbying to provide full British passports for the 8000 members of the South Asian ethnic minority community in Hong Kong. Like the now retired Secretary for Transport, they are predominantly from the Indian subcontinent, came with the garrison generations ago, and now find themselves trapped between the explicitly racist Chinese nationality law and the British Home Office's heavily rationed generosity over passports. We've moved the government and the Labour Party a small distance on the issue but still not far enough for Legco's liking, nor for mine.

Just before flying back to London, I did a mid-year phone-in programme on RTHK in Cantonese as well as English to mark my fourth anniversary as Governor. I took 21 questions, only two of which are hostile, after which there was apparently a big surge of supportive calls. Cheung Man Yee, the wise head of RTHK, says that 7.45 to 9 o'clock was not long enough. Apparently there was a huge backlog and they could have gone on until lunchtime.

Friday 5 July

We got back to the flat in Morpeth Terrace after the overnight flight. We are all going to be in London together for a bit, then after meetings in London and Brussels, and Kate's graduation in Newcastle, I will go back to Hong Kong. Kate will be much preoccupied with sending CVs to putative employers, Laura with her work at *Harper's* magazine. Lavender is going to take Alice to have a look at universities she may like to apply to and will start to look around London for the sort of area we want to live in when we return.

Saturday 6 July

We were taken by David Tang and his fiancée, Lucy, to the three tenors concert at Wembley. A miserable, cold and grey evening and awful traffic jams getting to the stadium. We are in the best seats when the clouds opened and like all the other nobs we were drenched. As ever there was a sort of eccentric English gallantry about open-air events in the summer. The concert gave us all the big arias, although I'm not sure why they insist on singing 'Moon River' and all those Neapolitan and showbiz ballads. But the great big Italian voices warm up a damp north London night. On the way out, we bumped into Jackie Stewart (the Formula One British racing driver) who asks about Whisky and Soda and the quarantine laws. He and his wife also have a Norfolk terrier. I fire off both barrels about quarantine and, needless to say, he agrees with me.

Sunday 7 July

At mass in the cathedral Cardinal Hume gave me a big wink on his processional exit at the end of mass; he is a great head of the Catholic Church in England for us to have at the moment, not only because he winks at Governors.

Monday 8 July

I've flown to Brussels and am staying with our ambassador to the EU, Stephen Wall, who used to be John's foreign affairs private secretary. He is a first-class guy, lean as a whippet, driven and clever. He and his wife have a nine-year-old long-haired dachshund which potters around their palatial house. I've worked with three ambassadors to the EU – David Hannay, John Kerr and now Stephen Wall, all outstanding. Lucky Britain.

After a speech at lunch to Belgium's equivalent of Chatham House, I took questions and get one tricky one from the *FT* about the position of SAR passport holders after 1997. There are some people who say that there is no legal basis for visa-free access for SAR passport holders and that we shall need to amend the visa list and add a new declaration, or at least reach some sort of political agreement. The trouble is that we are all nervous when we raise these questions. Some of the Schengen states (which coordinate their immigration policies closely) will seek to amend the visa list in the wrong way, excluding SAR passport holders because they don't trust China, don't believe in 'one country, two systems', think that the SAR passport will be abused, and that it could lead to a flood of Chinese immigrants. It's horribly complicated and we all know that we are walking on egg shells. If we had got the Home Office's agreement earlier on visa-free access, and if the Foreign Office had believed that we would succeed with the Home Office, maybe we'd have played the issue differently. We thrash around these issues together with other officials to no great effect. I'm able to make the point at a dinner that the Japanese, Australians, Canadians and Americans have a higher profile in Hong Kong than Europe and that they are more supportive of us.

Tuesday 9 July

A day packed with meetings, thanks in part to help from Leon Brittan, including lunch with Jacques Santer (the President of the European Commission), a long session with the European Parliament and an interesting meeting with the Belgian Finance Minister. He tells me a rather worrying story. Talking privately, he says that he is chairman of the IMF interim committee. He is worried by the fact that recently the Chinese government pressed for the inclusion of a particular Chinese official who works for the IMF in a delegation going back to Beijing. When the delegation arrived, the official was arrested immediately and then sentenced to 12 years for corruption. The IMF was outraged but is trying to play the issue quietly for fear of the publicity which it could trigger. The concern now is that if this is not satisfactorily resolved, some will argue that the IMF should not come to Hong Kong for its annual meeting in September 1997. This would be a disaster for the new SAR, not least because of the reason for the decision. Everybody has to try to find some way in which to get a tough message through to senior Chinese officials. But does sending of messages do any good? It's no surprise that the minister doesn't seem to have much confidence in 'one country, two systems'.

The press back home have beaten up my remarks on Europe to the Belgian Chatham House equivalent. 'Patten to crusade for soul of Tory Party', and so on. Leon, who is obviously the real heavyweight in the commission, talks to me about whether or not to return to British politics. He thinks that I should definitely go back if we win the election. If we lose then it would depend on who became leader. Right on both counts.

Wednesday 10 July

Lavender and I flew straight from Brussels to Newcastle for Kate's graduation. The Vice Chancellor gives the same speech about the squeeze on university funding that I've heard vice chancellors give for 20 years. Nothing seems to change despite the fact that the assembled mums and dads always seem to agree with what is said. Higher education just doesn't appear to have the salience which is needed in politics to make things happen, which says something about our priorities as a society. I went back to London to deliver a speech to the Centre for Policy Studies on Hong Kong, after which Lavender and I had a dinner with Malcolm and Edith Rifkind. As ever I have to get my act together to answer his sharp and forensic questions. He's got some good ideas about how to react to a provisional Legco, though I think he's on less firm ground in wanting to press the Chinese to make the membership of such a body as broad as possible. The Chinese wouldn't take any notice of us, but the argument would come very rapidly to focus on their body rather than the one which has actually been elected by the voters of Hong Kong.

Edward tells me that he had dinner with a crowd of journalists who were all very nice about me but argued that my views on Europe suggested that I'd never make a serious return to Conservative politics. What I find extraordinary is how far things have moved in four years. Ken Clarke is written off as a sort of fanatical extremist because of his views on Europe. He (and I) were mainstream a few years back. Ken is one of the main reasons why the government is still alive and he's an outstandingly successful Chancellor with a strong and audacious personality. He would be a good leader – if, that is, leadership consists of staking out your views and fighting for them.

Thursday 11 July

I had a private meeting with the foreign affairs select committee, which remains very helpful, and then a big meeting at the FCO covering the same sort of ground that Malcolm Rifkind and I covered at dinner. Malcolm thinks that if the Chinese set up a provisional Legco we should take them to the International Court of Justice (stopping off, I suggest, with the international jurists' group, Justice, en route). Officials shift rather nervously in their seats. They are sent off to write lots of papers. I ask whether the feeble recent one, which suggested that it would be very difficult ever to tell whether the Chinese had breached the JD and even more difficult to find anything appropriate to do about it if they had, was the sort of advice ministers had been given in the mid-'80s when we were negotiating this treaty. Sherard's response was that Sir S. Y. Chung had pressed at the time for an arbitration clause in the declaration, but ministers had concluded that this wasn't necessary, both because of the development of democracy in Hong Kong and because the JD was a binding treaty! This rather confirms my argument that throughout the mid-'80s the democratic development of Hong Kong was regularly seen (at least in public) as the buttress to the territory's freedoms and as the moral salve for the handover to Chinese communists.

I had half an hour with the Prime Minister, who had been involved in talks about the public spending round which he claimed (as usual) was the most troubling he could remember. He appeared quite cheerful. The polls have moved a bit in the government's direction, but there is still a long way to go. That evening we had a Balliol dinner at the Groucho club in memory of Richard Cobb. Richard Lambert, the editor of the *FT*, is there and says that they have held a page all evening on rumours that Deng has died. Again. Richard slipped out to phone the office to find out what's happened. Vivat. Deng is still alive.

Friday 12 July

After lots of official meetings we have dinner with Tristan and Alastair, who is doing a superb job in his present trench as Chief Whip dealing with some of the more ghastly Conservative MPs. Tristan has just written a piece about patriotism, taking Michael Portillo's Spanish Republican father as the model for his argument. No response from 'Little Gate', as Enoch Powell calls him, but his mother phoned Tristan and came to tea with him on the terrace of the House of Commons. Tristan says that she is charming and was pleased to read a serious appreciation of her husband and his poetry.

Saturday 13 July

After some not very serious house hunting, we went to the Royal Tournament in the evening, where I take the salute since the Royal Hong Kong Police and the Service Corps from Hong Kong are performing. We filled the royal box with family and friends. My former Commons PA, Freda, was there. She's just been accepted for the Anglican priesthood. It's nice to know that the churches still accept saints. Patrick Rock, who used to be my political adviser but now works for Michael Howard, was there as well. He clearly thinks my remarks about Europe are politically dopey and therefore assumes that I don't really wish to return to politics. Patrick invariably has excellent political sense.

Monday 15 July

I've returned on my own to Hong Kong. My first night back I had dinner with Martin Dinham. He remains a rock on which we have been able to build our defences, against both Beijing and from time to time – without any rancour on his part – London. He has impeccable judgement and works like a dog. People like him, too. I've been so lucky that he came here. He says that we're going to have to watch out for a tendency on the part of the FCO from the autumn onwards to sacrifice all else to a 'smooth transition'. (Why doesn't the world talk about a successful transition?)

They will want to avoid a fuss about the provisional Legco and will wriggle to avoid legislation on interceptions and all the things we want to do and are committed to do, bringing our laws into line with the Bill of Rights. We have to avoid, for example, last-minute 'I told you so' accusations that we have ratted on what we promised on interceptions, on which there are clear Law Reform Commission proposals. The view of some officials in the FCO is that we should simply veto any Legco private member's bill if one comes forward, which will probably happen if we fail to act ourselves. The idea that one of our last colonial acts might be to veto a bill on phone tapping is not one that attracts me. You need the political wit of a melon to think this feasible or desirable. Martin also takes the view that we will have more FCO London second- – and even first- – guessing the closer we get to the election and the possibility of a new government.

Wednesday 17 July

I've written an article this week for the *Daily Telegraph* on Hong Kong, not politics but the places, goods and shops that I like. I describe two walks – one urban and the other rural. The city walk covers ground with which I'm very familiar from my favourite baker's in Lyndhurst Terrace to my favourite ironmonger's in Possession Street by way of the antique shops in Hollywood Road and lots of other delights. Then I describe the actual walk we took on Lantau over a weekend back in March with the Cornishes and Kim Salkeld. There were two days of very good walking with the night between spent on the *Lady Maurine* and a final lunch at a jolly South African-owned restaurant, where we ate huge barbecued meals.

I'm playing quite a lot of tennis with Colin, whose unofficial designation is 'the man responsible for the Governor's sanity'. I spoke to Lavender, who is in rural France at our new home there. It's very hot but she is happy continuing to sort out the house. At a series of meetings this week, I become increasingly aware of growing if polite scepticism about what is going to happen after 1997. People keep on asking me what I really think.

Friday 19 July

I went this morning on one of my fairly regular unannounced visits to the black spots in a particular district. Today, it's the turn of Yuen Long, up on the north-western borders of the new territories. People here have lived on the very edge of the law for years. Does the Queen's writ actually run here? Barely. You notice it for instance in the chaotic planning with so many unauthorized container dumps. We are trying to deal with these environmental horrors. I set up a black-spots task force a couple of years ago. They've made some difference relocating a few unlawful activities and planting screens of trees along the roadsides. But it's an awful job – pushing a boulder slowly uphill inch by painful inch.

This afternoon I had a lot of American visitors, including Senators Feinstein and Helms. The former seems to think that everything will be okay after the handover because she was told so by Jiang Zemin when he was mayor of Shanghai. Best of all is Winston Lord, who is as smart and encouraging as ever. I also had a dinner with the Canadian Foreign Minister, Lloyd Axworthy. What plainly worries the Canadians most about Hong Kong is that if things go wrong after the handover, they'll suddenly have getting on for 150,000 Hong Kongers with Canadian passports arriving in . . . Hong-couver and all points east.

Tuesday 23 July

At quite a long Exco, with my departure on holiday imminent, the papers were all flooding in. The trickiest issue is about bringing the immigration status of Britons into line with that of other expats before the handover. The problem has been made more awkward by a small flood of British workers, including a few of the yobbo tendency, into Hong Kong in recent months. They work on building sites, in bars and so on, and give a bit of an impression of a reverse coolie class. This has become quite a sensitive political question, because the United Front trade unions, newspapers and politicians are claiming we are taking away jobs from locals at a time of higher unemployment by giving privileges to the blue-collar workers of the colonial power. Actually, unemployment figures remain exceptionally low (sometimes they look like a rounding error), and provided we can commit ourselves to sorting things out before the handover we should be all right. This may be an issue that I need to talk through with my successor.

Wednesday 24 July

The great escape is imminent. But before then, we're having a discussion on the two Foreign Office draft papers prepared for Malcolm Rifkind after our discussions in London on what he should say to his opposite number, Qian, when he sees him about the provisional Legco, and the second about whether establishing such a body would be a breach of the JD. We prepare a pretty tough and uncompromising form of words for Malcolm to use with Qian. I wonder if he'll use it. The rats will probably get at it over the summer before the meeting in New York at the UN. But it's important that the Chinese don't think that if they set up a provisional Legco we will simply look the other way. This and related questions will clearly dominate the autumn. We'll also have to work out with Anson exactly how she handles the next few months and how the rest of the civil service manage this difficult period as well. I spoke to her on the phone – she is at Liverpool University getting an honorary degree. We agreed that we will talk every Friday morning while I'm away in Europe.

I've had a very funny letter from Michael Pakenham, the number two – the Minister – in Paris. I knew him when I was aid minister and he was looking after the external relations portfolio in the UK delegation to the European Community. He told me that he accompanied Sir Christopher Mallaby, our departing ambassador, on his farewell call on President Chirac. On being introduced to the President, who clearly misheard his name, Michael was asked, 'Any relation to Chris Patten?' Michael replied, 'I'm afraid not. We are both Catholics, but otherwise we have no connections.' 'Ah well,' replied the President, 'No one is perfect.' Michael charitably concluded that this was a reference to the fact that he wasn't a Patten rather than that we were both Catholics. 'Well, no one's perfect' just happens to be my favourite last line in *Some Like It Hot* – actually it's my favourite film too.

Thursday 25 July

Before packing and the night plane, I had meetings with both Martin Lee and Emily Lau. I encouraged Martin, sating that if he wants to be effective in drumming up support in the international community for his position on the provisional legislature, it would be a good idea not to lambast foreign leaders like Winston Lord, who is after all the American Assistant Secretary of State for Asia, Alexander Downer and Lloyd Axworthy. They should be treated like important friends. Emily had a go at me on the position of dissidents and the selection of a Chief Executive. My own view is that the community would be very lucky if Anson was chosen. I'm not sure that elected politicians are very keen on the fact that Anson outstrips them all in the popularity polls.

On the plane back to London my incomparable PA, Jenny Best, will also be travelling, as will my former ADC Mike Ellis. Mike has now left the police force, done a law degree and got a job with a solicitors' firm in Hong Kong. He has told me a string of anecdotes about people leaving Hong Kong before the handover next year or planning to do so afterwards.

Thursday 1–Friday 30 August

Lavender and I went straight from London to Salzburg to stay with our great friends Lothar and Christina Wesseman. Travelling back through London, we flew to Toulouse and then drove up past Gaillac and Cordes to our new home. We came here for our first visit last year; it doesn't disappoint. The house consists of two converted tobacco farms and outbuildings around a courtyard, brought together in 1822 when the son from one farm married the daughter from the other. We spent much of our holiday knocking the house into shape, installing our furniture and preparing the garden for some serious later work. We were greatly helped by Jo and Binny Dimbleby, the gardening sons of the sculptor Nicholas, the youngest of the three sons of Richard Dimbleby. William and Caroline Waldegrave came to stay with their four children. We played lots of fiercely competitive tennis, had some good walks and picnics and did quite a lot of gardening. I'm determined to rescue from weeds and brambles what used to be a decent vegetable garden. Kate, Alice and Laura were with us and appeared to love the place as much as we do. It's not grand but very beautiful in lovely countryside with rolling hills and quite big rivers in which we swim. Looking west from the end of the vegetable garden, next to the walnut tree, I can see nothing except the distant white cliffs above a river gorge. The first morning I swear that I was woken up by the silence. We are going to love it here.

I have thought about Hong Kong from time to time. So much of the next year is going to be predictable. First, we – I – really will start to look more and more irrelevant. The days will be loud with the slap of coats turning. People will question the point of making a fuss about anything any more. To do so will risk the accusation that one is undermining confidence. The international community will be keen to avoid having to have a spat with China about Hong Kong. Alleged pragmatism will dictate turning a blind eye to bad Chinese behaviour, for example over the Legislative Council and the Bill of Rights. Any gesture of generosity, however slight and self-serving, from China will be seized on as a harbinger of hope for the future.

Second, as time ticks past we will lose our ability to extract a price for bad behaviour. So there will be snubs and imagined snubs and a disposition on the part of the unhelpful to be even less helpful.

Third, the press will either write stories saying that we in general and the Governor in particular are beleaguered and irrelevant, or else are selling out Hong Kong's interests. There will also be stories about human rights in Hong Kong being an irrelevant issue now. There won't be much applause for us as we take our bows.

Fourth, we will have more problems with the Foreign Office and the Beijing embassy as they all opt for neat tidying up, and an allegedly pragmatic look to future interests, the avoidance of any more rows and a way of distancing themselves from us. The imminence of a general election, with ministers' minds on other issues, and the likelihood of a change of government, with new ministers anxious to distance themselves from policy failures in Hong Kong made by their predecessors, will make critical and hostile officials even more difficult to deal with.

So what should we do?

I am determined to keep singing the same tunes. Don't give up now. Ask from time to time how will all this look in five years? The long term is what matters.

And, of course, we will have to do the packing! The fact that the sand is running so fast out of the glass may help to make the rest more bearable.

Sunday 1 September

We got back to Hong Kong this afternoon. On the way, I watched a rather dim James Bond movie, but woke with sufficient time to knock off 1100 words for the *Economist Yearbook*. Anson greeted me at the airport with Martin, Edward, Lance [Brown] and Irene Yau, the head of the government information services. It's been a pretty quiet August, the main flutter over reports that Sir T. L. Yang, the Chief Justice, is being pressed to run for the Chief Executive post. Emily Lau has spoken for many in criticizing this idea, given that – in her bowdlerized words — Sir T.L. is not a great administrator and has been supine over the Bill of Rights. He wants to speak to me. We get back to Government House; Elspeth, Ah Chak and all the staff greeted us, and Whisky and Soda are all over Lavender and Alice. They look quite sleek from the 'fur dresser' and are doubtless exhausted by their non-stop activity in the very funny daily cartoon strip in the *Hong Kong Economic Journal*, 'Fei Pang's Theatre', which records Fei Pang's (Fatty Patten's) life through their eyes and activities. Recently they have been discussing whether they should take French lessons.

During dinner, the Chief Justice phoned. He is on leave in London en route from Canada to Turkey and then on a cruise ship until October. That's the way to campaign. He told me that he's been approached by an old pro-Beijing supporter to see if he's a candidate for CE, doesn't of course wish to put himself forward, will do so if enough people want him, is quite prepared if necessary to resign as CJ, and go on paid or unpaid leave or merely withdraw from hearing cases. I purred my sympathy, said that we can work out exactly what he should do if he is really nominated, and suggested that we should clear a statement for him to make through his principal administration officer. From what I am told, she is the only person apart from his wife who is capable of managing him.

Sir T.L. is a slight, perky Shanghainese, trained in London. He has 'risen without trace' through the magistracy and the judiciary largely because he's clean (no bad thing) and local. He became the first local CJ partly as a result of a failure to bring on better local lawyers or to parachute a really top-class Chinese QC into the job: someone like Andrew Li or Denis Chang, but there are others too these days. He is a decent and well-read man, who translates Chinese novels into English as a pastime. There isn't an ounce of malevolence in him. I hope that the ambition of others doesn't press him on towards self-destruction. The Hong Kong leftists are probably running him, pushed on by T. S. Lo, whose own campaign is spluttering to a halt, and by business opponents of C. H. Tung. Or it may be that the Chinese merely want someone else in the field so that C.H. faces an allegedly contested election. Who knows? But if the Almighty is kind, she or he will spare Sir T.L., who would be crucified were he to get the job.

Monday 2 September

After a mountain of work, Anson talked to me about the pressure on her to become a candidate herself for CE. She is pressed by several perfectly decent people to throw her non-existent hat in the ring, but she is reluctant. I argue that she would probably find it easier to be number one than number two, but in either circumstance she will be faced with difficult decisions that may compromise her. Many will reckon that as long as she's there, they'll stay. But she worries about declaring her candidacy while C. H. Tung is still waiting to declare himself. She wouldn't want to run against him, any more than he'd like to run against her. Andrew Li, who has been increasingly close to Tung, has told her that Tung will declare in a couple of weeks. Tung articulates his very conservative views with courtesy and a degree of eloquence, but if she doesn't run and he doesn't run, what then? Will the Chinese really want her? Will the fact that the majority in Hong Kong really want her be helpful or provocative? And what of the fact that Archie, her straight as an arrow husband, doesn't – at least this is my guess – want her to be Chief Secretary let alone CE? He clearly loves her too much. I agonize away with her for half an hour. They way I see it is –

(a) I think she's terrific, wise and the best person for the job, a great and brave administrator with strong values – I have never worked with anyone better;
(b) the most cautious decent ticket might well be C.H. for the top job and Anson for the second;
(c) will she be able to avoid being compromised whichever job she does?
(d) the whole thing is a snakepit.

It's much easier if you want the job to lose your Parliamentary constituency.

My friends and advisers are completely divided. Simon Murray thinks it would be an awful job, likes and admires Anson hugely, and thinks she shouldn't touch it with a barge pole. Bob Peirce, a similar admirer, takes the opposite view. And me? In some respects I just like her too much to have a position.

Both Richard Hoare, my excellent (inherited) first private secretary, and Kerry have bought post-'97 houses during the summer holidays, Richard near Chichester and Kerry in Sydney. I find the news vaguely encouraging. The last act has started and there is life beyond next year.

Tuesday 3 September

At our first Ad Hoc meeting, we discussed two Foreign Office papers that we went over before the holidays. Would it be legal to set up a provisional Legco? Would it be a breach of the Joint Declaration? And how would it fit with Hong Kong's mini constitution, the Basic Law? What are the options for action? The FCO papers meander elegantly across the surface of these questions. For me, what is most interesting is the genesis of the whole debate. During the negotiations on the JD, Sir Philip Haddon Cave (then Chief Secretary) and – as I noted before – Sir S. Y. Cheung (the senior member on Exco) argued strongly that there should be some arbitration clause in the JD and some agreed remedial courses of action in order to deal with any abuses. Percy Cradock and his FCO acolytes persuaded the Cabinet that this wasn't necessary. The JD was a binding international agreement which China wouldn't breach. And anyway, they argued, the development of democracy would protect Hong Kong's position. So now here we are: if the Chinese breach the JD there is not much we can do about it except make clear that in our view a breach has happened and tell the world more or less noisily that the Chinese can't be trusted to keep their treaty obligations. The JD binds China to cooperate with our discharge of sovereign responsibilities before 1997, and the JD and the BL commit them to a legislature composed through elections. It's difficult to argue that setting up an alternative Legco before 1997 is in line with these requirements and almost as difficult to assert that setting up a selection committee of 400 to pick a Legco is what we all mean by an election.

I have three objectives. First, not to resile from our defence of democracy. Second, to be able to do this with the minimum fallout for Hong Kong and the minimum chance of isolating Britain from her friends. Third, to stick to a position which Anson and most of the administration can easily accept. I steered the committee quite gently towards accepting this as the basis of the briefing for Malcolm Rifkind before he sees Qian at the UNGA and raises the question of the establishment of a provisional Legco before 1997. We must sound tough enough to discourage the

Chinese from doing too much too long before the handover. Anyway, we are on pretty safe ground. On the principle of a provisional Legco we should say that we've lived up to our promises in the JD on democratization, that it's difficult (whatever the legalistic arguments) to argue that a selection committee of 400 represents what the JD promised on elections, that any provisional Legco so constituted should do as little as possible for as short a time as possible, and that Britain and the international community should press China to get back into compliance with the spirit and letter of the JD and the BL as soon as possible by holding free and fair elections. I'm also keen that we should ring one or two international bells. The FCO argue convincingly that we can't really go to the World Court, since this would involve hazardous diplomacy in the UN, but we could ask the International Commission of Jurists for their legal opinion on a provisional Legco, which might help increase pressure on China while allowing ministers to say they'd done something (at least when pressed by opinion in Congress in Washington). Of course, the attitude of the Democrats in Hong Kong will largely determine whether international opinion thinks we've simply thrown in the towel. My own judgement is that this approach would be more or less right and politically solid. It should also give some relief to the Hong Kong civil servants present. It is principled without committing us to a year of struggle.

We seem to be drifting towards an agreement on a joint handover ceremony in the new convention centre. But before that we will stage a farewell next to the harbour; the Chinese communists will doubtless have their own fun and frivolity a bit later. They are still being tricky about issues like the press, and may try to implicate us in various unsavoury aspects of the inauguration of the new SAR institutions, for example Legco. I was amused by an exchange today in Beijing between Jeremy Hanley, our relatively new Foreign Office minister, and Vice Minister Wang at their Foreign Ministry. Wang protested against any idea that the Chinese might behave badly at the ceremony: after all they were an ancient and courteous civilization, he said. I suspect they may have been thinking – what about that unspeakably badly behaved Governor in Hong Kong? A satisfactory outcome seems in sight, especially now that Britain looks likely to agree to cough up some money to pay for a farewell. The main problems now are organizational. I want a younger and competent Hong Kong civil servant called Stephen Lam to be in total charge of the whole operation and Anson agrees.

Wednesday 4 September

I make a point of seeing individual secretaries from time to time alongside the Chief Secretary in order to review their areas of responsibility. I have a very good discussion today with Nicholas Ng,* who has taken over the responsibility for Constitutional Affairs from Michael Sze, now the senior executive at the Trade Development Council. Nicholas has done this controversial job, seeing through our legislation and supervising the elections, extremely well. By instinct he is probably more conservative than Michael but he has a clear sense of the difference between right and wrong and a rocklike commitment to whatever is the agreed government line. I have huge respect for him, and there are a lot more like him.

Thursday 5 September

Lavender organized an extremely good reception for matrimonial lawyers at GH. She's been speaking at their conference and it's another opportunity to give them the standing in the legal profession and in wider social discussions that they deserve. She has also just launched an appeal for Eurasian bone marrow donors. She met a lovely little boy called Jasper Wong, who has a Chinese father and a Scottish mother. He has a serious form of leukaemia which can only be cured by a bone marrow transplant. The problem is that there is no match on the Chinese register and so far nothing back in Britain. It is thought that there is more likelihood of finding the right match among the Eurasian population here, so a Eurasian register is being set up. We hope that it will help Jasper and any other Eurasian children who need a transplant. There is in fact quite a sizeable Eurasian population in Hong Kong – there was a great deal of intermarriage between Eurasian families who often felt they were not fully accepted by either the Chinese or the British. They produced some extraordinarily talented individuals. Perhaps as Hong Kong becomes more cosmopolitan they won't feel as much like outsiders.

Wednesday 11 September

I'm spending a lot of time writing my last policy address. In the meantime, C. H. Tung has apparently been up to Beijing, presumably to get the once over, and there have also been reports of Chinese officials coming down to

* Nicholas Ng was a civil servant who moved up through senior positions becoming Secretary for Constitutional Affairs from 1994 to 1997. He was appointed Secretary for Transport from that year until 2002. He became chairman of the Public Service Commission in 2003 until his retirement in 2014.

Hong Kong to have a look at Anson. There has been growing concern in the legal profession about the rather anomalous position of the Chief Justice. After some public comments about whether he is now in the political game or not, he sent me a letter of resignation and I've appointed a very good Australian judge, Noel Power, as an interim CJ. I talk to him about improvements in court administration on which he makes a number of excellent points. I haven't had a chat like this since I arrived in Hong Kong. What on earth did Sir T. L. Yang* do? Australia also came to the rescue when we were looking for a restaurant to celebrate our wedding anniversary. We went to one called 'M at the Fringe' run by a splendid Australian woman.

Thursday 12 September

Some of the China watchers who talk to us suggest that the politburo concluded during their seaside talks in August that 'leftism' should be avoided over Hong Kong and Taiwan and that they should try to charm us to bits. Certainly, talks on the handover have been moving slowly towards a reasonably satisfactory conclusion. The Chinese have been giving way across a broad front and now there are suggestions (not least from the FCO and our Beijing embassy) that since they've fallen back on so many points, we should surrender a few castles ourselves. This is a return to old-style diplomacy with China. I think it gets you into trouble. I am insisting on digging in and only giving up points of little substance. Martin as ever is keeping me on the straight and narrow. But it won't make me particularly popular.

The CBF, Bryan Dutton, came in to talk about the garrison and the position of China on the future arrangements for their troops. We want to discuss with them what the legal situation will be in the future so far as their soldiers are concerned. Will they be subject to the laws of Hong Kong like everyone else? The Basic Law says 'yes', but evidently the Chinese military are having second thoughts. There will be a huge amount of concern here if Chinese soldiers are, literally, a law unto themselves. Until the Chinese talk to us about their intentions on this we'll find it 'too difficult' to find time to talk to them about the posting of Chinese advance

* Sir T. L. Yang was born in Shanghai and moved to Hong Kong after studying law in England. He climbed steadily up the judicial ladder from magistrate to District Judge to Justice of Appeal, and was finally appointed Chief Justice of Hong Kong by David Wilson in 1988. He was the only ethnic Chinese lawyer to hold this post during the period of Britain's colonial rule. He remained in that post until 1996. In the election by the specially appointed small committee to select the first Chief Executive of the SAR he was defeated by 320 to 42 by C. H. Tung. In retirement he pursued his interest in translating Chinese classics into English.

personnel here before the 1997 handover. Bryan tells me that there will be five Chinese generals to replace him. Both the commander and his deputy are generals and they will apparently require equal-rank officers to take political care of them.

Of course, in order to have the handover ceremony in the convention centre, we will need to have built the convention centre! There are some problems about this, particularly about the roof, which is being made elsewhere and brought here by ship. It seems as though it's likely to be a tight finish. At a meeting this afternoon with Anson, Donald [Tsang] and the Secretary for Trade and Industry, I simply made clear, in an example of triumph of the will leadership, that it has to be finished by next June. I don't want to listen to briefings saying how difficult this is going to be. It simply has to be done. So far the technique appears to be working – just about. Nietzsche would be proud of me. Given that this is Hong Kong, the impossible will probably happen. I don't think that any public administration anywhere in the world makes things happen so quickly.

Friday 13 September

We are having rather a tricky time getting agreement with China on international rights and obligations after 1997. What should happen according to the JD is that we agree with China what these are and then write to the UN Secretary General setting out a list of them. The Chinese have agreed on the list too, with the exception of two international covenants on human and civil rights. This is all of a piece with their refusal to accept that they have the obligation to report to the UN on the application of these covenants in Hong Kong, even though the JD binds them to accept the covenants here. I'm against the suggestion that we should agree on the list without the covenants while continuing to haggle over them. This would give Beijing what the communists want. I think it's better by far to send what we believe the list should be to the UN and draw attention to what the Chinese are doing. That might at least put some pressure on them. So much for the 'improved atmosphere' enabling us to make progress on all these issues. Whenever something comes up affecting political control the Chinese just dig in.

Saturday 14 September

I've pretty well written the Legco policy address myself, all 9000 words of it. Reactions to the draft are interesting: my British advisers think it's good strong stuff and needs to be said; local officials, including Anson, Donald and Nicholas, are worried that it will be regarded as too confrontational, too parliamentary and too difficult to translate. I'm not sure about the last point. Can it really be more difficult to translate what I have tried to make lively prose than slabs of bureaucratese? Anyway, I think I'll have to tone it down. I don't want to make life awkward for some very good senior civil servants. Jeremy Hanley is in Hong Kong for a couple of days. He has had a positive meeting with Exco but a more difficult time with the press and Legco. He doesn't really put a foot wrong but it's not easy bobbing and weaving when asked whether setting up a provisional legislature would represent a breach of the Joint Declaration. We need rather better answers than the ones we've got a present.

Wednesday 18 September

The JLG is getting busier than ever. The Chinese have at last signed up to a deal on the container terminal after holding it up for four years, perhaps because Jardine's was in one of the consortiums and had originally supported my political proposals. The main argument in the JLG is now over security during the handover ceremony. It's perfectly clear that even if we sign an agreement now, which makes plain that security is the responsibility of the Hong Kong Police, the Chinese will try to get their own armlock on the arrangements. We can offer them the same liaison that we would have with say British or American police if there was a high-level visitor from their country. The trouble is that for the Chinese security isn't just stopping leaders being killed – it also embraces saving them from any potential embarrassment. So we will have endless haggling over the carrying of weapons and the control of demonstrations. What we can't do – whatever the inevitability of these rows – is to give the Chinese now a hook on which they can subsequently hang an alleged entitlement to be consulted on all these things. Nor can we possibly sign up to anything next June which erodes the position of our police and appears to have given entrée to the Chinese security forces.

Thursday 19 September

C. H. Tung announced his candidature, sort of. What he actually said was that he is actively considering being a candidate and would make a proper announcement within two or three weeks. His press conference is disastrous. He is over an hour late. The press release is changed. The press crowd into a tiny boardroom. There are so many cameras and recorders on the boardroom table that it collapses. But C.H. comes across as a decent and sincere man, which he undoubtedly is, and he gets away with it through sheer niceness. I have shown my slightly redrafted Legco address to Malcolm and Jeremy Hanley and they have both given it their imprimatur.

Friday 20 September

I was reminded today of one of my most important encounters in Hong Kong. It has been raining hard but there's a break in the clouds after lunch when I went to open the new buildings at Castle Peak hospital for the mentally ill. It was a grim institution in the furthest part of the new territories and I made it a priority to rebuild it. The last time I visited I was stopped by one Chinese patient, who spoke beautiful and formal English. 'Excuse me, Governor. Would you claim that Britain is the oldest democracy in the world?' he asked. 'One could certainly claim that,' I replied. 'And would you also agree that China is the last great communist totalitarian state in the world?' 'Some people might say that,' I responded diplomatically. 'Well could you tell me, Governor,' he went on, 'why your democracy is handing Hong Kong, a fine and free city, over to a communist society without ever having consulted the people who live here about what they want?' Here was the sanest man in Hong Kong locked up in a hospital for the mentally ill. So we are rebuilding it!

That evening I had a foresight of what lies ahead. Lavender and I went to a dinner for the SmithKline Beecham board, one of whose directors is Christopher Hogg. He is there with his wife, Miriam Stoppard as was. We had a particularly jolly conversation with them when we realized that they have a house in France only about seven or eight miles from us. They use the same nursery and Miriam gives us good advice about watering systems. My main project for next year! From building an airport to buying hosepipes.

Tuesday 24 September

Hugh Davies has had an awful – 'grisly' was his word – encounter with his opposite number, Zhao, on the handover. The Chinese negotiating style is always the same. Others, while obviously wanting to get the best for their own side, do at least search for some acceptable compromise or accommodation. But the Chinese are only interested in getting their own way. They'll hold on, even if they intend to do a deal, until the 11th hour and beyond trying to extract last-minute concessions. And if they can win, they'll try to ensure that the text of an agreement gives them enough elbow room to reopen every matter they might want to change subsequently. That's what they did with us over the memorandum of understanding on the airport and that's what they are doing over the handover now. The rest of the world should really learn how to play hardball with them. At present they get away with a negotiating style that combines the tactics of the Mafia and those of every barrack room lawyer, with a good dollop of unvarnished duplicity thrown in for good measure.

In the evening I had a long though delayed telephone conversation with Malcolm, who is at the UN General Assembly in New York – delayed because he's been coping with a domestic drama (or pantomime). Sir Nicholas Bonsor, or Bonsoir as we used to know him, has called for Ken Clarke to shut up over EMU. You wouldn't normally trouble about such turnip head criticism except that Nicholas, not a bad soul, is a Foreign Office minister. Thus does the party prepare for opposition. Malcolm agrees that it would be wrong if the spin on his meeting with Qian was that he'd secured a 'dignified withdrawal' for Britain, that is a deal on the handover ceremony, in return for soft pedalling on the provisional Legco. He's got a tough line on the latter and intends to use it. I just hope they spin it the right way too. There's always a tendency to think that the only good spin after these meetings is to say that they were friendly and constructive and signify a warming up or (awful phrase) thickening up of relations. Sometimes the best politics is to have a really bad meeting.

Wednesday 25 September

Things here just became more difficult. The Chinese have pulled the plug on any further discussions in Hong Kong about our farewell ceremony next to the harbour. They clearly feel that Qian can get an agreement out of Malcolm personally at their meeting about issues like the policing of the handover. I spoke to Sherard in the evening saying that we cannot accept an agreement which would lead to Chinese-style policing in Hong Kong. 'But there wouldn't be any Chinese police controlling the crowds,' replies Sherard disingenuously. In fact, if the Chinese have a veto on how our police handle things, it will be a public relations disaster, getting the SAR off to the worst possible start and making a complete mockery of the JD. Beijing-style crowd control and swarms of Chinese Tonton Macoute-style bodyguards in mid-camera shot is not the impression we should wish to leave as we bow out. The Beijing embassy are naturally out for a quick surrender and they are claiming – wrongly, I think – that the Chinese will hold up agreement on privileges and immunities for our Consulate General until we come into line on the handover. We sent off telegrams to New York and London trying to stiffen backbones before tonight's meeting. London are all for offering 'consultation' to the Chinese to get an agreement. But 'consultation' to the Chinese means a veto, and that is well known in Hong Kong. Let's hope Malcolm keeps his nerve. So far as we can judge, the senior diplomat with him – Graham Fry – is standing firm in his customary gentlemanly way.

Thursday 26–Friday 27 September
All has gone swimmingly in New York. Malcolm stuck to his position and the Chinese blinked first. He and Qian quickly reached an agreement on totally acceptable wording regarding the media and security. So we got a deal. For the rest, Malcolm set out our position on the provisional legislature at length during the only somewhat tense part of the meeting. Qian listened but said little in response. Let's hope he may think again and return the Chinese position to where it was last April in The Hague, when Qian made it clear that there would only be one Legco before 30 June. We also got the deal we wanted on the Consulate General and announced a visit to London in November by the Chinese Vice Premier, Li Lanqing, who is in effect the minister for foreign economic relations and trade. That should please Hezza. And the moral? It's the usual one. If the Chinese want to do a deal badly enough, they'll do one – but until the 11th hour or even later they'll try to screw everything they can out of you. It's a lesson, alas, which has still to be learned by our Beijing embassy and by a number of other officials in London as well.

Hugh Davies and Zhou signed the agreed minute at noon, after a final attempt by the Chinese to make one or two changes (for example, giving 'the Hong Kong Police' a small 'p'). They are incorrigible. We also told them that we are planning our own farewell ceremony at dusk on 30 June next year, and we announced that here today as well.

Monday 30 September
Two rather disagreeable things today, but they can't subtract from the fact that it's Alice's birthday. She is a real joy to have with us, beautiful, cheerful and bright. (She's particularly cheerful at the moment because her boyfriend, Alex, has returned to Hong Kong from Europe before going to university in Sydney.) On the downside, however, Cradock (not so ubiquitous these days) has written an article two days before my policy address. He's turning into a bit of a stalker. On top of that I had to go to the NCNA reception for China National Day. I shook hands with the quisling aristocracy of Hong Kong and then with the NCNA senior staff, including the ever-grinning Zhang, the vice director charged with public Patten-bashing. I've always rather cared for him. He gives the impression that he and I know it's only a game and that chaps have to do what chaps have to do. In my remarks I referred as often as possible to a 'freely and fairly elected Legco'. We left as the Communist Patriots flooded out into the night, duty done for another year. Next June it will be the real McCoy – the patriotic embrace of the motherland.

Wednesday 2 October

My last big speech to Legco. At 2.20pm we all – Lavender and half the private office team – piled into the Daimlers and headed for the Legco building. As ever, there were cameras and demonstrations outside. The main demo this year involved construction workers who want us to abandon our plans to tighten up safety on building sites, which they think will cost some of them their jobs.

I began by saying that even though there were only a few months left, we did not intend to go into hibernation. I quoted the American lawyer Justice Holmes, who had said, 'We must sail sometimes with the wind, sometimes against it, but we must sail and not drift or lie at anchor.' I then reported on how well we had done in meeting the goals that I set out in my very first address to Legco in 1992, listing area by area exactly what we had achieved. I started with schools, teachers, computers in classrooms and places at tertiary institutions. I went on to list all the things we had done for the disadvantaged and disabled. I went through our achievements in healthcare from hospital beds to new clinics. I ticked off a similar list of achievements in relation to housing, the environment and crime. I pointed out that while there were 50,000 Vietnamese migrants in 1992, the number had now fallen to 12,000. Then there were the infrastructure investments – the new airport, the container terminals, the first river trade terminal and our advanced telecommunications system. I also observed that we had further reduced corporate profits tax, raised the exemption levels of business registration and reduced other taxes as well. I pointed out that our tax rates were among the lowest in the world. 60% of the working population paid no salaries tax at all and only 2% paid tax at the hardly onerous top rate of 15%. For most people the tax burden was lower than in 1992.

I mentioned the preparations made for the transition. Hong Kong's success was the result of all of the hard work by the Chinese men and women who lived in the city. I argued that the freedoms we took for granted at the moment reflected universal values. Our GDP per head was today US$23,200, even higher than Australia, Canada and the United Kingdom. We were the eighth-largest trading community in the world. Since the signing of the JD, Hong Kong's GDP had almost doubled in real terms and fiscal reserves had increased six-fold. By the end of the present financial year our fiscal reserves would total almost HK$150 billion.

I referred to the work done in the Joint Liaison Group and set out how we had tried with our proposals on democracy, accountability and elections to meet the obligations and promises made in the JD and the BL.

Outlining our attitude to the provisional Legco, I quoted what the JD had to say about the UK's responsibility for the administration of Hong Kong before 1997 with cooperation promised by China. Noting that some people argued that democratization would go hand in hand with unaffordable welfarism, I said that we spent on welfare about the same as on perfume and cosmetics each year. Public spending had gone up considerably but was still only about 18% of GDP and represented a lower proportion for 1997 than in the early 1980s.

We were completing our programme of bringing all our laws into line with the Bill of Rights and the two international covenants on human rights which were part of the BL. Setting out what was required to continue our competitiveness, I finished with a checklist which the world could apply to see whether Hong Kong remained fundamentally the same place. It covered 16 questions that we should be able to answer, from autonomy and the rule of law to freedom of the press and due process in our courts. My peroration quoted Jack London's credo:

'I would rather be ashes and dust, I would rather my spark should burn out in a brilliant blaze, Than it should be stifled in dry rot. I would rather be a superb meteor, With every atom of me in magnificent glow, Than a sleepy and permanent planet.'

Finally, this:

'Whatever the challenges ahead, nothing, nothing, should bring this meteor crashing to earth, nothing should snuff out its glow. I hope that Hong Kong will take tomorrow by storm. And when it does, history will stand and cheer.'

And then of course, as always in Legco, there was complete silence. I sat down. I guess I should have known by now not to perorate in purple.

Friday 4 October

For the remainder of the week I did the follow-ups which have become part of the post-speech routine. There was a question and answer session in Legco, a big press conference and a phone-in programme, and of course a public meeting with about 600 in the audience. It was quite a cheerful occasion, probably my last public meeting in Hong Kong. I was mobbed when I left and must have given at least 100 autographs. Looking back, it's difficult to remember just what a culture shock it was when I started doing these meetings four years ago. How much things have changed since then. The political reactions were as frustrating as ever. I've done too much on democracy. I've done too little. I've done nothing on welfare. I've done too much. Why don't I just keep quiet about democracy? Why do I sound so defeatist about the future? Why do I paint such a rosy picture?

Why don't I realize that British colonial government did some dreadful things? Why am I so British? Why did I quote Jack London?

Tuesday 8 October

There have been a couple of quite big polls – one in the *SCMP* shows that my address has a higher score than last year's and that my personal rating has gone up from 62 to 67%. The same paper had a poll the following day which indicates that a majority opposes the provisional legislature; another majority thinks that nevertheless we should cooperate with it; and yet a third majority is strongly opposed to it amending the Bill of Rights. So that's clear then. I got some fair press in Britain, a much more mixed one in Hong Kong (which makes the poll findings even more interesting), and a very nice letter from Winston Lord in which he said that I proved I was neither a lame duck nor a Peking duck.

Best thing was a quiet dinner with Alice. Lavender had gone out to the ballet. Alice and I talked about how much you needed to know about art or music in order to appreciate them. She's excellent company. I haven't had a talk like that (except with Lavender) for ages.

Wednesday 9 October

I've spent much of this week giving interviews to journalists and businessmen. Sometimes I look at my poor private secretary, pen poised listlessly over the pages as he pretends to be interested in what I'm saying once again. It's the same spiel, the same anecdotes – a new order occasionally for a new audience. My office should have a code and give my stories and arguments numbers. 'Governor – three, five, seven, nine, six' et cetera.

I had a district visit to Eastern today. It's the biggest district in Hong Kong – home to about 650,000 people, including about 50,000 recent immigrants from mainland China. Since I came to Hong Kong, it has been transformed. The squatter settlements which used to cover the hillsides are now replaced by blocks of high-rise flats. I had tea with a group of recent immigrants in a local café, where we eat delicious sugary buns and drink horrid sugary stewed tea. Then I emerged to a street packed with people. There must have been well over a thousand all pressing forward for a handshake or an autograph. I get worried about people's safety as we go on a walkabout with a squad of photographers shoving and pushing their way through the crowds. All this celebrity-spotting stuff will probably build up as we get closer to next June, unless the choice of a Chief Executive switches the spotlight completely to him or her, but I slightly doubt it. I assume the economic situation is helping to sustain an increase in the enthusiasm for the last Governor. Inflation is down. Unemployment is down. The Hang

Seng Index is booming. Crime is lower than it was 10 years ago. So much for catastrophe and a helicopter from the roof of Government House, as Max Hastings lugubriously warned.

Thursday 10 October

I spoke at lunchtime to the collected Chambers of Commerce – about 300 people or more at the Grand Hyatt. Without actually rubbing their noses in some of the nonsense their spokesmen have spouted (suborned by the United Front), I went through the fallacies which some in the business world have espoused but which – I argued – I can't for a moment believe represent the overall business view. What are the main fallacies? That the economy needs a 'kick-start' to revive it. That it's overregulated. That we are turning Hong Kong into a welfare state. That the rule of law doesn't really matter. Then I say how important it is for business leaders to speak up for Hong Kong's autonomy. Jimmy McGregor, a brave and independent-minded and genuinely liberal member of Legco who was a victim of the transformation of the General Chamber of Commerce into a United Front organization and was kicked off its board, is delighted with the speech. The chairman, James Tien, and the director, Brigadier Ian Christie, look rather sheepish and have some trouble finding anything to criticize. Christie is a real chump, a retired soldier who makes you wonder how we've ever won a war.

Friday 11–Sunday 13 October

Lord MacLehose is staying with us for a short visit and came with us to a party for Clare Hollingworth's 85th birthday. Talking to her about Second World War novels, I mention Olivia Manning. Clare says that she had once sacked Manning when she worked for Clare as a stringer on the *Daily Express*. We give my predecessor a good tour of everything that's happening in Hong Kong, a great deal of which was started by him. He tells me that he is pleased with what he's heard about the quality and morale of the police and civil service, but he's very concerned at the number of officials the Chinese are clearly intending to send to Hong Kong. After a trip we arranged for him around the territory by helicopter, he came back excited by all he's seen. 'All those things we dreamed about, all those things we were told were impossible, rising from the ground.' He told Lance, my ADC, who went with him, that while he didn't share my views or my way of expressing them, he was impressed by the way people regarded me and by how I'd managed to get things done. He's a dignified and gentlemanly figure. We just come from different generations and different backgrounds.

Monday 14 October

There have been two great stories in the British press this week. First, there's one in *The Times* suggesting that the government may look again at the quarantine regulations for dogs. The present ones involve locking up pets travelling back to the UK for months to protect it allegedly from rabies. Lavender and I are quoted attacking the existing controls as preposterous. The fate of Whisky and Soda looms large in the story. Kerry gets calls all day from British media and television programmes asking me to give my views. Kerry said it's the greatest display of British interest in anything I've ever said! So much for the place of Hong Kong in the pecking order of issues back home.

The second great story, which comes out of Andrew Neil's autobiography serialized in the *Daily Mail*, is that Rupert Murdoch doesn't like me because he thinks I am screwing up his business interests in China. Andrew Neil has interviewed me for an article for a magazine and told me that I can add Conrad Black to the list of press barons who can't stand me. At last, I have found a nasty Canadian.

Thursday 17 October

Qian Qichen has trampled all over the JD and the BL in an interview in the Asian *Wall Street Journal*. He says that there will be no vigil to commemorate 4 June after 1997 and no one will be allowed to criticize Chinese leaders. These things may not be against any particular law but they won't be allowed. There can't be any pretence that he didn't really say all this. The text printed in the paper was translated from the original by Chinese Foreign Ministry officials. There has been a lot of to-ing and fro-ing with London about what sort of protest we should make. Malcolm agreed to send a personal message himself to Qian. The first draft we see is robust stuff, then the usual watering down began. There was a typically pusillanimous telegram from the Beijing embassy, where the official who deals with Hong Kong normally appears to take the Chinese position on any delicate issue. References to the need not to spoil the atmosphere ahead of the visit to London by Li Lanquing made their first appearance. After a struggle, we got a reasonable draft agreed. But it's a bore, not least since we are also fighting Beijing and London about our proposal to go ahead unilaterally with legislation on the so-called Basic Law article 23 offences – treason, sedition, subversion and secession, plus bills on official secrets and telephone tapping. We're getting a large bucketful of London at its worst, second-guessing everything we want to do. The Hong Kong department – Sherard – is on the phone every five minutes sending new lists of questions, drafting telegrams which ministers tick through late at night, putting his arguments in their name. It's draining and bad for morale. The Governor is now home in London. The FCO suggest we are getting hysterical and imply that officials are swept along by the Governor's political will and charisma. Actually, we've wrung our hands for months before coming to these collective conclusions. London officials don't seem to understand that it's not just the Governor and FCO diplomats here who are concerned, but senior Hong Kong government officials who are starting to notice what they regard as a drift away from serious efforts to stand up for Hong Kong. Anson and her colleagues observe what is happening with more than raised eyebrows.

There are now some twists and turns in the CE race. The retired judge Simon Li, who helped to assess public opinion in the late 1980s and concluded that Hong Kong didn't want democracy and more directly elected legislators, has thrown his wig into the ring. He has Stone Age views and is very cross with Britain for not giving him a K despite all his lobbying. At the same time T. S. Lo has announced that he is pulling out of the race. Like for like, loser for loser. Another candidate has joined as well – Peter Woo, a very rich businessman who is married to one of Lavender's golf partners, Bessie, one of the daughters of the late shipping tycoon Y. K. Pao. Peter is not going to win, but I doubt that he wants to hear that.

Friday 18 October–Sunday 27 October

London and Scotland. This has turned into one of my most exhausting trips home, or maybe I'm just getting older. The first Monday began with Sue Lawley and *Desert Island Discs* and went on later in the day to meetings with Malcolm Rifkind and John Major. Sue Lawley conducted a surprisingly political and aggressive interview, but choosing the music has been great fun. Malcolm had been strongly briefed by officials to be unhelpful but – while largely ignoring their steer – gave me a rigorous and perfectly fair workout. We've got most of what we wanted; for example, trying to push on ahead with legislation on official secrets and article 23 of the BL on treason, sedition and so on, though leaving some space between these matters and the visit early in November by Vice Premier Li Lanqing. On interceptions, Malcolm is worried about us going further in Hong Kong than the law in the UK, but it's left open. For me what is important is judicial oversight of our decisions. The PM, on what is a busy day for him just before the Queen's Speech debate, spends 45 minutes going through our Hong Kong agenda. It went well. He was on very relaxed form, charming my entourage before the meeting. We talked on our own and gossiped a bit about politics. The economy is looking better. He seems at ease with himself. I wish the same could be said of the Conservative Party. With the Home Secretary, Michael Howard, we do Chinese asylum seekers (on which I think he will be helpful), Vietnamese refugees and the ethnic minorities. Afterwards, privately, he made it pretty clear that he doesn't think that Ken Clarke is being very helpful about a single currency. Since this is an issue for the next Parliament at the earliest, it seems to me that the priority should be to get through on this contentious question in as good shape as possible. I don't think that Michael would necessarily disagree with this.

I gave yards of speeches in London, Edinburgh and Glasgow, the main one of which was the annual Hong Kong Trade Development Council dinner. In the margins of this event I spoke to Michael Jones, who makes the rather obvious point that I wouldn't find a return to British politics a doddle. So I notice!

Saturday 26 October

We got back to Hong Kong, and while I've been away Anson has made a statement that she wasn't herself going to run for the CE post but that she and the civil service would serve happily under a Chief Executive who met a number of criteria, such as standing up for Hong Kong's freedoms and the promises set out in the JD. It was a good, brave statement, typical of her. She could have finished after stating her own position but she went on with a page of her benchmarks for the Chief Executive.

My main worry this week has been that C. H. Tung is sounding more and more hardline. Is this show or is it for real? He has just worried an American civil liberties campaigner, who has given him occasional advice over the years, by sounding so tough, saying that the new government will need to use the provisional legislature to put through tough restrictive legislation on civil liberties as soon as possible. When Anson spoke to Tung recently, he said that he wanted to keep her and Donald if he wins. He thought we needed a provisional Legco before next June, but apart from requiring it to help set up the Court of Final Appeal he didn't seem to know why it was necessary.

Thursday 31 October

We are in the middle of two or three bellyaching episodes of Somme-type diplomacy with London. It's a toss-up whether we have more difficulty with FCO officials or with Chinese apparatchiks in the JLG. London seems intent, if it can be managed, on clawing back the decisions which went against officials at my meeting with Malcolm on official secrets and on the treason and subversion proposals. Alan Paul has had a meeting with his JLG opposite number about official secrets in which the Chinese assured him that they were anxious to make progress. London regards this as a 'very hopeful' sign. There will shortly be pleas for postponement of final decisions on unilateral action so that more time can be devoted to seeking an agreement. We've been here of course before – again and again. London officials are also much distressed that the UN Human Rights Committee in Geneva, which has just conducted a further hearing on Hong Kong's compliance with the International Covenant, is suggesting that we have a legal obligation to press China after 1997 to report on compliance, and perhaps, if China won't do so, Britain should. Oh, what horror – a legal obligation! Not just moral or political waffle which will enable us to wriggle and run, to wash our hands of Hong Kong. FCO lawyers seem to be all of a heap. What exactly does it mean when we say that the JD is legally binding – on whom exactly to do what? And what if the legal bonds are snapped by one party? These are always the points that are obfuscated. Even if we have no legal obligation, the offer to report on non-compliance should things go wrong seems to me quite an attractive option which we shouldn't throw away without a political judgement. After all, the Prime Minister and Foreign Secretary have talked about 'exploring every legal avenue' if China appears to break its word under the JD.

Friday 1 November

Lavender and I went to a 'lump in the throat' evening with the Gurkhas at their camp at Shek Kong. They have been part of the history of Hong Kong for years. They leave in the middle of the month and are beating the retreat for the last time in Hong Kong. As dusk fell over the Chinese hills, a pipe and brass band played all the old favourites. We finished up with a speech by me, the playing of 'Sunset' as the flag is lowered, and a lone piper playing a lament. There were wickedly strong champagne cocktails in the mess afterwards; I try to stick to beer.

Wednesday 6 November

President Clinton was re-elected yesterday and in London the Prime Minister made all the right points to Vice Premier Li about the provisional Legco during the course of a good-natured meeting. Hezza seemed to be rather cross about the strength of the PM's briefing for this meeting, warning that we shouldn't put at risk the gains in trade made recently. FCO officials are keen to pass this on to us. Fact – exports to China fell 25% in the four years before I arrived in Hong Kong to wreck all our exporting prospects. Fact – exports to China rose by 75% in the four years since then. What does this prove? Not much. Only – maybe – that kowtowing doesn't make much difference.

Friday 8 November

At one of our Ad Hoc meetings, the members of the group looked at the timetable for introducing our bill on treason and related issues. We've agreed that as there seems to be a better chance of getting agreement on official secrets legislation, we should do that before taking a unilateral step on treason which could immediately scupper an agreement on the other. Yet we can't give ourselves too much time because we want to get this unpleasant stuff on the road well before a Chief Executive is selected.

A meeting with and dinner for the visiting Swedish Prime Minister, Göran Persson, who has just discovered in China how difficult it is to strike a balance between cuddling up to Beijing to try to win trade while satisfying his domestic press and voters on human rights issues.

Sunday 10 November

Lavender and I went with Lance in his full ADC kit complete with feathered helmet for our last Remembrance Sunday in Hong Kong. Bands, judges in scarlet, Exco and Legco members (not many), veterans, consular corps, poppy wreaths. We pledge 'never to forget' against the background hum of Hong Kong. And next year?

At lunch I injudiciously asked Alice whether she has decided yet about the university to which she wants to apply. During her visits in the summer I know that she found Oxford 'rather quaint' but very much liked Queens' College at Cambridge. They have their own theatre. I think part of her concern is that I might in some way influence an Oxford college to take her. Little does she know. Any suggestion of this, indeed any wafer-thin reminder of our relationship, would backfire with atomic force!

Tuesday 12 November

Although I'm only just back from London I had to go off again on the evening of Remembrance Sunday, this time to speak at the CBI conference in Harrogate on 11 November and then to visit Paris and Bonn. I enjoyed my first Eurostar trip to Paris, where I made a speech at the embassy and had a number of meetings with ministers and politicians. The Premier, Edouard Balladur, whose face gutters down into his suit like a melting candle, predictably asked whether anyone will be prepared to do anything to help Hong Kong if it jeopardizes their trade with China. This is done with a sad shrug about the ways of the world, but at least it's honest. The

Foreign Minister, Hervé de Charette, tested my Francophile sentiments by complaining about Hong Kong's ad valorem tax on wines and spirits. He said (I tell myself nervously that it must be a joke), 'Human rights are one thing, but the sale of cognac . . .' He was entirely noncommittal about whether or not he will support allowing visas for access to SAR and BNO passport holders. He wants me to press Britain to take the lead in the annual ritual of condemning China in Geneva for its human rights record. I think it would be rather difficult to do this in April and then applaud Hong Kong's return to China in July. I somehow think that this must have some relationship to Chirac's state visit to China in May!

My most interesting meeting was with the former president, Giscard d'Estaing, who was as courteously *de haut en bas* as ever. He began by saying that he'd recently been to Bath, recalled our past meetings, quizzed me gently about my Irish ancestry and my Catholicism, and conferred worldly advice of no special perceptiveness about China, to which he is a regular visitor. One of the 'old friends', I think. While there are no particular insights, the language and the performances, as the French might say, 'ça vaut le détour'. He is like a cardinal, wand thin, beautiful hands, old-fashioned suit and laced black brogues, a few strands of hair combed back hard from his high raised forehead. El Greco would have enjoyed painting him. Definitely a great patrician figure – but I'm not surprised that he wasn't re-elected.

Thursday 14 November

I gave a speech in Bonn yesterday to the main CDU think tank. The prevailing mood in Germany, as in France, seemed to be to avoid boat rocking in case China's golden favours were withdrawn. But I had a wonderful meeting with Chancellor Kohl today. It was supposed to last for 35 minutes but, despite periodic attempts by his secretary to end it, it went on for 2¼ hours. He listened patiently to what I had to say about Hong Kong and China, but most of his own remarks were about other Europeans, including John Major and the British royal family, and about how to manage a party. He has a habit of generalizing from very good anecdotes. In one, he told the Polish Interior Minister in Jaruzelski's time that he couldn't depend on the police to keep the people down in the wake of the Pope's visit to Poland because, when those same policemen went home for supper and bed, they were clambering under the sheets with wives who had spent the day either kneeling in church or on the cobbles waiting for a blessing from the Holy Father as he passed by. He also told me that he had asked Li Peng why he had ordered the massacre in Tiananmen Square. Li had lost his temper. 'It wasn't just me,' he said. 'I can prove it. I'll show you television film and documents.' Kohl politely declined. When he took me to the door at the end of our marathon meeting, he saw some officials waiting, including Herr Tietmeyer from the Federal Bank. He pulled me back from the door saying, 'If I'd known they were all waiting, I'd have gone on for longer.' I flew back from Berlin to London, did a rather tired interview for *Panorama* on quarantine, and then hopped on the plane for Hong Kong.

Friday 15 November
I got a quick briefing from Bob, Martin and Edward on what's been happening. C. H. Tung has all but won the CE race – 206 nominations (out of 400) in the first ballot with T. L. Yang and Peter Woo far behind and Simon Li eliminated. After going to an early evening Beating the Retreat by the police at Aberdeen, we went back to welcome a visit from Margaret Thatcher. She has just been in China, where she's made a brave speech at an *International Herald Tribune* conference calling for the release of Chinese dissidents and for China to keep its word on Hong Kong. Our late-night drinks with her were very jolly until I mention seeing Chancellor Kohl. This set her off on a diatribe about Europe and its history which neither Germany nor France came out of well. At the end she turned on Lavender and says to her rather fiercely, 'And you've bought a house in France.' This is clearly regarded as some sort of act of treason. Her admirable major domo, Julian Seymour, cut in, saying, 'But, Margaret, Peter Lilley, one of your closest political friends, has not just bought a house in France, he's bought a château.' She paused for a moment and then replied, 'But it's in *northern* France.'

Monday 18 November
We have finally reached agreement with the Chinese on the Official Secrets Bill. Can we now pocket that (as they'd say in the FCO) and go ahead with the treason and sedition legislation unilaterally, without Beijing going back on the Secrets agreement? I dare say we'll spend all week arguing this through with London. We do. Sherard and his colleagues are incorrigible and try at every stage to unpick the agreement I had with Malcolm.

Wednesday 20 November
There has been an appalling fire in Kowloon. Lance and I went to the scene as soon as we heard in the evening and the area of Kowloon, known as Jordan, looks as though it's been the scene of a battle. There are fire engines, police, ladders, hoses, emergency radio vans, TV lights and crowds held back behind barriers. The burned-out building itself looks like any other 20-odd-year-old building in Hong Kong. I'd guess about

15 storeys, undistinguished slab concrete, the windows and surrounds now blackened by smoke, which was still belching out of the upper floors. I splashed through water and was jostled through cameramen to get an impressive briefing from the chief fire officer. The fire service in Hong Kong was the first to be localized. It's a very competent and well-led force. The guess is that the fire started in the lift shaft; engineers had been repairing the lift and some sparks from the welding probably ignited rubbish at the bottom of the shaft. The fire then spread rapidly through the department store on the bottom four floors and was sucked up by the lift shaft, mushrooming out with terrifying effect on the upper floors. About 80 people have been taken to hospital. I went on to the Queen Elizabeth Hospital, swarms of press, large teams of doctors coping with burns and smoke victims, distraught relatives. They were unsurprisingly stunned, incoherent with grief and shock. They look poor, giving the lie to the average per capita GDP figures in Hong Kong. Most of the casualties I saw were young women – a lot of them worked for a paging company in the building.

Thursday 21 November

I'm told that at least 40 people may have died. The fire and police services are now combing the still smouldering building and finding charred corpses. Such a horror. I am black with depression. Hong Kong has a First World economy but we stagger from one Third World horror to another. In this case, the building of course had no modern fire preventing equipment like sprinklers. Ever since the last big fire in commercial premises two years ago, we have been trying to beef up the safety regulations and introduced a bill into Legco in May to tighten things up. Needless to say, one or two of those who call themselves liberals – especially Selina Chow, who represents the retail functional constituency, and Ronald Arculli, who represents property – have been asking questions about the additional costs we are imposing on commerce. The fire wouldn't have been prevented even if we had got the legislation through by now, and it will take years to deal with all our other buildings, but this is a typical bit of Hong Kong politics. Efforts to give Hong Kong the civilized standards we require are denounced as drags on our competitiveness and as examples of my Fabian socialism. We've been through all this with our attempts to improve Hong Kong's dreadful industrial-safety record. No wonder some people argue that this is a city grown rich on tragedy. When I went to Legco to answer questions, many of them now about the fire, the whole weight of discussion had swung from 'Why are you rushing and aren't you asking businesses to do too much?' to 'You must do more straight away.'

In the JLG, Alan Paul, the extremely competent deputy to Hugh Davies, has a complete stand-off with his Chinese opposite numbers on the Crimes Ordinance on sedition, treason and so on. They simply read out the 'get stuffed, it's none of your business' statement that they delivered when we last spoke to them in early October. Everyone agrees that we should go ahead with the bill and we draft a strong telegram. At the end of the week, we had a telegram from Malcolm Rifkind saying he supports our line and can go ahead. I really resent the way in which officials have stoked up this issue, just as they did with the negotiations last year over the Court of Final Appeal, so that it may put a strain on my relations with ministers.

Monday 25 November

We have started discussing guest lists for the handover. I really don't want to have to spend time dealing with this. What happens about wives? What about bodyguards? What about former diplomats like Percy Cradock? And so on, and so on. I'm looking forward to passing the buck comprehensively on all these important decisions in an implacably irresponsible way to those who have had years of training on how to decide them. To think that when he was Viceroy in India Lord Curzon used to supervise the placement for dinners and durbahs.

Tuesday 26 November

After a discussion in Exco we announced we are going ahead with the Crimes Ordinance which meets the obligations under article 23 of the BL. The United Front lay into us but the lawyers and the Democrats are strongly onside, and the reporting in the international press reflects this.

Tuesday 26 November–Sunday 1 December

Lavender and I have had three hectic days in Tokyo and Osaka and a fine Saturday doing Kyoto in a day, rather in the manner of Japanese tours of the world. I saw much of the political establishment: Prime Minister Hashimoto, the Foreign Minister, the Finance Minister, the Minister for International Trade and Industry, former prime ministers and the opposition leader. The meetings all took a predictable course. We exchange pleasantries through an interpreter, then I do my bit in interpreter-sized gobbets, and then my interlocutor – having listened politely – gives a reaction which usually contains a recognition of Hong Kong's success, its importance to Japan (there's Japanese investment equivalent to US$20 billion dollars in the city) and finally a mild scepticism or at least the need to be convinced about Hong Kong's future. Hashimoto is an interesting man who looks a bit sharp with an Elvis haircut and sideburns. He complained that his brief on the subject of visas and SAR passports is incomprehensible but gave me the assurance I need that SAR passports will be treated differently from and better than the PRC ones. A string of interviews, breakfasts, lunches, dinners and speeches. They know Hong Kong pretty well; they will be helpful in a quiet way; but they have no illusions about the way that China is likely to behave. We spent a ridiculously short time in Kyoto on a perfect autumn day. Everything was a blaze of colour – yellow ginkgo trees in the streets and bright-red maples in the formal gardens.

Monday 2 December

When I got back Anson wanted to talk to me about relations with the CE and the next administration. She may have been worried about how far I am prepared to cooperate. I make clear that I'm not prepared to be completely bypassed in any dialogue; though much of the detail can be sorted out with officials, C. H. Tung (we all assume it will be him) will have to talk to me about the broad thrust of our approach to his incoming team, as well of course as the 101 housekeeping issues that need to be resolved. I agree with Anson that we should offer good office staff to the CE elect. I made it clear that we can offer support in preparing policy, but we can't assist with drafting of any legislation which will be considered before 30 June and I don't expect to be involved in discussion about anything that will be done after the handover. I want to discuss how we can minimize friction between us, whether we can coordinate our programmes at all, whether C.H. will travel at least to Washington, Tokyo and London (he should), the arrangements for the handover ceremony, and the detailed household and housekeeping matters that will need to be resolved. I asked Anson to let me have a detailed paper on all this prepared and agreed by Nicholas Ng, the Secretary for Constitutional Affairs, Bob Peirce and Martin Dinham.

Tuesday 3rd December

After what has been a reasonably placid period we are suddenly facing an unnecessary firestorm over the British Nationality Selection Scheme [BNSS], introduced with the intention of preventing panic in, and mass migration from, Hong Kong after the Tiananmen massacres. This allowed the Governor to approve applications for passports from certain classes of permanent residents which would give them, if they wished, the opportunity to become registered as British citizens. The scheme covered about 50,000 heads of households with an additional 90,000 or so who were family members. The Chinese have always hated it, both because of its origins and because it has given an escape route to so many well-qualified Hong Kongers. Now the Chinese have suddenly made a fuss about this saying that they won't recognize that anyone ethnically Chinese is a British citizen unless they can prove that they have acquired their passport by living in Britain. This looks like an attempt to define to whom we can give citizenship. It raises a very difficult consequence, that is whether a British citizen who has dual nationality (in our view but not China's) can receive formal protection from a British consulate. Today, perhaps inadvertently, the Consulate in Hong Kong and the FCO in London put out a wishy-washy statement which makes it look as though people who are British nationals in Hong Kong won't get full consular protection after 1997. It takes outrage from Anson, Donald Tsang and the general Hong Kong public and furious phone calls from us to London to get a statement issued putting this right and making clear that we will of course continue to give protection after 1997 to anyone holding a BNSS or any other British passport.

Thursday 5 December

I had to go down to Legco to make a statement and answer questions for an hour about BNSS. I hammered away at the basic points. The BNSS passports are the same as any others. Even if we can be convinced that a British passport holder does have dual nationality, and that we cannot therefore offer formal protection, that does not mean that we will not offer any protection at all. Chinese nationality law, when aggressively asserted, already creates consular problems in China, and if the Chinese behave similarly in Hong Kong there will be a string of consular arguments with other countries as well as Britain. I flourish passports, wax indignant, and argue with as much passion as I can summon. I hope it does a bit of good, though it may be difficult to get the horse back into the stable. The situation isn't helped by the fact that an unnamed Chinese official is quoted in the papers saying that China will find out who has BNSS passports and deal with them in due course: chilling but believable. For those, not least among our most loyal supporters, who have doubts about how much faith they can place in British honour and promises, this has been a confirmation that they are perhaps right.

After a big reception at GH for 150 or so civil servants who have received 'best service' awards in their departments, we had dinner with Mike and Judith Hanson. Mike is about to leave Hong Kong and rejoin the civil service back in the UK. He is pretty demob happy. He assumes the worst, and that C.H. and Anson will be dispatched once they've served their time. The smart money, Mike says, is then on C. Y. Leung, a mildly sinister, long-time communist trustie here. Maybe Mike is just too cheerfully gloomy. He's been a great friend and was like a rock as my information coordinator during the hottest times from 1992 to '94. He never blinked and never lost his cool or his sense of humour. They are a grand couple and we will all miss them.

Friday 6 December
I said goodbye to Rod Eddington, who has been running Cathay Pacific. He is going back to his home in Australia to run the second airline there, Ansett. He will be a loss, a very smart Australian who was once a physics don in Oxford. He is also a very good cricketer. Rod says that his departure has nothing to do with the deal with Citic and the Chinese aviation authority which has given them a big stake in Cathay and Dragonair (the other airline owned by Swire's) at a sweetheart price. Maybe not. His boss, Swire's taipan, Peter Sutch, was named businessman of the year the other day for apparently placing Cathay skilfully before 1997 with one foot in China's commercial camp. I'm not sure myself whether the foot was placed or dragged! Time will tell whether Swire's strategy of trusting China is more sensible than Jardine's of not trusting China further than you (or the Chinese) can spit. Rod has been the best Swire's man here.

Saturday 7 December
Lavender and I attended the opening ceremony of the International Day for the Disabled. Harry Fang, who is Anson's uncle, the head of her clan, and a distinguished doctor who looked after Deng Xiaoping's son after he was defenestrated in the Cultural Revolution and left disabled, made a very kind and complimentary speech about the things that Lavender and I have done for the disabled and other needy groups. We then had a Christmas party for 100 or so disadvantaged kids, including the ones who were burned in the hillside fire earlier this year. Lavender has organized this brilliantly. Andy Lau comes to sing. There is a magician. Kerry dresses up as Santa Claus.

Sunday 8 December
Jonathan Dimbleby is here to do more filming and has dinner with us. A great blast of fresh air from London.

Monday 9 December
Lavender and I went to Kowloon for a moving ceremony to commemorate the fireman who died in the building disaster the other day. The hearse was an old fire engine, piled high with flowers. The police band played a slow march. There was a big photograph of the good-looking dead hero on the front of the hearse, and his coffin – wrapped in the Union Flag – was at the

back, surrounded by firemen. A squad of fire service officers in their big wellingtons marched either side in escort. One by one we walked forward to place wreaths in front of the hearse. Behind the cortège, the family, many dressed in Buddhist funeral white, watched and wept.

In the evening there are two marvellous events. First, we held a reception for one of Lavender's favourite small charities, Dr Dog, which encourages pet owners to take their creatures on morale-raising visits to hospitals, old people's homes and so on. 'Soda' Patten stars on this circuit. We went straight from there to a packed Catholic cathedral for the consecration of two new bishops for the diocese, one – Father Zen – is to be Bishop Coadjutor, which means that he will pretty well automatically succeed Cardinal Wu, the wise and stately figure with a face like a Big Apple, who has led the church here for over 20 years. There must be about 250,000 local Chinese Catholics (about half the total Christian community) in Hong Kong and getting on for another 140,000 Filipina domestic helpers. The church is very active in health and education provision, and a high proportion of senior civil servants are Catholics, Anson and Donald for example, and several politicians too. The church has to manage its relations with two sister churches in China – the patriotic church (state-controlled and therefore not in direct communion with Rome) and the underground church (persecuted, from time to time, by the authorities). Both are growing fast. The ceremony itself was spectacular and moving, about three hours long. Bishop Zen made a witty and moving speech at the end, partly about unity with the church in China, which brought things to a forward-looking and confident conclusion. At the end, as the line of priests rolls by, they shook my hand warmly one by one; many are old friends from parish and welfare visits. The day ended a lot more cheerfully than it began.

Wednesday 11 December

The big day of C. H. Tung's election (with Chinese characteristics). As it has crept up on us there has been more and more concern expressed, at least privately, about whether C.H. is really going to be his own man or whether he will be imprisoned by the Chinese communists in their own system from the start. The election committee is made up of 400 toadies, timeservers, tycoons, and members of the just keeping their noses clean brigade. Qian made a little speech in Mandarin welcoming this first step along the road to democracy in Hong Kong! Those who can understand him clap dutifully in the right places, and the others try to come in as quickly as they can. Then the voting started and C.H. wins by almost too much – he gets well over 300 votes. T. L. Yang and Peter Woo are miles behind. C.H. handled his victory – speeches, questions and so on – very well. I spoke to him on the phone after lunch and also sent a letter. He responds in a friendly way, recognizing that Hong Kong is mine to govern until the end of June and indicating that he hopes to see me when he's gone through the bustle and formalities of the next few days. It's all perfectly cordial. My guess, however, is that he'll actually be in no great hurry to see me, and that will be the public impression. Let's see.

There was one slightly unfortunate hitch in the proceedings. As the final vote was cast the organizers suddenly realized that the votes added up to 401. Lu Ping's face went pale. Would the whole thing be discredited as a cock-up? He was saved by C. Y. Leung, vice chairman of the selection committee, who declared that he'd seen a woman whose job was to keep a tally double-counting one vote. And with that, before any questions could be asked, the organizers of this first communist step in democracy in Hong Kong swept up their papers and fled the hall.

'When are they going to meet?' That is going to be the question until we do actually sit down together. C.H. will be under a lot of pressure to give me as little 'face' as possible. But what the hell. I'm certainly not going to run after him. His nice wife, Betty, turned up at a lunch which Lavender gave for the wives of the whole consular corps. She is very gracious and complimentary, and gave Lavender a handsome shawl and a kind letter. Lavender and I are both a little preoccupied with Alice's interviews at Cambridge (to read French and Spanish), where she has been this week. I hope that Queens' College will like her even a fraction as much as we do.

Saturday 14 December

The disbandment parade of the Hong Kong Military Service Corps, the only Chinese unit in the British Army. It's a sad occasion, and one stained by Britain's lack of generosity to these men. We haven't given passports to all who applied for them. Home Office honour doesn't run that far. It's no way to treat people who have been so loyal to Britain. At the insistence of members of the corps, we sang 'Abide With Me' and the national anthem. Then they marched off to whatever the future holds for them.

The European Council meeting in Dublin at the weekend has put out a statement supporting Hong Kong, including a sentence endorsing our representative institutions 'as already established'. This seems to be as near as we could get to them supporting the elected Legco. Apparently, Chirac wouldn't let them go any further. He has presumably got his state visit to China next May in mind. In addition, the French are trying to block the usual European support for a human rights resolution on China at Geneva. All this makes it slightly more difficult to swallow an attack in

Le Monde on Britain's handling of Hong Kong, saying that we will leave 'without glory'.

Thursday 19 December

C.H. has gone up to Beijing for the laying on of hands. I went on a cheerful district visit to Kowloon city, recorded my annual Christmas day music programme for RTHK and attended a pre-Christmas meeting and lunch, organized by Anson, with heads of department. I think she wants me to show them that I'm still alive and capable of kicking. I praised them for their work, noted the consequences of the selection of a Chief Executive, say that we have got to deliver good government right up to the handover because you can't switch public administration on and off like a car engine. I also remind them of our position on the provisional Legco.

Friday 20 December

There's a scathing editorial in the Chinese language *Economic Journal* (the best upmarket Chinese newspaper) taking C.H. to task for not saying anything substantial so far, for sounding like a mainland official and for refusing to commit himself to keeping all our senior officials in post. Anson is making it clear that she thinks it's important to reappoint all the senior officials even if some are later shifted. She worries about the effect on morale if the civil service gets the impression that political loyalties are what will count from now on in determining appointments. She notes wryly how many businessmen seem to think that I make all the appointments. The truth is that I've always left appointments largely to her or to David Ford.

C.H.'s office has phoned up to arrange a meeting and in London the FCO put out a statement on the provisional Legco making clear among other things that the process of selection for it can hardly be described as democratic. We won't allow it to undermine the government of Hong Kong before next June.

Saturday 21 December

Lavender and I went up to Fanling to open the flower bird, fish and insects show. Lavender used to do it on her own, but when I heard what fun it is I crashed her visits. It's a sort of Chinese version of a Wodehouse country flower and horticultural show. There are owls and snakes, tortoises and turtles, guppies and coral, orchids and bonsais; a glorious warm morning and huge fun. Kate and Laura came home this evening along with four of Lavender's nieces and nephews. Kate has got a job in TV and Laura has been given a contract at *Harper's*. I am so proud of how they have handled things while we've been in Hong Kong. All the girls are home for

Christmas. That's what really matters. Stuff the provisional Legco (rather a large number of whose members were defeated candidates in the 1995 elections for the real Legco).

Monday 23rd December

C.H. and I had an 85-minute talk in the afternoon on our own in my study. I began by setting out the arrangements we are happy to make to help the CE – office accommodation, staff – including a private secretary and an official at policy secretary level to coordinate preparatory work for the handover, a car and so on. I noted that we are already providing security (more than I get, actually). I also said that we'd like him to get in touch with the Chief Secretary and the Financial Secretary and individual policy secretaries to put in hand preparatory work. I told him that we've already prepared a big brief on every aspect of the government's work policies and problems and suggested he should sort out the details with Anson. I then made two points of principle. He knows our position on the provisional Legco that we can't and won't do anything to help it before the handover. As for legal drafting, we are not prepared to provide any help with bills that would be considered before 30th June but could do so for legislation that would be looked at after that date. We then had a rather repetitive exchange. He is impervious to the argument that the provisional Legco doesn't really have any work to do before July whatever the other arguments about its credibility. He's the same old C.H. He is perfectly likeable but his deeply conservative and anti-democratic views are probably rather more bolstered now than they were. It's clear that he will be Beijing's man while presenting a more acceptable face to Hong Kong for his communist bosses. Afterwards we went out and addressed a huge regiment of the media. I said that we had a good meeting. He said that he raised the question of the provisional Legco, hasn't been able to convince me to change my mind but will try again.

After that we had our usual annual carol concert, crowding around the big tree in the main hall led by the cathedral choir from St John's. I guess this may be the last carol concert here.

Tuesday 24 December.

On Christmas Eve I visited the civil servants in the constitutional affairs branch, whose party is held in the old colonial house in Kennedy Road where the JLG meetings happen. I was shown around the drab rooms where hours of drab meetings with Chinese officials take place. Despite these gloomy surroundings and duties, the CAB staff have a real esprit de corps. They have been led by decent, straight civil servants – first Michael

Sze and now Nicholas Ng – who have been under awful pressure to bend and trim but have declined to do so. We've been lucky to have them.

Thursday 26 December

We had a lovely Christmas, begun with a strange church sermon in rhyming couplets – 'And so, dear brethren, there's nothing stranger, than putting a baby in a manger' and so on. There has been a full house, lots of walks, too much food, some competitive tennis and a boat trip to Sai Kung.

Saturday 28 December

Anson has seen C.H. at his family home on the south of the island. He spoke of his optimism about China, which he foresees joining the G7 within 10 years. He wants Anson to stay on and doesn't want to replace anyone in our team of policy secretaries at present, but would obviously wish to see them all for himself. He is happy to take delivery of an office and staff and was grateful that I wasn't trying to make things more awkward for him. But he remained adamant about the provisional legislature – we should recognize it before 30 June – and is still talking about changing the Bill of Rights legislation. He didn't think that he would want to do the job for more than one five-year term and hoped that Anson would run for it after him. Many bridges and much water before then. Anson warned him against trying to do anything on the Bill of Rights before 1997. He said afterwards that he wants to retain the political neutrality of the civil service. Good.

Tuesday 31 December

New Year's Eve. Donald has had his meeting with C.H. He told the next CE how strong the economy is and set out his very modest budget proposals, envisaging a small tax and rates reduction and a whopping surplus of over HK$20 billion. C.H. said that he wants a Financial Secretary who is strong, by which he presumably means immune to commercial pressures. Donald faces opposition from three groups. First, Chinese officials don't much care for him because he was the civil servant who piloted through the British Nationality Selection Scheme. Second, United Front groupies don't like him because he's worked for the British. Third, some of the property developers and tycoons who form C.H.'s praetorian guard don't like him because of his toughness and determination. I tell him that he's only criticized by all these people because he's been doing his job well and with integrity.

The girls here headed off for various forms of midnight revelry. Lavender and I stayed in, had a quiet dinner, drank champagne and watched *Tin Cup*. There are 191 days to go. I will be counting.

Sunday 5 January 1997
C.H. has gone off to Beijing again. The main fruit appears to be an agreement that Beijing will pay for the provisional legislature before the end of July and that Hong Kong will repay the costs afterwards. How's that for a bargain? There's growing criticism of him, some saying that he is in Beijing too much. He appeared in a showbiz spectacular on TVB New Year's Eve spouting communist-sounding phrases. He makes it sound as though he's had to clear the appointment of Fanny Lau as his private secretary with Beijing.

Monday 6 January
Just before supper Alice got a letter from Cambridge. She went into our bedroom to open it on her own and we heard a little squeak of pleasure. She's got an offer from Queens' – three As required.

Geoffrey Howe and Bob Hawke are in town. Howe is clearly doing some work for Cable & Wireless, and Bob Hawke has all sorts of dubious interests here. Sadly, he knows rather a lot of seedy businessmen in Hong Kong. In an interview on the radio yesterday Geoffrey Howe called for compromise over the provisional legislature and said the people in Hong Kong should recognize the need for self-restraint and for not using the territory as a base for thwarting China. Today Bob Hawke told the radio audience that if Britain asks for international help in lobbying China over Hong Kong after July, no one will take any notice because they'll only be interested in trade with China. There's a pretty savage editorial later in the week in the *Asian Wall Street Journal* on Geoffrey, contrasting what he has said with what Anson and I have done and said.

Thursday 9–Thursday 16 January
I had to go back to London for the usual round of meetings and speeches. I had an awful cold, which wasn't improved by some foul-tasting herbal medicine that I was given by our director of health, Margaret Chan. I haven't seen any increasing disposition to say we've got it all wrong. My main lobbying has been focused on the question of passports, visa-free access and rights of abode for the ethnic minorities. The PM and Malcolm are onside; the blockage is of course Michael Howard. Even his Minister of State has apparently urged him to change course. I think he may be prepared to move at least on right of abode. He's an odd man, genuinely charming and kind in private, but unattractively narrow and hardline as a politician.

My meeting with Blair, Prescott and Cook was interesting. I tried to persuade them that it was unlikely that the handover would turn into the sort of foreign policy crisis they seem to fear in their early months of government. On the other hand, I said that they couldn't simply wash their hands of Hong Kong on 30 June and get on with building a more commercially successful relationship with China. Hong Kong issues would continue to cut across the China relationship, and the rest of the world (above all America) would be looking to Britain to put down markers if anything went wrong. I said that they wouldn't have to decide whether Tony Blair should attend the handover until May. I did not think myself that it would be too much of a risk.

I had lunch in the flat at No. 10 with John and Norma. He is trying to be helpful about ethnic minorities. We talked about domestic politics. What should he do if he lost? I said that the first thing that would happen would be that a delegation of grey-suited men would call on him. 'Yes,' said Norma, 'telling him to go?' 'No,' I said, 'telling him to stay – he's the only man who can unite the party – duty to see the party through a few difficult months – wait until an acceptable candidate emerged, et cetera et cetera.' 'Oh, no', said Norma. 'And what should I do?' asked John. 'Tell them to fuck off,' I replied. They both looked relieved. Both John and Norma were in excellent form. They look well, relaxed and happy. They have great strength of character, which has seen them through some hard times and they are both content to take whatever comes, confident that they have done their best. I have liked Norma more and more down the years; she's highly intelligent and astonishingly candid. She feels no pressure to pretend that she and John are other than they are, which is quite good enough, thank you very much.

Lavender and I ordered a car (a Volvo estate), more or less sold our flat to our next-door neighbours, and saw a house in Barnes that we greatly liked. We put in an offer. It would be so good to get that sorted out. The house has an Aga. What will Alice make of us acquiring a Volvo and an Aga? Can we handle the social statement this suggests?

Friday 17 January

Back in Hong Kong, the first meeting on the handover was about the ridiculously restrictive security arrangements being proposed by the police. They want to accredit, check out and give security badges to everyone with access to Tamar and the convention centre. That would mean about 30,000 people. They rather give the game away when the assistant commissioner speaks out on the importance of protecting guests from embarrassment. Chinese security already? I sent them away to think again. I'm not having Hong Kong turned into an armed camp on 30 June. What happens the next day is up to them.

I wasn't surprised when Jeremy Mathews, the Attorney General, later told me that he and the Director of Public Prosecutions watched the police video of the handling of a demonstration outside the convention centre at the time of the selection committee meeting there. They think the police were very heavy-handed with a small group of demonstrators and are not intending to prosecute. More sign of things to come.

C.H. has told one or two of our senior officials his choice of Exco. It includes four communists, and one guy, Paul Yip, whose background would set alarm bells ringing in every security agency in the world. C.H. has a gatekeeper called Andrew Lo who is helping to keep him away from the present civil service. We hear as well that a Preparatory Committee subgroup has proposed gutting the Bill of Rights, and reinstating some of the old colonial legislation, which limited the right to demonstrate and the activities of political groups. This legislation has not of course been used for years – if in some cases at all. At the very least there is bound to be a great deal of legal confusion. The JD and the BL state that the International Covenant on Civil and Political Rights (ICCPR) should be applied to Hong Kong. Yet what is being suggested now is that the Chinese would put back on the statute book laws which contravene the convention. This should certainly keep the courts busy. After a number of representations about his preferences for Exco members, it does seem as though C.H. may now be rowing back.

Tuesday 21 January

There's growing concern in the press about the threats to our human rights legislation. At Exco several members said that C.H. should get the Chinese to leave this issue to his administration after July. The main issue we discussed was housing. In our understandable response to the acute housing need of the 1940s and '50s, we set up a public housing authority on the model of municipal housing departments in the UK or, I guess, the Singaporean housing authority. We are now locked into a socialist housing policy which doesn't meet our needs. It is combined rather exotically with the dominance in the private sector of half a dozen big developers who control a large land bank and ensure that housing supply doesn't reduce prices or abate their rise. The result of all this is that despite high incomes, it's difficult for people to become homeowners, and if they are living in public flats there is no incentive for them to do so. Rents become politicized – tenants only pay about 9% of household income in rent, tenures are handed on from parents to children, and many of those who do buy privately sit tight on whatever public assets they might also have – between 12 and 14% of housing authority tenants own flats or property elsewhere. So really poor families find themselves on the waiting list for years, paying a higher proportion of their income on rotten private sector accommodation than is paid by often better-off tenants in heavily subsidized publicly owned property. The system leads to inequity and a huge misallocation of resources. I would have liked to have gone for some radical solutions years ago, but 1997 has always cast a shadow and now we are still looking at marginal adjustments to policy. And so it will go on.

Thursday 23rd January

Whisky has survived chewing a poisoned chicken bone on one of Lavender's favourite walks with him. What sort of malign individuals get their kicks out of trying to kill dogs?

Anson is off to the States. She will obviously have some difficulty dealing with the question of civil liberties when she is there. She phones me up just before she goes to tell me that the good news is that Paul Yip is not going to be on Exco; the bad news is that he is going to be named as a special adviser to C.H. I record one of my 'Letters to Hong Kong' in which I have another go on human rights.

Friday 24 January

I took the annual parade of the Correctional Services Department and then had to go to speak at the St Andrew's Society Burns Night dinner. There were five speakers and I was last up. All but the president's speech were filthy beyond measure. The room rocks to jokes about the most intimate sexual encounters and the lower regions of the body. No wonder no Governor has been for 30 years or more. I survive, managing to get through a more or less pubic hair-free speech and they give me a great ovation. I've now learned that provided you tell the Scots that they've done everything important in British history they appear quite content.

Saturday 25 January

I was woken up at 6.30 by a call from Lance to say that there's been a fire at a karaoke bar in Tsim Sha Tsui, a nightlife district in Kowloon. Fifteen people, mostly young, are dead. We had been planning a visit this weekend to Macau but we postponed our departure and drove over to the scene, then to the hospitals which have looked after the victims. It looks as though it was probably the result of arson, maybe a consequence of a Triad war. I spoke to the relatives at the hospitals. It's a harrowing experience. They are mostly parents about our age, with teenage kids. They are poor, battered, shocked. This is our third big fire disaster in less than a year. It's the worst part of my job, trying to take comfort to the ravaged.

Lavender is far better at it than I am. She never appears to be trying to get through it as quickly as possible, which is what I always feel I'm doing. What can you say – especially in a language which they don't understand? We still see the kids who were so badly burned in the country park fire last year. I find it easier to talk to them than to the bereaved.

Monday 27 January

An interesting talk with Sir Philip Haddon Cave, who was Financial Secretary and then Chief Secretary at the time of the Joint Declaration negotiations. He left in the mid-'80s and hasn't been back since then. He's a man of old-fashioned public service principle, repelled by the behaviour of other retired civil servants like Percy Cradock. He disliked the Foreign Office and didn't think they ever really understood the nature of colonial responsibilities. He believed that things really went wrong when the constitutional development of Hong Kong, planned by Teddy Youde in 1984–5, was aborted in 1987 with the phony consultation exercise which 'proved' that people didn't want a build-up in the number of directly elected seats in Legco until much later. This inevitably piled up trouble for the early '90s by which time – post-Tiananmen – China was more hostile to any faster democratic development. He says that Youde and Cradock got on very badly, partly chemistry, partly different views about our obligations to Hong Kong.

Tuesday 28 January

The chairman of the Bar Association, Audrey Eu, has written a withering letter to C.H. on human rights. The Bar's evidence to Legco called the proposal to amend the ordinances to seek to return them to their original shape an exercise in legal futility. Much the same points were made in a good Exco discussion, not least by Denis Chang, who referred as well to a speech by Zhou Nan to the provisional Legco in which he argued that Hong Kong would now be introduced to another legal tradition. This did not strengthen confidence in the future of the common law.

The Princess Royal has arrived to open the new consulate building. As ever, she's mastered her brief and works hard. She looks fit, dresses like a young headmistress, and doesn't tolerate an ounce of familiarity. As far as I'm concerned she behaves like 'royals' should. She is pre-eminently dutiful. At dinner, she cheered me up not least with a very funny story about how she was patronized during a recent visit to Delhi staying at the High Commission.

To be honest, I suspect that I'm also cheered in a perverse sort of way by the signs of the communists' behaviour. They're now doing what they wanted me to do on human rights, democracy and so on. How ghastly it would have been and what a mess would have resulted: a mess which would have brought obloquy down on our heads. Hong Kong deserved better than it is, I fear, likely to get.

Thursday 30 January

We've had a second Exco this week which was rather downcast. Jeremy Mathews, the Attorney General, said that the controversy over the legislation affecting civil liberties has shown the depth of commitment in the community to their adequate protection. He went on to note that it's encouraging so many people have been prepared to speak out even so close to the handover.

There's a mild fuss when one line in an interview I've given to AFP [Agence France-Presse] is ripped out of context and made to look as though it is an attack by me on Hong Kong's tycoons for betraying the community. Fortunately, Kerry – the Shane Warne of spin – deploys his arts with his usual skill and calms the whole thing down. I've really been lucky to have two terrific spokesmen in succession.

Saturday 1 February

Exactly 150 days to go. China's advisers on the Preparatory Committee have endorsed the decision to scrap the civil liberties laws and Alice has accepted her conditional offer from Cambridge.

Monday 3rd February

Anson has just got back from the US. She thinks it was very useful for her to be there to reassure people like George Shultz, George Bush, Bill Bradley and so on. There was a lot of concern about C.H. and what he was doing among his friends. Was he just a stooge for China? Anson appears to have done her best with the Americans, telling them that they must stay engaged and give C.H. fair advice. She's very much against his making an early visit to America, especially if he's just going to tell them to keep their noses out. Overall, she remains sparky even after a tough schedule and a long flight. Being told so often how vital she is for Hong Kong's well-being and success must be quite good for morale.

Tuesday 4–Wednesday 12 February

After going through some Chinese New Year rituals, handing out gifts to the children of the staff and recording a message for RTHK, we went off for a week's break to Bintan, an Indonesian island 40 minutes by fast ferry south of Singapore. We slept a lot and read a lot. I read *Heart of Darkness* largely because it is one of Alice's A level texts. I suppose one reason it has had such a following over the years is it was written at the onset of a century which demonstrated all too horribly his main thesis that civilization is a thin veneer over man's savagery. I read again recently some of Stefan Zweig's work which shows how that civilization was shredded in Europe. He should be known more widely in Britain.

Two bits of politics intruded. First, very early on the morning we were setting off, Martin phoned to say that he had a phone call in the middle of the night from the Home Secretary's private secretary to say that Michael Howard had seen the Prime Minister earlier in the day and had told him that he had decided to give the Hong Kong ethnic minorities full British nationality. A triumph – and a hat-trick! We have got passports for war widows and for the now ethnic minorities and visa-free access for SAR passport holders. It looks as though we will be able to sail away at the end of June without those stains on our record. It will be interesting to see how it's all reported. There is also a poll showing that, despite his honeymoon coverage, C.H.'s approval rating is well below mine. You have to be a PR genius to push the first local Chinese boss down below the last colonial oppressor within two months. It's a triumph for the Chinese understanding of politics.

Thursday 13 February

Before Malcolm Rifkind's meeting in Singapore with Qian Qichen and his visit to Hong Kong, FCO officials have produced a briefing which suggests that Tung's early days have gone pretty well and that Malcolm should negotiate a tolerable level of cooperation with the provisional Legco before 1 July. We agree that he should be told what is actually happening and that it would be intolerable if Hong Kong's senior civil servants were required to answer to the provisional Legco as well as to the real Legco before 1 July. Anson has had what she says is her best meeting with Tung, who confirms that he is going to reappoint all the principal officials. We will arrange for her to have a private meeting with Malcolm when he is in Hong Kong.

I'm told that Chancellor Kohl phoned President Clinton personally this week to try to get him to drop the annual motion criticizing China's human rights record at the UN Human Rights Commission. Presumably the Volkswagen sales department was in on the call.

Princess Alexandra has arrived the day before Malcolm. This will be her last visit to Hong Kong as Commandant General of the police. She has been a fantastic formal head of the police service. They love her to bits and she works incredibly hard whenever she is here.

Saturday 15 February

Malcolm had a long 'no progress' meeting with Qian yesterday. There was no give on their side and fortunately none on ours either. At least we haven't fallen into any of the elephant traps which London and our embassy in Beijing were so keen to dig for us. Malcolm is now in Hong Kong for a visit made more brief by the necessity of him returning to London for a vote on mad cows. Try explaining that to the Chinese. He never performs below par; he's always sharp, fluent and in intellectual command. I like and admire him the more I see him, and anyone whose best political friend is Richard Luce (now dispatched with plumes as Governor of Gibraltar) must be a good thing. He begins by having dinner with Anson, with whom he has an excellent talk and shows an accurate understanding on what is happening. Today he saw C.H., whom he thinks seems very self-confident, and tells him about his decision on reappointing senior civil servants. He has also seen both Exco and Legco. Exco gave him a rather gloomy readout, his fellow lawyers telling him that they fear that any change to the law on demonstrations is likely to lead to a challenge on the streets which will either show up the future government as toothless or else oblige it to be heavy-handed. At his closing press conference, the front row was composed of some of our most pessimistic foreign correspondents looking rather like the sinister birds in Hitchcock's film. Kerry always calls the most miserable of them 'the Laughing Cavalier'. They throw a lot of 'it will all end in tears' questions at him. Malcolm gives much better than he gets and leaves a few bloody noses behind. 'What do you suggest we should do that we're not doing already?' he asks to general silence.

Sunday 16 February

We gave a dinner for Malcolm and Princess Alexandra. Yeung Sum, one of the best and nicest of the Democrats, came with his pretty young wife. When I said that I'm looking forward to seeing her again with her young baby, she burst into tears. She is worried sick about the future. I imagine she is most concerned about what's going to happen to her brave and decent husband.

Tuesday 18 February

We discussed at Exco our proposals on phone tapping and suggested a system of judicial warrants to be contained in a so-called White Bill for public consultation. We're going to press forward when we can gauge reactions and see how the article 23 bill on subversion and secession goes.

There won't be much point in us pushing on with the ideas on interceptions if the other proposals are carved up in Legco by a combination of pro-Beijing legislators and liberal lawyers.

Wednesday 19 February

Rumours again that Deng is dead. Bob has phoned our embassy in Beijing, who report that there are no signs of an imminent Deng–Mao celestial meeting – no extra police on the streets, no solemn music on the radio. One of our senior officials, whom I invested with the CBE a few months ago, has suggested that, since a message for the disabled in our lifts is not yet available in Cantonese, we should stop the English message.

We also had a good district visit to Sham Shui Po in Kowloon. It's an old working-class area with a host of economic, housing and environmental problems. I'd been here last on an unpublicized visit to look at some black spots and I returned to the same block of really bad private housing that I looked at before. It's been tidied up a bit and the tenants are disarmingly grateful. But the conditions are still pretty awful. I climb up onto the roof and look across rooftops of similar buildings, covered in illegal shacks as though a raggle-taggle army had camped out on Kowloon's skyline. This is a long way from the marbled halls in mid-levels. Hardly surprisingly this district is a hotbed of political activism. The social problems find their safety valve in politics, petitioning, demonstrating, arguing – all pretty peacefully. When I see the problems in a place like this, it makes me realize how much Hong Kong needs another blast of social progress. I'd like to be building on what I started in 1992, which in some areas has only touched the surface of peoples' lives. I ran into a good-natured demo on the way into a shopping mall and I disarmed them by handing out the traditional New Year *lai see* packets. There is a mad scramble to get one of the little red envelopes, banners dropping as hands reach out for the packets. Edward heard a photographer on his mobile phone talking to his newsdesk. 'Did you get good photos of the demo?' he was asked. 'No – he started handing out bloody presents.'

Thursday 20 February

I was woken in the night by Kerry to tell me that Deng really has died; another triumph for our embassy's ear to the ground. None of us knows exactly how this will alter the balance in Beijing. How will he be judged? His opening up of China's economy was a spectacular achievement. But how do you weigh up the part he played in the anti-rightist campaign of the '50s and the Tiananmen killings? I turned on the BBC TV World Service first thing to see a bloated and aggressive Ted Heath lambasting

Martin Lee for believing in democracy and then going on to defend Tiananmen. What a despicable old bore he's become. I then went down to the New China News Agency headquarters in Happy Valley to sign the condolence book. Bob Peirce, who went with me, recalled the visit here by Percy Cradock and calls it our memorial visit. We are taken upstairs past mourning billionaires and their chauffeurs into a long room at the end of which, in front of a large photo of Deng and a mountain range of wreathes, stood Zhou Nan and three of his vice directors. I advanced with Bob and our director of protocol in tow, stopped, bowed three times to Deng's photo, exchanged grave words and handshakes (yes, they shook my hand) with Zhou and his buddies, turned on my heel and left.

Kerry tells me that C.H.'s office has demanded to see earlier articles written by foreign journalists who ask for an interviews before the request is accepted. Anson has been asked to find him a new office and house – he doesn't intend to live in GH because he doesn't like the feng shui.

Just before we said goodbye to Princess Alexandra and her husband, Angus Ogilvy, that evening, one of her policemen said to me, 'It's been really lovely; like spending a week with my favourite auntie.'

The reappointment of senior officials has been announced and gone down well. But the Paul Yip story is starting to emerge. No one quite says, 'this man is a Chinese agent', but they come close. It's pretty clear that he is Li Chuwen's man. Li is a sinister, urbane fellow with a spooky background, who posed as a Catholic priest in Shanghai back in the early days of the revolution in order to blow the whistle on genuine believers. Recently he's come out of semi-retirement as Jiang Zemin's eyes and ears in Hong Kong. A really bad man, I suspect, though sophisticated and intelligent.

David Ford is here and has had an argument at a dinner party with Michael Thomas, the former AG and the husband of Lydia Dunn. Michael Thomas thinks that we should have offered legal draughtsmen to C. H. Tung and argues with great passion that Hong Kong's success is all due to Chinese qualities and very little to Britain. The weather changes and the birds sing a new tune.

Friday 21 February

On the way to Exco, Lance said to me, '125 days to go.' He has his house and family in Canada to think about. Kerry had to go into hospital at the weekend. Early worries that he'd had a heart attack turned out to be untrue, thank heavens. But he's been under heavy pressure and was feeling the strain. He and his lovely wife, Jenny, think that come mid-year they may just head home to Sydney rather than stay on. Martin in my office is having terrible back problems and has had to go into hospital this week for traction. For all of us, time is almost up. We want to get on with the next stage of our lives, whatever it may be.

I gave a jolly lunch for our departing refugee coordinator and his wife. They are Irish and live near Sligo. He has necessarily had to spend a great deal of time dealing with civil liberties lawyers but doesn't resent it a bit. He has carried out a tough and unpleasant policy with competence and compassion. They are sailing home on the *Oriana*, which is a perk for retiring civil servants left over from the distant past. When his wife asked if they could be seated on a table without any other civil servants, they were told that everyone was asking for the same.

Wednesday 26 February

Michael Portillo, the Defence Secretary, is here for a brief visit. We know one another very well. I recruited him from Cambridge to the Conservative Research Department when I was director. He's clever and seems to be trying to re-invent himself as more right wing than he really is. We had a perfectly friendly discussion about the garrison and the handover. He told Lavender that it looks as though the ministers opposed to changes to the quarantine regulations will succeed in blocking any move towards liberalization before the election. Lavender's reaction prompts a mutter as he heads for the car that he is sorry he put his foot in it.

Our ambassador in Vietnam is staying so that we can say 'thank you' to him before he leaves his job and review what more can be done to deal with the migrant problem before the handover. What is remarkable is how many Vietnamese have passed through Hong Kong on their way to a new life – before being returned with difficulty to the old one. The figure must now exceed 200,000 and we are down to under 5000 still in Hong Kong. Over 15,000 went home last year. Many of those left are ethnically Chinese and, if the remaining problem is largely identified in this way, we should be reasonably well covered against criticism that we should take back to the UK any migrants left here at the time of the handover.

During the course of questions this week in Legco, I managed to get out a line which I've picked up from Bob. Hong Kong is a Rolls-Royce. C.H. and the Chinese are tinkering with the engine and trying to change the tyres. But all they really need to do is turn on the ignition and away she'll go. This week's metaphor takes the road.

We've published our proposals on phone tapping as a bill for consultation. There is to be a month's discussion time. We got ourselves into a silly position on this and will be criticized for not going straight for early legislation. Some assume that we are looking for ways of avoiding this bill.

It's the first time we have blinked so far as this legislative programme is concerned. Thank you, FCO.

Saturday 1 March

Martin has been in hospital for four days now. He's trying to cure the trapped nerve in his neck – if that's what it is – that's been giving him back and arm pains for so long. He is sedated in traction and having a ghastly and painful time. The treatment sounds medieval and is so far having bugger all effect. In the evening we went to the American Chamber of Commerce annual dinner and dance in the convention centre with 1200 cheerful Americans. AmCham [American Chamber of Commerce] have been much the most resolute members of the business community. They don't get too exposed on the more high-profile political issues, but they take a firm and eloquent line on corruption and the rule of law.

Monday 3rd March

Breakfast with C. H. Tung. He came in, smiling, his distinctive brush cut flattening the top of his head, his shoulders slightly hunched forward as he walked, giving him a very soft slippered glide. Affable, all-American. Well, probably ex-American now. It's a country for which, I am told, most of his family have passports. We discussed whether he should call in on the UK after he attends a business conference in the USA. I said that I'm sure a visit would be welcome but that the timing may be difficult in view of the upcoming general election.

C.H. strikes me these days as very different from the man I first met 4½ years ago. Anson thinks he's changed too. He's still got a genial manner, but behind it is a stubborn and rather insensitive character with the authoritarian tendencies of someone who has always got his own way. He knows best. When I say 'insensitive', I'm exposing one of the puzzles about him. There is such a jumble of opposites – he is both tactful and tactless, indecisive and impetuous, cautious and rash, sophisticated and naïve. This makes him very difficult to read, though it seems fairly clear that he will basically do whatever Beijing wants (or maybe whatever he thinks Beijing wants) on all the big things.

We covered familiar ground. Why am I so unhelpful about the provisional Legco? Why is he worried about the Bill of Rights? We don't connect on much except his living arrangements. I said that if he's not going to live in GH, we must work out as soon as possible an alternative use for the house that will guarantee the staff's jobs, to be announced when his own wishes are made clear. Otherwise it's unfair to our very loyal workers. He seems to take this point, says that Betty is cross with him for not agreeing to move into GH but that he does want to use Fanling. We are currently showing him all sorts of houses and sites. Presumably he's going to get the feng shui expert to look at wherever is proposed. We are working on a plan to use GH for government entertaining and accommodation.

At Exco we discussed the plans which Beijing's Preparatory Committee appear to be knocking about for a new election system. Denis Chang says that even though they can dismantle the legislation which produced the present electoral arrangements, they can't dismantle a benchmark. People know what a fair electoral system is like now, and they will be able to compare it with whatever China imposes on Hong Kong.

It's been helpful being able to talk to David Ford while he's been in town with the other heads of our overseas offices. He always has a very good feel for what's going on. He is impressed by the way that the civil service is still hanging together, despite all the pressures on them. He says that our overseas representatives were open with C. H. Tung when they saw him, pointing out that he was getting a bad press in their countries and would continue to be heavily criticized unless he changed some of his policies and language. On the other hand, David was rather dispirited about the speed at which the new political correctness is taking hold. While some leading Chinese businessmen are fed up at the demands on them to stump up large amounts of dosh for the handover celebrations in order to show their patriotism, there is generally a willingness to accept the inevitability of change in Hong Kong.

Thursday 6 March

We've had a readout from Madeleine Albright's recent visit to Beijing. She spoke very well on Hong Kong – focused and self-confident and very clear, especially on the legislature and human rights. The Chinese responded rationally, though they still put out statements warning other countries to keep their noses out and criticizing the US human rights record. A French minister came by who's been in China as the John the Baptist before Chirac's state visit. He doesn't behave out of character – in other words he doesn't utter a word of criticism about the Chinese Communist Party. I'm delighted but not surprised that Michel Camdessus,* who is hosting an IMF conference here, clearly understands all the dangers that lie ahead. – threats to autonomy, corruption, *guanxi*, meddling with the free market, political instability in China. Anson has wowed a group of American fund managers to whom she talks.

* Michel Camdessus was an economist who became Governor of the Bank of France and managing director of the International Monetary Fund from 1987 to 2000.

We've had a briefing on the farewell ceremony from our officials. The details are starting to come together. Thank heavens we're not having to negotiate the details now of our ceremony with the Chinese. Bryn Terfel can't now come and we are searching for an alternative. It looks as though we might be able to persuade Dame Gwyneth Jones.

Kenneth Clarke arrived in the evening, as ever cheerful, noisy, self-confident and intelligent. Lavender and I had to go to one of our three charity 'dos'of the week. So Ken was taken off on *Star Ferry* by Edward to eat in Kowloon. Edward says that a bright journalist on the boat would have been able to pick up a scoop as Ken delivered his views on the single currency at fortissimo.

Friday 7 March

I made the opening speech at the IMF conference this morning. The Governor of the Bank of China hid in a room off the hotel lobby to avoid having to shake hands with me along with the other members of the platform party. As we swept into the main auditorium, he scuttled out to join the back of the line of speakers. What a silly lot. I had lunch with Ken before he nips off to spend the afternoon birdwatching at Mai Po. He's gloomy about the election (who isn't?) and thinks that voters have simply had enough of us. He is adamant that he won't budge on Europe; to do so would ensure that the Conservatives fought an anti-European campaign and drifted into an increasingly hostile European policy. He doesn't believe that the Germans can endure politically or economically another dose of belt tightening. He's not convinced that the party will degenerate into civil war after the election, but admits this may be wishful thinking. He's not very optimistic about Hong Kong staying the same, mostly because he doesn't think that China really understands what has made it special.

I admire Ken greatly. He is a decent and wise man with swashbuckling charm, great wit and the self-confidence to deliver his views on anything and everything in a way which inevitably makes him 'unsafe' so far as party managers are concerned. But he is usually right. Challenged about Britain's colonial record by the press in the morning, he went in with both feet in a way which most people wouldn't have dared to do. He argued that Britain had a better colonial record than any other European power and it was difficult to think of any countries which had been British colonies that were now better governed or more free than in the past. When we tried to compile a list, we didn't get much further than Botswana and Singapore (and that with reservations). Ken is a Cavalier, the very opposite of a wimp, his own man, with generous but hard-headed instincts. He notes how much the party has been changing and how many rather unpleasant right-wingers (with the stress on the unpleasantness rather than the right-wingery) there are in it these days. For that reason, I don't suppose he will ever lead it. But he should. He belongs to the days when you had views yourself rather than waiting to discover from the latest market research or newspaper article what your views should be.

The US consul-general has told me that he not only warned Tung on Paul Yip, but also recommended strongly that he shouldn't appoint Ronnie Chan as the Hong Kong chairman of the US–Hong Kong Business Council. Chan is a dreadful but ubiquitous fellow with the sort of views which seem specially designed to put off Americans, and indeed anyone who believes in liberal democracy, a signed-up member of the 'no one cares about human rights' school. Last year after he addressed an AmCham meeting they received a number of letters of complaint. Needless to say, he has an American passport.

Monday 10 March

There are disturbing stories out of Beijing. It looks as though the Ministry of Posts and Telecommunications have told Cable & Wireless that they must sell off 51% of Hong Kong Telecom. This would conclude the story of C and W's brilliant handling of Hong Kong and China – kowtowing their way brainlessly and incompetently to disaster. It would also be another scalp for China as it marauds its way through British commercial interests in Hong Kong. Cathay and Swire. China Light and Power and the Kadoories. Now Cable & Wireless.

I saw Mrs Ogata, the UN High Commissioner for Refugees, who is reasonable and impressively well briefed, to discuss the difficulty of pushing the Vietnamese government to help us repatriate the last few thousand migrants. If we can reduce the number to a few hundred ethnic Chinese we will have done pretty well. She had to run the gauntlet on her way to the press club of a nasty crowd of communists shouting about the money that the UNHCR allegedly owes to Hong Kong. She was very philosophical about it, noting wryly that it may be difficult to persuade aid donors to cough up for Hong Kong when they are still being pressed for contributions to places like Rwanda. Bob Peirce is back from 10 days in the US. He reports a growing criticism of China right across the political spectrum and considerable scepticism about Hong Kong's prospects. Qian hasn't helped matters with a speech about the need after 1997 to rewrite school textbooks.

Tuesday 11 March

Jeremy Mathews made this practical point at Exco. He noted that lawyers have to do their best for their clients and are obliged to press every reasonable argument. Any laws which seem to have started their lives in the bowels of the provisional Legco before July will be challenged by lawyers who are actively pursuing their client's interests and will sometimes challenge the legality of these laws. Bob notes that the establishment of the provisional Legco, with its dubious membership (so many people who were defeated in the elections for the real Legco) demonstrates that you can clone not only Scottish sheep these days, you can also clone Chinese political institutions.

Dinner in the evening at the China Club with Jonathan Dimbleby, his production crew and my private office plus their spouses. It seems so long since the filming for the BBC began, back in our kitchen in Victoria – almost five long years. It was a jolly meal at the end of which I made Edward do the reply to Jonathan's toast. Edward is so long-suffering with me. Because he's really family, he is the only member of the team I'm ever grumpy with. He takes it very well, occasionally giving as good as he gets. He is pissed off at missing the upcoming general election in Britain. I'm not sure that sharing in the tragedy would actually be all that much fun.

Wednesday 12 March

When C.H. is challenged about Qian's remarks on textbooks, he agreed with Qian straight away, prompting an American journalist to ask him whether he'd ever said 'no' to China. He reacted angrily, enquiring when a British Governor had ever stood up to London. Where has he been all these years? Another journalist calls out – 'war widows, visas, ethnic minorities, passports', but he was ignored. And there was a time when Lord MacLehose used to be described as the second most unpopular foreign leader in the FCO after Dom Mintoff.

Thursday 13 March

With Lavender in the lead, we had dinner at the Society for AIDS Care's almost finished hospice at Tai Po. Lavender has worked on a number of projects, including this one with a marvellous Irish nun, Sister Maureen, and she'd organized a delightful supper out on the lawn of the house looking down over the sea for all the helpers, sponsors and staff. For the second time we meet someone whose child had haemophilia and was an early victim of AIDS. We helped the family four years ago when Lavender set up a fund to help all those who had suffered like this child. Every time the father sees us he bursts into tears. Tonight he brought us a present, a handsome traditional Chinese teapot. His wife has got a job at the hospice. They are courageous people.

The Transition Project, run by an academic at Baptist University, has produced another of their regular in-depth surveys of public opinion which they have called 'a golden sunset' for Empire. It shows that 90% of the sample are satisfied with their life in Hong Kong. 73% are satisfied with the government. 62% are satisfied with me, and 53% are satisfied with C. H. Tung. I hope the project survives the handover.

Sunday 16 March

We opened the gardens this weekend to the disabled. Mums and dads with badly handicapped children queue up for photos. These families have such heroic qualities, coping day and night with so many unrelenting physical and emotional challenges. Their only disappointment seemed to be that Whisky and Soda have already left for Fanling. On Sunday evening we give a dinner for Tony Kenny, the former Master of my old college, Balliol, and Warden of Rhodes House, his wife, Nancy, and son (who works in Hong Kong), a number of friends and Jeremy Irons, who is in Hong Kong making a film with Gong Li. Tony Kenny reminds him of the time that he was one of the actors in a Shakespearean performance put on after dinner for the visiting Chinese leader Hua Guofeng and his party. They were in Britain and visiting Oxford with Harold Macmillan. They were clearly bored to tears by the performance of what was billed as the 11 ages of man. So 11 had to be cut to 6 mid-show.

Tuesday 18 March

John Major has called the election in Britain allowing for a long six-week campaign. The first blow is that the *Sun* has endorsed Blair. One wonders what black deal he has done with Rupert Murdoch; presumably he's promised not to do anything to prohibit cross-media ownership. At Exco this morning, the Police Commissioner gave us some extraordinary crime figures. The numbers continue their steep decline. Over coffee afterwards, we were told that Victor Fung, who has just been in the USA, says that the mood there on Hong Kong is worse than he's ever known it. The general view seems to be that C.H. would be well advised to postpone any visit until after the handover, by which time he would (presumably) be able to demonstrate that civilized life had not ended in Hong Kong. The passage of time might also have seen the end of the snowballing 'Chinese connection' political-funding scandal in American politics.

Wednesday 19 March

I've just done my last university congregation. I must have distributed more university degrees – aggregating eight congregations a year over my five years – than any other human being. Perhaps I could claim a place in the *Guinness Book of Records*? Joseph Hotung gets a degree 'honoris causa' at this one. A very well-deserved honour for someone who has been so honourable. Talking of which Percy has been at it again, claiming that because of me Hong Kong will now have less freedom and democracy after 1997. He appears to suggest that what I have been trying to do here is to ensure that I can return to Westminster afterwards as a plausible candidate for the leadership of the Conservative Party. I wonder if he has ever talked to a Conservative MP.

Thursday 20 March

Our redoubtable warriors in the JLG, led by Hugh Davies and Alan Paul, are doing the business this week in London. Of all of us, I sometimes think that they are the ones who most deserve the medals. A small number of British officials, supported by members of the Hong Kong government, work away day after day and week after week in dealing with some of the biggest issues, but also with the real minutiae of the handover. They cope with a succession of Chinese officials, largely charmless, often rude and invariably difficult and mean-spirited. Of course, there are some exceptions. But I guess that even the nicer ones are reined in by the instruction to be as difficult as possible as often as possible. This week we have made some progress on air service agreements flying rights in and out of Hong Kong, but on the question of the right of abode the Chinese are determined to try to use the issue to get us to accept the legitimacy before 1997 of the provisional Legco. The issue doesn't affect Hong Kong Chinese residents in the city, but the status of Hong Kong citizens who had emigrated and that of foreigners who are resident in Hong Kong. It's more and more apparent that the Chinese want to sort out all the 'one country' matters, while we are more bothered about the 'two systems' agenda. We are not going to give way on legitimizing their gimcrack unelected legislature, nor on Chinese pressure to bring in large numbers of their soldiers before 30 June.

Saturday 22–Sunday 23rd March

We've had our last Sevens tournament. The rugby as ever is very exciting, and as always the crowd behaviour is part of the show in the south stand, demonstrating that we are never going to be like Singapore. The regular chants include, 'Who's the wanker on the mobile phone' and 'Stand up if you hate the French'.

I phoned up John to wish him luck in the election. He's pretty gloomy about the difficulties of focusing the campaign on the economic good news. Kate's birthday on 24 March is not spoilt by a long discussion about guest lists for the handover and farewell ceremonies. The Chinese are still refusing to say whether they will come to the handover banquet. It could be because, since the Hong Kong government is footing the bill, the invitation is going out in my name. The new security arrangements for the event look better. After I had said the previous plans risked appearing to turn Hong Kong into an armed camp, the police have had second thoughts. We are also making progress with the UNHCR and the Vietnamese to return most of the remaining immigrants home before the handover.

We all went out to dinner at the Peak café for Kate's birthday. Simon Murray came along and kept his end of the table enthralled and amused with jokes and tricks probably first performed in some desert fort in the Foreign Legion.

Monday 24 March

If the coming weeks are anything like the present one there will be legions of distinguished foreign visitors, other foreign visitors who think they are distinguished, their hangers on, academics and journalists who want to know what is going to happen after 1997 and who think that I know. Much of our negotiations are going to focus on China's attempts to give some credibility to the provisional Legco and on the final arrangements for the farewell ceremony. There are endless twists and turns but I can't just say, 'I'm going to bed.'

Wednesday 26 March

I'm in discussion with the director of protocol about the handover honours list. I can never bring myself to get very excited about this less than engrossing subject, and I'm therefore always worried that we may have excluded some deserving candidate. I wish we could have a dis-honours list, to claim back gongs and baubles from those who have behaved badly, like Rita Fan (the president of the provisional Legco), whose services are available to any passing or arriving colonial power. She can be guaranteed to horrify any foreign visitors who talk to her.

We had on a district visit to Tuen Mun, big, cheerful crowds in a working-class community trapped by bad planning in the far north-west of the territory with inadequate transport links to the rest of Hong Kong. We've been trying to respond over the last couple of years to some of the social problems there. I originally paid an incognito visit to see some of the drug, housing, welfare, planning and transport problems for myself, and then pursued their resolution (or at least amelioration) through a three-monthly report back system from government departments. I think it's had a small effect, and perhaps has rescued Tuen Mun from the bottom drawer of every departmental filing cabinet.

Anson and I had a chat before she goes off to Beijing for joint meetings with C.H. and both Li Peng and Lu Ping. She is wondering how outspoken she can be and how much C.H. will bridle at any indications of independence on her part. She is determined to speak out to Lu Ping on the right of abode, and the wisdom of signing up to our offer to produce a White Bill which the new administration can take forward with its own legislation after 1 July.

Friday 28– Monday 31 March

We've had a glorious Easter weekend in Fanling, including lunch in a big noisy restaurant in Sheung Shui followed by a bit of shopping in the local market afterwards. An old lady gives us some vegetables from her stall, including a lotus – she refused payment, which some of the onlookers thought unwise. 'Take the money,' one shouted. 'He'll only be here for another three months.'

Tuesday 1 April

Kate went home today along with our friends the Codringtons, who came originally for the Sevens. Anson has given me a readout of her meetings in Beijing. She says that Lu Ping was adamant about the right of abode and won't buy our White Bill formula. He is determined to give the provisional Legco something to do and C.H. simply went along. There is a general feeling that C.H. feels obliged to run absolutely everything past Lu. In Beijing he raised with him housing and education policy and welfare benefit rates. A high degree of autonomy indeed.

We've been clearing out files, either to send back to London or to destroy. We've discovered one fascinating file which has some of the characteristics of a 'smoking gun'. It contains telegrams between Hong Kong and London at around the time of the consultations in Hong Kong about the desired number of directly elected seats in Legco. It is not difficult to spot the cloven hoof of Percy Cradock. It seems that the principal objective at the time was not to find out what people in Hong Kong wanted but what Beijing might secretly accept. Since conspiracies of this kind are what many people in the territory assumed had happened, and since some journalists and commentators have claimed it for certain, I guess that it's no big revelation. But I suppose that I've always hoped that it wasn't true. The cloven hoof of Percy Cradrock is not difficult to spot, but even at my age I'm capable of being shocked.

Wednesday 2 April

We've had a telegram from London about the annual Geneva human rights resolution. It's proving difficult to find a European Union member to table it now that the French (with tacit German and Italian support) are opposing the whole exercise as part of their demeaning 'let's suck up to China' strategy. There is a draft submission to ministers advising against Britain taking the lead. We weigh in strongly on the other side, noting that our protestations of concern about post-handover Hong Kong will look pretty incredible if we chicken out of this. Needless to say, now that the Chinese can see that they are driving other countries off the crucial resolution, they are sitting on their hands as far as any relaxation on their attitude to human rights is concerned.

Thursday 3rd April

Geoffrey Howe is in town for C & W trying to help them find a strategy for Hong Kong Telecom, which makes the lion's share of their profits. Lord Young has certainly left C + W in a terrible mess. The company is being driven into flogging off a large chunk of their shares to Chinese interests. Geoffrey and I had a talk about Hong Kong, I noted that no one can argue that having occasional rows with China has greatly unsettled the territory. As for the proposition that as a result of my policies Hong Kong will have less freedom and democracy than would otherwise have been the case, this is by definition unprovable. But I don't find it very convincing. To get a smooth transition, I would have needed to do what C. H. Tung is setting his hand to now. This would have meant less freedom and democracy before 1997 under British sovereignty, local and international criticism, and protests in Hong Kong, with a British imprimatur on measures that would satisfy China's appetite for political control. I say that I think more attention in future will concentrate on what many people will see as the hollowing out of the JD by Britain between 1984 and 1992, and that in particular there will be a lot of interest in whether Britain made secret promises about direct elections to China before the allegedly fair and open consultation was completed in 1987. Geoffrey mumbles in response.

Friday 4 April

An awful meeting with a tetchy C.H. He banged on and on about the provisional Legco, rejected the proposal that we should provide a White Bill on right of abode, is very negative on civil liberties legislation and declines to attend the opening of the Lantau bridges on the grounds that – even if I invited him to take a role in the ceremony – he didn't like attending occasions at which I would be present because he would actually be attracting the limelight. Moreover, it was inappropriate to do anything with me while we were disagreeing about issues. So, yah boo from Mr Tung.

Sunday 6 April

Peter Barry's last 9.30 English mass at the cathedral. He's been doing it for about five years. There are obviously good reasons for replacing him with a full-time English priest in the parish, which is what the parish priest is doing, but there are some suspicions that his frequently expressed views on democracy and civil liberties may have something to do with it. He is a brave and forthright supporter of decency and he has been a terrific friend both to me and to Lavender.

Barry and Lizzie Humphries have been staying. He's doing a film for the BBC on Hong Kong, called not surprisingly *The Last Night of the Poms*. Some of our Chinese staff won't believe that he really is Dame Edna. 'But she's a woman,' they insist.

Tuesday 8 April

At Exco, when we talk about C.H.'s Exco designate, Andrew Li asked who we think is the most influential member. Several colleagues replied, 'Lu Ping.' There is an unpleasant racist storm triggered by remarks made by a local Neanderthal businessman called Philip Tose (he was the fellow who offered the Conservative Party £5 million to get rid of me – some reports suggested that shooting was one option), who is believed to have said at a meeting of Harvard Business School alumni that democracy had been all right in America until about 30 years ago, in other words when black citizens got the vote. He's a reminder that seriously stupid and unpleasant people can make a lot of money. C.H. has produced a consultation paper on civil liberties. Screw tightening all round – on demonstrations and political parties for instance. The words 'national security' appear frequently. I suspect that this document will bomb.

Friday 11 April

Another farewell ceremony, this one to decommission the Navy base at Tamar on Stonecutters Island. White ensigns. Eight bells. The First Sea Lord with sword, gongs and sash. Smart naval drill and speeches about duty. 'For Those in Peril on the Sea' sung to a steady beat from a Royal

Marines band. So the Royal Navy 'melts away' in the words of 'Recessional'. More lumps in the throat.

We've reached a first stage agreement with the Chinese on advanced military personnel, but will keep them hanging on further detachments. They are doing most of what we wanted on this, but we can go on using the issue to get a bit of leverage on other matters. There's no point in being too accommodating. Anson is back from a brief trip to London, being philosophical about the problems of working with C.H. She has been told by a lot of people that there is no longer any point in giving him advice because he doesn't listen. One or two have also reminded her that the fact that she seemed to Beijing to be reasonably well disposed to C.H. was pretty decisive when they in effect selected him. But what was the alternative? There's another poll giving Tung a 54% satisfaction rate and me 79%. The general view is that he has slipped so much because he's seen to be Beijing's stooge doing whatever they want. He has decided not to go to the USA this summer, which may be a result of Martin Lee being fêted there – the President has now agreed to see Martin.

Tuesday 15 April

At Exco we discussed whether there needs to be legislation to provide a statutory basis for the public holidays on 1 and 2 July. Some people are worried that this will provoke a row with China. But apparently it is required legally and both Anson and Donald strongly back my support for it. From the top down our civil service is continuing to behave with professional integrity, even though people must know that they may have to argue the case on the other side over some of these issues in the future.

On civil liberties, it seems more and more clear that business leaders have no notion of the obvious point that when you take away, say, Martin Lee's rights, sooner or later the rights of large corporations are filched too. Lavender has been making farewell calls on her charities and gets the impression that people are just starting to face up to the fact that the future is almost upon them. Leo Goodstadt is off soon. He has been an exceptionally valuable member of our team. His last contribution is to mark our cards about the communist past of some of Hong Kong's new political elite and the history of C. H. Tung's shipping business.

Thursday 17 April

The JLG are having an awful time in the negotiations on the handover ceremony. Even Hugh Davies, a man of legendary patience, lost his cool with the awful bullying and arrogant Chinese protocol boss. C.H. is apparently blaming me for his bad press and, in order to ensure that it continues, is insisting that new legislation on flags and emblems should oblige our offices around the world to fly the PRC flag as well as Hong Kong's.

I had my last two investitures. It's impressive to see Anson, Donald, Police Commissioner Eddie Hui and others warmly applauding their public service colleagues' achievements. There's a real sense of pride and corporate spirit, which is certainly one of our main successes here. I hope this won't be lost.

Monday 21 April

We had a dinner to say 'farewell and thank you' to Lance and his honorary ADCs, drawn from the disciplined services and the garrison. They all look splendid in summer mess kit, gleaming like Persil advertisements – white jackets, striped trousers, cummerbunds, lanyards and medals. They have done a wonderful job, helping at official occasions and sweeping up a succession of important foreign visitors at the airport. By common agreement, they give the President of Gabon and his entourage the prize for tiresomeness; but this group did apparently make a spectacular contribution to our consumer spending figures. Lance has been fantastic, tough when necessary and a great friend to Lavender and the girls. If they had ever got into any scrapes, I wouldn't have known about it and he would have rescued them. But naturally I don't believe that this could have happened!

Tuesday 22 April

I'm looking through my private papers and throwing most of them away. Lavender and Edward are horrified. But I don't much like accumulating clutter about myself. I've hung on to some of the really good letters but chucked the ones that flattered me from people who subsequently or even at the same time criticized me behind my back. Reading those after the event lowers the spirits.

Wednesday 23rd April

Lydia Dunn has made a speech of magnificent blandness at a conference in London which seems to be rather different from what she's been saying to people in private. She claimed that stories of problems in Hong Kong are all got up by the press; that the consultation on civil liberties is wholly genuine; and that Hong Kong's rights aren't about to be seriously constrained, and so on. Maybe this is a sensible thing to do and good for Hong Kong and Swire's.

We sent a telegram to London with a 'tongue in cheek' series of questions about the 'smoking gun' papers we found. London has responded at length with an exegesis of the telegrams in which they claim that there was no secret deal done at all about the number of directly elected legislators. But we seemed to have marked China's card at the time about the importance of maximizing the number of letters (as opposed to names on petitions) opposing direct elections. In other words, one petition with scores or hundreds of signatures favouring directly elected seats was given the same weight as a single letter on the other side of the argument. Afterwards we told the Chinese that they shouldn't underestimate the pressure for direct elections just because the consultation exercise purported to show that there wasn't great support for them. 'Don't believe the result just because it tells you what you want to hear.' I think that if we had done more then, we would have had almost a decade of developing representative government under our belts before the handover. I suppose that as ever it was all done to avoid a row with China. London unsurprisingly appears a little anxious about what we have discovered.

Thursday 24 April

I went to answer questions in Legco again on human rights and right of abode, and I asked rhetorically whether any Legco member would tell me any way in which our existing civil liberties legislation infringed the Basic Law. Silence. I allowed it to sink in.

We held our 70th charity dinner dance in the GH ballroom. We have also had about three dozen concerts and lots of other dinners there. I'm surprised that I don't have an even bigger problem with my weight.

Friday 25 April

Members of my Business Council gave me a farewell lunch, organized by Sir Q. W. Lee, the chairman of the Hang Seng Bank, a gracious adornment of the past British colonial establishment, and now inevitably to become an adornment of the coming establishment. I am not sure that his heart is really in this, and there are some aspects that clearly worry him – he's close to Anson. He is a very nice old boy, a slow-moving tortoise of a man with a deserved reputation for sagacity. I sit next to Larry Yung, the Citic boss, who is a real charmer and now the owner of Harold Macmillan's old home Birch Grove. He is passionate about both shooting and fishing as well as golf. Harold Macmillan would doubtless have had some drollery to sum it all up – not so much selling the family silver as turning one's house into a Chinese takeaway.

After lunch, I had a meeting with Margaret Ng. She said that it's pretty certain that there will be legal challenges to bills which began their life in the pre-July provisional Legco. She wanted assurance that the British government won't undermine any legal action by saying that they can't see any problem with what the provisional Legco has done. It's plainly not an assurance that I can give. Who knows what a (likely) new government will do?

Saturday 26 April

Margaret and Denis Thatcher arrived yesterday for the opening of the new Lantau bridges. We had a big dinner this evening for her, about 160 people in the ballroom, and marking tomorrow's opening of the two great new bridges, which together we call the Lantau Link. After our speeches, Margaret and Denis came upstairs for a drink in our sitting room with Francis Cornish and Sherard Cowper-Coles, who is on his last visit before the handover. Margaret saw C.H. this morning. 'He's just like all the other businessmen here,' she said.

Sunday 27 April

Except that C.H. chose not to come – he fixed up a last-minute trip to Guangdong as an excuse. I get a bit depressed by the graceless small-mindedness of Chinese communists and those who take their cue from them. It doesn't damage me particularly, but it's bad for Hong Kong.

The opening of the bridges went famously. We swept out on a motorcycle-led convoy through the new tunnel under the harbour and along the motorway to Tsing Yi. There, almost in the shadow of the bridge, there were 'march pasts' by community groups, bands, dragon dancers and choirs. Margaret and I both made speeches, she's looking wonderful in blue. The sun set in a dramatic orange glow over one shoulder and the bridge towered over the other. Then, with Anson, we light up the bridges with laser beams and garlands of lights along the cables. A convoy of cars with us leading in our open Rolls-Royce then drove onto the bridge, through a tape and under clouds of streamers and confetti. We drove across, did a U-turn (unusual for Lady T.) and came back again for a reception and the spectacular firework display. It's the best I've seen, with a waterfall of colour and sparks appearing to cascade off the bridge itself. The whole of the sound to the south is full of boats, big and small, with cameras flashing as the heavens are illuminated in silver, gold, purple, pink and green by the exploding fireworks. They cost the Kwok brothers HK$5 million. It couldn't have gone much better.

Monday 28 April

Denis has perfectly innocently been drawn into the election campaign. A 'friendly' journalist called out to him when he and Margaret were visiting one of David Tang's English-language centres, 'What do you think of John Major's chances in the election?' 'Absolutely nil,' he replied. How to get a mini-scoop. On the whole Denis is several guineas a minute – cheerful, funny, self-deprecating, generous. After sitting next to Lavender at dinner on Saturday night, he thanked her for being such a good hostess and added, 'It's so good of you to spend the whole evening talking to a boring old soul like me.' Margaret and Denis have been our last important official British visitors. As usual all the staff lined up in the hall in their white jackets with the red flashes and the crowns on their shoulders. Margaret is always so kind to them. I wonder what they were thinking. She said an especially warm thank you to one of our staff who was burned on *Sir Galahad* in the Falklands. Whisky and Soda were sorry to see them go. Margaret spoils them, feeding them biscuits in her room. 'Poor little things, they looked so hungry.'

Tuesday 29 April

We had a briefing at Exco on the handover celebrations. Andrew Li's first question was about the arrangements for the demonstrators. Everyone is very keen that they should have a reasonable place to demonstrate within sight of the convention centre. That's certainly the way to avoid trouble. I wonder if the future Exco will see things that way. My main worries now about the handover are – first, that we need to know soon whether or not senior Chinese officials will attend our handover banquet. Second, I'm pretty sure that they will try to ensure that no members of the public can say farewell to us as we embark on *Britannia*. We'll have to see whether we can finesse this.

I have a last discussion with Sherard. He is of course complimentary about how things have turned out. Among the usual unconvincing flattery, he observes that we've kept Hong Kong as an issue from bearing down on an increasingly weak government. That's only partly true. It was the Prime Minister and ministers who helped to keep the issue of Hong Kong off its own back; they supported this last major colonial territory, despite pressures from business and from their own advisers from time to time. If they had hesitated or backtracked, it would have been very different – politically hazardous both at home and internationally.

Wednesday 30 April

I spoke first thing at Alice's school prizegiving. She has been so happy at Island School with a good head, excellent teachers and very nice friends. It is a genuinely comprehensive school in the sense that there are mixed ethnicities, languages and abilities. Lavender and I feel enormously grateful to them.

Thursday 1 May

Polling day in Britain and the only question seems to be how big will the Tory defeat be. With political loyalties these days so much less deep, as the ideological divide narrows, the range of possible election outcomes almost everywhere seems to become much wider: a shallow but broad river. Similar things have happened in Canada, France and Australia.

Another good talk in the afternoon with the scholar Michael Yahuda. He is a bit more encouraged by the mood in Hong Kong, arguing that the reactions to Tung's proposals on civil liberties – by, for instance, the legal profession and academics – show a greater resilience in the community than he had expected. He says there's not much respect for Hong Kong in Beijing. People in the north only see the Hong Kong tycoon lobbyists, who they think are an unimpressive venal lot. They have no experience of Hong Kong's public service, its intellectuals and its cultural life. Maybe after the handover they'll learn about Hong Kong beyond the tycoons and come to respect it more. He thinks that Chinese communists live in their own ghetto world. There is no great admiration for those who cope with the outside world, though they know it has to be done by someone like Qian. In the evening we had our last public concert in the ballroom, given by the Stan Tracey Octet and featuring my favourite trumpeter, Guy Barker.

Friday 2 May

We woke up to news of the electoral disaster for the Conservatives. Landslide. Calamity. Earthquake. Avalanche. Wipeout. Slaughter of the not always so innocent. What a way to end 18 years in government. Tony Blair has stormed home with a crushing majority. Several of my friends have gone, including William Waldegrave. The majority looks set to give Blair a decade in office, though what goes up always comes down again. Eventually. It's a great triumph for Blair himself. He's turned Labour into an electable force with great skill and determination; at the same time some in our party have been assiduously making it unelectable. I'm still not convinced that he's got a great strategy or more than plastic principles, and reading some of the truly, deeply soppy stuff written about him doesn't convince me. St Anthony of Islington has come among us etc. We shall see. Sooner or later the shit will hit the fan even in Blair's Britain. Of course, one doesn't want things to go badly, quite the reverse. But it's difficult to imagine how they can possibly go as well as we have been promised. 'The crooked timber of humanity' and all that.

John Major has resigned with dignity as party leader as well as Prime Minister, defeated by Conservatives more than Labour. But the outlook is bleak. *No* seats in Scotland and Wales. Tactical voting in spades cutting down Tories everywhere and returning over 40 of the wretched Liberal Democrats. Is it really true, as Enoch Powell once said, that all political careers end in failure? Look at William, a very clever and public-spirited man: five years of misery because of the wretched Scott Inquiry, now defeat. I suspect we all preferred making the journey to ministerial office rather than arriving there. It's like Cavafy's poem, 'Ithaka':

> Ithaka gave you the marvellous journey.
> Without her you wouldn't have set out.
> She has nothing left to give you now.

The Tung entourage have started criticizing the civil service for being excessively in Britain's image and for not being more interventionist in economic policy. Local American businessmen confirmed the stories we've heard about the appalling effect that people like Ronnie Chan and other Tung groupies have on visitors. Gerald Segal was brought over from the Institute of Strategic Studies with a colleague this week to try to sort their image out, but they went away pretty horrified by what they'd heard from Tung.

Saturday 3rd May

Jim Prior and other businessmen in London have been in touch with John Coles to tell him that Li Peng and others in Beijing have told them that if I didn't start cooperating with Tung, it would be bad for British trade. They presumably think that I should be brought into line by the new government. Coles's reply undertakes to note what's been said, not perhaps the most robust defence. I spent much of Saturday afternoon phoning the fallen. Then Carl Bildt, an old friend, telephoned me about Bosnia. He wants to know whether, not least in the light of the election result, I would be interested in succeeding him as the EU special envoy to Bosnia. I told him what I've said to others, namely that after this post I think I need a bit of time to decompress.

Lavender and I went out to dinner with Emily Lau and her lawyer husband, who are great fun. They are flattering about Lavender, who they rightly say is admired and liked on all sides. They've watched one British betrayal after another, as we've comforted ourselves in the past that at least the old colonial establishment were on our side, their knighthoods and passports packed. Contemptible really.

Robin Cook has said that he wants me to stay on and has every confidence in me. Hezza has announced that he won't stand for the party leadership and has gone into hospital with an angina attack. He worked himself into the ground during the campaign. He's a great soldier. I imagine that William Hague's chances of getting the leadership increase by the hour. A very young man for a very long haul.

Monday 5 May

Lydia Dunn clambered noisily off the fence at the weekend, giving an interview on television criticizing the last Conservative government's policy on Hong Kong and China, bemoaning the fact that we are not 'cooperating' with China, and calling on us 'to face reality' and work with the provisional Legco. She's getting quite a lot of flak on the phone-in programmes for quitting Hong Kong and offering pro-Beijing advice from a convenient distance – Knightsbridge or the Cotswolds. I suppose she's just singing from the Swire's songsheet. But it's quite a change to see her off the fence on which she normally perches so skilfully. On this occasion she might have got slightly ahead of the breeze, which appears to have turned, the opinion polls souring further on Tung. It was Lydia who sold me most of my original ideas on the composition of Exco, and Lydia who enthusiastically applauded in private during my early months and after my election proposals were first announced. I also know that she's been very critical of C.H. in private, despairing of ever being able to convince him about anything he doesn't want to hear. I didn't want to think that Lydia would behave as she is now. She was such a firm supporter in my first two difficult years. This makes me even more grateful for those who've been brave, decent and principled right the way through – Anson, Donald, Michael Sze, Nicholas Ng and Peter Lai to name just a few. These are Chinese public servants who believe in values and not just what they are told might be their short-term interest. Peter Lai did a brilliant job as Michael Sze's deputy at Constitutional Affairs, and he has done just as well as Secretary for Security. Their values are universal, not Asian or Western, and they know the difference between right and wrong, between loyalty and its reverse. All of them – like Michael when he was piloting our reforms through Legco – have often been under huge pressure from China and its bully boys in Hong Kong. I know that without these fine public servants I – we – would have been shipwrecked.

Having already let the media know that I am to stay, Robin Cook phoned me. He's on his first day in the Foreign Office, even though it's a bank holiday, and he wanted to talk about Hong Kong. He assured me that there would be continuity of policy and that he would welcome me staying at my post. We discussed C. H. Tung, whose behaviour is clearly worrying him ('Well,' he says, 'what more can you expect of a contributor to Tory funds?'), and he asked my advice on whether Tony Blair should come out for the handover. I said that I hoped on balance that he would, provided he was able to say some reassuring things to Hong Kong which would underline Britain's continuing commitment. I think that Robin Cook is an impressive man – clear, sharp-witted and (I would guess) decisive. He may well be nicer than he seems, even though he has a visceral dislike of Tories. It's legal. When we briefly discussed the election results, he observed that there will presumably be more Conservative supporters of proportional representation now. I surprised him by saying that, like him, I've been a supporter for years.

Tuesday 6 May

We had our team photograph taken before Exco. They've been a good group, with few changes over the 4½ years since I put David Wilson's crowd to the sword. They are intelligent, decent, rational people and have worked very well together. Rosanna Wong has done extremely well as the senior member; she is straight with me. The consensus is that Tung will go ahead with most of his civil liberties changes. He is off to see Qian tomorrow, presumably to get the Chinese chop on his plans. It will look awful here, but he doesn't seem to take much account of these sorts of political perception. Yeung Sum, vice chairman of the Democratic Party, his wife, Eileen, and their toddler son, Gabriel, all came to lunch . He's encouraged by gestures of public support for his party and thinks that they can do well enough even with rigged elections to establish a reasonably solid powerbase in Legco. He is pretty scathing about Lydia's call to 'face reality'. What would have happened, he asked rhetorically, if China had 'faced reality' and given in to Japan after being invaded? He says that the Democrats have voted unanimously to invite me to dinner, apparently not something they have ever done for an outgoing Governor before.

We went out in the evening to eat with Jonathan Mirsky and his clever partner, Deborah Glass. He's just done an interview with Tung and thinks there's nothing there except saloon bar vapidities. When pressed about the difference between Asian values and the Judaeo-Christian tradition, C.H. responded that some of his best friends were Jewish.

Thursday 8 May

News from England on screen (I've been given a lesson on the Internet by Kim Salkeld and can now switch it on to read *The Times*). Mr Mandelson in London has taken the helm – a minister without portfolio whose portfolio will actually embrace the whole of government, perhaps, if he has his way, the whole of the country. I wonder if he's wise to take on a sort of super Machiavelli job – won't it just confirm in trumps all the prejudices and hatreds about him? My confident prediction is that it will all end in tears. But I suspect he's smart enough to rise from the sodden handkerchiefs. He's a very talented man and (Lavender says) rather nice, an insight which has so far been denied me.

We're getting a little worried about the boom in red-chip shares – companies set up in Hong Kong by Chinese public sector organizations which offer the prospect of a share of the Chinese action. It's a form of privatization of state assets, but hardly one that should commend itself to socialists. Some are doubtless kosher; others are simply a wild punt attracting mostly small investors rather than big institutional funds. When the chips turn into mashed potato, it will be the little guys who get gobbled up.

We went to an evening service with the Carossian nuns, a mixture of mostly ancient Italians from the north and predominantly younger Chinese. We wanted to thank them for all their work in the community, mostly in schools. I so like nuns like these, full of grace and practical worldliness, by which I mean that they know more about and see more of the world than most of the rest of us put together. Moreover, they are far from judgemental. After that it's dinner with a group of columnists from the Chinese-language newspapers. They invited me some time ago and I had rather dreaded the encounter. In fact, it turns out to be enjoyable; nearly all of them are on the side of decency.

A few lessons today in Chinese bullying and Western kowtowing. First, we learned from Canadian diplomats that when Lloyd Axworthy, the Canadian Foreign Minister, went to China earlier in the spring, Li Peng told him that if Canada supported the Geneva human rights resolution, Beijing would consider cancelling two power station contracts awarded to Canadian firms. To his credit, Axworthy returned to Ottawa determined to stick to his guns and support the resolution – but he was overruled by the Cabinet. Second, the Australians have convinced themselves that they are now on the commercial inside track with China, having withdrawn their support for the Geneva resolution. Third, the Foreign Office are already trying to claim ground lost to the Governor and our team here – 'Perhaps we should try for a fresh start with China, Foreign Secretary.' There's been an exchange between Li Peng and Tony Blair without us being consulted on the draft of Blair's reply. This would have been inconceivable two weeks ago. Our embassy in Beijing is already into 'thickening up mode'. Time to press hard on the appeasement pedal. We learned by accident about the Blair letter and by the same accident that Qian has written to Cook. I doubt whether we will be consulted on the reply.

Friday 9 May
Chancellor Kohl is in Hong Kong again. After seeing C.H. he says that he is confident China will stand up for Hong Kong's democratic development and promised freedoms, although I don't think he believes this for one moment. We talk mostly about the British election and Europe, and as usual we had a frank conversation. I then took him off with four of his aides and Lavender, John Tsang, Bob Peirce and Edward Llewellyn to Yung Kee restaurant, famous for its geese. We worked our way through about 14 courses washed down with Tsingtao beer, one of Germany's gifts to China. The Chancellor does not let Germany down. The only problem comes after a liberal splash of chili sauce on his steamed fish, when for a moment I think that the single currency was going to peg out in a Chinese restaurant, surrounded by dragons with flashing bulbs in their eyes and yellow pyjamaed waiters. Since we plainly hadn't eaten enough, I took him afterwards to my favourite baker to get some custard tarts for tea. He is in every sense a big figure. I then went down to inspect the site for the farewell ceremony with the stands almost completed. Not long now.

Sunday 11 May
Lavender and I went to see a cricket match with a group of Australian tourists who are en route to England. On my way out, after I presented the cup to the winners, I was confronted by a seemingly unwashed, tattooed young Englishman, full of beer, who snarls, 'You Tory piece of shit' at me. I suppose the recent election has focused his eyes and energy. But it's interesting how seldom I've been abused in Hong Kong. I can think of a drunk Indian, also at a cricket match (clearly a very dangerous game), and about three Chinese who have been or looked this disobliging. After all those walkabouts, that's the full score. Otherwise people are cheerful and courteous. Anyway, the 'Tory piece of shit' is sufficiently unfazed to respond, 'Ah, New Labour, I suppose.'

In the evening, we gave dinner to the head of Alice's school and about 20 of the staff. We wanted to say 'thank you' for all they've done for Alice, who refused to show up on the grounds that it would be inappropriate. It's a corker of a school. The teachers present us with a photo album showing Alice in various school activities – not many of them athletic, I notice. Lavender got a bit weepy.

Monday 12 May
I am 53. We had a nice party with the private office. They've arranged a piper from the police to play 'Happy Birthday to you'. Lavender has given

me a wonderful Chinese grave figure. The added bonus is that all the girls have remembered my birthday. Kate has written on her card, 'Yippie, you'll be home soon'.

Lee Kuan Yew has given an interview to the *FT* saying the usual stuff, though when I say 'usual' I recall that he gave an interview shortly after my first policy speech in which he applauded my deepening of democracy and the ingenious way that I'd filled in the spaces left in the Basic Law and the Joint Declaration. Why did he bother?

Tuesday 13 May

Andrew Li had a talk with me after Exco. He is perfectly reasonably preparing the ground in case he is chosen as Chief Justice, which I think and hope will now happen. If it does, then C.H. can be congratulated on choosing Andrew as well as Anson and Donald. The only question is how much they will be able to do on their own.

Tony Blair seems likely to come to the handover, which is pleasing. However, I keep as far away as I possibly can from all the lobbying that is going on about the guest lists for the final receptions, dinners, parties and other events. I hate this sort of thing at the best of times but also admit I'm starting to become a bit demob happy.

Thursday 15 May

I recorded a 'Letter to Hong Kong' for RTHK criticizing those who suggest that Hong Kong should adopt a more 'proactive' industrial policy with subsidies, government intervention and all the rest of that clapped-out malarkey. I hope that C.H. will be smart and knowledgeable enough to resist pressure to go down this road. It's all based on the specious argument that wealth creation in Hong Kong has been hollowed out as manufacturing employment and processing have moved to the mainland or offshore. What actually happened is that we've retained the higher value-added aspects of manufacturing – design, quality control, marketing, financing – and exported the lower value. We made stupendous economic switches with little social and economic dislocation and minimum economic interference. But the whingers and free lunchers are circling the new administration looking for an opening and a tax break or back-hander. Some of the textile magnates and others are pressing for this sort of interventionism. It would damage our reputation with the international financial community and damage our economy too.

Friday 16 May

My morning tennis knock with Colin is memorialized by ITN and a photographer from *Time*. The most serious matter they record is that my forehand is having to be rebuilt with painful slowness – cocked wrist, full swing, racquet low to high. The trouble is that age has taken its toll of my ability to transfer signals from brain to body. Colin patiently keeps trying to get it all right. He is my friend, my shrink, my cardiac specialist. We never talk about politics. What would I have done without him?

Another friend, Bob Rae, the former Premier of Ontario, a genuinely good man and another reminder of just how intelligently decent Canadians can be, told me in the afternoon that last night he went to a lecture given by C.H. to the Asia Society and had bristled at the comparisons C.H. made between Asian and Western values. C.H. seems to have bought lock, stock and barrel from the egregious Ronnie Chan, his most damagingly talkative adviser, nonsense about Asian supremacy.

Invited out to dinner with Martin Lee and the Democratic Party legislators, all 18 of them, at a spectacular fish restaurant in Lei Yue Mun. Excellent food. A lot of Tsingtao beer. Jokes. Autographs. Photographs. More photographs. Speeches. Presentations. Szeto Wah, the veteran campaigner for democracy in Hong Kong and China, is also a famous calligrapher and has done a fine piece of calligraphy for me, cleverly playing on Lu Ping's denunciation of 'the sinner condemned for a thousand years' which he has turned into a similar-sounding description of 'the man who made Hong Kong drunk' (with freedom). They also gave me cartoons of themselves, and in return I signed lots of first-day covers for them with a variety of topical observations, e.g. 'from Rita Fan' s favourite Governor'. They love all this knockabout but were apparently puzzled and slightly alarmed when I said in my 'thank you' speech that I was pleased to be able to fit this engagement in before my dinner with the (communist) DABHK. When I was outside having a pee, they anxiously asked John Tsang, who was with me, 'Is he really having dinner with them?' They are good and brave people. We have let them and others down. We should have delivered more explicitly what was promised in the Joint Declaration and given greater protection for the values which the great majority of Hong Kong Chinese citizens believe in and want to survive. In many respects these men and women represent the very best of China.

Saturday 17–Sunday 25 May

Lavender and I have been back in London. We spent much of the week observing the scale of the electoral disaster for the Conservative Party and talking to our friends about it. One mark of the rout is the problem of remembering who has survived. Lavender and I took John and Norma out to dinner at Green's on Monday night. Sir Peter Tapsell was eating at the bar on his own. I could not remember whether he was still in the House of Commons. John thought (rightly) that he probably is; otherwise, why would he be eating in central London on his own? John and Norma are relieved to be shot of the grinding battle with Conservatives intent on suicide. He is sad about the friends who lost. He has been through a ghastly seven years and did his utmost, but the Tory Party was unmanageable. Later in the week I had a drink with Ken Clarke at the Garrick. The party would be mad not to vote for him, the only candidate who can rally it through his performances in the House and lead it back to the firm middle ground. We didn't, as he points out, lose because we were insufficiently right-wing and Eurosceptic. But I think that William Hague will probably get it, as do most of those to whom I speak. William is clever and certainly not a rabid right-winger. I sometimes felt, as the week went past, that we are moving through occupied territory from one safe house to another, from Tristan's for dinner to poor Alastair's – poor because he's still the Chief Whip with an even tougher job in opposition than in government.

Tony Blair asked me to go and see him at No. 10 to talk about Hong Kong and whether he should come to the handover. Relaxed, without his jacket, he seemed very much in control of events. Who wouldn't be, with a recently acquired majority like that behind him? I quite like him, though his amiability requires a palace guard of real thugs to allow it to be paraded so conspicuously. If I was younger, I can imagine settling down with enthusiasm to the job of trying to turf them out – provided that the Conservative Party offered more congenial company than now seems likely.

Robin Cook gave me a dinner preceded by a meeting at Carlton House Terrace. He is very impressive, on top of his subject, and with good instincts on China and Hong Kong. He understandably wants a better relationship with China but not at Hong Kong's expense. But you can see officials manoeuvring around him to downgrade our commitments to Hong Kong. They've started, for example, to put in submissions to him and draft messages to Chinese leaders without showing them to any of us in Hong Kong first for our comments. There's always an excuse, but now it forms a pretty clear pattern. Ah well, only thirty-odd days to go. When I saw John Coles, the permanent secretary at the FCO, he gave a real Sir Humphrey performance. The new ministers were very impressive, especially the PM, he said. He'd come to address the meeting of permanent secretaries and given a superb presentation. Et cetera et cetera et cetera. I guess they've got to do it, but yuck. And why bother doing it to me? As far as the media are concerned, the honeymoon tale continues with Mills and Boon still writing most of the copy.

It looks as though we may finally have agreed the purchase of a pretty house Lavender and I saw in Barnes in January. I hope that it gives us the same joy as our place in France. We flew down to Toulouse at the weekend with Kate and Laura – it was looking beautiful, covered in roses. On Sunday morning, I stood in the vegetable garden looking west to the farthest horizon listening to the birds. I realized how much the thought of this home has kept me going during some of the most testing days in the last couple of years.

Tuesday 27 May

We got back to the very welcome news that Andrew Li has been nominated by C. H. Tung to be Chief Justice. Andrew is a moderate – clever, cautious, clean and decent. He will stand up for the independence of the judiciary and for the rule of law. C.H.'s best decisions have been the appointment of Anson, Donald, the other senior civil servants and now Andrew. He should be congratulated for doing what is plainly in the community's interest. I hope he will let them get on with their jobs.

The question of when Chinese troops will arrive is still dominating everything. There seems to be a degree of embarrassment on the Chinese side that Jiang Zemin is so determined part of the Chinese garrison should be in place before the actual handover, whatever we say. In the JLG and elsewhere we present a catalogue of quotes and promises about the arrival of Chinese forces only happening once sovereignty has changed. There is of course a tendency in our Beijing embassy to suggest that perhaps we can negotiate with the Chinese about a small number of the garrison arriving early, and officials in London are starting to sniff out prospects of a compromise (i.e. modified surrender). But so far, ministers' lines seem to be holding firm.

Discussion with Bob, John Ashton, Hugh Davies, Alan Paul and Martin and Edward about a paper for the FCO on the lessons we've learned over the years on dealing with China, and on what negotiating with China has told us about what that country is like. There's so much hogwash talked about the Chinese. The Chinese communists always act solely in what they believe to be their own best interests, and regard any agreement as a stage in a relationship not as an immutable conclusion to a negotiation. I have never used the line that used to appear in all the briefs, that the Chinese always keep their word even though negotiating with them is hard pounding. This is simply untrue. Nor is it correct to suggest that if you do more or less what the Chinese want, they'll give you a fair crack of the whip. They want to define both the crack and the whip. Look at the problems the Portuguese have still over Macau, even after throwing in the towel to China at every turn. Our negotiations have shown that the Chinese system is fundamentally unstable and this is one of the reasons why it is so difficult to construct a permanent policy of engagement with the Chinese Communist Party. The current leadership is erratic, nervous and bloody-minded. Yet the likelihood is that despite our experience in the trenches, the mush school of diplomacy will be listened to on China rather than us. So China will continue to get away with bad behaviour and will therefore go on behaving badly.

Wednesday 28 May

By mistake we received from Francis Cornish's office a copy of a submission last week from the FCO to No. 10 about the PM's proposed visit to, and performance in, Hong Kong. The covering letter from Sherard to Francis says that we aren't to see the submission because it doesn't agree with our advice on the length of Blair's proposed visit and on the importance of him delivering some sort of message or speech. I don't think this is the result of any conscious decision by ministers. For five years, we've been in the driving seat over policy because of my relationship with ministers. But since 1 May that has changed, so in a petty-minded way officials (with Sherard in the lead) are trying to 'get things back to normal' for the last few weeks. The sort of thing that happens is that we sit around with the JLG team, Anson and Hong Kong government officials to work out a negotiating position on this or that relatively minor issue. Then we get a letter from Sherard substituting his own judgement, without any ministerial endorsement. It's crazy and brings out the worst bossy-boots fusspot side of one or two FCO officials. My colleagues have to cope directly with all this interference and it makes them even angrier than it does me.

Thursday 29 May

Our press office have found out that C. H. Tung's office are issuing a press release on the future use of Government House as an official guesthouse and entertainment complex. C.H. is intending to stay in his own flat. It's nice to be told. John Tsang quickly got the staff together to assure them that their jobs and accommodation are safe. We can't answer all their questions. Who can? Maybe the Chinese Ministry of State Security.

The JLG has been meeting this week and predictably getting nowhere. For most of yesterday and today, the Chinese banged on about sending the garrison in early in increasingly shrill and minatory terms.

Friday 30 May

I had lunch with Robin Munro of Human Rights Watch Asia and Han Dong-Fan and his family. Han was the leading young trade unionist involved in Tiananmen. He was locked up, caught TB, released for medical treatment in the USA, and then refused re-entry to China when he tried to return. Since then, despite protests from the Chinese, he has lived in Hong Kong and wishes to do so after 1 July. We'll see whether they let him stay. Han is a very handsome young man with real grace and authority. I hope that the future of China will one day rest with people like him. Robin says that, with every sign of dissident activity snuffed out, and with would-be dissidents thoroughly depressed about the prospects for peaceful political change and evolution in China (the West's behaviour doesn't help morale), there is a growing and miserable realization that if change comes at all it may well be violent and erratic.

Saturday 31 May

I worked all day. John Coles has written to apologize for not keeping us in the picture about the PM's visit and so on. Perhaps we have done enough to prevent any further drift in London before the end of next month. No. 10 have given a briefing to the *Sunday Times* suggesting that, if the Chinese insist on swearing in the provisional Legco at the same time as the Chief Executive, Tony Blair won't come to Hong Kong for the handover ceremony. That may mean that the Chinese dig in and we'll have knock-on boycotts of the banquet and so on. Maybe it doesn't much matter. But I'm sure the PM has done the right thing. We got telegrams today about the meeting between Blair and Clinton. They both spoke very well on Hong Kong.

Sunday 1 June

Not just the last lap, but the final straight. We gave a barbecue for present and past private office staff, bodyguards and families at Fanling. We will miss them all a lot. I can just about get through my 'ta v. m.' speech. Just about.

Monday 2 June

Anson has given an interview to *Newsweek* and they put her on the cover. It's full of spirited stuff about standing up for Hong Kong's freedoms and the importance of acting according to your conscience. It looks like the drawing of a line in the sand. Coincidentally, *Time* have done a cover story on me for their international edition. I am sure that one of the things that most worries Anson is the feel already of a drift in standards. I know that she makes this point to C.H. But does he take any notice? Today he gave Hong Kong a lecture about how everyone should forget about 4 June.

We are starting to get a series of white-flag telegrams from the Beijing embassy and from London (I doubt whether they are all agreed with ministers) about the negotiations on the garrison and the handover ceremony in general. There is mucho panico by Sherard and his groupies in London about all this. It makes life particularly difficult for Hugh Davies and his colleagues in the JLG if every time they try to take a reasonably firm line with their Chinese opposite numbers they have their legs cut from under them. It doesn't bode well for the work they have to continue to do for some time after 1997 in the JLG. The impact of these limp arguments from London and the Beijing embassy is also starting to have an effect on any lingering confidence which civil servants like Anson and her colleagues may have on the dependability of British understanding (and, if necessary, action) after July. One or two of our senior Hong Kong civil servants have been saying that they sympathize more and more with Emily Lau's frequently expressed view that you can never trust the Brits. As head of the Hong Kong civil service, Anson is sufficiently worried about the way things are going that she has fired off a personal telegram herself to Robin Cook.

Tuesday 3rd June

Among the many farewell lunches and dinners I went for a meal with the EU consuls-general. I gave the assembled diplomats a working over about how pathetic most European countries have been over Hong Kong, telling them that my Chinese officials who are staying on after the handover aren't going to take declarations of European concern over Hong Kong remotely seriously. I suppose the flavour of these remarks may get back to capitals, though it won't make any difference. In the meantime, we will continue to hear high-flown sentiments about a common European foreign and security policy.

Thursday 5 June

There's a final meeting with the heads of civil service departments and a lunch at which Anson makes a lovely speech. Lots of tears all round. I only managed to avoid a lump in my throat by making a controlled and dry little response. In the evening, Exco gave me a dinner at the Grand Hyatt. When I look back on nearly five years with (mostly) this team of advisers, what is most surprising is that we've never had a really ill-natured discussion, despite all the problems. I must say that I've been much more relaxed with this group since Willie Purves left and Rosanna

Wong became the senior member. There has never been a sense that any of the present Exco members brought their own agenda to the table or were pursuing all sorts of serpentine activities outside.

London seems to be panicking even more because of Anson's telegram. Robin Cook has replied with oodles of reassurance. But the hunt for any bottom line in the negotiating positions of FCO officials and the Beijing embassy continues.

Saturday 7 June

Nury Vittachi, the very humorous columnist, sent me a copy of his latest book with a tear-jerking inscription.

We had a barbecue supper on the terrace of GH for our best friends here. There are lots of hugs from Father Barry and Father Lambertoni – I'll miss them, the best of Irish American and the best of Italian, and the best of the Catholic Church. I've had more nice letters, including one from Hamish McLeod, who recalled how most of my local and expat advisers back in 1992 and 1993, including him, argued that we should stand fast on our bottom line having negotiated for years without one and seen the consequences. His conclusion was that whether you have a bottom line or not, the Chinese behave in the same way – the struggle school of diplomacy. But at least if you have a bottom line, you keep your respect and make it easier to govern Hong Kong.

Tuesday 10 June

The administrative service officers, the crack regiment in the civil service, gave me a farewell dinner. There was a record turnout of about 350. Nicholas Ng and Anson make nice speeches. Afterwards, Martin and Edward said that Hong Kong civil servants are watching the drift back to the usual FCO ways with, unsurprisingly, mild contempt. They've seen it all before – for example, when the Beijing embassy in 1989 refused to open its gates to Hong Kong citizens who went there for refuge after the Tiananmen massacre.

Wednesday 11 June

Just over a fortnight to go. GH seems to be full of packing cases and there is a loud noise of strips of sticky tape being ripped. Elspeth and Louise are helping to organize everything with their usual superb competence. Lavender conducts the orchestra and Alice does her exams!

The slither and slide in London continues. They don't really take any notice at all now of what we have to say. Here we are, leaving Hong Kong in pretty good shape without years of domestic rows, demonstrations, turbulence, shaking fists, and you'd think this had been accomplished by the sort of diplomacy that came so naturally to some of those officials. It's also worth pointing out that we are leaving our last major colony without the rest of the world thinking we have behaved badly. But there is no last ditch that some officials wouldn't abandon. I don't blame ministers. I think they believe that if we have a better relationship with the Chinese themselves, they will be able to do more for Hong Kong. But they'll be advised the whole time that if they do or say anything about Hong Kong's freedoms and democracy, they will annoy the Chinese leaders. Officials have slipped effortlessly into the vacuum created after the election. Anyway, Tony Blair has announced he is coming for the handover and I don't imagine that he will want to be any part of Britain seeming to be humiliated by Beijing.

I made my last visit before the end of the month to the convention centre and the airport. They are both astonishing examples of what Hong Kong is able to do in a short time. When Lavender and I went on holiday in July 1994, work on creating the island base for the convention centre had only just been started. Now the whole spectacular edifice is complete. And work on the airport had only just begun when we arrived in 1992; it will be opened next April despite all the rows with China. The half a million square metre terminal, designed by Norman Foster, has been more or less finished in 29 months.

Kate has arrived from London in excellent form, a boost for morale for all of us, not least Alice (despite having to complete her A levels). Laura will be with us soon. Lords Howe and MacLehose have made disobliging speeches in a Lords debate saying that there wasn't much wrong with the provisional Legco. I wonder if Geoffrey, who is not at all a bad egg, ever goes back and looks at what was promised, not least by him, in the House of Commons and in Hong Kong about democracy and the Joint Declaration in the mid-1980s.

Thursday 12 June

There's been a so-called experts' meeting on the early arrival of the garrison. The Chinese JLG leader started the meeting by saying that they would like our ideas about how they could best get 3000 soldiers into position on 30 June. This is what they take from their meetings with our ambassador in Beijing. Hugh Davies tells them that it had surely been agreed that Chinese experts would brief us on their own plans. When was the briefing to be? Stalemate. End of meeting. We're also told that they're intending that Jiang Zemin and other senior leaders should arrive in a huge new yacht which is presumably intended to win the 'ours is bigger than yours' competition. Meantime, Bryan Dutton [Commander British Forces] is quietly getting on with organizing the departure of our own garrison. He has done an excellent job, probably helped by the fact that he doesn't have to clear every decision with the FCO.

Monday 16 June

Donald and Selina Tsang gave us a farewell dinner and a lovely piece of calligraphy by Selina. It's a Tang poem, 'Farewell to Minister Zhu':

> Farewell to a travelling friend returning to capital.
> My precious sword worth thousand gold.
> I readily part for my friend,
> Together with my eternal friendship and a faithful heart.

Tuesday 17 June

Can I do another fortnight of farewells, emotional speeches and interviews about the future? Lavender and I flew to Macau for a farewell dinner with the Governor, Vieira, and his wife, Leonor. They have become good friends. He's greyer than he was with big black bags under his eyes – and he's still got 2½ years to go. I guess we know more about the impossibilities of our respective positions than anyone else. Here we are, on this strange Chinese shore, trying to bring a decent end to our respective countries' colonial histories.

I had an enjoyable lunch on that day with a group of trade unionists who are members of Legco. It's better to have praise from them than from a bunch of property developers. They gave me a cartoon and a delicious meal. I much appreciate the tribute from these guys who are not habitually social lunchers. After my last Legco Q and A session today, there was a lunch with Legco members past and present where I was presented with a pewter tankard. Asked in the chamber what I would have done if I'd been Prime Minister, I reply that the way things have turned out in the UK, I'd certainly have appointed myself Governor of Hong Kong. Tsang Yok-sing, the leader of the DABHK, makes a characteristically brave speech paying tribute to some aspects of British administration and of my governorship. There is even applause in the chamber, something I haven't heard before. Our last formal dinner at GH was another goodbye to Exco. They have stuck by me through thick and thin. They will remain friends – mine and one another's. They are planning to meet for dinner from time to time. Those who are going to serve on C. H. Tung's Exco won't have too much of a problem spotting the difference.

Friday 20 June

JLG experts are still locking horns over the advance arrival of Chinese troops. The Chinese are now looking for some sort of face-saving formula. We've obviously managed to beat them down quite a long way. I think we should be able to get the numbers down to about 500, with a few at Prince of Wales barracks in the middle of Central and the rest at Stanley and in the new territories. It won't look very good, but it could be much worse.

An engaging conversation with Henry Kissinger on Friday afternoon. He's had a talk to C.H., whom he found 'cocky'.

Saturday 21 June

This afternoon I opened the new town near Chek Lap Kok airport. It has gone up in an astonishingly short time. I suspect that Rosanna Wong and Sally Lau, the Director of Home Affairs – a bubbly extrovert who gets things done – brought the opening forward so that I could do it.

Sunday 22 June

Lavender told me to prepare myself for a secret treat. We were driven off after breakfast and fetched up at the Catholic church at Shatin. We battled through a horde of cameramen and got into the church, to be confronted with a surprise. It was packed and the congregation gave us a great ovation. At the front were the Hong Kong Sinfonia, its full choir and four soloists. What was this all about? Then I saw David Tang, his girlfriend, Lucy, Simon Murray, Dominic Lawson and his wife, Rosa (they are staying with David again), and Cheung Man Yee. David handed me a sheet of paper with notes on the Haydn Nelson Mass. So here we were, Sunday mass with the full Haydn works. Most of our favourite priests had been recruited to come to concelebrate the occasion – Peter Barry, Peter Newberry, Jim Huvane, Sean Burke – and the parish priest Father Ahearne. It was completely wonderful. The parish priest simply announced that my friends had wanted to give me a prayer. Some prayer. In my emotional thanks, I avoided saying that this mass – long one of my favourites – was called 'In Angustiis', a mass for troubled or perilous times. Let's hope not.

Then we went to David's for lunch with more surprises. When we had finished, the pipes and drums of the Black Watch suddenly appeared on the lawn and banged away for us, then Simon Murray read a tear-jerker of a poem he had written, and to cap everything a tall-masted French sailing boat appeared in the bay to take us back to Central. We arrived home exhausted with emotion. Unbelievable. What great friends. Lucky old Guv.

Monday 23rd June

It's a 'lasts of everything' week. And planning and organization for the farewell, the departure and the launching of the SAR government are becoming ever more demanding and even more frenetic. Chinese secretiveness and bureaucratic incompetence risk throwing everything into chaos. The Chinese are still producing lists of guests whom they want invited to events. Their plans for the arrival of senior leaders change by the day, but they seem to have given up on the idea of the vast yacht. What a mess. Our team of officials is working literally around the clock and are all dog-tired.

The weather is awful, leaden skies, rolls of thunder and swampy heat. At Exco, the main issue was about de-registering a company called Rex, which is involved in weapons proliferation, especially chemical weapons. It's plainly a front for the main Chinese arms dealer and manufacturer, Noninco. The papers have all come through for this decision to be taken this week, and I'm also being pressed to close down an Iranian bank which has been funding the proliferation exercise along with the Bank of China. I'm prepared to act against the company even though it is so late in the day. But to hit the bank, which has local creditors, risks provoking an 11th-hour bank run that would look to the Chinese like a final British 'petty trick'. We can fire a shot across their bows, setting the government on course to close them down later if they don't give satisfactory answers to our questions. It will be an interesting test of the new SAR government's resolve to protect Hong Kong's reputation as a reliable partner in the strategic trade field.

Tuesday 24 June

Last night we had a big reception for all our Government House and Fanling staff and their families: gardeners, cooks, stewards, laundry workers, cleaners, electricians and so on. Autographs, photos, tears and dim sum. Tonight it was a final dinner given by Anson at Victoria Lodge, her official residence, for some of our closest friends and their spouses. We ate a delicious Chinese meal. The greatest stroke of luck that I've enjoyed here is having Anson as my number two. She is one of the nicest and bravest people I've ever known, and she's become a firm friend. The dogs trotted out to greet us when we got home and Whisky made his customary diversion to bark at the policeman who was saluting his good night. The *Economic Journal* strip cartoon which stars the dogs had them learning French today. 'Why are we doing this?' says one. 'Is there another British dog in France?' Luckily, as I note too regularly, they have been taking French lessons.

Wednesday 25 June

A day full of interviews and a rather unpleasant meeting with Lee Kuan Yew. He berated Anson for her *Newsweek* interview suggesting that C.H. didn't know very much about the way government works. I pointed out that civil servants in Hong Kong have always had a more public role than in Britain for example. Anson in particular is regarded by the public as the main custodian of their liberties and the standards and integrity of government. He brushed all this aside and slid into the mode he likes best – monologue. I increasingly wonder whether Lee would know a civil liberty if it hit him over the head with a truncheon. Edward told me that Margaret Thatcher had once said to him, 'Harry's become much more extreme since he was in government. I suppose there's a lesson in that for all of us!' A highly intelligent man, he's also become a bit of a bore.

Thursday 26 June

Alice did her last A level today. She's been incredibly relaxed about having to do her exams while we prepare for our departure, which can't have been easy for her. She's a remarkably mature kid. My monthly radio talks on the radio – 'Letters to Hong Kong' – have been published today. I've attempted in them to encourage Hong Kong people to stand up for themselves, and for the values which have made Hong Kong such a special and successful place. They are an example of what Denis Chang, my clever and funny Exco colleague, calls tutorial government.

Between all my interviews today was a call from the bully of the Lower Remove, Henry Keswick, to grumble again that we haven't given sufficient help to Jardine's, specifically in freeing them from the ambit of the Hong Kong takeover code. Actually we expended huge quantities of effort on this issue – Martin has a file on it like the *Encyclopaedia Britannica*. It's lucky nobody's ever dropped it off the back of a lorry. I steadfastly refused to overrule the independent regulator or try to push him to do what he believed would be contrary to the law. It would have been disastrous for me and disastrous for Jardine's as well had we done so, a point completely lost on Keswick. We go round the same old bushes, both keeping our tempers more or less. Henry departed, full of anecdotes about C. H. Tung's alleged commercial dishonesty. All this means is that they had some kind of a row over money. For perhaps understandable reasons, while knowing nothing about all this, I feel an instinctive sympathy for the CE designate.

Like some other big men, Henry wears soft little slippers and moves light-footed, heading off down the hill to abuse me again – and I assume as a vocation for evermore – once he is off the premises. I am sure that he will try to exact a price for the fact that I failed to comprehend that the whole purpose of the British Empire was to increase his personal fortune. Jardine's is pretty well managed by competent people both here and in other countries – it doesn't need special favours to make its lavish profits.

Friday 27 June

I rose early and went to the RTHK Studios for my last phone-in programme. There was only one hostile question in an hour and a quarter. We had our last district visit, this one to Kowloon, which goes as well as ever. Lance arrived this evening to take Whisky and Soda for their flight to France, but their departure has been delayed for 48 hours because of an airstrike. The stewards are delighted. One says, 'We'll miss them. They are like our children.' After a drinks party which Simon Murray gives for Jennifer's latest helicopter adventure, we went to a splendid concert at the theatre of the Academy of Performing Arts. This really is the last night of the Poms – Jerusalem, Elgar, flag-waving and of course 'I Vow to Thee My Country'. I can't sing the second verse of this great hymn at any time without choking up. And this isn't 'any time'.

Saturday 28 June

I went to the airport this morning to meet the Prince of Wales and Robin Cook, and escorted the Prince, who is as ever charming, to *Britannia*, which arrived earlier in the week. She is moored at Tamar along with the Type 22 frigate *Chatham*, which is really a light cruiser, both looking very handsome.

We still haven't resolved all the outstanding issues with the Chinese about the handover and departure. They are pressing for the Prime Minister and Foreign Secretary to go and visit Jiang Zemin and Li Peng at their hotel on Kowloon side, and also for the Prince of Wales to call on Jiang at the convention centre since he is junior in protocol terms. But, of course, I insist that he should take precedence since Britain is sovereign until midnight. We are working on a compromise under which they both arrive at the same room at the same time. As for the arrival of their garrison, they've told us that 21 armoured cars will arrive with 4000 troops, warships and helicopters at dawn on 1 July. Armoured cars! So much for the argument that if we were accommodating about a pre-midnight arrival, they would scale down their post-midnight plans.

The Prince of Wales did an investiture before the Queen's Birthday

Party reception in the late afternoon. Everyone was there, including the Democrats for a change. The Royal Hong Kong Police Force band beat the retreat on the lawn at the back of the house. As the Union Flag came down to the sound of 'The Last Post', strong men bit their lips. Then the Prince gave a grand dinner on *Britannia* for the great and good of Hong Kong, with my Exco and senior officials as the core guests. The ship itself is a real beauty, elegant salons without any of the gin palace excess of so many big yachts. It is all perfectly done and gently understated. The Prince works hard, making a real effort with C. H. Tung and his wife. I wrote to Tung today wishing him well. I do. I got him into this in the first place.

Sunday 29 June

I did several interviews, including *Breakfast With Frost* before we went off to our last 9.30 mass at the Catholic cathedral. It's the feast of St Peter and St Paul. Lavender and I are asked to do the readings. The second reading is from Paul to Timothy and is all about 'fighting the good fight' and 'winning one's crown'. I ask Lavender to do that one! The priest, Father Hanley (with whom Peter Barry concelebrates), preaches a nice sermon about love and service and ends with a story which is his response to questions about the future of Hong Kong. A small boy approaches an old man with cupped hands held in front of him and says, 'I have a small bird here. Is it alive or dead?' The old man knows that if he answers 'alive', the boy will crush the bird, if 'dead' the boy will open his hands and that the bird will fly free. So the old man says, 'You have the life of the bird in your hands. You can crush it. Or if you want, it can fly.' Thus the responsibilities that belong to the people of Hong Kong. At the end of mass the parish priest, Father Tsang, makes a nice short speech about Lavender and me which, as they say, my father would have enjoyed and my mother would have believed. Applause and photographs as we left.

Either side of lunch the Prince of Wales does another investiture and Lavender and I continue our face-to-face farewells with all the GH staff. Before dinner there was a reception for a cross-section of Hong Kong's great and mostly good, especially those who run Hong Kong's main charities. Louise has done such a brilliant job helping Lavender in her work with so many of them. On *Britannia* in the evening there is a dinner for the international grandees. I watched Ted Heath, who was with the Russian Foreign Minister, Primakov. So far as I can tell, he says nothing all evening sitting like an Easter Island statue. The high spot of my evening was a chat before dinner to Madeleine Albright, who said all the right things about decency and freedom. She's clearly somewhat sceptical about Hong Kong's prospects. Tonight will be my last night's sleep in Hong

Kong. Before turning in, I look out through the curtains of my dressing room at the wall of lights beyond. Five years not just to remember, five years branded on my mind.

Monday 30 June
I woke as I have for weeks at about 4.15am, my arms and hands rigid with adrenaline. I snoozed fitfully and manically until about 6.30. I was cross to discover that my early TV interview was being held outside, where I worked up a sweat, returning for an interview with Jim Naughtie, who was as friendly as ever – a nice person with whom to start the day. Madeleine Albright came in at 9 o'clock and we had a good round-the-houses talk about benchmarks for the future. She will keep the State Department switched on to Hong Kong, though I think they are anyway predisposed that way. We then rushed off to the airport to greet the Blairs and their entourage. I travel back to Central with the Prime Minister, Cherie and Lavender. He seemed once again the epitome of bright charm, quite an amicable and certainly an intelligent man – keen to do his best. They had brought along his brother and sister-in-law.

We got back for a briefing at Francis Cornish's apartment. There were still some complex negotiations about the formal meetings. I warned that they would be completely vacuous occasions, but I don't suppose that matters. The message for the day was, 'we are making a fresh start with China', as Robin Cook made clear when he joined us. The Prime Minister took me on one side and said that he hoped they could square this message with the expression of a lasting commitment to Hong Kong. I think he's genuine about this and that he is trying to be courteous to me as well.

We organized a walkabout in the Pacific Place shopping mall afterwards for the Blairs, Lavender and me. I'm not sure that his officials, especially his press man, Alastair Campbell, quite knew what to expect. I suspect they thought that sometime during the day I'd try to cart them. Anyway, Pacific Place should have gone far to reassure them in a pretty gobsmacking way. There were huge crowds of well-wishers all pressing forward to be touched or spoken to. Spontaneous applause welled up through the galleried mall as we waved and pressed the flesh. There were shouts of 'we'll miss you' – which the Blairs clearly think was directed at them. We stomped and stormed our way through the crowds with Tony and Cherie in the lead. They appeared delighted and surprised by the reception. It should make good television pictures back home, which will doubtless please Campbell. And that of course is what matters!

Back at GH, we bade farewell one by one to the stewards. 'I've been bad. You've been good master,' said my excellent and sweet-dispositioned valet. ('But surely,' said Prince Charles later, 'no man is a hero to his valet?') The senior steward, Ah Chak, who saw the dogs off to France last night, was woeful, wondering about the differences of working for Chinese rather than British employers. The staff were then all drawn up in a mighty circle in the hall and we went as a family person to person shaking hands. Tears dripped freely onto what will soon be Mrs Tung's carpets. Then, everyone left for the ceremony outside, before Lavender, Kate, Laura, Alice and I – one glance back at a home where we'd been so happy – stepped outside this into a light drizzle for the last ceremony at the house.

It was simple and moving. I left the house through an honour guard of police, stepped onto a dais, accepted a royal salute with the National Anthem playing, watched a display of silent drill and then stepped down to say farewell to all my honorary ADCs. Back on the dais, the band played 'Sunset' and 'The Last Post' as the Union Flag on the balcony over the front porch was lowered for the last time. As the flag was folded and brought down to me, the pipes of the police band played my favourite 'Highland Cathedral'. Lance, my tough and very competent ADC, who's been like a friend and brother to me, handed me the flag, my flag. The band began playing 'Auld Lang Syne' and we stepped into the car, circled the front drive once and left to tears inside the garden, where all our staff and their families were drawn up and to tumultuous applause from the huge crowds outside. We drove down through the rain to the quayside, cheered on our way.

Changing on *Britannia*, and watching the crowds gather for the farewell, sporting thousands of umbrellas, the rain set in – by now very heavy drizzle. The farewell ceremony itself went well, despite or maybe because of the weather – children, choirs, 'Nimrod', bands, 21-gun salutes, marching, dancing and Hong Kong's best rain. It tipped down harder and harder but everyone kept going cheerfully. In the front row of the main stand, we weren't properly covered and got wetter and wetter. Despite the attempt by Laura, sitting beside him, to shield the Prime Minister with her umbrella, by the time he went off for his bilateral with Jiang he was completely drenched. I made a speech halfway through and cut short the ovation. The Prince of Wales was the real man of the hour. Shortly before he got up to speak, the rain began to pelt down even harder, monsoon style. 'Oh no,' he said, 'I knew this would happen.' But he stepped bravely and uncovered to the lectern, the rain cascading from his cap onto his naval uniform. He was barely able to turn the sodden pages of his speech. He deserved 10 out of 10 for sangfroid.

We then drove back to *Britannia* as the heavens began to explode with the grand firework display. After getting into some dry clothes, we returned to join the pre-dinner reception at the convention centre. I was able to shake hands with one sheepish Chinese official after another. Those who had declined to come near me for years were obliged – embarrassed, slightly crestfallen, even nervous – to accept the cheery salutations of the triple violator. All my pals from the north were there – Qian Qichen, Lu Ping, Zhou Nan, (former Ambassador) Ma Yuzhen. For the banquet I sat at the top table between Cherie Blair and Madeleine Albright. Mrs Blair was chatty company. We had a jolly conversation about education on which we didn't seem to disagree. I thought her a smart woman. Madeleine Albright asked me about dealing with China, and I was able to give my usual spiel about obliging them to separate trade from politics and about getting better coordination between Europe and the USA, based on the realization that in practice kowtowing to China was not the only key to the tradesman's entrance.

At the end of the banquet, served and eaten in record time, I joined Robin Cook to go and meet Jiang Zemin at the entrance. As we rushed down to meet him, we met Li Peng and his heavies on the way up. The entrance hall to the centre was surrounded by Chinese security men, with plastic pieces in their ears, but even their numbers and furious squawking into telephones did not stop Jiang's car missing the entrance and having to reverse. He clambered slowly out of the Mercedes, Ronnie Corbett with trousers at half-mast. We took him upstairs for a meeting of fatuous irrelevance. Jiang, Li Peng , Zhou Nan, C. H. Tung and others sat in a line opposite the Prince, Blair, Cook, the Chief of the Defence Staff and me. Loads of photographers, officials and journalists stood at either end of the room. Jiang then read some bloviate stuff about 'one country, two systems'. As the Prince replied rather well, without any script (partly about the agreement we had made in the Joint Declaration), Tony Blair whispered to me, 'Shall I speak?' 'Yes,' I said, 'go next.' And he did with a suitable follow-up to the Prince's off-the-cuff remarks. At which point, Li Peng said that Hong Kong should be 'a bridge not a barrier', a phrase which the Chinese have picked up from Robin Cook as the new mantra.

And that was it. Meeting over. Apparently, the earlier bilateral wasn't much better. As I looked at these clapped-out old tyrants, I thought to myself, 'Why do we allow ourselves to be bullied by these people? Most of them are not remotely impressive and are scared stiff of the world. All they can do is bully.' There weren't many signs of grace and natural authority. I am sure that we would have felt differently if I'd been looking at Qiao Shi or Zhu Rongji.

And last, the handover itself. A stiff little ceremony, best got over with as quickly as possible. I looked back at the senior guests on the Chinese side, arranged in their egg box stand, the coelacanths of Leninism, rich, mighty, a bit seedy, cruel, corrupt, depressingly unimpressive. I turned to my left to wink at my girls. Jiang shouted his guttural speech, clapping himself and being clapped dutifully in all the right places by the Chinese guests. Then the Chinese honour guards goose-stepped about and, with our flag lowered and theirs raised, it was time for us all to shake hands and for us to get out as quickly as we could, leaving Heath, Howe and Heseltine to salute the new order and the provisional Legco. Howe has been phoning up journalists saying what a tragedy it is that I chose not to be de Klerk to Mandela. What does this crap mean? Who is Mandela? Jiang or Li Peng?

At the quayside, lots of our friends had gathered to give Lavender and even me a last hug. ('They all said they played tennis with you,' said the Prince.) All my policy secretaries and Exco members, and a number of other senior officials, had hurried to the quay by coach, which can't have been a very politically correct thing to do. We hugged them too. I kissed Anson for the first time and wished her luck. I could only cope with the emotion by being brisk and gauntly cheerful. A few handshakes with a bemused group of Chinese officials led by their Vice Foreign Minister, and then a last goodbye to Robin Cook and his cheerful doctor wife, Margaret, who kissed me on both cheeks. Lavender and the girls, who all looked fantastic, went up the royal ramp ahead of me, faces crumpled with emotion and streaked with tears. I walked up last, just behind the Prince, turning to wave as the band on *Britannia* played 'Auld Lang Syne'.

And so it ended. We pulled away from the quay, the crowd cheered and waved, singing 'Rule Britannia'. Followed by *Chatham* and our escorting patrol craft, we pulled into midstream and drove down the harbour through a canyon of light, every window seeming to explode with the flashbulbs of cameras. A flotilla of small vessels followed as far as the Lei Yue Mun gap, where crowds lined the shore and cheered the departing oppressors. Then we sailed off into the night and the empty sea. Lavender and I gave the girls a hug, and went down to bed. I was tired. Tired but more deeply happy than I have ever been. The job was done. Lavender and I were going home.

Postscript

We spent two and a half days on *Britannia*, arriving in Manila just after lunch on Thursday 3 July. It was an extraordinary experience. Living in this elegant old ship is rather like spending a weekend in a very agreeable country house. Big cooked breakfasts, delicious Bloody Marys, cold lunches, Sancerre, fruitcake, dry martinis, good claret, excellent company. The Prince of Wales was a charming host, kind, courteous, amusing. He was particularly good with our girls, who sparkled. He spent some of the journey painting, and some reading poems by Rilke. He speaks enormous sense about the environment, for which he is frequently mocked. I fear that he will have the last laugh.

Unfortunately, the weather on the first day was pretty rough, which laid most of the family low for part of the time. I appeared to have good sea legs. Edward, who was with us and is the son of a naval officer, said it's the result of a finely balanced middle ear, whatever that may mean. As the first morning wore on, so the ships of the Royal Navy's task force, 'Ocean Waves', appeared all around us. There were 16 in all, the largest British fleet in these waters for years. At the end of an elaborate manoeuvre, we led the two-file convoy, then completed a half-circle to port and steamed up between the two columns, with the crews of each vessel drawn up on deck to cheer us as we passed through: the last time that a royal yacht will pass through the fleet. It was an extraordinary occasion – the Prince, Lavender and me on the royal deck at *Britannia's* stern moving from port to starboard rail and back again to acknowledge the cheers of each vessel – Type 22 and 23 frigates, patrol ships, fleet auxiliaries, a nuclear submarine and the light aircraft carrier *Illustrious*. The Chinese intelligence ships which had followed us at a distance from Hong Kong must have been mystified by the amount of 'face' being given to the departed colonial Governor.

On the second day, with the sea mill pond calm under blue skies and fluffy clouds, there was a fly past as *Illustrious* pulled alongside and her complement of Sea Harriers tore off into the heavens. Later, the fleet's helicopters and Sea Harriers joined together to salute us as the western sky turned pink, yellow and blood orange with the setting sun. I doubt whether a Governor and his wife have ever left before in such style: a pardonable way to bring down the curtain on Britain's old Empire.

I'll never forget my very first afternoon out of brave and decent Hong Kong, hanging over the prow of *Britannia*, watching the dolphins leaping alongside us through the waves, flying fish behind them by the dozen, skimming the water for a hundred yards or more. Dolphins and sunsets, that's the real world now. Isn't it?

The Destruction of Hong Kong: What Happened after 1997?

Many had always been dubious about the sustainability of Deng Xiaoping's pledge that Hong Kong would continue to be itself for 50 years after 1997. The pledge, which was written explicitly into an international treaty signed by both Britain and China and lodged at the UN (the Joint Declaration), was encapsulated in the mantra 'one country, two systems'. For a start, many questioned whether the leadership of the Chinese Communist Party had any idea what Hong Kong being itself actually meant. As I noted in the diary, I had a problem explaining to Lu Ping the difference between the rule of law and rule by law. He found it difficult to accept that when I had been a government minister, my decisions could be subject to successful challenge in the courts. The distinguished barrister and pro-democracy legislator Margaret Ng put the point very well when speaking in her own defence in court against charges brought against her for civil disobedience. She said this: 'Your honour, I came late to the law. I have grown old in the service of the rule of law. I understand that Sir Thomas More is the patron saint of the legal profession. He was tried for treason because he would not bend the law to the King's will. His famous last words are well authenticated. I beg to slightly adapt and amend them: I stand the law's good servant but the People's first. For the law must serve the people, not the people the law' (*Hong Kong Free Press*, 16 April 2021).

The economist Milton Friedman thought the whole idea of a free market economy under the rule of law living happily within the control and jurisdiction of a communist totalitarian state was preposterous. It was an oxymoronic contradiction on stilts. Others, including many Chinese business leaders in Hong Kong, plainly had their doubts as well, albeit kept close to their chests. Why otherwise would they make sure that they had foreign passports in their back pockets before British rule came to an end? Each of my successors, chief executives for the communist colonial power in the Hong Kong Special Administrative Region (SAR), either themselves had foreign passports or had ensured that members of their families had them. And, of course, there were some (for example, members of the United

Front) who knew the Chinese Communist Party and its ways all too well and accepted as a pardonable necessity the bloody brutalities that had for years kept China in Leninist hands. There were also some people like my visitor (in May 1995), the former Labour Party Prime Minister Jim Callaghan, who thought that Beijing's bosses would probably behave badly but there was not much the rest of us could do about it, so why bother making a fuss now? That was simply what China's communists were like. You would have to 'get real', shrug and move on.

What of those who were optimists? Some had read or at least noted the main message of the book by Francis Fukuyama on the so-called 'end of history'. China would change, as had happened elsewhere as economics and technology perforated its thick political hide. Both arriving in and exiting what economists call the middle-income trap would produce political change in China as it had elsewhere. Maybe, they hoped, Hong Kong would change China rather than the other way around. While there was a large dollop of delusion about this, it had some effects on many of us. Although never myself believing that there was an umbilical relationship between economic development and political change, I hoped that there was at least some connection, even if it was not mechanistic, between politics and economics. On top of this, I found it impossible to believe that nothing we had tried to do would last and that Hong Kong's citizens would come to the point of defining their patriotism first and foremost as loving the Communist Party. After all, the majority of them were in Hong Kong as refugees from some of the worst excesses of communism. They knew better than most of us what the distinction was in practice between a free society and a dictatorship.

Such were the cautious hopes that I held when I left Hong Kong, buttressed by the thoughts of one of my most experienced Foreign Office officials that surely the Communist Party had not spent more than 20 years negotiating with us about every pinhead only to walk away as soon as they could from what they had helped to create. This degree of modest optimism, admittedly constrained within the bounds of public decorum, was strengthened by a sense of relief that we seemed to have come through critical years in Hong Kong with its structures and practices more or less safely in place.

As all who asked knew from my answers to their regular questions about Hong Kong's future, I never for one moment reckoned that Hong Kong was too successful for China to risk its future well-being. Yes, it may be a 'golden goose', but history is full of examples of this large, valuable bird being killed off by the farmer supposedly responsible for its welfare. Hong Kong's success in comparison to China's was bound to decline proportionately because of the rapdily growing Chinese economy. Moreover – crucially – communist bosses did not distinguish between the interests of the country and those of the party. People very often talked with another avian metaphor about Hong Kong as the canary in the coal mine: its treatment would give a clear signal of what China was really like and what its intentions would inevitably be. I never believed that the Communist Party would hesitate for a second to throttle the canary if they thought this was important to the party's continued control of the country. They would not be deterred by the signal this would send to the region and the rest of the world.

Why had so many Chinese men, women and children sought refuge in a British colony? The journalist Tsang Ki-fan described Hong Kong as 'the only Chinese society that, for a brief span of 100 years, lived through an ideal never realized at any time in the history of Chinese societies. A time when no man had to live in fear of the midnight knock on the door.' Hong Kong enjoyed the separation of powers between executive, judiciary and legislature; executive accountability to a partially elected legislature; due process and an independent judiciary; the rule of law; disciplined services operating within strict rules according to a Bill of Rights (or at least explicit legislation governing their behaviour); a clean, respected and competent civil service operating within the traditions of public integrity; fierce measures against corruption; freedom of assembly and worship; a free and outspoken media; and schools and universities that were not given political directions from the government or its apparatchiks.

None of us who left in 1997 would pretend that Hong Kong was perfect. Although considerable progress had been made to encourage the creation of a socially responsible market economy, to develop welfare, health and education, and to limit the worst extremes of income and wealth distribution, the gap between rich and poor remained excessive, especially in housing. The casual and infrequent patronizing racism probably institutionalized in every colony had mostly disappeared; but it had left some understandable resentments. Overall, however, Hong Kong was a good place to live, to bring up a family, to thrive, aspire and prosper. And, probably above all, there were no midnight knocks on the door, feared in every totalitarian society, and the sound of a police siren did not occasion quiet prayer. What price do you put on all this? How do you explain its importance to a communist hack?

I used to wonder occasionally how much the rest of China liked or admired Hong Kong with its own language – Cantonese – and its (not always disguised) disdain for its northern cousins. The communist leadership, I am sure, regarded with a degree of contempt the rich Hong Kong tycoons who paid court to them. How much respect did those tycoons attract by bowing quite so low? Perhaps their wealth and behaviour sometimes brought out, if only for a fleeting moment, a few residual communist sentiments in the attitude of those whose approval was being sought or purchased. Yet many of the communist hierarchy and their families were of course very happy themselves to loot their own economy and stash away the proceeds in colonial Hong Kong, the laundromat for their corruption. In addition many communist officials undoubtedly believed, with limited historical understanding, that the material success of Hong Kong resulted from piggybacking on China's own economic resurgence. For many mainland visitors to the city there must have also been a palpable sense that they were being looked down on, criticized for their intermittent crude public behaviour and tastes. Hong Kong's growing sense of its own identity must have become apparent to those who could tell that in this southern city people did not think of themselves as simply Chinese. They were more than that: they were a unique hybrid, Hong Kong Chinese.

Yet for all this, for a dozen or so years after 1997, Hong Kong did seem able largely to retain its civic personality. Not everything went well. Beijing went back on the promises it had made about the development of Hong Kong's modest democracy, commitments made before and after 1997 by both Lu Ping and the Foreign Ministry. The debate about this was choked off whenever it arose. And it was of significance that in C. H. Tung's first term as Chief Executive, his deputy, Anson Chan, resigned after only four years. She had attempted to get Tung to stand up for Hong Kong's autonomy, to protect the integrity of the Hong Kong civil service and gradually to strengthen Hong Kong's democratic institutions. She had become known as 'the conscience of Hong Kong'. Needless to say this had not gone down well with leaders in Beijing, who criticized her and let it be known that she should do no more than loyally support Tung. His behaviour set in motion a process of weakening Hong Kong's autonomy which gathered pace over the years. Hong Kong's government began in time to suffer the exhaustion of servility. Public service standards and morale slipped and the search for Beijing's approval became the city government's default position.

Tung was not at all a bad man but was too malleable with Beijing. He combined a curious mix of indecision and stubbornness. He was also politically tone deaf. He set out in his second term in 2003 to legislate on the issues raised in article 23 of Hong Kong's Basic Law governing secession, sedition and other public order offences. Before 1997, we had offered Chinese officials assistance in drafting legislation on these matters in ways consistent with the Basic Law obligations, the common law and Hong

Kong's international human rights commitments. When Tung himself attempted to legislate on these matters in 2003 the result was a disaster. Many legislators objected, not only the Democrats, and there were public demonstrations involving up to half a million people. The result weakened and discredited Tung. He had to withdraw the legislation.

This failure cut short Tung's second term. He was succeeded by Sir Donald Tsang, who had been an exemplary Financial Secretary in the last period of my governorship and had then, under Tung, succeeded Anson Chan as Chief Secretary for Administration. He served for seven years and made at least some effort to revive discussion of universal suffrage for the Legislative Council and for choosing the Chief Executive. But he was stopped in his tracks by Beijing. He ended his term criticized for alleged corruption but was eventually acquitted by the courts after serving a short term of imprisonment.

Meanwhile, year by year, Beijing's interference in Hong Kong's affairs became increasingly pronounced. When the United Kingdom, with considerable diplomatic circumspection, pointed out that there was a danger of infringement of the Joint Declaration, Chinese officials argued with apparently growing confidence that this was simply a historical document and of no further relevance: an extraordinary way of talking about an international treaty. Presumably any past treaty could be described in such a way. So, I suppose, could the 99-year lease covering the New Territories, the termination of which had rightly led to the change of sovereignty in 1997. It would have been helpful if the Hong Kong government had also criticized this argument, which might have encouraged the UK government itself to be rather more robust on the matter. But with the Cameron government we were moving into the so-called 'golden age' of relations between Britain and China. Nothing could be allowed to cool the ardour of affection sustained by often imaginary, fictionalized or quietly aborted trade and investment deals.

Nevertheless, while first Jiang Zemin and then Hu Jintao ran China, Hong Kong remained identifiably what it had been before 1997. The rule of law was still based on due process, with an independent judiciary and a police service which operated within legal constraints defined by human rights principles. Freedom of assembly was still guaranteed, one prominent civil rights group commendably organizing protests with government and police approval and largely without violence or disorder. There was manifestly an increasing degree of self-censorship, but there were still some independent newspapers, particularly *Apple Daily*, owned by a notable refugee from mainland China, Jimmy Lai, and a public service broadcaster, Radio Television Hong Kong, which regularly broadcast BBC news coverage of world affairs including those in mainland China. Hong Kong seemed to have survived reasonably well, if not without some knocks and bruises: an extraordinary mixture of Chinese and Western attitudes, a great international trade and cultural hub acting as the principal conduit for investment in and out of China, and a part of China with its own personality which had managed to safeguard China's knowledge of its own history. Books were published and sold in Hong Kong which told the story of modern China with honesty. They could not be published and sold on the mainland. Perhaps the most notable example of this aspect of Hong Kong's contribution to China's Memory Palace was that every 4 June thousands of people commemorated, with a solemn vigil in the centre of the city, the murders of students and others in 1989 in and around Tiananmen Square. The Chinese Communist Party might be able, so it thought, to whitewash the past, but that was not something that could or would happen in Hong Kong. In the future this itself will be regarded as a major contribution to the history and culture of China. Hong Kong would not 'burn the books and bury the scholars' like an early Qin emperor and like modern China's communist dynasty.

It is interesting that the next dramatic twist in Hong Kong's history was largely triggered by an attempt to counter what communists call historical nihilism, or what most others call the search for the evidence-based truth. This was the attempt in 2012 to impose a Chinese communist version of civic education on the Hong Kong public school curriculum. There were huge protests against this involving more than 90,000 people in street demonstrations. A group of secondary students called Scholarism, organized by a 15-year-old school pupil named Joshua Wong, helped to lead and organize protests against what they regarded as brainwashing. Opposition to these plans was so fierce that they were dropped, though the whole experience paved the way for further protests during the disastrous period of office of the third Chief Executive, C. Y. Leung.

After higher education in Britain, Leung had been a commercial property developer, very often in China. He was an enthusiastic fellow traveller with an eye for the main chance and a hint of racism in his attitude to the West. Whether he had actually been a closet member of the Communist Party was a matter of some debate. According to the polls, the public (who often have excellent judgement in these matters) clearly thought he was a nasty piece of work. Leung's period of office, which mined new depths of disapproval, coincided with the emergence of Xi Jinping as China's leader.

Following the successful campaign against trying to browbeat children and students in Hong Kong to accept the Chinese Communist Party's narrative about its history and aims, Joshua Wong and those who had led the protests turned their attention in 2014 to proposals made by the National People's Congress in Beijing in a document which claimed 'comprehensive jurisdiction' over Hong Kong. It defined local autonomy as simply the power to run local affairs as the central leadership of China laid down. Within this approach there would be limits determined by Communist Party leaders for the next Legislative Council elections in 2016 and for the election of a Chief Executive in 2017. This election would allow for universal suffrage, but the choice of candidates would in effect be determined by a selection committee chosen by Beijing. This is similar to the process for electing a president in Iran.

Beijing's announcement produced an extraordinary series of city and street protests, sometimes called the Umbrella Revolution (the demonstrators carried yellow umbrellas to attempt to ward off tear gas and pepper spray) or the Occupy Movement (the demonstrations blocked the centre of the city) from late September to mid-December 2014. The organization of the demonstrations was extraordinarily successful despite increasingly heavy-handed policing. The demonstrators, many of them students, could be seen in the evenings helping one another with their homework. After each day's events they would help to clear up any rubbish left behind. The demonstrations caused disruption and inconvenience in the heart of the city but also attracted global media coverage, both for the cause espoused and for the manner in which it was pursued. The same could not be said for the position of the Beijing and Hong Kong authorities – not that there was now any obvious difference between them. The Hong Kong government had become simply the transmission mechanism for Beijing's political judgement about how best to crush dissent and democracy in the city.

Attempts to engage the protesters in discussion and debate got nowhere. As with demonstrations in later years, tear gas and pepper spray replaced any attempt to find agreement or compromise. Eventually the demonstrations fizzled out, leaving behind considerable bitterness among many of the pro-democracy activists and a nascent movement arguing that the issue should not be just about democracy in Hong Kong but the liberation of Hong Kong from China's yoke. This was not a wise political development on the part of those, a minority, who advocated it. I visited Hong Kong twice in the years after the Occupy Movement had ground to a halt, and on the first of these occasions, in 2016, made a speech to the Foreign Correspondents' Club in which I said that I would always support the movement for greater democracy in Hong Kong and for protection of the rule of law, but that I could never support a campaign for Hong Kong's independence from China, desirable as some people might regard it. That had never been possible within the terms of Britain's historic agreements with China.

The first time that I made this speech Joshua Wong and other student leaders asked if I would go and say the same things to students themselves. I agreed and spoke in a packed main hall to 700–800 students at Hong Kong University. I set out my reasons for not being prepared to go along with the argument for Hong Kong's independence. I was listened to politely but there were some very tough questions. I was asked for example what supporters of democracy outside Hong Kong would do if Beijing attempted to destroy the democratic cause. It was a very good question which I answered with some well-meaning remarks about the indestructible case for freedom, the concern of most of the world, and the courageous spirit of Hong Kong. I did everything except sing 'Kumbaya'. But I am not sure that my answer convinced even me. A year later I was back in Hong Kong and I was asked again if I was prepared to talk to students on the same subject. I did, and to my amazement was told that in the intervening period no one from the government, let alone from Beijing, had tried to talk to them to try to persuade them to take a less confrontational position. What happened then was of course entirely predictable. Calls made by a small minority for independence were used by hardline communist officials and propagandists to disparage all the efforts of the democracy movement to promote greater accountability and respect for Hong Kong's local autonomy. A Rubicon had been crossed, and the die was cast.

Leung's deep unpopularity ensured that, even given the political insensitivity of Beijing, he was only a one-term Chief Executive. The election for his successor pitched the very successful Financial Secretary, John Tsang (who had been my private secretary), against Carrie Lam, the Chief Secretary for Administration, who had been given responsibility by Leung for constitutional development (not that there was any) during the period of the Umbrella Movement protests. Tsang had a huge opinion poll lead. He had favoured talking to the leaders of the democracy movements, not least the students, whereas Lam's selling point with communist apparatchiks was that she either refused to communicate with them or else simply put up a stone wall to all their requests or demands. So Lam got Beijing's nod. She was a career civil servant who had risen without notable trace through the administration through hard work and, latterly, a willingness to carry out unquestioningly the political decisions taken by the Chinese communist politburo. A Chinese Vice Premier, Han Zheng, was given responsibility for Hong Kong and Macau affairs; in effect he took all the big decisions affecting these territories. Senior Hong Kong government officials, particularly those with any responsibilities for security, would frequently (especially during increasingly numerous periods of tension) travel to Shenzhen to a residence there called Bauhinia Lodge to take instructions from Han Zheng and those who were really running their community – a community once, of course, promised a high degree of local autonomy.

The first major protests against Lam took place in the summer of 2019, when she attempted to introduce an Extradition Bill on a spurious justification built around a real argument for extradition unhappily involving a crime committed in Taiwan. How could a subservient Hong Kong deal with Taiwan? These cases had been dealt with in the past with discrete legal and administrative competence. But Lam plainly saw the opportunity of winning support in Beijing for the way that she dealt with the matter. One well-known and experienced journalist, Melinda Liu, argued convincingly (*Foreign Policy*, October 2019) that 'Lam was in a rush because she'd hoped to curry favour with senior officials in Beijing around the time of the PRC's 70th anniversary.' Opposition to the bill came from right across the community, including business: there was a widespread perception that the bill would be used by Beijing to secure the arrest and trial on the mainland of Hong Kong citizens not least for political offences. One of Lam's closest advisers gave the game away when he said that a main reason for the legislation was that it would save Beijing from having to abduct people from Hong Kong, as had happened in 2015 in the case of five men involved in the publication and sale of books which the Communist Party did not like, and the abduction also of a very rich Chinese citizen who had obviously been a bag carrier for corrupt senior officials on the mainland. He had evidently known too much about the corruption of senior party leaders for his own good. The demonstrations built to almost a million people by June 2019 and later to double that figure. The police dealt with them using increasingly violent methods which plainly well went well beyond the normal limits placed on public order policing. As the protests grew in size, the young demonstrators, who were in the vanguard, appeared to be taking their tactics explicitly from the martial artist Bruce Lee, who had talked about acting like water, without obviously organized tactics or strategy. Using social media and mobile phones, they moved almost formlessly from one target to another. The roughhouse police response inevitably produced occasional violent reactions by the demonstrators. There was no excuse for this behaviour; this was not civil disobedience. It was used by the government and its friends – and particularly Beijing – to discredit the protests as a whole. But keeping civil disobedience civil is always difficult when it is not regarded as a legitimate form of protest by the authorities. It was not just the incontinent use of pepper spray and tear gas, along with the wielding of batons, which provoked anger. There were some specific incidents which outraged public opinion well beyond the ranks of the demonstrators. For example, in one incident at Yuen Long Metro station, people who were travelling home after demonstrating were beaten up by Triads. This was plainly done with the complicity of the police, who turned a blind eye to what was going on. Calls for an enquiry into the handling of the demonstrations, as well as the behaviour of the demonstrators themselves, were rejected out of hand. Moreover, the authority of the police complaints body was filleted by the government. It became readily apparent that the police were not accountable to anyone except their own leadership, clearly under the thumb of Beijing security officials. Radicalization of young demonstrators was also inevitably the result of the disenfranchisement by the government of Legco members whom they had helped to elect.

The initial demand for the withdrawal of the Extradition Bill (which was eventually conceded in September 2019 with a bad grace) grew into a wider political agenda which became known as 'the five demands'. In addition to full withdrawal of the Extradition Bill the protesters insisted on the establishment of a commission of enquiry into alleged police brutality, the retraction of the classification of protesters as rioters, an amnesty for arrested protesters and, perhaps most fundamental, universal suffrage both for the election of the Legislative Council and for that of the Chief Executive.

Probably the greatest violence was seen on university campuses, particularly with what amounted to a state of siege in some cases. During the course of the violence in and around these campuses, and in other demonstrations, there were credible reports of the police manhandling and even arresting professional medical staff who were trying to help those who had been injured. Overall during these and some later demonstrations more than 10,000 people were arrested and over 2300 charged. Hardly a single police officer was charged at the same time for excessive use of force.

The Hong Kong government and the United Front as a whole regularly bragged that the demonstrations were unpopular with the public at large, who would give the causes advocated by the demonstrators a big thumbs down in the district council elections in November 2019. In fact the reverse happened, as could have perhaps been predicted by looking at the opinion polls which showed overwhelming support for the demonstrations – and suggested that more than one third of all those in the territory had actually attended at least one demonstration. The council elections proved to be an overwhelming success for the pro-democracy camp, with a high level of voter participation and victory in 86% of all the seats up for election. The response of Carrie Lam to the results was not to meet the newly elected councillors but to invite the defeated candidates to a meeting. Her government, which really meant Beijing's communist leaders, refused to accept the reality which was staring them bravely in the face. Hong Kong wanted its autonomy, its way of life and a greater share in the way it was governed: all these things were anathema to Beijing.

Another consequence of the events of 2019 was a collapse of public respect and trust in the police service. In a survey in the autumn of that year conducted by the Chinese University of Hong Kong, almost half of those questioned had zero trust in the police. On a scale of 1 to 10 with 10 points indicating 'complete trust' the average score given was 2.89. This was a police service which had been called before 1997 'Asia's finest' and which had deserved the epithet.

The lesson which Beijing's communist leaders plainly took from all this was that they could not believe those who told them there was a silent majority in the city for acquiescence in Beijing's demands; they needed to act comprehensively and directly to destroy what they disliked about the city, to run it themselves and to bury the idea of 'one country, two systems'. The macabre joke was all too obvious: 'one country, two cisterns'. From now on, anything resembling another system was to be a facade or masquerade. Above all they had to avoid the holding of the Legislative Council elections in the autumn of 2020, which would, on the basis of those held in 2019 for the district councils, produce a large pan-democratic majority. They now moved to destroy the autonomy and way of life of Hong Kong with a National Security Law enacted in time for the July celebrations of Chinese National Day in 2020. Needless to say it was neither enacted by the Legislative Council in Hong Kong nor as the result of consultations in the territory.

This law gave the notorious mainland security police the right to work in Hong Kong without being answerable to local laws. Soon after the National Security Law was passed by the National People's Congress in Beijing, the Chinese security services moved into a 33-storey hotel in the centre of Hong Kong, which became known as the new National Security Office. Hong Kong's new rulers were headed by Zheng Yanxiong, a former party boss in the neighbouring province of Guangdong with a reputation as a hard-line enforcer of the party's will. Formal responsibility for implementing the National Security Law was given to a new committee for safeguarding national security which in theory was headed by the Chief Executive, Carrie Lam. It consisted in the most part of officials from the discipline services, particularly the police. The real power lay with Beijing's National Security Adviser, who acted as a commissar directing the committee's activities. This was Luo Huining, the head of the Chinese government's liaison office in Hong Kong, who had increasingly been the power behind the local administration.

The National Security Law was based on the Chinese legal system. The main judicial authority in Hong Kong was in practice to be the Communist Party. Special courts with harsh sentencing powers were to try cases under the new legislation. The nature of potential offences was defined in only the broadest terms and in practice it soon became apparent that the prosecuting authorities were free to define your criminality in pretty well whatever way they wanted. These broad powers, exercised without the safeguards and transparency which are a fundamental part of the common law, dealt with what were deemed acts of subversion, terrorism, secession and collusion with a foreign country in any way which might endanger national security. A panel of judges selected by Carrie Lam, under the guidance of Beijing, presided over this new judicial system, and in exceptional cases suspects were to be pushed across the border to face Chinese courts, where no one really doubts what will happen in trials. In practice it soon became apparent that bail, jury trials and open courts would be set aside at will even when the offence was covered by the common law. The procedures and approach under the National Security Law leached into the common law: for example, over bail. One of the more unusual aspects of this National Security Law was, as Amnesty International pointed out, that it applied to the whole planet: it asserted jurisdiction over people who are not residents of Hong Kong and who may never have set foot in the city. Amnesty International noted that 'social media companies for example can be asked to remove content deemed unacceptable by the Chinese government, even if these were posted outside of Hong Kong or if the companies' offices and servers are located in other countries'.

Well over a hundred pro-democracy activists have already been arrested under this draconian law and face up to 10 years to life in prison for a range of vague and dramatic charges. In February 2021, 47 pro-democracy leaders were arrested on suspicion of 'subversion' because they had participated in democratic primaries organized by various civil groups to select the best candidates for the Legislative Council elections in 2020. The free press has been attacked, most infamously with the closure of *Apple Daily* and the arrest of its proprietor, Jimmy Lai. The Chinese communist leadership hates Mr Lai, who is an example of a refugee from communism who made a huge success of his life in Hong Kong and was bravely determined to try to protect it from the heavy hand of Chinese communism, which, like so many others, he had personally experienced.

Other well-known democratic leaders have been charged and sentenced, like Martin Lee, under old public order legislation as well as under the new law. The full horror story of what has happened has been very well told by Stephen Vines in *Defying the Dragon*. Vines is a brave and distinguished journalist who has lived and worked in Hong Kong for over 30 years and has also run a business there. In August 2021 he left Hong Kong for the United Kingdom fearing what he called the WhiteTerror – a combination of the new national security legislation and the activities of United Front thugs. He had been threatened because of his views and argued that his most suspect activity was that he loved Hong Kong. He believed that 'the near-term prospects of things getting better are simply non-existent'.

Apart from those jailed or threatened with imprisonment, civil servants have been purged, academics thrown out of their jobs, teachers sacked, professional bodies attacked and, in the case of the main teachers' union, closed down. Schools are obliged to teach the sort of communist curriculum against which they protested successfully in 2012–13; this is called using education as 'an engineer of the soul'. The whole notion of separation of powers between the executive, legislature and the judiciary has been dismissed, even though it is fundamental to the Basic Law and the Joint Declaration. How much of the rule of law still exists is moot; most of whatever confidence remains seems to be based on the fact that judges still wear wigs. What we have witnessed, and are still witnessing, is the destruction of one of the freest societies in Asia by communist tyranny with the complicity of some local leaders and against the manifest wishes of the majority of the public. The world has criticized, but the Chinese leadership has been oblivious. No one can now pretend that they don't understand the reality of Chinese communism, and no one can surely base their approach to China any more on the Cradock proposition that, while the Chinese leadership may be thugs, they are men of their word.

Many countries have offered to take emigrants from Hong Kong, where the number seeking to leave has reached record levels. As I write these words, I have just finished reading a farewell statement to Hong Kong from the owner of an independent bookshop who is closing it down, and with his university professor wife and young family quitting the city they all love. Neither the owner nor his wife is overtly political, but given the state of politics in Hong Kong, they said, they could no longer see a life for themselves and their children in the city. This is a fairly typical story. But Beijing seems prepared to tolerate the flight of so many Hong Kongers. Its leaders hope that they can create a Hong Kong fit for bankers and other financial executives with many of the jobs in the sector filled by mainlanders: their ideal city will be Hong Kong without Hong Kongers, they want Hong Kong with political lobotomy. Early signs show many medical professionals and teachers among the emigrants.

In the United Kingdom, the BNO Visa scheme was announced after passage of the National Security Law in 2020 and began in January 2021. This gives Hong Kongers with BNO passports and their dependants the opportunity to work in the United Kingdom as a pathway to gaining citizenship. The scheme covers 2.9 million Hong Kongers who have BNO status. The estimates of how many are likely to take advantage of this are inevitably uncertain but run up to over 300,000. One mark of changes in attitudes to China, and perhaps a recognition of the vigour and entrepreneurial enthusiasm of Hong Kong citizens, is that overwhelmingly they have been welcomed so far in the United Kingdom.

With Hong Kong in handcuffs and the building blocks of a police state now in place, we should perhaps consider briefly how and why this happened. I go back to the nature of communist tyranny and to what I said earlier about the relationship between economics and politics. The bloody events in Tiananmen Square in 1989 seemed to many to be just a blip on the great arc of history. It was argued, with a good deal of liberal hubris, that the fall of the Berlin Wall would presage a comprehensive defeat for authoritarianism all around the world. These sentiments were turbocharged by China's entry into the WTO in 2001 (on terms which it has regularly abused). Tony Blair confidently predicted that there was now in China 'unstoppable momentum to democracy'. He was not the only person to utter these sorts of wishful sentiments. So what happened?

The momentum might of course always have been illusory. But such momentum as might have existed was halted in its tracks by the present leader of the Chinese Communist Party and the subject of its latest personality cult, Xi Jinping, who assumed power in 2013. He took over the leadership at a time when he and his colleagues had been badly spooked by the attempts of the aggressive and talented Bo Xilai to elbow his way to the top of the party with the support of Zhou Yongkang, who combined both power and patronage in the energy sector and in the security field. Party leaders were even more worried by the threats to their ability to hold on to power posed by globalization with its economic consequences, by urbanization with the flood of rural workers into the cities and by the development of the Internet. They also evidently recognized that some of the increasingly successful and wealthy tycoons in the technology sector posed a threat to the party's control of economic policy. Their conclusion was that the party had to tighten its grip on every aspect of national life, not least education and the private sector, even though the latter was a much more productive contributor to the economy than the State Owned Enterprises.

The more I have known about contemporary China and its leaders, the more I have asked myself why we accept its description of its all-powerful party as a communist organization following a socialist path. Its own definition of socialism has little to do with the usual meaning. Confucius believed that things should be what they were called and should act as they were described. But how does Chinese communism or socialism explain the fact that the inequalities in the country are greater than in the United States of America? Inequality is the Achilles heel of the party in China's totalitarian state. Inequality can only be confronted by removing many of the privileges of the governing class. To do this in a way which has much of an effect would require the dismantling of China's governing cadre.

Shortly after taking power, Xi Jinping ordered party and government officials to recognize that they needed to conduct an 'intense struggle' against liberal democracy. The existential threat, the enemy, was itemized: Western constitutional democracy, the allegation that human rights were universally applicable and valid, civil society, the West's idea of journalism, and open historical enquiry. This began the crackdown across society from the concentration camps, forced abortions and sterilization in Xinjiang to the incarceration of Hong Kong's freedoms, from locking up dissidents to attacking faith groups including Muslims, Buddhists and Christians, from closing down swathes of civil society to stamping out free enquiry at universities, to greater control of the internet to try to prevent any foreign news or ideas polluting China's story. Xi Jinping has made clear what Chinese communists oppose; to discover what the Communist Party under Xi favours, you need to attempt to penetrate the vacuous waffle of 'Xi Jinping Thought', which was officially made an integral part of China's constitution. It has also been turned into a series of brainwashing books for students and children of all ages. What does it all mean? A former US President, Warren Harding, used to talk contemptuously of bloviation – 'the art of speaking as long as the occasion warrants and saying nothing'. This is 'Xi Jinping Thought'.

This blether, from a man described by those who polish his cult of personality as someone almost super-human, with the wisdom of Solomon and the eloquence of Lincoln, boils down to three positions: first, grievance-infused nationalism; second, the notion that the Communist Party embodies all that is best in China's history and culture; third, obey Xi at all times and everywhere. China is a great country with some hugely talented citizens. Surely it can do better than this (admittedly the same could have been said of Trump and America). If you want to know more, why not sign up – it's possible – to do a weekend study course in Xi Jinping Thought. Monday morning won't come quickly enough. Hong Kong represented an amalgam of precisely the sort of values which Xi Jinping and his colleagues regarded as posing an existential threat to their ability to hold on to power. They hated free enquiry; they were scared stiff of political accountability; they were suspicious of civil society; they felt threatened by a free press; they were in short scared stiff of free citizens; and they felt no obligation to abide by agreements they had made if this meant (for instance) allowing the values of an open society to continue to flourish in Hong Kong. It may also be the case that nervousness about their ability to cling to power was aggravated by understanding the huge challenges which have started to hit them: first, the falling and ageing population; second, the severe water shortages in parts of the country, the most serious consequence of climate change in China; and third, the growing debt burden, each unit of growth now requiring twice as much debt as was the case only a decade ago.

China's behaviour over the outbreak of the coronavirus is a reminder of how untrustworthy it is as an international partner and citizen, and how its institutionalized commitment to secrecy threatens all of us in a world so interconnected. We have to see Hong Kong in relation to all this.

In 2021 Xi added a further defensive trench around the Communist Party's absolute control of the totalitarian Chinese state. It was dug by a member of the seven-man standing committee of the party politburo, Wang Huning. He is regarded by some as the present 'court philosopher' in Beijing. An academic intellectual, Wang has risen with little fanfare (having been a senior adviser to both China's previous presidents) and is now the focus of attention as an *éminence grise*. In 2017 he was made chairman of the Central Guidance Commission on Building Spiritual Civilization. Could George Orwell have made up this title? His 'spiritual guidance' is based on his experience of a single visit to America, a country which he clearly loathed, and which became the subject of a widely read book in China, *America Against America*. From his comprehensive critique of America, he has cobbled together an assault on liberal values, which in his judgement combine to destroy social solidarity, high personal moral standards and national purpose. That liberal values, or a distant reflection of them in economics, have been the principal engines of economic growth in China as elsewhere is a fact which he appears to reject or of which he is perhaps ignorant. Wang's perspective has been transformed into a justification for an assault on the very rich, especially the high-tech billionaires who represent a challenge to the party's monopoly control of China's national narrative. But millionaires are caught in the net as well as billionaires, especially if they have a flashy lifestyle. This provides the pretence of a campaign for greater social equity and also can be advantageously used to take down any critics of Xi Jinping. Yet the fundamental reason for gaping inequity is ignored. The party's absolute and comprehensive powers put its leaders on top of everything everywhere, accountable to no one but themselves. That is of course in part a result of the lack of any rule of law and the total absence of a free press. Moreover, attacking gambling in Macau, proscribing videogames, lashing out against so-called 'sissy boys', as well as those with large cars and glamorous mistresses, does not offer a very convincing or profound alternative to the spirituality absent from Marxism/Leninism but still offered in China by faith groups. The idea of a return to Maoism in order to discover a contemporary moral code ignores the lechery of the former party leader, though perhaps lechery is the part of Mao's legacy which has survived among party bosses, and not just in relation to female tennis players!

However badly China behaves, we do not want to return to the Cold War years. But Chinese communist leaders sometimes behave as though that is exactly what they want. We don't wish to build a wall of containment around China. Nevertheless, we should recognize the truth today, in relation to the Chinese Communist Party, of what George Kennan said in his famous long telegram in 1946 about the Soviet Union: 'our respective views of reality are simply incompatible'. Our views of the treatment of Muslims in Xinjiang and Buddhists in Tibet are incompatible with those of Beijing's leaders. Our views on the trade in body parts are incompatible. Our views on forced labour are incompatible. Our views on freedom of religion and freedom of expression are incompatible. Our views on military threats to Taiwan and even India are incompatible. Our views on Hong Kong are certainly incompatible. The list goes on and on, and it is alas Hong Kong's ill-fortune to be included.

There are a few other factors which have sabotaged Hong Kong's chances. First, as many Hong Kong citizens recognized at the time, the guarantee of Hong Kong's way of life contained in the Joint Declaration was not supported by any arbitration mechanism. It was said by British ministers and officials – this was the sales pitch to Hong Kong, to the United Kingdom and around the world – that this was unnecessary, since it was the intention to develop more rapidly Hong Kong's own democratic institutions. In the event, this promise was left rather limply dangling in the wind. China's leaders recognized that breaking an international agreement such as the Joint Declaration would trigger criticisms from many countries. But they thought they could get away with it, just as they have got away with their behaviour in the South China Sea (militarizing reefs and islands against international law and against all their commitments to America and others) and with the breach of the International health regulations in relation to the coronavirus.

Second, totalitarian bosses, sometimes with good reason, take a cynical view of the limited extent to which many of the more prosperous members of any society are prepared to take risks to stand up for the values which probably helped to make them prosperous in the first place. While I am a huge admirer of the bravery of the majority of people in Hong Kong in fighting and speaking out for what they believe in, I still find myself shocked from time to time by the attitudes of some of the better off. I recall one friend whose main comment on the activities of demonstrators was that their presence on the streets made it more difficult to get to the golf course. I recall another conversation with a very prosperous lawyer who argued, as though it were a certain truth, that the demonstrations had all been funded and organized by organizations from outside Hong Kong. I remember being assured, by a wealthy Hong Kong friend who prided himself on being a man of the left, that there were no threats to freedoms and the rule of law in Hong Kong; he went on to tell me about the new boat he had just purchased. I suppose I am naïve. I suppose these are just expressions of human nature as it has always been. Perhaps in their position I would have behaved in exactly the same way; perhaps I should not feel so personally aggrieved by usually amiable people who act in such a self-deluding and spineless way when the consequences of behaving well are likely to be uncomfortable. This is true on the national scale as well. China thinks it can get away with almost anything because of the attractions of access to its market. Moreover, so far as Hong Kong is concerned, it doesn't really care if it has to squash the city's openness, competitiveness and commercial sophistication in order to keep a grip on power on the mainland.

Third, the leadership of the public service in Hong Kong, renowned at one time for its integrity and professionalism, has gradually been squeezed into acquiescent servility. Hong Kong has produced its own quisling class drawn not only from the ranks of the United Front. I suppose that Carrie Lam and some of those like her, including some lawyers, who are happy to implement the National Security Law and Beijing's other diktats, may be outlived by the totalitarian Chinese Communist Party. They may not confront therefore the infamy which history will surely load on them for the part they have played in destroying a great city and its way of life.

Finally, we should recognize the part that the values and bravery of the people of Hong Kong have played in determining their own fate. They heroically and understandably refused to accept that to love China they had to love the Communist Party, a piece of Leninist political consubstantiality. Indeed, the opposite is plainly true. How do people in Hong Kong see and define themselves? In a public opinion survey by Hong Kong University in 2019, part of a programme which has been tracking the question of identity for many years, it was found that a majority of people identified themselves as Hong Kongers – 53%. Two years earlier the figure had been 37%. There was also a drop in the number who regarded themselves as being of mixed identity. Worst of all for Beijing was that the number who identified themselves as simply Chinese had dropped to 11% in 2019. Were the people of Hong Kong proud of becoming citizens of China in 1997? 71% said no. In the youngest age group, from 18 to 29 years of age, only 9% said they were proud of being Chinese nationals, and indeed hardly any in the same age group identified themselves as Chinese at all. One might think that it would be something of a wake-up call to Chinese communist leaders to recognize that the handover of 1997 reduced rather than increased the sense of being Chinese in Hong Kong. Insofar as this is recognized by Xi Jinping and his acolytes it only apparently encourages them to hammer Hong Kong for being so ungrateful for the benefits of living in a totalitarian surveillance state. If you can't convince or win over their hearts and minds, hammer them or lock them up.

Who can know what comes next? Will the story of the 21st century be one in which freedom and liberal values are snuffed out around the planet one by one as they have been in Hong Kong? Is Hong Kong and what it has always stood for now doomed? I refuse to accept this, refuse to accept that the sort of world I have taken for granted is doomed to disappear long before my grandchildren are my age. I learned more about the relationship between economic and political freedom in Hong Kong than I've ever learned from any books, and more about the importance of the rule of law. Maybe I learned too about the extent to which very often some people get the system of governance they deserve. But I'm not sure that this last point was entirely true in Hong Kong, certainly not for the majority. They deserved better than we bequeathed them, and I cannot give up hope that they will get a better deal in due course through their own courage, despite these recent depressing and tawdry events.

Hong Kong was an important part of my public life, perhaps the most important part of it. I think what happens there will be crucial for all of us over the next few years. We have to go on caring about Hong Kong, speaking up for Hong Kong, making clear that we share the values for which Hong Kong citizens are courageously fighting. As we know from what has happened in Hong Kong, we cannot take the survival of those values for granted. Hong Kong's fight for freedom, for individual liberty and decency, is our fight as well. That is why I read again and again the words of the anthem that Hong Kongers – young and old, students and pensioners, men and women in wheelchairs and parents pushing prams – sang at their demonstrations with passion and belief:

> We pledge. No more tears on our land
> In wrath, doubts dispelled we make our stand
> May people reign, proud and free, now and ever more
> Glory be to thee Hong Kong.

The Chinese dissident artist Ai Weiwei, when asked how Hong Kong can bear fighting for democracy in a climate of fear, described the cause as an 'eternal struggle'. He went on: 'Hong Kong's glory and true victory are going to be defined by history and not by the regime.' From a historical perspective, people won't forget the price that Hong Kongers have paid for Hong Kong's own autonomous and free spirit, and the price they continue to pay for democracy, dignity and freedom. The struggle continues for Hong Kong. And for the rest of us. It is surely a cause that will define us all.

Who was Who and Where are They Now?

The Governor's staff at Government House (GH) was run by the private secretary. Richard Hoare was private secretary when I arrived; he moved on to become the government's Head of Administration, and then retired from the Hong Kong civil service to England before the handover. He was succeeded by Bowen Leung, who became Secretary for Planning, Environment and Lands from 1995 to 1998. He was then made the head of the Hong Kong government's office in Beijing. Bowen was followed by John Tsang. He was appointed Secretary for Commerce, Industry and Technology in 2003 and was Financial Secretary from 2007 to 2017, a job in which he was very successful. He stood in the pseudo-election to become Chief Executive in 2017, and despite fighting an excellent campaign and having opinion poll leads of up to 40% he was defeated in the Beijing-picked election committee by Carrie Lam, and received only 365 votes out of the 1194-member election committee. He had won the support of those who wanted greater democracy, or at least a dialogue on the subject between the members of Hong Kong's different parties, the Hong Kong government and Beijing officials. His fault was plainly to favour trying to build a consensus in Hong Kong rather than to steamroller opponents. He has subsequently set up a fund to help young entrepreneurs and taught at university. His election would have changed Hong Kong's history, but instead Beijing got their hand-picked committee to rubberstamp the person they wanted.

My chief spokesman in GH was first Mike Hanson, a British civil servant on secondment who returned to the civil service in the UK and was succeeded by an Australian former journalist, Kerry McGlynn. They were both open with the press, politically savvy and very competent. I trusted them completely and I cannot think of a single occasion when they got anything wrong in dealing with an endless barrage of questions from the local and international press. I assumed that they were both slightly left of centre but never asked. I still see Kerry, now alas widowed, on my occasional visits to Sydney. I once introduced him at a meeting with Michael Howard as the

Australian ambassador (a touch of humour on a dull morning), which rather flummoxed the Home Secretary.

I have described my political advisers at the beginning of the diary. After Hong Kong, Martin Dinham (a brilliant and thoroughly decent civil servant) went back to work in the overseas development field, and Edward Llewellyn came to work in my Cabinet in Brussels and then, after working with Paddy Ashdown in Bosnia, returned to London to become David Cameron's chief of staff. After Cameron's resignation as Prime Minister, Edward became British ambassador in France and then Italy, and was made a member of the House of Lords in 2016. Readers of this diary will know how much I relied on his and Martin's advice, good humour and friendship in Hong Kong.

My main Foreign Office officials in Hong Kong were first Sir Anthony Galsworthy, who ran the British side of the Joint Liaison Group (JLG) until 1993. He became the ambassador to the People's Republic of China from 1997 to 2002 after the retirement of Sir Len Appleyard. Sir William Ehrman, my political adviser, was ambassador to Luxembourg from 1998 to 2000 and ambassador to China from 2006 to 2010. Bob Peirce, who replaced Ehrman as political adviser in Hong Kong in 1993, went from there to a post in the British embassy in Washington after the handover, and I requested his secondment to the UK to be Secretary to the Independent Commission on Policing in Northern Ireland, which I chaired after the Good Friday Agreement in 1998. He then became British consul-general in Los Angeles, and left that post for a career in business. Witty, forceful and a superb draughtsman, he was a loss to the diplomatic service.

Hugh Davies followed Tony Galsworthy running our JLG operations. With only about a year to go before the handover, the FCO tried to persuade him to take on a big Asian embassy which suddenly fell vacant. Honourably, Davies declined on the grounds – correctly – that his job on the JLG was one of the most important diplomatic posts for Britain. He was an extraordinarily patient and courteous man with an excellent deputy, Alan Paul, and a first-class team. They did much of the heavy lifting in dealing with the PRC. Davies has privately published his diaries of his experiences dealing with the Chinese. Paul stayed in Hong Kong after the JLG was wound up at the end of 1999 and started a consultancy there.

The two deputy FCO political advisers in Hong Kong were Stephen Bradley, who later became consul-general there from 2003 to 2008, and John Ashton, who was to become the special representative for climate change at the Foreign Office.

The Hong Kong government itself was led when I arrived in Hong Kong by the Chief Secretary, Sir David Ford, who then went on to run the Hong

Kong office in London. After retirement, he became a director of the campaign to protect rural England and to breed rare cattle and sheep in Devon. He died in 2017. His successor as Chief Secretary was Anson Chan, who continued in that role after the handover in 1997 until 2001. During this period, working under C. H. Tung, she became known (as I have noted) as Hong Kong's conscience. She withdrew completely from public life in 2020 after years in which she had spoken out bravely about events in the city. The choice of Tung rather than Chan as the first Chief Executive of the Hong Kong Special Administrative Region (SAR) was one of Beijing's biggest errors, as some of their leaders probably soon realized.

The Financial Secretary, Sir Hamish McLeod, held this post from 1991 to 1995, when he retired to Scotland and a private sector career. He was succeeded by Sir Donald Tsang, who himself followed C. H. Tung as the second Chief Executive of the SAR from 2005 to 2012. He was followed in the job by C. Y. Leung, a long-time United Front supporter who had a probably deserved reputation for being mildly sinister. He was hugely unpopular: another triumph for Beijing's political judgement.

The main FCO officials who worked for us on Hong Kong matters in London were first of all Peter Ricketts, who later became ambassador to NATO and France, head of the Foreign Office and the UK's National Security Adviser from 2006 to 2012. Ricketts, who is now a cross-bench member of the House of Lords, is a real class act. He was succeeded as head of the Hong Kong department by Sherard Cowper-Coles who later became private secretary to Labour's Foreign Secretary, Robin Cook, and then ambassador to Israel, Saudi Arabia and Afghanistan, a post which ended with his reported clashes with NATO and US officials. Sir Sherard, as he of course became, always had strong personal opinions. He worked in the FCO for Sir Christopher Hum, who was the ambassador to the PRC between Galsworthy and Ehrman. On retirement from the diplomatic service he became Master of Gonville and Caius College, Cambridge.

The list of those with political responsibilities on Hong Kong is much shorter. Douglas Hurd was Foreign Secretary from 1989 to 1995, followed by Malcolm Rifkind from then to the handover. The Minister of State was first Alastair Goodlad, who later became Conservative Chief Whip, High Commissioner in Australia and a member of the House of Lords, and then Sir Jeremy Hanley, who was – lucky man – MP for Richmond and Barnes for 14 years until 1997, before pursuing a career in business.

The main players on the Chinese side were first the Chinese Foreign Minister, Qian Qichen (1988 to 1998), who was also a member of the Communist Party politburo. A good linguist – Russian, English and French – he probably had more influence in the party than any other diplomat since then. No 'wolf warrior', he was nevertheless tough without being rude or abrasive, as readers of the diary will have seen. He did seem to believe that diplomacy sometimes involved give as well as take. He died in 2017.

In Hong Kong itself the PRC's day-to-day interests were the responsibility of the New China News Agency, in practice more a cover for and a co-ordinator of United Front activities than a media organization. Its director was Zhou Nan. He was a Foreign Ministry official who had spent a short time in 1980–81 as ambassador to the UN, after which he became a vice minister of the PRC. He spent the rest of his political career involved in negotiations with the UK over Hong Kong. He spoke fluent English, apparently improved by his time interrogating prisoners of war in Korea. Admired by Sir Percy Cradock but not by anyone else whom I've ever met, he retired shortly after the handover and was succeeded by Jiang Enzhou.

The head of the Hong Kong and Macau Affairs Office of the PRC State Council was Lu Ping, a major figure in the diary. He had joined the office in 1978 and left as its head shortly after the handover. It was interesting that both Lu and Zhou left their jobs not long after I sailed away from Hong Kong. I would have liked to know Lu better and could never ascertain how much control he was able to exercise over the main policy issues regarding Hong Kong, or even over some of the smaller ones. I once promised to send him some CDs of English composers – mainly Elgar and Vaughan Williams. I did send them but I was told that he later complained that he had never received them. I guess it was the same story as the interception of the ties which Margaret Thatcher used to send as a gift to Zhao Ziyang every time she was in Hong Kong. Lu Ping died in 2015.

Finally, three post-diary stories about the author which are relevant to the events recounted there.

After leaving Hong Kong I wrote a book called *East and West* about my experiences there and more generally about the relationship between Asia and the rest of the world. It was commissioned by HarperCollins, which was owned by Rupert Murdoch. When he heard the news that his firm was publishing a book by me, partly about China, at a time when he was trying to curry favour with Beijing in order to develop his media interests there, he intervened to prevent its publication. The spurious grounds for doing this led to a generous financial settlement and the publication of the book by Macmillan with a sticker on the front in the United States saying 'the book that Rupert Murdoch tried to stop'. Perhaps partly as a result of this, it sold extremely well. The book's editor, who played a brave role in this affair, has worked for many years since then for Penguin Allen Lane. His behaviour defined publishing integrity.

I like the story told by one of Mr Murdoch's principal associates in his business empire of his trip to Beijing to try to persuade the Premier, Zhu Rongji, that he should be allowed to run satellite TV channels in China. Zhu apparently asked him, 'Is it true, Mr Murdoch, that you were born an Australian citizen?' Mr Murdoch said it was indeed true. 'And is it also true, Mr Murdoch, that you became an American citizen in order to buy an American newspaper and American TV channels?' Murdoch replied in the affirmative. 'So is it the case, Mr Murdoch,' Zhu continued, 'that in order to run TV channels in our country you would like to become a Chinese citizen?' Zhu's officials could hardly contain their amusement.

The second tale followed hard on the heels of our departure from Hong Kong. It has been told in detail in a book by Peter Oborne, *The Rise of Political Lying*. At about the time that I left Hong Kong, Jonathan Dimbleby wrote a very carefully researched book about the handover and the last years of British sovereignty. It drew on extensive interviews with most of those in and out of both the Hong Kong and the British governments and was critical of some Foreign Office officials and attitudes. It was also very positive about others. I had of course myself been interviewed on camera by Dimbleby for a TV documentary that he produced alongside the book. It was not hagiographical about me; indeed, it was particularly critical of the position I took on the Court of Final Appeal. The book and the documentary clearly annoyed some UK diplomats, present and retired, who blamed me for the criticisms.

A few weeks after the handover, the *News of the World* found out that Robin Cook, Labour's Foreign Secretary, had a mistress. To distract attention from the story, and from Robin Cook's rapid decision to divorce his wife (all of which looked like the first example of sleaze under New and clean-as-a-whistle Labour), the government launched a number of eye-catching stories to divert attention over the weekend of 2 and 3 August. The first was that the government was intending to save the Royal Yacht *Britannia* from being mothballed, and the second was a carefully leaked story that I was about to be investigated by the security services for breaches of the Official Secrets Act because of the Dimbleby book. Jon Sopel, the senior BBC journalist, described at the time how the story was sedulously given credibility without anyone from No. 10 or the Foreign Office actually confirming it. The Labour government's spin-meister Peter Mandelson was thought to have more than a hand in this piece of black propaganda. I was on holiday at the time with my family when the story broke and they and my friends learnt that I was apparently about to be investigated by Special Branch and – who knows? – perhaps committed to the Tower of London, or at least Wormwood Scrubs. They were understandably upset by what Oborne describes as 'reckless and irresponsible' behaviour. I was in fact never interviewed by the security services, Special Branch or any other law enforcers, and nor was Dimbleby.

In the autumn of that year, the government's Attorney General answered a written question in the House of Lords about the affair saying that in the public interest no further action was being taken. I suppose this was an unpleasant early example of the way that the often sanctimonious Blair administration was prepared to do business. As I pointed out to Oborne, the irony was that in the following year, after the signing of the Good Friday Agreement about Northern Ireland, I was asked by the Prime Minister (presumably with no worries about breaches of the Official Secrets Act) to chair the Independent Commission on Policing in Northern Ireland. We had of course to cover a number of sensitive security issues during the course of this work. I'm glad that I was asked – it was one of the most difficult assignments that I have had. But I had not forgotten the attempt to tarnish my reputation in order to take attention away from an embarrassing weekend media story.

Finally, in 1999 I became European Commissioner for External Relations. China was of course part of my beat. The first time that I met the Foreign Minister who had succeeded Qian Qichen, at the UN General Assembly in 1999, he said to me, 'This time, Governor Patten, we must cooperate.' I replied, 'But that is what I wanted to do last time.' The minister, Tang Jiaxuan, whom I rather liked, gave me a little smile. He visited me in Brussels on one occasion, and as he came into my office he noticed pictures of my daughters on the wall. Sitting down he asked, 'How come that such beautiful daughters have such an ugly father?' His ambassador to the EU, greatly embarrassed, said very quickly, 'My minister is telling a joke.' Towards the end of the meeting, he very solemnly read out a sentence from his brief, which announced that senior leaders had concluded that 'I was an element of concord not of discord.' So, once a sinner condemned for a thousand years, I had earned remission. Indeed, throughout my negotiations with Chinese officials over the next five years we had perfectly amicable discussions, albeit we were often in disagreement. This was particularly the case since the member states of the European Union usually turned to the Commission to deal with the most sensitive issues over which it actually had no responsibility, such as the EU's refusal to sell arms to the PRC or the treatment of human rights. I particularly enjoyed my encounters with Zhu Rongji during discussions about China's access to the WTO. I thought he was one of the most impressive public servants I had ever met.

I was invited by President Jiang Zemin to go on a semi-official visit with my family to China. My wife and I went and at the end had a long meeting with the President himself. As we left the room, his interpreter sidled up to me carrying a copy of *East and West* – plainly a pirated edition – and asked if I could sign it for him. The President quoted a lot of Shakespeare and was enthusiastic about British films from the 1940s and '50s. I gave him a collection of Shakespeare's plays and said that I thought he would particularly enjoy the history plays. Our only disagreement was that he wanted me to spend more time in China.

All this happened without me ever changing my views on Chinese communism or the way I behaved. I am interested in China and admire much about its culture. The same is not true of my vision of the Communist Party. But, once pardoned, I suspect that I may now again be regarded as a recidivist sinner speaking out against China's bullying behaviour around the world, and in particular its systematic destruction under Xi Jinping of the freedom and promised autonomy of Hong Kong. What the Chinese communist regime has done there is wrong and wicked. We should say that clearly.

Index